Wealth of a Nation to Be

ALICE HANSON JONES

WEALTH
OF A
NATION
TO BE

*The American Colonies on the
Eve of the Revolution*

New York COLUMBIA UNIVERSITY PRESS *1980*

Columbia University Press
New York   Guildford, Surrey

Library of Congress Cataloging in Publication Data

Jones, Alice Hanson, 1904–
Wealth of a nation to be.

Bibliography: p.
Includes index.
1. United States—Economic conditions—To 1865.
2. Wealth—United States—History.   I. Title.
HC104.J67   330.973′027   79-28543
ISBN 0-231-03659-0

To
Homer, Robert, Richard, and Douglas

Contents

Preface and Acknowledgments

THIS book is the culmination of work done over more than a dozen years. Yet it still leaves many questions unanswered, as will become evident to the reader. I hope these will be a challenge to other scholars. The work also reflects and focuses my long-time interest in economic consumption and well-being (long before the era of "consumerism" fashionable today) that runs as a thread through my academic preparation and job experience.

My initial interest in the topic "social and economic standards of living" as she phrased it, was aroused by the brilliant Professor Theresa S. McMahon in my undergraduate and early graduate days at the University of Washington in Seattle. She had taken her Ph.D. degree under John R. Commons at Wisconsin, and under her iconoclastic, witty, and stimulating guidance I read, avidly discussed, and at least partially digested, among other works in labor and economics, Thorstein Veblen's *Theory of the Leisure Class,* Hazel Kyrk's *Theory of Consumption,* and A. C. Pigou's *Economics of Welfare.* The first two, in particular, profoundly affected my subsequent professional interests. In further graduate study at the University of Chicago, where Homer Jones and I met as economics fellows, in addition to studies in labor and required statistics, I took courses with Kyrk in the economics of consumption, with Frank H. Knight and Jacob Viner in economic theory, with Paul H. Douglas in comparative economic systems, and with Chester W. Wright and John U. Nef in American and English economic history. I was attracted by Wright's capsulation of economic history as appraisal of how well, at various cross-sections in time, an economic system has met the needs of the consumer, i.e., what level of living it has permitted for the "common man."

Graduate study was interrupted by two financially and professionally tempting editing and research jobs in New York, involving consumption. I married Homer Jones in New York in 1930. After a summer's European sojourn in 1932, to learn French and German language, we returned for two more graduate student years at the University of Chicago, where I served as a research assistant, the first year in economic theory to Frank H. Knight, the second year in consumption to Hazel Kyrk. In the fall of 1934, I laid aside, I thought only temporarily, a partially researched Ph.D. dissertation on "the standard of living in the northern American colonies, ca. 1770." Homer went that fall as a fellow to the Brookings Institution in Washington and I took a three-month job in the Bureau of Labor Statistics, helping to direct field studies of workers' family expenditures to furnish revised weights for the cost of living index, now known as the Consumer Price Index. That job was extended, rapidly placed me as assistant chief of the Cost of Living Division, and lasted for ten years. It included three special assignments, one to help design an interagency nationwide study of consumer purchases (consumption by income, occupation, and family type), one to set up and advise the first island-wide study of workers' family incomes and expenditures in Puerto Rico, and one to collaborate in Geneva on a report of the International Labor Office on workers' standards of living. Jerome Cornfield was a colleague in the Cost of Living Division of the Bureau of Labor Statistics in those years and contributed substantially to the effectiveness of our interagency studies of wartime consumer expenditures and savings with his important theoretical work on small samples. His exacting standards of survey sampling formed an important link to my present study, and he was the person to whom I turned as technical consultant for the design of an appropriate sample for my dissertation, when I resumed it in 1965.

Some months after the arrival of our third son, I resigned from BLS, but with World War II on, I was soon induced to take a half-time job at the Office of Statistical Standards, Bureau of the Budget, as economist dealing with government statistics on prices and research in consumption adequacy.

After 1948, when I experienced a severe viral illness, I put aside professional work for the next ten years to be at home with a growing family. In 1957, things changed when Raymond W. Goldsmith invited me to take a part-time job with the committee he chaired, appointed by the National Bureau of Economic Research at the request and with the support of the U.S. Bureau of the Budget. The function of the committee was to evaluate and make a report on recommended revisions in the national economic account statistics, which were assembled by the U.S. Department of Commerce. This experience refreshed my interest in national estimates, which had developed earlier at the BLS. The NBER job was followed by a full-time appointment in the Food and Consumer Research Division of the U.S. Department of Agriculture, but this job was cut short when, in 1958, Homer and I decided he should accept an offer to become Senior Vice President in Charge of Research at the Federal Reserve Bank of St. Louis. In St. Louis, for the next seven years, I resumed the role of wife and mother of two teenagers and one college student, except for completing, as a consultant, a report for the U.S. Department of Agriculture on helping families manage their finances. (The USDA position to which I had been appointed was formerly held by Margaret Reid, and she had done an earlier version of the family spending guidance bulletin.)

As an indirect result of some attempts to dust off and proceed with my old notes on colonial standards of living, I was asked, in the fall of 1963, by Professor Werner Hochwald, chairman of the economics department at Washington University, St. Louis, to teach a course in the growth of the American economy. That led to a push from his successor chairman, Professor Harold J. Barnett, to complete my Ph.D. at the University of Chicago, where I had long before, in 1934, finished all requirements but the dissertation. In 1968, under the thesis committee chairmanship of Professor Robert W. Fogel, then in the economics department at the University of Chicago, I obtained the Ph.D. degree in economics, with the dissertation "Wealth Estimates for the American Middle Colonies, 1774" (hereafter referred to as Jones 1970 and cited in full in the bibliography). When I first had a conference in 1965 with Professor Fogel regarding the possibility of being reinstated as a graduate candidate and completing the old thesis on "colonial standards of living," I confessed, in answer to his question, that I considered the available colonial wage and price statistics very poor. I was able, however, to show him some interesting detail I had found in a few published probate inventories. His next question, with his eyes glistening, was "Where are these things?" To my reply, "I think in county courthouses," after about three minutes of reflection, he next asked, "Why couldn't you take a cluster sample of counties, take a subsample of inventories from those counties for a certain date or dates, and why couldn't you made a wealth estimate?" My rather astonished reaction was "Why not?" The idea of sampling fitted in with my BLS experience with Cornfield, the wealth with my work with Goldsmith's committee, and the consumption implications with my long-term interest in the well-being of the "common man." And so the study in its present form was cast. When the dissertation was finished, it was Professor Fogel's urging to "Go on and do it for all thirteen colonies" that has been my undoing for the past ten years.

The foregoing account implies deep roots in and indebtedness for my stimulating academic training and experiences in private research and writing and in government survey and statistical work. Beginning with 1965, I am indebted to another and extensive set of institutions, people, and agencies who have facilitated, encouraged, and supported my specific work on colonial wealth estimates. These include, besides the other two members of my thesis committee at the University of Chicago, John G. Cragg and Robert F. Dernberger, the other people and agencies acknowledged in my dissertation. Among them are county courthouse and state archive officials in New Jersey, Pennsylvania, and Delaware, genealogists, and student and other assistants. Their names are detailed in the dissertation preface and also in the acknowledgments section in volume 1 of my three-volume work *American Colonial Wealth: Documents and Methods,* published in 1977 by Arno Press, Inc., New York. A second, revised edition appeared in 1978. This publication is cited hereafter as *American Colonial Wealth*[1] 1977 or 1978, as the case may be. I am indebted also to the Economics Department, the Libraries, the Social Science Institute, and the Computing Facilities of Washington University, and for a grant-in-aid from the Council on Research in Economic History and for National Science Foundation Grant G-22296. Among my Washington University colleagues who were particularly helpful in the launching or completion of the dissertation phase of the study were, besides Werner Hochwald and Harold J. Barnett, Sam Bass Warner, Theodore C. Bergstrom, Edward Greenberg, and Fredric Q. Raines. Ben Bloxham, then librarian for the Genealogical Society of the Church of Latter Day Saints, Salt Lake

City, made materials available, and his student at Brigham Young University, Miss Karen Williams, made helpful genealogical searches for names in the sample.

Starting with 1969, through January 1975, I acknowledge National Science Foundation grants GS-2457, GS-2457A1 and A2. Starting with 1970, extending through May 1976, I acknowledge supplementary grants from the National Endowment for the Humanities RO-258-70-4429, RO-6136-72-127, and RO-1059-74-101. Harold Barnett, Murray L. Weidenbaum, and David J. Pittman helped to obtain the first grant. Subsequent Washington University Economics Department chairmen Edward Greenberg, Edward Kalachek, and Charles L. Leven helped later to provide matching university support. For the extension of the study to New England, New York, and the South, which those funds permitted, I am indebted to Professors Stephen E. Fienberg and F. Kinley Larntz, now of the Department of Applied Statistics of the University of Minnesota, for sampling and other statistical guidance. I also profited from discussions with my Washington University colleagues Edward Greenberg and Robert P. Parks on problems of regressions and measurement of inequality, with J. Trout Rader on general theory, with David Felix on development theory, with John M. Murrin, Rowland Berthoff, and David T. Konig on various colonial topics, and with William T. Alpert on comparison with the English inventories, generously supplied to me by Peter H. Lindert of the University of California at Davis. The genealogists, student assistants, courthouse, archival, and state library personnel to whom I am indebted for the New England data are listed in my New England article (see Jones 1972 in the bibliography). I should also mention Kenneth G. Carroll, Jr., who helped me to locate the 1774 inventories on the lists in the registries of deeds or courthouses of Essex and Plymouth counties, Massachusetts.

For New York and the South, the state library, courthouse, and state archive officials, the student assistants, genealogists, and others to whom I am obliged for data collection and processing are listed in the acknowledgments section in volume 1 of *American Colonial Wealth,* either edition. To them should be added Richard J. Jones, who assisted at the courthouse of Fairfax County, Virginia by identifying the names of decedents whose estates were probated there in 1773 and 1774.

Two particularly outstanding assistants were Sharon DeSha in regression and other data analyses and Russell Glenn in computer programming. Acknowledgments also appear in *American Colonial Wealth,* "Preface to the Second Edition," to Kenneth B. Schechtman for additional computer programming and to Linda M. Beck for statistical checking and manuscript typing. Others who have been extremely helpful in manuscript typing include Katherine H. Larson, Mary E. Kastens, and Sarah M. Garner.

The graphs were drawn by artists of the Washington University School of Medicine, Department of Illustration, and the maps by cartographer Janice Holt. The illustrations at the beginnings of chapters were drawn by Janice Lindstrom and Frank Ossman for the 1974 reprint of Alice Morse Earle's *Home Life in Colonial Days,* published by the Berkshire Traveller Press, whose permission to copy the drawings is acknowledged with thanks. The coins illustrated at the beginning of chapter 5 are from Thomas Snelling, *A View of the Coins at This Time Current Throughout Europe* (London, 1766). I first saw them photographed in John J. McCusker, *Money and Exchange in Europe and America, 1600–1775: A Handbook* (University of North Carolina Press for the Institute of Early American History and Culture, 1978); John McCusker kindly lent me his photograph to use here.

There is another group of readers or critics who have made helpful suggestions on various drafts of these chapters, or responded to questions from the author. High on this list is Stuart Bruchey, who read the entire manuscript twice, helped reduce its awkwardness at various points, and took a warm personal interest in the outcome. Stanley L. Engerman responded promptly, chapter by chapter, with excellent suggestions and significant questions. Stanley Lebergott and Raymond W. Goldsmith also gave helpful comments on early chapters. Lois Green Carr caught an important error in an early version of the southern paper and has answered numerous inquiries. Peter H. Lindert was particularly helpful on chapters 6 and 8 and encouraged me in the difficult decision to make the retabulations with the revised Charleston weights. Robert E. Gallman commented on several chapters and was particularly helpful with respect to chapter 3. Richard N. Bean as well as Stanley L. Engerman supplied comment and material on slave prices, David W. Galenson and Lois

Carr on indentured servants. Charles H. Feinstein and Simon Kuznets made helpful comments regarding capital-output ratios. Kinley Larntz' review of appendix A was invaluable, and Robert Hanson Jones' and Edward Greenberg's comments on and clarifications of it were helpful. Homer Jones has not only editorially and critically reviewed drafts almost ad infinitum, but has engaged in helpful substantive discussions through the years, and accompanied me on portions of data gathering trips to courthouses in Pennsylvania, Connecticut, and Massachusetts. He has also been supportive and understanding at the many times when the research and writing have taken precedence over household chores, meal preparation, or entertaining.

I owe much of such intellectual curiosity and disciplined work habits as I may have to my totally deaf parents, Olof and Agatha Tiegel Hanson, both graduates of Gallaudet College for the Deaf in Washington, D.C. She was the first woman to receive a Bachelor of Arts degree and graduated first in a class of twelve in 1893, giving a stirring address on "The Intellect of Women" that reads as if it were written yesterday. He was an architect in Seattle, and received an honorary doctorate from Gallaudet recognizing his architectural work and his national leadership among the deaf. In his later years he was ordained an Episcopal minister.

I enjoyed and benefited from presentations of aspects of this study at various professional association meetings, as well as at seminars or workshops in economic history at the University of Illinois, Urbana, the University of Indiana, the Newberry Library in Chicago, the University of Chicago, and Harvard University.

There are many others to whom I am indebted, some of whom are named in the acknowledgment section of *American Colonial Wealth*. They have answered queries, engaged in discussion, supplied useful data or copies of their related research, or assisted me in checking data or reaching solutions to certain technical problems. To all of these, named or unnamed in footnotes or acknowledgment sections, I wish here to express my gratitude and appreciation. Obviously the study has benefited from the discussions and many suggestions, not all of which I accepted. Needless to say the remaining errors, whether of omission or commission, are mine.

Finally, I wish to thank Bernard Gronert of Columbia University Press for his tolerance of my slowness in pulling the pieces together and Karen Mitchell of that press for her skillful editing to soften the rough edges.

ALICE HANSON JONES

Washington University
St. Louis, Missouri

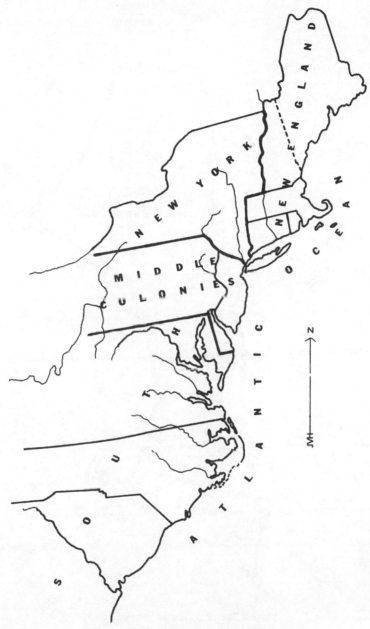

Figure 1.
Map of the Thirteen Colonies

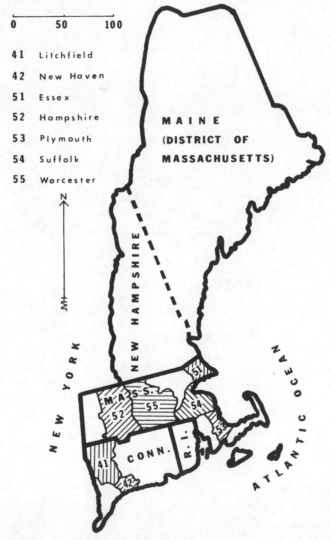

Figure 2.
Map of Sample Counties, New England

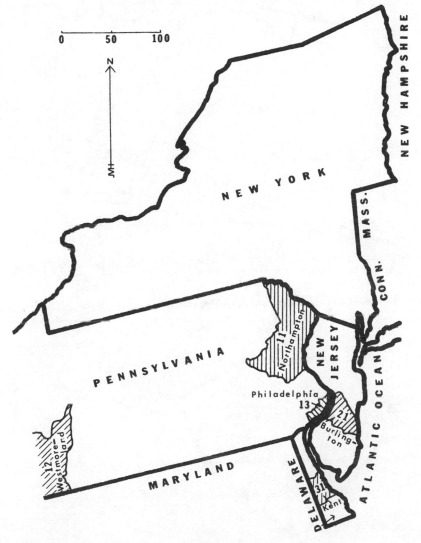

Figure 3.
Map of Sample Counties, Middle Colonies

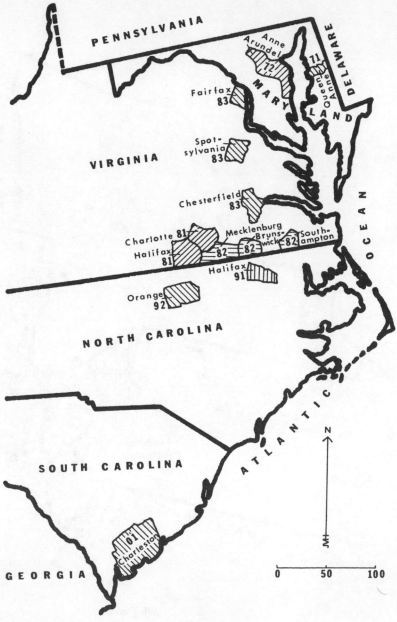

Figure 4.
Map of Sample Counties, South

Introduction:
A Note on Method

As geographers . . . crowd into the edges of their
maps parts of the world which they do not know about,
adding notes in the margin to the effect,
that beyond this lies nothing but the sandy deserts
full of wild beasts, unapproachable bogs,
Scythian ice or frozen sea,
so . . . after passing through those periods
which probable reasoning can reach to
and real history find a footing in,
I might very well say of those that are farther off:
"Beyond this there is nothing but prodigies and fictions,
the only inhabitants are the poets and inventors of fables;
there is no credit or certainty any farther."
. . . Yet . . . let us hope that Fable may,
in what shall follow, so submit to the
purifying processes of reason as to take the character
of exact history.
—Plutarch, *Lives: Theseus*

THIS is the first study, so far as I am aware, to apply modern
statistical sampling techniques to probate records in order to
analyze American colonial wealth patterns. I believe it is also the first
to attempt to analyze such data by age class and the first to fit
American colonial wealth data into the conceptual framework and
categories of our present-day wealth analysis.

Although a wealth estimate for one time and place can stand on
its own feet, it gains in interest and value when and if it can be compared with other somewhat similar estimates for the same place at
other times, or with those for other places at the same time. This
study tests a method that can be replicated for other times and places.

The more nearly comparable the methods used to estimate amounts and composition of capital at various benchmark points in time, the narrower should be the area of unknowns with which economic historians must wrestle in formulating hypotheses concerning growth rates in the "statistical dark age" prior to 1840.[1]

The reader concerned only with results will find them beginning with chapter 3. Others may wonder how wealth of the dying can inform us about that of the living, and whether a small sample is adequate for the job. I attempt in this note and in appendix A to answer these questions affirmatively in nontechnical jargon in the hope that this will add depth and focus to the interpretation of my results. At the same time, I feel an obligation to point to frailties in some parts of the estimates that arise for a variety of reasons. Among them are such facts of life as that historical records are not always preserved with the orderly perfection the statistician would prefer. Those preserved are not always complete. Records made for purposes quite different from our present interest do not fully answer our questions at some crucial points. Probate records do not tell us the wealth of nonprobates. I faced many questions for whose answers there was no precedent and for which alternative options were frequently open. Yet, sampling experts recognize the complexities of the real world and are prepared to make some controlled compromises. I kept in touch with my consultants at each stage from initial sample design to numbers of surviving cases found, and to proper final weights. With their help at important points, I believe I made the best possible decisions in light of the practical difficulties encountered and the desired end result.

Although I did not succeed in getting what is known as an automatically self-weighting unbiased sample, my statistical advisers and I believe that, through the use of weights, discussed in appendix A, I still have the end result of an unbiased sample[2] of probate inventories. Beyond the inventories lie still other practical obstacles that I believe I surmounted in ways calculated to further the main purposes of the study and minimize its frailties. The latter stem chiefly from assumptions required to account for wealth of nonprobates and from estimating from related data the real estate assets and financial liabilities of probates whose records did not contain this information. I believe the reader who is candidly informed of their nature can better interpret my results and judge their acceptability for some specific purposes he may have in mind. I am also aware that continuing research, as the recent burgeoning interest in colonial demography illustrates, may yield new data on some aspects, e.g., on death rates or the age structure of the living population, the use of which might somewhat alter my findings. It is with the possibility in mind of alternate results under some alternate assumptions that I have deposited the computer tape of my sample observations at the University of Michigan, deposited my files of decedent data at the Newberry Library, and detailed my methods more fully in *American Colonial Wealth,* two editions, 1977, 1978. For the reader who does not have access to that work or does not wish its detail, I sketch these matters partly in the pages that follow, and partly in appendix A.

BASIS OF WEALTH ESTIMATES: THE SAMPLE OF INVENTORIES

The key to this entire study is the use of a small, rigorously selected, statistical sample of historical records. The elements selected, that is, the sample cases, are probate inventories of people who died two hundred years ago. I call them "sample decedents."[3] I used a probability sample[4] to select them randomly from the universe of probate inventories in the thirteen colonies. The inventories are preserved to this day, mainly in county courthouses and state archives. The inventories, together with supplementary data[5] on land and financial liabilities of the sample decedents, are the basis of more extended estimates of the wealth of the living population in 1774. The estimates for the middle colonies of Pennsylvania, New Jersey, and Delaware are based on a small sample first reported on in Jones (1970). Those for New England, New York, and the South are based on a subsequent drawing of congruent small samples.

The study can be likened to a survey such as the Gallup poll, or to the U.S. Census Bureau's monthly survey of households, the reliance being placed on sworn valuations of the property of the sample decedents rather than on answers to a questionnaire. The total sample, shown in table 1, consists of 919 cases from 21 counties (or groups of counties in the South and in New York),[6] drawn from all the counties in existence in 1774 in all thirteen colonies. The counties were arranged in sample frames in such a way that ran-

Table 1
Sample

Thirteen Colonies, Region, Province	County or Group of Counties, Number of Cases		Total
Thirteen Colonies			919
New England, total			381
Conn.	Litchfield	31	
,,	New Haven	37	
Mass.	Essex	102	
,,	Hampshire	27	
,,	Plymouth	35	
,,	Suffolk	100	
,,	Worcester	49	
New York, any county,	Total		23
N.Y.	Albany 1, Ulster 1, New York City 6,		
,,	Dutchess 3, Kings 2, Orange 1,		
,,	Westchester 6, County not stated 3	23	
Middle Colonies of Pennsylvania, New Jersey, Delaware, total			217
Pa.	Northampton	21	
,,	Westmoreland	7	
,,	Philadelphia	135	
N.J.	Burlington	25	
Del.	Kent	29	
South, total			298
Md.	Queen Anne's	38	
,,	Anne Arundel	27	
Va.	Charlotte 10, Halifax 15	25	
,,	Southampton 11, Brunswick 9,		
,,	Mecklenburg 3	23	
,,	Chesterfield 16, Fairfax 6,		
,,	Spotsylvania 8	30	
N.C.	Halifax	39	
,,	Orange	32	
S.C.	Charleston District	84	

SOURCE: Original sample for this study. See *American Colonial Wealth*, table 5.7 and, for complete sampling frame, its tables 5.2 through 5.6.

NOTE: Each county or group of counties was drawn to represent a stratum of approximately 20,000 living white "wealthholders." In the case of New York, data were desired from two counties (see second paragraph of note 6) representing two strata totaling 41,575 white "wealthholders." For the South, a post-weighting of Charleston District, discussed in part 2 of appendix A, limits the representativeness I attribute to its cluster of probate inventories. No counties from Maine (which was a district of Massachusetts in 1774), New Hampshire, Rhode Island, or Georgia were drawn into the sample, but each county in those areas had its due chance to be drawn. It just happened that the luck of the draw did not bring them in.

domly drawn numbers could determine which counties be chosen, when each had a chance to be drawn proportionate to the best proxy[7] for its number of probate inventories. One county (or group of counties in the South) was chosen by random number from a stratum[8] of approximately 20,000 living white "wealthholders."[9] Of the selected sample counties or county groups, seven were in New England, six in the Middle Colonies,[10] and eight in the South. This distribution is in proportion to the numbers of living white "wealthholders" in the respective regions. Each county or county group in the sample yields a cluster of probate inventories.[11]

REASONS FOR A SMALL UNBIASED SAMPLE

Cost, in time as well as money, is a strong reason for taking a sample rather than making a complete count or census of every probated inventory. But it is not the determining one. A second, and positive, reason for using a small sample is that we can get sufficiently reliable answers from it,[12] so long as it is unbiased. A third strong reason for opting for a small sample is the greater ease of processing the data. With fewer numbers of cases to be checked for additional documents and supplementary data, the data summarization is speedier and more flexible. The target sample size is determined by balancing considerations of cost, of both data gathering and data processing, against the number of regional and other breakdowns of the data envisaged and the degree of accuracy to be attained. At times the cost of obtaining additional cases does not improve accuracy sufficiently to justify it. It was the judgment of Mr. Cornfield regarding the first sampling, concurred in by Mr. Fienberg and Mr. Larntz for the second, that the objective of an unbiased sample must take precedence over increasing sample size. The latter was a desirable but secondary objective, should time and funds permit.[13]

If a sample is unbiased, its results can be generalized to the universe from which it is drawn, in this case all the probate inventories taken in 1774. Confidence intervals[14] can also be estimated that indicate approximately how certain we are of the findings. Of course, we can never be altogether certain unless we have all the elements in the universe (and even then we canot be 100 percent certain because of measurement errors, in this case the question of whether the inventories give the correct wealth values). To justify generalization, it is of the utmost importance that the sample be drawn in accord with principles of randomness, that is, the sample must be unbiased.[15] It is not necessary that elements from every part of the larger statistical population actually be drawn into the sample, but it is indispensable that they all have their proper chance to be drawn. A much larger sample, if it is biased because it fails to meet this test, does not yield correct results—i.e., ones which can properly be attributed to the entire statistical universe—and the difficulty can never be remedied by adding more cases, selected on the same basis.[16]

The great importance of this objective explains the care devoted to drawing sample counties and to obtaining the particular inventories from them strictly in accordance with choices dictated by the random numbers within the sample design. It also explains the care devoted to weighting procedures that subsequently became necessary to preserve the unbiased character of the sample of inventories. This point is elaborated in appendix A. Reduction of measurement error, that is, obtaining values of wealth as nearly correct as possible for each sample decedent, explains the care spent in obtaining supplementary data for gaps in the wealth information found in the probate inventories.

WEALTH OF THE LIVING

As to the wealth of the living, the small unbiased sample of probated inventories is only a first step. It yields us a reasonably close approximation to the true wealth of all decedents whose estates were probated in 1774 in each region and in the thirteen colonies combined. Additional steps transform the figures for decedents' wealth into estimates of the wealth of all living free wealthholders. These latter figures can be reduced to a per capita basis for the total population, free and nonfree, or for the total free population, or the total white population, the free adult male population, or other population variants.

The transformation from decedent wealth to wealth of the living involves parameters from outside the sample and is achieved by further weighting. Because I use parameters based on other than sample data, I cannot state confidence intervals for the final esti- mates[17] of wealth of the living. Their credibility depends both upon the unbiased decedent sample and upon the acceptability of the assumptions underlying the parameters.

More specific comments on how the sample was drawn and how I generalize from it to the wealth of the living are presented in parts one and two of appendix A.

DATA FROM OTHER SOURCES

My primary data source is inventories of all estates probated in each sample county in 1774,[18] with the exception of New York counties, which present a special problem discussed later. A few cases as early as 1773 or as late as 1775 were used to complete small clusters. Significant information needed for wealth analysis but not found in the probate inventories or in the subsequent accounts filed by the estate administrator or executor includes: (1) age at death, (2) frequently occupation, (3) valuation of inventory items in a substantial number of the inventories in the two sample counties of Orange and Halifax, North Carolina, (4) value of real estate in the Middle Colonies and in the South, (5) amount of financial liabilities[19] for those cases for which no estate account could be located.

To close these data gaps I undertook a variety of searches and analyses. Age at death was found by search of genealogists, case by case. When occupation was not indicated in the probate documents, the genealogists also kept an eye out for clues or evidence on this point as well. In the middle colonies they also searched tax lists, and in the South wills, deeds, and land grants for evidence of land ownership by sample decedents. Our debt to the hard-working genealogists is very great. The values obtained from tallies of estate sales were used for some cases of unvalued inventories in the two counties of Orange and Halifax, North Carolina.[20]

I consider further here only some highlights of these data sup- plementation matters that affect data interpretation in the chapters to follow. Some qualifications are particularly important with respect to figures for financial liabilities in all regions, and with respect to those for real estate in the South. Since financial liabilities are required to compute net worth, the qualifications regarding them also affect the interpretation of net worth.

Valuations in North Carolina

The problem of unvalued inventories in North Carolina was met by use of two-county means computed from tallied values from estate sales. These values are shown in table 1.6 and in greater detail in *American Colonial Wealth,* either edition (table 3.1). Such values were used, when there was no other figure, matching them as closely as possible to the wording of the unvalued items on the incomplete inventories. In 37 cases, there was both an account of sale and an unvalued inventory for the same estate. For these cases, the sale value from the decedent's own sale was the first choice and the two-county mean was used only for those of his unvalued items which did not appear on his sale. I observed that, in some instances where the same decedent had both an unvalued inventory and one or more accounts of sale, sometimes not all the inventoried items were sold and, conversely, some items were sold that had not originally appeared in the inventory.

These latter were included in the sample decedent's wealth totals, added to his originally inventoried items, with care exercised not to double-count the same item. For a few tag-end unvalued items not found in any North Carolina estate sale, I used the value for the nearest comparable item in the middle colonies of Pennsylvania, New Jersey, and Delaware, for which I had an itemized computer printout. I observed that many item values in those middle colonies seemed rather closely in line with North Carolina item values, and also that exchange rates with sterling were close in the two areas. (Sales of items omitted in inventories reinforces my opinion that the inventories, in all regions, may be rather understatements than overstatements of wealth, because of occasional omissions, oversights, etc. on the part of the appraisers or those who assembled the objects for their inspection.) On the whole, I conclude that my valuations of the unvalued items in North Carolina inventories are reasonably close to correct values and am satisfied to have the reader believe them approximately as accurate as the valuations for other counties. The basis of the valuations is given, however, for those readers who might be inclined to question the procedure.

Real Estate Valuations in the Middle Colonies and the South

New Jersey, Pennsylvania, Delaware Although most inventories in the Middle Colonies did not value real estate, it so happened that nine inventories in Northampton County, Pennsylvania and one in Philadelphia gave real estate values, and I used these. For the other cases in Pennsylvania, New Jersey, and Delaware, I determined valuation of real estate principally from tax lists. Wills and estate accounts also were scanned for evidence of land ownership, even though values thereof were not shown. Where decedents' names could be located on 1774 tax lists, the annual rental valuation implied by the real property assessment was capitalized at 6 percent and used as a minimum real estate value for the decedent. The valued observations, together with some personal and wealth characteristics of those owning the valued real estate, were used as inputs in a resort to a commonly used statistical technique known as regression analysis. The purpose is to fit equations to data for known variables, for each of which the analysis yields a coefficient; then the values of the unknown variables can be estimated by ascertaining, through the coefficients, their relationship to the known variables.

From the best equation, coefficients associated with the personal and wealth characteristics were derived. For the cases for which I had no information on real estate value, I nevertheless knew their personal and wealth characteristics, and sometimes knew they owned real estate. Using the regression coefficients for the known characteristics, I assigned the estimated values of real estate associated with them in the equation, including the possibility of zero value, to the appropriate cases for which I lacked direct evidence of value. I conclude that I have an approximation of the true real estate values of the sample decedents in the middle colonies of New Jersey, Pennsylvania, and Delaware, which is substantially better than assuming zero real estate value or average real estate value for all the real estate unknown cases. It was not possible, from information available, to separate value of land from value of buildings or other improvements.

South For the southern sample counties, I not only lacked information on real estate values from probate inventories, but there were no tax lists for 1774 or a few years prior thereto. Here, also, I was unwilling to assign, by default, zero real estate values to all cases. Therefore I requested the genealogists to search deed and land grant records for the names of the sample decedents. Additionally, I asked them to scan wills for evidence of land ownership, and in Maryland to search the Debt Books, which record quit rents paid to the colonial proprietors; there they sometimes found additional information in the exemplary files in the Maryland Hall of Records for testamentary papers, county court records, parish records, Chancery Court records, and "Tract Names." Although such search fairly often turned up information of land ownership, it was frequently in the form of number of acres without a value and often for a date considerably earlier than 1774. Deed data sometimes showed land sold or transferred as a gift, and hence no longer owned in 1774 by the decedent in question. Assistants under my supervision reviewed all real estate information assembled, case by case, for the southern sample, to eliminate land sold or no longer possessed in 1774. To determine the value in 1774 of the numbers of acres I believed a decedent then possessed, several steps were necessary. Where possible from the wording of individual land observations, assistants determined the geographical location of the land, whether on a lesser river, creek, or major river, coastal, marsh, or lower pine belt, "town lot," etc. From these descriptions, the land plots were located on maps so far as possible. When a value, for any date, of such a plot was known, this information was used. To increase the number of land/price observations, I had the genealogists draw additional deeds, following a carefully specified random procedure, from the same sample counties. These, with their dates, values, and locations,[21] were also used as inputs. In consultation with Kinley Larntz, and me, and occasionally with my colleagues at Washington University, Sharon De Sha worked out regression equations expressing relations of land price over time, taking account of location and other variables, for the South, province by province. The equation results were used to "predict" the most probable price per acre in 1774 of land of the kind that the decedent held in 1774. These prices are, of course, at best only approximations, but I believe reasonable and internally consistent ones, which accord with the scant external data on land prices we could find. Although sale prices reflect improvements on the land, we had insufficient information about the improvements to do other than treat the analysis as if it were simply price determination of "land."

The values in 1774 per acre of land of various kinds, that is, by location or types of crop grown, determined from the regression analysis, were finally multiplied, for each sample decedent in the South, by the number of such acres we figured, from our inspection of evidence, was held by a decedent in 1774 (unless we had some better positive information, as from a recent deed). The result is my estimate of the value of land he held at death. I may have missed some other land, especially if it was received by inheritance or in other ways not recorded.

I assigned zero land values to all the remaining southern sample decedents for whom we found no positive evidence of land ownership. That is, if I had no estimate of number of acres a decedent owned in 1774, I treated him as having zero land value.[22] Hence there are, in the southern sample, a large number of cases of zero land values, in default of better data. I consider it likely that the true figures for percentage of southern "probate-type" wealthholders owning land may be considerably higher than the 59 percent I found, compared with around 80 percent in the North. Correspondingly, I may have only a lower limit on the probable aggregate value of land held by those in the sample in the South. This is a very important measurement limitation that I ask the reader to bear in mind when, in subsequent chapters, he compares the proportions of landowners and of wealth in real estate in the various regions.

Determination of Financial Liabilities

I was able to locate estate accounts, or in some cases "lists of debts," which yield data on financial liabilities, for only a fraction of the sample decedents. The numbers were 170 out of 381 sample cases in New England, 101 of the 217 middle colonies' cases in Pennsylvania, New Jersey, and Delaware, 9 of the 23 New York cases, and in the South for the following numbers of sample cases: Maryland, 39 out of 65; Virginia, 11 out of 78; North Carolina, 12 out of 71; South Carolina, 1 out of 84. For the South as a whole, the number is 63 out of 298. Most historians dealing with probate inventories have ignored debts owed[23] even for the cases for which the information was available from accounts. This is understandable, because merely locating the accounts requires additional search. I, however, summarized the appropriate totals from the available accounts, and again, as in the case of real estate information, sought to utilize the known data to give a "predicted" estimate for each of the cases for which the liabilities figure is completely lacking.

Northern Regions   For the northern regions, Sharon De Sha was able to calculate useful and statistically significant regression equations, following the same general principles as for the middle colonies' real estate regression, for which I am indebted to Fredric Raines. Details are presented in *American Colonial Wealth,* either edition, pages 1756–59. Using the coefficients from these regressions, I "predicted" the most probable financial liabilities for the liabilities-unknown cases, including the possibility of zero financial liabilities, that is, that the decedent owed no debts at his death. For the middle colonies of New Jersey, Pennsylvania, Delaware, the equation accepted yielded coefficients related to some personal and wealth characteristics of the decedent. Their use, to "predict" financial liabilities, gave some amount of financial liability for 81 of the 116 liabilities-unknown cases, and found zero financial liabilities for 35 of them.

For New England, the personal characteristics of the liabilities-known cases explain so little of the variance of the financial liabilities that they were not found useful in the equation. The equation accepted as best for New England "predicts" or estimates liabilities for the unknown cases as a function of simply their holdings of financial assets, real estate, and portable physical wealth. This equation gave some, even though sometimes very small, financial liabilities to all but four of the liabilities-unknown New England sample cases, one each in Plymouth and Worcester counties and two in Suffolk County.

For New York, the special procedure followed, analogous to that used to estimate real estate for the unknown cases there, gave some liabilities for each of the 14 New York cases of unknown liabilities. None of these was calculated as zero liability.

South   For the South, no satisfactory regression equation for financial liabilities could be developed. Experiments with possible equations, based on the 63 cases of known financial liabilities, were disappointing. No acceptable equation involving more than one variable could be developed from the few cases. That is, of the various personal and wealth characteristics regressed, only one, namely portable physical wealth, showed a significant relationship to size of financial liabilities. Portable physical wealth had, in work previously completed, proved to be a highly significant variable in the financial liabilities equations developed for the middle colonies and for New England. My best estimate of financial liabilities for the southern decedents with unknown liabilities is accordingly a function of only their portable physical wealth. From the 63 decedent cases with known liabilities in the South, I found that such decedents, on average, had liabilities in amount equal to 22 percent of their portable physical wealth, and this is the basis of my estimate for all the liabilities-unknown cases there. Its value was available for every case in the South from the probate inventory. Accordingly, I estimate that all the southern sample decedents have some liabilities values, albeit small values in many cases. The procedure gives an estimate of fairly large liabilities for the cases with high portable wealth assets, a relationship that is consistent with credit extension to credit-worthy borrowers. Yet, since no account is taken in the South of landholding as a variable affecting liabilities, the method followed may understate the financial liabilities of some large holders. The procedure gives no cases of zero financial liabilities in the South and consequently almost surely overstates the percentage of sample decedents there who were indebted. Available data, however, permitted no further refinement.

Financial Liabilities and Net Worth

In summary, my estimates of financial liabilities may be somewhat on the high side for New England, New York, and the South, since some liabilities are assigned in New England to virtually all, and in New York and in the South to all the liabilities-unknown cases. I place greatest reliance in the estimate of financial liabilities for the middle colonies, and am least satisfied with those for the South.

This ranking is repeated in my evaluation of the reliability of my net worth figures by region, since net worth is computed as the sum of total physical wealth plus financial assets minus financial liabilities. In New England, the subtraction for liabilities, including estimates for the liabilities-unknown cases, brings it to the position shown in chapter 5 of poorest in net worth among all the regions, as it is also in total physical wealth. Its relative poverty in physical wealth is shown in chapter 4, and that figure is firm, since for New England both land and portable physical wealth, the two principal components of total physical wealth, are based on figures from the probate inventories. However, even if I had cut the estimates of their financial liabilities by as much as half, the average net worth of New England's sample decedents would still have been markedly below that of the Middle Colonies and very far below that of the South.

Admittedly, the reeds we lean upon are slender, and the exact amounts subtracted as financial liabilities for the cases of liabilities-unknown in each region could have been greater or less under alternative procedures. However, I believe the ones finally used, after careful consideration of various possibilities, are the most reasonable approximations to the truth presently available to us. I am satisfied that these estimates are better than having treated all the liabilities-unknown cases as having zero liabilities. We can be sure that failure to subtract some reasonable amounts for debts probably owed would yield too high a net worth figure for a large proportion of the cases for which accounts could not be located. This failure would be particularly indefensible in the South, where the highest total physical wealth was found, but where very few accounts could be located. It follows from the foregoing discussion that, despite the tremendous efforts made in this study to estimate financial liabilities, the problems of their estimation remain sufficiently great that chief reliance should probably be placed on the measure of total physical wealth rather than of net worth. Hence I present, in chapter 6, size distributions by total physical wealth, as well as by the more interesting but less reliable net worth.

NEW YORK HYBRID WEALTH PATTERN

Before we can leave the subject of data gaps, I must mention the thorny problem of severe data sparsity for New York, which required very careful consideration. As shown in table 1 and note 6, after extended search for all counties in the province, I could locate only 23 decedent cases, though my target was a total of two clusters, or at least 50 cases, to represent over 40,000 living white "wealthholders." This is a case of failure of inventories to survive. The 23 cases are insufficient to represent all of New York, the more so since they showed wealth unusually high in comparison with the results found in the other middle colonies and in New England.[24] Accordingly, it does not appear reasonable to attribute such high wealth to the probate inventories for New York that failed to survive. The solution adopted was to create a New York hybrid wealth pattern.[25] This is used only for incorporation with results from the other middle colonies to get a regional Middle Colonies' estimate for purposes of chapters 3, 4, and 5 in the present volume, and incorporated in the thirteen colonies' results in both the present volume and *American Colonial Wealth*, in order to reach my best estimate from all available data.

The hybrid New York pattern uses the 23 cases, but with a weight of only 10 percent, combined with the pattern for the other middle colonies, given a weight of 60 percent, and that of New England, given a weight of 30 percent. The values for this pattern are found in *American Colonial Wealth*, either edition, table 7.11.

To estimate land and financial liabilities information not found in the probate inventories or estate accounts of the 23 cases, Sharon De Sha developed coefficients based one-third on New England data and two-thirds on other middle colonies' data. Details are stated in *American Colonial Wealth*, either edition, pp. 1754–56, 1759.

The New York hybrid results are included in all tables for the thirteen colonies as a whole, both in this volume and in *American Colonial Wealth*. They are included in this volume in all tables for the "Middle Colonies," except, as in some tables in chapters 5, 6, and 7, where the omission is indicated by column headings or notes. In the text of the present volume, when I refer to the "middle colonies," without initial capital letters, I mean only New Jersey, Pennsylvania, and Delaware, without the New York hybrid. When I speak of the "Middle Colonies"[26] in capital letters, I mean the combination of these colonies plus the New York hybrid pattern.

INTERPRETATION OF DATA AND INTERNAL CONSISTENCY

The value of these wealth estimate depends, in the most fundamental sense, upon the validity of my sample design and of the weights I was obliged to assign the data in my effort to achieve the closest possible approximation between the sample and the larger statistical universe that it represents. At one level, weighting was essential in order to obtain unbiased regional estimates of the wealth of probated decedents. At other levels, it was required in order to expand the data beyond the bounds of the decedent sample to estimates of the wealth of living free wealthholders. Finally, I saw no way to avoid the need for a post-weighting of data for the Charleston District to bring results for the South into conformity with independent data on the numbers of blacks in the South.

Decisions at every level were complex and difficult, as will be clear from the further discussion of these matters in appendix A, and, in even greater detail, in *American Colonial Wealth*. Yet it has been my persistent effort to reach the best and most reasonable wealth estimates obtainable from an unbiased sample of probate inventories, with the introduction of the minimum of additional assumptions and supplementary data. Not many independent checks with outside data are available to prove this. One, the check on number of blacks, forced the development of the Variant Two weights for the South discussed in appendix A.

For other wealth values, at various places in ensuing chapters, the reader will see evidence of the convincing internal consistency of the wealth patterns and the character of the regional differences observed, which accord very well with recent scholarly work on foreign trade (Shepherd and Walton 1972), as well as with classic studies of colonial agriculture. I believe the high degree of internal consistency and congruence with such external evidence as we have, as well as the reasonableness of the regional comparisons, indicate that this small sample, after my post-weighting adjustments, gives us a rather close approximation to the true wealth picture of the thirteen colonies.

Wealth of a Nation to Be

CHAPTER ONE

Measures of Wealth

There are no colonies of which the progress has been
more rapid than that of the English in
North America. Plenty of good land, and liberty to manage
their affairs their own way, seem to be the two
great causes of the prosperity.

—Adam Smith[1]

THAT the American colonists lived well for their times has been
asserted by many historians on the basis of impressionistic data.
Others have inferred scant margins above simple subsistence needs
for many, and that wealth accumulation came only painfully and
slowly. Hard data to confirm statements such as Adam Smith's or
more pessimistic views have been lacking. It is just such information
that this study attempts to provide. What was the total wealth of the
thirteen colonies on the eve of the Revolution, approximately in the
year 1774, and what was per capita wealth? Did per capita wealth
vary by region? What were the characteristics of the wealthholders?
Did the composition and distribution of wealth vary by region? I cannot hope to answer these questions definitively, but the estimates
offered here may narrow the bounds of our ignorance and supply
data useful to others attempting more precise answers. Some reasons
for undertaking such an investigation have been well stated by Stuart
Bruchey:

Everyone wants to know what was the wealth of the American people on the
eve of the Revolution. If average levels were low, it follows that the rate of
economic growth must have been slow indeed for a century and a half. In
that case, scholarly inquiry should turn, and quite properly, to an examina-

tion not only of economic and social conditions unfavorable to productivity advance but also to the possibility of British imperial constraint upon opportunities for individual betterment. Furthermore, post-colonial growth would be seen as somewhat more rapid because of the relatively low level extant at the time of the Revolution. If, on the other hand, average levels of well-being appeared quite favorable in 1774 a different focus upon both previous and subsequent activity would be in order. The difficulty has been that we have known too little to speak in terms of averages. Instead, impressions have ranged from those founded on the existence of urban almshouses to those suggested by increasing trade and population and evidence of affluence associated with the life styles of the landed and maritime gentry. Neither basis is generalizable. What we have needed is information derived from a carefully-drawn sample that permits legitimate inferences about the population as a whole.[2]

My estimates are based on an unbiased statistical sample drawn from probate inventories in the thirteen colonies in the year 1774. Of course, not everyone who died had his estate inventoried. How this is taken into account, how the sample was drawn, and other technical questions are discussed in an appendix on techniques (appendix A). That appendix also states the assumptions and procedures required to move from a sample of probate inventories to generalized estimates concerning all possible living wealthholders. The data permit estimates of the total wealth of the living population of the thirteen colonies, as a whole and by regional groupings. They afford a basis for comparative evaluations of the wealth held by different segments of society and for a testing of the notion sometimes advanced that the society was egalitarian. Regional variations in wealthholding are highly suggestive of different rates of economic development, and the same is true of urban and rural sectors. In addition, the rich detail in the probate inventories throws much light on comparative life-styles.[3]

I have selected 1774 as the base year for these estimates for several reasons. In that year wholesale prices (measured either by the Warren and Pearson or the Bezanson index) were at about the average level for the preceding decade, not yet reflecting wartime price increases. Population estimates, county by county, are available for about that date. Detailed tax data for that year exist in manuscript for Philadelphia County, which contained the largest city in the colonies; for Burlington County, New Jersey; and for many towns in Essex County, Massachusetts. The last year of the colonial period makes a reasonably good benchmark for comparison with earlier colonial dates and with economic estimates for some dates in the nineteenth[4] and twentieth[5] centuries.

POSSIBLE DATA SOURCES

Clues to wealth of the colonists may be sought in a variety of sources. Some property tax lists[6] are available, as are reports of Provincial Governors to the lords of the Council for Trade and Plantations in London, answering queries as to the number of inhabitants[7] and the nature of commodities produced. Export records[8] are preserved in reports of Inspectors General in the Public Records Office at London. Probate inventories,[9] as well as abstracts of wills, histories of wages and prices or of agriculture and manufacture, contemporary newspaper advertisements, account books, diaries, travelers' observations, all provide some indications of wealth.[10]

While such sources have their advantages, these are outweighed by their limitations.[11] None except the probate inventories give detailed, sworn wealth appraisals, person by person. None of the other sources is available year by year and county by county. The near-universal availability of probate inventories in all counties permits the designing of the unbiased sample described in appendix A in such a way as to yield a consistent across-the-board examination of private wealth in all the colonies at a single date. The completeness of wealth itemization in each inventory makes it possible to summarize the kinds of wealth held by each deceased person included in the study (hereafter called a "sample decedent"). Because the inventories contribute so basically to my wealth estimates, something should be said of their origin and character.

PROBATE INVENTORIES AND OTHER PROBATE DOCUMENTS

Detailed probate inventories of the personal property owned at time of death have a long history. They were made in England and Europe at least as far back as the twelfth century, and in Brazil and other Latin American countries at least as early as the eighteenth.[12] They are still made in the United States today for probate courts. In colonial America, there were no inheritance, gift, or estate taxes, although estate administration costs included court fees.

A principal reason for filing inventories of assets with the court, so far as I can determine, was to protect creditors and heirs by preventing assets from being dissipated before claims were settled. In New England, a second reason was to establish clear land titles. There, a probate court record generally had to be produced when inherited land was sold, and an executor or administrator had to obtain court approval to sell land if personal estate assets were not large enough to settle debts. In the Middle Colonies and in the South, however, land titles appear to have passed validly by inheritance without any entry in probate inventories. Wills were used in the South to provide for equal division of land among sons—at least in Virginia, where primogeniture in case of intestacy still prevailed until after the Revolution. An additional reason for making a will in the South, I believe, was to insure the passing on of Negroes to designated heirs. In the Middle Colonies and New England, where a double portion for the eldest son still tended to prevail in case of intestacy, wills were filed to alter that proportion. However, in all regions whether or not the deceased left a valid will, estate inventories were made. Hence the cases included in this study are not limited to testate cases, with wills; they include a large proportion of intestate cases. Nor were probate inventories limited to the well-to-do; the sample includes many cases where possessions are very scanty, others of middling wealth, and still others of the rich.

Exact probate procedures varied slightly in different provinces and different courts, but in general the following steps were taken that yielded the documents on which this study is based.[13] Usually within a few days or weeks after a death, but occasionally after a much longer interval, one or more persons who had known the deceased appeared in court and exhibited the will, or if there was no will testified that the deceased had indeed died. The person(s) who appeared was frequently the widow, son, or other heir or a relative. Often this person was named in the will as executor or executrix; sometimes he or she was a principal creditor. The court, after the will was "proved"—found valid—formally appointed the executor(s), sometimes in a document called "letter testamentary." When there was no will, but the fact of death had been established, and also in cases where the named executor or executrix had declined to serve, the court appointed an estate administrator or administratrix in a "letter of administration" or in a simple court order. The executor/ administrator was usually required to furnish bond for the faithful performance of duty, and sometimes, as in many of the sample cases in Connecticut, a document survives showing the amount of the bond required and the duties to be performed. The court further, usually at the same time it named the executor/administrator, appointed three appraisers (one or more of whom might also have been named executor/administrator) and charged them to make and bring to the court, in from thirty to usually not more than ninety days, a true and perfect inventory of all the "goods and chattels, rights and credits" of the deceased. The appraisers personally visited the deceased's dwelling place and listed, usually in great detail, although sometimes with regrettable lumping, the portable wealth, and gave each listed item an appraised value. Both physical and financial assets were enumerated; the latter might include cash and credit claims held against others in such forms as bonds, notes, or "book accounts." Only in New England was land also listed and appraised. The appraisers signed the probate inventory, often before witnesses, and then exhibited[14] it in court, swearing that it was true and correct to the best of their knowledge and belief. In some counties, notably in Maryland, the same names appear as appraisers for various estates, which suggests that by 1774 there may have been, at least in some localities, a group of near-professional appraisers used regularly by the courts.

That the appraised values in the probate inventories were neither perfunctory nor conventional is shown by their meticulous variation from inventory to inventory. That they were not greatly understated, as might be suspected if tax avoidance were involved, is apparent from the closeness with which they approximate actual sales values in those cases where the goods were subsequently auctioned at an advertised "publick vendue" and an account of the sale survives as an additional probate document presented in court. Furthermore, the subsequent account of an estate executor/administrator sometimes carries such an entry as "what the goods sold for more than appraised" or "what the goods sold for less than appraised," and the differences between appraisal and sales values were usually small. No reason appears for suspecting that values were overstated. If anything, the inventory total may, at times, be on the low side, because of a few omissions of items overlooked, considered not worth the bother of listing, or perhaps already taken by heirs. That there were such occasional omissions is sometimes indicated in a subsequent "additional inventory" filed with the court or in items so reported in the account of the estate executor/administrator. Where such additions were reported for the cases in the sample, they have been included in the wealth figures of this book.

For many estates there are no probate documents beyond the inventory (and the will if one was made). For some, however, one or more accounts were subsequently presented to the court and sworn to by the executor(s)/administrator(s). These reported, besides the total value shown in the inventory, any additional assets found or debts owed to the deceased that had been or were to be collected by the executor/administrator. As offsetting items, they reported payments made to creditors, by name with receipt exhibited, for debts owed by the deceased, as well as payment of taxes or "rates" the decedent had owed. In some cases a new administrator *de bonis non* was appointed, when a previous executor/administrator had failed to complete the job. In such cases, which are fairly rare and chiefly in New England, there might be a second and later "inventory d.b.n,"[15] and there might be further accounts by the new administrator. Sometimes the final estate account was not made until many years after the death, though most commonly accounts were made within a year or two. Occasionally they were made within a few months after the inventory or filed at the same time.

These accounts furnish the data used in this study for the financial liabilities of the sample decedent at the time of death or just prior to the last illness. The correct items must be selected discerningly from these handwritten accounts, for it would be inappropriate to include such items as costs of last illness, of estate administration, of bequests to relatives or maintenance of dependents after the deceased's death, costs of running his farm or business, or interest charges against him that had accrued after his death. The proper components of "financial liabilities" are sums paid to the deceased's creditors or still owed them at the date of the account. I have extracted these figures from the accounts available.

In cases for which we find no account of the estate executor/ administrator or any other "list of debts owed by the estate," a question arises. Did the deceased owe nothing? Or did he owe some debt whose amount is unknown to the researcher today? I have assumed the latter. My method of inferring a plausible amount of debt owed by the deceased, which probably comes closer to the truth than assuming he had zero debt, is explained in the Note on Method. An estimate of liabilities is required to compute the net worth for each decedent and, from these figures, the most meaningful distribution of wealth.

For some cases, particularly in North Carolina, there exists no probate inventory, but there is an "account of sale" of goods at public auction. In those cases the account of sale has been used as the inventory of wealth. Also, quite a number of the inventories, found for the North Carolina sample decedents merely listed such items as "six hogs" or "eighty bushels of corn" without giving a value for them. To solve this problem, an average price was calculated from the fairly numerous sales in Orange and Halifax counties, item by item. That mean value was then used to assign values to unvalued inventory entries.

All the documents I have mentioned were presented in courts, held sometimes monthly, sometimes quarterly or semiannually, in various county or district seats. In New England they were called Court of Probate and Insolvency, or sometimes just Probate Court. In New York the term was Surrogate Court. In Pennsylvania, New Jersey, and Delaware it was the Orphans' Court. In Maryland in 1774 the Prerogative Court was a central agency and the Commissary General had deputies in the counties.[16] In Virginia and in North and South Carolina it was simply called the Court or General Court or sometimes Inferior Court of the respective county or district. These courts were presided over by a judge, and documents were countersigned as sworn to before the judge, or sometimes before a clerk of the court or a "Register of Probate" in New England and Pennsylvania, or before the Deputy Commissary General in Maryland counties.

A number of other probate documents of tangential interest to an estimation of wealth are sometimes encountered, especially in the New England and Pennsylvania county courthouses, where all papers for one estate are gathered in one file. These include, but only in New England, warrants appointing Insolvency Commissioners when it appeared that assets were insufficient to maintain the widow and orphans and pay debts, and occasionally a report of the Insolvency

Commissioners recommending that creditors be paid on a reduced scale. There are occasional documents referring to premarital property agreements and to widow's dower rights. Sometimes documents survive concerning litigation. Some petitions to court were made in New England for permission to sell land from an estate— authorized only if movable assets were insufficient to meet obligations. For some cases in New England there are documents showing divisions or final allotments of land to heirs.

A great merit of the probate inventories as a source of information about wealth for the colonial economy, in a pre-census era, is that they clearly show the accumulated possessions and holdings. These include not only items purchased in a market but also many produced within the household, or received in kind as a result of barter or "country pay."

MONEY VALUATIONS AND EQUIVALENTS

Values in the probate inventories are stated in pounds, shillings, and pence of the particular colony or province. The local circulating medium often consisted of notes or "bills" of the provincial government.[17] They were backed in most cases by the taxing power of the provincial government. In the absence of ready money, many transactions were settled by commodity exchange, or simply by "book accounts"—that is, by credit and debit entries—once again valued in pounds, shillings, and pence of the particular colony. Personally signed notes, bearing interest, were also used as payments. Coinage within the colonies was not allowed by the crown in 1774, and coins, especially British coins, were usually in short supply. Some Spanish, Portuguese, Dutch, and other foreign coins appear in the sample probate inventories, and some inventories, especially in Maryland, indicate the value of the local currency in terms of the number of shillings and pence to the Spanish dollar. I have converted the entries in all the sample inventories to pounds sterling, the common denominator for all colonial monies in this study. The conversion rates I have used are set forth in table 1.1.

The reader may still wish to know how much a 1774 pound sterling is worth in today's money. The question is deceptively simple. The route to an answer is complex and involves philosophical

Table 1.1
Exchange Rates by Colony, 1774

	Mass. *Conn.*	*N.Y.*	*Pa.* *N.J.* *Del.*	*Va.*	*Md.*	*N.C.*	*S.C.*
British pound sterling	1.00	1.00	1.00	1.00	1.00	1.00	1.00
Value of one pound sterling in local pounds	1.33	1.79	1.70	1.32	1.67[a]	1.77[b]	7.00
Value of one local pound in pounds sterling	0.750	0.559	0.588	0.758	0.599	0.565	0.143
Local shillings and pence per Spanish dollar	6	8	7/6	5/8	7/6	8	32/8

SOURCE: *American Colonial Wealth*, table 3.3.

[a] For Maryland "common" money, the money of ordinary transactions, in which estate accounts were usually stated. Maryland "current" money, used for inventory valuations, exchanged at 1.33 or 0.750.

[b] For "North Carolina money," used for ordinary transactions and for inventory valuations. For North Carolina "proclamation money," in which many land deed values were stated, I used an exchange rate of 1.33 or 0.750.

questions about the meaning to be attached to very long-term price indexes.[18] I have given in table 1.2 what seems to me the most sensible estimate of the purchasing power of a 1774 pound sterling at various other dates.

For the modern reader to get some "feel" of relative prices, that is, of what money would buy in 1774, I have given some selected, rather typical values of items from probate inventories in several regions. The items shown in tables 1.3 through 1.7 convey not only some sense of relative values but also a feeling for the kinds of eighteenth-century tools, equipment, livestock, crops, apparel, house furnishings, and miscellaneous items that comprised the material levels of living of the colonists and their productive assets. Many of the values are surprisingly in line with prices today, but the relationships portray 1774 relative prices. Quality range is suggested by a few instances of several actual values from different inventories for the same item.

In table 1.3, we see the items that went to the widow Gordon at the sale of the personal estate of a low-wealth farmer in Burlington County, New Jersey. Interestingly, the items she got come to just about one-third of the value of all items sold.[19] The values, which in present dollars may appear low, reflect second-hand sale prices from

Table 1.2
Price Trends, 1774–1978
U.S. Private Wealth

Year	Linked Index 1774 = 100	Linked Index 1976 = 100	Current Dollars Equal to £1 Sterling in 1774
1774	100.0	8.7	"4.15"
1792	110.0	9.5	4.56
1805	159.0	13.8	6.60
1850	95.6	8.3	3.97
1900	109.2	9.5	4.53
1929	220.9	19.2	9.17
1940	198.0	17.2	8.22
1950	411.6	35.8	17.08
1958	521.0	45.3	21.62
1960	546.0	47.4	22.66
1965	617.9	53.7	25.64
1967	665.8	57.8	27.63
1970	771.6	67.0	32.02
1972	859.6	74.7	35.67
1973	912.3	79.3	37.86
1974	997.4	86.6	41.39
1975	1,093.6	95.0	45.38
1976	*1,151.1*[a]	*100.0*	47.77 (47.84)[a]
1977	1.217.3	105.8	50.52
1978	1,307.5	113.6	54.26

SOURCE: Computed by the author, using for 1774 to 1805 the Warren and Pearson wholesale price index, for 1805 to 1929 the implicit private wealth price deflator of Raymond W. Goldsmith, from 1929 thru 1973 the price index of Dale W. Jorgenson for "total private domestic tangible wealth," after 1973 the implicit price deflator for the gross national product shown in the *Survey of Current Business* for July 1977 and June 1979. See full citations in *American Colonial Wealth*, table 3.5.

NOTE: The "$4.15" for 1774 is placed in quotation marks since the American dollar was not created until 1792. The $4.15 may be thought of as the number of dollars at 1774 prices which a pound sterling would have brought if the American dollar had then existed with the same gold content as the one of 1792.

To obtain equivalent dollars for intermediate years prior to 1929, one may use, as a proxy, the relationships found in *American Colonial Wealth,* table 3.6, based on the Warren and Pearson index to 1871 (ser. E-1 in *Historical Statistics,* 1960) and thereafter on the implicit deflator for the gross national product (ser. F-5). These would yield in the second column linked indexes of 116.2, 113.7, and 165.1 for 1840, 1860, and 1870 respectively, and values in the last column of $4.82, $4.72 and $6.85 respectively. On that basis, for 1914 the corresponding figures would be 143.9 and $5.97.

Though I have nothing better for the eighteenth century component than the Warren and Pearson index, based on prices in New York, it should be noted that this is a fairly flimsy index, which covered only between 11 and 19 items for the years 1740–82 and about 71 for the years 1783–96.

[a] In an earlier version of this table, based on preliminary figures for 1976 from the U.S. Department of Commerce, the values for that year in columns 2 and 4 were 1,152.7 and $47.84. These numbers, which differ trivially from the final ones in this table, were generally used in the translations to 1976 dollars in subsequent tables, figures, and text throughout the book.

Table 1.3
Appraised Values of Items of the Widow Martha Gordon
Burlington County, New Jersey, 1774

Item	In New Jersey Pounds, Shillings, and Pence			In Pounds Sterling and Decimal Parts Thereof	In Dollars of 1976 Purchasing Power
	£	*s*	*d*	£	$
Cow	6	0	1	3.53	168.88
Shoat		5	1	.15	7.18
Pork and barrel		5	1	.15	7.18
Small washing tub			7	.02	0.96
Loom	1	12	7	.96	45.93
Iron pot		5	3	.15	7.18
Iron pot			6	.01	0.48
Skillet		1	–	.03	1.44
Coffee pot		1	4	.04	1.91
2 Tea pots etc.			3	.01	0.48
4 Tea cups, 5 saucers			9	.02	0.96
2 Tea pots, bowl, cream jug		1	1	.03	1.44
Bed etc.	3	0	1	1.77	84.68
Bedstead cord		3	1	.09	4.31
Case of drawers etc., dressing table	1	–	–	.59	28.23
Table		3	3	.10	4.78
4 Chairs		7	7	.22	10.52
Total	13	7	7	7.87	376.54

Source: "Account of the Goods of William Gordon, Deceased, Sold this 2nd Day of May, 1774." New Jersey. Wills, Burlington County, 1773–74, pp. 9664–70. Decedent case 21007 in this study. Martha Gordon's name appears opposite these items in the account of sale of her husband's estate.

an estate whose total appraised value was only £16.2 sterling, or £27.5 in New Jersey pounds. There were, of course, other, higher-valued estates in the New Jersey sample with more expensive items. Table 1.4 shows values selected from various inventories in Plymouth, Massachusetts. There the majority were farmers; several were esquires or gentlemen, several were mariners, one a captain, and some were artisans. Most of the items in these inventories show somewhat higher values than corresponding items of the widow Gordon. In table 1.5 we see selected values from inventories of farmers in Northampton County, Pennsylvania, many of whom had German names and some of whom had substantial assets. Many of these values seem "reasonable" in present dollars and some are higher than the Plymouth values.

Table 1.4
Appraised Values of Some Individual Wealth Items
Plymouth County, Massachusetts, 1774

Item	In Massachusetts Pounds, Shillings, and Pence			In Pounds Sterling and Decimal Parts Thereof	In Dollars of 1976 Purchasing Power
	£	s	d	£	$
10 Bushels of oats		15	–	.56	26.79
Year old colt	3	–	–	2.25	107.64
Cow	4	–	–	3.00	143.52
Heifer	2	–	–	1.50	71.76
3 Calves	3	12	–	2.70	129.17
3 Swine	3	–	–	2.25	107.64
26 Gallons molasses	2	3	–	1.61	77.02
3 Pounds coffee		3	–	.11	5.26
Grindstone		1	4	.05	2.39
Loom and tackling	2	13	4	2.00	95.68
Loom		16	–	.60	28.70
3 Old barrels		3	–	.11	5.26
Meat tub		6	–	.23	11.00
Bread trough		1	–	.04	1.91
One-third part of a schooner	66	–	–	49.50	2,368.08
A quarter of a sloop	53	6	8	40.00	1,913.60
Gun		12	–	.45	21.53
Clock	4	16	–	3.60	172.22
Skillet		1	–	.04	1.91
Brass kettle		12	–	.45	21.53
Pr. andirons		6	–	.23	11.00
Pr. steelyards		3	–	.11	5.26
Brass kettle		12	–	.45	21.53
6 Silver teaspoons		8	–	.30	14.35
Silver spoon		7	4	.28	13.40
Best bed and furniture	5	–	–	3.75	179.40
Bed	1	–	–	.75	35.88
New blanket		10	8	.40	19.14
Chest of drawers		12	–	.45	21.53
Maple desk		8	–	.30	14.35
11 Chairs	1	2	8	.85	40.66
6 Common chairs		8	–	.30	14.35
Round about chair		3	4	.13	6.22
Small looking glass		5	–	.19	9.09
Bible		2	8	.10	4.78
Case of razors		2	–	.08	3.83
Watch	3	6	–	2.48	118.64
Fine shirt		6	–	.23	11.00
Woolen shirt		2	–	.08	3.83
2 Pr. shoes		4	–	.15	7.18
25 Skeins of tow yarn		5	–	.19	9.09

SOURCE: Selected from sample inventories in Plymouth.

Tables 1.6 and 1.7 introduce the South. The North Carolina figures are mean values from actual sales from 47 estates of farmers in Halifax and Orange counties. The South Carolina figures are from probate inventories in the Charleston District, outstandingly the richest component of our entire sample. Here we have predominantly farmers and planters, but also esquires, gentlemen, lawyers, merchants, and a sprinkling of mariners and artisans. Over four-fifths of the Charleston District sample decedents held slaves, a few of them large numbers of slaves. Some, as can be seen from the table, had fine furniture and apparel or other consumers' goods of considerable value. Further fascinating details on many items that can illuminate different facets of colonial history, depending on the focus of interest of the scanner, can be found in *American Colonial Wealth* (section II), where all the sample inventories are reproduced verbatim.

The colonial items and their appraised values are quite similar to ones described in probate records from Cambridgeshire, England some thirty-five years earlier. This can be seen from the illustrative valuations in table 1.8 for 1739, the nearest date for which we have comparable English data. Since the general price level in Britain rose relatively little between these years,[20] direct comparisons would seem to be in order, after allowance is made for differences in exchange rates of colonial money to sterling. Most of the differences seem hardly more than those to be expected between one inventory and another in the condition or quality of the particular items appraised. There are, of course, no slaves in the Cambridge inventories.

The most notable difference we find in appraised values between the English and colonial inventories is the much higher values of wheat and rye crops per acre in England. The average value of an acre of wheat (i.e., the value of the crop standing in the field) in five of the Cambridge inventories was £2.50 sterling, compared with a typical example of only £0.65 sterling in Pennsylvania in 1774, shown in table 1.5. For an acre of rye, the value in one Cambridge-shire inventory was £1.50 sterling, compared with only £0.29 in Pennsylvania in 1774. These differences can be explained partly by higher prices per bushel in England, where the corn laws were in effect. Wheat, for instance, was around £0.22 to £0.25 sterling per bushel in 1739 and £0.32 to £0.35 in 1774 in England,[21] compared with £0.15 in Pennsylvania and £0.18 in North Carolina, as shown in tables 1.5 and 1.6. The rest of the difference probably could be

Table 1.5
Appraised Values of Some Individual Wealth Items
Northampton County, Pennsylvania, 1774

Item	In Pennsylvania Pounds, Shillings, and Pence			In Pounds Sterling and Decimal Parts Thereof	In Dollars of 1976 Purchasing Power
	£	s	d	£	$
Bushel of wheat		5	–	.15	7.18
Acre of wheat	1	2	–	.65	31.10
Bushel of rye		3	6	.10	4.78
Acre of rye		10	–	.29	13.87
Bushel of oats		2	–	.06	2.87
Horse	10	–	–	5.88	281.30
Cow	3	–	–	1.76	84.20
Hive of bees		7	6	.22	10.52
Wagon	15	–	–	8.82	421.95
Plow	1	–	–	.59	28.23
Plow and harrow	1	10	–	.88	42.10
Grindstone		8	–	.24	11.48
Grindstone		3	–	.09	4.31
Grubbing hoe			3	.01	0.48
Cutting box and cutting knife		12	–	.35	16.74
Windmill	1	10	–	.88	42.10
Barrel		2	–	.06	2.87
Gun	1	10	–	.88	42.10
Wool spinning wheel		8	–	.24	11.48
Loom	2	10	–	1.47	70.32
Loom		7	6	.22	10.52
Ten plate pipe stove	4	10	–	2.65	126.78
Iron stove	4	–	–	2.35	112.42
Iron stove	2	4	–	1.29	61.71
Eight day clock with case	12	–	–	7.06	337.75
Copper kettle	1	15	–	1.03	49.28

explained by differences in the number of bushels produced per acre, because of the relative scarcity of arable land in England and the related use there of greater amounts per acre of labor and manure.[22]

WEALTH, CAPITAL, INCOME, AND PROPERTY DISTINGUISHED

Four closely related concepts, wealth, capital, income, and property, may be usefully distinguished and their relation to

Table 1.5   (Continued)

Item	In Pennsylvania Pounds, Shillings, and Pence			In Pounds Sterling and Decimal Parts Thereof	In Dollars of 1976 Purchasing Power
	£	s	d	£	$
Iron kettle	1	–	–	.59	28.23
Iron kettle		15	–	.44	21.05
Iron pot		4	–	.12	5.74
Steelyard		7	6	.22	10.52
Pewter dish		3	–	.09	4.31
8 Pewter spoons		2	6	.07	3.35
12 Wooden plates		3	–	.09	4.31
Bed and bedstead	4	10	3	2.65	126.78
Bed and bedstead	1	10	2	.89	42.58
Bedstead and upper bed and tick for peas		1	5	.04	1.91
Old bedstead, straw and two pillows		3	–	.09	4.31
Walnut chest		15	–	.44	21.05
Old chest		2	–	.06	2.87
Table		5	–	.15	7.18
Large Bible	3	–	–	1.76	84.20
Fine hat		10	–	.29	13.87
Pair of boots		2	6	.07	3.35
Pair of leather breeches		10	–	.29	13.87
Petticoat		10	–	.29	13.87
Woman's cloak		12	–	.35	16.74
Greatcoat	1	2	6	.66	31.57
Jacket	1	2	6	.66	31.57
Jacket		1	–	.03	1.44
3 Pounds flaxen yarn		7	6	.22	10.52
Negro woman and negro male child	40	–	–	23.52	1,125.20

SOURCE: Selected from sample inventories in Northampton County.

consumption noted before we turn to the categories used in this study to group the many individual items of wealth for analysis. *Wealth* is anything that has market value. It is usually measured as a stock, not a flow. It includes such physical assets as (1) land, (2) tangible, man-made goods used both for production and for final consumption, and (3) intangible assets such as good will or claims against others. Its value is determined by what it brings on the market.

Capital, as economists use the term, has various meanings. One is a stock of physical goods used to promote the production of further goods. Such a capital good is reproducible, that is, man-made, and

Table 1.6
Sale Values of Some Wealth Items
Halifax and Orange Counties, North Carolina, 1774

Item	In North Carolina Pounds, Shillings and Pence			In Pounds Sterling and Decimal Parts thereof	In Dollars of 1976 Purchasing Power
	£	s	d	£	$
Barrel of corn		9	5	.27	12.92
Bushel of oats		2	1	.06	2.87
Bushel of wheat		6	4	.18	8.61
Horse	19	17	7	11.23	537.24
Mare	9	15	8	5.53	264.56
Steer	2	5	–	1.27	60.76
Cow	2	14	8	1.54	73.67
Sheep		9	10	.28	13.40
Hog		7	3	.21	10.05
Hoe		1	6	.04	1.91
Weeding hoe		4	2	.12	5.74
Axe		4	9	.13	6.22
Barrel		1	1	.03	1.44
Gun	1	8	6	.81	38.75
Iron pot		6	3	.18	8.61
Pot		5	5	.15	7.18
Butter pot		2	8	.08	3.83
Bed and furniture	6	2	5	3.46	165.53
Chest		9	3	.26	12.44
Chair		2	10	.08	3.83
Side of leather		13	4	.38	18.18
Hide		8	6	.24	11.48
Negro man	91	3	8	51.52	2,464.72
Negro woman	76	17	–	43.42	2,077.21
Negro boy	49	17	11	28.19	1,348.61
Negro girl	52	2	8	30.02	1,436.16
Plank built boat with tackle, etc.	200	–	–	113.00	5,405.92
Cyprus canoe	10	–	–	5.65	270.30

SOURCE: *American Colonial Wealth* table 3.1, based on mean values for which goods sold at "public vendue" in 1774 from 47 estates in the sample in Halifax and Orange Counties.

usually durable. Capital goods include such tangible assets as tools, equipment, buildings, and improvements to land. Wealth in this form wears out with use; the depreciation must be replaced or augmented by current production over and above current consumption if the capital stock is to remain the same or to increase. Another meaning of capital is a stock of money value resulting from saving. It may be held in liquid form as currency—or today in deposit credits, although in the colonies there were no banks or deposit institutions in our modern sense. Or it may be loaned out to others and a claim for repayment held in the form of a note, bond, or other financial claim, whose ultimate value depends generally on physical wealth. Because the rate of physical wear and tear on a capital good and rates of depreciation that accountants use do not always synchronize perfectly, there are sometimes differing views as to the precise way to calculate the present value of a specific piece of capital. In principle, capital is anything that yields a discountable stream of future income, against which are offset the discountable future costs of its maintenance (Fisher 1906:chap. 3). In this sense we have human capital as well as nonhuman capital (terms that will be dealt with below);[23] futhermore, land is not excluded from the definition of capital.

Income is a current flow (in money or in kind) during a period, as a quarter or a year, from use of capital or such other wealth as consumers' durable goods; or it may be received as payment for current services of land in the form of rent, or of labor in the form of wages or salary.

Property is a matter of legal right or claim to the particular asset.

A person's claim to wealth may indicate right to the use of, income from, or control over, assets. The meaning of wealth ownership is the subject of property law. In the earliest statements of legal theory a property right was conceived of as absolute control over a tangible object such as land, a building, an animal, or a human being. This absolute control included the right to direct the use of the object, the right to receive any income produced by such use, and the right to sell or otherwise dispose of the object. . . . the liability for loss and responsibility for damages resided with the person who held title.

In the course of centuries, the legal concept of property has undergone many changes. By common law, statute, and constitutional amendment, the meaning and content of the term 'property' have been under constant revision. Thus, the right to hold certain things as personal property has been withdrawn, as in the case of ownership of a human person. . . . the opportunity to claim new property rights has been expanded. [Lampman 1962:2–3]

Net worth, or equity, is the difference between assets and liabilities. It is calculated for an individual as the sum of all the wealth

Table 1.7
Appraised Values of Some Individual Wealth Items
Charleston District, South Carolina, 1774

Item	In South Carolina Pounds, Shillings, and Pence			In Pounds Sterling and Decimal Parts Thereof	In Dollars of 1976 Purchasing Power
	£	*s*	*d*	**£**	**$**
7 Barrels rice 500 lb. @ 45/	82	5	–	11.76	562.60
Horse	3	5	–	.46	22.01
Horse	10	–	–	1.43	68.41
Mare	20	–	–	2.86	136.82
3 Head of sheep	6	15	–	.97	46.40
Grindstone	1	–	–	.14	6.70
Grindstone	1	12	6	.23	11.00
Loom and tackling	9	–	–	1.29	61.71
Wind fan	40	–	–	5.72	273.64
10 Rice hooks	1	–	–	.14	6.70
2 Rice sieves	1	–	–	.14	6.70
Gun and a shotbag	4	–	–	.57	27.26
3 Iron pots	3	10	–	.50	23.92
2 Iron pots	8	–	–	1.14	54.54
Pr. steelyards	1	10	–	.21	10.05
Spinning wheel and cards	3	–	–	.43	20.57
Eight day clock	50	–	–	7.15	342.06
Copper tea kettle	3	–	–	.43	20.57
Silver coffee pot	10	–	–	1.43	68.41
Silver tea pot	35	8	9	5.07	242.55
Case with silver handled knives and forks	3	5	–	.46	22.01
3 China cups and saucers		5	–	.04	1.91
Bed and furniture	25	–	–	3.58	171.27
Bedstead	5	–	–	.72	34.44

assets to which he has legal claim minus all the claims others have on him.

For many purposes wealth and capital may be considered as virtually interchangeable terms, although wealth is the broader term and both may contribute to future consumption. Both may be considered as a stock of physical or financial assets—that is, financial claims—or a combination of the two. Both, conceptually, may also include wealth in the form of human capital. In classical and neoclassical economic thought, capital is considered one of the principal factors of production, or, as economists would say today, inputs, which in combination with the other factors, land and labor, yields a

Table 1.7   (Continued)

Item	In South Carolina Pounds, Shillings, and Pence			In Pounds Sterling and Decimal Parts Thereof	In Dollars of 1976 Purchasing Power
	£	s	d	£	$
Chest drawers	15	–	–	2.15	102.86
Old chest		12	6	.09	4.31
Desk	20	–	–	2.86	136.82
Mahogany desk	30	–	–	4.29	205.23
Tea table	8	–	–	1.14	54.54
Mahogany stand and tea urn	20	–	–	2.86	136.82
Backgammon table		12	6	.09	4.31
Backgammon table	3	–	–	.43	20.57
Backgammon table	10	–	–	1.43	68.41
15 Chairs	7	10	–	1.07	51.19
12 Mahogany chairs, hair bottoms	50	–	–	7.15	342.06
Looking glass		15	–	.11	5.26
Large family Bible	6	–	–	.86	41.14
Pr. leather breeches	1	10	–	.21	10.05
Pr. silver buckles	1	10	–	.21	10.05
Scotch carpet	15	–	–	2.15	102.86
Diamond ring	70	–	–	10.01	478.88
Amethyst ring	3	–	–	.43	20.57
Negro man	420	–	–	60.06	2,873.27
Negro wench	325	–	–	46.48	2,223.60
Negro boy	250	–	–	35.75	1,708.37
Negro girl	200	–	–	28.60	1,368.22
Young mulatto male child	50	–	–	7.15	342.06

SOURCE: Selected from sample inventories in Charleston District.

flow of product, or output. Over a span of time this output is the physical income for that period. The physical income may be consumed immediately, or its proceeds invested, saved in financial form, or used to pay taxes to the government, which in turn uses tax revenue to command goods and services. It seems clear that a high present level of wealth implies past production that yielded a surplus above consumption that was saved or invested. Likewise, a high present level of wealth promises a relatively high future consumption, in that it will yield future income that, after replacement of wear and tear, can be used for future immediate consumption or for future investment in durable consumers' goods, producers' goods, or land.

Measures of Wealth

Table 1.8
Appraised Values of Some Individual Wealth Items
Cambridgeshire, England, ca. 1739

Item	In Pounds Sterling, Shillings, and Pence			In Pounds Sterling and Decimal Parts Thereof	In Dollars of 1976 Purchasing Power
	£	s	d	£	$
Acre of wheat (range from £1.5 to £3)	2	10	–	2.50	119.60
Acre of rye	1	10	–	1.50	71.76
Acre of oats	1	10	–	1.50	71.76
Horse (range from £4 to £12)	7	–	–	7.00	334.88
Mare (range from £3 to £7)	5	6	–	5.30	253.55
Cow (range from £1.5 to £3)	2	3	–	2.15	102.86
Sheep		6	4	0.32	15.31
Hog		17	6	0.88	42.10
3 Geese		3	–	0.15	7.18
Wagon	8	–	–	8.00	382.72
2 Wagons	10	10		10.50	502.32
Cart (range from £1 to £3.5)	2	4	–	2.20	105.25
Plow and harrow	2	–	–	2.00	95.68
5 Forks in barn		2	6	0.13	6.22
1 Dung rake		4	–	0.20	9.57
1 Gun	1	10	–	1.50	71.76
1 Wheel and reel (indoors)		1	6	0.08	3.83
Clock (in the staircase)	2	2	–	2.10	100.46
Clock	4	4	–	4.20	200.93
1 Iron pot		1	–	0.05	2.39
2 Iron dripping pans		15	–	0.75	35.88
1 Brewing copper	1	–	–	1.00	47.84
Frying pan and Pr. of bellows		1	–	0.05	2.39
2 Frying pans, 1 warming pan		4	6	0.23	10.90
1 Pot and a warming pan		5	–	0.25	11.96
Cheese press		10	–	0.50	23.92
2 Cheese presses, 20 cheese vats	2	–	–	2.00	95.68

Wealth in final consumers' goods has traditionally been less clearly identified as capital than have producers' goods, although consumers' durable goods clearly yield services (real income) over a considerable time period, and thus come within the foregoing definition of capital. Consumers' perishable goods were recognized as wealth by Adam Smith (1776:329). However, he noted that as soon as they were consumed their value was entirely gone, whereas the purchaser of durable goods had at least some value in them left at the

Table 1.8   (Continued)

Item	In Pounds Sterling, Shillings, and Pence			In Pounds Sterling and Decimal Parts Thereof	In Dollars of 1976 Purchasing Power
	£	s	d	£	$
1 Silver tankard, 22½ ounces	5	12	6	5.63	269.34
1 Silver cup & spoons, 33½ ounces	8	7	6	8.38	400.90
10 Pewter dishes	1	10	–	1.50	71.76
6 Dishes		14	–	0.70	33.49
4 dozen Plates	1	8	–	1.40	66.98
14 Plates		7	–	0.35	16.74
Feather bed and bedding	1	10	–	1.50	71.76
Bed and beding in the parlour	5	–	–	5.00	239.20
Bed, bedstead and all things belonging to it	1	10	–	1.50	71.76
1 Old flock bed		3	–	0.15	7.18
12 Chairs		6	–	0.30	14.35
2 Tables		5	–	0.25	11.96
Pr. of Drawers in the parlour		2	–	0.10	4.78
5 Gold rings	3	–	–	3.00	143.52
Watch	2	2	–	2.10	100.46
Watch	3	3	–	3.15	150.70
2 Wigs		10	–	0.50	23.92
2 Hats		4	–	0.20	9.57
10 Pr. Shoes	2	–	–	2.00	95.68
Breeches, buckskin		6	–	0.30	14.35
Gown, camlot		6	–	0.30	14.35
Gown, pople		4	6	0.23	11.00
Greatcoat		7	–	0.35	16.74
Coat and waistcoat		12	–	0.60	28.70

SOURCE: Selected from the first 21 inventories of a 1739–41 sample from Cambridgeshire (Cambridge County), England drawn by Peter H. Lindert, who generously shared them with the author. He obtained copies from the Manuscript Room of Cambridge University Library. One case was appraised in 1736, one in 1737, three in 1738, and sixteen in 1739.

end of the period. Alfred Marshall (1920:81), writing in the 1890s, asserted there was a clear tradition that we should speak of "capital" when considering things as agents of production and "wealth" when considering them as goods consumed or yielding the pleasures of possession. He avoided the topic of human capital values, treating labor only as a factor of production; to him the efficiency of labor and the value of its product were in proportion to the amount of land and capital equipment available to it.

National Wealth

The physical assets of all the individuals in a nation can be usefully summed to estimate a national total. The same is not true of net worth, which takes financial assets into account. The financial asset of one person is the financial obligation of another, and in national summation these cancel out, except for foreign assets or claims. This can be illustrated by the logic of John Stuart Mill (1848:7) who argued that a mortgage on land of a thousand pounds is wealth to the person who has the claim,

> to whom it brings in a revenue, and who could perhaps sell it in the market for the full amount of the debt. But it is not wealth to the country; if the engagement were annulled, the country would be neither poorer nor richer. The mortgagee would have lost a thousand pounds, and the owner of the land would have gained it. Speaking nationally, the mortgage was not itself wealth, but merely gave A a claim to a portion of the wealth of B. It was wealth to A, and wealth which he could transfer to a third person; but what he so transferred was in fact a joint ownership, to the extent of a thousand pounds, in the land of which B was nominally the sole proprietor.[24]

The same point, that domestic financial assets cancel domestic financial liabilities, is made by Raymond W. Goldsmith (1968). He includes in his estimates of national wealth land, tangible and reproducible physical wealth, and net foreign assets held by nationals. Essentially the same inclusions have been followed by John Kendrick (1967; Kendrick, Lee, and Lomask 1976) and by Christensen and Jorgenson (1973) in estimating U.S. national wealth for dates since 1929. All these estimators include in national wealth not only that held in the private sector by individual households, unincorporated businesses, corporations, and nonprofit institutions, but also tangible wealth in the government sector. This latter takes the form of government-owned lands and other physical assets, including monetary metals.

Human Capital

Most estimates of national wealth have not included human capital, although Gregory King (1936:32) as early as 1688 added £330 million in human capital to other forms of physical wealth to reach a total estimate of £650 million for the wealth of England and Wales.[25] John Kendrick (1974) has made a beginning at estimating this for the United States in the twentieth century.[26] In the case of historical periods when slaves or indentured servants play an important role, some consideration of such capital is necessary and practical. The American colonies and the subsequent United States from the seventeenth century to about 1860, some two hundred years, are a case in which human capital demands consideration.[27]

John Stuart Mill (1848:9) debated whether the "skill of a workman, or any other natural or acquired power of body or mind, shall be called wealth, or not." He evidently did not find useful or was not aware of Gregory King's capitalization of the annual product over 11 years of the skills of the English people. He argued that

an example of a possession which is wealth to the person holding it, but not wealth to the nation, or to mankind, is slaves. It is by a strange confusion of ideas that slave property (as it is termed) is counted, at so much per head, in an estimate of the wealth, or of the capital, of the country which tolerates the existence of such property. If a human being, considered as an object possessing productive powers, is part of the national wealth when his powers are owned by another man, he cannot be less a part of it when they are owned by himself. Whatever he is worth to his master is so much property abstracted from himself, and its abstraction cannot augment the possessions of the two together, or of the country to which they both belong. In propriety of classification, however, the people of a country are not to be counted in its wealth. They are that for the sake of which its wealth exists. The term wealth is wanted to denote the desirable objects which they possess, not inclusive of, but in contradistinction to, their own persons. They are not wealth to themselves, though they are means of acquiring it. [1848:8][28]

From a slightly different standpoint, the same problem was wrestled with by those who debated and drafted the Articles of Confederation in 1780.

The first important dispute arose over the drafting committee's plan to apportion taxes according to the gross number of inhabitants, the Southern States disclaiming against the enumeration of slaves in rating the State quotas. Chase asserted that slaves were property, not population. Lynch of South Carolina also compared them with land, or dumb animals. But John Adams argued that slaves, like freemen, produced wealth, and should be reckoned when preparing an index of the wealth of the country. . . . [Nevins 1927:625]

Nearly a century later, President Abraham Lincoln recognized that freeing the slaves would deprive their owners of property and proposed to Congress in 1862 that the nation as a whole should reimburse them.

In a certain sense the liberation of slaves is the destruction of property— property acquired by descent, or by purchase, the same as any other property. It is no less true for having been often said, that the people of the South are not more responsible for the original introduction of this property, than are the people of the North; and when it is remembered how unhesitatingly we all use cotton and sugar, and share the profits of dealing in them, it may not be quite safe to say, that the South has been more responsible than the North for its continuance. If then, for a common object, this property is to be sacrificed, is it not just that it be done at a common charge? [Basler 1946:681]

Ownership claims to black or mulatto slaves were clearly legal in the colonies by the eighteenth century.[29] The same was true of the services of an indentured servant, usually white, for the contract period.[30] The owner had a legal claim to the product of their work, and his responsibility for their maintenance was recognized. He could sell a slave or an indenture contract. For our estimation of wealth in 1774 on a basis of inventories of estates, the market values of slaves and servants are available just as consistently and reliably as the values of other forms of tangible wealth. In the creation of wealth, they were clearly productive agents, whose value can be added to that of other producers' goods as part of capital used in production.[31] Inclusion of the value of owned nonfree human capital is necessary in considering the distribution of wealth.[32] Clearly the people who owned slaves and servants, who had legal claim to the product of their services, with no cost after initial purchase other than their maintenance, enjoyed a substantial real income from such services.[33] This income is the reason for the capitalized wealth value of the slaves and servants. In arraying the free wealthholders by the size of their wealth, those who possessed this type of wealth undeniably were richer than those who did not. The owning of slaves and servants by people in some regions may contribute, through the slaves' productivity, to high nonhuman wealth in those regions. This would follow if, as some have suggested (Fogel and Engerman 1977), the slaves were required or induced to work harder and more productively than did free persons.

Yet as Mill pointed out, there is no more real wealth in the nation whether the productive worker owns himself or does not. The real capital of the United States was not reduced[34] by the direct effect of the emancipation proclamation, although ownership claims were greatly altered. If the people over six feet tall tomorrow enslaved the people under six feet, the wealth of the nation would not be increased. The answer to this dilemma is that both free and nonfree humans have capital value, and it is illogical to include in national wealth the value of the nonfree without adding an estimate of the value of free human capital (see the discussion in chapter 4). As a consequence, except insofar as attention may be given to total human plus nonhuman wealth, this study is in the main concerned with nonhuman wealth. When the structure of wealth is analyzed, in chapter 4, nonhuman wealth is separated from the value of privately owned slaves and servants, since the latter are only the nonfree part of the total human capital of the colonies. Nonhuman physical wealth is the wealth most economically meaningful and most usefully considered on an aggregate and per capita basis for a nation or a region. It is especially appropriate for the colonies when we wish to compare their wealth with that for the nation at later dates when slavery no longer existed. However, because of the legal existence of servitude in the colonies, and the necessity for including such nonfree human capital in distribution of wealth, I also offer in chapter 3 some alternative aggregate figures including the monetary value of slaves and servants.

WEALTH AS DEFINED IN THIS STUDY

The definitions of wealth and its subcategories adopted in this study aim at usefulness for economic analysis and at comparability, so far as the data permit, with later wealth estimates, particularly the studies of Goldsmith, Kendrick, and Christensen and Jorgenson. The objective has been to include (in addition to the nonfree human wealth that forces its attention upon us by its presence in the estate inventories) all forms of privately held nonhuman physical wealth and also, for certain purposes, financial claims as well. The physical items include land (real estate) and portable items both durable and perishable, both consumers' goods and capital used for production.

"Real estate" values (as opposed to "personal estate" or portable wealth) cannot be separated for the colonial period into the value of land per se and the value of buildings, structures, and other improvements to the land. In this respect we cannot achieve complete comparability with later wealth estimates because of the data limitations.

The possible combinations of wealth subcategories yield several measures of total wealth that I have found useful. The suitability of each depends on where the interest is focused and on how hard the data are required to be. In later chapters the totals appropriate to the particular discussion will be indicated. The most inclusive measure, "net worth," includes all privately owned assets of every kind, nonhuman physical and financial, nonfree human, minus financial liabilities. A size distribution by "net worth" places at the top those who command, clear of debt, the most assets of every form, and at the bottom those with negative wealth who owe more than their assets. The next most inclusive measure, "total physical wealth," is equal to "net worth" except that it omits both financial assets and financial liabilities. Its smallest possible wealth value for a "wealthholder" is zero. I include in the totals for both "net worth" and "total physical wealth" land (real estate) and nonfree human wealth in slaves and servants, as well as other portable physical wealth; in "net worth" only, I include financial wealth, which includes currency.

A third measure, "total nonhuman physical wealth," omits slaves and servants but otherwise is identical with "total physical wealth."

A fourth total, "portable physical wealth," is equal to "total physical wealth" except that it excludes real estate, the value of which is generally not available from probate inventories outside New England. Since this total is restricted to physical wealth, it does not include financial assets. It does include slaves and servants, unless it is specified as "nonhuman portable physical wealth."

To complete the roster of wealth terms, we might refer to one more which earlier (Jones 1970) I called "gross portable wealth." This, in the middle and southern colonies, is the total of all the items found in the probate inventories, that is, the portable physical wealth, including nonfree human wealth, plus the financial assets. It does not include real estate, and it does not subtract the financial liabilities nor make corrections for additions or reductions to wealth reported in the estate accounts. I have not given totals of "gross portable wealth" in

Table 1.9
Summary of Wealth Definitions

Net Worth	*Total Physical Wealth*	*Total Nonhuman Physical Wealth*
Land (real estate)	Land (real estate)	Land (real estate)
Slaves and servants	Slaves and servants	—
Nonhuman portable physical	Nonhuman portable physical	Nonhuman portable physical
Financial assets	—	—
Financial liabilities	—	—

Gross Portable Wealth	*Portable Physical Wealth*	*Nonhuman Portable Physical Wealth*
Slaves and servants	Slaves and servants	—
Nonhuman portable physical	Nonhuman portable physical	Nonhuman portable physical, i.e.
Financial assets	—	livestock
		other producers' durables
		crops
		nonfarm business inventories
		other producers' perishables
		consumers' durables
		consumers' perishables

this book because it was more useful to separate the financial from the physical assets, except, of course, in the calculation of net worth.

The firmest wealth figures are those found in the probate inventories—that is to say, in all regions the portable wealth figures, including physical and financial assets and slaves and servants, and in New England real estate. The least firm are the figures for financial liabilities and for real estate estimated from other documents and sources.

Table 1.9 summarizes the foregoing definitions of wealth for which measures are available and indicates the components of each of the major wealth totals for which figures will be presented in subsequent chapters. It may serve to remind the reader that differing definitions of wealth, in addition to differing portions of the population included in studies made for various times and places, for various purposes, and based on various data, may actually account for a considerable part of the observed differences in wealth (Hoenack 1964).

CHAPTER TWO

Human and Land Resources

THE story of colonial wealth creation is a tale of the interaction of people, land, capital, and know-how. The wealth existing in 1774 resulted from people's work with the colonial land and resources, together with the capital equipment brought from Europe or accumulated in the colonies. The immigrants also brought, in their heads and in books, knowledge of western European science and technology, to which they added some arts learned from the native Indians. Economic activities took place within the setting of the political and social institutions brought from England but modified by the conditions encountered in the colonies. A treatment of the technologies and the institutional settings of the colonies, which were undoubtedly influential in their economic development, lies outside the scope of this work. A consideration of the numbers and characteristics of the population, however, is indispensable to the task of wealth measurement and interpretation, as is some understanding of the land available to them.

THE USES OF POPULATION FIGURES

Population figures are vital to this study for a number of reasons. One is to enable us to move from sample estimates of wealth of decedents to estimates of the wealth of the living, by region and for the thirteen colonies. A second is to allow the presentation of wealth estimates in the most useful forms, such as aggregate, per capita, or per adult male. Third, figures on location of population by region and on regional growth rates form a backdrop for judging economic development of the various regions, a theme that recurs throughout this work. Fourth, people have important relationships to wealth, as producers and as users as well as owners of it, and people themselves are human wealth. My definition of a wealthholder, which is basic to all the estimates, depends upon consideration of which groups in the population were legal owners and controllers of wealth.

To compare the American colonists' wealth, even roughly, with that in other times or places, as well as from region to region within the thirteen colonies, we need per capita figures to allow for differences in numbers of inhabitants. Clearly, this measure depends on two numbers in a fraction, the society's aggregate wealth in the numerator and, in the denominator, its population size, the number of persons using that wealth.

We may also prefer, for other viewpoints, to consider various categories of population in relation to the magnitude of the society's wealth. Since there were proportionately more children in the colonial population than in the present-day United States, one may wish to compare wealth per adult or per adult male. For another comparison, the wealth per free family or household, one needs an estimate of the number of heads of free households in the colonies.

In order to inflate our figures from a sample of probated wealthholders, we need the total number of wealthholders in the entire colonial population. In the colonies, as in virtually all times and places, people were both producers of new wealth and users of existing wealth, and usually heads of families were the owners of the family's wealth. We have also the anomaly, which lasted for some two centuries, of nonfree persons as a form of wealth owned and controlled by others. The presence of the native Indians, of black slaves, and of some nonfree white persons, as well as of women and children, bears on the question of who were wealthholders and on the question of the appropriate population divisor. We further need information on the age and sex composition of the living population of wealthholders to make the adjustments required to move from estimates of decedents' wealth to that of the living. Before considering the specific demographic estimates required for our wealth calculation, I shall briefly sketch the colonial population of 1774 and its origins.

POPULATION ORIGINS AND GROWTH

On the eve of the American Revolution, the eastern fringe of the North American continent was populated principally by white settlers and their descendants. The Indians had in general moved westward. The whites had also, especially after 1690, imported black slaves from Africa or the West Indies, and these in turn had produced American-born offspring. By 1774 the black population comprised about a fifth of the total of 2.35 million non-Indian people in the areas that later became the thirteen original states. The whites had come from Europe—principally the British Isles, though many Germans had reached the Middle Colonies, as well as some French Huguenots, who also settled in the southern colonies. Still others had come from Sweden, Switzerland, or Holland, and a sprinkling from other European countries.

Many of the whites, or their ancestors, had come voluntarily, as free settlers who had financed their own expensive passage from Europe. Some had arrived in companies of free men, women, and children (as in New England), financed at least in part by British stockholders to whom they planned to remit payments from the results of their labor combined with the resources they expected to find in the New World. Others, as in the early years of some proprietary colonies such as Pennsylvania and Maryland, were induced to come at the expense of a sponsor or promoter, who might receive a "headright" of fifty or so acres of land for each "head" he brought over. Some, before leaving Europe, signed "indentures" to serve for a specified number of years as servant to the person who financed the passage or to a third party who had acquired the contract.[1] Some of these were called "redemptioners," i.e., persons who voluntarily agreed to serve to redeem the cost of their passage. Other whites, mostly single males, were lured or tricked into coming on shipboard, or in a few cases were actually kidnapped; upon arrival, lacking means to pay their passage, they were sold into involuntary servitude for a number of years by the ship's captain or by an agent or promoter. The term of servitude, whether voluntary or involuntary, varied, depending, in part, upon age.[2] Indentured servitude generally lasted from three to seven years.

By 1774, most of the population was native-born and, especially in New England, often had been for several generations. Much of the rapid population growth was coming from natural increase. This is believed to be true of blacks[3] as well as whites, although the slave trade was not outlawed until 1808. The rate of increase in total population, about 3 percent per year, compounded, up to 1770 (see table 2.1), was higher than was being experienced in England and European countries. This rapid rate of population growth, noted by Benjamin Franklin and other contemporary observers, was one of the factors that disturbed Thomas Malthus (1798) and led to his gloomy analysis of the propensity of population to outrun food supply. But in the colonies, after the few initial years of hardship before crops were well established, there was adequate food to sustain overall population growth. The rate varied from region to region and colony to colony and by 1774 was slowing in New England—especially in the older colonies of Massachusetts and Connecticut—to under 2 percent. Such relatively new areas as those that later became Maine and Ver-

Table 2.1
Population Growth Rates
Thirteen Colonies and Three Regions 1650–1780
(*Percent*)

	Thirteen Colonies	New England	Middle Colonies	South
1650–1670	4.1	4.2	2.8	4.2
1670–1690	3.2	2.6	8.0	2.6
1690–1710	2.3	1.4	3.5	2.6
1710–1730	3.2	3.2	3.8	3.0
1730–1750	3.2	3.0	3.6	3.4
1750–1770	3.1	1.9	3.3	3.4
1770–1780	2.6	1.5	3.1	2.6
1670–1770	3.0	2.4	4.4	3.0

SOURCE: Calculated from population figures in Census, *Historical Statistics* (1960, 1975), ser. Z 1-17, and shown by decade in *American Colonial Wealth*, tables 4.1, 4.3, 4.4, 4.6. Population includes whites and blacks and excludes native Indians. Rates are compound annual rates of growth during the periods indicated.

NOTE: "Middle Colonies" include New York, Pennsylvania, New Jersey, and Delaware throughout the tables and text in this book unless New York is specifically excluded (see appendix A and the Introduction for an explanation of the problems with New York figures). For middle colonies excluding New York see *American Colonial Wealth*, table 4.5. For corresponding figures for the United States 1780 to 1970 see its table 4.2; for individual colonies to 1780 see its tables 4.7 through 4.20.

mont, as well as Georgia, were growing much more rapidly as new settlers moved in. The rate around 1774 in Georgia was 9.1 percent.

Indentured servants and apprenticed boys or girls, who were mostly white, became free members of society after completion of their terms of service (or sometimes earlier if they ran away successfully) and made their ways economically in a variety of ways. Some of them served a while as farm laborers or mariners, others as assistants to artisans, and some eventually acquired land, particularly when they moved to newer western counties.

Blacks, on the other hand, except for those who ran away successfully, usually remained slaves for their lifetimes, and their descendants were born into lifetime slavery. Running away was not easy because of their obvious color and because there were legal penalties for harboring them[4] and owners offered rewards for their capture and return. However, there were instances of manumission. For example, some owners provided in their wills that upon the owner's death certain favorite slaves (and sometimes their issue if any) should be given their freedom. Others provided that certain slaves were to serve certain of the owner's children until the child became 21 and then were to be freed. There was fairly strong Quaker sentiment against slavery, especially in Pennsylvania and New Jersey, and it seems likely that the proportion of free blacks was greatest there.[5] Cities like Philadelphia may have been something of a haven for runaway slaves.[6] The nature of diversified crops on relatively small farms in the Middle Colonies and of even less favorable farming conditions in New England probably accounts for the relatively small proportions of slaves there.

PEOPLE AS PRODUCERS AND AS USERS OF WEALTH

People are important not only as users of existing wealth but also as producers of more wealth. Men, women, and children are the source of the society's labor force, including the managers. Depending on custom and the legal environment, a person might be free or bound to another. If he is free, the product of his labor belongs to him or the family or the head of the family; if he is indentured or a slave, his product belongs to his legal master or owner. The anticipated product, capitalized, minus costs of rearing and maintenance, equals the value of human capital. The heads of free families and the owners or masters of nonfree persons provided for the sustenance of their dependents from their own stores of wealth, their own current production, or production by their dependents, to which they had legal claim. These human resources, whether free or nonfree, and the skill and vigor with which talents and abilities are combined with available capital and natural resources are major inputs of economic product in current and future periods. The surplus above consumption and replacement of wear and tear represents real saving, or an addition to the stock of physical wealth. Travelers and contemporary writers such as Crevecoeur (1782) and Peter Kalm (1750) attested to the restless energy and vigor of the free colonists in the North. The productive efficiency of the slaves has recently aroused intense debate among economic historians following the publication of *Time on the Cross* (Fogel and Engerman 1974a,b, 1977).

WHO WERE WEALTHHOLDERS?

Which groups among the human beings in the colonies are properly defined as wealthholders? I consider as wealthholders in this study only those who could, legally or by social convention, hold wealth. These include all free adult males; a small proportion of free adult females; all free black men; and a small proportion of free black women in New England and the Middle Colonies, but no free black women in the South. The females included are widows and a few single women. All these groups will hereafter be called "wealthholders," though in some instances the value of their actual wealth was zero or even negative. All other groups are considered nonwealthholders. Many of these, except for small children, were producers of wealth. All of them, even slaves to some extent, were users of wealth owned by others. We exclude them, however, as wealthholders because they did not or could not legally hold wealth or, economically, control its use, for reasons inhering in the mores as well as the laws of the time.

This concept of a wealthholder can be related to the more familiar notion of head-of-household. For simplicity, wealth per wealthholder may be thought of as roughly approximating wealth per free family. However, the equating of free families or households with wealthholders overstates the number of the former. There could be two or more free adult males in the same household, or a free adult son or other male in the household of a free adult widow or single female wealthholder. Consequently, wealth calculated per wealthholder is undoubtedly somewhat lower than the unknown wealth per free household or family, but is our closest available approximation, as we do not have a basis for estimating the number of households.

I shall consider in the following paragraphs the groups excluded as wealthholders and the reasons they do not qualify. The order follows the operations required to arrive at my estimates of the numbers of wealthholders by region, discussed more fully following presentation of tables.

Children and Youths Excluded

Children and youths aged 20 and under, though they generally worked, usually did not legally control their own wealth. Those aged 21 and over are considered adult wealthholders if they also qualify on the remaining requirements. In the colonies in 1774, the age at marriage of males was generally 21 or over. Until marriage, youths commonly remained in their parents' homes and had little, if any, separate personal wealth. They, like younger children, contributed the product of their work to the family and in turn were sustained by the family product or use of some of its accumulated wealth, both of which were owned and controlled by the family head.

Married Women Excluded

We know from the fact that I drew no inventories of married women with husbands living that such women were not allowed legal claim to wealth. This is confirmed by the specific bequests in wills, by husbands to their wives, of the wives' clothing and the like. Since, however, I drew a considerable number of inventories of widows in all regions and of a few "singlewomen" in New England and the South, it seems improper to exclude all women from the category of wealthholders.[7] Clearly widows were wealthholding women in the society, though usually their wealth was less than that of their deceased husbands. Remarriage was frequent,[8] but there were always some widows in the population. Accordingly, a very large proportion of the women must be considered single or married non-wealth-holders.

Under English law, which was the colonial model, land usually descended from father to son and was rarely held by women. Sometimes, by virtue of her husband's will, a woman received the use of the land for her natural lifetime or "so long as she remains my widow, but no longer." In a few wills, widows received the specific right to hold land for their lifetimes and to bequeath it upon their deaths. Also, occasionally fathers willed land to daughters, though the more common pattern was to will it to sons and to mention amounts of money for daughters—sometimes to be paid to them by their brothers—or personal property such as silverware or slaves. Sometimes a husband's will provided that the widow have access to certain specified rooms of the house and that her sons provide her with specified annual amounts of garden produce.[9] As to personal estate, sometimes a husband's will left to his wife her bed and bedding, her choice of cow, and similar specifics.[10] Sometimes, by virtue of their husbands' wills, women received the full personal estate. Widows had dower rights and under usual colonial intestacy laws received one-third of the personal or movable estate, the children two-thirds; and the real estate descended to the male heirs. In Virginia, in event of no will, primogeniture still prevailed; in New England the eldest son received a double portion. The name of Sarah Harper, a widow in my Philadelphia sample, appeared as the owner of several pieces of land on the Philadelphia County manuscript tax list, though she had an adult son. In Maryland (indicated in a letter to the author from Lois Carr dated October 26, 1977), and I believe in most colonies, a widow could renounce her legacy and take her third of the movables instead if she wished.

All Nonfree Adults and Free Black Women in the South Excluded

Among both men and women, nonfree persons are excluded as wealthholders since they could not legally or economically control or own wealth. The nonfree include the black slaves and the indentured whites. Their subtraction leaves us only free white or black men and women as wealthholders. It seems conceptually reasonable that free black men and women in the North could hold property, although I drew no such cases in the sample. That some free blacks in the South held wealth is confirmed by the case in the sample of "Cyrus, a free Negro" in St. Andrews Parish in the Charleston District of South Carolina. His inventory shows that he owned six slaves and five horses, and his will named a man of the same surname as his former owner to be executor of his estate. However, in the South, I very much suspect that the combination of then-existing attitudes toward blacks and toward women, reflected in the southern laws and mores regarding property holding, mean that southern black widows or single women who might have attained their freedom had no real estate and probably so little personal estate that for all practical purposes it may be considered zero in our overall wealth estimates. Hence I exclude as wealthholders the tiny number of black widows and single women who would comprise a small percentage of living free black women in the South.

Indians Excluded

The native Indians are omitted conceptually as wealthholders for several reasons. White mens' laws at that time did not sustain their land ownership claims. The white settlers had successfully preempted their land (Hughes 1976:chap. 4) and driven or maneuvered them to the west. The sample of probate inventories gives no clue to their movable property; I drew no inventories of Indians. If one had reliable estimates of their numbers and of the nature of their movable wealth[11] and its value on the white man's market, one might conceptually add the Indians to the denominator and their wealth to the numerator of the fraction by which we compute per capita wealth in the colonies. In view of the cultural differences which then prevailed, however, and the differing concepts of values, it does not seem useful to conceive of the Indians as participating in the use of the portable wealth accumulated by the colonists, nor of the colonists as sharing in the use of the Indians' movable possessions.[12]

Probate and Nonprobate Wealthholders

The separation of wealthholders into two types, the "probate" and the "nonprobate," is a necessary concession to the fact that estates of wealthholders did not always go through the legal process when they died. It is for the "probate type" that our sample probate inventories give us accurate wealth information. But in order to estimate the total wealth, we must also allow for the holdings of the "nonprobate type," the living counterparts of those who died in 1774 but whose estates never reached the probate courts and for whom probate inventories were never made. Otherwise, we cannot have meaningful wealth estimates for the total population.

NUMBERS AND LOCATION OF WEALTHHOLDERS

For the reasons suggested by the foregoing discussion, this study begins with a determination, so far as available data permit, of the numbers of the total colonial population and its significant categories in around 1774. The results are presented in table 2.2 and subsequent tables of this chapter. Table 2.2 shows that of a total population of over 2.35 million, excluding Indians, almost 19 percent, or about 435 thousand, were possible legal holders of wealth. Most of these were heads of free families or households, although, as we noted earlier, some households could have had two or more wealthholders. They were chiefly free whites (431 thousand), but included nearly 4 thousand free blacks, and were chiefly adult males (396 thousand), but included nearly 39 thousand adult females.

Table 2.2
Colonial Population, 1774

	Thirteen Colonies	New England	Middle Colonies	South
Total population	2,353,967	607,795	640,695	1,105,477
Nonfree population	533,948	25,510	55,546	452,892
Free population, total	1,820,019	582,285	585,149	652,585
Men	396,158	124,534	131,351	140,273
Women	389,405	134,001	122,244	133,160
Children and youths	1,034,456	323,750	331,554	379,152
Free wealthholders	434,835	137,934	143,576	153,325

SOURCE: Tables 2.4 through 2.7.

NOTE: Population includes whites and blacks and excludes native Indians.

Of the total population, somewhat more than half were in the North (slightly fewer in New England than in the Middle Colonies, including New York), whereas almost half (1,105 thousand), 47 percent, were in the South (see table 2.3). New England was the only region where women outnumbered men, and in all regions children and youths through age 20 outnumbered adults, most strikingly in the South. Of the over half a million (534 thousand) nonfree population, the South had an overwhelming 85 percent, the Middle Colonies 10 percent, and New England 5 percent or about 26 thousand. The 1.8 million free population, both white and black, were distributed much more evenly by regions, 32 percent in New England, 32 percent in the Middle Colonies, including New York, and 36 percent in the South. When the focus is on the location of the wealthholders, they divide regionally by thirds; New England had 32 percent, the Middle Colonies 33, and the South 35 percent. However, as proportions of the total populations in their respective regions (see tables 2.5 through 2.7), the wealthholders formed 23 percent of the inhabitants both of New England and of the Middle Colonies, but only about 14 percent of all persons living in the South. The much lower proportion of the southern population who were wealthholders is explained partly by relatively more children there, but principally by the large concentration of the nonfree population. Black slaves and indentured whites made up almost 41 percent of total population in the South, whereas free blacks formed an estimated less than 2

Table 2.3
Colonial Population, Regional Distribution, 1774
(*Percent*)

	Thirteen Colonies	*New England*	*Middle Colonies*	*South*
Total population	100.0	25.8	27.2	47.0
Nonfree population	100.0	4.8	10.4	84.8
Free population, total	100.0	32.0	32.1	35.9
Men	100.0	31.4	33.2	35.4
Women	100.0	34.4	31.4	34.2
Children and youths	100.0	31.3	32.0	36.7
Free wealthholders	100.0	31.7	33.0	35.3

SOURCE: Table 2.2.

Table 2.4
Thirteen Colonies, Population Composition, 1774

	Estimated number (1)	Percentage		
		Total Pop. (2)	Free Pop. (3)	Wealth-holders (4)
(1) Total population, free and nonfree	2,353,967	100.0		
(2) Total white	1,855,274	78.8		
(3) Free	1,802,258	76.6		
(4) Indentured	53,016	2.3		
(5) Total black	498,693	21.2		
(6) Free	17,761	0.8		
(7) Slave	480,932	20.4		
(8) Men	511,487	21.7		
(9) Women	499,299	21.2		
(10) Children and youths (under 21)	1,343,181	57.1		
(11) Free population, white and black	1,820,019	77.3	100.0	
(12) Total men	396,158	16.8	21.8	
(13) Aged 21–25	87,087	3.7	4.8	
(14) Aged 26–44	189,673	8.1	10.4	
(15) Aged 45 and over	119,398	5.1	6.6	
(16) Total women	389,405	16.5	21.4	
(17) Aged 21–25	89,933	3.8	4.9	
(18) Aged 26–44	180,941	7.7	9.9	
(19) Aged 45 and over	118,531	5.0	6.5	
(20) Children and youths (under 21)	1,034,456	43.9	56.8	
(21) All wealthholders	434,835	18.5	23.9	100.0
(22) White	430,872	18.3		99.1
(23) Men	392,305	16.7		90.2
(24) Women	38,567	1.6		8.9
(25) Black	3,963	0.2		0.9
(26) Men	3,857	0.2		0.9
(27) Women	106	0.0		0.0
(28) Probate-type	241,243	10.3		55.5
(29) Nonprobate-type	193,592	8.2		44.5

SOURCE: See text and section IV.C of *American Colonial Wealth,* either edition. This table corresponds to table 4.21 of *American Colonial Wealth.*

NOTE: Column 1 here is the sum of the corresponding columns in tables 2.5, 2.6, and 2.7. The sum of the regional totals gives the overall totals for each population subgroup (line of column 1). Columns 2, 3, and 4 in each line are computed from its column 1. The use of unrounded numbers is required to preserve underlying percentage relationships and to permit additions to subtotals horizontally by region or vertically by subgroups of population. For most purposes the user should not hesitate to round them.

The per capita wealth figures shown in chapters 3, 4, and 5 are most simply obtained by multiplying the w^*-weighted sample mean wealth figure (see chapter 3) by (line 21 ÷ line 1).

percent of all wealthholders there. Black slaves greatly outnumbered indentured whites in the South, but in the North their numbers were approximately equal.

Relevant subclasses of population used to arrive at estimates of numbers of wealthholders, by region, are shown in tables 2.5 through

Table 2.5
New England, Population Composition, 1774

			Percentage		
		Estimated number	Total Pop.	Free Pop.	Wealth-holders
		(1)	(2)	(3)	(4)
(1) Total population, free and nonfree		607,795	100.0		
(2)	Total white	592,791	97.5		
(3)	Free	580,935	95.6		
(4)	Indentured	11,856	2.0		
(5)	Total black	15,004	2.5		
(6)	Free	1,350	0.2		
(7)	Slave	13,654	2.2		
(8)	Men	129,989	21.4		
(9)	Women	139,872	23.0		
(10)	Children and youths (under 21)	337,934	55.6		
(11) Free population, white and black		582,285	95.8	100.0	
(12)	Total men	124,534	20.5	21.4	
(13)	Aged 21–25	26,311	4.3	4.5	
(14)	Aged 26–44	56,424	9.3	9.7	
(15)	Aged 45 and over	41,799	6.9	7.2	
(16)	Total women	134,001	22.0	23.0	
(17)	Aged 21–25	28,034	4.6	4.8	
(18)	Aged 26–44	60,430	9.9	10.4	
(19)	Aged 45 and over	45,537	7.5	7.8	
(20)	Children and youths (under 21)	323,750	53.3	55.6	
(21) All wealthholders		137,934	22.7	23.7	100.0
(22)	White	137,614	22.6		99.8
(23)	Men	124,247	20.4		90.1
(24)	Women	13,367	2.2		9.7
(25)	Black	320	0.1		0.2
(26)	Men	289	0.1		0.2
(27)	Women	31	0.0		0.0
(28)	Probate-type	46,898	7.7		34.0
(29)	Nonprobate-type	91,036	15.0		66.0

SOURCE: See text and section IV.C of *American Colonial Wealth,* 2nd edition. This table corresponds to table 4.22 of *American Colonial Wealth.*

Table 2.6
Middle Colonies, Population Composition, 1774

	Estimated number (*1*)	Percentage		
		Total Pop. (*2*)	Free Pop. (*3*)	Wealth-holders (*4*)
(1) Total population, free and nonfree	640,695	100.0		
(2) Total white	602,947	94.1		
(3) Free	581,573	90.8		
(4) Indentured	21,374	3.3		
(5) Total black	37,748	5.9		
(6) Free	3,576	0.6		
(7) Slave	34,172	5.3		
(8) Men	143,870	22.5		
(9) Women	133,860	20.9		
(10) Children and youths (under 21)	362,965	56.7		
(11) Free population, white and black	585,149	91.3	100.0	
(12) Total men	131,351	20.5	22.4	
(13) Aged 21–25	28,097	4.4	4.8	
(14) Aged 26–44	64,835	10.1	11.1	
(15) Aged 45 and over	38,419	6.0	6.6	
(16) Total women	122,244	19.1	20.9	
(17) Aged 21–25	28,030	4.4	4.8	
(18) Aged 26–44	60,030	9.4	10.3	
(19) Aged 45 and over	34,184	5.3	5.8	
(20) Children and youths (under 21)	331,554	51.7	56.7	
(21) All wealthholders	143,576	22.4	24.5	100.0
(22) White	142,693	22.3	24.4	99.4
(23) Men	130,545	20.4	22.3	90.9
(24) Women	12,148	1.9	2.1	8.5
(25) Black	883	0.1	0.2	0.6
(26) Men	808	0.1	0.1	0.6
(27) Women	75	0.0	0.0	0.0
(28) Probate-type	90,084	14.1	15.4	62.7
(29) Nonprobate-type	53,492	8.3	9.1	37.3

Source: See text and Section IV.C of *American Colonial Wealth,* 2d edition. This table corresponds to table 4.24 of *American Colonial Wealth,* which also gives separate figures for New York in table 4.23 and for Pennsylvania, New Jersey, and Delaware in table 4.25.

Note: The percentage of "blacks, free" used for the Middle Colonies in this book is 9.5 and the corresponding figure for "whites, indentured" is 3.5. For New York separately the figures are 9.0 and 2.5. For Pennsylvania, New Jersey, and Delaware they are 10.0 and 4.0.

2.7. They culminate in the estimates of total wealthholders on lines 21 of each table, and further subclasses of wealthholders are shown on lines 22 through 29. The subclasses by sex and color on lines 23, 24, 26, and 27 are required to reach the count of total wealthholders on line 21. Summations for the thirteen colonies appear in table 2.4.

Table 2.7
South, Population Composition, 1774

			Percentage		
		Estimated number (*1*)	Total Pop. (*2*)	Free Pop. (*3*)	Wealth-holders (*4*)
(1) Total population, free and nonfree		1,105,477	100.0		
(2)	Total white	659,536	59.7		
(3)	Free	639,750	57.9		
(4)	Indentured	19,786	1.8		
(5)	Total black	445,941	40.3		
(6)	Free	12,835	1.2		
(7)	Slave	433,106	39.1		
(8)	Men	237,628	21.5		
(9)	Women	225,567	20.4		
(10)	Children and youths (under 21)	642,282	58.1		
(11) Free population, white and black		652,585	59.0	100.0	
(12)	Total men	140,273	12.7	21.5	
(13)	Aged 21–25	32,679	3.0	5.0	
(14)	Aged 25–44	68,414	6.2	10.5	
(15)	Aged 45 and over	39,180	3.5	6.0	
(16)	Total women	133,160	12.0	20.4	
(17)	Aged 21–25	33,869	3.1	5.2	
(18)	Aged 25–44	60,481	5.5	9.3	
(19)	Aged 45 and over	38,810	3.5	5.9	
(20)	Children and youths (under 21)	379,152	34.3	58.1	
(21) All wealthholders		153,325	13.9	23.5	100.0
(22)	White	150,565	13.6		98.2
(23)	Men	137,513	12.4		89.7
(24)	Women	13,052	1.2		8.5
(25)	Black	2,760	0.2		1.8
(26)	Men	2,760	0.2		1.8
(27)	Women	—	—		—
(28)	Probate-type	104,261	9.4		68.0
(29)	Nonprobate-type	49,064	4.4		32.0

SOURCE: See text and section IV.C of *American Colonial Wealth*, 2d edition. This table corresponds to table 4.26 of *American Colonial Wealth*.

SOURCES AND METHODS FOR POPULATION STATISTICS

Since the first complete census for the United States was not taken until 1790 and it does not give sufficient age detail, the figures in these tables are drawn from a variety of sources. For earlier dates, scholars have approximated population size from provincial censuses taken in some colonies,[13] militia lists, tax lists at varying dates, and the like. These are synthesized and presented by decades up to 1780, by colony, for total white plus black population and separately for blacks as series Z, 1–17 of *Historical Statistics*. These numbers for 1770 and 1780 were used as the starting point for total population, with interpolation at 1774, colony by colony. They do not give the sex and age composition, nor the proportions of blacks who were free, nor of whites who were indentured, and we must seek this information elsewhere. The U.S. census of 1800 was the first to give adequate detail on sex and age structure. I followed its relationships,[14] calculated for the appropriate states arranged in the regional groupings of this study except for slight modification in the proportion of children. For my proportions of free blacks and indentured whites around 1774, the various secondary sources consulted are cited in *American Colonial Wealth,* pp. 1798–1800. The proportions I use for each region respectively are: New England, 9.0, 2.0; Middle Colonies, 9.5, 3.5; Maryland, 5.0, 3.0; Virginia and North Carolina, 3.0, 3.0; South Carolina and Georgia, 1.0, 3.0. (For New York separately see the note to table 2.6.) The estimate that 10 percent of free women in 1774 were wealthholders is derived from my estimate that about 10 percent of women aged 21 and over were widows.[15]

The reader will observe that a narrowing process goes on in tables 2.5, 2.6, and 2.7 from lines 1 to lines 21 as subgroups are eliminated. I separate the free men and women by age classes[16] because the age breakdown of free wealthholders is needed for weighting adjustments. Finally, I include as wealthholders all the free white[17] and black men and 10 percent of all the free white women in all regions, and 10 percent of the free black women in New England and the Middle Colonies. The percentages in columns 2, 3, and 4 show the relative frequencies of various subgroups of the total population, the free population, and the wealthholders respectively.

Probate- and Nonprobate-type Ratios

Not all living wealthholders could be expected to have wealth corresponding to that of probates (even of the same age), because not all who died were probated. Nonprobate types may very well have held different wealth, and some fraction of living wealthholders must have been like them. To estimate their number, I considered the following.

How many wealthholders (i.e., free people who might have held wealth) died in 1774 in the various regions without having their estates probated? Death records do not tell us, and indeed do not exist for many places. Court files and records tell us how many estates were probated, and that not always with the clarity desired.[18] If the estates probated in one year were fewer than the expected wealthholder deaths, the difference would have to be an estimate of the number of nonprobated wealthholder decedents in the year. Their proportion might be expected to pertain also to living wealthholders. Despite the lack of good mortality statistics for each region,[19] I saw no escape from an estimate, even if only a crude one, of wealthholder deaths to check on this point. I made the check in the sample counties.

I counted the total number of 1774 probate cases[20] in each of the sample counties that I had visited or whose records I had obtained from a state archives or library. This count was compared with my best estimate of the number of wealthholder deaths expected in one year in the same county. Expected deaths were derived from my estimate of the number of free wealthholders, by age groups, in the county,[21] multiplied by adult death rates.[22] For each sample county, the percentage of expected wealthholder deaths formed by the number of probated estates was calculated. This yields the proportion of wealthholder deaths probated. Since these counties were randomly drawn in accordance with the sample design discussed in appendix A, it seems reasonable to estimate overall regional probate ratios from these samples. Accordingly, I combined these percentages with equal weights,[23] and the resulting percentage is my probate ratio for the region. One hundred percent minus that percentage is the nonprobate ratio.

The regional percentages so determined were as follows:

	Probate ratio	*Nonprobate ratio*
New England[24]	.34	.66
New York[25]	.60	.40
Middle Colonies		
(Pa. N.J., Del.)	.64	.36
South[26]	.68	.32

These percentages, multiplied by the estimated total numbers of living wealthholders on lines 21, give us the numbers of living wealthholders of probate and nonprobate type on lines 28 and 29 of tables 2.4 through 2.7. (Estimation of the wealth of living "nonprobate-type" wealthholders is discussed in appendix A.)

LAND

Land in the colonies by 1774 was virtually all privately owned except for such things as some remaining "common lands" in New England towns, sites of courthouses, town halls, jails, churches, customs houses. The form and conditions of tenure had evolved from English feudal law (see Hughes 1976:chap. 5), with such vestiges as annual ground rent, still paid in Pennsylvania and Maryland to the proprietary government, representing the crown. For those who owned it, land[27] was a considerable proportion of total wealth.

Free or cheap land was an important attraction to early immigrants who arrived under grants or arrangements with the crown or crown-chartered companies. They settled principally at sites on the seacoast, or short distances up navigable rivers. In 1774 the densely settled areas were primarily along the coast or in major river valleys,[28] with a slight penetration west of the Appalachian mountains. In the South, where many navigable rivers and creeks gave access to good land in the coastal plains and westward into the Piedmont, the population was more dispersed than in the North. There were substantial areas of cleared land east of the Adirondack and Appalachian mountains devoted to crops and raising of livestock. The initial tasks of wresting land from the Indians and of clearing sites for agriculture and dwellings had already been accomplished to a considerable extent, particularly in the older counties. In the newer counties, usually the more western ones, a higher proportion of the land remained woodland or marshland. Samuel Blodget, writing in 1806, estimated that in 1774 there were 20.8 million acres of "cultivated" or "improved" land in the colonies that later became the United States (1806:60). This is about 8 percent of the 249.3 million acres within the present boundaries of the eastern seaboard states, including West Virginia, subsequently formed from the territories of the thirteen colonies.

It was from the land that the colonists and their families created products to sustain themselves and add to wealth. And it was for the intensive cultivation required for certain valuable crops such as tobacco and rice that they turned to augmenting the sparse labor force with slaves when the supply of indentured servants proved inadequate. Production above the needs of personal sustenance and maintenance of capital was the source of wealth accumulation. This occurred directly in the accretion of homemade furnishings, equipment, livestock, and stores of food and fiber. Accumulation was also facilitated indirectly by exchange within the locality and by coastal and overseas trade.

Regional Specialization

Regional specialization had developed to a marked degree by 1774, as table 2.8 shows. In Virginia and Maryland the main crop was tobacco, highly valued in Europe, which formed the principal market for tobacco exports. In this pre-cotton-gin era, cotton was not yet a significant southern crop. In South Carolina and Georgia rice and indigo used for dying cloth were the most valuable crops and ones for which England paid bounties. Tobacco, rice, and indigo formed three of the five highest-valued commodities exported from the British North American colonies in the five-year period 1768–72. (Shepherd and Walton 1972:98, 1976:408–9). In North Carolina there was relatively more cattle and grain raising, with exports of forest products. The Middle Colonies, sometimes known as the bread basket, had significant exports of flour, meat, grains, flax seed, and some tobacco, chiefly from Delaware. In New England, where soil was poorer and the climate less favorable, livelihoods often depended on a combination of the sea, the forest, and to some extent minerals. Fishing, whaling, shipping, and shipbuilding were sea related and furnished such exports as whale oil, dried fish, ships, and shipping services. The forest yielded such exports as timber for masts, shingles, boards, barrel staves, and potash. Of the five highest-valued commodities exported in the period 1768–72, "bread and flour" ranked second and came preponderantly from the Middle Colonies and the upper South, and "dried fish," which ranked fourth, came chiefly from New England (ibid.). Some pig and bar iron, made from bog iron, were exported from New England, New York, Pennsylvania, and Maryland. Coastal shipping, moving products between the colonies, as well as trade with the West Indies and Europe (Shepherd 1970:13–21) were important to the regional economies.

The comparative values for some major commodity exports in the year 1770, for which exports by region have been tabulated by Shepherd, are summarized in table 2.8. The regions presented coincide with those used in this study, except that figures for the South are shown separately for the upper and lower South. For New England, the table clearly shows that exportable products came principally from the sea and forests, and only to a much smaller degree—in beef and pork, for example—from agriculture. For the South, the tobacco came principally from Virginia and Maryland and the indigo and rice chiefly from South Carolina, with smaller amounts from Georgia. For the lower South, the lesser-valued exports of pitch, tar, and turpentine, boards and staves came in large part from North Carolina.

Urbanization

While most of the land was rural, cities had grown at sites of good harbors (Bridenbaugh 1955; Warner 1968:3–21). There was Rockingham in New Hampshire, Boston, Salem, Plymouth, Newburyport, and Marblehead in Massachusetts, Newport and Providence in Rhode Island, New Haven and New London in Connecticut, New York City, Philadelphia, Wilmington in Delaware, Baltimore and Annapolis in Maryland, Norfolk and Virginia City in Virginia, Charleston in South Carolina, Savannah in Georgia. The largest city, Philadelphia, had a population of about 25,000; Charleston's population was around 16,000 and Boston's about 12,000. County seats and towns or cities that were regional market centers had developed, usually on navigable river sites, and ranged in size from a few hundred to several thousand persons. Such places as

Table 2.8
Major Commodity Exports by Region, 1770
(*In Pounds Sterling*)

	Thirteen Colonies	New England	Middle Colonies	Upper South	Lower South
Tobacco	724,186	—	—	723,286	900
Bread and flour	467,166	20,800	346,101	96,019	4,246
Rice	266,708	1,697	4,427	—	260,584
Dried fish	147,342	145,099	1,673	557	13
Wheat	138,674	218	35,435	101,657	1,364
Pine, oak and cedar boards; staves and headings	135,132	61,014	28,607	20,201	25,310
Indigo	103,925	—	—	495	103,430
Whale oil and spermacetti candles	79,289	73,282	5,670	17	320
Indian corn	70,487	2,895	16,933	40,632	10,027
Iron, pig and bar	66,134	1,552	38,249	26,209	124
Beef and pork	57,039	16,938	17,942	14,863	7,296
Flaxseed	50,178	1,700	43,398	5,065	15
Deerskins	48,940	—	2,927	14,282	31,731
Pitch, tar, turpentine	38,498	2,160	2,050	5,428	28,860
Potash	31,687	21,294	10,228	165	—
Rum, American	21,745	19,088	2,658	—	—
Bees wax	5,668	434	3,850	639	745

SOURCE: Shepherd and Walton (1972), appendix tables 2–6, based on the American Inspector-General's Ledgers (London, Public Records Office, Customs 16/1) for quantities, valued at prices from Benzanson, Gray and Hussey (1935), Benzanson, Daley, Dennison and Hussey (1951), Cole (1938), G. Taylor (1931–32 for rice) and a few miscellaneous contemporary sources. Figures are totals for exports to Great Britain, Ireland, southern Europe, West Indies, Africa.

NOTE: Corresponding figures by individual colony for each year 1768 through 1762 are found in table 3 of Shepherd (1970:13–21). Upper South includes Maryland and Virginia. Lower South includes North Carolina, South Carolina, Georgia.

Worcester City, Massachusetts, Hartford, Connecticut, Albany, New York, Harrisburg, Pennsylvania, Burlington City, New Jersey were known as cities. Among market or county-seat towns were such places as Springfield and Northampton in Massachusetts, Litchfield in Connecticut, Easton, Chestertown, and York in Pennsylvania, Trenton in New Jersey, Dover in Delaware, Hillsboro in North Carolina. All had market days if not continuous markets and most had an inn, some artisan shops, and general traders or storekeepers.

About three-quarters of the wealthholders in the sample held land and buildings (real estate) as a major and highly significant asset. Since the population resided predominantly in rural areas, it follows that the bulk of the land they held was rural. However, the urban cases in our sample, found chiefly in the North, frequently owned their own houses and town lots, and sometimes those who were well-off had another house or two that they rented out. Such a town-dweller sometimes held in addition one or more farms or "plantations" or "tracts of land" in rural areas. Some rural inhabitants held, in addition to their farmland, a "town lot in Annapolis" (Maryland) or a "town lot in Hillsboro" (North Carolina), though this was rarer.

Land Tenancy

Land tenancy existed, for example, in Maryland and in Pennsylvania. A man in our sample might own livestock and farming tools, yet not be a landowner. He paid rent to the owner of the land he farmed. Likewise, a merchant might have a substantial inventory of merchant goods in a shop attached to or in one or more rooms of his house, or an artisan might have a considerable stock of materials and tools in the shop part of his house, yet each might be an urban renter rather than a property owner. This was found in this study particularly in cities such as Philadelphia, Boston, and Salem.

We have now examined the colonial population on the eve of the Revolution, the wealthholders, and the land resources available to them for the creation of wealth. We now go to chapter 3 for the story of colonial wealth itself.

CHAPTER THREE

 Aggregate and Per
Capita Private Physical
Wealth for Thirteen
Colonies and Three
Regions

O N the eve of the American Revolution, how much private wealth
had been accumulated by the 2.35 million people[1] who
inhabited the thirteen colonies? Of what did their wealth consist?
Were the various regions equally well off? How many of the colonists
were rich and how many poor? How did their wealth compare with
that of other times and places? Answers to these questions are basic
to analyses of the economic growth and welfare and appraisal of the
social structure of the colonies, as well as to comparisons with the
later United States. This chapter and the next two attempt answers
to the first three and last questions. Discussion of the rich and poor is
the subject of chapters 6 and 7.

TOTAL PHYSICAL WEALTH

The aggregate private physical wealth of all thirteen colonies in
1774, according to my estimate, was around 110 million in British
pounds sterling, or about five and a quarter billion dollars in 1976
values. Of this total over one-half was in the South, about one-fourth

Table 3.1
Private Physical Wealth, 1774
(*Aggregates in Thousands of Pounds Sterling*)

	Total (1)	Nonhuman (2)	Slaves and Servants (3)
(1) Thirteen colonies combined	109,570	88,106	21,463
(2) New England	22,238	22,136	101
(3) Middle Colonies	26,814	25,782	1,032
(4) South	60,518	40,188	20,330

SOURCE: Sample data, w^*-weighted averages per wealthholder, Variant Two for the South (see appendix A), multiplied by the total numbers of wealthholders on lines 21 of tables 2.4 through 2.7 respectively.

NOTE: Private physical wealth excludes that of the government sector, which I believe was negligible. Components may not add precisely to totals owing to rounding. To approximate the equivalent in dollars of 1976 purchasing power, multiply by $47.77 (or a rounded $48); see table 1.2. For exchange rates of local money of the various provinces to the pound sterling in 1774, see table 1.1.

in the Middle Colonies, and the balance in New England (tables 3.1 and 3.2). This total includes a valuation of nearly £21.5 million sterling of nonfree human capital in the form of slaves and indentured servants, found predominantly in the South. Value of "real estate" (land, structures, and other improvements thereon) is included, as well as all forms of portable physical nonhuman wealth, such as livestock, crops, tools and equipment, and other producers' and consumers' goods, both durable and perishable. Financial assets are excluded from the totals of aggregate physical wealth. Data on financial assets and liabilities, along with some inferences on the foreign indebtedness of the colonies, will be presented in chapter 5.

Table 3.2
Regional Distribution of Private Physical Wealth and of Wealth
in Slaves and Servants, 1774
(*Percent*)

	Thirteen Colonies	New England	Middle Colonies	South
(1) Total physical wealth (2 + 3)	100.0	20.3	24.5	55.2
(2) Slaves and servants	100.0	0.5	4.8	94.7
(3) Nonhuman	100.0	25.1	29.3	45.6

SOURCE: Table 3.1.

Human Physical Wealth

The economic reasons for restricting the concept of physical "national wealth" to nonhuman wealth are particularly cogent when, as in the case of the colonies, valuation data available for human capital pertain only to a nonfree segment. As I noted earlier, if nonfree human capital were to be included in the analysis of colonial "national wealth," a parallel estimate of the human capital value embodied in the free persons of the colonies would be needed to round out the estimate. The fragmentary colonial data on age, wages, income, and living costs scarcely justify an attempt to estimate the capital value of free colonists as their lifetime earnings minus their lifetime maintenance and rearing costs. However, a crude minimum estimate might be made, on the assumption that a free person was worth at least as much as a slave. Likewise, an indentured servant's lifetime value—as opposed to the valuation for remaining time of servitude, which is the only value that appears in the probate inventories—might be assumed to have been at least as much as that of a slave. On this basis, we might add a minimum of £63.2 million to the aggregate totals of table 3.1. This addition values the free population at £34.0 per head and white servants at a differential of £25.0 more than their values shown in the probate inventories.[2] Such an addition of £63.2 million in free human capital to table 3.1 would quadruple the human wealth shown in its column 3 and increase all physical wealth shown in column 1 by almost 58 percent, to a total of almost £173 million.

The absolute increase would be shared almost equally in the three regions, since the free population was roughly so divided (see table 3.3). Such an addition would substantially reduce but still not eliminate the southern wealth advantage over the northern regions. Such valuation of free human capital would also solve the paradox debated by John Stuart Mill.[3] For the major thrust of this chapter, I will consider the most meaningful analysis to be that of nonhuman physical wealth; but contributions of slaves and servants to differences in methods of production and to consumption patterns in the several regions seem relevant to the present study. Hence total estimates are presented both including and excluding nonfree human capital; the reader may select the figure most relevant to the particular problem or question he may wish to pursue. The topic of

Table 3.3
Distribution of Population by Region, 1774
(*Percent*)

	Thirteen Colonies	New England	Middle Colonies	South
(1) Total population	100.0	25.8	27.2	47.0
(2) Whites	100.0	32.0	32.5	35.5
(3) Blacks	100.0	3.0	7.6	89.4
(4) Men	100.0	25.4	28.1	46.5
(5) Women	100.0	28.0	26.8	45.2
(6) Adults	100.0	26.7	27.4	46.8
(7) Children	100.0	25.2	27.0	47.8
(8) Free	100.0	32.0	32.2	35.9
(9) Nonfree	100.0	4.8	10.4	84.8
(10) Free men	100.0	31.4	33.1	35.4
(11) Free adults	100.0	32.9	32.3	34.8
(12) Wealthholders	100.0	31.7	33.0	35.3

SOURCE: Tables 2.4, 2.5, 2.6, and 2.7.

NOTE: For separate population figures for New York and the other Middle Colonies see *American Colonial Wealth*, tables 4.23 and 4.25.

slaves and servants as wealth will inevitably arise again, from time to time, as we consider in succeeding chapters the components of private wealth and wealth distribution.

Nonhuman Physical Wealth

When we look at only the nonhuman physical capital of the thirteen colonies, excluding the £21.5 million in nonfree human capital (table 3.1), the aggregate private physical wealth of the colonies drops from £110 million sterling to a rounded £88 million sterling. This is equivalent to roughly $4.2 billion in 1976 prices. Of this total nearly half was found in the South (table 3.2), which also had nearly half the total population, including blacks and whites, and somewhat over a third of the wealthholders (table 3.3). Over a quarter of this nonhuman wealth was in the Middle Colonies including New York, which together had slightly over a quarter of the population. Less than a quarter was held in New England, which had a fourth of the population and nearly a third of the wealthholders of the colonies. Percentages of total population and of various subgroups by region are summarized in tables 3.3 and 3.4 as an aid

Table 3.4
Distribution of Population Within Regions, 1774
(*Percent*)

	Thirteen Colonies	New England	Middle Colonies	South
(1) Total population	100.0	100.0	100.0	100.0
(2) Whites	78.8	97.5	94.1	59.7
(3) Blacks	21.2	2.5	5.9	40.3
(4) Men	21.7	21.4	22.5	21.5
(5) Women	21.2	23.0	20.9	20.4
(6) Adults	42.9	44.4	43.4	41.9
(7) Children	57.1	55.6	56.6	58.1
(8) Free	77.3	95.8	91.3	59.0
(9) Nonfree	22.7	4.2	8.7	41.0
(10) Free men	16.8	20.5	20.5	12.7
(11) Free adults	33.4	42.5	43.3	24.7
(12) Wealthholders	18.5	22.7	22.4	13.9

SOURCE: Tables 2.4, 2.5, 2.6, and 2.7.

in visualizing the location of various kinds of people as a background to the regional location of wealth.

Both wealth and total population are taken account of in the per capita figures in table 3.5. The total physical wealth, excluding the value of slaves and servants, conceptually divided among the entire 2.35 million population—men, women, and children, free and

Table 3.5
Private Physical Wealth Per Capita
(*In Pounds Sterling*)

	Total (1)	Nonhuman (2)
(1) Thirteen colonies combined	46.5	37.4
(2) New England	36.6	36.4
(3) Middle Colonies	41.9	40.2
(4) South	54.7	36.4

SOURCE: Aggregates from table 3.1 divided by the numbers of total populations on lines 1 of tables 2.4, 2.5, 2.6, and 2.7 respectively.

NOTE: The note to table 3.1 pertains to this table also. Per capita values of total physical wealth, which includes the value of slaves and servants, are presented in column 1 only for comparison with relative magnitudes in column 2 and in subsequent tables. See the text discussion.

nonfree—yields a per capita figure of £37.4 sterling in 1774 for non-human physical wealth. This amount is roughly equivalent in purchasing power to about $155 current if the dollar had existed in 1774 or to about $1,782 in 1976 dollars ($2,029 in 1978 dollars) (see table 3.15 and notes). It compares with per capita private domestic tangible wealth of approximately $16,714 in the United States in 1973, equivalent to $21,120 in 1976 dollars ($23,950 in 1978 dollars). This is an increase of about twelvefold in real wealth per head in two hundred years. Later in this chapter I show comparable estimates for the United States for some intervening benchmark years and discuss economic growth rates and welfare implied. Later I will also show some comparisons with other countries. For a four-person family, the 1774 per capita figure implies an average wealth per family in the colonies of about £150, or over $8,100 in 1978 dollars.

SHARING OF WEALTH

As today or at any other time or place in history, per capita wealth, of course, tells nothing as to how the wealth was shared. There were striking differences in wealth of the colonists not only among geographical regions, apparent in tables in this chapter, but also among wealthholders within each region. The regional differences in total and in nonhuman physical wealth are discussed in this chapter, and differences by types of physical assets in chapter 4.

Nonhuman Wealth Per Adult

In considering the economic implications of £37.4 sterling per capita (or about $1,780 in 1976 purchasing power, $2,030 in 1978 dollars) of physical nonhuman capital for the colonies as a whole, it is important to recall that there was a much higher proportion of children in the colonial population (57.1 percent, table 3.4) than in the United States at the last decennial census of 1970 (38 percent). To the extent that we think of the physical nonhuman wealth as predominantly land and producers' goods, which it was (see chapter 4),[4] it is useful to look at the amount of wealth per worker, or, in today's terms, per member of the "labor force." The colonial labor force might be defined to include most adult men and women, most youths from 16 to 21 and considerable numbers of younger children. In the absence of specific information on proportions of nonworking men and women who would not be in the labor force, as well as incomplete knowledge of proportions of working children and youths, we may take the total number of adults, both men and women, as a very rough approximation of the size of the equivalent full-time labor force. Here I am using "labor force" to mean productive workers, whether self-employed working for the family or for others, and whether producing for household consumption or for sale in the market. Since so much of colonial production was by self-employed farmers and artisans and much of the product of both men and women (as well as of youths and children) was for household use rather than for the market, such a broad concept of labor force seems useful in thinking of colonial output. If we then exclude the children from our divisor, but use the same numerator of £88 million sterling of aggregate private nonhuman physical wealth, the new per adult figure of £87.2 sterling (table 3.6) is more than double the per capita figure. This wealth per adult, about $4,730 in 1978 purchasing power, may be thought of as roughly the capital, including land, available for combination with each member of the colonial labor force, both free and nonfree, for the colonies as a whole. If we subtract 9 percent for consumers' durable goods, the figure is lowered only to £79.4 or about $4,300 per adult in 1978 dollars.

Table 3.6
Private Nonhuman Physical Wealth Per Man,
Per Adult, Per White Capita, 1774
(*In Pounds Sterling*)

	Per White Capita (1)	Per Man (2)	Per Adult (3)
(1) Thirteen Colonies	47.5	172.3	87.2
(2) New England	37.3	170.3	82.0
(3) Middle Colonies	42.8	179.2	92.8
(4) South	60.9	169.1	86.8

SOURCE: Column 1: Aggregates from table 3.1 divided by the total white population on lines 2 of tables 2.4 through 2.7 respectively. Column 2: Same divided by the number of all men on lines 8 of the same tables. Column 3: Same divided by the number of all adults, the sum of lines 8 and 9 of those tables.

NOTE: The note to table 3.1 pertains to this table also.

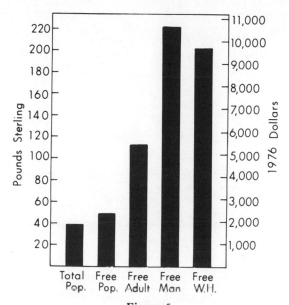

Figure 5.
Per Capita Private, Tangible, Nonhuman Wealth,
Total Population and Subgroups, Thirteen Colonies, 1774
SOURCE: Tables 3.5, 3.7, 3.9

Nonhuman Wealth Per Free Capita and Per Free Adult

In considering the social implications of the amount of non-human capital available to either the total colonial population or to the working population, we immediately confront the legal realities of the time. Not all of the people were free. The more than 480,000 slaves, and to a considerable extent as well the more than 53,000 indentured servants did not have the right to their own persons, nor to the income they produced, and hence may be viewed for all practical purposes as nonwealthholders, even though they may have used some of their owners' capital in productive activities. If we accordingly exclude all the nonfree persons from our divisor, and keep the same numerator for nonhuman wealth as above, the new per-free-capita figure rises to £48.4 (table 3.7) as compared with the £37.4 for the total population (table 3.5). If we further exclude the free children, the same physical wealth conceptually divided only among free adults (roughly about equal to the free labor force) yields

Table 3.7
Private Physical Wealth Per Free Capita, Per Wealthholder, 1774
(In Pounds Sterling)

	Per Free Capita		Per Wealthholder	
	Total	*Nonhuman*	*Total*	*Nonhuman*
	(1)	*(2)*	*(3)*	*(4)*
(1) Thirteen Colonies	60.2	48.4	252.0	202.6
(2) New England	38.2	38.0	161.2	160.5
(3) Middle Colonies	45.8	44.1	186.8	179.6
(4) South	92.7	61.6	394.7	262.1

SOURCE: Columns 1 and 2: Aggregates from table 3.1 divided by the numbers of free populations on lines 11 of tables 2.4 through 2.7 respectively. Columns 3 and 4: Sample data, average w^*-weighted.

NOTE: The note to table 3.1 pertains to this table also.

the considerably larger figure of about £112.2 sterling (table 3.9), or about $6,090 in 1978 purchasing power.

Nonhuman Wealth Per Free Man, Per Free Wealthholder

To visualize the amount of nonhuman wealth controlled by an average free family or free household, we may wish to drop the women as well as the children from the divisor, which brings us to an estimate of private nonhuman physical wealth per free man of £222.4 sterling (table 3.9) or over $12,000 in dollars of 1978 purchasing power. A free man may be thought of as roughly the head of a family or free household (see chapter 2). This figure is for stock of all physical nonhuman wealth including house, land, personal goods and is not an annual income figure. Besides the free men who held wealth, there were, as indicated in table 2.4, some free women, chiefly widows but also some single women, who held wealth in their own right. When we add our estimate of the numbers of wealthholding women to the numbers of free men in our divisor, and keep the same aggregate nonhuman physical wealth as above, the estimate of physical nonhuman wealth per free wealthholder in the thirteen colonies is reduced only slightly to £203 sterling (table 3.7) or roughly $11,000 in 1978 dollars.

REGIONAL DIFFERENCES

Wealth was far from equally divided among the three regions in 1774, although the numbers of free wealthholders in the regions were roughly the same. (In the ensuing discussion, I am including within the Middle Colonies' figures my best estimate for New York.[5] The South was the richest region in aggregate physical wealth, whether or not slaves and servants are included, but including them gives the South about 55 percent of the wealth of all the colonies, making that region almost three times richer than New England and over twice as rich as the Middle Colonies (table 3.1, column 1). This was due in part to the role that slavery played in the South, which gives a distorted impression of the wealth of that region in the most significant economic sense. The fact that part of a population owns another part does not necessarily make the region richer in total productive capacity, although it makes a big difference in comparative wealth of those who hold claim to the services of others.

Even without counting slaves (table 3.1, column 2) the South had nearly twice the wealth of New England and almost one and a half times that of the Middle Colonies. But on a per capita basis, free and nonfree, and counting only nonhuman wealth, New England was on a par with the South and both were topped by the Middle Colonies. Here the value of slaves and servants is excluded from consideration as physical wealth, but they are counted in the divisor as people sharing the wealth (table 3.5, column 2). This figure for the total population (black and white, free and nonfree, men, women, and children) was £36.4 sterling for the South, the same for New England, and was highest at £40.2 for the Middle Colonies. In terms of 1978 purchasing power, this was $2,181 for the Middle Colonies and $1,975 each for New England and the South.

The same aggregate wealth may be conceptually divided among other groups of the population to help us understand the relation of wealth to groups who may have made varying productive contributions to its creation and accumulation. When nonhuman physical wealth is calculated per adult or per man, both free and nonfree (table 3.6, columns 2 and 3), the same relative wealths (as in table 3.5, column 2) are found among the three regions, but at higher abolute amounts per head; that is, the South is again about on a par with New England and slightly below the Middle Colonies. When the nonhuman wealth is conceptually divided among only the white population (removing a much larger number of blacks from the denominator of the fraction in the South than in the other two regions—table 3.6, column 1), the wealth of the South, at £60.9 per white head, is 63 percent greater than that of New England and 42 percent greater than that of the Middle Colonies.

The southern advantage is roughly similar to the per-white comparison when nonhuman physical wealth is considered per free person or per free wealthholder, white or black (table 3.7, columns 2 and 4); or per free man or per free adult, white or black (table 3.9, columns 2 and 4). On this basis the wealth of the South is again over one and a half (1.6 or 1.7) times that of New England and almost half again as great as (over 1.4 times) that of the Middle Colonies. Per wealthholder, the figure is £262.1 for the South, as against £160.5 in New England and £179.6 in the Middle Colonies. This means that the average free wealthholder in the southern colonies drew upon approximately one and a half times the nonhuman wealth of wealthholders in New England and the Middle Colonies. In terms of 1978 dollars, these figures approximate $14,220, $8,710, and $9,745, respectively. A more unequal distribution of real income in the South probably stimulated saving and a consequent high per capita wealth accumulation.

Table 3.8
Value of Slaves and Servants Per Capita, Per Free Capita,
Per Wealthholder, 1774
(*In Pounds Sterling*)

	Per Capita (*1*)	Per Free Capita (*2*)	Per Wealthholder (*3*)
(1) Thirteen Colonies	9.1	11.8	49.4
(2) New England	0.2	0.2	0.7
(3) Middle Colonies	1.6	1.8	7.2
(4) South	18.4	31.2	132.6

SOURCE: Column 1: Aggregates from table 3.1 divided by the numbers of total population shown on lines 1 of tables 2.4 through 2.7 respectively. Column 2: Same divided by the numbers of free population on lines 11 of the same tables. Column 3: Sample data, w^*-weighted.

NOTE: The note to table 3.1 pertains to this table also. See also text discussion of limited usefulness of the "per capita" measure of wealth in slaves.

Table 3.9
Private Physical Wealth Per Free Man, Per Free Adult, 1774
(*In Pounds Sterling*)

	Per Free Man		Per Free Adult	
	Total (1)	Nonhuman (2)	Total (3)	Nonhuman (4)
(1) Thirteen Colonies	276.6	222.4	139.5	112.2
(2) New England	178.6	177.8	86.0	85.6
(3) Middle Colonies	204.1	196.3	105.7	101.7
(4) South	431.4	286.5	221.3	147.0

SOURCE: Columns 1 and 2: Aggregates from table 3.1 divided by the numbers of total free men in lines 12 of tables 2.4 through 2.7 respectively. Columns 3 and 4: Same divided by number of free adults, the sum of lines 12 and 16 on the same tables.

NOTE: The note to table 3.1 pertains to this table also.

If the value of slaves and servants is added to the numerator as a part of the wealth available to the free wealthholders (table 3.7, column 3), the advantage of the South is accented, both absolutely and relatively. The average £391.7 for the free southern wealthholder is almost two and a half times New England's £161.2 and over twice the Middle Colonies' £186.8. In terms of the 1978 dollar, the corresponding figures are $21,416 for the South, $8,747 for New England and $10,136 for the Middle Colonies. The tremendously greater wealth in slaves and servants held in the South is indicated not only by their aggregate value of £20 million pounds for the South (shown in table 3.1, column 3), as compared with only £1 million for the Middle Colonies and £100,000 for New England, but by the per-wealthholder figures of table 3.8, column 3. There we see that the average free wealthholder in the South held about 190 times as much slave wealth as a New Englander, and 18 times as much as a wealthholder of the Middle Colonies. In pounds sterling per wealthholder, the figures are £132.6 for the South, £0.7 for New England, and £7.2 for the Middle Colonies, or $7,195, $38, and $391 respectively, in 1978 dollars.

RELATION BETWEEN WEALTH AND INCOME

For comparison with other times and places, it is sometimes useful to have income rather than wealth figures. We lack substantial estimates of annual product or income for the colonies. However, a conversion of our figures to income can be made by way of a capital-output ratio (wealth-income ratio) that may reasonably be applied to the American colonies. The basis for such a ratio is less clear than we might wish (see part five of appendix A). U.S. observations for the nineteenth century by Goldsmith and Gallman and ratios observed in recent decades in some developing countries suggest a figure as low as three, or even two and a half, to one. On the other hand, work by various English estimators in the late seventeenth, eighteenth, and nineteenth centuries suggest ratios there of six, seven, or even more to one. A recent estimate by Feinstein for Britain in 1760 is ten to one when land is included, five to one when it is excluded from the definition of capital.

Some of the differences in ratios may be due to differing definitions of wealth and of output and some to other factors mentioned in a note to appendix A, part five. For the colonies we are dealing with a bundle of capital that in many ways was more medieval than modern, being comprised in large part of land, livestock, and household goods, with very little infrastructure, a tiny component of industrial capital but a somewhat larger component of commercial capital. The income included a large component of income in kind.[6] Selection of the particular ratio appropriate to the colonies in 1774 seems to me a very chancy matter. However, the reasonableness of the resulting income figure can be judged, in part, by viewing it in relation to export figures, where we have fairly good data, and to some plausible food consumption estimates.[7] For the purposes of a very rough comparison of colonial incomes with other times and places, I hazard that ratios of three or three and a half to one may be reasonable—that is to say, nonhuman wealth, including land, may have equaled three to three and a half times annual income or product.

Table 3.10 shows the range of per capita yearly income or product computed on this basis, and table 3.11 shows figures on per capita exports. The income figures may be considered roughly comparable to today's figures on per capita gross national product, or, since the government sector was almost nonexistent in the colonies in 1774, as somewhat more closely approximating today's figures on per capita personal income. They imply from £10.7 to £12.5 sterling. The low estimate is roughly equivalent to $231 at the 1958 price

Table 3.10

Range in Income Per Capita

Thirteen Colonies and Three Regions, 1774

	In Pounds Sterling		In 1976 Dollars	
	(1)	*(2)*	*(3)*	*(4)*
Thirteen Colonies	10.7–12.5		512–598	
New England	10.4–12.1		498–579	
Middle Colonies	11.5–13.4		551–641	
South	10.4–12.1		498–579	

SOURCE: Column 1 from table 3.5 column 2 divided by 3.5 (i.e., capital-output ratio of 3.5 to 1). Column 2 from same divided by 3.0. Columns 3 and 4 from columns 1 and 2, respectively, times $47.84 (see table 1.2).

NOTE: The income estimates are tenuous because of inadequate knowledge from which to determine the correct capital-output ratio (see appendix A, part five). Consumer durables comprise about 9 percent of the wealth in table 3.5. If they were excluded from the wealth concept, both in computing the ratio and then in dividing wealth by the ratio, the income figures shown here would change negligibly. In dollars at 1958 purchasing power, the multiple is $21.62 and figures in column 3 become $231, $225, $249, and $225. In dollars at 1973, 1977, or 1978 purchasing powers, the multiples to convert the figures in columns 1 or 2 to the desired year are, respectively: $37.86, $50.52, and $54.26. For some alternate capital-output ratios, ranging from a possible high to a possible low ratio, the figures on line 1 column 1 would become: at 5 to 1 (table 3.5 column 2 divided by 5), £7.5 or $359 in 1976 dollars; at 2.5 to 1, £15.0 or $718.

level, or to $512 in 1976 dollars and $580 in 1978 dollars per head. For a family of four, this would mean an annual income of over $2,300 in 1978 purchasing power. The $231 is substantially larger than the approximately $145 around 1776 (at 1958 prices) implied in Goldsmith's[8] projection backward to the seventeenth century of the 1.6 percent annual growth in per capita income in the United States for the entire period 1839–1959, discussed later in this chapter. The $231 is more than double the speculation of Albert Fishlow[9] that around $100 in per capita income (at 1958 prices) would have been a minimum for the United States in the 1780s, a decade of war and recovery from war. This level of income would place per capita commodity exports at about 12.3 percent of total product. It is near the middle of the per capita income range estimated by Klingaman (shown in note 7) on the basis of food consumption. The high estimate of £12.5 sterling is equivalent to $270 at the 1958 price level, or almost twice the $145 projection that Goldsmith considered too low. And it is nearly three times Fishlow's speculated minimum, and toward the upper range of Klingaman's preferred income estimates. At 1978 prices, it implies $678 per head, or about $2,700 for a family of four. I conclude that from £10.7 to £12.5 is a fair guess at per capita income in 1774.

In considering the meaning, in terms of purchasing power in the late colonial era, of an income of roughly £11 to £13 sterling, I refer the reader to tables 1.3 through 1.7 and to B. Smith (1979) for values in the city of Philadelphia. We should also bear in mind the larger component in 1774 of home production for home consumption (non-monetary production), and the availability to many colonists, on a free basis except for the real cost of gathering, of items that have since become scarce "economic goods," such as wood for fuel,[10] wild berries, fish, fowl, and game. Also the colonists had ready access to simple outdoor recreation and unpolluted clean air.

The southern income figure, though seemingly on a par with that for New England, would be much higher, 17.4 to 20.3 pounds, or $944 to $1,101 in 1978 purchasing power, if the income were figured as shared by the white population only (see table 3.6). The corresponding calculation would scarcely change the New England figures, and the Middle Colonies' figure would rise only to £12.2 or £14.3, or $662 to $776, distinctly below that of the South. Although I have included all the nonfree population, both black and white, in the divisors for table 3.10, their access to the yearly income was in fact limited, though of course they shared in food and had the use of some clothing and minimal shelter.

Export Earnings

The magnitude of the income numbers may be better sensed if they are viewed in the perspective of one year's export earnings of the colonists. The work of James Shepherd gives us that information, which is summarized in table 3.11. As exporters of commodities, the southern colonists, with their highly valued staples of tobacco, rice, and indigo, were better off than their northern counterparts. However, the "invisible earnings" from shipping services were an important source of compensation to New England for its relatively

Table 3.11
Value of Exports Per Capita
Thirteen Colonies and Three Regions, 1770
(*In Pounds Sterling*)

	Commodities	*Total*
Thirteen Colonies	1.32	1.70
New England	0.85	1.56
Middle Colonies	1.10	1.57
Upper South	1.80 ⎱	1.85
Lower South	1.55 ⎰	

SOURCE: Column 1, Shepherd (1970:68); Shepherd and Walton (1972:101). Column 2 Shepherd (1970:70); Shepherd and Walton (1972:102).

NOTE: Column 2 includes value of "invisible earnings" from shipping services. Upper South includes Maryland and Virginia. Lower South includes North Carolina, South Carolina, Georgia.

poor agricultural output. When these values are included, New England and the Middle Colonies are on a par with each other and not far behind the South, on a per capita basis. The export advantage of the South would be substantially increased if the figures were stated on the basis of whites only, or were calculated per free family or per free wealthholder. That commodity exports alone contributed something like 10.6 to 12.3 percent of the colonists' per-capita income around 1770 (depending on which capital-output ratio one chooses) suggests the great economic importance of the Atlantic community of nations.[11] Although revolutionary sentiment was rising, and colonists were chafing under monetary and other restrictions of the British crown, they profited from the economic advantages of operating within the imperial shelter. The bounties on rice and indigo were a boon to the lower South. The regulations restricting shipping to British ships, which included those of the colonies, were advantageous to northern colonial shipbuilders and suppliers of shipping services.

Although much of colonial production was sold within the colonies[12] or consumed directly in the home, earnings from exports of goods and shipping services were substantial, and, conversely, imported goods were available, particularly in the larger centers and to the well-to-do. The colonists also received services, such as protec-

tion by the British navy, that aided colonial commerce as well as pro-
viding security.

COMPARISON WITH OTHER TIMES
AND PLACES

How did the wealth or the income of the colonies compare with
that of England or some other European countries at somewhere
near the same time? How does it compare with that of some
underdeveloped countries today? How had it grown through the
colonial period, and what has been its subsequent growth in the
United States? These questions are not readily answered, but in
following sections I give some approaches toward answers, drawing
on data from other studies.

Contemporary England and Europe

We turn to estimates of varying reliability by contemporaries for
an idea of magnitude of wealth and income in the United Kingdom
and Europe. Figures by Gregory King (1936:31, 61) pertaining to
the close of the seventeenth century and by Arthur Young (1771:389–
93) for around 1770, as well as estimates for some later dates by
other authors for Great Britain or the United Kingdom have been
critically compared and set forth by Phyllis Deane[13] and by Deane
and Cole (1967:82, 156), subsequently reviewed by Sidney Pollard
(1968:336 ff), and discussed by François Crouzet (1972:19–30). The
most recent estimates are by C. H. Feinstein (1978a,b). Convenient
summaries and evaluations are found in Studenski (1961:30–36, 41–
43, 51). Comparisons can be only approximate because of differences
in methods and in definitions of wealth or income. For France[14] and
Holland, I have found no reliable eighteenth-century figures; for
them we are limited to the 1695 estimate of King (table 3.12). From
the King estimate, I conclude, as did Phyllis Deane, that at the close
of the seventeenth century, England was only slightly behind Holland
and ahead of probably all other countries of the world in material
welfare. It was also ahead of many Third World countries of today.
The English per capita income figure of £7.8 is lower than our very
rough estimate of that for the colonies in 1774. (If we exclude gold

Table 3.12
Income Per Capita, England, France, Holland, 1695
(*In Pounds Sterling*)

England and Wales	7.8
France	5.9
Holland	8.1

SOURCE: G. King (1936:55). Cited also in Deane (1955). Both King and Deane show the figures in pounds, shillings, and pence, which I have reduced to pounds and decimal equivalents. The figures for 1688 were substantially the same as for 1695. Population figures shown by King are: England and Wales, 5.5 million; France, close to 14 million; Holland, around 2.2 million.

and silver coin, bullion, etc., King's figure would be lowered by 5 percent, to £7.4.)[15] However, our colonial wealth figure of £37.4 is lower than Britain's three quarters of a century earlier (table 3.13). This reversal reflects my choice of capital-output ratio, discussed in appendix A. King's 1688 per capita wealth figure for England and Wales, which corresponds, as closely as I can judge, to my estimate of nonhuman physical colonial wealth, is £55 sterling, and may be somewhat high. Closer to our 1774 date there is Arthur Young's estimate for 1770 for England and Wales, which, figured to correspond to our definition of private nonhuman physical wealth, yields an amount of £135 wealth of £15.4 income per capita[16] (table 3.13). This estimate is considered less reliable than King's and has been criticized as being too high, particularly in its agricultural component.

Revised estimates for Britain (excluding Ireland) of wealth and income by C. H. Feinstein became available to the author rather late in the preparation of this book. They are discussed briefly and are shown in table 3.13. They are lower, both for wealth and for income, than Young's estimates, but substantially higher in wealth than our colonial estimate. Whether the true colonial income was actually as close to Feinstein's figure of £10 per capita for Britain as the low estimate in the table shows hinges on the reasonableness of the 3.0 to 1 capital-output ratio for the colonies.

I find it difficult to believe, in view of the continuing migration to the colonies, usually in search of economic betterment, and the rapid rate of natural population increase, surely facilitated by ample food, that average income in the colonies could have been greatly

Table 3.13
Income and Wealth Per Capita, England and Colonies,
1688, 1774
(*In Pounds Sterling*)

		ca. 1770	
	1688	Low	High
Income:			
England and Wales	7.4	10.0[a]	15.4[b]
Thirteen Colonies	—	10.7[c]	12.5[d]
Wealth:			
England and Wales	55.0	108.9[e]	135.0[b]
Thirteen Colonies	—	37.4	—

SOURCE: For England and Wales, 1688, G. King (1936); for 1770, Feinstein (1978a) and A. Young (1771). For thirteen colonies, income from table 3.10, nonhuman physical wealth from table 3.5.

NOTE: Relative prices in England and Wales were not substantially changed from 1688 to 1770. See Deane (1966:36) and Deane and Cole (1967), long-term trend in British prices, 1661–1959, pullout at end of book. Hence I conclude we can compare directly, without need for price correction, the above English figures and our colonial figures calculated in pounds sterling as of 1774.

[a] Feinstein (1978a:84). Great Britain (excluding Ireland), £11 in 1760 at prices of 1851–60, or £10 at prices of 1761–70, using Feinstein's price indexes cited in table A.5. He uses a population figure of 7.87 million.
[b] A. Young (1771). I am dubious about these estimates. See note 16.
[c] Using a wealth-income ratio of 3.5 to 1. See appendix A, part five.
[d] Using a wealth-income ratio of 3.0 to 1.
[e] Feinstein (1978a) estimate for 1760. We should bear in mind that my study includes consumers' durable goods in estimates of wealth whereas the Feinstein estimates for Britain do not. They comprise 9 percent of nonhuman physical wealth in the colonies. I am indebted to Stanley Engerman (1979) for a rough calculation to move from Feinstein's wealth estimate (1978a:84 and passim.), valued at 1851–60 prices, to one at 1761–70 prices (see table A.5).

lower than in England. I also believe that, with documented colonial export income as high as shown in table 3.11, per capita income from all sources, including production for the domestic market and by families for their own consumption, could not reasonably be placed much below the lower bound of £10.7, or $512 at 1976 prices ($581 in 1978), of table 3.10. Hence I conclude that, if we had the true figures for both sides of the Atlantic, we might find the colonies in 1774 very nearly on a par in per capita income with England, but somewhat lower in wealth.

Is there an explanation for the wide gap between Feinstein's £109 and my £37? Appendix A gives various reasons for believing that the colonial wealth estimates presented here may be on the low side. There are also, despite his careful work, many uncertainties in the Feinstein estimates, suggested both by the definition he quotes in his opening headnote for the chapter and his remark on page 82. The former reads delightfully: "Conjecture: an opinion formed on slight or defective evidence or none." The latter reads: "As will be painfully clear to anyone who has studied the preceding pages, there have been very few items for which precise, objective, and comprehensive data could be found. . . ." The Feinstein estimates include several items for which I have no colonial counterpart: "public works and buildings," "roads and highways," "docks and harbours," "ships." The first two and "harbours" are conceptually not in my estimates. "Docks" and "ships" are undoubtedly understated by my relatively few inventory entries for "wharf" and for such items as "one-third of a sloop," "one-twentieth of a schooner." However, their deletion from Feinstein's estimates, at 1761–70 prices, would reduce his wealth figure only about 3.5 percent to around £105 per capita.

We are left with the possibility that British wealth per capita, which includes the wealth of the barons, lords, etc. and of other great landed estates, was considerably higher than that of the colonists, including the slave population. Income may have been higher in relation to wealth in the colonies because of the much lower value of land here, the importance of "free" income (gathered from the countryside), the lesser elegance of the finer private buildings, the relatively fewer "carriages and coaches," the as yet relatively small amounts of fixed industrial capital. Further work on capital-output ratios may bring more clarification.

The comparison is complicated by the existence of slave wealth in the South but not in England. Slave wealth has been excluded in the foregoing discussion from the numerator, although slaves are counted as population in the divisor. If we were to add the slave wealth and drop the slaves from the denominator, the colonial wealth figure of £60.2 per free capita (table 3.7, column 1) comes considerably closer to that of England than does the £37.4 of table 3.13. For the South alone, the figure is still higher at £92.7. Income per free capita, on this basis, would be something like £17.2 to £20.1 or $823 to $961 at 1976 prices ($933–$1,091 in 1978), for the thirteen colonies, and for the South would be from £26.5 to £30.9, or $1,268 to $1,478 ($1,438–$1,677 in 1978).

Some Other Countries Today

Our estimate of the income of the colonies may be very roughly compared with recent estimates of gross national product (GNP) per capita in a number of the lesser developed and more developed countries of the world.[17] The comparisons at best are only approximate because of many technical difficulties of measurement and should be used with caution, particularly the comparisons of centrally planned with relatively free-market economies. Our lower estimate for 1774 of $581 income per capita at 1978 purchasing power would be about $444 in 1974 dollars (or $382 in 1972 dollars), by the index of table 1.2. Our upper estimate for 1774 of $678 in 1978 dollars would be $519 in 1974 dollars (and $446 in 1972 dollars). The $444 to $519 in 1974 dollars may be compared with the numbers in the body of table 3.14, and the $382 to $446 in 1972 dollars with those in its note. If our colonial income range is somewhere near the correct mark, and to the extent that the present-day estimators of GNP for developing countries succeed in including allowances for value of items in the nonmonetary sector—such as food, cloth, and tools produced in households, whether or not they reach a market—it would seem that the thirteen colonies were at over twice the level of the group at $200 or less per capita, into which over a third of the world population today falls, and near the top of the level of the group at $200 to $499, which presently comprises more than another third of the world's inhabitants. Many of these present-day underdeveloped countries with low per capita GNP lie in Asia or Africa. Of countries in Central and South America, only three in 1974 had GNP per capita below $500. Factors favoring the North American colonies in 1774 and lacking in many of the present-day Asian and African low-income countries are the following: (1) the favorable ratio of land to population, the heritage of (2) European culture, including (3) literacy, (4) scientific knowledge, and (5) a long tradition of stable governmental institutions, all conducive to relatively high productivity in the important agricultural sector and to encouragement of commercial ventures. Simon Kuznets (1965:176–85 ff.) in a discussion, without the specific data we now have for the American colonies, argued that such factors as the foregoing would lead one to expect that the past growth patterns of present developed countries were not the same as those in prospect for many countries

Table 3.14
Gross National Product Per Capita
Average by Continents, and for Selected Countries, 1974
(*In U.S. Dollars of 1974*)

North America	$6,630	Oceania	$4,110
United States	6,670	Australia	5,330
		Indonesia	170
Europe[a]	3,580		
Sweden	7,240	Central America[c]	960
Switzerland	7,870	Mexico	1,090
Germany, Federal		Honduras	340
Republic of	6,260		
France	5,440	South America	950
United Kingdom	3,590	Argentine	1,520
Poland	2,510	Brazil	920
USSR	2,380	Colombia	500
Hungary	2,180	Bolivia	280
Asia[b]	230	Africa	403
Japan	4,070	Congo, People's	
Korea, Republic of	480	Republic of	470
Philippines	330	Kenya	200
Viet Nam, Socialist		Tanzania	120
Republic of	150		
India	140		

SOURCE: World Bank (1976:10–20)

NOTE: My estimate (table 3.10) of the private per capita income in 1774 of the thirteen colonies, in 1974 dollars, is $444; in 1972 dollars, $382. The World Bank *Atlas* of 1974, pp. 7, 8, gives the following summaries for 1972 (which are not presented for 1974 in the 1976 *Atlas*): Averages in 1972 U.S. dollars, for industrial countries, $3,670; for developing countries, $280; for centrally planned economies, $580. Within the developing countries, averages are shown for petroleum exporters, $270; higher income, $740; middle income, $260; and lower income, $110. Corresponding figures for 1974 would differ because of continuing inflation of the U.S. dollar (see table 1.2) and changes in relative exchange rates and in the income effects of increases in petroleum prices 1973. See the World Bank (1976:21–22) re. continuous updating of its methodology and re. limitations of intercountry comparisons that depend on exchange rate conversions. To convert to dollars of other years see note 24.

[a] Average excluding USSR.
[b] Average excluding Japan.
[c] Average including Mexico.

with low per capita income today. For the American colonists there was more than sufficient food for all, plenty of wood for fuel and building, and resources highly valued in export trade that, with ingenuity and work, could be transformed into income-producing items.

Nonetheless, although the average American colonist may have fared quite well, even by today's standards in underdeveloped countries, there was, of course, nothing like the wide diversity and richness of modern industrial product available in advanced industrial countries of today to many of their inhabitants of modest income. A literal comparison of the $444 to $519 per capita income (in 1974 dollars) for 1774 with the $6,670 shown in table 3.14 for the United States would indicate real income per capita in 1974 13 to 15 times as great as two centuries earlier. However, this is an overstatement of increase in private income, since the $6,670 includes (as, generally, do the other figures in table 3.14) the government sector. Gross national product per capita in 1974 for the United States, excluding the government sector, was something like $5,238. Personal income, which includes some government transfer payments to individuals, was $5,443 per capita. These figures seem to us conceptually more comparable with our colonial figures, and suggest real incomes per capita around 10 to 12 times as great as 200 years ago. The latter is the same increase as we find in real wealth in 200 years (discussed in a later section). Wealth figures are not available for the present for enough other countries to offer, instead of table 3.14, a comparison of their wealth with colonial figures. However, some estimates by Mulhall[18] are available for around 1880 and show the United States of that date comparing favorably in wealth with other industrial countries.

The Thirteen Colonies in Earlier Periods

We cannot determine with much certainty whether, when, or at what rates the wealth and income of the American colonies grew in the century and more before the Revolution. A number of quantitative studies of the period, based largely on probate inventories, have appeared in recent years and somewhat reduce the bounds of our ignorance. It would be most desirable if we could use these studies to find what was happening to the wealth and income of the colonies as a whole and for each of the major regions.[19] But most of the studies are of particular localities or limited areas, their methods vary, and the results of one are often inconsistent with those of another. So far as I can judge, income and wealth per capita appear to have reached rather high levels within 25 or 30 years of settlement; thereafter, for all regions combined, growth in per capita real nonhuman wealth was slow and fairly steady. Because of crop and European price conditions, weather and epidemics in certain years and places, and immigration and other factors making for differences, some colonies certainly moved ahead faster than others in some decades or shorter periods. But for the colonies as a whole, I suggest that the average increase for the first 75 year period following 1650 was most likely at around 0.3 percent per year, rising to perhaps 0.4 percent in the 1725–50 period and to 0.5 percent per annum in the last quarter-century before the Revolution. The rationale for these estimates and comparison of them with growth rates subsequent to the Revolution will follow some references to previous estimates of overall growth rates during the colonial period, and a brief summary of some of the individual studies.

Some Previous Estimates of Overall Colonial Growth Rates Raymond Goldsmith (1959, 1965) speculated as to whether a 1.6 percent annual rate for per capita real product growth in the United States, estimated for 1839–1959,[20] could have been attained in earlier years as well by considering whether the incomes per capita which that rate would imply for the seventeenth and eighteenth centuries seem plausible. He concluded that, in terms of 1958 dollars, incomes per capita of $145 in 1776, $80 in 1739, and less than $30 in 1676 were insufficient, even in the simpler conditions of the colonial economy, to keep body and soul together and were implausibly low. He argued further that one need not rely on that judgment alone, but may recall that average real income per head around 1958, in current American prices of that year, was "in the order of $200 in countries such as Mexico, Turkey and Portugal whose present standard of living for the mass of the population is hardly higher than that prevailing in colonial America" (Goldsmith 1965:355). He concluded that the growth of real product per head must have been at some slower rate prior to the nineteenth century, and that such a slower rate is consistent with the secular growth of real national income per head at that time in Great Britain, for which the trend has been estimated for a period of over 300 years (ibid:360, chart VI).

Following Goldsmith's opening of the question, there have been several subsequent speculations as to possible slower rates of growth of real product or income during the colonial period. These have included: a projection back from 1840 to a date somewhere late in the eighteenth century and perhaps earlier of an average rate of 1.3 percent per year (David 1967a,b); a suggested rate of 1 percent from around 1710 to about 1770–74, preceded and followed by periods of slower growth (G. Taylor 1964); and an estimate of an average rate of 0.3 to 0.5 percent per year for the entire period 1720 to 1840 (Gallman 1972:21–22). The difficulty with all these estimates has been the lack of empirical data, for either verification or rejection. A further serious problem that underlies all estimates of per capita income or output over such changing centuries as the seventeenth to the twentieth is the extent to which the measure captures home-produced goods and services consumed without money payment (Stark 1961:13–16), production and consumption that played a heavier role in the earlier centuries.

Recent Quantitative Studies The recent studies are usually of wealth and usually based on single counties, though Gloria Main (1972, 1973) covered several counties in Massachusetts, and in Maryland, for the period 1650–1720 and Anderson (1975a,b, 1979) studied probate inventories from five counties in Massachusetts and Connecticut plus some for New Hampshire to provide his New England estimates for 1650–1709. Menard, Harris, and Carr (1974) reported on four counties on the lower western shore of Maryland from 1638 to 1705. To adjust for possible cyclical or trend price changes Anderson and Main each deflated their findings by price indexes each derived from values in the inventories. Carr's group has also experimented with deflation by a consumer price index derived from inventory data. Anderson further made corrections for decedent age structure and assumptions as to wealth of nonprobates to estimate wealth of the living. Duane Ball (1976) studied Chester, a Pennsylvania county near Philadelphia, and Allan Kulikoff[21] gives an eighteenth-century wealth series for Prince Georges County, a relatively rich county on the lower western shore of Maryland. These by no means exhaust the list of recent studies.

Productivity estimates have also been made from inventory data. Ball and Walton (1976) for Chester County, and Anderson (1979) for Hampshire County, Massachusetts, measured factor productivity in agriculture during the eighteenth century. For some lower western shore counties in Maryland, Menard[22] has calculated that output of tobacco per hand doubled from around 1630 to 1670, but showed little productivity gain thereafter.

Productivity gains in shipping, through such means as reduction in piracy, reduced turnaround time in ports, and increased vessel size, have been estimated by North (1971) and Shepherd and Walton

(1972), and records of Philadelphia shipping activities over considerable time periods have been summarized by McCusker (1971, 1972). Egnal (1975) has computed a kind of composite measure of per capita exports and per capita imports, by region and for the thirteen colonies, in four time periods from 1720 to 1775.

From these individual studies, differing and sometimes conflicting answers as to the pacing of growth are not surprising, in view of the varying locations, differences in record survival in various counties, different sampling procedures, varying inclusions in wealth totals, and different procedures of price deflation and other adjustments to compensate for lack of coverage of the living population.

Anderson (1975a:171, table 11) finds very high growth rates for per capita real wealth (including land and capital, price deflated) for New England in the seventeenth century, particularly up to 1680, but thereafter a slower rate to 1710. I calculate his average rate from 1650–59 to 1680–89 at 2.5 percent and at 1.5 percent a year for the fifty year period from 1650–59 to 1700–9. He finds negative growth or economic stagnation through much of the eighteenth century in New England (Anderson 1979: table 3),[23] on the basis of productivity calculations from inventories of farmers taken during crop months in Hampshire County, Massachusetts, an inland county in the Connecticut River valley. His early high rates of growth correspond to the Essex County findings of Davisson (1967b:312–13), from which I calculate a 2.6 percent average rate of growth in mean probated estate value (including land, and I think not price deflated), from 1641–50 to 1671–79. Anderson's rate to 1680–89 and Davisson's rate are strikingly similar to a 2.5 percent rate roughly calculated by Menard (1976:124) for real physical wealth per capita (excluding land and price deflated) in Maryland from about 1655 to about 1685. However, G. Main's (1973) figures, calculated from decadal mean estate values in personal wealth (excluding land and price deflated), show negative growth in Boston for thirty years from 1650–60 to 1680–89. They also show negative or flat growth in rural Massachusetts through the whole fifty years from 1650–69 to 1700–9. But her means yield a 1.3 rate for Boston for the later thirty years from 1680–89 to 1710–19 and a rate of 1.8 for rural Massachusetts for the ten years from 1700–9 to 1710–19. Only for Maryland, where her figures start with the decade 1670–79, are her early rates of growth of personal estate (excluding land) high, and even there they are lower than Menard's for a part of the same period. I calculate from her means a rate of 0.9 percent for the ten years from 1670–79 to 1680–89, followed by virtually no growth to the decade of 1690–99, then growth at 1.3 percent from that decade to 1700–9. There followed negative growth from 1700–9 to the succeeding decade, 1710–19. The overall growth rate in personal estate shown by her Maryland figures averages 0.8 percent in the approximately forty years from 1670–79 to 1700–19. There are sharp year-to-year variations both above and below Main's trend lines, as is true of Davisson's and Nash's (1976a:569–71) for Boston and Philadelphia. These may reflect cyclical fluctuations in economic conditions to some extent. It seems more likely that they reflect principally the chance factor of whether or not a particularly poor or particularly rich person happened to be included among the fairly small numbers of cases probated in the particular year and place. In eighteenth-century Prince George's County, Maryland, Kulikoff (1979:table 1) found negative growth rates in per capita real wealth (personal wealth plus land, deflated) from 1705 to 1755, and then a strong growth period from 1755 to 1776, at the average rate of 2.7 percent per year.

Ball found slow increments in wealth in Chester County, Pennsylvania, during the eighteenth century. The analysis by Ball and Walton for that county concluded that the productivity increase could not be placed higher than at a rate of 0.2 or 0.3 percent per year through the eighteenth century. Higher efficiencies in shipping served to bring the figures up only slightly, since a much larger part of the population was engaged in farming than in shipping.

Egnal's (1975:200) composite index of imports and exports per capita, which he curiously calls income per capita, showed an overall increase of 0.5 percent per annum for the thirteen colonies from 1720 to 1775. This was heavily influenced by a high 3.0 rate in the period 1745–60, while he found negative or zero growth rates in the three other periods for the colonies as a whole. But among the regions, he found wide variations, with a strong period of 5.0 percent growth in the lower South from 1720 to 1735, and lower positive rates there in 1745–60 (from 1.0 to 2.5) and in 1760–75 (from 1.5 to 3.0). For the upper South, he found a positive rate of 1.0 for the period 1735–45, one of 2.0 to 3.0 in 1745–60, but negative rates in other subperiods. For the northern colonies (New England plus the Middle Colonies) his growth rates were zero or negative from 1720 to 1745, but then registered a strong 3.0 to 5.0 for the period 1745–60, followed by a drop for the 1760–75 period (minus 1.0 to plus 1.0). McCusker (1971, 1972:155) found a rate of 1.6 for per capita imports plus exports from Pennsylvania from the period 1725–29 to 1770–74. Egnal found that commodity imports, which fluctuated above and below £1.0 sterling per capita in all the regions analyzed, were pretty well matched in value by the commodity exports per capita until 1745. He observed that longer terms of credit were extended to the colonists by British exporters from 1745 to 1760, but not subsequently. T. Cochran (1975) suggests the need for careful reconsideration of estimates of American economic growth.

My Interpretation The size of probate wealth found by other scholars seems to indicate that by as early as 1650 per capita wealth was substantial. I suggest a plausible guess of £24 for nonhuman wealth in that year, a figure only about a third below my estimate for 1774. The £24 seems reasonably consistent with values in early probate inventories reduced to a per-person-in-household basis and consonant with implications of early estimates of needs of settling colonists shown in appendix E. This early colonial prosperity in the seventeenth century is attested not only by the research findings from the probate inventories and statistics of English trade with the colonies, but also by attraction of immigrants and by one of the greatest known natural rates of increase of population in the history of the world. Despite possible local or area spurts or lags or even negative economic growth in some periods following 1650, as suggested by some of the local studies I have mentioned, I perceive from consideration of their findings no synchronized upswings or downswings and no consensus as to a general trend that pertained to entire regions or to the colonies as a whole. I conclude that, despite wide ranges in year-to-year prices for tobacco, which seem to have been a particular problem from about 1680 onward, and despite possibly varying European demand for other colonial commodities, the great dominance of agricultural production, much of it for home consumption, and the counterbalancing effects of the wide variety of products exported from the several regions would tend to produce, for the colonies as a whole, a rather steady and not spectacular growth rate for the next century and a quarter after 1650. I suggest that a most likely trend of per capita wealth in the thirteen colonies may have been as follows:

Year	*Nonhuman Wealth Per Capita*	
	In Pounds Sterling	*In 1976 Dollars*[24]
1650	£24	$1,148
1700	28	1,340
1725	30	1,435
1750	33	1,579
1774	37.4	1,782

The 1774 figure, my estimate for the present study, is not far behind that of contemporary England or Europe and compares favorably with wealth of many underdeveloped countries today. The values in pounds sterling are presumed to be at the price level prevailing in the colonies in 1774. Since available indexes of prices in Britain show little or no long-term trend over this period (see note to table 3.13), and the available indexes of prices in the colonies are scanty, are fraught with technical weaknesses, and show no clear trends consistent from region to region, I conclude that the wealth in nominal pounds—that is, in pounds sterling at the purchasing powers of the respective years shown above—may not have differed greatly from the above figures. If there was a price inflation over the period, then real growth rates would have been somewhat smaller. That is, if the above figures were approximately correct nominal values, but prices rose over time, then the nominal pounds in the earlier years would have purchased relatively more goods than in the later years, and the growth rate would be correspondingly reduced.

If the 3.5 or 3.0 to 1 ratio of wealth to income, discussed in an earlier section and in appendix A, is used, the above figures would imply, at 1774 prices, colonial per capita incomes of £6.9–£8.0 in 1650, £8.0–£9.3 in 1700, £8.6–£10.0 in 1725, £9.4–£11.0 in 1750. These figures, whether expressed as per capita wealth or as per capita income, imply the following rates of economic growth for the indicated periods:

1650 to 1700	0.3 percent per annum
1700 to 1725	0.3
1725 to 1750	0.4
1750 to 1774	0.5

I conclude that from 1650 on there was overall a fairly steady rate of intensive growth for all regions combined. This may be said to have resulted from accumulated experience in the New World, learning by doing, from more knowhow in shipping within the Atlantic community, and from the increasing size of the market, all of which resulted in some increases in output per head that permitted savings embodied in agricultural and shipping capital, as well as some rise in ownership of livestock, in consumption goods, and in the quality of housing—in short, in the level of living. Improvements in agricultural efficiency were important in the Chesapeake area before 1660, as Menard has shown, and may have occurred again there in the eighteenth century with the shift from tobacco to wheat (Klingaman 1969). In the lower South, there were improvements in the production of rice when the crops were moved from relatively high lands to coastal marshes and tidelands; and the introduction of indigo as a new crop, with English bounties, around 1740 was an important addition to output. The Middle Colonies were engaged in a flourishing export business in grains and cattle in the mid-eighteenth century. Perhaps it was in New England, which, from the 1774 wealth figures, appears to have done the least well of any of the regions, that the slowest productivity gains in the eighteenth century were made. Even there, although the shipping benefits from reduction in piracy came by 1710, and greatest benefits of larger size of ships came after 1774, some of the benefits of reduction in shipping turnaround time and some of the income-multiplying effects of growth of urban services must have been taking place throughout the eighteenth century.

In the next section I compare the foregoing view of the early, preindustrial growth of wealth in the colonies with the course of American wealth growth at later dates.

United States Wealth at Benchmark Dates since 1774

To examine American economic growth for the two centuries since 1774, I believe the most useful measure is nonhuman physical wealth. I omit from the numerator the value of slaves and servants and I count all persons in the denominator at each date. To reduce the money values at the various dates to constant dollars I use the price index in table 1.2. In real per capita terms expressed in 1976 dollars, nonhuman physical wealth per person increased from $1,782 to $21,130 (table 3.15), a twelvefold increase in two hundred years.

(In 1978 dollars the figures are $2,021 and $23,966.)[25] This increase is at a compounded annual growth rate of 1.3 percent (table 3.16) for the entire period, and the rate was higher from the mid-nineteenth century to about 1929.

The reference dates for tables 3.15 and 3.16 are determined by the availability of conceptually comparable and fairly reliable wealth estimates, briefly summarized as follows:

1774: the findings of this study;

1805: the contemporary estimate of Samuel Blodget made in 1806;

1850 and 1900: estimates of Raymond W. Goldsmith based principally on U.S. census data;

1929 to 1973: Annual data series commencing in 1929 furnished by Dale W. Jorgenson, based principally on official estimates from the U.S. Department of Commerce. Figures from the Jorgenson series are closely consistent with aggregate estimates by Goldsmith for 1929 and the selected subsequent dates (Goldsmith, 1965, 1968) and by John Kendrick (1967; Kendrick, Lee and Lomask 1976), who extended Goldsmith's earlier estimates to 1966 and subsequently to 1975.

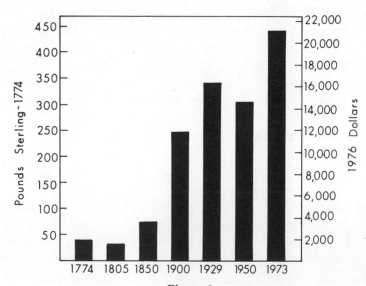

Figure 6.
Per Capita Private, Tangible, Nonhuman Wealth,
United States, Benchmark Dates, 1774–1973

Source: Table 3.15

Table 3.15
Private Tangible Nonhuman Wealth, Per Capita, United States
Benchmark Dates, 1774–1973

Year	Population (millions) (1)	Current Dollars (2)	Constant Dollars at 1976 Prices (3)
1774	2.35	"155"	1,782
1805	6.35	211	1,529
1850	23.67	298	3,590
1900	76.8	1,116	11,747
1929	122.	3,127	16,286
1940	133.	2,365	13,750
1950	154.	5,213	14,602
1960	182.	7,874	16,612
1970	206.	13,173	19,691
1973	211.	16,714	21,130

SOURCE: *Column 1*: 1774 from table 2.4. Other years, population at end of year, averages of two mid-year figures: 1805 from *Historical Statistics* (1960), ser. A-2; 1850 through 1929 from Goldsmith (1968:56; table 2, line IX); 1940 and later from *Historical Statistics* (1960), ser. A-2 and U.S. Office of the President (1975:275; table C-23).

Column 2: Figures for all years include private land and civilian structures; they exclude values of slaves and servants, financial assets, monetary gold and silver, and net foreign assets. Specific sources are:

For 1774: Per capita nonhuman wealth of 37.4 pounds sterling from table 3.5 multiplied by "$4.15" from table 1.2. The American dollar was not created until 1792.

For 1805: Wealth from Blodget (1806:196), divided by population in column 1. Total wealth includes for land $760 million of cultivated lands and "acres adjoining and near the cultivated lands," for structures and producers' durables $420 million, but excludes $20 million in "public buildings, churches . . . etc." and excludes $200 million in slaves; other components of Blodget's estimate are totaled by Goldsmith (1968:56, table 2) and described in greater detail in Goldsmith (1952:315–316).

For 1850, 1900: Goldsmith (1968:56), table 2, line VI, "National wealth in current prices" minus "Public civilian structures."

For 1929 and subsequent years: Computer printout for "Private domestic tangible wealth" supplied to the author by Dale W. Jorgenson, Harvard University; see also Christensen and Jorgenson (1973)

Column 3: U.S. dollar figures from column 2 divided by the linked price index, 1976 = 100, in table 1.2. The difference between $1,782 for 1774 derived in this way and the $1,787 for 1774 that results from £37.4 multiplied by the $47.77 ($1,789 by the preliminary $47.84) in the last column of table 1.2 is due to rounding. I consider $1,782 the better figure. For values in U.S. dollars at prices of other years, all numbers in column 3 may be multiplied by the factors shown in note 24.

NOTE: Pitkin (1817:367–68) found that execution of the Act of July 14, 1798 for the first direct tax of the United States yielded an estimate for 1799 of $620 million for land plus dwelling houses valued at over $100. His figures are 163,746,688 acres of land valued at $479,293,263 and 276,695 dwelling houses, valued including their lots at more than $100, at a total of $140,683,984. If population in 1798 was approximately 5,021,000, the $620 million averages $124 per capita in 1798 dollars.

Aggregate and Per Capita Wealth

Table 3.16
Growth Rates of Private Wealth Per Capita, United States
Benchmark Dates, 1774–1973
(Compound Annual Rates of Change)

To Terminal Year	Average Wealth[a] Per Capita (1976 $)	From Initial Year							
		1774	1805	1850	1900	1929	1940	1950	1960
1774	1,782	—	—	—	—	—	—	—	—
1805	1,529	−0.5	—	—	—	—	—	—	—
1850	3.590	0.9	1.9	—	—	—	—	—	—
1900	11,747	1.5	2.2	2.4	—	—	—	—	—
1929	16,286	1.4	1.9	1.9	1.1	—	—	—	—
1940	13,750	1.2	1.6	1.5	0.4	−1.5	—	—	—
1950	14,602	1.2	1.6	1.4	0.4	−0.5	0.6	—	—
1960	16,612	1.2	1.6	1.4	0.6	0.1	0.9	1.3	—
1973	21,130	1.3	1.6	1.5	0.8	0.6	1.3	1.6	1.9

SOURCE: Column 2 from table 3.15 in constant 1976 dollars. Other columns computed from values in column 2.

NOTE: I computed an alternate table, using for 1774 the $w*B$-weighted figure (under assumptions of Variant One in appendix A) of $2,024 in 1976 dollars (£42.3 in 1774 pounds sterling), which derives from the $w*B$-weighted average nonhuman wealth per wealthholder of £228.9 in table 7.7 of *American Colonial Wealth*. Figures in all columns in the alternate table, except column 3 headed 1774, are identical with those in the above table. The alternate values, using the Variant One initial figure for 1774, reading down in column 3 are: 1805, −0.9; 1850, 0.8; 1900, 1.4; 1929, 1.4; 1940, 1.2; 1950, 1.1; 1960, 1.1; 1973, 1.2.

[a] Private, domestic, tangible, nonhuman wealth.

Real private nonhuman physical wealth per person declined from the findings of my study in 1774 to Blodget's estimate in 1805. If we take the figures at face value, private real wealth per head declined at a rate of 0.5 percent annually over the period (table 3.16). The wartime disturbances of the Revolution and the political confusions of the confederation period may have set back real wealth accumulation more than it was enhanced by the profits from neutral shipping services during the early years of the Napoleonic Wars and from uneven success in regaining export markets in England and opening new markets in Europe. Although it must be recognized that the Blodget estimates of 1805 were a heroic one-man undertaking with weak statistical underpinnings, the decline over a war decade followed by a period of readjustment seems inherently sensible and consonant with the experience of the decade of the Civil War and its aftermath. A closely parallel decline in wealth from 1860 to 1870 has been found by Soltow, and in output by Kuznets and Gallman.[26]

The wealth decline to 1805 may be compared with the sharply criticized and much discussed estimates of Robert Martin that real per capita national income declined from 1799 to the 1810s and failed to rise enough to reach the 1800 level by 1839.[27] The possibility of decline to 1805 is further consonant with Stanley Lebergott's (1960:468 and his appendix C) estimate that farm real wages probably declined from 1800 to 1819 by less than 5 percent but non-farm real wages by from 10 to 20 percent during that period.

Rates of Growth   If we choose to ignore the 1805 Blodget estimate, we find that the per capita growth rate of wealth from 1774 to 1850 was 0.9 percent annually, bringing per capita wealth in constant 1976 dollars from about $1,800 just before the Revolution to nearly $3,600 prior to the Civil War.[28] By 1900 wealth reached $11,747 in 1976 dollars, and the average growth rate from 1774 to 1900 was 1.5 percent per year. The period to 1850[29] saw not only the Revolutionary War and the emergence of a national government but also the introduction of turnpikes, steamboats, steam engines, railroads, acquisition and settlement of western lands, growth of new cities, development of a substantial manufacturing sector, creation of banks and insurance companies, and the emergence of the corporation as a form of business organization. I believe that the wealth estimates for 1850 and 1900 are reasonably accurate, and that the per capita growth rate of private wealth in that half century was the greatest in the history of the country, with an average rate of 2.4 percent for the period. This period includes the decade preceding the Civil War, the war period, and the last third of the nineteenth century. In this half century came the ascendancy of mining and manufacturing, completion of transcontinental railroads, and pushing of the frontier to the Pacific coast, together with rise of trust companies and varied financial institutions, a national banking system, growth of large corporations, excess of manufactured exports over raw material exports, and other signs of the transformation from a relatively simple, dominantly agricultural economy to a modern industrial and financial giant.

We do not know when this great rate of wealth increase per head came to an end. Possibly it lasted up to World War I, during which a slowdown in the rate if not an actual decrease probably occurred. In any case, the average rate of growth for the first twenty-nine years of the present century, including the War I period, was

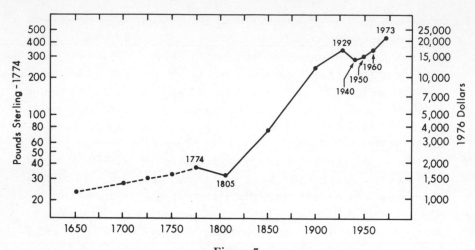

Figure 7.
Growth of Private, Tangible, Nonhuman Wealth,
Per Capita, United States, 1650–1973

SOURCE: 1650–1750, see text. 1774–1973, table 3.15
NOTE: To convert 1976 dollars to 1958 dollars, divide by 1152.7/521.0 = 2.21.
To convert 1976 dollars to 1840 dollars, divide by 1152.7/116.2 = 9.92.

1.1 percent, less than half that of the preceding half century, which included the Civil War period. Another absolute decline in real wealth occurred between 1929 and 1940, which had been only partially made up by 1950. The decline from $16,286 in 1976 dollars in 1929 to $13,750 in 1940 was an aspect of the Great Depression. By 1950, in spite of World War II, which terminated in 1946, per capita wealth was again growing and by 1960 exceeded the 1929 level, although the growth rate was much below nineteenth-century rates. For the entire forty-four years, 1929 to 1973, a period of recession, two wars, and inflation, the annual real growth rate in per capita wealth was further halved in comparison with the first twenty-nine years to 0.6 percent. For the thirteen years from 1950 to 1973, the rate improved to 1.6 percent, but still remained far below the impressive rate of the last half of the nineteenth century.

These figures on growth of real wealth, as opposed to the more often seen figures of national income or national product, have the advantages of wealth estimates pointed out in chapter 1. They are less subject to extremes of cyclical variation from year to year. In addition, with particular reference to dates in the seventeenth and eighteenth centuries and the years 1774, 1805, and 1850, they give at least some basis for judging economic growth when complete annual income or product figures are not available.

The figures for benchmark dates over a span of three hundred years are plotted in figure 7 on a ratio scale, such that relative steepness of the lines indicates relative growth rates. The dip to 1805 is less steep than that during the great recession years 1929–40, and there was no growth from 1950 to 1960. If we had comparable estimates for 1860 and 1870, it is quite possible that we would see a flattening, if not actual downturn, between those two dates. If the 1805 estimate should prove to be too low, a direct connecting of the points for 1774 and 1850 would show a relatively smooth growth rate for two centuries, accelerating in the latter half of the nineteenth. The trend of the poorer performance of the twentieth century until 1960, in comparison with the latter part of the nineteenth century is suggestive of the rates I find plausible for the seventeenth and three quarters of the eighteenth century. After 1960 the rate improved, but did not regain the extraordinarily high rate of the last half of the nineteenth century.

CHAPTER FOUR

Structure of Physical Wealth in Thirteen Colonies and Three Regions

O UR peering, as it were, into the households of the colonists by way of the probate inventories of their belongings offers clues to various aspects of their lives. Among these are their modes of production, implying the character of economic development, and their consumption goods, implying life styles made possible by the economic development. The appraised listings also reveal their ownership claims, including legally recognized rights in slaves or indentured servants. The treatment of legal claims to human beings, when viewed from the standpoint of relative command over and direction of the use of resources, belongs logically in a consideration of wealth distribution among various holders. From the standpoint of comparative modes of production and consumption in the different regions, however, they are pertinent to an analysis of types of assets held; therefore classifications both including and excluding human capital are offered in this chapter. I reserve to chapter 5 the discussion of net worth, which involves, in addition to physical wealth, the nature of financial claims, whether assets or liabilities. These claims also affect wealth distribution among various holders.

The three terms wealth, capital, and property, distinguished in chapter 1, are pertinent here. Without adopting any rigid definitions, I have attempted to arrange the data in such a way that the user can adapt them to his needs for the particular problem or analysis that may interest him. I tend to treat wealth as the broader term, one which includes land and other capital, both human and nonhuman, both producers' and consumers' goods. I view property as the legal aspect of ownership rights to specific forms of wealth.

WEALTH ANALYSIS

In this chapter we examine the components of the physical, nonfinancial wealth of the colonists. The tables arrange the data in ways to illuminate our understanding of the level of economic development and consumption attained by the eve of the American Revolution. For such economic analysis, various meaningful breakdowns of wealth are possible (Goldsmith 1952:275–76). Ideally, for economic (or social) analysis, cross-classifications by as many criteria as possible are desired, but they are usually not available for the full range of wealth items, and only a few one-way breakdowns are available.[1]

We may list the following breakdowns, all but one of which (item 2.f.) have been made in this study.

1 Characteristics of owners or wealthholders.
   a. By location (New England; Middle Colonies; South; urban; rural; county).
   b. By age class (younger—21–25, 26–44; older—45 and over).
   c. By sex (men; women).
   d. By occupation (farmers and planters; farmers with outside activity; esquires, gentlemen, officials; professionals; merchants; shopkeepers and innholders; artisans; mariners and laborers; etc.).
   e. By wealth class (high; middle; low).
   f. By testacy (testate; intestate).
2. Kinds of physical asset.
   a. By human capital and nonhuman capital (slaves and servants; all other physical assets).
   b. Nonhuman capital by portability (land, including structures and improvements thereon; portable nonhuman physical wealth).
   c. By purpose (producers' goods; consumers' goods).
   d. By industry (agriculture, not separated from household; clearly separable nonfarm business).

    e. By length of useful life (durable goods; perishable goods).

    f. By origin (imported; purchased on the market from colonial sources; or produced within the household for household consumption).

    g. Portable nonhuman physical wealth, by subclasses or types of physical assets (livestock, equipment, materials, crops, apparel, furnishings, etc.).

Characteristics of Owners

In studying colonial wealth from a sample of free wealthholders, we are actually in a better position than are present-day constructors of wealth estimates, who work from various national aggregates, to break down the amounts and kinds of property held by free owners with various characteristics. We are also forced to consider the wealthholding status of the nonfree population of the time.

Location   We will look separately at the total amounts and also the various forms of wealth held by the free owners, classified as to their location in major regions, as well as a composite for the thirteen colonies as a whole. The data also permit examination of wealth held by owners in specific sample counties within regions.[2]

Age, Sex, Occupation, Urban/Rural, Testacy, Wealth Class   Amounts and kinds of wealth held by owners grouped by age, sex, occupation, urban or rural residence, testacy, and wealth class are offered in subsequent chapters. These breakdowns afford inferences regarding social structure as well as life styles of various groups. They provide a general framework within which the increasing numbers of recent excellent studies[3] in social history may be placed in perspective. These in turn can supplement the present study with depth in time.

Sector of Ownership   One breakdown often made in current wealth estimates[4] but not feasible for colonial data is that by sector of ownership (private individuals or households; corporations; nonprofit institutions; governments; foreigners). This study is limited to private wealth held by individuals or households; no wealth held by governments is included. However, as compared with the present day, the government sector was small; its physical assets included chiefly such items as county courthouses, town meeting houses (which were combined with churches), town jails, town wharves, town common lands (which by 1774 had increasingly been divided up) and the like. States and their claims to western lands had not yet come into existence.

The data from probated estates do not indicate whether there was foreign ownership of some of the land or other physical assets. I believe such absentee ownership was relatively small by 1774.[5] It is well known that many original subscribers to stock in overseas settlement companies never received the returns anticipated from colonial undertakings. There were business partnerships in the colonial period, particularly in shipping ventures, but no limited liability corporations.

There were very few nonprofit institutions other than a hospital at Philadelphia, a few colleges such as William and Mary, Harvard, and King's College (which later became Columbia University), and a few academies. The data, coming as they do from probate inventories, give us coverage of the wealth held by private individuals most of whom in effect shared that wealth with members of their households. These wealthholders, individually or in partnerships, engaged in various kinds of business undertakings, of which by far the predominant one was agriculture. The wealth estimates therefore correspond to what in present-day estimates would be considered the private household and corporate sectors.

Kinds of Physical Asset

For insight into the processes of production and style of consumption of the colonists, breakdowns by type of asset are an important clue. (See table 4.1.) Human capital needs to be separated from nonhuman and, of the latter, the assets devoted to production need to be separated from those used directly for consumption.

(Nonfree) Human Capital A first and crucial breakdown for the colonial data, that by (nonfree) human and nonhuman capital (lines 2 and 3 of table 4.1), accommodates consideration of the economic meaning of the valuations of slaves and indentured servants. Such values were found in the probate inventories of all regions and need to be separated from other forms of "personal estate" listed there. For the purpose of viewing the real productive capacity of society as a whole (of all the colonies or of each region), as I noted earlier, the values of nonfree persons are best excluded from

Structure of Physical Wealth

Table 4.1

Components of Private Physical Wealth

(*Aggregates in Thousands of Pounds Sterling*)

		Thirteen Colonies	New England	Middle Colonies[a]	South
(1)	Total physical wealth (2 + 3)	109,570	22,238	26,814	60,518
(2)	Slaves and servants	21,463	101	1,032	20,330
(3)	Nonhuman, total (4 + 5)	88,106	22,136	25,782	40,188
(4)	Land (real estate)	60,221	15,874	16,584	27,763[b]
(5)	Nonhuman portable, total (6 + 15)	27,886	6,262	9,199	12,425
(6)	Producers' capital, total (7 + 11)	19,209	3,614	6,609	8,986
(7)	Durable, total (8 + 9 + 10)	13,781	2,674	4,125	6,982
(8)	Livestock	10,114	1,703	3,059	5,352
(9)	Equipment of farm and household	3,210	760	883	1,567
(10)	Equipment of nonfarm business	456	211	183	62
(11)	Perishable, total (12 + 13 + 14)	5,428	940	2,484	2,004
(12)	Crops	3,141	134	1,333	1,674
(13)	Materials in household	575	222	198	155
(14)	Business (nonfarm) inventory	1,712	584	953	175
(15)	Consumers' goods, total (16 + 19)	8,677	2,648	2,590	3,439
(16)	Durable, total (17 + 18)	8,007	2,520	2,407	3,080
(17)	Apparel	1,638	502	694	442
(18)	Equipment, furniture, other	6,370	2,018	1,713	2,639
(19)	Perishable	670	128	183	359

SOURCE: Sample data, w^*-weighted, Variant Two, averages per wealthholder, multiplied by the total numbers of wealthholders on lines 21 of tables 2.4 through 2.7 respectively. "Mixed categories" of nonhuman portable wealth are allocated in accordance with table 7.6 of *American Colonial Wealth*.

NOTE: Components may not add precisely to totals because of rounding.

Lines 10 + 14, business equipment plus business inventory, yield a total for the nonfarm business sector. All other lines pertain to the household sector, which includes farm business.

Lines 8 + 12, livestock plus crops, yield a total that may be conceived of as agricultural inventory.

Line 13, producers' materials in household, may be conceived of as household producers' inventory, analogous for the household sector to the nonfarm business inventory. The former includes producers' materials of relatively short life, such as shot, lime, tallow, salt, materials for making cloth and mattresses, as well as producers' materials of somewhat longer useful life, such as leather, cloth, boards, nails, glass. It combines two items shown separately in *American Colonial Wealth* (see its table 7.6) as "producers' durable materials" and "producers' perishables other than crops."

[a] Middle Colonies include New York. For corresponding separate figures for the middle colonies of Pennsylvania, New Jersey, and Delaware, and for the New York estimate see *American Colonial Wealth*, vol. 3, table 7.186. See also Introduction and Note on Method, section on New York hybrid.

[b] For the possibility that my southern land estimate is low see appendix A.

consideration unless a corresponding valuation is added for the human capital value of the free population. On the other hand, even without this balancing item, their inclusion is required for analysis of wealth distribution among individual wealthholders (chapter 6), and is certainly relevant to comparative analysis of modes of production and consumption in the various regions that are examined in this chapter.

Nonhuman Capital Aside from wealth claims to human beings, we have all the other forms of physical and financial assets. The physical assets may be further subdivided into "real estate" (line 4 of table 4.1), and portable nonhuman wealth[6] (lines 5 through 19 of table 4.1) and its components.

Portability: Land "Real estate" in this study includes structures and improvements to land. A distinction between land (considered a nonreproducible form of wealth in the tradition of the classical economists) and structures and improvements to it (considered as reproducible, tangible nonhuman wealth) is made in some wealth estimates of today.[7] Their relative proportions can be useful for assessing advancement; the higher the proportion of reproducible structures and improvements, the more advanced is the economy. Such further separations of "real estate" on line 4 are not possible for the colonial data for reasons discussed in appendix A. The combination of land plus structures and improvements into one item of "real estate" does not, however, preclude analysis of its importance and function as a category of wealth in the several regions, or held by various kinds of owners.

Purpose: Producers' and Consumers' Goods The third asset breakdown, according to purpose for production (table 4.1, line 6) or for consumption (line 15), is highly significant for analysis of economic development and style of life. To this separation the colonial data lend themselves well. The items of portable physical nonhuman wealth (lines 5 through 19) in the probate inventories can be assigned, after careful consideration of each, its meaning,[8] and its use, to one or the other class and to the appropriate subcategories within them. Included as forms of producers' capital are livestock; producers' vehicles such as wagons, sleds; farming tools and equipment; artisan tools and equipment; equipment of nonfarm business; equipment within the house for use in production, such as the spinning wheel, cheese press, cabbage plane, apple mill, barrel, keg, tub, scale,[9] and materials to be used in production, such as leather, yarn, lumber, tallow. Included in the consumers' goods list are such items as carriage or riding chair; house furnishings and equipment used for consumption, as cooking and dining equipment; apparel (watches, jewelry); such miscellaneous consumers' durables as clocks, books, sculpture, etc.; and such perishables as foodstuffs, liquors.

Industry For the fourth breakdown, by industry, the only separation feasible, in a colonial sample of the present size and with the wealth items found, is that of equipment and materials for agriculture or farm business from those of nonfarm business (table 4.1 line 10). It is not feasible to separate the kinds of nonfarm business, nor is it feasible to separate the equipment or materials used for farming from those for family use. Nonfarm equipment and business inventory are so classified only when they are clearly separable from production items of the family as household (examples are items used in trade by merchants, shopkeepers, or artisans, or provided by professionals, innkeepers; etc.).

The data do not permit separation of real estate (line 4) according to industry or purpose. That is, we have insufficient data to determine whether land and structures were used for agriculture or for nonfarm business, and whether the structures were used for production or for direct consumption or both. We know in a general way, however, that, outside of cities and towns, in which dwelt something less than a tenth of the total population, land was used primarily for agriculture or forestry activities and that farm dwellings served both as family shelter and for production. We know also that many shops of artisans, shopkeepers, and even merchants were housed in one or more rooms of the family dwelling.

Length of Useful Life The fifth breakdown, by durability or perishability, is usefully applied to the component items of nonhuman portable physical wealth. Our classification provides for this separation within both the producers' and the consumers' goods categories. In the producers' durable category (table 4.1 line 7) I place livestock. The logic is that livestock consisted in large part of horses and oxen used as draft animals over a long period of years, and that other forms of livestock such as sheep, swine, and fowls reproduced themselves. Crops, on the other hand, are considered producers' perishables, since they would generally be used up within a year, and only the seed carried over.

Equipment used for further production, whether by the (farm) household or by the separable nonfarm business, is treated as a producers' durable. Producer's materials, usually stored in the house, were separated by durability in the tabulations.[10] Examples of the more durable materials are leather, cloth, lumber, boards, iron, and glass. Examples of the relatively more perishable materials are shot, lamp oil, fuel, lime, tallow, salt, materials for making cloth and mattresses, paints. Since, however, the dividing line between durable and perishable useful life is a somewhat arbitrary one, for the tables in this volume, it is more useful for analysis to combine all the household producers' materials as perishables (table 4.1, line 13). Correspondingly, nonfarm business inventories (table 4.1, line 14) also come under the heading of producers' perishables.[11]

The separation by durability of consumers' goods is essential to a wealth estimate, since the durable items give a product or service (real consumer income) over a much longer period of time than do the perishable ones. As Adam Smith argued (1776:329), an individual who spends on durable commodities will be richer than one who spends on perishable ones, for the latter goods will be consumed and gone at the end of a period, but the former, though not worth fully what they originally cost, will still remain and be worth something. Consumers' durables include apparel and jewelry, consumer household equipment, furnishings, and such miscellaneous items as books. Consumers' perishables include materials such as meal, meat, flour, sugar, coffee, tea, cheese, fruits, vegetables, liquors, candles, firewood, etc.

Origin The sixth breakdown, as to origin of the wealth items, is not feasible for this study. The available colonial data do not permit consistent separation of portable physical wealth by whether items were imported, locally purchased at a market or from another household, or produced within the household.[12] For that very reason, however, the probate inventory data give a complete wealth estimate by virtue of including the home-produced articles. Some of the items appraised in the estate inventories were surely imported, such items as "Queensware plates" and "silk stockings." Others, such as "cutting box," "feather bed," "feather bolster," shoes, "linen cloth," or "Negro cloth," were quite possibly made within the household or almost surely within the colonies, probably within a geographic area fairly close to the owner. Locally produced items could have been paid for by cash, by book credit, by labor, or in "country pay," produce such as corn, wheat, tobacco, or rice. But perusal of the individual probate inventory items[13] suggests that a substantial part of portable physical wealth was household produced. Some of these items were in turn used for further household production, while others were directly consumed. I believe that the household produced items were important contributors to the colonial level of living, which would be seriously understated if defined chiefly in terms of quantity of imported items, as Egnal (1975) seems to recommend. Raymond Goldsmith (1952:276) suggests that for the twentieth-century United States, a breakdown of wealth by origin (imported or domestically produced) is probably not significant. It may be quite significant with regard to capital equipment in some developing nations today. Their patterns of development, however, are considerably more affected by the advanced technology that may be imported than was the case with the American colonies in the era before the advent of the cotton gin and spinning jenny.

Subclasses of Portable Nonhuman Assets The seventh asset breakdown, that of subclasses of portable nonhuman physical wealth, has already been touched on in the discussion of separation into producers' and consumers' durables and perishables. We have such producers' goods subclasses as livestock, crops, equipment of the household including farm equipment, equipment of nonfarm business, materials in the household, nonfarm business inventory. Consumers' goods have been divided into three meaningful categories: apparel; durable equipment and furnishings of the household; and perishables. Equipment and furnishings include not only furniture and cooking equipment but also bedding and curtains, household linens, dishes, looking glasses, clocks, wax works, sculpture, books, and other miscellaneous items. Included with apparel are jewelry, wigs, watches (sometimes specified as gold or silver), canes and similar accessories. In the North such items as coats, greatcoats,[14] jackets, velvet jackets, worsted stockings, silk stockings, beaver hats, leather breeches, silver buckles, silver sleeve buttons, gold sleeve buttons were sometimes listed. Similar items were found in the South, with the heavy and warmer items less frequently mentioned.

For a comparison of the colonial economic structure with that of today, not all the asset breakdowns of table 4.1 are relevant, and some slight rearrangements of its classifications are made later in the chapter to facilitate the comparison of wealth structure over time. For example, crops and livestock are combined into what is today called agricultural inventory. When, in chapter 7, data are separated by socioeconomic groupings of owners, subdivisions by kind of asset are somewhat truncated to keep the number and length of tables manageable.

MAJOR OUTLINES OF PHYSICAL WEALTH

We now turn to thumbnail sketches of the colonial economies revealed by the physical asset classifications of tables 4.1, 4.2, and 4.3. The major interest will be in the composition of the nearly £90 million sterling in nonhuman physical wealth, the approximately

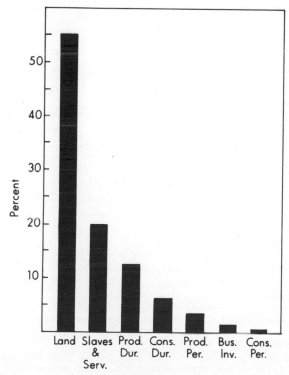

Figure 8.
Composition of Total Physical Wealth, Percentage,
Thirteen Colonies, 1774

SOURCE: Table 4.3

£37.4 per capita in the thirteen colonies (lines 3 of tables 4.1 and 4.2); but we must also deal with nonfree human capital. One way to view the latter is in the relation of value of slaves and servants to total physical wealth when the nonfree human capital of nearly £21.5 million (lines 2 of the same tables) is added to the total of real estate and portable physical wealth. The proportionate contribution made by value of slaves and servants to the larger total of physical wealth defined to include them is about a fifth (20 percent) for the colonies as

Table 4.2
Components of Private Physical Wealth, 1774
(*Average Per Capita, In Pounds Sterling*)

	Thirteen Colonies	New England	Middle Colonies	South
(1) Total physical wealth (2 + 3)	46.5	36.6	41.9	54.7
(2) Slaves and servants	9.1	0.2	1.6	18.4
(3) Nonhuman, total (4 + 5)	37.4	36.4	40.2	36.4
(4) Land (real estate)	25.6	26.1	25.9	25.1
(5) Nonhuman portable, total (6 + 15)	11.8	10.3	14.4	11.2
(6) Producers' capital, total (7 + 11)	8.2	5.9	10.3	8.1
(7) Durable, total (8 + 9 + 10)	5.9	4.4	6.4	6.3
(8) Livestock	4.3	2.8	4.8	4.8
(9) Equipment (including farm) of household	1.4	1.3	1.4	1.4
(10) Equipment of nonfarm business	0.2	0.4	0.3	0.1
(11) Perishable, total (12 + 13 + 14)	2.3	1.5	3.9	1.8
(12) Crops	1.3	0.2	2.1	1.5
(13) Materials in household	0.2	0.4	0.3	0.1
(14) Business (nonfarm) inventory	0.7	1.0	1.5	0.2
(15) Consumers' goods, total (16 + 19)	3.7	4.4	4.0	3.1
(16) Durable, total (17 + 18)	3.4	4.1	3.8	2.8
(17) Apparel	0.7	0.8	1.1	0.4
(18) Equipment, furniture, other	2.7	3.3	2.7	2.4
(19) Perishable	0.3	0.2	0.3	0.3

SOURCE: Aggregates from table 4.1 divided by the appropriate numbers of total living population, including the nonfree, shown in tables 2.1, 2.2, 2.3, and 2.4 on their lines 1 respectively. Components may not add precisely to totals because of rounding.

NOTE: Notes to table 4.1 pertain to this table also. The averages on lines 1 and 2 are presented only for comparison of relative magnitudes. The fractions to compute per capita averages for these two lines include in the numerators the value of slaves and indentured servants as wealth and in the denominators their numbers as holders or users of that wealth, a dubious conception under the laws of the day. However, I find the idea of their sharing, at least conceptually, in the economic use of nonhuman wealth, along with free women and children, considerably more plausible.

Table 4.3
Major Components of Private Physical Wealth 1774
(*Percentage by Asset Category*)

	Thirteen Colonies	New England	Middle Colonies	South
(1) Total physical wealth (2 + 3)	100.0	100.0	100.0	100.0
(2) Slaves and servants	19.6	0.5	3.8	33.6
(3) Nonhuman, total (4 + 5)	80.4	99.5	96.2	66.4
(4) Land (real estate)	55.0	71.4	61.8	45.9
(5) Portable, total	25.5	28.2	34.3	20.5
(6) Producers' durables, total	12.6	12.0	15.4	11.5
(7) Producers' perishables, total	5.0	4.2	9.3	3.3
(8) Business (nonfarm) inventory	1.2	2.6	3.6	0.3
(9) Consumers' durables, total	7.3	11.3	9.0	5.1
(10) Consumers' perishables	0.6	0.6	0.7	0.6

SOURCE: Table 4.1

NOTE: Components may not add precisely to totals because of rounding. For percentages based on only nonhuman wealth as 100 percent see table 4.7.

Table 4.4
Selected Components of Private Physical Wealth, 1774
(*Average Per Free Capita, in Pounds Sterling*)

	Thirteen Colonies	New England	Middle Colonies	South
(1) Slaves and servants	11.8	0.2	1.8	31.2
(2) Land	33.1	27.3	28.3	42.5
(3) Producers' capital, total	10.6	6.2	11.3	13.8
(4) Durable, total	7.6	4.6	7.1	10.7
(5) Perishable	3.0	1.6	4.2	3.1
(6) Consumers' goods, total	4.8	4.5	4.4	5.3
(7) Durable, total	4.4	4.3	4.1	4.7
(8) Apparel	0.9	0.9	1.2	0.7
(9) Equipment, furniture, other	3.5	3.5	2.9	4.0
(10) Perishable	0.4	0.2	0.3	0.6

SOURCE: Aggregates from lines 2 and 4 through 19 of table 4.1 divided by the appropriate numbers of living free population shown on lines 11 of tables 2.4 through 2.7, respectively.

a whole (table 4.3), but this reflects almost entirely the southern influence. For the South alone the proportion is 33.6 percent, for the Middle Colonies under 4 percent and for New England only 0.5 percent. Thus the wealth advantage of the South is dramatically heightened by inclusion of nonfree human capital. It seems clear that the use of slaves and servants was an integral part of the southern economy.

On the eve of the Revolution, the southern colonies, as a group, clearly had the highest total physical wealth of any region in the American continental colonies. The statement holds whether such wealth is considered in the aggregate (table 4.1) or is averaged per free capita (tables 3.7 and 4.4), per free wealthholder (tables 3.7 and

Table 4.5
Components of Private Wealth, 1774
(*Average Per Wealthholder, in Pounds Sterling*)

		Thirteen Colonies	New England	Middle Colonies	South
(1)	Total physical wealth (2 + 3)	252.0	161.2	186.8	394.7
(2)	Slaves and servants	49.4	0.7	7.2	132.6
(3)	Nonhuman, total (4 + 5)	202.6	160.5	179.6	262.1
(4)	Land (real estate)	138.5	115.1	115.5	181.1
(5)	Nonhuman portable, total (6 + 15)	64.1	45.4	64.1	81.0
(6)	Producers' capital, total (7 + 11)	44.2	26.2	46.0	58.6
(7)	Durable, total (8 + 9 + 10)	31.7	19.4	28.7	45.5
(8)	Livestock	23.3	12.3	21.3	34.9
(9)	Equipment of farm and household	7.4	5.5	6.1	10.2
(10)	Equipment of nonfarm business	1.0	1.5	1.3	0.4
(11)	Perishable, total (12 + 13 + 14)	12.5	6.8	17.3	13.1
(12)	Crops	7.2	1.0	9.3	10.9
(13)	Materials in household	1.3	1.6	1.4	1.0
(14)	Business (nonfarm) inventory	3.9	4.2	6.6	1.1
(15)	Consumers' goods, total (16 + 19)	20.0	19.2	18.0	22.4
(16)	Durable, total (17 + 18)	18.4	18.3	16.8	20.1
(17)	Apparel	3.8	3.7	4.9	2.9
(18)	Equipment, furniture, other	14.6	14.6	11.6	17.2
(19)	Perishable	1.5	0.9	1.3	2.3

SOURCE: Sample data, w^*-weighted, Variant Two, adjusted to allocate mixed categories of nonhuman portable wealth—see table 7.6 of *American Colonial Wealth*.

NOTE: The notes to table 4.1 pertain here also.

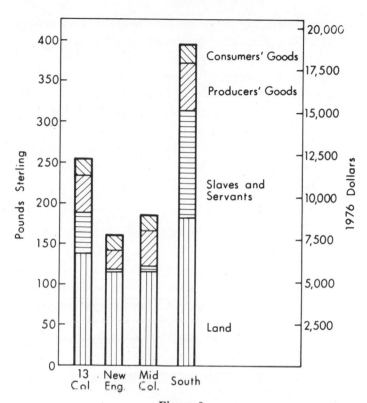

Figure 9.
Composition of Total Physical Wealth,
Per Free Wealthholder,
Thirteen Colonies and Three Regions, 1774

SOURCE: Table 4.7

4.5), or by the conceptually more dubious per capita measure (table 4.2, line 1; see also the note to that table). The South, as we shall see in chapter 5, also led all regions on the basis of estimated net worth, when financial assets and liabilities are taken into account. At the other extreme among the regions, New England held the lowest total physical wealth whether calculated per capita, per free capita, or per free wealthholder. It also had the lowest net worth.

The southern predominance contrasts, however, with what we saw for nonhuman wealth in chapter 3. There, when the comparison excluded wealth in slaves and servants, the South was outdistanced by the Middle Colonies and equaled by New England in per capita nonhuman physical wealth (tables 3.5 and 4.2, line 3). The Middle

Colonies also led the South in nonhuman physical wealth averaged per man, and New England was nearly on a par with the South in this respect (table 3.6). The composition of wealth, by region, is an important key to these regional differences in major wealth totals. In terms of amounts available per head of the free population (table 4.4), we see not only a southern predominance in wealth in slaves but also in real estate values and in producers' capital. Additionally, it had a slight superiority over the other regions in consumers' goods per free inhabitant.

HUMAN CAPITAL

Nonfree human capital, that is, the value of slaves and servants, is the principal item that, when included, gave the South its wealth advantage. For the thirteen colonies as a whole, to which total the South contributed heavily (see table 3.2) this item alone exceeded that of nonhuman producers' capital (table 4.1, lines 2 and 6). In the South it was more than double. While slavery was clearly an important social and economic factor, we must be clear and consistent in our thinking about it in the most important sense of wealth as capital. A parallel source of real annual product, and, to the extent that such product was not fully consumed, of contribution to accumulated nonhuman wealth was also the labor of free men, women, and children. Such product of free labor could be capitalized as I noted in chapters 1 and 3. Free human capitalized value does not appear as an item of wealth in tables of this chapter, partly because in 1774 it was not customary to think in terms of the value of free human capital.

Rough Estimate of Value of Free Human Capital, Thirteen Colonies

An additional reason for the omission of free human capital value is the limited facts we presently have for creating such an estimate. I suggested in chapter 3 that one might take as a minimum estimate of the capitalized value of a free person in the colonies the £34 value per slave shown later, in table 4.9. This happens, coincidentally, to be not far below the £37.4 per capita nonhuman physical wealth shown in table 4.2. If we were to add, on this basis, some £63 million in free human capital to the over £21 million of slave and servant value shown in table 4.1, we would reach some £84 million in total human capital, free and nonfree. This is not far below the estimated £88 million in all kinds of nonhuman physical capital, including real estate. However, an alternative approach, if we had better data, could be to capitalize the value of the estimated annual product of a free person.[15] Such an alternative calculation, while highly interesting, does not seem warranted by the facts presently at our disposal.

Nonfree Human Capital
(Values of Slaves and Servants) by Region

When we look at human wealth in the form of slaves and servants, the pattern is utterly different than the moderately close correspondence by region (tables 3.5 and 4.2, line 3) of per capita wealth in nonhuman assets. On a per capita basis, and even more strikingly on a free capita basis, the southerners held many times more slave wealth than did northerners:

	Value of Slaves and Servants	
	Per Capita	*Per Free Capita*
New England	£ 0.2	£ 0.2
Middle Colonies	1.6	1.8
South	18.4	31.2

I cautioned earlier that including nonfree persons in both numerator and denominator to arrive at a per capita figure is conceptually dubious. Yet such a figure dramatizes the heavy role of slaves in the South. If we rather divide the slave and servant values (the same numerator) among only the free persons, which is the more sensible construct, the New England figure is unchanged at 0.2 but that for the South rises to £31.2. When we further eliminate from the denominator of the fraction all the free children and 90 percent of the free women as nonholders of wealth, but keep the same aggregate value of slaves and servants in the numerator (table 3.8 column 3 and table 4.5), the comparative figure per wealthholder for the South is still more striking, at £132.6. The figures for the northern regions rise, but far less dramatically.

	Value of Slaves and Servants Per Wealthholder
New England	£ 0.7
Middle Colonies	7.2
South	132.6

Overall (lines 2 of tables 4.1 and 4.6), the South held a whopping 95 percent of the total value of slaves and servants in the colonies. With only 36 percent of the free population (table 3.3 line 8), it held over half the total physical wealth (table 4.6 line 1), more than the other regions combined. In contrast, the Middle Colonies held only 25 percent and New England 20 percent. The South held better than half the crops and livestock and nearly half the total real estate values.

The consequence of the relatively small slave and servant holdings in the northern regions is that their addition in line 2 in tables 4.1 (aggregate) and 4.2 (per capita) makes comparatively little difference in the total physical wealth (line 1), as compared with the nonhuman total (line 3), for New England or the Middle Colonies. The same addition in the South, however, makes a stunning difference between the two totals. There, the total value of slaves and servants is not far behind that of real estate. As a percentage, southern land values drop from 69 percent of total nonhuman

---

Table 4.6
Selected Components of Private Physical Wealth, 1774
(*Percentage by Region*)

	Thirteen Colonies	New England	Middle Colonies	South
(1) Total physical wealth (2 + 3)	100.0	20.3	24.5	55.2
(2) Slaves and servants	100.0	0.5	4.8	94.7
(3) Nonhuman, total (4 + 5)	100.0	25.1	29.3	45.6
(4) Land (real estate)	100.0	26.4	27.5	46.1
(5) Portable, total (6 + 9)	100.0	22.5	33.0	44.6
(6) Producers' capital, total	100.0	18.8	34.4	46.8
(7) Livestock	100.0	16.8	30.2	53.0
(8) Crops	100.0	4.3	42.4	53.3
(9) Consumers' goods, total	100.0	30.5	29.8	39.6

Source: Table 4.1.

Note: Components may not add precisely to totals because of rounding.

Table 4.7
Components of Private Physical Nonhuman Wealth, 1774
(*Percentage by Asset Category*)

	Thirteen Colonies	New England	Middle Colonies	South
(1) Nonhuman physical wealth, total (2 + 3)	100.0	100.0	100.0	100.0
(2) Land (real estate)	68.3	71.7	64.3	69.1
(3) Nonhuman portable, total (4 + 13)	31.7	28.3	35.7	30.9
(4) Producers' capital, total (5 + 9)	21.8	16.3	25.6	22.4
(5) Durable, total (6 + 7 + 8)	15.6	12.1	16.0	17.4
(6) Livestock	11.5	7.7	11.9	13.3
(7) Equipment (including farm) of household	3.6	3.4	3.4	3.9
(8) Equipment of nonfarm business	0.5	1.0	0.7	0.2
(9) Perishable, total (10 + 11 + 12)	6.2	4.2	9.6	5.0
(10) Crops	3.6	0.6	5.2	4.2
(11) Materials in household	0.7	1.0	0.8	0.4
(12) Business (nonfarm) inventory	1.9	2.6	3.7	0.4
(13) Consumers' goods, total (14 + 17)	9.8	12.0	10.0	8.6
(14) Durable, total (15 + 16)	9.1	11.4	9.3	7.7
(15) Apparel	1.9	2.3	2.7	1.1
(16) Equipment, furniture, other	7.2	9.1	6.6	6.6
(17) Perishable	0.8	0.6	0.7	0.9

SOURCE: Table 4.1. Nonhuman physical wealth excludes value of slaves and servants.

NOTE: Components may not add precisely to totals because of rounding.

physical wealth (table 4.7 line 2) to only 46 percent of physical wealth when the value of slaves and servants is included in the total (table 4.3 line 4).

There can be no gainsaying the general order of magnitude of these figures, which suggest that in 1774 the economies of the southern colonies were closely geared to slave labor. The case was quite different to the north, except to a very much smaller extent in the Middle Colonies, most particularly Delaware. The figures on standard deviations and confidence intervals for values of slaves and servants show that there was a statistically significant difference not only between northern regions and the South, but also as between New England and the Middle Colonies.[16] For those many fewer wealthholders in the northern regions who had slaves and servants,

16 percent in the Middle Colonies and 3 percent in New England, as against 60 percent in the South (table 4.8, line 1), the mean value per wealthholder having them was £22 in New England and £45 in the Middle Colonies as against £223 in the South.

In New England and the Middle Colonies slaves were used for different purposes than in the South. They were used chiefly as domestic servants, and also to some extent for help at loading and unloading cargo. The somewhat larger numbers of "Negroes" in Delaware, where a significant amount of tobacco as well as wheat was raised, were employed chiefly in the fields.

Table 4.8
Percentages of Wealthholders Having Various Forms of Physical Wealth 1774

	Thirteen Colonies	New England	Middle Colonies	South
(1) Slaves and servants	33.2	3.3	16.0	59.6
(2) Nonhuman, total	99.7	100.0	99.9	99.3
(3) Land[a]	70.4	79.9	79.7	58.9
(4) Nonhuman portable, total	99.4	99.8	99.9	99.9
(5) Producers' capital	95.2	91.3	95.5	96.4
(6) Durable, total	94.3	91.3	93.8	96.0
(7) Livestock	82.2	75.8	79.6	87.1
(8) Equipment of farm and household	91.0	87.4	90.3	93.1
(9) Equipment of nonfarm business	9.8	10.6	17.2	3.5
(10) Perishable, total	73.0	56.9	80.5	68.9
(11) Crops	48.1	17.7	58.2	51.8
(12) Materials in household	54.4	50.7	69.2	45.0
(13) Business (nonfarm) inventory	6.4	6.7	11.1	2.4
(14) Consumers' goods, total	98.5	98.1	99.8	97.6
(15) Durable, total	98.5	98.1	99.8	97.6
(16) Apparel	72.1	90.8	86.7	52.5
(17) Equipment, furniture, other	93.2	97.2	93.0	91.7
(18) Perishable	38.7	34.8	44.4	35.5

SOURCE: Sample data *w*-weighted, Variant Two, percentages of probate-type wealthholders. These are used as my estimate of percentages of all wealthholders having various types of wealth (see appendix A).

[a] Land (real estate) includes cases in the Middle Colonies that were assigned positive real estate values by regression equations. For the South, it includes only cases for which positive evidence of land ownership was found from search of deeds and land grants. Hence the southern figure is a lower bound for the true figure (see appendix A).

Indentured service in New England was quite rare by 1774, and no "servants" were found there in our sample of probate inventories. It was somewhat more common in the Middle Colonies and not often found in the southern probate inventories where the values of "slaves and servants" were chiefly for lists of "Negroes" or sometimes "Mulattos" by name, whom I interpret to have been slaves.[17] The substantial use in the seventeenth century[18] of indentured servants in the Chesapeake area in Virginia and South Carolina appears, from the inventory evidence, by 1774 to have largely given way to use of slaves.

Some children in New England, as in all the regions, were apprenticed by their parents or guardians to craftsmen, as was customary also in Great Britain in the late eighteenth century, but the inventories do not suggest that apprenticed children were among the "servants" whose capital values were appraised in the inventories. For New England, and to a slightly lesser extent in the Middle Colonies, I conclude that the work of farms, fisheries, and forests by 1774 was performed chiefly by the members of the free families themselves, with occasional hiring of laborers for seasonal work. In many tasks in the household and chores of the farm and woods, free children in New England and the Middle Colonies contributed substantially to production. Likewise in those regions the women's work in the households, and to some extent also in gardens and fields, was extremely important in the production, preserving, and preparing of food; in preparing yarns and threads for cloth; in preparing feathers, straw, or other stuffing materials for pillows and bedding; in making cloth and fashioning it into bedding, curtains, and floor coverings as well as apparel. The free men in New England, in the well-known tradition of Yankee ingenuity, and in many cases in Pennsylvania with skills brought from Germany, not only performed the work of farms, fisheries, and forests, but also constructed ships and buildings, cleared fields, erected fences, made drains, dug wells, fashioned much of the household furniture, and made containers, tools, and equipment from the abundant wood. They also used leather, supplemented with iron, tin, copper, brass, and occasionally steel or silver, to make harness, apparel, and other equipment.

Similar activities were, of course, performed by free men,

women, and children in the South, with the exception that much less shipbuilding was done, even in Charleston (Sellers 1934:62–63). A further exception arises from the much smaller proportion of southern households that did not have servants and slaves. These tasks must have been also performed in the South by Negro and Mulatto slaves, of whom there were so many. Additionally, the slaves, as is well known from other literature (Gray 1932:chaps. 10, 13, 16), were the principal labor force in the production of tobacco in Virginia and Maryland, of rice and indigo in South Carolina. Despite the fact that none of these crops was of major significance in North Carolina, I found substantial numbers of slaves in the North Carolina inventories. There the economy resembled somewhat more that of Pennsylvania, with large amounts of livestock, corn, oats, and rye, frequently mentioned, as well as lumber and skins and resin. My surmise from the probate inventories is that in North Carolina the Negroes assisted to a considerably greater extent than in the Middle Colonies and New England with general farming and forestry tasks, besides serving as domestic servants in households of the wealthier farmers.

The offspring of slaves in all regions were the legal property of the owners and were frequently appraised along with the mother, as "Negro woman and child." From sources other than this study, we know that the Negro children worked in the fields at a fairly early age and thereafter brought in produce above the cost of their maintenance, an income that was reflected in their capital value.

A few of the southern inventories specifically indicate skilled occupations for Negroes. They show a blacksmith in Queen Anne's County, Maryland (*American Colonial Wealth,* p. 1245); and among the slaves of Peter Manigault in South Carolina (*ibid,* pp. 1544–71) we find several coopers and carpenters, one a "jobbing carpenter," a bricklayer, several "boat Negroes," "a girl learning to sew," a gardener, and a cook. Some secondary literature suggests Negro skills (Sellers 1934:143).

The secondary literature leaves no doubt that, for slaveowning families, some Negro women served as cooks and domestic servants, whereas others were "field hands." From the numbers of slaves owned by one household in the sample inventories, the impression is that many more women were engaged in field work than in housework.

NONHUMAN PHYSICAL WEALTH

From the viewpoint of only the nonhuman physical wealth (tables 4.1 and 4.7), real estate was the dominant component. It formed 68 percent of the total for the colonies as a whole, and a rather similar percentage for each of the regions. Producers' capital (table 4.7, line 4) formed about 22 percent in the colonies as a whole, but a much lower percentage in New England and the highest in the Middle Colonies. These figures suggest that New England was at a disadvantage in production, owing to less capital per worker. Smaller capital may have contributed to lower production, less saving, and so on about the circle, and hence to the likelihood of a lower rate of economic growth. For the colonies as a whole, consumers' durable goods formed 9 percent and consumers' perishables less than 1 percent of the total. Consumer's durables took a larger share of New England's smaller total than was true of the other regions.

The dominant role of real estate as a colonial asset is consistent with the colonies' basically agricultural character. It accords with much past work in American economic history that emphasized the availability of land as an important magnet for immigrants, and as the principal source of their sustenance and development of products for export. It suggests that well-located land by 1774 was relatively scarce and valuable. It was clearly a major source of products that contributed to the relatively high colonial level of living I believe our data will establish. To the extent that such products were not fully consumed in a given period, their accumulation added to the stockpile of wealth. Land yielded staple crops and garden produce, supported livestock, furnished fuel, lumber, and forest products of great importance to shipping and building, minerals such as bog iron, fish from lakes and streams, sites for dwellings, barns, mills, warehouses, wharves, shops and other structures.

The predominant role of agriculture in all the colonies is revealed in the fact that livestock alone (table 4.1, line 8; table 4.7, line 6) formed about half of the total producers' capital, and crops (table 4.1, line 12; table 4.7, line 10) about a fifth of it.

Equipment for production, both of the household and of separable nonfarm business (table 4.7 lines 7, and 8), came close in value to the total of crops, forming about a fifth of the total producers' capital for the thirteen colonies. The balance, of producers' capital, a little over a tenth, was in the form of perishable producers' goods in the household (line 11) plus nonfarm business inventory (line 12). The former were used up in the creation of many kinds of products to be consumed directly or exchanged for products of other households or of artisans, shopkeepers, or merchants. In the business inventory figures we find the iron supplies and products of a forge, the flour of a miller, and the finished goods as well as materials offered for sale by merchants, shopkeepers, and artisans. The smallness of the business inventories, in aggregate, reminds us of the relatively small role as yet attained by commerce and industry in the colonies, even at the close of a period of over 150 years since the earliest settlements. It was relatively much more important in the northern regions than in the South (tables 4.1 and 4.7). The value of the producers' equipment and materials, though exceeded by that of livestock, suggests substantial past accruals of still useful farming and other implements, equipment, and materials for production.

Of the consumers' goods total for the colonies as a whole (table 4.7, line 13) over a fifth was apparel (line 15), over three-quarters consumers' equipment, furniture, and household furnishings (line 16), and less then one-twelfth the consumers' perishables of the cellar and larder (line 17). It may be that this last figure is somewhat low, if some consumers' perishables in cupboards or cellars were omitted as not worth the bother by some inventory appraisers. Yet the consistency of the figures on consumers' perishables from region to region (tables 4.2 and 4.7) suggests that if there was such understating, it was fairly uniform across the regions. These stores of consumers' goods attest to a fairly high level of living for the American colonists, on average (table 4.2), and even more so for the free population (tables 4.4 and 4.5). Their accumulation is testimonial that past production had been sufficiently in excess of past consumption requirements that a significant stock of consumers' goods could be built up, and the colonists of 1774 had the services of these stocks to draw upon in coming periods.

Let us consider further the constituents of physical wealth in the various regions in 1774. In so doing, we seek to understand more of the implications they suggest as to the production methods established—hence the kind of economic development attained—and as to the consumption levels of the several regions.

Land (Real Estate) by Region

Land was by far the largest component of total physical wealth in the northern colonies, and likewise in the South when slaves are not considered. The relative regional importance of various forms of wealth can be judged from either of tables 4.3 and 4.7, where percentages are given in two ways. It is also apparent from the relative per capita magnitudes shown in table 4.2, where the numbers possess the additional merit of being comparable on an absolute basis from region to region. Our findings show land (including buildings and other improvements) to be about the same in New England and in the Middle Colonies, at about £26 per capita (table 4.2) or about £115 per wealthholder (table 4.5). In the South our findings show a slightly lower value of land per capita (both free and nonfree). But the figure per wealthholder is £181, substantially greater[19] than in other regions. This is so, despite the concern discussed in the introduction that our southern land estimate may be an understatement. As a percentage of nonhuman physical wealth, the South's 69.1 percent for real estate is very close to New England's 71.7 and somewhat above the Middle Colonies' 64.3 percent.

I believe that the greater value of land held per wealthholder in the South is explained by higher values per acre of agricultural land,[20] rather than by urban land values. Cities and towns were more infrequent in the South (see Sellers 1934:3–5) than in New England and the Middle Colonies. The land of the South was probably inherently superior in climate and location on creeks and rivers with outlets to the sea. It had also had the benefit by 1774, in the settled areas, of great amounts of improvement, not only in buildings but in drainage and other improvements on the tobacco, rice, and indigo land. Slave labor in large amounts had been invested in these improvements. The high investment and the high sale value reflect the fact that the southern provinces of Maryland, Virginia, and South Carolina had valuable export products—tobacco, rice, and indigo—for which there were substantial markets and high demand in Europe.

The measures of standard deviation and confidence intervals[21] suggest that there is not a significant statistical difference in land values per wealthholder in any of the regions, but the measures are closer together for New England and the Middle Colonies than between either northern region and the South.

Portable Physical Wealth by Region

Nearly half the aggregate amount of physical wealth other than land or slaves and servants (tables 4.1 and 4.6, line 5) was found in the South, about a third in the Middle Colonies, and over a fifth in New England. Such wealth, including all producers' goods and consumers' goods, averaged less than half the value of land on either an aggregate (table 4.1) or a per capita (table 4.2) basis, except in the Middle Colonies, where the ratio of such wealth to land was the highest of any region.

The Middle Colonies excelled in portable nonhuman physical wealth per capita. Such holdings were £14.4 per capita in that region compared with £11.2 in the South and only £10.3 in New England. Per wealthholder, however, the South was again much the richest, with £81.0 compared with £64.1 for the Middle Colonies and only £45.4 for the New Englanders. The low wealth of New England appears to be accounted for by a smaller amount of producers' goods per capita.

Consumers' goods accounted for about £4 per capita in each region, although on a per free wealthholder basis, the South, with £22.4 per wealthholder, had somewhat more than the northern colonies (Middle Colonies £18.0 and New England £19.2). In the consumers' durables of household furnishings and equipment for consumer use (aside from apparel, where the amount was lower), New Englanders had larger amounts[22] than did those in the Middle Colonies, on either a per capita or a per wealthholder basis. They were ahead of the South in this respect per capita, but not per wealthholder. In the area of producers' durables, the New Englanders ranked dismally low on either basis.

What elements of producers' capital goods accounted for this depressing of New England? In almost every subcategory the holdings were less in New England than in other regions. Livestock amounted to only about £3 per capita compared with about £5 in the Middle Colonies and the South; a smaller percentage of New England wealthholders held livestock (table 4.8), and the average amount held per wealthholder (roughly per free family or household) was only £12.3 compared with £21.3 in the Middle Colonies and £34.9 in the South. Crops in the field and in storage after harvest amounted to only about £0.2 per capita in New England compared with £2.1 in the Middle Colonies and £1.5 in the South. On the per wealthholder basis the average was only £1.0 in New England, compared with the much larger £9.3 in the Middle Colonies and £10.9 in the South. One wonders whether in the case of crops there was widespread underreporting in inventories in New England. It seems more likely, however, that our data, as well as table 3.11, confirm the well-known facts that difficulties of climate and soil made farm produce in New England much more meager than that raised to the south, and that New Englanders were forced to rely much more heavily on products of sea and forest than were the other regions. We cannot escape the conclusion, so far as our data go, that accumulation of total production goods by New Englanders was relatively meager and that most kinds of goods available to facilitate further production were limited. The tradition of great thrift among the Yankees is not borne out by our data, but the facts may reflect relatively low production and income, both money and real, from which to save. Alternatively, perhaps we should infer that because New Englanders had relatively so little, they prized what they were able to save the more. The southern wealthholders, on the other hand, in addition to achieving relatively high consumption, appear to have accumulated substantial producers' capital. This accumulation may reflect, in part, relatively high returns on advantageous land, acquired by land grant, inheritance, or purchase.

Producers' equipment of the household, including farming, fishing, forestry equipment as well as containers, spinning wheels, and other tools of household production were about the same in all regions (£1.3 or £1.4). Per free family (wealthholder), there was no statistically significant difference[23] between New England and the Middle Colonies, but there was for the South's higher £10.2 per wealthholder figure as compared with those for the northern regions.

The total of nonhuman production capital was some two pounds greater in amount per capita in the Middle Colonies than in the South, and we can observe some possibly significant differences in the character of such wealth. While livestock, crops, and production equipment of the household (including farm, fishing, forestry) were about the same in each of our two more southerly regions, there was a marked difference in business inventories held per capita, and still more markedly so per wealthholder. Such inventories were £1.5 per capita in the Middle Colonies but only £0.2 in the South; per wealthholder the figures were £6.6 and £1.1. This is consistent with a greater role of merchants, processors, and shippers in the Middle Colonies. Business inventories in New England were five times as large per capita as in the South, but were apparently not so high as in the Middle Colonies. Philadelphia was at this time the largest city in the colonies, with much shipping and exporting of flour and meats going on, and some of the richest cases in the sample there were merchants, as was also the case in New England.[24] The very few merchants in the sample from Charleston were far less wealthy than the large planters in our sample there. The low business inventories of the South may be in part due to the importance in Maryland, Virginia, and Charleston of factors who, as agents of British merchants, handled most of the import and export trade and furnished goods to shopkeepers or retailers on credit terms similar to the credits allowed them by their British principals.[25] The data on measures of statistical significance (*American Colonial Wealth,* tables 7.163–7.164, A.7.165) show that there is no significant difference in the figures for business equipment or for business inventories as between any two of the regions. On the perishable producers' materials, the Middle Colonies again were highest on a per capita basis and also outranked the South on the per wealthholder basis.

Apparel by Region   In the colonies as a whole consumers' goods were found to amount to £3.7 per capita, of which £0.7 was apparel, £2.7 was equipment and furnishings, and £0.3 was perishables. Regionally, the value of apparel per capita was the greatest in the Middle Colonies (£1.1) and next in New England (£0.8). In the South apparel was only £0.4 per capita, probably accounted for by the warmer weather and the general failure of slave clothing, (which in any case would have been of fairly low value) to be included in the estate inventories. On the basis of per free capita (table 4.4) or per wealthholder (table 4.5) the southern figures for apparel were still the lowest, and those of the Middle Colonies the highest; however the differences between regions are not statistically significant (ibid.).

Household Equipment and Furnishings by Region   The figure for other consumers' durable goods, consisting primarily of household furniture equipment and similar goods, was remarkably similar in all the regions on a per capita basis, ranging from the high of £3.3 for New England to £2.4 for the South. Here again, I believe that the southern probate inventories failed to list to any significant extent the equipment used by slaves for their own consumption. If we consider that the listed consumers' durables were used only by the free population, we come to the figures of tables 4.4 and 4.5. They show much larger amounts per wealthholder household or per free capita in the South, and this is probably the more accurate picture with respect to levels of living actually achieved by the free population. The southern figure per wealthholder is significantly higher (ibid.) than in the northern regions.

Consumers' Perishables by Region As might be expected, consumers' perishables were relatively small. At £0.3 per capita for all the colonies, they amounted to only 8 percent of all consumer wealth. Here we have the meal and flour, vegetables, meats, fish, liquors, etc. stored for household use. Differences found between regions were minor and were not significant. It seems possible that here also the inventories may have understated some of these perishables; yet the remarkable consistency from region to region suggests that, if so, the understatement was also consistent.

SLAVE AND SERVANT INDIVIDUAL VALUES

We turn now to a discussion of values of individual slaves and of individual indentured servants. This special analysis was precipitated by the problem of the atypical extremely high wealth of Charleston district, treated in appendix A. This presentation is based on a simple unweighted[26] tally of the numbers of slaves and servants and their respective individual values as shown in the inventories of the sample decedents. In 1774, values per black slave in our sample in the thirteen colonies averaged about £34 sterling, or a little over $1,600 in 1976 dollars (table 4.9). For the few white indentured servants in the Middle Colonies' inventories, average value of "remaining time to serve" was £7.9 and in the South £9.9 (table 4.10). making a value for the thirteen colonies of about £9 per servant, or about $430 in 1976 dollars. The "remaining time to serve" for the white servants was for much less than their lifetimes; the individual values in the table footnotes suggest that one year's service by an indentured white

Table 4.9
Slaves in Sample, by Region and Province, 1774
(Average Value Per Slave, in Pounds Sterling)

	Number of Slaves	Number of Owners	Average No. of Slaves Per Owner	Average Value Per Slave
Thirteen Colonies, total	3,556	250	14.2	34.0
New England, total	37	20	1.9	18.4
New Haven, Co., Conn.[a]	7	3	2.3	18.0
Three Counties in Mass.[b]	30	17	1.8	18.5[c]
Middle Colonies, total	97	33	2.9	21.8
23 Wealthholders, in ten Counties, N.Y.	22	7	3.1	23.1
Two Counties in Pa.[d]	34	15	2.3	22.5
Burlington Co., N.J.	9	3	3.0	19.3
Kent Co., Del.	32	8	4.0	20.9
South, total	3,422	197	17.4	35.5
Two Counties in Md.[e]	325	41	8.0	25.9
Three County Groups in Va.[f]	428	49	8.7	32.7
Two Counties in N.C.[g]	323	37	8.7	37.9
Charleston District, S.C.[h]	2,346	70	33.5	45.8

SOURCE: Tally of unweighted figures in sample inventories.

NOTE: Values reflect the skills, health conditions, age, and sex of the particular slaves held by the sample decedents. Number of slaves in this table exceeds the sum of those in tables 4.11 through 4.13 because tables 4.11 and 4.12 exclude lumped values for 49 cases of "man and wife" valued jointly at an average value of £44.7 per person; 37 cases of "man, wife, and child(ren)" valued jointly at an average value of £34.9 per person; and 157 cases of "female and child(ren)" valued jointly at an average value of £32.2 per person. They also exclude 83 cases of jointly valued groups regardless of family group or sex at an average value of £38.9 per person. The average value per slave (column 4) for the thirteen colonies is composed of the three regional averages, with relative weights proportionate to total slave populations by region in 1774. The percentages are New England, 3; Middle Colonies, 7; and South, 90. The average slave value for New England is a simple average of the few cases. The same is true for the Middle Colonies. For the South, to prevent the large number of Charleston District cases from dominating it, the average value per slave is composed of the tallied averages for each of the four province groups, with relative weights proportionate to total slave population in the entire province. These percentages are: Maryland, 15.4; Virginia, 44.9; North Carolina, 17.4; and Charleston District, 22.3.

[a] No slaves were owned by Litchfield County sample decedents.

[b] Massachusetts cases occurred by county as follows: Suffolk, 12 owners of 24 slaves at an average value of £17.7 sterling; Essex, 4 owners of 5 slaves, average value of £28.7; Worcester, 1 owner of 1 slave valued at £18.0. No slaves were owned by sample decedents in Hampshire or Plymouth Counties.

[c] Includes two old men valued at zero. Inventory wording for one is "1 old Negro man paid his Labour £0." If the two were excluded, the average value for Massachusetts would rise to £19.8, and for New England to £18.9.

[d] Includes one owner in Northampton County of one Negro woman with child, valued together at £23.5 sterling; all other Pennsylvania cases were in Philadelphia County. No slaves were owned by Westmoreland County sample decedents.

[e] In Maryland, cases occurred by county as follows: Queen Anne, 23 owners of 144 slaves, average value £25.2 sterling; Anne Arundel, 18 owners of 181 slaves, average value £26.4 sterling.

[f] Virginia cases occurred by county groups as follows: Charlotte-Halifax, 20 owners of 169 slaves, average value £32.1 sterling; Southampton-Brunswick-Mecklenburg, 10 owners of 63 slaves, average value £33.4 sterling; Chesterfield-Fairfax-Spotsylvania, 19 owners of 196 slaves, average value £33.0 sterling.

[g] North Carolina cases by county were: Orange, in the Piedmont, 12 owners of 69 slaves, average value £36.6; Halifax, a coastal plains county, 25 owners of 255 slaves, average value £37.8. These include 297 slaves listed without values in some North Carolina inventories; they are valued in column 4 at the sale values shown in table 1.6. These values at actual sales were higher, on average, then values for the 26 slaves for whom the slave value figure was found in the North Carolina inventories.

[h] Includes 49 cases of "man and wife" valued jointly at an average of £89.4 per couple. Also includes 37 cases of "man, wife and child(ren)" valued jointly at a total of 144 persons with an average value of £34.9 per person.

TABLE 4.10
Indentured Servants in Sample
Middle Colonies and South, by Province, 1774
(Average Value Per Servant, in Pounds Sterling)

	Number of Masters	Number of Servants	Value Per Servant
Middle Colonies, total	13	23	7.9
New York	0	0	—
Pennsylvania	11	21	7.9
New Jersey	1	1	8.8
Delaware	1	1	6.9
South, Total	9	14	9.9
Maryland	8	10	8.6
Virginia	1	4	13.3
North Carolina	0	0	—
South Carolina	0	0	—

SOURCE: Tally of unweighted figures in sample inventories.

NOTE: The sample counties within the named provinces are the same as shown for the Middle Colonies and South in table 4 9. Values reflect skills, health conditions, age, sex, and remaining time of the particular servants bound to the sample decedents. No indentured servants were found in the sample for New England. The wording in the documents for some individual cases follow.

In Pennsylvania pounds (multiply by .588 for pounds sterling):

"8 years and 8 months of a servant girl's time"	£20
"Unexpired time of a servant man"	14
"Unexpired time of servitude of two servant maids"	40
"Two servant men's time"	20
"Time of a servant man"	18
"Remaining part of a mulatto lad named Will on time who has 9 years to serve from Nov. 11, 1774"	30
"Time of a Dutch servant man named Jacob Saunders 3 (yrs.) 8 (mo.) & 20 days"	£18
"Time of Patrick Connally, a servant man 4 mo. & 20 days"	1 shilling
"Time of Wm. McGwen, a boy, for 5 (yrs.) 11 (mo.) & 22 days"	3
"Time of a Dutch servant woman named Katherine Sobst 4 (yrs.) 6 (mo.) & 2 days"	15

The New Jersey case, in New Jersey pounds (multiply by .588 for pounds sterling):

"Time of a Dutch servant"	£15

The Delaware case, in Delaware pounds (multiply by .588 for pounds sterling):

"a mullato Boy named John Dyer that has Ten years and About five or six months to Serve"	£11.8

In Maryland (for pounds sterling, multiply by .750, the rate for current money in which inventories were appraised):

"Mulatto man who has about seven years to serve"	£25
"Man named Morris Jones, 16 months to serve"	4
"White servant named John Akerlin"	20
"White servant woman named Martha Pitts"	10
"White woman"	9
"James Brady"	12
"John Sarders"	16

In Virginia pounds (multiply by .758 for pounds sterling):

"James Nash, a white servant"	£10
"Thos. Ogleby, a white servant"	20
"Thos. Landrhen, a white servant"	20
"Jno. Hevens, a white servant"	20

or mulatto man was worth £2.2 to £2.9 sterling, roughly $105 to $140 in 1976 dollars. Corresponding values suggested for a "mulatto lad" are £2, for a "mulatto boy" £0.7, and for a "boy" £0.3. A year's service of a "Dutch woman" was valued at £2 and of a "servant girl" at £1.4. In dollars of 1976 purchasing power the indentured mulatto boy's year of service was worth $33, the boy's $14, and the servant girl's $67. The white or mulatto indentured servants were found in the sample tally chiefly in Pennsylvania, second most frequently in Maryland, and negligibly elsewhere. I judge that their economic importance in 1774 was far less than that of slaves who were vital to the production of southern tobacco, rice, and indigo.

The £34 average value estimated for all slaves in the thirteen colonies, as would be expected, is considerably lower than the sale price of a male slave in his prime years, say ages 16 to 30.[27] Slave values were generally lower for women and girls than for men and boys (tables 4.11 and 4.12), with "wenches" of childbearing capacity frequently, but not always, higher valued than "women." The all-slave average of table 4.9, as compared with sale values of newly arriving prime-aged males, reflects both the upward influence of seasoning or experience and the downward influence of inclusion of children, women, and old men, some occasionally noted as "crippled," "sickly," or simply "old." This average is not dominated by Charleston sample slave values.[28]

Belief that our sample of slaves has no undue proportion of the old or very young to pull down the average is supported by a tally of their ages in Maryland,[29] compared with the age structure of whites in Maryland in the 1800 census. There is insufficient age information on slaves in the inventories to calculate value of a prime-aged male for the thirteen colonies as a whole; for the Maryland sample, where the age data are unusually complete, taking "prime aged" as 16–30, the figure is £42.7, about 65 percent greater than the average for all sample Maryland slaves in table 4.9. If that ratio is valid elsewhere, we can estimate from the £34 of table 4.9 that the prime-aged male figure for all the colonies might average £56. This is higher than the average for all ages of £53.2 for male names or the £47.7 for "Negro man or Fellow" of table 4.11. The latter figures, as all the "sample totals" in tables 4.11 through 4.13, are high, since they reflect the heavy Charleston District dominance indicated by the unweighted

Table 4.11
Male Slaves in Sample, by Province, 1774
(*Average Value Per Slave, in Pounds Sterling*)

	All Males		Male Name Only		Negro Man or Fellow		Negro Boy or Lad	
	No.	Val.	No.	Val.	No.	Val.	No.	Val.
Connecticut	2	24.8	—	—	2	24.8	—	—
Massachusetts	20	18.8	6	18.7	12	16.7	2	31.9
New York	11	24.7	—	—	9	27.6	2	11.7
Pennsylvania	14	25.3	—	—	9	28.2[a]	5	20.0[b]
New Jersey	4	25.0	—	—	2	35.3	2	14.7
Delaware	13	27.8	2	0.6	7	35.7	4	27.6[c]
Maryland	161	28.4	63	33.7	33	35.6[d]	65	19.7[e]
Viginia	177	36.2	63	39.0	67	43.5	47	21.9
North Carolina[f]	100	42.6	68	42.5	23	46.6	9	32.7
South Carolina	820	55.1	527	59.2	179	56.5[g]	114	34.2[h]
Sample Total	1,322	46.9	729	53.2	343	47.7	250	27.3

SOURCE: Tally of unweighted figures in sample inventories.

NOTE: The sample counties within the named provinces are the same as shown in the stub of table 4.9.

[a] Includes one mulatto man valued at £23.5 sterling.
[b] Includes one mulatto boy valued at £23.5 sterling.
[c] Includes one mulatto boy valued at £32.3 sterling.
[d] Includes one mulatto man valued at £45.0 sterling.
[e] Includes one mulatto lad valued at £51.0 sterling.
[f] Includes unvalued slaves, assigned values as indicated in table 1.6 and *American Colonial Wealth*, pp. 1691 ff.
[g] Includes one mulatto fellow valued at £64.4 sterling.
[h] Includes two mulatto boys, one valued at £42.9 the other at £7.2 (young child).

numbers of cases in the number columns. Accordingly, the absolute values in these tables are most useful for the samples within the respective provinces; the unweighted "sample total" is, despite the large influence of Charleston, useful not for its absolute value but to indicate relative values between and within the sex groups.

There is a general pattern[30] in table 4.9, repeated less clearly in tables 4.11 and 4.12, of relatively low slave values in New England and the Middle Colonies, but with higher values as we proceed farther south. Whether this is merely a chance result of the characteristics of the particular slaves of our sample or a true relationship that would be confirmed by a larger sample can be answered only by additional data. Such a pattern does seem reasonable. In the North, the slaves were used principally as house servants or for work around

Table 4.12

Female Slaves in Sample, by Province, 1774

(Average Value Per Slave, in Pounds Sterling)

	All Females		Female Name Only		Negro Woman		Negro Wench		Negro Girl	
	No.	Val.	No.	Val.	No.	Val.	No.	Val.	No.	Val.
Connecticut	4	15.8	—	—	1	2.3	—	—	3	20.3[a]
Massachusetts	6	15.0	—	—	5	14.4	—	—	1	18.0
New York	6	23.6	—	—	4	22.8	2	25.2	—	—
Pennsylvania	12	27.2	—	—	4	30.1	2	29.4[b]	6	24.5[c]
New Jersey	4	16.9	—	—	—	—	2	19.1	2	14.7
Delaware	12	14.8	—	—	5	9.3	1	35.3	6	16.0
Maryland	151	22.5	56	24.7	28	28.6	4	18.8	63	19.0
Virginia	184	30.7	61	31.1	36	37.1	20	37.9	67	24.7[d]
North Carolina[e]	94	34.2	66	35.9	6	29.8[f]	3	31.4[g]	19	30.2[h]
South Carolina	446	47.5	295	47.5	41	48.3	105	47.8[i]	5	31.6
Sample Total	919	37.3	478	41.1	130	35.6	139	44.1	172	22.9

SOURCE: Tally of unweighted figures in sample inventories.

[a] Includes one mulatto girl valued at £19.5 sterling.
[b] Includes one mulatto wench valued at £29.4 sterling.
[c] Includes one mulatto girl valued at £29.4 sterling.
[d] Includes one mulatto girl valued at £3.8 sterling.
[e] The general note and note f to table 4.11 pertain to this table also.
[f] Includes three inventory valued at £43.4 sterling each.
[g] Includes two inventory valued at £43.4 sterling each.
[h] Includes one mulatto girl, inventory valued at £29.5 sterling.
[i] Includes two mulatto wenches, one valued at £68.6, the other at £20 or an average value of £44.3 sterling.

wharves and the like, and may well not have been so highly valued as slaves working primarily in tobacco, rice, and indigo. That the Maryland slave values in our sample are the lowest in the South may be due to the tendencies of farmers in that province to shift from tobacco to wheat and other grains (Klingaman 1969).

The number of slaves held per individual owner in New England and the Middle Colonies was very small, mostly only one or two. This can be judged from table 4.9. Only in Kent County, Delaware, the Middle Colony sample county with the most slaves and the most tobacco production, did it exceed 3 slaves per owner. In the South, however, the average numbers were far higher, with 8 or more per owner in the Maryland, Virginia, and North Carolina sample counties, and about 33 in Charleston District, South Carolina. To find out whether these average numbers are strongly

Table 4.13
Sex-Unknown Slaves in Sample, by Province, 1774
(*Average Value Per Slave, in Pounds Sterling*)

	"Negro" Only		Child	
	No.	*Val.*	*No.*	*Val.*
Connecticut	—	—	1	13.5
Massachusetts	5	21.6	—	—
New York	—	—	—	—
Pennsylvania	—	—	2	4.4
New Jersey	—	—	1	5.9
Delaware	—	—	—	—
Maryland	—	—	—	—
Virginia	18	36.7	1	11.4
North Carolina	4	25.5	—	—
South Carolina	51	40.5	2	28.6
Sample Total	78	37.6	7	13.8

SOURCE: Tally of unweighted figures in sample inventories.

NOTE: The general note to table 4.9 pertains to this table also.

influenced by a relatively few owners in the South with extraordinarily large slave holdings, I made the tally shown in table 4.14. Here we see that, with the exception of the Charleston District, this does not seem to be the case. There over half of the owners held between 3 and 18 slaves, and nearly a third held 26 or more.[31] In the

Table 4.14
Distribution of Owners by Number of Slaves, South, by Province, 1774
(*Percent of Owners*)

Number of Slaves	Maryland	Virginia	North Carolina	South Carolina
1	15.4	8.2	24.3	5.7
2	10.3	10.2	5.4	2.9
3–5	20.5	28.6	13.5	15.7
6–12	23.1	28.6	32.4	24.3
13–18	25.6	10.2	10.8	14.3
19–25	5.1	10.2	10.8	7.1
26 and over	0.0	4.1	2.7	30.0

SOURCE: Tally of unweighted figures in sample inventories.

NOTE: Percentages in vertical columns may not sum to 100.0 because of rounding. The samples of counties within the named provinces are the same as shown for the South in table 4.9.

three other southern provinces, the concentrations were chiefly among holders of 3 to 18 slaves, with substantial numbers holding 19 to 25.

The pattern of slave values by age is given in table 4.15 and figure 10 for the sample cases in Maryland where exact age in years was noted in the probate inventories. The shape of the curve for males is close to that noted by other observers (Fogel and Engermon 1974a:73, 1974b:82) for somewhat later periods, with a rise from infancy to adulthood and a tapering off in later years. The prime age for males seems to be from 16 to 30, and the peak value is reached at

Table 4.15
Slaves by Sex and Age, Maryland Sample, 1774
(*Average Value Per Slave, in Pounds Sterling*)

	All		Males		Females	
Age	*No.*	*Val.*	*No.*	*Val.*	*No.*	*Val.*
Under 1	8	6.1	3	4.0	5	7.4
1–3	25	10.5	16	10.6	9	10.2
4–6	24	15.6	11	14.7	13	16.4
7–9	27	19.9	13	19.4	14	20.5
10–12	18	27.3	10	28.9	8	25.4
13–15	19	32.3	13	32.8	6	31.2
16–20	28	36.7	16	40.1	12	32.2
21–25	20	44.3	12	49.8	8	36.1
26–27	5	41.7	3	45.0	2	36.8
28–30	13	35.3	4	39.2	9	33.5
31–35	13	32.6	6	36.4	7	29.4
36–40	13	31.3	8	34.9	5	25.5
41–44	3	23.7	2	31.1	1	9.0
45–50	16	18.7	7	25.3	9	13.5
51–60	13	14.9	7	15.1	6	14.7[a]
61–79	1	0	0	—	1	0[b]
80	2	0	1	0[c]	1	0[c]
Sample Total	248	25.4	132	27.9	116	22.6

SOURCE: Tally of unweighted figures in sample inventories for Queen Anne's and Anne Arundel Counties, Maryland.

NOTE: Average for prime-aged males, 16–30, is £43.7.

[a] The slight upturn for female prices at age 51–60 is not significant, in view of the small number of cases, whose individual values were in local pounds £30, 25, 25, 20, 15, and 3 (sterling £22.5, 18.75, 18.75, 15.0, 11.25, and 2.25).

[b] The female was valued at 1 shilling in local money, which rounds to less than 0.05 pounds sterling, or in effect a zero value.

[c] No values were shown for either the male or the female.

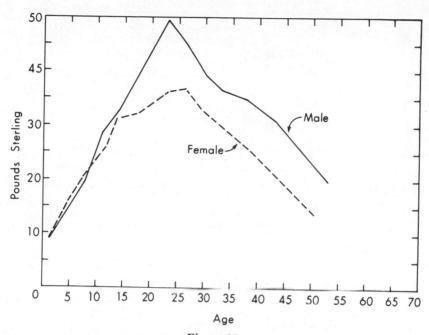

Figure 10.
Slave Values by Age and Sex, Maryland, 1774
SOURCE: Tally underlying table 4.15
NOTE: Points plotted at average value of cases in age interval. Last point is average of cases aged 45–60

about age 23. For women the peak value comes a bit later at about age 26, and the curve drops off somewhat more precipitately after age 30 than for males. The age values reflect the costs of maintenance for the remaining years of expected life subtracted from the anticipated productivity of those years. Virtually zero values are reached after age 60. We now leave the specifics of slave values for a general overview of the structure of late colonial wealth compared with that of our day.

CHANGES IN THE STRUCTURE OF WEALTH
1774 TO 1973

Further insight into probable consumption levels and production functions of the colonial period is afforded by the wealth profile of table 4.16, which compares the relative sizes of the major categories

Table 4.16
Structure of Physical Wealth
Thirteen Colonies 1774, United States 1973

Kind of Wealth	Thirteen Colonies 1774	United States 1973
Total private domestic tangible nonhuman wealth:		
In pounds sterling, thousands	£88,106	—
In 1973 dollars, millions	$ 3,336	$3,526,755
In 1976 dollars, millions	$ 4,215	$4,449,711
Number of inhabitants	2,400,000	211,000,000
Total private domestic tangible nonhuman wealth, Percentage:	100.0	100.0
Land and structures (real estate)	68.4	64.1
Agricultural inventories (livestock and crops)	15.0	1.4
Nonfarm business inventories	1.9	7.0
Other producers' durables	4.2	13.2
Producers' perishables	0.7	—
Consumers' durables	9.1	14.3
Consumers' perishables	0.8	—

SOURCE: For 1774, table 4.1. For 1973, computer printout, aggregate data supplied to author by Dale W. Jorgenson, Harvard University.

NOTE: Figures for 1774 exclude £21,463,000 in value of slaves and servants which, if included, would add 24.4 percent more to the total used here. Figures for both dates exclude net foreign assets. Producers' perishables and consumers' perishables in 1973 were included in business inventories of processing plants and retail businesses to a much greater extent than was the case in 1774, when such items were commonly stored in households.

of wealth in 1774 with those in 1973.[32] The absolute amount of non-human physical wealth in the United States of America, a nation of 211 million persons in 1973, was of course enormously greater, almost four and a half trillion dollars in 1976 purchasing power, than the near four and a quarter billion dollars in such purchasing power possessed by the 2.35 million inhabitants of the thirteen colonies in 1774. In the aggregate, 1973 wealth was over a thousand times greater than that of the colonies, but on a per capita basis (chapter 3 and table 4.2) the figure is only some 12 times greater. Before considering the specifics of this table, let us review some facts that set such a two-hundred-year comparison in perspective.

The United States today, at the national level, is under a single federal government, whereas each of the thirteen colonies was a separate political entity, only loosely joined by their individual ties to the British crown. The 1774 wealth content reflects economies that ranged from frontier regions with substantial segments of production in the household for home consumption to areas of commercial agriculture and fishing. It also reflected accumulations from artisans' production, output of mills and iron forges, service of taverns, inns, and shopkeepers, teachers, doctors, lawyers, and some rather sophisticated commercial operations by merchants who engaged in a variety of local buying, selling, and financing services and overseas shipping. The 1973 content reflects the highly intertwined and complex industrial, agricultural, and commercial economy that undergirds our "affluent society."

In comparing wealth two centuries apart, we are handicapped by the incommensurability of the institutional arrangements of the two centuries with respect to privately owned, nonfree human wealth. Investment in slaves, or in time of indentured servants, was an alternative form of holding wealth, particularly in the southern colonies, which competed in 1774 with land, livestock, and other producers' and consumers' goods. Yet, with the disappearance of indentured servants by some time in the early nineteenth century, if not sooner, and of slavery at the close of the Civil War, this alternative was legally removed and there is no place in the 1973 wealth profile for such an item. This change, of course, has profound economic as well as social overtones. The comparison without the servants and slaves for either date in table 4.16 eliminates trying to "compare apples and oranges"; yet it thereby somewhat increases the proportions of all the other components in the total of physical wealth for 1774 from the proportions they would form of the substantially larger total that included slave values. Other complex changes in the whole economic fabric of society accompanied the economic growth and industrialization that took place in the two centuries.[33]

An additional incommensurability is that the kinds of goods which make up the major wealth categories have drastically changed over time, in many instances. Foods have changed from dried and preserved to canned, frozen, and convenience packaged. Commercial buildings, which in the colonial period were seldom more than three storeys at most, and usually of wood and brick, are now frequently gleaming glass and steel skyscrapers, or tremendous cement structures. Housing has changed from single-family dwellings without central heat, plumbing, or electricity to many instances of insulated and centrally heated and air-conditioned apartments or condominiums. Colonial horses, oxen, wagons, carriages, canoes, sloops, and schooners are replaced by powerful automobiles, trucks, trains, airplanes, jetliners, tremendous barges, and ocean liners. Apparel, shoes, jewelry, and furniture, instead of being hand fashioned, are mass produced, yet meet whims of fashion. Cloths and fibers that were often of homespun wool and flax, more rarely of imported silk, are replaced by factory-produced cloth of cotton, wool, and synthetic blends, nylons, and acetates. Tasks then undertaken with wooden and iron plows and harrows, scythes, and sickles are now performed with tractors, mechanical cultivators, harvesting and threshing machines. Business inventories, instead of consisting of the sides of leather and partly-finished shoes of a shoemaker, or the goods for sale by a shopkeeper or merchant, or some "old iron" at an iron works, comprise tremendous quantities of metals, chemicals, and intermediate products of industry, as well as stocks in wholesale and retail establishments. Consumers' durables today include refrigerators, televisions, radios, tape recorders, cameras, and many more items unknown two centuries ago. .

Though the bare figures in table 4.16 by major categories of wealth at two points so distant in time mask many specific details of the kind just suggested, I believe that inspection of their relative sizes reveals significant changes in wealth patterns and implied consumption levels. In part, they reflect real changes in the economy, such as the shift from a predominantly agricultural economy to a complex industrial one. This is evident in the sharp drop in relative importance of agricultural inventories. In part they reflect the relative shift of some activities from the household to the market. This is apparent in the much greater present-day importance of nonfarm business inventories and other producers' durables. In part they reveal a rise in the level of living. Land and structures remained very close to two thirds of the total at the two widely separated dates.

The rise in consumers' durables betokens a higher relative as well as absolute level of consumption. Undoubtedly Americans had many more creature comforts in 1973 than had the colonists, and held a larger portion of their wealth in this form. This has been the great achievement of our competitive, relatively free enterprise economy.

The presently much lower proportion of wealth in agricultural inventories, particularly livestock, which was a heavy component in 1774, testifies not to absolute smallness of the farm sector today,[34] which not only turns out food to support this nation's population but produces a surplus for export. It is explained rather by the relatively much larger industrial and trade sectors of the modern economy. This same industrial and commercial dominance today is evident in the much higher proportions than in 1774 of wealth in the form of nonbusiness inventories. This difference is less sharp if we add to the colonial nonfarm business inventories those parts of wealth in the form of producers' and consumers' perishables that were then commonly stored in households. Our 1973 source does not give separate figures for producers' perishables, nor for consumers' perishables. I consider it appropriate to combine those perishable figures in 1774 with the nonfarm business inventories to reach the 1774 figure of 3.4 percent, which is reasonable, compared with the 7.0 percent in nonfarm business inventories of 1973. In the colonial figures for producers' and consumers' perishables were such items as the grease, tallow, feathers, yarn, cloth, meats, meal, flour, dried and salted vegetables, cider, liquors, fruits found in the colonial probate inventories. In 1774, these goods were stored in households, whereas today they or their equivalents in our current production and consumption patterns are found on the shelves of retail or wholesale establishments, or as part of the supplies of processing establishments, fuel suppliers, and similar businesses.

The closeness in the proportions two centuries apart for "land and structures" (which we are unable to separate for 1774) is best explained by opposite movements of its two components. A decreasing proportion in the value of private land itself as a fraction of total physical wealth, has been more than offset by the relatively great increase in structures. The former is to be expected with the shift from predominance of the agricultural sector to increase in more capital-intensive sectors, particularly noticeable since World War II (Goldsmith 1968). A significant part of that increased capital has taken the form of structures of many sorts: commercial, industrial, mercantile, and farming, as well as residential. The skyscrapers, industrial park complexes, suburban shopping centers and housing developments, as well as urban downtown business centers old and renewed, established housing neighborhoods, and extensions of megalopolis (Gottman 1957), have brought the values of private structures to impressive totals and a relative importance far beyond that of the private structures of the colonial period. The urban and suburban structures more than offset some failures to maintain farm buildings in midwestern states such as Iowa, where some family-sized farms are being operated in larger units to make efficient use of the new fertilization techniques and expensive capital equipment required, for example, in corn raising.

All in all, the two-century comparison shows us a much larger present-day population with much more sophisticated land uses and structures, and technologically more elaborated producers' and consumers' goods that permit a wide range in life styles. If the total (excluding the wealth in slaves) per capita, man, woman, and child, black and white, free and nonfree, in the colonies in the 1770s was one-twelfth in real terms that of Americans in the 1970s, that was surely a substantial accomplishment for that era. Whether the "average American" today is actually twelve times better off than his "average colonist" forebear is still another question, discussion of which I reserve for the concluding chapter.

CHAPTER FIVE

Net Worth,
Financial Assets
and Liabilities

SOME colonists held financial assets, in addition to the physical assets we looked at in chapters 3 and 4. Others owed debts. Many simultaneously held financial assets and owed debts.[1] To round out the overall colonial wealth picture we need to bring in financial assets and liabilities.

When we add financial assets to the total physical wealth (including the value of slaves and servants) of an individual or family and subtract debts owed, we have the measure of the person's or family's net worth. Conceptually, this is the best measure of wealth for determining who is richer or poorer than whom, which will be the subject of chapter 6. But the approximations concerning assets and liabilities, despite the problems with the liability figures discussed in the Note on Method and in appendix A, have another utility: they give us some information regarding credit and financial transactions in this pre-banking era, and hence further clues to the development of the colonial economies.

Some overall wealth relationships involving financial assets and liabilities are summarized in their aggregate amounts in table 5.1 and on a per capita and per wealthholder basis in table 5.2. Subsequent tables distinguish various subcategories of wealthholders with respect to amounts of financial assets and liabilities they held.

NATURE OF FINANCIAL ASSETS
AND LIABILITIES

The financial assets consisted, in relatively small part, of cash and, in much larger part, of claims on debtors. The collectibility

Table 5.1
Net Worth, Major Components, 1774
(*Aggregates in Thousands of Pounds Sterling*)

	Thirteen Colonies	New England	Middle Colonies[a]	South
(1) Net worth, total (2 + 3 − 7)	105,777	19,040	29,730	57,006
(2) Physical wealth, total	109,570	22,238	26,814	60,518
(3) Financial assets, total (4 + 5 + 6)	17,640	3,926	9,375	4,339
(4) Cash	2,558	248	1,160	1,150
(5) Claims, good	14,002	3,647	8,101	2,254
(6) Claims, doubtful	1,080	30	115	935
(7) Financial liabilities	21,433	7,123	6,460	7,850

SOURCE: Line 2 from table 4.1. Lines 3 through 7: Sample data w^*-weighted, Variant Two, from table 5.2, lines 11 through 15 multiplied by total numbers of wealthholders on lines 21 of tables 2.4, 2.5, 2.6, and 2.7, respectively.

NOTE: For limited significance of the concept of aggregate net worth see the text. Components may not add to totals because of rounding. For components of line 2 see table 4.1. Figures for lines 1, 3, and 7 per free capita, per free man, per white capita, etc., may be calculated in the manner indicated in the source notes for tables 3.6, 3.7, 3.8, and 3.9. Sample data do not yield information sufficiently specific to determine whether or what amounts of the financial assets or liabilities might represent claims against foreigners or debts owed to foreigners.

[a] In this chapter, as elsewhere, "Middle Colonies" figures include an estimate for New York (see Introduction). Where New York is excluded, figures will be given for "New Jersey, Pennsylvania, and Delaware."

of some of these claims was considered doubtful, dubious, or "desperate" by the inventory appraisers; yet since they nevertheless listed them as assets, they are shown here as such, with the warning "doubtful." Detail as to the composition of the cash and of the "good" claims, of whose collectibility no questions were raised by the appraisers, were tabulated only for the pilot study in the middle colonies. The results, shown in table 5.3, suggest that cash was much more often in paper money than in coin, and that the great bulk of "good" claims were in book accounts, bonds, notes, and interest due thereon.

Because the sustainable economic interpretations depend heavily upon understanding of what the particular kinds of assets and liabilities consisted, I devote some space to presenting my rather limited understanding of them[2] before discussing the results shown in the tables.

There were in the colonies in 1774 no banks or savings institutions with the exception of public provincial loan offices, which functioned in the 1770s and earlier in some colonies. Funds were loaned on an individual basis (e.g., Gwyn 1971, 1974) from lender to borrower, sometimes secured by a note or bond; or credit was extended by an artisan, shopkeeper, merchant or his agent to a purchaser of his goods, often simply by an entry in his books, that is, a "book account." Despite the absence of institutional facilities, a web of financial interrelationships existed in 1774 among individuals, creating financial claims. The evidence from the probate inventories and estate accounts indicates that this was almost entirely on a person-to-person basis, or occasionally a partnership was the creditor. There were notes and bonds payable with interest, usually at 6 percent,

Table 5.2
Overall Wealth, 1774
(*Average Per Capita and Per Wealthholder, in Pounds Sterling*)

	Thirteen Colonies	New England	Middle Colonies	South
Average per capita:				
(1) Net worth (2 + 5 − 6)	44.9	31.3	46.4	51.6
(2) Total physical wealth (3 + 4)	46.5	36.6	41.9	54.8
(3) Land (real estate)	25.6	26.1	25.9	25.1
(4) Portable, human and nonhuman	20.9	10.5	16.0	29.6
(5) Financial assets	7.5	6.5	14.6	3.9
(6) Financial liabilities	9.1	11.7	10.1	7.1
Average per wealthholder:				
(7) Net worth (8 + 11 − 15)	243.2	138.0	207.1	371.8
(8) Total physical wealth (9 + 10)	252.0	161.2	186.8	394.7
(9) Land (real estate)	138.5	115.1	115.5	181.1
(10) Portable, human and nonhuman	113.5	46.1	71.2	213.6
(11) Financial assets (12 + 13 + 14)	40.6	28.5	65.3	28.3
(12) Cash	5.9	1.8	8.1	7.5
(13) Claims, good	32.2	26.4	56.4	14.7
(14) Claims, doubtful	2.5	0.2	0.8	6.1
(15) Financial liabilities	49.3	51.6	45.0	51.2

SOURCE: Lines 1, 5, 6: aggregates from table 5.1, lines 1, 3, 7 divided by the appropriate numbers of living populations on lines 1 of tables 2.4, 2.5, 2.6, and 2.7, respectively. Lines 2, 3, 4: from table 4.2, lines 1, 4, and 5 + 2, respectively. Lines 7 through 15: sample data, w^*-weighted, Variant Two.

NOTE: For limited significance of the concept of net worth per capita see the text. Components may not add to totals because of rounding. Lines 3, 6, 9, and 15 include values estimated from regression analysis (see Introduction). Lines 4 and 10, and hence lines 1, 2, 7, and 8, include value of slaves and servants. Lines 5, 6, 11, and 15 include no specific calculation of net foreign assets, although unknown portions may have been due to or from foreigners.

Table 5.3
Gross Financial Assets, Detailed Components
New Jersey, Pennsylvania, Delaware, 1774
(Sample Decedents, Not Age Adjusted)

	Percentage of Sample Decedents Having	Average Value in Pounds Sterling	Value as Percentage of Gross Financial Assets
(1) Gross financial assets, total	59.5	95	100.0
(2) Cash, total	38.0	9	9.5
(3) In gold	0.1	—[a]	—[b]
(4) In silver	0.1	—[a]	—[b]
(5) Not specified	37.9	9	9.5
(6) Claims, total	—	86	90.5
(7) Mortgage	0.9	1	0.6
(8) Rents due to decedent	0.9	—[a]	—[b]
(9) Bonds, notes, interest thereon	27.0	21	22.1
(10) Book accounts, credits, etc.	36.5	62	65.3
(11) Claims, "doubtful"	1.7	2	2.1

Source: Jones (1970), table 21. Data are for sample decedents only, not weighted. Data are from five counties combined, giving each county equal weight, that is 0.2 weight in the regional total. (See appendix A.)

Note: Gross financial assets are figures as given in probate inventories, without adjustments from supplementary data in estate accounts and without allocations for lumped items not separable (see appendix A and *American Colonial Wealth,* pp. 1688–89). "Doubtful" or "bad" claims are ones identified as such by contemporary appraisers at the time they made the probate inventory yet which they included as assets. The percentages in the third column are computed from the unrounded numbers underlying the second column.

[a] Less than one-half pound.
[b] Less than 0.05 percent.

signed by the debtor in favor of the creditor. "Rents due" appeared in the inventory as assets of the landlord, who might be a farmer with several pieces of property. There were frequently simply "accounts due" or "book accounts" or "book debt" due from one person to another. An artisan such as a tailor or shoemaker might have book accounts owing him from his customers, and he in turn might owe accounts to his suppliers. Merchants' account books recorded debts owed for purchases from suppliers and amounts due from customers. In merchants', artisans', or farmers' account books,[3] one finds occasional entries showing that, as of a certain date, the "accounts were balanced" with one particular customer or supplier, and that, as of that date, the new balance owing or due was a specified amount duly entered in the book. Farmers often had notes or book debts due them and in turn owed such debt to others. A farmer might sell a spare cow or hog or some bushels of rye to a neighbor, but in turn owe him for some milling, or he might have lent his son-in-law money to buy land or slaves. Or he might have money due him for part or all of a crop, or meat, timber, or potash he had turned over to a storekeeper, merchant, factor, or shipper for sale or export. He might buy some cloth, needles, ribbons from a city merchant, giving a note, and sell them to others. He might occasionally sign a note as part owner of a vessel; or accept a bond to secure back payments of rent due on land he rented out. The purpose of the credit or debt was rarely stated in the probate documents, which usually had just the name of the debtor or creditor and the amount. Location of the debtor or creditor was very rarely indicated. Occasionally a "mortgage" appeared as a debt owed or an asset held, though I observed these in probate documents much less frequently than the terms "bond" or "note" or "account" (table 5.3).

Account book entries and the appraisals in probate documents of financial assets or debts were almost always in the local pounds of the particular province. Occasionally, but quite rarely, amounts due were specified to be paid in sterling, or in money of another province. When not otherwise stated, the amounts due were in local pounds of the province. In Maryland and Virginia, taxes and other debts were often settled in pounds of tobacco at an accepted valuation. Settlements in other colonies were also fairly often made in kind at accepted valuations in local money. To compare the financial asset and liabilities figures from region to region, the common denominator of English pounds sterling has been used, at the exchange rates with local pounds shown in table 1.1.

The "doubtful" financial claims were judged as such by the contemporary appraisers. Terms often found in the New Jersey, Pennsylvania, and Delaware inventories were "doubtful" or "bad" notes, book accounts, or other claims. In New England and in the South, particularly in Maryland, a term more commonly used was "desperate debts" owed to the decedent. In Maryland I also encountered the term "sperate debts." *The Oxford English Dictionary* defines "sperate" pertaining to debts as "having some likelihood of being recovered; not desperate." Hence "sperate debts" were ones whose collection was hoped for, and I classed them as "good." "Desperate debts" were not hoped for, and I classified them as "doubtful."

In estate accounts filed with the court at subsequent dates by estate executors or administrators, sometimes financial claims that had been previously listed in the probate inventory as assets were finally written off as uncollectible, with such notations as "worthless," or "cannot collect." When I compared such individual account entries with the corresponding original probate inventory entries, in the cases where sufficient identification of the item made it possible, it was evident that, for a particular decedent, the amounts of his "doubtful" claims and the amounts subsequently written off by his executor often did not coincide. Some "doubtful" or "desperate" debts were eventually collected by estate administrators or executors, and some not initially so judged had occasionally to be written off. So the practice of listing doubtful claims as financial assets of their holder proved in fact reasonable at least some of the time.

The meaning of "cash" as a financial asset is not entirely clear. I found in the inventories such wording as "cash in the house" or "his purse." In cases of the latter, the amounts stated were sometimes much too large to mean the value of a wallet or purse in today's language, so I treated "purse" as meaning cash. Whether the cash was in coin or paper was rarely stated. In New Jersey, Pennsylvania and Delaware, I coded separately for gold and silver coins (table 5.3) but found so few cases that I gave up the separation for the other regions. An attempt to watch the wording in the probate inventories in other regions for evidence as to gold or silver coins, at the time that data were being summarized for tabulation, turned up few instances of such mention. Hence I believe that the inventoried cash was largely in the form of current local money, in paper, of the particular province.

Contemporary comments on trade are full of complaints about the scarcity of "hard money" or coins,[4] the supply of which was often inadequate to meet the needs of shopkeepers' or merchants' transactions. Coinage in the colonies was prohibited by England, following a few early attempts (such as the minting in Massachusetts of a lightweight silver pine tree shilling). Some Spanish, Portuguese, and Dutch coins entered the colonies as a result of the West Indian trade, and these supplemented the meager supply of English coins, though all tended to flow out in payment of trade balances. The Spanish dollar or "piece of eight" is the coin meant by references in the probate inventories to "dollars." A few names of such coins as florin, joe, half joe, appear in the colonial inventories of the sample. "Joe" is an abbreviation of Johannes, a Portuguese gold coin worth about 36 shillings sterling.

Paper money circulating in the colonies was occasionally pound sterling notes issued in England, but much more commonly paper money issued by the province and payable in "current money" or "lawful money" of the province.[5] These note issues were authorized by the provincial legislatures and took the form of promises to pay, sometimes with specified interest, at a date in the future. The first issues originated in needs to pay returning soliders who had participated as British subjects in military campaigns in provinces that later became Canada. The taxing capacity of the provincial governments was the source of value for these notes, and their large issue in some colonies was, in part, the reason for their lower rate of exchange for pounds sterling, as in the case of South Carolina's exchange rate of seven local pounds to one sterling in 1774. The money of one colony was not always acceptable, except at a discount that varied from time to time, in another colony. However, by 1774 the paper money of Connecticut and Massachussets was interchangeable and stable at 1.33 local pounds for one pound sterling, as was also the paper money of New Jersey, Pennsylvania, and Delaware at 1.70 or 1.67 local pounds for one of sterling (table 1.1).

Attempts at private note issues in Massachusetts and South Carolina, backed by land, had been discouraged by England in the 1740s. Subsequently some public provincial loan offices lent to individuals by issuing notes, backed by land of the borrower as security. Some private paper, as of English merchants in London, reached colonial shippers or merchants. Examples are bills of exchange (McCusker 1978:19–23), drawn by a colonial shipper on an English consignee at the time of shipment, ordering the latter to pay in London a stipulated amount, and sometimes accepted by the factor serving as representative of a London merchant house in such ports as Charleston[6] or Philadelphia.

In this situation of shortage of coins and a not-too-plentiful supply of reliable paper money, transaction settlements were often handled by means of signing notes or making entries in book accounts.

"Book accounts and credits" are the dominant form of claim shown in table 5.3, both in percentage of decedents in the sample in New Jersey, Pennsylvania, and Delaware holding such claims and in their average amount. Their average per decedent, 62 pounds at sterling equivalent, was three times greater than that for "bonds, notes and interest thereon," which comprise the second largest financial asset form for which I am able to present figures separately. Mortgages were a much rarer asset, held by less than 1 percent of the probated decedents, and averaging only one pound sterling for those in the New Jersey, Pennsylvania, and Delaware sample. Rents due, to an even smaller percentage of decedents, averaged less than a pound. "Bad" or "doubtful" claims held by a little under 2 percent of these decedents averaged two pounds sterling for all in the middle colonies' sample (table 5.3).[7]

The specific evidences of financial claims in New England and New York were rather similar to those found in New Jersey, Pennsylvania, and Delaware.[8] They consisted of occasional entries in probate inventories concerning mortgages and rents due, but many more for bonds, notes, book accounts, or just "account due" or other indications of credit extended. In the South, despite the greater dominance of farmers and planters in the sample and relatively fewer artisans and merchants, and financial assets noted in a smaller percentage of the probate inventories, there were nonetheless many entries for accounts, notes, and bonds. These suggest both the use of accounts in lieu of cash or produce to settle claims, and that some farmers and planters, sometimes even those of only moderate wealth, carried on a wide variety of activities, some of them supplemental to farming and some of which verged on money lending or financing ventures of one sort or another (Land 1965; Brock 1975:4).

The Total Debt Picture

The aggregate domestic financial claims of the colonists in principle should equal their domestic financial liabilities. This is so because for each claim there are two equal and canceling entries, the amount the debtor owes and the amount of the creditor's claim against him. This means that in table 5.1 the aggregate of financial claims (line 5 plus line 6) would be expected to approximate closely aggregate financial liabilities on line 7, if overseas obligations were minor. Similarly, financial claims per wealthholder in the lower panel of table 5.2 (line 13 plus line 14) would be expected to equal the financial liabilities per wealthholder on line 15, if these were all internal obligations within the colonies. This would occur, however, only if our sample were large enough, more nearly approximating a complete census, if our liabilities estimates were on the nose, and if any large amounts that might be owing to or from abroad were excepted. Given our small sample and our problems of estimating liabilities, the correspondence between £15,082,000 in financial claims and £21,433,000 in financial liabilities is reasonably close.

Whether there was a net foreign debt, that is, a true excess of financial liabilities in the colonies as a whole, suggested by the difference between these two figures, is not fully discernible from our present data. The individual component items of financial assets and liabilities of sample decedents are not sufficiently specific as to the locations of the persons or agents on whom they had claims, or to whom they owed the stated amounts, to permit a separation by foreign or domestic claims and obligations. We must keep in mind that obligations to or from persons in another colony were perceived as foreign obligations by individual colonists, although they would be domestic obligations as we are using the term. It is possible that the colonists as a whole did have an external debt approaching £6 million sterling in 1774, although the figure is tenuous, derived merely from the difference between the two figures in the preceding paragraph. There could also have been interregional balances owing. If £6 million were netted out from colonial wealth (subtracted from total physical wealth shown in chapter 3), the total would be reduced by 5 percent. The reduction would presumably be greater in New England and the South than in the Middle Colonies.

By region (table 5.1), the Middle Colonies appear to have been a net creditor and New England and the South net debtor regions. We saw in table 3.11 that New England's "invisible earnings" from shipping services helped its relatively low commodity export earnings, bringing its estimated export earnings per capita to a par with those for the Middle Colonies. Despite this, the gap between aggregate financial claims and financial assets was much greater for New England than for the Middle Colonies, and as large as the gap in the South. Since the physical wealth per wealthholder in New England was so much lower than in the South, and somewhat lower than in the Middle Colonies, this, combined with its high financial liabilities, gave it the lowest net worth of any region.

In view of the considerable literary tradition[9] that southern planters owed large debts to English or Scottish creditors for consumption goods or plantation supplies, I assume that some, but unknown portions, of the amount I estimate as southern financial liabilities were due abroad.[10] Perhaps the liabilities were chiefly short term. Whether the same is true of the excess of New England financial liabilities is more questionable, in view of the much lower New England figures for portable wealth. A possibility is that there were considerable regional debts for food owed from New England to the Middle Colonies,[11] and that Middle Colonists sent their exports (Kalm 1770:103) in their own rather than in New England ships, so that New England had little source of revenue from the Middle Colonies. Shepherd and Walton, from their study of export and import data, conclude that long-term foreign investments in the thirteen colonies were nil in the period 1768–72.[12] They suggest that the relatively small size of foreign capital inflows means that the growing stock of capital in the colonies was due to domestic saving rather than to foreign investment in the colonies. They find that "invisible" earnings offset 62 percent of the commodity trade deficits and that there were further offsets from sales of ships abroad and salaries paid to British civil servants and army and navy personnel stationed in the colonies. More complete answers as to interregional and foreign balances owing depend on additional research.

NET WORTH AND ITS COMPONENTS

For the thirteen colonies, when financial assets of £40.6 per free wealthholder are added to total physical wealth, and offset by £49.3 of liabilities, the resulting net worth figure is £243 (table 5.2). This is lower than total physical wealth of £252 by the £9 excess of liabilities over financial assets. In other words, total physical wealth was nearly 104 percent of net worth. Or conversely, net worth was 97 percent as large as physical wealth. This is true in the aggregate (table 5.1) and per wealthholder (table 5.2). Because of the canceling effect of domestic financial claims and liabilities in the aggregate, and because slaves as well as most free women and children did not hold assets, I do not find the concepts of aggregate net worth, per capita net worth, or per capita financial assets or liabilities to be particularly meaningful. An aggregate net worth figure differs from an aggregate physical wealth figure only if the amounts of financial claims plus cash fail to equal financial liabilities. Such a figure divided by total population is not much more informative. Despite their limited meaning, per capita figures are shown in table 5.2 chiefly for symmetry with table 4.2.

The more meaningful average is that per free wealthholder shown in the lower panel of table 5.2, where the numbers are comparable with the physical wealth components shown in table 4.5. The free wealthholders were the individuals who held the financial claims and cash or who owed the acknowledged financial liabilities, and it is the relative sizes of their holdings and obligations that are of economic interest. Their net worth may be meaningfully compared by region, or by other subgroups of wealthholders.

On the per wealthholder basis for the thirteen colonies (table 5.2, lower panel) the financial assets contributed one sixth to total net worth. They were nearly one fourth of land values and over a third as large as all kinds of portable wealth, including slaves. But they were more than offset by the subtraction of £49.3 in financial liabilities owed by the average free wealthholder.

Net Worth by Region

In aggregate net worth, insofar as that concept has meaning, the South was the richest region (tables 5.1 and 5.4). This continues the pattern of its superiority in physical wealth seen in chapters 3 and 4. Per wealthholder, the South's net worth was, however, smaller than its physical wealth, because of the excess of estimated financial liabilities over the financial assets we found there. Net worth was also smaller than physical wealth in New England. Financial liabilities there averaged about the same amount per wealthholder as in the South, though the physical wealth was very much smaller. Only in the Middle Colonies did net worth per wealthholder exceed physical wealth (tables 5.2 and 5.5), because the average wealthholder there held substantially more financial assets than he owed in liabilities. Despite this, the aggregate net worth and that per wealthholder in the Middle Colonies were much lower than in the South. Per capita net

Table 5.4
Components of Net Worth, Financial Assets and Liabilities, 1774
(*Percentage by Region*)

	Thirteen Colonies	New England	Middle Colonies	South
(1) Net worth, total	100.0	18.0	28.1	53.8
(2) Physical wealth, total	100.0	20.3	24.5	55.2
(3) Financial assets, total	100.0	22.3	53.2	24.6
(4) Cash	100.0	9.7	45.5	44.9
(5) Claims, good	100.0	26.0	57.8	16.1
(6) Claims, "doubtful"	100.0	2.8	10.7	86.4
(7) Financial liabilities	100.0	33.2	30.1	36.6

SOURCE: Table 5.1.

NOTE: Regional figures may not add to thirteen colonies' total because of rounding.

worth, if that average has meaning, in the Middle Colonies was only slightly lower than in the South, since so many southern slaves enter into the per capita divisor for the South.

Financial Assets and Liabilities, by Region

The relative leadership of the Middle Colonies in financial assets is apparent in tables 5.4 and 5.5. Although table 5.1 shows the

Table 5.5
Components of Net Worth, Financial Assets and Liabilities, 1774
(*Percentage by Asset Category*)

	Thirteen Colonies	New England	Middle Colonies	South
(1) Percentage of net worth (2 + 3 − 7)	100.0	100.0	100.0	100.0
(2) Physical wealth, total	103.6	116.8	90.2	106.2
(3) Financial assets, total (4 + 5 + 6)	16.7	20.6	31.5	7.6
(4) Cash	2.4	1.3	3.9	2.0
(5) Claims, good	13.2	19.2	27.2	4.0
(6) Claims, "doubtful"	1.0	0.2	0.4	1.6
(7) Financial liabilities	20.3	37.4	21.8	13.8
(8) Percentage of total physical wealth	100.0	100.0	100.0	100.0
(9) Financial assets, total	16.1	17.7	35.0	7.2
(10) Financial liabilities	19.6	32.0	24.1	13.0

SOURCE: Table 5.1.

South had over twice the Middle Colonies' aggregate physical wealth (slaves comprising a third of the South's £60 million, as may be seen in table 4.1), it had less than half the financial assets held in the Middle Colonies and only slightly more financial assets than New England (table 5.4). Per wealthholder, the financial assets averaged substantially highest in the Middle Colonies, and very much lower in New England, where they were about the same as in the South.

Among the New England sample counties, Suffolk, in which lay Boston, and Essex, which included Salem, led the other counties in size of financial assets (see appendix table B.1). In the Middle Colonies Burlington County in New Jersey and Philadelphia County in Pennsylvania had the largest financial assets (table B.2). Charleston, an important shipping center for the lower South, had much higher average financial assets per wealthholder than the other southern sample counties (table B.3). As a percentage of the South's much larger physical wealth figure, financial assets were much lower, 7 percent, than the near 18 percent in New England and the 35 percent in the Middle Colonies (table 5.5, line 9).

Financial liabilities likewise were the lowest as a proportion of physical wealth, only 13 percent, in the South (table 5.5, line 10). Stated in average values per wealthholder (table 5.2), the New England liabilities were at about the same level as those of the wealthier South, and larger than those of the slightly wealthier Middle Colonies. The liabilities were estimated at nearly twice the financial claims per wealthholder for New England and the South, but only at four-fifths of those in Middle Colonies.

From table 5.6 I conclude that financial assets were held by greater percentages of wealthholders in the northern regions than in the South and by more in the Middle Colonies than in New England. By this measure, Charleston was not the leader among the southern sample counties. Higher percentages of the wealthholders in the two Maryland counties, followed by those in the two North Carolina counties, held financial assets than did those in the Charleston District.[13] Good financial claims were reported for an estimated 71 percent of wealthholders in the Middle Colonies, 52 percent in New England, but only 25 percent in the South, whereas cash was reported by only 21 and 24 percent in New England and the South as against 44 percent in the Middle Colonies. "Doubtful" claims or "desperate debts" were held relatively twice as frequently by

Table 5.6

Percentages of Wealthholders Having Major Forms of Financial Assets, 1774

	Thirteen Colonies	New England	Middle Colonies	South
(1) Financial assets, total	56.3	61.4	77.9	36.8
(2) Cash	31.0	21.4	44.4	24.2
(3) Claims, good	46.8	52.1	71.3	24.9
(4) Claims, "doubtful"	3.9	3.3	1.1	6.5

SOURCE: Percentages of probate-type wealthholders having various forms of assets (sample data *w*-weighted, Variant Two; see appendix A).

NOTE: Percentages of wealthholders owing financial liabilities are not shown for reasons discussed in the Introduction. I have assumed that virtually all New Englanders and southerners in the sample owed financial liabilities. I estimate from a regression equation that 87 percent of the sample decedents in New Jersey, Pennsylvania, and Delaware owed them.

southerners as compared with New Englanders, and six times as frequently as Middle Colonies' wealthholders.

Both New England and the Middle Colonies were sites of great port cities with a variety of commercial transactions taking place in them.[14] The South had Charleston, Baltimore, and some lesser ports. More of the southern obligations may have been owed abroad than was true of the other regions. If we were to allocate to the South the larger part of the £6 million discrepancy in table 5.1 between claims and liabilities, the effect would be to lower that region's superiority in net worth over the other regions. However, most of the specific amounts owing that I observed in the relatively few actual estate accounts found in the southern sample were stated in local pounds rather than in sterling. The Middle Colonies' figures include assets of a number of wealthy merchants as well as farmers engaged in multiple activities, and doubtless reflect growing commercial and shipping activities of this region. Possibly New England's low financial assets were tied to the relatively low producers' wealth noted in chapter 4 and to the necessity to import foods from other regions. Its very high financial liabilities may imply not so much poverty as a wide range of commercial activities or transactions.

Southern wealthholders had an average of only a fifth as much financial assets as wealth in slaves and servants, and a sixth as much as wealth in land (tables 4.5 and 5.2), a situation far different from that in the northern regions. In the northern regions land, though averaging lower per wealthholder (only about three-fifths as much as in the South), came much closer to amounts of financial assets. In New England the ratio was about four to one. In the Middle Colonies, the ratio of real estate to the larger absolute financial assets was about two to one.

There seems to be a pattern here (tables 5.1, 5.2, and 5.4) of an overall richer South holding absolutely much more of its capital in the form of slaves and land, and relatively much less in financial assets. In the North, slaves and servants formed negligible to very small proportions of net worth. Real estate, on the other hand, formed smaller absolute amounts but larger relative proportions than in the South. The Middle Colonies appear to have accumulated the greatest amounts of financial assets. This, together with their high portable wealth, much of which was highly liquid, may have made this region the most nearly ready with capital for future industrial development. New England, though it was to show significant development characteristics by the 1810s and 1820s, seemingly had the most dismal outlook of any region in 1774, not only with respect to physical capital, as noted in chapters 3 and 4, but also in financial capital.

Although I do not subscribe to the interpretation of James Henretta (1973) that the mere existence of financial assets means that they were invested in industrial enterprise, their existence certainly implies economic transactions of one sort and another whose meaning calls for exploration. Possibly a surplus of financial assets over liabilities in a region (if the measures are sufficiently accurate) implies some commercialization, and that the region was a net supplier of capital to other regions.

WHO WERE THE DEBTORS AND WHO THE CREDITORS?

There are many questions on which we would like firmer answers and to which this study brings at least some light. To what extent was there a creditor class, to what extent a debtor class? A great deal of historical interpretation has assumed there were such classes (Brock 1975:528–32). Who were the debtors and who were the creditors? Did the debtors have high or low net worth, high or low physical wealth? Were they primarily the farmers? Were the debtors poor? Were the creditors rich? I find in this study that "debtor" and "poor" were not synonymous, nor "creditor" and "rich." Rather, as today, the holding of significant assets in physical forms and cash made one credit-worthy, and high debt was very apt to go hand in hand with high assets. High debt was in large part an indication of developing business and commercial relations, merely incidental to financing the purchase of land, slaves, livestock, farm tools, shipping equipment, or producer's durables. It was not necessarily an indication of borrowing for consumption needs or survival.

By individual decedent there is a wide range in the ratio between a man's financial assets and his financial liabilities.[15] Though there were many cases of large financial liabilities, either actually reported or estimated,[16] there were not many cases of negative net worth among the sample decedents. The largest number of such cases, 19, was found in the New England sample, and it so happened that there were fairly numerous instances there of Insolvent Commissioners' having been appointed to make a report to the court on the case.[17] In New York there was one case of negative net worth. In New Jersey, Pennsylvania, and Delaware there were just two, one of a young man under 25 years old who owned two slaves and substantial physical assets as a carriage maker, but who also had very large debts. In the South there were only two such cases in the sample.

By subclasses of wealthholders, the data in tables 5.7 through 5.14 suggest that some of the stereotypes of colonial debtors and creditors need revision.

Financial Assets and Liabilities Held and Owed by the Richer and the Poorer

The richer owed more debts than the poorer and also had more financial assets. Whether we use total physical wealth, as in table 5.7, or net worth, as in table 5.8, as the scale to measure relative richness, the data show, for each region and for the thirteen colonies combined, that the high-wealth class had not only the highest average financial assets, as one would expect, but also the highest average debts. Financial assets and liabilities averaged less in the middle-wealth class and least in the low-wealth class. In the high-wealth class, the regional findings in table 5.2, line 11 are confirmed.

Whether by total physical wealth (table 5.7) or net worth (table 5.8) measure, the rich of New Jersey, Pennsylvania, and Delaware on average had larger financial assets than the rich New England wealthholders, who in turn held greater financial assets than those in the South. At the low-wealth level, New Jersey, Pennsylvania, and Delaware wealthholders again had the highest financial assets of any region, but low-wealth New Englanders outclassed low-wealth southerners in this respect. Just why, at all wealth levels, the wealthholders of New Jersey, Pennsylvania, and Delaware held more financial assets than those in other regions is a question to which only tentative answers may be suggested here. Perhaps the higher proportions of merchants and of urban dwellers in the North who had relatively high financial assets (see tables 5.11 and 5.12) was a factor. We shall see in chapter 7 that even low-wealth farmers in the middle colonies held considerable financial assets.

To look for the debtors, we turn to the financial liabilities, and

Table 5.7
Financial Assets and Liabilities
Held by Wealthholders of High to Low Total Physical Wealth, 1774
(*Average Value in Pounds Sterling*)

	Thirteen Colonies[a]	New England	New Jersey Pennsylv. Delaware	South
Financial assets held by those with total physical wealth of:				
£400 and over	88.1	89.9	179.7	54.8
£100–399	35.4	19.7	56.6	18.6
£99 and under	12.7	10.4	30.4	4.2
Financial liabilities owed by those with total physical wealth of:				
£400 and over	112.5	112.2	147.1	103.2
£100–399	41.2	55.3	38.1	24.5
£99 and under	13.7	21.1	4.5	10.4

SOURCE: Sample data, w^*-weighted, Variant Two; liabilities estimated from regression analysis (see the Note on Method).

NOTE: The wealth divisions at £400 and £100 roughly break the combined sample of all thirteen colonies into thirds. However, because of their relative wealths, a higher proportion of the southern cases than of the New Engand cases fall in the high wealth class, and conversely a higher proportion of the New England sample falls in the low wealth class. See chapter 6 and tables 7.1–7.4.

[a] The thirteen colonies' figures include the New York estimate.

Table 5.8
Financial Assets and Liabilities
Held by Wealthholders of High to Low Net Worth, 1774
(*Average Value in Pounds Sterling*)

	Thirteen Colonies[a]	New England	New Jersey Pennsylv. Delaware	South
Financial assets held by those with net worth of:				
£400 and over	130.2	129.3	239.2	69.0
£100–399	18.7	21.2	24.2	7.3
£99 and under	6.0	6.8	9.4	2.6
Financial liabilities owed by those with net worth of:				
£400 and over	99.2	99.8	78.2	108.5
£100–399	39.3	51.9	36.9	26.6
£99 and under	27.8	38.5	30.1	10.7

SOURCE: Sample data, w^*-weighted, Variant Two; liabilities estimated from regression analysis (see Introduction).

[a] The thirteen colonies' figures include the New York estimate.

we do not find average debt high at the low-wealth levels. Rather, in all three regions and for the thirteen colonies as a whole our estimates give us a pattern of large average liabilities at high-wealth classes (whether by physical wealth or by net worth), dropping steadily to middle liabilities at the middle-wealth class and low liabilities at the low-wealth class. There is a difference, however, in amount of liabilities, when we compare the classifications by net worth (table 5.8) and by total physical wealth (table 5.7). That is to say, the average size of liabilities is greater at the high–physical wealth class than at the high–net worth class, except in the South. It is smaller at the low–physical wealth class in all regions. For instance, for New England the comparison was £112.2 at high physical wealth compared with £99.8 at high net worth, but £21.1 and £38.5 respectively at the low classes. It is not surprising that debt levels were great for people of high physical wealth; they held financial assets less frequently and in smaller amount than people of high net worth, and hence needed credit for some of their transactions. The "notes," "book debts," or other evidences of obligation which they furnished to their creditors were good because they were, in effect, backed by substantial average assets in land, producers' goods and consumers' goods in the North, and in the South by those items plus slaves. I do not show figures on percentages of wealth-holders owing debts, by wealth class, for the same reasons that they were omitted from table 5.6.[18]

To find the creditors, we look at holders of financial assets. Highest average claims were held by those at high-wealth levels (whether by physical wealth or by net worth). The pattern for amounts, when we compare holders classified by net worth and by total physical wealth, is reversed, however, from that for financial lia-bilities. That is, the average amount of financial assets is greater at the high–net worth class than at the high–physical wealth class. The decline in amounts held from high to low wealth class is sharper in the net worth classification. For example, in New England average financial assets were £129.3 at the high and £6.8 at the low net worth class, but £89.9 and £10.4 at the corresponding physical wealth classes. Since financial assets as well as liabilities enter into calculation of net worth, it is not surprising that high net worth and high financial assets go hand in hand.

The proportion or percentage of wealthholders having financial assets (table 5.9) followed the same pattern that we found for the average amounts. That is, the percentages holding some financial assets were highest in the high-wealth class and lowest in the low-wealth class, whether wealth is measured by total physical wealth or by net worth. Only in the South among those in the middle–physical wealth class was there an exception. There 44.7 percent held financial assets as compared with 37.3 percent at the high level, and this abberation resulted in a similar alteration of the pattern in the figures for thirteen colonies. On the other hand, when wealth is measured by net worth, the percentages having financial assets in the South declined consistently, though not markedly, from the high level to the low. These figures indicate that, though more creditors were richer than poorer, yet there were substantial numbers of creditors among people whose wealth was less than £100.

Financial Assets and Liabilities by Age, Sex, Residence, Occupation, Testacy

Creditors were not predominatly urban, and they included a considerable proportion of the relatively few women wealthholders and of younger wealthholders. I conclude from table 5.10 that older

Table 5.9
Financial Assets
Held by Wealthholders of High to Low Wealth, 1774
(*Percent of Wealthholders*)

	Thirteen Colonies[a]	New England	New Jersey Pennsylv. Delaware	South
Financial assets held by those with total physical wealth of:				
£400 and over	51.2	74.7	88.0	37.3
£100–399	66.8	68.2	80.2	44.7
£99 and under	46.7	48.2	76.5	29.9
Financial assets held by those with net worth of:				
£400 and over	61.4	79.9	97.9	42.5
£100–399	62.6	73.1	76.5	40.4
£99 and under	45.7	47.5	73.7	27.5

SOURCE: Sample data *w*-weighted, Variant Two.

   [a] Thirteen colonies' figures include the New York estimate.

wealthholders had larger financial assets and also larger liabilities than the younger. However, a large percentage of younger ones held some financial assets. By sex, men outdistanced the women in amount of financial assets and of liabilities, although the percentage of women wealthholders holding financial assets, well over half at 56.5, slightly exceeded the percentage of men who held them. I observed, rather often, that widows, if they were fairly well off, held financial assets more often than land or livestock, but not more often than they held slaves in the South. Some may wonder at the finding that slightly more rural dwellers than urban held financial assets, although the average amount held by the urban was very much larger on average, as was also the average size of urban liabilties, compared with those of rural dwellers. But many farmers held financial claims of the sort mentioned earlier in the chapter, which probably accounts for the high rural percentages.

When we look at occupational status groups, also in table 5.10, the two with outstandingly highest financial assets as well as liabilities were "esquires, gentlemen and officials" and merchants.[19] The designation of "esquire" or "gentleman" or "gentlewoman" as an occupation is not entirely satisfactory. It arose from terms used in the probate inventories to identify decedents and was incorporated in the coding at an early stage. In retrospect, I see it as rather a term of rank or social status than of occupation. Many "gentlemen" were also farmers, and occasionally successful artisans[20] or professionals. Some "esquires" were merchants, officials, attorneys or, especially in the South, planters. As a warning against too literal interpretation of

Table 5.10
Financial Assets and Liabilities
Held by Wealthholders, by Socioeconomic Group
Thirteen Colonies, 1774
(*Average Value in Pounds Sterling*)

Wealthholder Group	Average Value of Financial Assets	Average Value of Financial Liabilities	Percentage having Financial Assets
All Wealthholders	40.6	49.3	56.3
Younger (age 44 and under)	36.9	51.9	62.9
Older (age 45 and above)	62.8	60.5	49.6
Men	41.2	51.4	56.3
Women	31.2	18.8	56.5
Urban	73.7	77.3	55.2
Rural	35.3	44.6	56.3
Esquires, gentlemen, officials	192.5	135.3	78.3
Merchants	110.1	173.8	28.6[a]
Professionals (including sea captains)	54.8	50.1	31.3
Farmers only and planters	27.8	43.2	53.3
Farmers plus other activity, vessel owners, fishermen	89.4	91.6	73.8
Shopkeepers, innkeepers	83.4	92.9	75.5
Artisans, chandlers	28.2	33.2	63.6
Mariners (not captains), laborers	20.1	31.8	49.3
Widows, single women	16.2	20.5	43.2
Men, occupation not determined	37.4	17.2	68.1

SOURCE: Columns 1 and 2: sample data, w*-weighted, Variant Two. Liabilities from regression analysis (see the Note on Method). Column 3: sample data, w-weighted, Variant Two, percentage of probate-type wealthholders.

NOTE: For relative frequency of groups, see table 7.1. For further detail on financial assets see *American Colonial Wealth*, 2d ed., relevant tables from A.7.39 through A.7.83.

[a] The merchant percentages by region are New England, 51.5; Middle Colonies, 95.4; South, 0.9 (see tables 5.11, 5.12, 5.13). The ages and large-county locations of the northern merchants contribute to pull down their influence in the combined thirteen colonies' figure (see appendix A, part one).

the occupational and residential categories assigned in this study, I give a rather extreme example of the difficulty of assigning specific codes. Peter Manigault, the richest case in the sample, had extensive consumer goods listed in inventories both at Charleston and at Goose Creek, South Carolina. He was variously designated as barrister at law, esquire, gentleman, and held office as provincial treasurer. He also owned several plantations in addition to the place at Goose Creek, with many Negroes and farm implements. I coded his residence as urban and his occupation as "esquire, gentleman."[21] In general, the occupational designation in this study of a case as "esquire," "gentleman," or "gentlewoman" stems from its being so designated on its probate inventory and there being no other clear-cut evidence to place it in a specific single occupation. It is likely that more of the "esquires" and "gentlemen" could have been alternatively assigned as "farmers" than to any other occupation (J. Main 1965:215–20; Brown 1955:18–19).

A much larger percentage of those coded as "esquire" or "gentleman" or "official" held financial assets than those coded "merchant." The seeming anomaly in table 5.10 of the low percentage of merchants holding financial assets is explained in its note a. It was true only of the southern merchants in the sample. Farmers, especially those with side occupations,[22] frequently held financial assets. These amounts for both farmer groups were considerably below the averages for merchants. Other occupational groups that were creditors relatively frequently were shopkeepers, artisans, and chandlers. Though over two-fifths of widows held financial assets, their average amount was the lowest of any of the occupation/status groups. In every occupation group, with the exception of "esquires, gentlemen, officials," and "professionals," average financial liabilities exceeded average financial assets.

Persons who left valid wills (testates) held financial assets slightly less often than did the intestates, but their average amounts were much higher, as were their average liabilities (table 5.14).

Regional Differences for Subgroups of Wealthholders

Corresponding figures by separate region in tables 5.11 through 5.13 bear out the foregoing generalizations, with a few trivial excep-

Table 5.11
Financial Assets and Liabilities Held by Wealthholders
by Socioeconomic Group
New England, 1774
(*Average Value in Pounds Sterling*)

Wealthholder Group	Average Value of Financial Assets	Average Value of Financial Liabilities	Percentage Having Financial Assets
All Wealthholders	28.5	51.6	61.4
Younger (age 44 and under)	21.9	47.4	66.3
Older (age 45 and above)	45.7	63.3	54.2
Men	29.8	53.9	61.1
Women	7.5	16.0	65.0
Urban	57.4	63.9	44.4
Rural	19.0	47.7	67.1
Esquires, gentlemen, officials	112.5	99.2	80.1
Merchants	85.0	227.3	51.5
Professionals (including sea captains)	84.4	51.6	64.4
Farmers only and planters	16.2	42.3	58.5
Farmers plus other activity, fishermen	18.7	54.1	78.8
Shopkeepers, innkeepers	118.5	169.1	86.8
Artisans, chandlers	12.8	38.8	50.7
Mariners (not captains), laborers	6.5	38.1	44.8
Widows, single women	7.7	13.6	66.7
Men, occupation not determined	27.7	31.8	55.1

SOURCE: Columns 1 and 2: sample data, w^*-weighted; liabilities from regression analysis (see the Note on Method). Column 3: sample data, w-weighted percentage of probate-type wealthholders.

NOTE: For relative frequency of groups, see table 7.2. For further detail on financial assets see *American Colonial Wealth,* either edition, appropriate tables 7.43 through 7.93.

tions that are chiefly to be explained by small numbers of cases in some subcells of the samples.

No "creditor class" or "debtor class" is discernible in the regional figures, although we find some interesting regional differences among some wealthholder subgroups. In each region more of the younger than of the older held financial assets, although the younger in the North held smaller average amounts than the older. The financial liabilities were somewhat but not substantially greater for the older. In both New England and the middle colonies of New Jersey, Pennsylvania, and Delaware, relatively more of the few women wealthholders held financial assets than did the men, and in

Table 5.12
Financial Assets and Liabilities Held by Wealthholders
by Socioeconomic Group
New Jersey, Pennsylvania, and Delaware, 1774
(Average Value in Pounds Sterling)

Wealthholder Group	Average Value of Financial Assets	Average Value of Financial Liabilities	Percentage Having Financial Assets
All Wealthholders[a]	65.3	45.0	77.9
Younger (age 44 and under)	50.3	47.6	87.2
Older (age 45 and above)	116.8	54.9	70.1
Men	65.1	45.7	79.4
Women	77.7	10.7	94.4
Urban	102.5	102.3	73.5
Rural	61.1	33.0	81.5
Esquires, gentlemen, officials	199.9	310.5	100.0
Merchants	357.5	243.3	95.4
Professionals (including sea captains)	37.0	49.0	81.5
Farmers only and planters	67.9	34.2	80.3
Farmers plus other activity, vessel owners	39.4	79.4	73.1
Shopkeepers, innkeepers	42.1	73.3	64.6
Artisans, chandlers	38.5	56.3	82.1
Mariners (not captains), laborers	77.1	5.3	72.5
Widows, single women	79.3	3.2	94.2
Men, occupation not determined	30.3	1.5	59.6

SOURCE: Columns 1 and 2: sample data, w*-weighted; liabilities from regression analysis (see the Note on Method). Column 3: sample data, w-weighted percentage of probate-type wealthholders.

NOTE: For relative frequency of groups, see table 7.3 and Jones (1970), table 38. For further detail on financial assets see *American Colonial Wealth,* either edition, appropriate tables 7.47 through 7.103.

[a] For this line only, the values include estimates for New York.

those middle colonies they held a larger average amount than the men. As debtors, on the other hand, men averaged much larger amounts, here reinforcing the commercial interpretation of debt. Urban dwellers in all three regions emerge as substantially the greater holders of financial assets judged by average amounts, but the percentages holding financial assets were in each case greater among rural dwellers. We can hardly say that country dwellers were indebted to the town residents. As debtors, the relatively fewer urban dwellers far outranked the more numerous rural dwellers in amount of debt in the South. This was also true in the middle colonies of

New Jersey, Pennsylvania, and Delaware, and substantially so in New England.

Testates averaged larger amounts of financial assets and larger debts than did the intestates in all three regions. There were no striking regional differences in percentages of testates and intestates holding such assets or having debts (table 5.14).

By occupation by region, we find that for New England the largest creditors, judging by amount of financial assets, were notably "shopkeepers," "esquires, gentlemen, officials," "merchants," and "professionals including sea captains." In New Jersey, Pennsylvania,

Table 5.13
Financial Assets and Liabilities Held by Wealthholders
by Socioeconomic Group
South, 1774
(*Average Value in Pounds Sterling*)

Wealthholder Group	Average Value of Financial Assets	Average Value of Financial Liabilities	Percentage Having Financial Assets
All Wealthholders	28.3	51.2	36.8
Younger (age 44 and under)	34.7	57.4	42.9
Older (age 45 and above)	32.2	61.3	29.1
Men	28.8	53.4	37.0
Women	22.3	25.6	34.7
Urban	180.1	128.0	28.2
Rural	26.5	50.3	37.0
Esquires, gentlemen, officials	424.7	183.0	71.9
Merchants	5.4	52.7	0.9
Professionals	0.0	31.0	0.0
Farmers only and planters	14.4	47.2	34.8
Farmers plus other activity	83.0	159.0	62.0
Shopkeepers, innkeepers	0.0	10.5	0.0
Artisans, chandlers	11.8	17.5	23.1
Mariners (not captains), laborers	18.3	23.5	6.8
Widows, single women	22.3	25.6	34.7
Men, occupation not determined	18.5	12.4	66.7

SOURCE: Columns 1 and 2: sample data, w^*-weighted, Variant Two; liabilities from regression analysis (see the Note on Method). Column 3: sample data, w-weighted, Variant Two, percentage of probate-type wealthholders.

NOTE: For relative frequency of groups, see table 7.4. For further detail regarding financial assets, see *American Colonial Wealth*, 2d ed., appropriate tables A.7.51 through A.7.113.

Table 5.14
Financial Assets and Liabilities
Held by Wealthholders by Testacy,
Thirteen Colonies and Three Regions, 1774
(*Average Value in Pounds Sterling*)

	Average Value of Financial Assets	Average Value of Financial Liabilities	Percentage Having Financial Assets
Testate			
Thirteen Colonies[a]	61.8	64.4	53.4
New England	50.6	63.1	62.6
New Jersey, Pennsylvania, Delaware	96.4	52.7	80.9
South	37.5	72.6	34.1
Intestate			
Thirteen Colonies[a]	25.8	39.0	59.9
New England	21.0	47.8	60.9
New Jersey, Pennsylvania, Delaware	40.1	36.2	79.7
South	19.0	27.8	41.9

SOURCE: Columns 1 and 2: sample data, w*-weighted, Variant Two; liabilities from regression analysis (see Introduction). Column 3: sample data, w-weighted, Variant Two, percentage of probate-type wealthholders (see appendix A, part three).

NOTE: For further detail on financial assets see *American Colonial Wealth,* either edition, tables 7.116 through 7.119, and 2d ed., tables A.7.114, A.7.115, A.7.120, A.7.121.

[a] The thirteen colonies' figures include the New York estimate.

and Delaware, "merchants" were the holders of largest financial assets, followed by "esquires, gentlemen, officials". Debtors in New England who owed largest amounts as a group were "merchants," followed by "shopkeepers," then "esquires, gentlemen and officials." In New Jersey, Pennsylvania, and Delaware, the heaviest debtor occupation group was the "esquires, gentlemen, and officials," followed not far behind by "merchants." Next came "farmers with side occupations plus vessel owners," then "shopkeepers," then "artisans and chandlers" with "professionals" closely on their heels. These occupation groups as principal debtors, both in New England and the middle colonies, support the commercial hypothesis of the character of much of the debt in those regions.

For the South, the holders of far and away the largest amounts of financial assets, and at the same time debtors with largest financial liabilities, were the "esquires, gentlemen, and officials." They also were the most frequent holders of financial assets. Distinctions between esquires, gentlemen, planters, farmers are unclear. Many planters were designated as "esquire" or "gentleman." Those coded in this study as "planter" (see note 22) are included with the "farmer only" group, meaning farmers without side occupation. The occupation group in the South with second largest amounts both of financial assets and of liabilities was the group of farmers with side activities. The lowest debt values there were found for "shopkeepers" and "men, occupation not determined."

It would seem that in the South, merchants played a much smaller financial role than merchants of the middle colonies and New England, probably because English mercantile houses played a more dominant role in the South than elsewhere.[23] Southern farmers with side activities and "farmers only and planters" owed substantial debt, but the farmers, especially those with side activities, held considerable financial assets (Gray 1932:413–17).

FINANCING OF ENTERPRISES

The general conclusion I draw is that, depite the seeming handicaps of absence of banking institutions, shortage of coins, and varying local paper currency, the colonists proved very enterprising. They engaged in a wide variety of credit transactions with each other as well as with agents or purchasers or suppliers in Europe and the West Indies. These transactions met their day-to-day, month-to-month, or year-to-year needs for purchasing supplies, equipment, land, livestock, slaves, and selling their products or services. Many kinds of people extended credit to many other kinds of people, and were repaid sometimes in kind, sometimes in paper currency, and sometimes by a "note" or "book account" that its owner might, in turn, use in settling another debt he owed to some third party (Baxter 1945:31 and passim).

We do not find a clear creditor class nor a debtor class. Claims on others were held by people of low as well as of high wealth, and debts were owed by the wealthy to a greater extent than by the less well off.

There does appear some difference among occupation groups, with merchants in the North serving actively as both creditors and debtors, followed by "esquires, gentlemen, and officials." The Philadelphia merchants of the middle colonies were outstanding holders of financial assets and also had high debt. Northern farmers, including those in New England, also frequently held creditor claims. In the South, the relatively few merchants played lesser financial roles, secondary to those played by "esquires, gentlemen, officials" and by "farmers with side activities."

The relatively few women wealthholders often had money out "at interest," especially in the middle colonies, as did "men, occupation not determined." Testates were creditors no more frequently than the intestates, although they held larger amounts of financial assets and owed larger amounts of financial liabilities.

There is insufficient evidence to claim that accumulated financial assets were used for industrial enterprises, of which there were as yet relatively few in the colonies. It seems clear, however, that financial assets were accumulating for some individuals in the North from "money at interest" and commercial activities and in the South from slave-produced export crops, combined with a variety of other activities. Some of these contributed to overall fortunes and substantial wealth for some individuals, which in subsequent decades became available as capital for industrial enterprise.

CHAPTER SIX

Distribution of Wealth: The Rich and the Poor

EARLY observers from England and Europe saw society in the northern colonies as egalitarian by European standards. They found many leveling influences in a country where economic opportunities and land were abundant and the contrasts between rags and riches seen in the old world were not painfully displayed.[1] Alexis de Tocqueville,[2] visiting in the 1830s, gained much the same impression.

American historians have not always agreed with these conclusions. They have long debated whether American colonial society was one of relative equality of opportunity, at least for white adult males. Here two questions may be separated: the amount of inequality in a given cross-section of society, and changes in the position of any individual or family over time (mobility). Was there plenty of room for upward mobility and no great cross-sectional inequality of wealth until the coming of industrialization in the nineteenth century? Or were there in fact strong concentrations of wealth, social status, and political power in the hands of privileged groups at the onset of the Revolution and even much earlier? Among those supporting the idea of status, power, and entrenched wealth are Charles Beard[3] and Carl Becker, who is cited by Bernard Bailyn (1962:341) in an interpretive summary of new studies that he found constituted a fundamental revision of early American history under way in the 1960s. John Murrin (1965–66, 1972) also illuminated important new interpretations emerging from recent studies.

Some of the local quantitative studies of the past two decades have found important "middle-class" elements in the society of both New England and the Middle Colonies, while at the same time noting some great wealth disparities and conflicting evidence as to time trends. Convenient summaries of them, focused on the issue of inequality trends, are found in Williamson and Lindert (1977) and in Gloria Main (1977a). The former observe that the comparison of (cross-sectional) levels of inequality with those of England and Europe has never been seriously debated by historians. They suggest (1977:7) that the modern quantitative evidence is effectively summarized by Allan Kulikoff's (1971:87, 98–100) statement that "in the seventeenth century wealth in the American towns was typically less concentrated than in sixteenth-century English towns, where . . . the richest tenth owned between half and seven-tenths. . . ." Modern social historians, according to Williamson and Lindert, have done nothing to upset the early impressionist judgments as to greater cross-sectional equality than in England and Europe, but they are engaged in a lively debate regarding trends over time during the colonial period. Williamson and Lindert (1977:8–10) discern three competing hypotheses in this ongoing debate.

The first, following Jackson T. Main (1976:54), is that the seventeenth century saw exported to America a European class structure and highly concentrated wealth distribution. The frontier made short work of the European model, however, and the Revolution eventually insured its demise. This hypothesis suggests an egalitarian trend for the overall colonial economy.

The second thesis argues that a very equal distribution of land, and thus wealth, was achieved right at the start. A trend to inequality and wealth concentration set in, however, as the readily accessible land became exhausted. The Revolution served only to halt the retrogression. Williamson and Lindert label the many proponents of this thesis, such as Kenneth Lockridge,[4] "the revisionists." Others of the revisionists[5] find increasing poverty and intensification of wealth disparity in colonial cities—particularly Boston, Philadelphia, and New York City—the key to wealth concentration trends at work prior to the Revolution. Gloria Main (1977a:566–67, 573) sees as significant early emergence of urban wealth concentration and high early inequality in six Maryland counties. She finds that the evidence from probate studies does not support the thesis that as the eighteenth century wore on, inexorable forces widened the gap between rich and poor.

The third hypothesis, favored by Williamson and Lindert after their intensive review of many of the quantitative studies, is that the general overall trend in cross-sectional inequality for the colonies was one either of no change or of a slight upward drift in inequality. They do not deny rising inequality in large cities, particularly Philadelphia, although they raise questions as to whether data revision similar to that by Warden[6] for Boston tax data may be in order for Philadelphia and New York. Nor do they deny possibly increasing concentration in older eastern settled areas, although the evidence here is not always clear cut. However, they argue that, in proportion to population, the existing studies concentrate too heavily on large cities and older areas, and do not represent the expanding wealth-getting opportunities in the newer counties, which were steadily developing both extensively and intensively. They note relatively slow urban population growth except in Philadelphia, as compared to burgeoning populations to the west, where equalities were greater. They conclude that a reasonable population weighting would yield a combined pattern of highly stable wealth inequality during the colonial period.

My own hypothesis makes a further allowance for the cumulative impact of slavery in the South and the fact that half the total population of the colonies was in that region by the time of the Revolution. This hypothesis is that there may have been sufficient upward trend in cross-sectional wealth inequality in the South in the eighteenth century to more than counterbalance the fairly stable or moderately updrifting general trend in the two northern regions. Hence it seems likely that a composite tendency to substantial cross-sectional wealth inequality is the best characterization of overall colonial wealth trends. This thesis will be further dealt with in the section on trends in chapter 8.

Economists also have long been interested in the size distribution of wealth and income in contemporary society and in the question of whether inequality has increased or decreased over time. Even before the beginnings of modern economics with Adam Smith in 1776, they have sought to understand the causes of the growth of wealth of nations, which have always been related to the distribution of income and wealth.[7] Greater precision in measurement of size distribution, whether of wealth or of income, came with work by Gini (1912), Lorenz (1905), Paglin, (1975, 1977) and others.[8] Economists' interest in size distribution concerns not only equity and opportunity, but also the functioning and growth of the economic system. The propensity to consume may vary with size of present income and expected lifetime income, family size, and shape of the utility function, to name at least some of the major variables, and affects the portion of income saved. Individual savings, in turn, are reflected in the society's accumulation of savings and the growth of capital stock for use in further production, both of which affect size of output (income) in the next period, and hence are parts of the recurring interrelationship between income, consumption, savings, investment, and growth of wealth.

All of the foregoing facets, in particular both income and wealth, bear directly upon the issue of inequality. In terms of well-being, income and consumption also tie in with the question of who shared what. First I will attempt to untangle some of these facets as they affect the way in which I present and interpret the data found on cross-sectional wealth inequality in the colonies in 1774. I will next discuss the several measures of inequality that I offer and then present the data results here and in chapter 7.

POPULATION AMONG WHOM THE WEALTH DISTRIBUTION IS MEASURED

How well off various portions of the colonial population were depends, in part, on the household's share of aggregate wealth. Well-being was also affected by how the income or product flowing from the use of that wealth was shared within the household. Here, the close relationship between wealth and the income yielded by its use is apparent. Wealth in such forms as land, slaves, furnishings and equipment, crops and other producers' or consumers' goods, as well as financial assets, remained the property of the free family head or single wealthholder for his or her lifetime, unless he/she used them up, exchanged them for other forms of wealth, or made gifts before death. We may safely assume, however, that the head of a free family shared the income flow or produce from his wealth to support his family and other dependants. In all likelihood, these household sharings, especially of food, varied with need, depending on age, sex, and activity. Also they were almost certainly more generous, in quality if not in quantity, for family members than for slaves and servants. Undoubtedly the wealthholder also shared the use of such forms of wealth as land, furnishings, and equipment with family members and to some extent with slaves and servants. An example of the latter was the cultivation of the land by slaves with tools of the owner, to produce not only export staples such as tobacco but also such subsistence foods as corn and vegetables, at least part of which were for their own consumption. Our data cover the capital aspects of wealth ownership, from which we can only indirectly infer who, other than the owner, may have shared in its use or enjoyed part of the product / income yielded by its use.

For reasons such as the foregoing, I shall appraise wealth distribution not among all persons but among free wealthholders, most of whom were heads of families.[9] These were chiefly males but included some females. I also offer two alternative tables that include, at the bottom of the array of free wealthholders, all the nonfree adult males, whose actual wealth was zero, as potential wealthholders.

COMPOSITION OF THE WEALTH WHOSE DISTRIBUTION IS CONSIDERED

Differences in definitions of wealth sometimes impede meaningful comparisons of various studies of wealth concentration. We might use any one of the totals of wealth defined in chapters 1, 3, and 5 to rank wealthholders. Here I prefer the concept of net worth, which includes financial assets and liabilities,[10] to determine who is richer than whom. However, since the data on ownership of physical assets are more firmly grounded, I also show tables for wealthholders ranked by size of total physical wealth. The tables and graphs by net worth generally show a higher degree of inequality than those by total physical wealth. However, with the exception of net worth for New England, the general conclusions as to amount of wealth concentration do not differ greatly, whichever measure is used.[11]

Although my emphasis in chapters 3 and 4 was on nonhuman physical wealth, I consider inappropriate the exclusion of assets in the form of slave and servant values when we are looking at relative command over wealth by individual holders. The slaveowner did, by that fact, have more wealth. His legally enforceable claim to the product of slave services in the present and future was an important asset and source of income that it would be unrealistic to ignore. I therefore include these values in most instances in the present chapter. This inclusion appears to be a major contributing factor to wealth inequality in the South, but not to that of the comparably high inequality in New England. To check this last statement, and because of the great interest in the subject of slavery, I also offer, for the South only, a table (6.11) of free wealthholders distributed by size of nonhuman physical wealth assets, that is, excluding slave values.

This chapter presents the wealth concentration pattern by deciles (tenths) and for the two top percentiles (the richest 1 and 2 percent) of all free wealthholders, as it existed in 1774 in the thirteen colonies. With the exception noted in the preceding paragraph, these calculations include the assets in slaves and servants as part of the wealth of their owners, but exclude the slaves and servants in the count of wealth-owning members of the society. Corresponding wealth concentration patterns are shown for each of the three regions, insofar as the data justify separate analysis.[12] Two final tables (6.14 and 6.15) consider the effect of including slaves as zero-wealthholding members of the society.

MEASURES OF INEQUALITY

Different observers of data for various times and places have used various measures of inequality. Some are impressed by the large proportions or the absolute amounts of wealth controlled by an elite few, or by an arbitrary fraction such as the upper 10 percent of wealthholders. Some are interested in changes somewhat lower on the scale, for example, in what fraction holds 50 percent of the wealth. Others are concerned with the smallness of holdings of a large bottom segment, or with the proportion of possible wealth-holders who hold no property of discernible value. Still others prefer one succinct number to summarize the degree of inequality of one distribution as compared with another. I provide, as in tables 6.1 and 6.2, data with which the reader may focus on the aspect of the inequality that interests him. I summarize briefly the several measures offered and some of their respective merits and limitations. These measures include: (1) the spread between the mean and the median wealth; (2) the percentages of total wealth held by those in certain percentiles or deciles; (3) these percentages cumulated upward and graphed in the form of a Lorenz curve; and (4) the single summarizing measure, Gini's coefficient of concentration derived from the areas graphed in the Lorenz curve.

Mean and Median Wealth

The divergence between mean and median wealth is readily understood, as indicating departure from the bell-shaped curve of a normal distribution. Since wealth distributions are typically skewed, with many more cases of low wealth than of high, the two measures diverge and the median is smaller. The median is the midway value, below and above which half the cases lie. It has the virtue of not being influenced by the extremes at either end of the wealth scale, whereas the mean is pulled up by large individual values toward the top. The wider the divergence, the greater the indication of large wealthholdings toward the upper end of the distribution, and conversely, of small ones toward the lower end.

Percentage of Total Wealth Held

Another readily understood measure of concentration is the proportion of total wealth held at the upper end, as by the richest 1 or 2, or 10 or 20 percent. Or, one may wish to know the proportions of wealth held by the poorest half, or 30 or 20 percent. The absolute amounts they held are indicated by the boundaries of the wealth brackets examined. The differences between the lower bounds of the wealth brackets suggest the scope of differences, among individual families in levels of wealth. The monetary value can be visualized as the real estate, slaves, producers' goods, and consumers' goods (as well as financial assets or liabilities, if the wealth measure is net worth) purchaseable with that amount of wealth. In interpreting table 6.1 and figures 11, and 13 the reader should bear in mind that I found especially large financial liabilities in New England.

Table 6.1
Net Worth Distribution by Decile
Free Wealthholders, 1774

	Thirteen Colonies	New England	N. Jersey Pennsylv. Delaware	South
			Percentage	
Percentage share held by:				
100th percentile (richest 1%)	14.6	20.9	13.7	11.3
99th percentile (next richest 1%)	8.0	6.6	4.0	7.0
Tenth decile (richest 10%)	54.8	56.8	42.1	48.8
Ninth decile	18.4	19.9	18.6	21.3
Eighth decile	11.1	12.2	12.0	13.1
Seventh decile	7.4	7.6	10.9	6.9
Sixth decile	4.8	5.0	7.1	4.6
Fifth decile	2.7	2.3	4.5	2.9
Fourth decile	1.5	0.9	3.3	1.5
Third decile	0.8	0.6	1.3	0.8
Second decile	0.3	0.2	1.1	0.4
First decile (poorest 10%)	−1.7	−5.6	−0.8	−0.3
Gini coefficient	0.73	0.80	0.60	0.68

SOURCE: Sample data, $w*B$-weighted, Variant Two, pertaining to all free wealthholders. For tables showing distribution of only probate-type wealthholders (sample data, w-weighted) and of all wealthholders under an alternate assumption A, which places all nonprobate-type wealthholders in the lower deciles (sample data, $w*A$-weighted, Variant One), see *American Colonial Wealth.*

NOTE: Includes value of slaves and servants, financial assets; subtracts financial liabilities. Percentages may not add to 100 because of rounding. The New York figures are not shown separately but are incorporated in the thirteen colonies' total. Estimates include probate-type and nonprobate-type wealthholders in the respective proportions shown in appendix A. Nonprobate-type wealthholders are distributed according to assumption B explained in that appendix. The exact weights used for nonprobate adjustment by decile for this table are:

	New England	N. Jersey Pennsylv. Delaware	South
Decile 10	0.040	0.005	0.010
9	0.048	0.007	0.015
8	0.057	0.012	0.022
7	0.068	0.020	0.033
6	0.081	0.033	0.048
5	0.096	0.054	0.071
4	0.115	0.089	0.103
3	0.137	0.146	0.151
2	0.164	0.240	0.221
1	0.195	0.394	0.324

The seeming inconsistency of a higher percentage of wealth held by the next-richest percentile in the thirteen colonies than in the constituent regions is explained by examining the right panel of the table, and

Table 6.1 (Continued)
Net Worth Distribution by Decile
Free Wealthholders, 1774

	Thirteen Colonies	New England	N. Jersey Pennsylv. Delaware	South
	Value in Pounds Sterling			
Value at lower bound of:				
100th percentile (richest 1%)	2,271.6	1,150.9	1,544.2	2,645.9
99th percentile (next richest 1%)	1,763.3	846.0	839.4	2,225.8
Tenth decile (richest 10%)	591.2	352.7	472.3	1,011.9
Ninth decile	335.5	207.5	316.3	624.8
Eighth decile	209.6	142.6	240.1	366.8
Seventh decile	146.7	91.6	192.5	201.6
Sixth decile	84.6	45.5	123.8	157.7
Fifth decile	45.9	19.8	77.7	65.3
Fourth decile	25.8	10.9	45.1	42.0
Third decile	11.3	4.8	28.7	20.5
Second decile	4.3	−3.3	13.9	8.4
First decile (poorest 10%)	−199.8	−199.8	−59.6	−101.0
Mean	237.3	138.0	211.2	371.8
Median	83.8	45.0	119.1	157.7

recognizing that the first column involved a complete reordering from high to low unweighted wealth of all 919 sample cases, using for counts their regional w^* weights (rw^*), explained in section VI on weighting in *American Colonial Wealth*, either edition. See also appendix A. Those in the top 1 and next 1 percent in the ranking by thirteen colonies are not a direct combination by rw^* weights of those in the top 1 percent and next 1 percent in each region. Rather, as indicated by the values at the lower bounds, the consolidated sample list brings predominantly southerners and their wealth to the top of the ordered ranking. With the unweighted wealths and the corresponding weighted numbers of cases being differently ordered than at corresponding portions of the decile scales in the regions, there is no reason to expect the percentage shares applicable to the thirteen colonies always to stay within the range of those for individual regions in the size distribution tables.

Lorenz Curve and Gini Coefficient
of Concentration

The Lorenz curve,[13] such as figure 11, gives a graphic presentation. It shows the cumulative percentages of wealth owned from the poorest to the wealthiest, in comparison with a 45 degree line of hypothetical perfect equality. If each wealthholder had the same wealth, all points would lie on this 45 degree line. When differing

Table 6.2
Total Physical Wealth Distribution by Decile
Free Wealthholders, 1774

	Thirteen Colonies	New England	N. Jersey Pennsylv. Delaware	South
			Percentage	
Percentage share held by:				
100th percentile (richest 1%)	12.9[a]	11.6	12.0	10.4
99th percentile (next richest 1%)	6.7	7.2	4.0	6.5
Tenth decile	50.7[a]	46.8	35.1	46.9
Ninth decile	17.2[a]	19.1	17.6	22.7
Eighth decile	11.3[a]	12.7	14.5	12.8
Seventh decile	8.2	8.1	12.7	7.0
Sixth decile	5.9	5.7	8.9	4.8
Fifth decile	3.1	3.6	6.7	2.7
Fourth decile	1.8	1.9	2.3	1.5
Third decile	1.0	1.2	1.1	0.9
Second decile	0.6	0.7	0.8	0.5
First decile (poorest 10%)	0.2	0.3	0.4	0.2
Gini coefficient	0.66	0.64	0.54	0.67

SOURCE: Source note to table 6.1 pertains also to this table.

NOTE: Includes value of slaves and servants; excludes financial assets and financial liabilities. The zero value for the first (poorest) decile in the middle colonies is a true case of zero physical wealth of sample decedent no. 13100. Balance of general note to table 6.1 pertains to this table, except that the exact weights used for nonprobate adjustment by decile for this table are:

	New England	N. Jersey Pennsylv. Delaware	South
Decile 10	0.031	0.002	0.010
9	0.039	0.004	0.014
8	0.048	0.007	0.021
7	0.060	0.013	0.031
6	0.074	0.023	0.046
5	0.092	0.041	0.069
4	0.115	0.075	0.102
3	0.143	0.137	0.151
2	0.178	0.248	0.224
1	0.221	0.451	0.333

amounts of wealth are held, the extent to which the curve bows out from the line is a measure of the inequality. Gini's coefficient of concentration summarizes this area of inequality in a single convenient number, ranging from 0.0 to 1.0. It is the ratio of the inequality area lying between the 45 degree line and the concave or

Table 6.2 (Continued)
Total Physical Wealth Distribution by Decile
Free Wealthholders, 1774

	Thirteen Colonies	*New England*	*N. Jersey Pennsylv. Delaware*	*South*
		Value in Pounds Sterling		
Value at lower bound of:				
100th percentile (richest 1%)	2,027.5	1,174.7	1,087.2	2,646.8
99th percentile (next richest 1%)	1,644.3	992.1	690.1	2,113.3
Tenth decile	609.4	401.6	379.9	1,140.1
Ninth decile	333.8	251.4	283.9	673.7
Eighth decile	241.7	163.6	246.8	390.5
Seventh decile	178.2	111.3	207.6	222.4
Sixth decile	110.6	74.5	154.9	148.1
Fifth decile	58.2	41.6	58.6	73.4
Fourth decile	31.4	25.8	31.1	53.9
Third decile	18.1	15.9	16.5	24.2
Second decile	10.2	7.6	11.2	14.8
First decile (poorest 10%)	0.0	3.0	0.0	2.6
Mean	252.0	161.2	189.2	394.7
Median	108.7	74.4	152.5	144.5

[a] That the percentage of wealth held by the 100th percentile and by the tenth decile for the thirteen colonies exceeds that of any region, and that the percentages held by the ninth and eighth deciles are less than those of any region, are not errors. The computation for the thirteen colonies is done by a reordering of all sample cases, appropriately weighted, into a single distribution, and is not a weighted combination of the three separate distributions. Accordingly, different cases, differently weighted, make up the deciles in each of the four distributions. See appendix A.

upper side of the Lorenz curve to the total triangular area enclosed by the 45 degree line and the two boundary lines at the base and right side of the graph. A zero value indicates perfect equality. A value of 1.0 indicates maximum inequality, when, for an extreme example, one person holds all the wealth and the others have none, or when the top 1 percent holds all the wealth and the other 99 percent hold zero wealth. Hence, the closer the value of the Gini coefficient is to 1.0, the more unequal is the wealth distribution, and graphically, the greater is the area of inequality bounded by the Lorenz curve. The Gini coefficient has both virtues and limitations.[14] It has been widely used for sixty years to compare income as well as

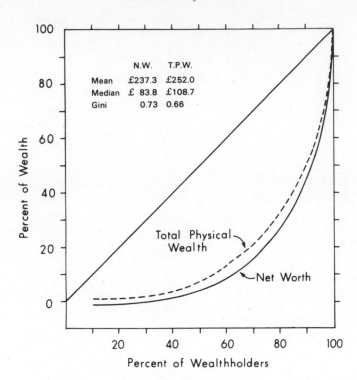

Figure 11.
Distribution of Net Worth, Total Physical Wealth,
Thirteen Colonies, 1774

SOURCE: Tables 6.1 and 6.2, data $w*B$-weighted

wealth concentration at various times and places, and it is independent of the monetary units in which the income or wealth is
expressed.

No Allowance for Age   A very important recent criticism by
Paglin[15] was foreshadowed by Allyn A. Young[16] as long ago as
1916. It is that the conditions of absolute equality specified by the 45
degree line are socially unrealistic. Unless they received substantial
wealth as a parental gift or by early inheritance, we would not expect
young wealthholders to have accumulated as much wealth as older
ones. This fact, in itself, is a reason to accept some inequality among
households as equitable and, indeed, to consider perfect equality of
holdings, with no regard for past years of work and saving, as in-
equitable.[17] The conventional Gini coefficient substantially overstates
inequality as compared with a similar measure that takes into

account the age of the family head or wealthholder. In graphic form, the appropriate base from which to measure inequality becomes not the straight 45 degree line, but a curving line that reflects the age-wealth profile of the society. Only a portion of the total area of inequality can be attributed to inequality of wealthholdings of family heads of comparable age.

The portion not so attributable, that is to say, the area of inequality that may be attributed to age-wealth differences, is shown hatched in figure 12 for net worth by age. It may be compared with Paglin's graph for 1962 Federal Reserve data[18] on wealth in the United States, presented as figure 20 in chapter 8. The P-curve in figure 12 is based on the percentages of aggregate net worth held by free wealthholders in three age classes.[19] If data were available to

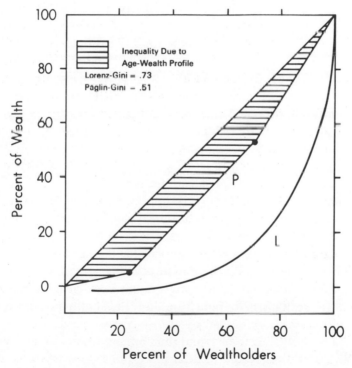

Figure 12.
Distribution of Net Worth and Net Worth by Age,
Thirteen Colonies, 1774

SOURCE: Line L, same as figure 11 for Net Worth. Line P, sample data, w^*B-weighted, by three age classes, and population by age class from table 2.4

subdivide the second and third age classes into somewhat finer age intervals, the P-curve would be slightly more rounded. The hatched area, which Paglin calls the area of inequality due to the age-wealth profile, would resemble even more closely its stunning approximation to the shape Paglin found for 1962, for which five age classes were available. The Gini coefficient that I call our Paglin-Gini for 1774, based on the data graphed in line P where allowance is made for age-wealth differences, is a low 0.51 as opposed to the much higher conventional Lorenz-Gini of 0.73 for line L, shown in both figures 11 and 12. Paglin notes a similar difference for 1962 data between the Lorenz-Gini of 0.76 and a Paglin-Gini of 0.50, and believes that the Lorenz-Gini overstates interfamily wealth inequality by about 52 percent (see note 15). I interpret the corresponding comparison of our two 1774 Ginis to mean that the conventional coefficient overstates the degree of interwealthholder inequality in 1774 by about 43 percent (22/51). Accordingly, to reach more meaningful figures, a reduction would be in order of something like 30 percent (22/73) in the degree of inequality we find in tables 6.1 and 6.2,[20] if allowance were made for that portion of the wealth inequality that can be attributed to age-wealth differences. The percentage reduction would vary slightly by region, owing to slight differences in the age frequencies of living wealthholders in the various regions and in the particular age-wealth relationships by region. Somewhat similar reductions would apparently be in order for all other wealth studies that calculate a Gini coefficient without regard to age of family head. The reader is asked to bear this important qualification in mind when considering the presentation in the balance of this chapter and in chapter 8. In appendix C, I trace the age-wealth profile in the colonial data by smaller wealth intervals for the age-known decedent cases. This profile supports the Paglin position.

Paglin's criticism of the conventional coefficient is especially pertinent to wealth distribution. Equality is generally presumed to be good and inequality to be bad or unjust. Yet we need to think carefully what "wealth" is to be equal, and among whom, to achieve justice. Who would argue that a desirable equality of wealth would be achieved if every man, woman, and child in a society held the same amount? Would equality be achieved if all heads of families, regardless of their stage in the life cycle, held the same wealth? Is it not reasonable and just to allow for greater accumulation of wealth, derived from past savings and from higher income gained from experience and work, as the head of the household approaches the prime of life? Are equality and justice achieved when all family heads of the same age bracket hold the same wealth? What of differing preferences for choosing children over physical assets, and for choosing to consume rather than to save? Are equality and justice more nearly achieved if the 21-year-old, other things being equal, attains at age 45 the same relative wealth held at that age by his father or the 45-year-olds who preceded him? I suggest the last-named possibility may come closer to reasonable equality, yet such is not compatible with the assumptions of the 45 degree line. Though debate may long continue on the best method of finding a norm for wealth by age, I fully concur with Paglin that age should be considered in the measure of wealth inequality. Possibly also family size should be considered, as suggested by Kuznets (1976) in his important article exploring the demographic implications of income inequality (see note 16) And possibly the whole issue of sex differentials should be faced before the area of debate is closed.

CONCENTRATION AMONG FREE WEALTHHOLDERS, THIRTEEN COLONIES

The colonial era came to a close in a preindustrial age, but one with widening commerical opportunities. The colonists were exploiting their natural advantages and developing some fairly complex forms of credit and productive arrangements. Wealth was distributed quite unequally among the free wealthholders. Although holdings may have been as or more unequal in England[21] or some other countries at the time, there was surely not egalitarianism. Judged by net worth in the colonies as a whole, the Lorenz-Gini coefficient was a rather high .73 (table 6.1, column 1). In a ranking by total physical wealth, it was somewhat lower at .66 (table 6.2, column 1), but this is still fairly high, as indicated by some comparisons later in the chapter. There was very large disparity between mean and median net worth, as those in the poorest group owed debts in excess of their assets. When we examine the age patterns of debt (*American Colonial Wealth*, tables A.7.39, A.7.40 and A.7.41), financial liabilities per wealthholder substantially exceeded financial assets through the 26–44 age group, and were overbalanced by financial assets only in the wealthholder group aged 45 and over. Even without the disturbing effects of debts owed, we also find in table 6.2 a substantial divergence between mean and median total physical wealth. Mean physical wealth also reached higher values in higher age brackets.

The inequality is very noticeably influenced by high wealth toward the upper end and low wealth in the poorer deciles, with half of all free wealthholders having net worth below £84 sterling and physical wealth below £109.

In the colonies as a whole, the top 1 percent had 15 percent of net worth. Their mean net worth was £3,560, or over $193,000 in 1978 money. This class comprised all who had £2,272 or more of net worth. Its upper bound, the wealth of the richest case in the sample (Peter Manigault of Charleston, S.C.), was £32,738 in net worth (table 6.3), or over one and three quarter million dollars in money at the 1978 price level. In physical wealth, the top 1 percent each held £2,028 or more (about $110,000 dollars in 1978), and as a group, held 13 percent of the total; Peter Manigault was also the richest by this measure (table 6.7) with £27,960. A fifth of all the physical wealth in the colonies and nearly a quarter of the net worth was in the hands of the top 2 percent of free wealthholders, and more than half of both forms of wealth was claimed by the richest 10 percent, many of whom were located in the South. Toward the lower end of the scale by net worth, the poorest half, relatively more of whom were from New England, held only 4 percent of the net worth (table 6.1 and figure 11). Only the bottom 10 percent held negative net worth, but the cumulative share of the bottom 30 percent was negative (figures 11 and 13). In the array by total physical wealth (table 6.2), the bottom half of wealthholders held only 7 percent of the wealth, and the poorest 30 percent only 2 percent (figures 11 and 14). The wealth boundary at the bottom of the second decile, the second poorest 10 percent, was £10 for physical wealth and only £4 for net worth. Physical wealth of over £200 was achieved only in the eighth decile and above, that is, by the top 30 percent of wealthholders in the colonies as a whole.

Some feeling for the kinds of person and probable nature of wealth found at the tops and bottoms of the wealth scales are found

Table 6.3
Ten Richest and Poorest by Net Worth
Thirteen Colonies, 1774

Occupation	Net Worth (Pounds Sterling)	Age	Place of Residence
Esq., planter, attorney	32,737.8	42	Goose Creek, S.C.
Esquire	15,303.2	58	Boston, Suffolk Co., Mass.
Planter	12,704.9	50	Dorchester, S.C.
Planter	11,707.0	(3)	Charles Town, S.C.
Esquire	9,625.2	(2)	Charles Town, S.C.
Esquire	8,534.6	(3)	St. Andrews Parish, S.C.
Esquire	7,425.3	n.d.	St. Pauls Parish, S.C.
Farmer	7,214.1	42	Christ Church Parish, S.C.
Physician	7,173.0	(2)	St. Georges Parish, S.C.
Planter	6,891.0	(2)	Edisto Island, S.C.
Gentleman	−41.3	30	Plymouth Co., Mass.
Cooper	−42.6	40	Danvers, Essex Co., Mass.
Chaisemaker	−59.6	18	Kent Co., Delaware
Yeoman	−78.3	41	Plymouth Co., Mass.
Merchant, captain	−90.6	51	Salem Co., Mass.
Farmer	−101.0	44	Chesterfield Co., Va.
Mariner	−117.6	52	Essex Co., Mass.
Cordwainer	−152.3	63	Salem Co., Mass.
Farmer, Fisherman	−180.5	(2)	New Haven Co., Conn.
Gentleman[a]	199.8	n.d.	Kingston, Plymouth Co., Mass.

SOURCE: Unweighted array of sample of probated decedents in twenty-six counties plus New York. See appendix A.

NOTE: Net worth includes value of servants and slaves, financial assets; subtracts financial liabilities. Decedent I.D. numbers and names, reading from top down, are: 01043 Peter Manigault, Esq.; 54096 William White; 01056 Elijah Postele, Esq.; 01053 Alexander Peronneau; 01001 John Ainslie, Esq.; 01014 John Cattell; 01073 Benjamin Williamson; 01012 Richard Capers; 01042 Dr. Archibald McNeill; 01032 Christopher Jenkins; 53024 Eliphalet Phillips; 51058 James Johnson; 31015 Isaac Cox; 53001 Israel Bailey; 51082 Jonathan Orne; 82014 Benjamin Walthall; 51029 Thomas Dixey; 51012 John Bullock; 42021 Thomas Grannis; 53004 Samuel Brewster. Number within parenthesis indicates age class: class 2 = age 26–44; class 3 = age 45 or over; n.d. = not determined. For caution in interpretation of occupational classification see chapter 5, text and notes.

[a] Samuel Brewster was shown as "gentleman" on a second "de bonis non" inventory of 1787 reporting real estate valued at £142 sterling and on an estate account of 1787; from his first inventory he seemed to be a laborer and he is so coded in table 8.1 of *American Colonial Wealth*. His debts exceeded the value of his land and other assets.

in tables 6.3 through 6.10, showing the locations, occupations, and ages when determined, of the ten richest and ten poorest decedents drawn in the sample. These are presented first for net worth and second by physical wealth, in part to show that not necessarily the same persons are at tops and bottoms by these two definitions of wealth. The tables also show the prevalence of esquires, planters, and professionals from the South among the top wealthholders and of women, some artisans, laborers, and small farmers from New England and the middle colonies among the lower wealth ranks. However, the poorest in net worth in New England was the case of Samuel Brewster, a gentleman from Plymouth county, Massachusetts. His estate was not settled until 1787, when Insolvent Commissioners and an administrator "de bonis non" reported debts owed in excess of his moveable assets and what his land sold for.

We see in tables 6.3 and 6.7 some evidence that the richest were usually middle aged or older, and we find, not too surprisingly, among individual cases of the very poor not only some young but also some old people. This corresponds with the age-wealth profile presented in appendix C.

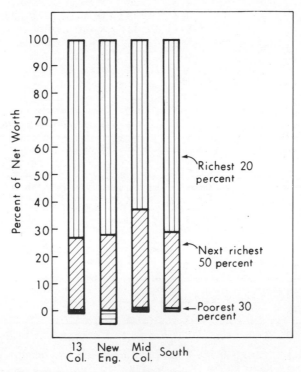

Figure 13.
Net Worth of Richest, Middle, Poorest Wealthholders,
Percentage, Thirteen Colonies and Three Regions, 1774
Source: Table 6.1, data *w*B*-weighted

Table 6.4
Ten Richest and Poorest by Net Worth
New England, 1774

Occupation	Net Worth (Pounds Sterling)	Age	Place of Residence
Esquire	15,303.2	58	Boston, Suffolk Co., Mass.
Merchant	5,786.2	72	Marblehead, Essex Co., Mass.
Physician	4,071.2	42	Marblehead, Essex Co., Mass.
Esquire	3,235.2	67	Boston, Suffolk Co., Mass.
Yeoman	2,271.6	(3)	Marshfield, Plymouth Co., Mass.
Shopkeeper	2,176.1	53	Boston, Suffolk Co., Mass.
Esquire	2,077.6	(3)	Salem, Essex Co., Mass.
Yeoman, cooper	1,868.8	75	Hingham, Suffolk Co., Mass.
Captain	1,763.3	75	Milford, New Haven Co., Conn.
Gentleman	1,694.3	49	Leicester, Worcester Co., Mass.
Mariner, fisherman	−25.0	45	Gloucester, Essex Co., Mass.
Yeoman, blacksmith	−26.7	55	Abington, Plymouth Co., Mass.
Gentleman	−41.3	30+	Bridgewater, Plymouth Co., Mass.
Cooper	−42.6	40	Danvers, Essex Co., Mass.
Yeoman	−78.3	41	Bridgewater, Plymouth Co., Mass.
Merchant, captain	−90.7	51	Salem, Essex Co., Mass.
Mariner	−117.6	52	Marblehead, Essex Co., Mass.
Cordwainer	−152.3	63	Salem, Essex Co., Mass.
Farmer, fisherman	−180.5	(2)	New Haven Co., Conn.
Gentleman[a]	199.0	n.d.	Kingston, Plymouth Co., Mass.

SOURCE: Unweighted array of sample of probated decedents in seven counties. See appendix A.

NOTE: General note to table 6.3 pertains to this table also, except that decedent I.D. numbers and names, reading from top down, are: 54096 William White; 51040 Thomas Gerry; 51028 Humphrey Devereaux, Jr.; 54063 Andrew Oliver; 53029 Samuel Tilden; 54034 Thomas Gray; 51006 Samuel Barton, Sr.; 54097 Enoch Whitten; 42015 Thomas Clark, III; 55006 Thomas Denny; 51055 Paul Hughes; 53012 Adam Cushing; 53024 Eliphalet Phillips; 51058 James Johnson; 53001 Israel Bailey; 51082 Jonathan Orne; 51029 Thomas Dixey; 51012 John Bullock; 42021 Thomas Grannis; 53004 Samuel Brewster.

[a] Footnote a to table 6.3 pertains to this table also.

Assertions that wealth and political power in the form of office-holding went hand in hand in the colonies have not yet been well documented in quantitative studies. A number of studies in individual towns or places[22] have traced connections between occupation or family status and office-holding, and frequently the powerful individuals have been of middle age or older. In the sample Peter Manigault held important office in the province of South Carolina (Crouse 1964), as did Lynford Lardner in Pennsylvania,[23] one of the ten richest in the middle colonies' sample.

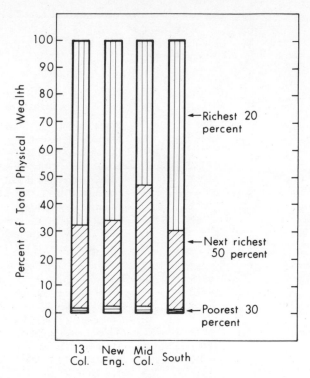

Figure 14.
Total Physical Wealth of Richest, Middle, Poorest Wealthholders,
Percentage, Thirteen Colonies and Three Regions, 1774
SOURCE: Table 6.2, data *w*B*-weighted*

CONCENTRATION AMONG FREE
WEALTHHOLDERS,
BY REGION

Regional differences[24] in wealth concentration among free
wealthholders were pronounced, with New England and the South
vying for greatest inequality, and with the middle colonies the most
egalitarian by every measure (tables 6.1 and 6.2 columns 2, 3 and 4;
tables 6.4 through 6.6, 6.8 through 6.10). Measured by the Lorenz
curve and the Gini coefficient for net worth, New England's wealth
distribution was the most unequal (figures 15 through 17). The
South had that dubious distinction when the measure is the coefficient
for physical wealth. The coefficient was lowest in the middle colonies

for both these definitions of wealth, and their Lorenz curves were the least bowed.

The spread between mean and median net worth was relatively greatest in New England, where I found much individual indebtedness. It was next greatest in the South and least in the more egalitarian middle colonies. When the effects of debts owed and financial assets held are removed, in the measure of total physical wealth,[25] the inequalities were generally less pronounced but were still notable. The mean/median spread in the South showed relatively more inequality than in New England, while that for the middle colonies

Table 6.5
Ten Richest and Poorest by Net Worth
New Jersey, Pennsylvania, Delaware, 1774

Occupation	Net Worth (Pounds Sterling)	Age	Place of Residence
Merchant	6,646.7	(3)	Philadelphia, Pa.
Merchant	6,167.5	55	Philadelphia, Pa.
Provincial officer	4,981.1	59	Philadelphia, Pa.
Farmer	3,647.8	64	Lower Solford Twp., Phil., Pa.
Widow	3,412.2	(3)	Radner, Philadelphia, Pa.
Captain	3,137.3	(3)	Philadelphia, Pa.
Merchant	3,005.9	60	Philadelphia, Pa.
Farmer, landowner	2,710.8	(3)	Little Egg Harbour, Burl., N.J.
Tallowchandler	2,111.4	51	Philadelphia, Pa.
Officer Royal Navy	2,072.2	(3)	Philadelphia, Pa.
Schoolmaster	8.6	(3)	Hannover, Burlington, N.J.
n.d.	6.9	n.d.	Philadelphia, Pa.
n.d.	6.9	65	Philadelphia, Pa.
Pilot, mariner	6.6	42	Upper Del., Phil. City, Pa.
Shopkeeper	5.7	n.d.	Philadelphia, Pa.
Laborer	4.4	n.d.	Allen, Northampton, Pa.
Laborer	4.2	63	Philadelphia, Pa.
Shoemaker	2.4	47	New Garden, Phil., Pa.
Widow	−30.1	36	Philadelphia, Pa.
Chaisemaker	−59.6	18	Jones Hundred, Kent, Del.

SOURCE: Unweighted array of sample of probated decedents in five counties. See appendix A.

NOTE: General note to table 6.3 pertains to this table also, except that decedent I.D. numbers and names, reading from top down, are: 13048 Samuel Neave; 13072 Stephen Carmick; 13059 Lynford Lardner; 13069 John Isaac Klein; 13049 Margaret Williams; 13066 James Miller; 13020 Jacob Lewis; 21013 John Ridgway; 13010 John Johnston; 13030 Valentine Puff; 21006 Joseph Goldy; 13100 William Janney; 13124 Frederick Wolf; 13073 John Adams; 13082 Thomas Dowell; 11013 George Reichert; 13122 John Thomas; 13080 Henry Bile; 13035 Mary Catherine Richerts; 31015 Isaac Cox.

Table 6.6
Ten Richest and Poorest by Net Worth
South, 1774

Occupation	Net Worth (Pounds Sterling)	Age	Place of Residence
Esq., planter, attorney	32,737.8	42	Goose Creek, S.C.
Esq., planter	12,704.9	(3)	St. George's Parish, S.C.
Planter	11,707.0	(3)	St. Andrew's Parish, S.C.
Planter	9,625.2	(2)	Charles Town, S.C.
Esquire	8,534.6	(3)	St. Andrew's Parish, S.C.
Esquire	7,425.3	n.d.	St. Paul's Parish, S.C.
Farmer	7,214.1	42	Christ Church Parish, S.C.
Physician	7,173.0	(2)	St. George's Parish, S.C.
Planter	6,891.0	(2)	Edisto Island, S.C.
Planter	6,772.3	(3)	St. Bartholomew's Parish, S.C.
Farmer	5.1	n.d.	Queen Anne's Co., Md.
Farmer	4.4	n.d.	Halifax Co., N.C.
Tailor	4.2	n.d.	Orange Co., N.C.
Farmer	4.0	n.d.	Queen Anne's Co., Md.
n.d.	3.6	n.d.	Halifax Co., N.C.
n.d.	2.7	n.d.	Queen Anne's Co., Md.
Carpenter	2.5	n.d.	Anne Arundel Co., Md.
n.d.	2.3	n.d.	Queen Anne's Co., Md.
Merchant	−19.5	n.d.	Chesterfield Co., Va.
Farmer	−101.0	(2)	Brunswick Co., Va.

SOURCE: Unweighted array of sample of probated decedents in fourteen counties grouped in eight clusters. See appendix A.

NOTE: General note to table 6.3 pertains to this table also, except that the decedent I.D. numbers and names, reading from top down, are: 01043 Peter Manigault, Esq.; 01056 Elijah Postele, Esq.; 01053 Alexander Peronneau; 01001 John Ainslie, Esq.; 01014 John Cattell; 01073 Benjamin Williamson; 01012 Richard Capers, 01042 Dr. Archibald McNeill; 01032 Christopher Jenkins; 01036 Capt. Thomas Jones, Sr., 71014 Isaac Ewen; 91008 Daniel Carter; 92029 Hope Taylor (a male); 71007 Humphrey Cleave; 91032 Solomon Powell; 71028 Philip St. Tee; 72006 Francis Crickmore; 71036 Moses Wootters; 83006 William Donald; 82014 Charles Gordon.

was very narrow, again reflecting more egalitarianism there. In mean net worth, the average free wealthholder in the South was almost twice as wealthy as his counterpart in the middle colonies and nearly three times as wealthy as such in New England. At the median, below which half of the wealthholders fell, net worth was £158 in the South, three and a half times greater than New England's £45, but only about a third greater than in the middle colonies, £119. In total physical wealth, the mean values for New England and the middle colonies were much closer together and less than half as great as the

South's £395. The middle colonies' median physical wealth, however, exceeded that of the South and was strikingly close to its own mean. Thus we find New England was poor with unequal wealth distribution, the South was rich with unequal wealth distribution, and the middle colonies were much closer to poor New England than to the rich South in average amount of wealth, but those assets were much more evenly distributed. This is of interest, since a number of early visitors went to the middle colonies.

Table 6.7
Ten Richest and Poorest by Total Physical Wealth
Thirteen Colonies, 1774

Occupation	Total Physical Wealth (Pounds Sterling)	Age	Place of Residence
Esq., planter, attorney	27,959.7	42	Goose Creek, S.C.
Esquire, planter	15,561.3	50?	St. George's Parish, S.C.
Planter	11,795.9	(2)	Charles Town, S.C.
Farmer	8,758.1	42	Christ Church Parish, S.C.
Merchant	8,335.6	(3)	Philadelphia, Pa.
Esquire	8,225.4	n.d.	St. Paul's Parish, S.C.
Esquire	8,128.1	(3)	St. Andrew's Parish, S.C.
Physician	8,063.9	(?)	St. George's Parish, S.C.
Planter	7,959.8	(3)	St. Bartholomew's Parish, S.C.
Planter	7,679.9	(2)	Edisto Island, S.C.
Tailor	3.9	n.d.	Boston, Suffolk Co., Mass.
Shoemaker	3.8	47	New Garden, Phil. Co., Pa.
Yeoman	3.8	88	Shrewsbury, Worcester Co., Mass.
Widow	3.6	n.d.	Brodefield, Worcester Co., Mass.
Single woman	3.6	19	Waterbury, New Haven Co., Conn.
n.d.	3.5	n.d.	Queen Anne's Co., Md.
Widow	3.2	n.d.	Kent Co., Delaware
Yeoman	3.0	30+	Sutton, Worcester Co., Mass.
Farmer	2.6	65	Halifax Co., N.C.
n.d.	0.0	n.d.	Philadelphia, Pa.

SOURCE: Unweighted array of sample of probated decedents in twenty-six counties plus New York. See appendix A.

NOTE: Total physical wealth includes value of slaves and servants. It taken no account of financial assets or liabilities. Decedent I.D. numbers and names, reading from top down, are: 01043 Peter Manigault, Esq.; 01056 Elijah Postele, Esq.; 01001 John Ainslie, Esq.; 01012 Richard Capers; 13048 Samuel Neave; 01073 Benjamin Williamson; 01014 John Cattell; 01042 Dr. Archibald McNeill; 01036 Capt. Thomas Jones; 01032 Christopher Jenkins; 54044 Isaac Herault; 13080 Henry Bile; 55007 Jabez Dodge; 55017 Anne Haskell; 42016 Sarah Cole; 71028 Philip St. Tee; 31021 Ann King; 55037 Jabez Pratt; 91008 Daniel Carter; 13100 William Janney. Number within parenthesis indicates age class: class 2 = 26–44; class 3 = age 45 or over; n.d. indicates not determined.

Table 6.8
Ten Richest and Poorest by Total Physical Wealth
New England, 1774

Occupation	Total Physical Wealth (Pounds Sterling)	Age	Place of Residence
Merchant	4,188.1	72	Marblehead, Essex Co., Mass.
Esquire	3,793.4	58	Boston, Suffolk Co., Mass.
Esquire	2,915.7	67	Boston, Suffolk Co., Mass.
Physician	2,252.6	42	Marblehead, Essex Co., Mass.
Shopkeeper	2,176.1	53	Boston, Suffolk Co., Mass.
Yeoman	1,850.6	75	Hingham, Suffolk Co., Mass.
Yeoman	1,845.3	(3)	Marshfield, Plymouth Co., Mass.
Captain	1,760.2	75	Milford, New Haven Co., Conn.
Esquire	1,750.6	(3)	Salem, Essex Co., Mass.
Gentleman	1,436.3	35?	Roxbury, Suffolk Co., Mass.
Widow	6.8	90	Topsfield, Essex Co., Mass.
Fisherman	5.6	36?	Marblehead, Essex Co., Mass.
Husbandman, chairmaker	4.6	40	Boston, Suffolk Co., Mass.
Widow	4.6	89	Springfield, Hampshire Co., Mass.
Single woman	4.0	24	Rowley, Essex Co., Mass.
Mariner	4.9	27	Plymouth Co., Mass.
Tailor	3.9	n.d.	Boston, Suffolk Co., Mass.
Yeoman	3.8	88	Shrewsbury, Worcester Co., Mass.
Single woman	3.7	19	Waterbury, New Haven Co., Conn.
Widow	3.6	n.d.	Brookfield, Worcester Co., Mass.

SOURCE: Unweighted array of sample of probated decedents in seven counties. See appendix A.

NOTE: General note to table 6.7 pertains to this table also, except that question mark following age in years indicates genealogist's best opinion but with some doubt; and that decedent I.D. numbers and names, reading from top down are: 51040 Thomas Gerry; 54096 William White; 54063 Andrew Oliver; 51028 Humphrey Devereaux; 54034 Thomas Gray; 54097 Enoch Whitten; 53029 Samuel Tilden; 42015 Thomas Clark, III; 51006 Samuel Barton, Sr.; 54011 Edward Bridge; 51030 Mary Dwinell; 51051 George Hyter; 54067 Edmund Perkins; 52019 Sarah Leonard; 51015 Mehitabel Burpe; 53023 Seth Nickerson; 54044 Isaac Herault; 55007 Jabez Dodge; 42016 Sarah Cole, 55017 Anne Haskell.

The foregoing generalization is confirmed in tables 6.1 and 6.2 by the value amounts and proportions of wealth held at the upper, middle, and bottom portions of the wealth ranges and by the proportions shown in figures 13 and 14. It is further reinforced by tables 6.4 through 6.6 and 6.8 through 6.10, which show the characteristics and amounts of wealth of the ten richest and ten poorest free wealthholders in each region. These tables show far greatest wealth range from lowest to highest in the South, where Peter Manigault again tops both lists. New England's sample case with highest net worth was William White, Esquire, of Boston, with £15,303, or about $830,000 in 1978 purchasing power. He was followed by Thomas Gerry, a merchant at Marblehead, with £5,786, whose son Elbridge Gerry (Billias 1976) was subsequently a signer of the Declaration of Independence. In the ranking by physical wealth (table 6.8), these two men reversed positions, with Gerry's £4,188 exceeding White's total physical wealth. The richest wealthholder in the middle

Table 6.9
Ten Richest and Poorest by Total Physical Wealth
New Jersey, Pennsylvania, Delaware, 1774

Occupation	Total Physical Wealth (Pounds Sterling)	Age	Place of Residence
Merchant	8,335.6	67	Philadelphia, Pa.
Prov. officer, landholder	7,601.8	59	Philadelphia, Pa.
Merchant	3,045.9	55	Philadelphia, Pa.
Merchant	2,395.7	60	Philadelphia, Pa.
Farmer and miller	1,697.9	(2)	Lower Merion, Philadelphia Co., Pa.
Esquire	1,661.7	61	Kent Co., Delaware
Farmer	1,579.5	64	Upper Dublin Township, Philadelphia Co., Pa.
Captain	1,566.8	50	Philadelphia, Pa.
Tailor	1,500.9	43	Philadelphia, Pa.
Merchant	1,459.8	(3)	Philadelphia, Pa.
Widow	7.6	36	Philadelphia, Pa.
Widow	7.5	(3)	Horsham, Philadelphia Co., Pa.
Laborer	7.3	(2)	Abington, Philadelphia Co., Pa.
n.d.	6.9	n.d.	New Hannon, Philadelphia Co., Pa.
n.d.	6.9	n.d.	Philadelphia, Pa.
Pilot	6.6	42	Philadelphia, Pa.
Laborer	4.2	63	Philadelphia, Pa.
Shoemaker	3.8	47	New Garden, Philadelphia, Co., Pa.
Widow	3.3	n.d.	Kent Co., Delaware
n.d.	0.0	64	Kent Co., Maryland (probated in Philadelphia)

SOURCE: Unweighted array of sample of probated decedents in five counties. See appendix A.

NOTE: General note to table 6.7 pertains to this table also, except that decedent I.D. numbers and names, reading down from top, are: 13048 Samuel Neave; 13059 Lynford Lardner; 13072 Stephen Carmick; 13020 Jacob Lewis; 13099 Charles Jolley; 31012 Andrew Caldwell; 13030 Valentine Puff; 13066 Capt. James Miller; 13012 Jacob Chrystler; 13054 James Maccubbins; 13035 Mary Catherine Richerts; 13037 Mary Hardy; 13058 Alexander Dunlope; 13132 George Mecklein; 13124 Frederick Wolf; 13073 John Adams; 13122 John Thomas; 13080 Henry Bile, 31021 Ann King; 13100 William Janney.

Table 6.10
Ten Richest and Poorest by Total Physical Wealth
South, 1774

Occupation	Total Physical Wealth (Pounds Sterling)	Age	Place of Residence
Esq., planter, attorney	27,959.7	42	Goose Creek, S.C.
Esq., planter	15,561.3	(3)	St. George's Parish, S.C.
Esq., planter	11,795.9	(2)	Charles Town, S.C.
Farmer	8,758.1	42	Christ Church Parish, S.C.
Esquire	8,225.4	n.d.	St. Paul's Parish, S.C.
Esquire	8,128.1	(3)	St. Andrew's Parish, S.C.
Physician	8,063.9	(2)	St. George's Parish, S.C.
Planter	7,959.8	(3)	St. Bartholomew's Parish, S.C.
Planter	7,679.9	(2)	Edisto Island, S.C.
Clerk	5,845.4	(2)	Charles Town, S.C.
Shopkeeper	7.0	(3)	Charles Town, S.C.
Farmer	6.8	n.d.	Orange Co., N.C.
n.d.	6.6	n.d.	Charles Town, S.C.
Tailor	5.5	n.d.	Orange Co., N.C.
Farmer	5.5	(3)	Queen Anne's Co., Md.
n.d.	5.2	n.d.	Anne Arundel Co., Md.
n.d.	4.6	n.d.	Halifax Co., N.C.
n.d.	4.6	n.d.	Queen Anne's Co., Md.
n.d.	3.5	n.d.	Queen Anne's Co., Md.
Farmer	2.6	n.d.	Halifax Co., N.C.

SOURCE: Unweighted array of sample of probated decedents in fourteen counties grouped in eight clusters. See appendix A.

NOTE: General note to table 6.7 pertains to this table also, except that decedent I.D. numbers and names, reading from top down, are: 01043 Peter Manigault, Esq.; 01056 Elijah Postele, Esq.; 01001 John Ainslie, Esq.; 01012 Richard Capers; 01073 Benjamin Williamson; 01014 John Cattell; 01042 Dr. Archibald McNeill; 01036 Capt. Thomas Jones, Sr.; 01032 Christopher Jenkins; 01070 Rev. John Tonge; 01076 John Brynan; 92027 John Sample; 01009 Peter Boura; 92029 Hope Taylor; 71007 Humphrey Cleave; 72014 Daniel Kent; 91032 Solomon Powell; 71036 Moses Wootters; 71028 Philip St. Tee; 91008 Daniel Carter.

colonies' sample, Philadelphia merchant Samuel Neave, with £8,336 (table 6.9), topped the New England high in physical wealth. He was followed closely by Lynford Lardner of Philadelphia, a province official and large landholder. In net worth, however (table 6.5), the two Philadelphia merchants at the top of the list, Samuel Neave and Stephen Carmick, were well below White's £15,303, but somewhat richer than Thomas Gerry, the richest merchant drawn into the New England sample.

The comparative richness of the South stands out again when

we look, in tables 6.1 and 6.2, at the boundaries of wealth expressed in pounds sterling for the top two percentiles and the upper deciles. These are much higher than in the other two regions down through the eighth decile, for both net worth and total physical wealth. The net worth value at the lower bound of the top 1 pecent was £2,646 for the relatively wealthy South, compared with the much lower £1,151 for New England and £1,544 for the middle colonies. But the greater equality of the middle colonies shows in its higher net worth boundaries for the first decile through the fifth (from the bottom). In the third through fifth deciles by physical wealth, the southern wealthholders were, however, still better off than both the New Englanders and middle colonists, judged by values at the lower bound of the class. At the sixth decile, however, the middle colonists' holdings were of higher value than the South's. In the ninth decile, the New

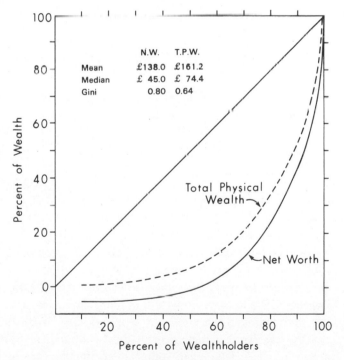

Figure 15.
Distribution of Net Worth, Total Physical Wealth,
New England, 1774
SOURCE: Tables 6.1 and 6.2, data $w*B$-weighted

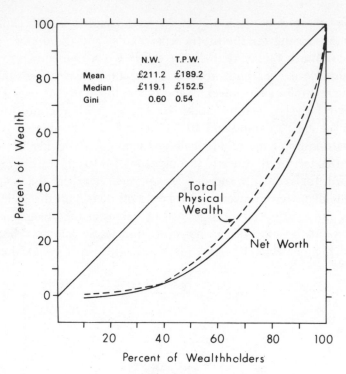

Figure 16.
Distribution of Net Worth, Total Physical Wealth,
New Jersey, Pennsylvania, Delaware, 1774
SOURCE: Tables 6.1 and 6.2, data w^*B-weighted

Englanders were close in value of physical wealth as compared with the middle colonists and at the tenth exceeded them, but both were far outclassed in these deciles by the southern wealthy. Without the disturbing effects of debts owed (table 6.2), we find that the lower bounds of absolute physical wealth of the bottom 20 percent were not greatly different, regardless of region. The lower bound values of even the poorest decile, in all but one case of zero value in the middle colonies, were sufficient to provide a few pots, pans, and utensils, a few articles of bedding, furniture, and apparel, and some geese or pigs, as can be seen from values of individual commodities shown in tables 1.3 through 1.7. Likewise, the scale of living permitted by a thousand pounds or more of physical wealth found in the richest decile in the South can be envisioned by some of the more expensive items, in sterling, in those same tables, such as mahogany desk, eight-day clock, silver teapot, silver buckles, Scotch carpet, diamond ring, Negro slaves.

A summary view of the relative holdings of the richest 20 percent, the next richest 50 percent, and the poorest 30 percent is given in figures 13 and 14. The great dominance in wealth of the top 20 percent is clear. In percentages of wealth held at the highest and lowest deciles, New England had the greatest extremes in net worth and the middle colonies the least. In total physical wealth, New England's percentages in the seventh, eighth, and ninth deciles approximated those of the South, whereas the middle colonies showed the least disparity between the first and the tenth decile. The richest 10 percent held only 42 percent of the net worth in the middle colonies, compared with 57 and 49 percent respectively in New England and the South. At the bottom of the net worth scale, the poorest

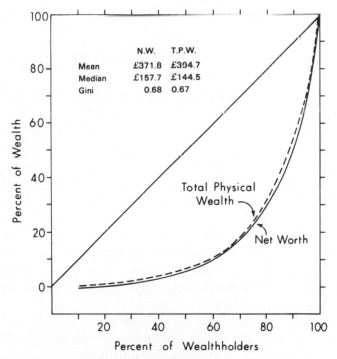

Figure 17.
Distribution of Net Worth, Total Physical Wealth, South, 1774

SOURCE: Tables 6.1 and 6.2, data *w*B*-weighted

had negative net worth, i.e., greater debts than assets, strikingly so in New England. There the poorest 10 percent combined had negative net worth equal to 5.6 percent of all the net worth of the region. When we look at the second to fifth deciles (from the bottom) inclusive, we find New England and the South to be rather similar in the small percentages of net worth held, while in the middle colonies relatively greater equality of distribution stands out. Looking at the bottom half of the wealthholders, the first five deciles as a group, this lower segment held 9 percent of the wealth in the middle colonies, but only 5 percent in the South and −2 percent in New England, where the small positive net worth in deciles two through five was overwhelmed by the debts of the poorest tenth.

The reasons for the relatively great inequality in New England do not lie in possession of slaves, which were of negligible significance in that region. The explanation may lie more in the relative harshness of climate, and poor soil that made wringing a living from the land or developing an export product difficult for small farmers. On the other hand, substantial wealth was gained in New England by merchants, sea captains, distillers, shipbuilders, and those who were able to take advantage of possibilities in trade, shipping, sending supplies to the West Indies, and the like. Our sample is too small to test, within New England, the hypothesis of Jackson Main that inequality was greatest in urban places and greater in areas of commercial farming than in ones that produced only for subsistence. The spreads in wealth of our sample cases in Boston, Salem, Philadelphia,[26] and Charleston support the idea of urban inequality. In chapter 7 I deal with urban-rural and occupational wealth differences for the samples by three wealth classes. Farmers dominate all the regional samples, more conspicuously so in the southern and middle colonies. I have no basis for separating the farmers in our samples by whether they engaged in commercial or "subsistence" operations. It seems evident, however, from the nature of the crops and livestock holdings that relatively more of our middle colonies' than New England farmers sold at least a considerable portion of their product and might be classed as commercial farmers. On this reasoning I suggest, although admittedly the evidence is not clear cut, that the lesser inequality of the total middle colonies' sample, as compared with that of New England, does not lend support to the hypothesis of greater wealth inequality in commercial farming areas.

In the middle colonies, although slaves and servants were slightly more important than in New England, they definitely were inconsequential in explaining relative wealth. In these provinces family-operated farms were the principal source of livelihood and wealthbuilding. Many in Pennsylvania came from German stock and were industrious, thrifty farmers. Quakers were important both in Pennsylvania and New Jersey. The farm land was richer, the climate better for farming than in New England. Substantial wealth also built up in Philadelphia, the largest city of that time in the colonies, where there was some shipbuilding as well as shop manufacturing, many artisan trades, and the many services connected with assembling the farm products from the interior and exporting them, bringing in the imports of Europe and the West Indies, and dealing in goods from other colonies. The relatively great equality of wealth in the middle colonies may have helped to create an important internal market in the region, which contributed to its economic growth.[27]

Size Distribution of Nonhuman Physical Wealth, South

There can be no gainsaying, from the evidence of chapters 3, 4, and 5, that ownership of slaves contributed to the high wealth of the South, but it is not the sole explanation of inequality in distribution there. To see the effect of subtracting slave values from the wealth figures of their owners, I present tables 6.11 and 6.12 and figure 18, showing distribution of free wealthholders in the South by the size of their nonhuman physical wealth. The result, at first blush, is surprising. When compared with the 4th column of table 6.2, the Gini coefficient in table 6.11 is unchanged, and the Lorenz curve in figure 18 is almost indistinguishable from that for total physical wealth in figure 17. The percentage shares of the top 2 percent are slightly greater, as well as the share for the entire tenth decile that includes them. The richest 5 percent held 33 percent out of the 50 percent of nonhuman wealth held by the entire tenth decile. This increase in shares at the top came principally at the expense of the ninth decile, whose share dropped from 23 percent in table 6.2 to 21 percent in table 6.11. The eighth decile loses more than 1 percentage point. From there on down, the changes in percentage shares by decile are relatively small, but with slight increases in the fourth, third, and second deciles.

Distribution of Wealth

A more notable difference between tables 6.2 and 6.11 is that, as expected, both mean and median drop by large amounts, as do the values at lower bounds of the top two percentiles and every decile from the tenth through the first. The difference between mean and median is relatively greater for table 6.11.

We must realize that we do not have here a complete measure of what the effect of removal of slaves from their owners might have implied in the long run for the owners' wealth. For much of the value of the land owned, and such physical possessions as fine furniture and clothing of the owners, whose total values appear in nonhuman physical wealth, were due to past product of the slaves owned. And such wealth, in turn, contributes to keeping up the relative inequality

---

Table 6.11
Nonhuman Physical Wealth Distribution by Decile
Free Wealthholders, South, 1774

	Value at Lower Bound (Pounds Sterling)	Share Held (Percentages)
100th percentile (richest 1%)	2,124.5	12.0
99th percentile (next richest 1%)	1,521.6	7.1
Tenth decile (richest 10%)	705.4	49.7
Ninth decile	404.2	20.7
Eighth decile	242.9	11.4
Seventh decile	148.3	7.4
Sixth decile	85.9	4.7
Fifth decile	59.5	2.6
Fourth decile	34.2	1.8
Third decile	22.2	1.0
Second decile	8.4	0.6
First decile (poorest 10%)	0.0	0.2
Gini Coefficient	0.67	
Mean	£262.1	
Median	85.3	

SOURCE: Sample data, $w*B$-weighted, Variant Two, pertaining to all free wealthholders.

NOTE: Wealth excludes value of slaves and servants, financial assets, and financial liabilities. Nonprobate-type wealthholders form 32 percent of all free wealthholders, and they are distributed according to assumption B defined in appendix A, part one. The exact weights used for nonprobate adjustments by decile for this table, proceeding from tenth to first decile are: 0.010, 0.014, 0.021, 0.031, 0.046, 0.069, 0.102, 0.151, 0.224, 0.332. For a corresponding distribution computed with w-weights, Variant Two, the median is £176.8, the mean £344.9, and the Gini coefficient 0.62. With $w*A$-weights, Variant Two, the median is £122.8, the mean £262.2, and the Gini coefficient 0.64.

Table 6.12
Ten Richest and Ten Poorest by Nonhuman Physical Wealth
South, 1774

Occupation	Total Nonhuman Physical Wealth (Pounds Sterling)	Age	Place of Residence
Esq., planter, attorney	16,107.9	42	Goose Creek, S.C.
Physician	5,126.7	(2)	St. George's Parish, S.C.
Planter	4,177.1	(3)	St. George's Parish, S.C.
Esquire	3,600.8	n.d.	St. Paul's Parish, S.C.
Planter	3,573.4	(3)	St. Bartholomew's Parish, S.C.
Planter	3,540.4	36	Chesterfield, Va.
Planter	3,306.8	(2)	Charles Town, S.C.
Planter	3,162.2	(3)	St. Bartholomew's Parish, S.C.
Esquire	3,013.0	(3)	St. Andrew's Parish, S.C.
Farmer	2,646.3	42	Christ Church Parish, S.C.
Tailor	5.5	n.d.	Orange Co., N.C.
Farmer	5.5	(3)	Queen Anne's Co., Md.
n.d.	5.2	n.d.	Anne Arundel Co., Md.
n.d.	4.6	n.d.	Halifax Co., N.C.
n.d.	4.6	n.d.	Queen Anne's Co., Md.
n.d.	3.5	n.d.	Queen Anne's Co., Md.
Farmer	2.6	n.d.	Halifax Co., N.C.
n.d.	0.5	n.d.	Orange Co., N.C.
Widow	0.0	n.d.	Halifax Co., N.C.
n.d.	0.0	n.d.	Halifax Co., N.C.

SOURCE: Unweighted array of sample of probated decedents in fourteen counties grouped in eight clusters. See appendix A, part one.

NOTE: Decedent I.D. numbers and names, reading from top down, are: 01043 Peter Manigault, Esq.; 01042 Dr. Archibald McNeill; 01056 Elijah Postele, Esq.; 01073 Benjamin Williamson; 01003 James Atkins; 83016 Henry Walthall; 01001 John Ainslie, Esq.; 01036 Capt. Thomas Jones, Sr.; 01014 John Cattell; 01012 Richard Capers; 92029 Hope Taylor; 71007 Humphrey Cleave; 72014 Daniel Kent; 91032 Solomon Powell; 71036 Moses Wootters; 71028 Philip St. Tee; 91008 Daniel Carter; 92005 George Josias Doyle; 91001 Mary Baker; 91011 Daniel Eelbank. For age class see note to table 6.7.

shown in table 6.11. In table 6.12, for instance, seven of the richest ten in table 6.10 reappear, with Manigault still in the number one position. Likewise, among the bottom ten, six of the same ten names reappear, although in somewhat revised order.

The relatively high proportion of southern farmers who did not own land[28] may be another explanation of the relatively high southern inequality, but this is economically closely allied to not owning slaves (Kulikoff 1975:chap. 5). Perhaps, after all, the ownership of slaves and the wealthbuilding possibilities which that implied is the principal explanation for the relatively high wealth inequality in the South on the eve of the Revolution. Some might argue that more wealth permitted more slaves.[29] In any case, the figures clearly tell us that the South, as compared with the other regions, had higher wealth that was distributed considerably more unequally among its free population than the lesser wealth of the middle colonies, and about as unequally as the still lesser wealth of New England.

Slaves and Servants as Holders of No Wealth

Since the nonfree held little or no wealth, I have omitted them entirely as wealthholders in our discussion and tables up to this point. Consequently, the wealth inequality considered does not reflect the plight of the slaves, nor, during their years of servitude, the indentured servants. They not only owned no land or personal possessions of any consequence, but had not even the right to the

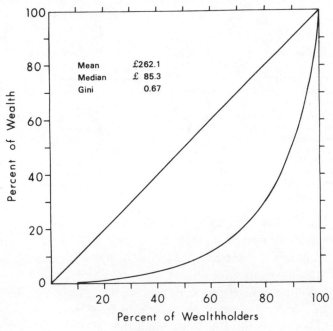

Mean	£262.1
Median	£ 85.3
Gini	0.67

Figure 18.
Distribution of Nonhuman Physical Wealth, South, 1774
Source: Table 6.11, data *w*B*-weighted

Table 6.13
Nonfree Adult Males as Proportion of Total
"Potential Wealthholders" 1774

	Percentage
Thirteen Colonies	21.0
New England	3.8
N. Jersey, Pennsylv., Delaware	6.9
South	38.8

SOURCE: Table 2.4–2.7. The corresponding figure for New York is 10.3.

NOTE: Total "potential wealthholders" include free wealthholders plus nonfree adult males. Inclusion of 10 percent of nonfree adult females would have a trivial effect in tables 6.14 and 6.15.

capital value of their own persons. Yet they certainly existed in the colonies, most numerously in the South. Their numbers were comparatively so few in the northern regions, as indicated in table 6.13, that their omission there might be defended as not making much difference in the results. But this is not the case in the South.

CONCENTRATION AMONG ALL POTENTIAL WEALTHHOLDERS

To consider how much this nonownership of wealth by slaves and servants increased the overall inequality of wealth, I offer a total physical wealth distribution in which they are included as "potential wealthholders." All non-free adult males[30] are included, but placed at the bottom of the range as holders of no, or zero, wealth. I still include the human capital value of all the slaves and servants as part of the wealth of their free owners or masters, who fall in the higher portions of the wealth array.[31] This makes economic sense, since we are interested, for size distribution analysis, in understanding what amounts of wealth were actually owned by and the use thereof controlled by the various population segments. The results for the South are shown in table 6.14, which may be compared with table 6.2, column 4, and in figure 19, which compares with total physical wealth in figures 11 and 17. Corresponding results for New England and the middle colonies are given in *American Colonial Wealth* (tables 7.181 and 7.182 and figures 11 and 12). For New England, the

Gini coefficient dropped only from 0.65 to 0.64, and for the middle colonies from 0.57 to 0.54. The overall results for the entire thirteen colonies are shown in table 6.15 and also in figure 19. For the South in particular, and as a consequence in the thirteen colonies, the inequality increase is more substantial when the nonfree are included within the universe we consider.

It can be seen at a glance in table 6.13 that, for New England and the middle colonies, in an array of all "potential wealthholders" by size of their actual wealth, the nonfree fill up only a part of the bottom decile (over a third of it in New England, two-thirds of it in the middle colonies). The wealth held in that decile becomes correspondingly smaller than in table 6.2, columns 2 and 3. Similarly, it is readily apparent that for the South, the impact is much more strik-

---

Table 6.14
Distribution of Total Physical Wealth, by Decile
Free and Nonfree Potential Wealthholders, South, 1774

	Value at Lower Bound (Pounds Sterling)	Share Held (Percentages)
100th percentile (richest 1%)	4,021.7	28.9
99th percentile (next richest 1%)	2,423.6	7.4
Tenth decile (richest 10%)	903.7	69.2
Ninth decile	390.8	18.2
Eighth decile	184.0	7.6
Seventh decile	65.4	3.3
Sixth decile	23.1	1.3
Fifth decile	4.6	0.4
Fourth decile	2.6	0.0
Third decile	0.0	0.0
Second decile	0.0	0.0
First decile (poorest 10%)	0.0	0.0

Gini Coefficient	0.83
Mean	£335.1
Median	22.7

SOURCE: Sample data, $w*B$-weighted, Variant Two, for all free wealthholders in the top deciles and nonfree adult males included in the bottom four deciles as "potential wealthholders" having zero wealth.

NOTE: The exact weights used for nonprobate adjustment by decile for this table, proceeding from tenth to first decile, are: 0.010, 0.014, 0.021, 0.031, 0.046, 0.069, 0.102, 0.151, 0.224, 0.333. Value of slaves and servants is included as part of wealth of their free owners and masters in the fourth and higher deciles. For comparable tables for New England and the middle colonies, see *American Colonial Wealth,* tables 7.181 and 7.182, where the Gini coefficients are, respectively, 0.65 and 0.57.

Table 6.15
Distribution of Total Physical Wealth, by Decile
Free and Nonfree Potential Wealthholders, Thirteen Colonies, 1774

	Value at Lower Bound (Pounds Sterling)	Share Held (Percentages)
100th percentile (richest 1%)	1946.2	14.5
99th percentile (next richest 1%)	1459.8	8.5
Tenth decile (richest 10%)	482.1	56.4
Ninth decile	279.6	18.0
Eighth decile	190.7	11.5
Seventh decile	107.6	7.6
Sixth decile	48.9	3.6
Fifth decile	23.8	1.7
Fourth decile	11.3	0.8
Third decile	0.0	0.3
Second decile	0.0	0.0
First decile (poorest 10%)	0.0	0.0

Gini Coefficient   0.73

Mean   £199.1
Median   £ 47.7

SOURCE: Sample data, $w*B$-weighted, Variant Two, for all free wealthholders in the top deciles and nonfree adult males included in the bottom three deciles as "potential wealthholders" having zero wealth.

NOTE: Value of slaves and servants is included as part of wealth of their free owners and masters in the fourth and higher deciles.

ing. There the nonfree fill up all of the first three deciles and most of the fourth, as shown in table 6.14. For the colonies as a whole, table 6.15, the nonfree fill all of the first two deciles and a small portion of the third. For New York if we showed a separate wealth distribution for it, the entire bottom decile would hold zero wealth.

As a consequence of placing the nonfree adult males in the South in the bottom deciles of its distribution, the same wealth that is spread out among ten deciles in table 6.2, column 4, is now bunched in table 6.14 from the top of the fourth through the tenth deciles. The wealth values at the lower bounds of those deciles are all thereby reduced. Similarly, for the thirteen colonies, in table 6.15, the same wealth that was spread over ten deciles in table 6.2, column 1, is bunched into the third through tenth deciles. The Gini coefficient for the South rises dramatically from 0.67 to 0.83 and that for the thirteen colonies from 0.66 to 0.73. Means fall, because of the many

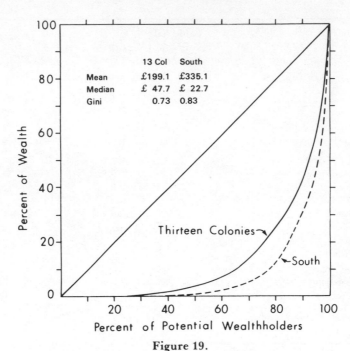

Figure 19.
Distribution of Total Physical Wealth, All Potential Wealthholders,
Free and Nonfree, Thirteen Colonies, South, 1774
SOURCE: Tables 6.15 and 6.14, data $w*B$-weighted

zero wealths. Median wealths fall even more drastically. The percentages of wealth held by the upper groups are all correspondingly increased. The spreads between mean and median wealth, at their reduced levels, are very much greater, relatively, than in table 6.2.

Thus, in a very real sense, we have, in table 6.15 and figure 19, the nearest approximation to a size distribution of wealth for the entire population of the colonies in 1774, free and nonfree. It gives us a Gini coefficient of 0.73 and shows that over half of all the physical wealth (including nonfree human wealth) was held by the top 10 percent. Only 3 percent was held by the entire poorer half of the universe, including all free wealthholders and the nonfree males who might conceptually have been possible wealthholders. This was surely not egalitarianism.

SOURCES OF WEALTH INEQUALITY

Slavery in the colonial South was one of the major contributors to wealth disparity there and hence to inequality in the colonies as a whole. However, we find inequality among free weathholders as great or greater in New England, where slavery played an insignificant role. Local studies, to be considered in chapter 8, indicate substantial and perhaps increasing wealth inequality in large northern cities such as Boston, New York, and Philadelphia. However, the populations of these cities were relatively small compared to the total population of their regions and are not a sufficient explanation of northern wealth inequalities.

It seems more likely that after slavery, and perhaps more important than large-city wealth as explanatory factors, came the spreads in wealth among and within occupational and other socioeconomic groups to be discussed in chapter 7. The individuals within these groups sometimes had widely varying wealth holdings. The individual differences may have stemmed in part from access to large land holdings, in part from commercial opportunities of varying sorts, in part from variations in risk-taking resulting sometimes in large debt.

Our sample size is not large enough to permit detailed size distributions for the many population subgroups. The differing wealth figures for such groups, however, may give important clues as to the sources of regional and total wealth inequality. Such information as the data permit on these groups is marshaled in chapter 7.

Another possibility, which we cannot entirely exclude, is that some of the technical difficulties of wealth measurement discussed in appendix A, particularly with respect to real estate and debts owed, may appear to give us sharper differences in regional wealth equality than actually existed, particularly as between the middle colonies and New England. Since land information was reported in detail for New England on the probate inventories but only estimated in other ways for the Middle Colonies and the South, we may have missed some of the inequality due to this factor in those two regions. In anticipation of chapter 7, the reader should consider this possibility, as suggested perhaps by the higher percentage of wealth in real estate (shown in tables 7.23 and 7.24) of high- and middle-wealth farmers in New England than in the other regions. Real estate is included in the totals for both net worth and total physical wealth.

Likewise, the fact that in New England the probate courts placed so much emphasis on insolvency as to be called courts of probate and insolvency and to appoint "Insolvency Commissioners" to report on certain estates may mean that there was greater zeal in New England to record debts owed by the estate than was the case in the other two regions.[32] If so, this might have caused an overstatement of financial liabilities and hence of net worth inequality in New England. If it were true, which we cannot know for sure, that we have relatively overstated both New England's land wealth and it's financial liabilities, that region might not stand out as quite so unequal in distribution, in particular of net worth. Any possible financial liabilities overstatement for New England affects only its net worth and has no effect on the measure of its total physical wealth. This fact is a major reason why I have presented size distributions for both these wealth totals in this chapter.

CHAPTER SEVEN

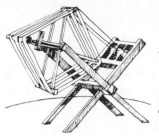

Wealth Distribution and Composition Among Various Socioeconomic Groups

THE diversity in characteristics between the ten richest and the ten poorest wealthholders seen in chapter 6 arouses one's curiosity. May some systematic wealth patterns be discerned when we classify the sample cases into groups on the basis of some of their more interesting socioeconomic characteristics? Our desire is to discover whether or not total wealthholdings, and some of their major components, differ significantly or interestingly for wealthholders grouped by such characteristics as age, sex, occupation, and urban or rural residence. Are certain of these characteristics more associated with high wealth than others? Whether the answers are yes or no, for each comparison,[1] such information affords a factual basis for further interpretation regarding the social structure and economic functioning of colonial society.

We can get an impression of relative richness or poorness within some socioeconomic groups by looking at the distribution when probate-type wealthholders[2] in these groups are classified, in tables 7.1 through 7.4 (see the end of the chapter for the tables), into three wealth intervals.[3] These we may designate for convenience as relatively high, middle, and low wealth. We can also compare some of the most significant components of wealth for the socioeconomic groups.[4]

For consistency of comparison, I prefer to use the same wealth class bounds for the thirteen colonies as a whole and from one region to another. It would also be desirable to have wealth bounds divide all the sample cases in each region approximately into thirds, to maximize the numbers of cases within intervals, but the very nature of the regional wealth distributions[5] precludes this neat approach. We are faced here with a choice between using the same class bounds for all regions, to facilitate interregional comparisons, or selecting different intervals for each region that divide its own probate-type wealthholders into thirds, which might imply differing regional standards of richness or poverty. In view of the findings of chapters 3 and 6 one could justify a higher standard of richness for the South than for the northern regions. However, the first choice seems best for our present purpose, as it permits comparison of the same absolute intervals from region to region, and thus keeps the same definitions of relatively high and relatively low wealth.

DEFINITION OF RICHNESS AND POORNESS AMONG ALL WEALTHHOLDERS

Unfortunately, there is a problem with those definitions. There was insufficient data on nonprobate-type wealthholders to perform any kind of socioeconomic analysis, and so the three class divisions were made for probate-type wealthholders, who were richer as a group than "all wealthholders." The lower and upper bounds used for tables 7.1 through 7.4, dividing the probate-type sample roughly into thirds, are £100 and £400; for all free wealthholders, the division by thirds would come at near £30 and £240, keeping to round numbers.[6] Accordingly, a more reasonable definition of "poor" would include those with wealth under £30, and of "rich" those £240 and above. Between would be the "middle-wealth" class. We did not analyze a probate-type group under £30 because our sample there was too small, and the over £240 group would have been unduly large. But I believe that such differences by socioeconomic groups as our probate-type data can reveal are of sufficient interest to warrant presentation.

It is a truism that all rankings of wealth are relative. To the extent that we find a pattern of wealth variation among the probate types for the intervals chosen, we might reasonably expect to find the same pattern continued on, perhaps in a slightly more pronounced form,[7] to the still lower group of "poor," if we had more precise information on the nonprobate-type living wealthholder cases toward the lower end of the scale.

RELATIVE SIZES OF WEALTHHOLDER GROUPS AND SOME HYPOTHESES

The composition of the probate-type wealthholding population, based on our good though small sample, mirrors in many ways the economic society of the period. The relative frequencies of certain characteristics of the wealthholders themselves (roughly household heads), indicated in columns 1 of tables 7.1 through 7.4, are a rough approximation for a nonexistent census of the free wealthholding population and its characteristics. This is true only insofar as we can assume that the nonprobate-type wealthholders might have had the same socioeconomic characteristics, if we could determine them, as the probate types. However, as shown by the comparison between table 6.2 column 1 and table 7.1 line 1, and the discussion in appendix A, I assume that their total wealth was in most cases somewhat lower than that of the probate types. Many particular circumstances contribute to explain where an individual householder fell on the wealth scale, among them age, health, and skills, sex, race, place of residence, and occcupation. We lack data on health, skills, and race[8] of our sample cases. However, tables 7.1 through 7.4 group the probate-type wealthholders by the other factors named, and show which proportions in each group fell into the three classes. The relation of the various lines within each of these tables to its line 1 tells us the extent to which the pattern of size distribution of wealth for the particular group diverges from the general pattern of all probate-type wealthholders for the area. The relative proportions for each group at low- or high-wealth levels also help to explain the size of the average wealth figure for the entire group, shown in table 7.5. Regional differences for the same socioeconomic group at the same absolute wealth level can be discerned from comparisons of the same line from one table to another. Some of the more interesting differences are summarized in succeeding sections.

Age

Older household heads were, on average, richer than younger. The adult free population in the colonies was much younger than the corresponding population of the United States today and such distribution is reflected in the w weights used to move the sample decedent data to the level of living wealthholders of the probate type. Their ages suggest that productive energies were relatively greater than among today's wealthholders. However, a considerable part of the energies of the women were expended in childbearing and child raising, and many men among our wealthholders were fathers of growing children with a strong incentive to produce and provide for their futures. Among the sample wealthholders, after age adjustment to the probate-type living (see appendix A), those aged 21–44 outnumbered those 45 and over by better than two to one for the colonies as a whole (table 7.1). The proportion of younger wealthholders was highest in the South, and lowest in New England (tables 7.2, 7.3, 7.4). Here we find the basis for a hypothesis that might explain the lower wealth accumulation of New England, which is a persistent finding of this study. Might this lowest percentage of younger adult family heads, in combination with our estimate in table 2.5 that New England was the only region with more women than men,[9] possibly explain lower total wealth production, and hence a lower base for wealth accumulation? I suggest that this possibility merits serious consideration and is not incompatible with higher average accumulated wealth of the older age groups, as seen in table 7.5.

Sex

As independent wealthholders, colonial women were far outnumbered and outranked by men. However, the proportions of cases of women drawn in the sample[10] were not inconsequential, and the wealth of a few of them was substantial (see table 7.32). Miriam Potts, a Philadelphia shopkeeper, had total physical wealth of £690, and

Abigail Townsend, a widow in Charleston District, had £2,559. As a group, the women wealthholders held substantially lower amounts than men (table 7.5), especially in New England. The colonial legal and social climate clearly gave men the principal property rights.

The itemization of some women's clothing in some men's probate inventories suggests that his wife's clothing belonged to the husband even though she survived him. This fact is further made clear by some wills in which a man specifically stated that he desired that his widow be allowed to keep her own clothing. Likewise, a generous husband sometimes stated in his will that his wife should be allowed to take her choice of a bed and chest, sometimes of a horse, sometimes of other specified items of his personal estate. Without such specification they clearly became a part of his probated estate, subject to sale to meet his debts. Some of the "accounts of vendue" or "accounts of sale" held by estate administrators list the "items bought by the widow," and in the research for this study I noted in several such cases in the sample that the items "bought" by the widow amounted to about one-third of the total proceeds of the sale.

Often a man's will stated that a woman should have the right to occupy the "dwelling house so long as she remains my widow but no longer." Some others, more unusual, gave the privilege for the duration of her natural life, with no limitation if she remarried, but without the right to bequeath it at death. In a few cases in the sample a man's will directed that his widow should receive the real estate with full right to its use during her natural lifetime and then to be disposed of as she should decide. These seemed to be cases where there were no children. In disposing of land in their wills, men usually left it to sons, sometimes subject to the mother's use for her lifetime or until remarriage, and gave daughters sums of money or such items as one or more Negroes, silverware, named pieces of furniture, or named horses. Occasionally they gave land to daughters.

That New England had no larger a weighted proportion of cases of women in the sample than did the middle colonies and a slightly lower proportion than in the South, despite its greater proportion of women (table 2.5) may suggest that New England had relatively more women with no wealth of their own. These women, if they remained unmarried, as the term "spinster" suggests, probably lived in the household of a relative and contributed to production of wealth through household tasks, but perhaps not ones of high market value or high wealth-creating value. Here is a second hypothesis as to a contributing factor toward New England's lower average wealth.

Urban or Rural Location

With respect to residential location, our small sample confirms gratifyingly well the known fact that New England was the region with the most urban population, the South least so, but that in every region the rural population far outnumbered the urban. The weighted sample proportions among probate-type wealthholders were 25 percent urban in New England, 14 percent in the middle colonies of New Jersey, Pennsylvania, and Delaware, and only 1 percent in the South. The high rural proportion is to be expected, as the colonies even as late as 1774 remained essentially agricultural. There were more towns and cities in New England, but in the decades preceding 1774, growth in Philadelphia and Charleston was at a faster rate than in Boston (Bridenbaugh 1955). Our particular rural/ urban comparison for New England compares rural populations in all seven sample counties with a fair number of residents of Boston and Salem, such secondary urban centers as Marblehead, New-buryport, Ipswich, and Gloucester in Essex County, Bridge-water, Middleborough, and Scituate in Plymouth County, Spring-field in Hampshire County, and Worcester City in Worcester County. The rural/urban comparison for the middle colonies is essentially limited to a comparison of residents of Philadelphia and its suburbs of Southwark, Germantown, and Northern Liberties with the rest of the middle colonies' sample, virtually all rural, in five counties in three provinces. There were only three additional urban dwellers drawn in the sample outside of the Philadelphia metro-politan area, two in the city of Burlington, New Jersey, and one, a yeoman, in the town of Easton in Northampton County. None of the Kent County, Delaware sample cases lived in its county seat of Dover. In the South, the comparison offered is essentially that between residents of Charleston and the rest of the sample. Outside of that city only two other urban residents were drawn in the southern sample, both in Annapolis, Maryland, one a widow and one a cooper. Although at least one sample case owned a "town lot" in Hillsboro, Halifax County, North Carolina, his residence was not in the town and he is classed as rural. No cases in the Virginia sample counties lived in towns.

In comparing rural/urban wealth in the various regions, the fewness of the urban dwellers, especially in other regions than New England, and the large-city emphasis in our sample cases in the middle colonies and the South, need to be kept in mind. In all regions urban physical wealth averaged higher than rural (table 7.5), but the averages were closer together in New England than in the other two regions. New England's urban wealth averaged distinctly lower than that of the middle colonies (essentially Philadelphia) and much lower than that of the South (essentially Charleston). These facts suggest that although New England was the most heavily urban of the regions, relatively more of its nonrural people lived in smaller towns, and those in Boston and Salem as examples of larger port cities often did not have wealth equal to that of residents of Philadelphia or Charleston. This is not to deny that there were some large fortunes in Boston in 1774, but in our cross section sample of deaths probated in that year, they did not appear as frequently or with such large wealth as did cases probated in the same year in the more southerly cities.

Occupation and Industry Sectors

The dominance of the agricultural sector in all the regional economies is confirmed by the major proportions shown in tables 7.1 through 7.4 of farmers[11] as well as of rural dwellers. New England, where the soil and climate were relatively unfavorable to farming and the sea was an important alternate source of livelihood, had the only fishermen drawn in the sample[12] and the highest proportion of farmers who were also fishermen, coopers, millers, or merchants. Correlatively, it had the largest proportion of the relatively small numbers of mariners and laborers, most of whom were urban, and relatively as many of the more numerous artisans and chandlers as the other regions. The proportions of farmers only or planters only among the probate-type wealthholders were greatest in the South, followed closely by the middle colonies, fitting in well with our general knowledge of the dominantly agricultural character of these two regions.

Commerce, on the other hand, was a much smaller though relatively buoyant sector of the colonial economies in 1774.[13] This can be inferred in part from the proportion of merchants and shopkeepers and their relatively high wealth (table 7.5), particularly that of the merchants in the North. Secondarily it may be partially inferred from the higher wealth of the group of farmers who had side activities[14] than of those who seemed to be solely farmers or planters, and from their higher financial assets and liabilities, noted in table 5.10. Such side activities ranged from combinations of merchant functions with farming, to coopering, milling, tanning, blacksmithing, weaving, serving as wheelwright, or other artisan activities.

A manufacturing and selling sector, as yet embryonic in a modern sense, may be considered to have consisted of the output of the artisans and chandlers, found principally in the cities, and the side activities by farmers just mentioned. The following list of artisan activity used in the occupational codes suggests the specialized skills and managerial abilities often involved: baker, blacksmith, brewer, brickmaker, butcher, cabinet maker, carriage maker, carpenter, clockmaker, cooper, cordmaker, cordwainer, caulker, distiller, fuller, harness maker, hatter, hosier, joiner, mason, miller, painter, potter, printer, ropemaker, saddler, sailmaker, shipwright, shoemaker, smith (blacksmith, whitesmith), tailor, tallow chandler, tanner, waggoner, wagon maker, watch maker, weaver, wheelwright.

These specialized activities were found mostly in Philadelphia in the middle colonies, in Charleston in the South, and in Boston, Salem, and some of the smaller cities and towns of New England. Nonfarm business inventories, some indication of a commercial or manufacturing sector, were held far most frequently by merchants and shopkeepers (table 7.12), second by artisans and chandlers, third in the middle colonies and South by farmers with side activities. Such inventories were held also by a sprinkling of "esquires, gentlemen, and officials" in New England, of professionals in New England and the South, and of mariners in Philadelphia.

The remaining occupational categories of table 7.1 might be conceptually grouped into two last sectors to round out the picture of the colonial economy. The first would be called, in present day terms, a service sector. In it we would place the officials and professionals, if one wished a different combination[15] than the ones presented in this chapter. The service sector might also incorporate the few innkeepers. In a final lumping of the remaining groups, "esquires, gentlemen",[16] "women with occupation not determined" and "men with occupation not determined," we have not so much an industry sector as a group possibly to be thought of as akin to people today "not in the labor force." Such designation would be correct only to the extent that they truly had no economically paying occupations. Actually some of them may have had occupations that I was unable to ascertain. Some of the men may have been retired. Others may have been drifters. Both possibilities are suggested by their low average wealth (table 7.5), lower in every region except New England than for the women whose occupations were not determined. Some of the women may have operated farms, or had them operated by others on their behalf. Of the "esquires" and "gentlemen," some may have been "gentlemen of lesiure," but more likely most of them pursued a variety of activities, some definitely economic.

It is the very lack of clarity at the margins of the colonial occupational profile which again reminds us that we are trying to analyze a preindustrial economy, to which our neat twentieth century categories of industrial sectors are simply not applicable. The rising commercial activities were fitted in wherever they found accommodation; with a merchant, an enterprising farmer, a sea captain, a mariner, or perhaps an attorney.

COMPOSITION OF WEALTH HELD BY SOCIOECONOMIC GROUP

It is in looking at the composition of wealth itself, in considering how much land and other property they held and what things were found in peoples homes at the ends of their lives that we get our most vivid insight into how colonial wealth was produced and consumed. The kinds of producers' goods, many hand fashioned, together with information on land and slaves and servants, tell the story of production processes and kind of economic growth they made possible before the Industrial Revolution. The kinds of consumers' goods, also hand fashioned for clothing and shoes as well as for household furnishings and for the rare carriage or riding chaise, tell the story of the amenities of daily life, the consumption life style of the people whose surviving records, never originally intended for such a purpose, have laid bare their economic lives for our examination. The verbatim descriptions of possessions in the probate inventories[17] give rich and illuminating detail.

The consumers' goods are the closest approximation I have been able to locate of a description of the colonial level of living. Yet, since they are wealth items and exclude current food consumption, they give only the part of the story told by the consumers' durables, whose use yielded current income, and by the consumers' perishables, whose use depleted capital stocks.

Here we wish to discover the differences in ownership of some major forms of wealth among the various socioeconomic groups in the several regions, as a further key to understanding their relative positions on the wealth scale and in colonial society. Summary[18] tables 7.6 through 7.31 present highlights with respect to ownership of real estate, slaves and servants, business inventories and equipment (non-farm), other producers' goods, and consumers' goods[19] for each of the socioeconomic groups we have been considering. Each of these wealth forms is fraught with economic and sometimes social implications, only some of which can be suggested here. How differently did the relatively "rich" live, what kinds and how much wealth did they hold, as compared with the relatively "poor"?

Figures on percentages of wealthholders in the group having the given kind of wealth under consideration, as in table 7.6 and subsequent tables, in themselves testify to the commoness or uncommonness of such holdings.

Consumers' and Producers' Goods

Virtually everyone had some consumers' goods, usually at least some pots and pans and a few articles of clothing or bedding. Likewise virtually everyone, with the occasional exception of a widow, a mariner, or a man whose occupation I could not determine, had some form of producers' goods—an axe or tool, equipment items such as wool cards or harness, a bushel or quart container, if not crops and livestock.[20]

Land and Slave Ownership

However, we find land ownership for a much smaller percentage at the low-wealth level;[21] it rises steadily as wealth increases (table 7.6). This is consistent with the fact that real estate was the single major form of physical wealth in the North (tables 4.2 and 4.3). The mere fact of possessing land is a major clue in assessing not only wealth, but correlated social status. On the other hand, for the South, ownership of slaves and servants may have been of even greater economic significance. They exceeded land in value (table 7.10 compared with 7.7) among the women and the urban group. We see in table 7.9 that in every socioeconomic category, not merely among farmers, far more southerners held slaves then did northerners; only among "esquires, gentlemen, and officials" in the middle colonies and merchants in New England was slave ownership relatively high in the North. The percentages holding slaves were particularly high in the South at the highest wealth class, and among the "esquires, gentlemen, and officials," as well as quite high among farmers, merchants, and shopkeepers. Women wealthholders held them almost as frequently as men and more frequently than men whose occupation was not determined. Only in New England was the urban percentage holding slaves greater than the rural. In the South, women or other owners of slaves not in a position to direct their work themselves rented them principally to planters. As is well known from other literature, some were used as house servants, most as field hands, and some did artisan work.[22]

Business Inventories

In nonfarm business inventory, shown in table 7.12, the interest lies in the very smallness[23] of most of the numbers. I deduce that the commercial or nonfarm business sector of the colonial economy was relatively tiny from the small percentages of wealthholders involved. Yet that it could involve significant absolute amounts in some areas is suggested by the large percentages found with such holdings among some economically strategic groups: merchants, shopkeepers, artisans and chandlers, farmers with side activities. This suggestion seems to be confirmed by the figures in table 7.13 showing large business inventory and equipment values, especially for merchants and shopkeepers in the North. That domestic commerce (other than the export of the great staples, and import of some consumer goods and slaves) was not taking hold in the South to a comparable degree is suggested by the much lower average values there of the business inventory and equipment of the few merchants and shopkeepers drawn in the sample. That occasionally in either the North or the South anyone in a position of access to a particular supply or market might take on small commercial ventures is suggested by the spotty small figures[24] in table 7.12 on percentages having business inventory in other economic groups than those we think of as primarily commercial. Some irregular business value figures for minor economic groups in table 7.13 accord with this interpretation.

Average Values and Some Patterns of Wealth

Values in pound amounts, as shown in table 7.5 and subsequent tables, permit direct comparisons both from region to region and from one wealth category to another of average values. This is useful to help us to visualize that the absolute values of some kinds of wealth of New England's upper third of wealthholders were substantially below those of the South, but not so far below and sometimes above those of the middle colonies.

Since New England groups' total physical wealth is usually much lower on the average than that in the South, and often some lower than in the middle colonies, the relative importance of its smaller absolute amounts for a particular wealth category, such as other producers' goods or consumers' goods (tables 7.15, 7.17) may more readily be discerned when they are considered in proportion to the size of total wealth (tables 7.16, 7.18). Even though absolute amounts for certain categories of wealth vary region to region, there are often interestingly consistent patterns in the percentages of total wealth found in certain categories from region to region.[25]

Examination of the tables shows some regularities in patterns of wealth that reflect basic relationships. Some of these have economic and perhaps even psychological explanations that we might dub, in old-fashioned terminology, "laws" of wealth. Some of these are as valid for the twentieth-century United States and other western countries as for the colonists.

Age   One example is the pattern of wealth accumulation and age, shown in appendix C. The pattern coincides with that for Guilford, Connecticut found by Waters (1976:156–59).

Consumers' Goods   Another is the pattern of wealth in consumers' goods, which, consistently for every region, rises in absolute amount from low to high wealth class (table 7.17) and just as consistently declines as a percentage of total physical wealth (table

7.18). This pattern has similarity to the "law," rooted in diminishing marginal utility, that Engel (1883) observed in the nineteenth century from family budget data: percentages spent for food decline as income rises. It is consistent with more sophisticated modern statements of the consumption function (see Friedman 1957) that relate consumers' choices between current consumption and investment to their anticipated lifetime incomes, and where the consumption-income ratio declines as expected income becomes high. Though we are dealing here with accumulated consumer durables and perishables (wealth), not with current consumption of them (income), still we can surely infer that the larger such stocks of wealth, the larger had been the colonists' use during their lifetimes of (income from) such wealth by their owners. Hence it is reasonable to conclude, as a general tendency, that though consumption increased absolutely as a colonial free household grew richer in total wealth, its accumulation in other forms of investments took a larger part of the greater wealth. That is to say, the totals of savings in forms other than consumers' goods showed definite wealth-elastic tendencies.

Other Producers' Goods   Other regularities in basic relationships for certain forms of wealth are rooted in the peculiar economic circumstances of the colonies. For example, "other producers' goods" (not counting land, slaves, or nonfarm business equipment and inventory, tables 7.15 and 7.16) consistently rises in absolute value at higher wealth levels but declines as a percentage of total physical wealth. The rising average amounts of such producers' goods (which include livestock and crops) suggest greater wealth-producing capacity at higher wealth levels. The falling proportion has a different explanation in the northern regions, where land is the expansive factor (table 7.8), from the South, where slaves also claim an expanding share of total wealth (table 7.11).

Slaves   In the South where the institution was widespread, ownership of slaves and servants was wealth elastic—that is to say, such wealth increased with complete regularity both absolutely (table 7.10), as a percentage of total wealth (table 7.11), and as a percentage of wealthholders having such wealth (table 7.9) from low- to high-wealth level. Except for a wobble in New England, explainable by one or a few exceptional cases among the much smaller percentages of wealthholders involved, the same general pattern holds for both New England and middle colonies for absolute value (table 7.10), and for percentages owning slaves (table 7.9),[26] except that the numbers involved are so very much smaller.

Business Equipment and Inventory   Another instance where the character of regional colonial economic development was very different from present-day conditions concerns nonfarm business equipment and inventory. Here the pattern, dominated by prevailing local opportunities and conditions, is mixed. We note wealth elasticity for New England in all three measures, percentage having such inventory (table 7.12), average value (table 7.13), and percentage of total wealth (table 7.14). For the middle colonies we find progression from low to high, however, only for average value (table 7.13), and for the South we find only spottiness in the nonfarm business pattern. An interpretation that appeals to me as plausible is that in more urban and lower-wealth New England, where farming returns were less attractive than elsewhere, there was greatest incentive, or we might say necessity, to turn to other alternatives, and a more regular pattern of greater acquisition of commercial wealth occurred. Yet this was exceeded, especially at the high wealth class, in the bustling middle colonies, where heavy volume of shipping in and out of the port of Philadelphia may have contributed to more or better nonfarm opportunities than ones turned up in New England by merchants, artisans, shopkeepers, or some of the other groups. For the South, with many creek and river connections leading to ocean ports, and with relatively high prices in Europe in 1774 for tobacco, rice, indigo, and naval stores, fewer incentives and fewer opportunities arose for varied commercial enterprises, and the agricultural sector maintained dominance.

Land   The very great economic role played by land (real estate) in the colonies is evident (table 7.7) in its high value among the wealthy, the "esquires, gentlemen, and officials" everywhere, the merchants in the North, and the professionals in the South. These groups on average owned more land than those classified as farmers, or "farmers plus other activity," although in the South, the farmers with side activities were very close behind the professionals in land ownership. In New England, however, greater real estate was held by farmers in the upper wealth bracket (table 7.20) than by all "esquires, gentlemen, and officials," but not so in the middle colonies and the South. A much lower percentage of total physical wealth in land in the South (table 7.8) than the other regions (despite its higher absolute value there, table 7.7) is explained chiefly by the high absolute and relative values there of slaves (tables 7.10 and 7.11).

Real estate may be said to be strongly wealth elastic. It shows completely consistent patterns of increase with higher wealth in tables 7.6, 7.7, and 7.8.

Though the percentages of the older people holding real estate were higher only in New England and the South (table 7.6), their holdings were of greater value than those of younger wealthholders in all regions, both in average amount (table 7.7) and as a percentage of total physical wealth (table 7.8).

As between the sexes, we find relatively more men holding land (table 7.6) of higher value in every region both absolutely (table 7.7) and relatively (table 7.8). Yet the interesting fact is that substantial numbers of women wealthholders (widows, or single women) did legally hold land in their own names in the colonies. My estimate is 11 percent in the South, but 29 percent in the middle colonies and 39 percent in New England[27] (table 7.6).

As between urban and rural dwellers, there were significant contrasts. Larger proportions of rural dwellers, except in the South, owned real estate (table 7.6) but of lower average value (table 7.7). It formed a higher proportion for urban than rural of total physical wealth (table 7.8) only in the middle colonies, where the large absolute and percentage amounts held by both merchants and "esquires, gentlemen, and officials" contributed. Its lower corresponding proportion in the South is, I believe, chiefly explained by the large urban percentage there of wealth in slaves (table 7.11).

By occupation the greatest frequency of land ownership (table 7.6) was among "esquires, gentlemen, and officials"; the lowest, after women and men of no determined occupation, was among mariners and laborers. Second place was taken by merchants in both northern regions, but in the South merchants were outranked in land-holding frequency by all other groups except those of undetermined occupation. Professionals in New England owned land only slightly less often than farmers, shopkeepers, and artisans; in the middle colonies an even higher proportion of professionals (found chiefly in Philadelphia county) owned land, outranking farmers with side activities, shopkeepers, and artisans in this respect. Seventy-nine percent of farmers with side activities in the South owned land, as did

75 percent of the professionals and 66 percent of farmers-only. A strikingly high proportion (95 percent) of men in New England of no determined occupation owned land, suggesting they may have been retirees and not drifters.

As we might by now expect, the average values of land held (table 7.7) were highest for the merchants in New England and for "esquires, gentlemen, and officials" in the two other regions. They were of intermediate value for farmers, but much higher for high-wealth than for low-wealth farmers (tables 7.20, 7.21, and 7.22) and high in the South for high-wealth farmers with side activity (table 7.26). They were of lower value among artisans, mariners,[28] laborers, and men and women of undetermined occupation. As proportions of physical wealth (table 7.8) land played a lesser role in the southern prestige occupations than in the North, owing to the greater role there of wealth in slaves.

Wealth Composition of Farmers and Merchants of High and Lower Wealth

A simplistic populist interpretation attributes common interests to farmers and laborers, antithetical to the commercial interests of merchants in the colonial as well as some later periods. Our data cannot answer questions of motives of these groups in the late colonial period, but we may draw some inferences as to their economic interests and consumption levels from the kinds and amounts of their wealth, when they are subdivided by wealth level. Differences in holdings of some key wealth categories, including financial assets and liabilities, are shown in tables 7.19 through 7.26 for the most numerous occupational group, farmers and planters. Corresponding tables for a smaller but highly interesting and economically vital occupation group, the merchants, are shown so far as the data permit,[29] in tables 7.27 through 7.31.

Certainly farmers were not monolithic in the size and character of their wealth. Those in the high-wealth groups in the North (table 7.20) held, on average, more than ten times the net worth of those in the low (table 7.22), and the contrast was still sharper in the South, with average net worth of £708 in the high-, contrasted with £32 in the low-wealth group. The discrepancy was somewhat greater for southern farmers having side activities (table 7.26), £755 as against £33.

The merchant group was so much smaller that we can compare merchants at separate wealth levels only for the two northern regions and the two upper wealth levels. The very absence of many cases of low-wealth merchants helps to explain the high average merchant wealth shown in table 7.5. High-wealth merchants substantially out-classed the high-wealth farmers, most notably in the middle colonies. Yet the differences in average wealth, whether of net worth or of total physical wealth, of merchants at middle and high levels (tables 7.28 and 7.29) show a far wider spread than farmers at those two levels (tables 7.20 and 7.21). Middle-wealth merchants, on average, were poorer than middle-wealth farmers. An exception is in physical wealth in New England, where middle-wealth merchants' business inventory was of greater value than middle-wealth farmers' land plus livestock and producers' goods.

High or low consumption levels are suggested by the values placed on the total amount of consumers' goods owned. These include items of house furnishings, apparel, jewelry, books, etc. At compara-ble high- and middle-wealth levels, northern merchants exceeded northern and also southern farmers in this respect. For low-wealth farmers, the similarity of the consumers' goods figures, averaging bet-ter than half that of middle-wealth farmers (table 7.21) in all regions, and a third that of high-wealth farmers (table 7.20) in the North and a fourth in the South, suggests that their consumption levels were not so far below those of their higher-wealth counterparts as was their disparity in land ownership, producers' goods, and financial assets. Consumers' goods of low-wealth farmers averaged in New England about two-thirds the figure for all mariners and laborers or for all artisans there (table 7.17). In the middle colonies, consumers' goods of low-wealth farmers averaged about a half those of all mariners and laborers and over half that of artisans. For the South, the consumers' goods of low-wealth farmers were less than half the average value of those of mariners and laborers and of artisans.

Judged by their total wealth, low-wealth farmers might have had economic interests somewhat akin to laborers and mariners (table 7.5), who, in turn, had less than artisans and chandlers had as a group. Land and livestock holdings of low-wealth farmers were small, suggesting that may of them were tenant farmers. Their slave and servant holdings were nil in the North and less than £2 average in the South. Their crops were of very small value, even in the South, where they reached an average value of £3. That their farm tools and equipment were rudimentary is suggested by the lower value of their producers' goods than of their consumers' goods, which latter amounted to about a quarter of their total physical wealth.

Yet these low-wealth farmers in the northern regions held substantial financial assets, approaching the value of their total physical assets. In New England, however, the financial assets were about equally offset by financial liabilities. Only in the middle colonies did low-wealth farmers' financial assets substantially top their financial liabilities. In the South, our less reliable evidence on financial liabilities indicates that they were greater for low-wealth farmers than our firmer figure of their financial assets.

Middle and high-wealth farmers also held substantial financial assets in the North, particularly so in the middle colonies, where the assets were much larger than the financial liabilities. But the New England middle- and high-wealth farmers owed financial liabilities in excess of their financial assets, pulling down their net worth. High-wealth merchants' financial assets topped those of high-wealth farmers in both regions, but at the middle-wealth level, merchants' holdings of financial assets were distinctly lower than those of farmers: however, I do not place strong reliance on this comparison because of the small number of merchant cases.

As landowners in the two northern regions high-wealth farmers trailed high-wealth merchants, as they did in ownership of slaves. At middle-wealth levels, the land pattern was reversed, with middle-wealth farmers' land values exceeding those of middle-wealth merchants in both regions. Ownership of crops and livestock was not limited to farmers, although they held larger amounts than did merchants at corresponding wealth levels.

As we would expect, wealth in the form of nonfarm business inventory was a major asset for merchants and a very small one for farmers, even the high-wealth farmers (tables 7.20 and 7.26). For both high- and middle-wealth merchants, this asset exceeded average financial assets, with the exception of the high-wealth merchants in the middle colonies, whose financial assets outweighed their business inventory.

Producers' goods, other than livestock, crops, and business inventories, were a major asset for farmers. At both the high- and middle-wealth levels, farmers held more of these assets than did merchants, and the average amounts among farmers were greater at each successively higher wealth level. However, these items, being indispensable to farming activities, took a larger share of the total physical wealth of low-wealth than of high-wealth farmers (tables 7.23 through 7.25).

I suggest a general conclusion from this analysis by wealth levels that neither colonial farmers nor colonial merchants on the eve of the Revolution were solid groups with united interests. At any rate, there was substantial variety in the levels and composition of their wealth. Variations among farmers from rich to poor were great. Rich merchants were much richer than middle-wealth merchants. Although rich merchants outclassed rich farmers in the North, the middle-wealth farmers, particularly in the middle colonies, were richer and held more financial assets than did middle-wealth merchants. At least in this region, farmers' assets rather than, or in addition to, merchants' may have been important sources of savings accumulations from which in future decades the financing of industrial expansion and stimulus to economic growth was to come.

WEALTH SIZE DISTRIBUTION BY SOCIOECONOMIC GROUPS

We now consider what additional light is shed on the wealth size distributions for all free wealthholders, presented in chapter 6, when we focus attention on the size distribution differences within smaller socioeconomic groups. These differences, shown in tables 7.1 through 7.4[30] for probate-type wealthholders and three wealth intervals, are at least suggestive.

Distribution by Age

Wealth is acquired by saving or inheritance, both of which are more likely to have been achieved by older persons than by the young. Among our probate-type wealthholders, we find a general tendency for the young to fall in the low- or middle-wealth brackets and for the older to appear more in the middle- and high-wealth intervals. That not all young were poor, nor old better off, however, is indicated by cases all the way from low to high within each of the two categories. In New England, the older were almost evenly divided between the two upper-wealth intervals; in the middle colonies, their greatest concentration was in the middle-wealth bracket; in the South it was in the upper. The younger in New England fell most heavily toward low-wealth, in the more egalitarian middle colonies more toward middle-wealth, and only in the rich South fell preponderantly in the high-wealth class.

The two broad age categories mask interesting differences for finer age groups. Tables and graphs based on fewer cases,[31] by ten- and five-year intervals, are presented in appendix C. These show a pattern of rising wealth, starting from a low point under age 25, up to a peak around age 60, or a plateau from about age 60 to 65 or even older. Thereafter, there is some dropping off in average wealth in later years to successively lower levels. This pattern accords with a general one[32] that has been observed by economists and historians for other times and places. It is consistent with progression through the life cycle of a young man who leaves his parents' household to make his own start and gradually acquires more possessions through work and saving. He may acquire land as his family expands and his experience grows, and perhaps he receives an inheritance upon the death of his father. His wealth reaches a maximum somewhere in late middle age or old age. Thereafter, as his energy declines and his children leave home, he may engage less actively in farming or other productive activities and may dispose of some of his assets to meet his current needs, or may tranfer some of them, as land to sons, to help them get a start. This wealth-age relationship, in conjunction with the relatively large proportion of young men in the colonies, may explain in part why colonial wealth size distributions of chapter 6 seem to be less unequal than those of around 1860.[33]

Distribution by Sex

Men probate-type wealthholders were much more strongly represented than women in the two upper-wealth groups, and they had higher average wealth in each region. The women fell most heavily in the low-wealth interval in all regions, most strikingly so in

New England. However, the women holding wealth in the South on average were richer in total physical wealth than were the men in New England and the middle colonies. There were also some wealthy women in the northern samples as well as the southern.

Since the proportion of wealthholders who were women was small in all regions, the sex factor is not major in explaining wealth inequality among all wealthholders shown in chapter 6. However, some of the individual cases of women wealthholders and the pattern of women's wealth are of intrinsic interest. Some women appeared for all regions among the ten poorest in the samples shown in chapter 6. Table 7.32 gives information on the richest women in the various regional samples.

Abigail Townsend, a widow who had grandchildren, from Wadmellow Island, Colleton County, near Charleston in the Charleston District of North Carolina, was the richest woman in the sample by total physical wealth, of which she had £2,559. It consisted very heavily of slaves, but she also had a large boat and two small ones, a riding chair and harness, horses, cattle, indigo vats, indigo seed, 270 bushels of rough rice, 298 bushels of corn, rice sieves, carpenters' tools, coopers' tools, a gold ring, a "chest with shop goods," apparel, household goods, books, 3 bags of cotton, a keg of powder, and various stored foods and liquors. The richest by net worth was Elizabeth Smith, a widow from Charleston, whose £2,229 in financial assets and £86 in slaves together with £183 in other physical assets brought her net worth, after a subtraction for financial liabilities, up to £2,439. These figures are much below those of Peter Manigault and the nine other richest men in the southern sample, yet they are considerably larger than the highest wealths we found for women in the two northern regions.

The richest woman in New England, both by net worth, £501, and by total physical wealth, £657, was Kathran Upham, a "gentlewoman" from Brookfield in Worcester County, Massachusetts. She was richer than all the men wealthholders in that county sample. She had substantial land, consisting of the "homestead, about two acres with the building," two farms, one "in Brookfield known by the name of Woocott farm" (*sic*) and one "known by the name the Nelson farm," and "one lot of land about 80 acres bought of Mr. John Rich." She owned one Negro slave. She had some livestock and farm equipment, books, silver plate, pewter and tinware, Delft ware, a chaise and harness, pictures, furniture, and apparel. The richest woman in the middle colonies, by total physical wealth, £690, was Miriam Potts, a widowed shopkeeper, age 34. She owned a house in High Street ward and another lot in Chestnut ward, according to the 1774 Philadelphia tax list, giving her an estimated real estate value of £287. She had £23 in financial assets, walnut furniture, an eight-day clock, a watch, pewterware, pictures, and a very large inventory of shop goods in Philadelphia and "in the Jerseys," which totaled £336 out of her portable physical wealth of £403. Potts' net worth of £475 was considerably topped by the £3,412 of Margaret Williams, a widow from Radnor in Chester County, Pennsylvania, whose estate was probated in Philadelphia County. This net worth consisted of very large financial assets, £3,383 in "several mortgages, bonds, bills and promissory notes, together with the interest due thereon," and in her "purse." She owned a cow and a gray mare, some lumber, household equipment, pewter, apparel, and two books, worth a total of £29.

When we look at average wealth patterns as a percentage of total physical wealth, women held relatively less land than men, especially in the middle colonies and the South. They also held less business inventory except in the middle colonies, where the inventory of Miriam Potts the shopkeeper pulls up the women's average. They held more consumers' goods in relation to their total wealth than did the men and relatively less in such producers' goods as livestock, crops, and producers' durable equipment. Women in the South and in the middle colonies held more slaves, as a percentage of total physical wealth, than the men, and also had relatively higher financial assets. As between those two regions, the middle colonies' women held relatively more financial assets than the southern, while the southern held a higher proportion of wealth in slaves.

Distribution by Location

Our data lend only partial support to the hypothesis of Jackson Main (1965) and New England findings of Bruce Daniels (1973–74) that there was greater urban inequality than rural. In the most urban region, New England, there was no relative predominance of urban cases over the rural in the high- or middle-wealth grouping; indeed most urban were in the low-wealth group. There was such predominance in the middle colonies in the high-wealth bracket and the low. In the South, among the much smaller proportion of urban cases there, relatively the most fell in the middle-wealth bracket. To judge wealth inequality within socioeconomic groups such as urban/rural one must consider the size distributions of tables 7.1 through 7.4 against the backdrop shown in table 7.5 of the average wealth within the three wealth brackets for the group. Thus one might conclude from tables 7.1 through 7.4 that there was not a marked wealth distribution difference between urban and rural; but the greater average wealth of the urban shown in table 7.5, especially in the middle colonies and the South, suggests that there may be greater divergences from the higher urban mean.[34] The average wealth of New England's urban (table 7.5) was closer to that of its rural wealthholders than was the case in the other two regions and it had the highest proportion of any region of "urban poor" (tables 7.2, 7.3, 7.4), but only a slightly higher such proportion than of its "rural poor". These two relationships suggest that New England's urban wealth inequality was only slightly greater than its rural inequality. Its urban inequality was rather akin to that of the middle colonies (principally Philadelphia), but less severe than that found in the South (principally Charleston). The egalitarianism of the middle colonies' wealthholders as a whole seems heavily due to its very large rural component, chiefly farmers, in the middle-wealth bracket (table 7.3).

Our regional data do not lend clear support to Main's hypothesis that second greatest inequality after urban areas was found in areas of commercial farming. In the South, our sample is dominated by tobacco raising counties in Virginia and Maryland and rice and indigo growing areas around Charleston, all commodities heavily exported, with only the North Carolina counties having more corn, livestock, and timber produce. Yet the southern rural wealthholders were quite equally distributed among the three wealth classes. Further, in the middle colonies, where the farming was more geared to exportable grain and cattle products and hence was more "commercial" than in New England, rural wealthholders were more, not less, equally distributed among the three wealth intervals than in New England.

Distribution by Occupation

The strikingly richest occupation classes were "esquires, gentlemen, and officials" in all regions and merchants in the two northern regions. Their predominance in the top-wealth classification with more than £400 sterling was conspicuous. These were found more generally in the towns in New England and in Philadelphia in the middle colonies. In the South, as farmers or planters, they often lived in rural places, though considerable numbers of "esquires, gentlemen, officials" were found in Charleston. Of the six southern merchants only three lived in Charleston and the others in rural Virginia.[35] Only in New England did merchants exceed in average wealth (table 7.5) the "esquires, gentlemen, and officials," who frequently, especially in the middle colonies and South, were large landholders. In the South farmers with side activity came second, and merchants were pushed down to fifth place in average wealth among occupation groups, exceeded also by professionals and by farmers and planters only. At the other extreme were most mariners (excluding captains) and laborers, who generally held less than £100, but a few mariners held large financial assets and had substantial physical wealth. In between, in the northern regions, were the professionals, farmers, "shopkeepers and artisans," who were spread more nearly equally among the three wealth intervals. Fishermen and farmer-fishermen in New England were predominantly of middle or low wealth, whereas farmers there who had dual or side occupations tended to have higher wealths; the grouping for farmer with side activities hence showed greater extremes in New England than those whose sole occupation appeared to be farming, and New England showed more of these as low-wealth than did the other regions. No fishermen appeared in the samples for the middle colonies or for the South. The farmers in those regions who had other occupations more frequently attained wealth of £400 or over than did those classed as farmers only or planters only. The higher wealths often associated with multiple occupations suggests that these side occupations of farmers may frequently have had commercial aspects. They would tend to involve production or merchandising for use other than within the household, and would tend to expand external contacts, thus stimulating economic development.

That not all people of an occupation group had similar wealth is evident in tables 7.32 and 7.33. We see there differences in kinds of wealth of some selected individual merchants, farmers, artisans, mariners, laborers and widows in various regions. The merchants tended to have large amounts of consumers' durable goods, but they were matched or followed closely in that respect by some of the wealthy farmers, artisans and widows. Among the merchants, Neave had over £6,100 in business inventory, Gerry over £1,000, William White only £155, and Coats and Michel had none, whereas the shopkeeper Miriam Potts had over £300. Ownership of livestock was found not only among farmers but rather frequently among artisans, widows, and also among some merchants, mariners and laborers. There were many more farmers in the colonies than artisans, but examples of the latter at both relatively high as well as low wealth are shown in table 7.33. Not all mariners were poor, although all the laborers I found in the sample were poor. Almost everyone, including widows, had some producers' durable goods. Servants and slaves were owned by the northern as well as southern merchants, but only by the richest of the northern farmers, whereas the middle- to low-wealth southern farmers in table 7.33 had some slaves. Some further details of the possessions of these selected decedents are shown at the close of chapter 9.

Table 7.1
Percentage Distribution of Probate-type Wealthholders by Socioeconomic Group and by Total Physical Wealth Class
Thirteen Colonies, 1774

| | | *In Wealth Interval* | | |
Wealthholder Group	In Sample (1)	£400 and over (2)	£100–399 (3)	£99 or less (4)
(1) All probate-type wealthholders	100	26	42	32
(2) Younger (age 44 and under)	57	22	51	27
(3) Older (age 45 and above)	25	43	35	23
(4) Men	93	27	44	29
(5) Women	7	16	19	65
(6) Urban	11	26	39	35
(7) Rural	89	25	40	34
(8) Esquires, gentlemen, officials	3	66	22	13
(9) Merchants	2	64	20	16
(10) Professionals (including sea captains)	3	27	47	26
(11) Farmers only and planters	61	27	51	22
(12) Farmers plus other activity, vessel owners, fishermen	7	41	34	25
(13) Shopkeepers, innkeepers	1	29	38	34
(14) Artisans, chandlers	10	14	31	55
(15) Mariners, laborers	2	4	34	62
(16) Women, occupation not determined	7	14	20	66
(17) Men, occupation not determined	4	6	9	85

SOURCE: Sample data w-weighted, Variant Two. Sample size is 919. Figures include New York estimate. Since I do not know the age, sex, occupational characteristics of the wealthholders who were not probated, I limit this and subsequent tables of this chapter to the probate-type wealthholders. See appendix A.

NOTE: Columns 2, 3 and 4 do not always sum to 100 percent because of rounding. In column 1, totals for subgroups by age do not sum vertically to 100 because data for age class 4 (age not determined) are incorporated in the total but are not allocated to age classes 1 and 2 (age 44 and younger) or age class 3 (age 45 and older). Of those with age not determined, 59 percent had less than £99, 25 percent had £100–£399, and 15 percent had £400 and over.

Information on socioeconomic characteristics such as age, sex, occupation, is available only for sample decedents. The w-weighted distributions of these characteristics, in columns 1 through 4 of tables 7.1 through 7.4, underlie all subsequent tables in this chapter, i.e., comprise the subsamples analyzed in the three wealth intervals. The subsequent tables, as 7.6 and 7.9, that show percentages of wealthholders having various forms of wealth, are w-weighted. The w-weighting brings the results to the level of probate-type living wealthholders, explained in appendix A. The reader will note that there is a divergence between the wealth distributions of lines 1 of tables 7.1 through 7.4 from those of table 6.2, for which w*B weights are used. For all living wealthholders, I prefer the w*B weighted distribution, using assumption B as to the wealth distribution of the nonprobate-type wealthholders for whom we lack specific data, explained in appendix A. However, the limited numbers of cases, especially in the smaller socioeconomic subgroups, and the complexity of the calculation of w*B weights for each make their use not feasible in tables 7.1 through 7.4 or to determine wealth boundaries for the analysis of this chapter. Their use would yield varying wealth boundaries for every subgroup. I consider more useful the bounds selected, using w weights, which place more nearly equal groups of probate-type wealthholders, particularly for the thirteen colonies as a whole, into each of the three wealth classes selected for analysis. See text discussion regarding wealth intervals.

However, in table 7.5 and subsequent tables that show values of various kinds of wealth, I use w*-weighted figures, to reduce values to levels consistent with value figures in previous chapters. See note to table 7.5.

Table 7.2

Percentage Distribution of Probate-type Wealthholders by
Socioeconomic Group and by Total Physical Wealth Class
New England, 1774

		In Wealth Interval		
Wealthholder Group	*In Sample* (1)	*£400 and over* (2)	*£100–399* (3)	*£99 or less* (4)
(1) All probate-type wealthholders	100	18	42	40
(2) Younger (age 44 and under)	62	11	47	42
(3) Older (age 45 and above)	31	35	36	29
(4) Men	94	19	44	38
(5) Women	6	4	12	85
(6) Urban	25	18	39	43
(7) Rural	75	18	43	39
(8) Esquires, gentlemen, officials	8	43	39	18
(9) Merchants	2	77	13	10
(10) Professionals (including sea captains)	5	29	37	35
(11) Farmers only and planters	45	16	52	32
(12) Farmers plus other activity, fishermen	11	19	37	44
(13) Shopkeepers, innkeepers	1	21	50	29
(14) Artisans, chandlers	14	13	33	54
(15) Mariners, laborers	7	0	43	57
(16) Women, occupation not determined	6	—[a]	12	87
(17) Men, occupation not determined	2	0	35	65

SOURCE: Sample data *un*-weighted. Sample size is 381.

NOTE: General note to table 7.1 pertains also to this table.

[a] Less than 0.05 percent.

Table 7.3

Percentage Distribution of Probate-type Wealthholders by
Socioeconomic Group and by Total Physical Wealth Class
New Jersey, Pennsylvania, Delaware, 1774

		In Wealth Interval		
Wealthholder Group	In Sample (1)	£400 and over (2)	£100–399 (3)	£99 or less (4)
(1) All probate-type wealthholders	100	13	63	24
(2) Younger (age 44 and under)	58	9	77	14
(3) Older (age 45 and above)	25	25	51	24
(4) Men	94	13	65	22
(5) Women	6	6	45	49
(6) Urban	14	22	41	37
(7) Rural	86	10	68	22
(8) Esquires, gentlemen, officials	1	91	0	9
(9) Merchants[a]	2	91	9	0
(10) Professionals (including sea captains)	3	17	63	21
(11) Farmers only and planters	62	8	83	9
(12) Farmers plus other activity, vessel owners	6	42	34	25
(13) Shopkeepers, innkeepers	2	32	32	35
(14) Artisans, chandlers	14	13	32	55
(15) Mariners, laborers	2	4	19	77
(16) Women, occupation not determined	5	1	46	53
(17) Men, occupation not determined	3	0	0	100

Source: Sample data *w*-weighted. Sample size is 217.

Note: General note to table 7.1 pertains also to this table.

[a] There were nine merchants in the middle colony sample, eight from Philadelphia, which receives a relatively low county-weight in the computation of *w*-weights. See appendix A.

Table 7.4
Percentage Distribution of Probate-type Wealthholders by
Socioeconomic Group and by Total Physical Wealth Class
South, 1774

		In Wealth Interval		
Wealthholder Group	In Sample (1)	£400 and over (2)	£100–399 (3)	£99 or less (4)
(1) All probate-type wealthholders	100	40	27	33
(2) Younger (age 44 and under)	56	38	33	29
(3) Older (age 45 and above)	22	62	20	18
(4) Men	92	41	28	30
(5) Women	8	25	10	65
(6) Urban	1	36	56	8
(7) Rural	99	40	27	33
(8) Esquires, gentlemen, officials	2	93	1	6
(9) Merchants	1	25	37	37
(10) Professionals	2	41	34	25
(11) Farmers only and planters	69	43	31	26
(12) Farmers plus other activity	6	59	28	13
(13) Shopkeepers, innkeepers	—ᵃ	15	62	23
(14) Artisans, chandlers	6	18	22	60
(15) Mariners, laborers	—ᵃ	86	7	7
(16) Women, occupation not determined	8	25	10	65
(17) Men, occupation not determined	5	8	9	84

SOURCE: Sample data, *w*-weighted, Variant Two. Sample size is 298.

NOTE: General note to table 7.1 pertains also to this table.

   ᵃ Less than 0.05 percent.

Table 7.5
Total Physical Wealth, Average Value, Held by Socioeconomic Group, 1774
(In Pounds Sterling)

Wealthholder Group	Thirteen Colonies	New England	Middle Colonies	South
All Wealthholders	252.0	161.2	186.8	394.7
Total physical wealth £400 and over	710.5	507.8	538.4	845.2
Total physical wealth £100–399	168.2	145.1	183.7	143.9
Total physical wealth £99 and under	27.0	25.1	21.0	32.8
Younger (age 44 and under)	236.9	129.2	185.1	399.0
Older (age 45 and above)	360.7	251.8	273.8	595.2
Men	260.4	168.9	194.3	410.5
Women	131.9	42.4	103.0	214.8
Urban	232.9	191.4	287.2	640.8
Rural	255.2	151.5	172.9	391.8
Esquires, gentlemen, officials	572.4	313.4	1,223.0	1,281.3
Merchants	497.1	563.1	858.0	314.0
Professionals (including sea captains)	341.0	270.6	240.6	512.2
Farmers only and planters	262.3	155.3	179.8	396.1
Farmers plus other activity, vessel owners, fishermen	410.5	144.2	257.3	801.7
Shopkeepers, innkeepers	204.3	219.0	221.7	194.7
Artisans, chandlers	122.5	114.5	144.5	137.8
Mariners, laborers	62.0	52.2	66.8	383.4[a]
Women, occupation not determined	138.0	31.8	82.3	214.8
Men, occupation not determined	56.8	54.2	15.7	54.6

SOURCE: Sample data, w*-weighted, Variant Two. Averages for thirteen colonies and line 1 for the Middle Colonies include the New York hybrid estimate. All other Middle Colonies' lines include only New Jersey, Pennsylvania and Delaware.

NOTE: This table deals with wealth values, which would be distinctly higher if limited only to probate-type wealthholders, for reasons discussed in appendix A. To keep values consistent in level with figures in previous chapters, I reduce them to all-wealthholder levels, which reflect lower estimated wealth of nonprobate-type wealthholders. Such incorporation requires an assumption that the socioeconomic characteristics of the nonprobate types may have been distributed approximately as were those of the probate types. Actually, the proportions may have varied, and possibly somewhat more for certain characteristics than for others, say more for urban/rural than for occupational characteristics. Given the limited state of our present knowledge as to the socioeconomic characteristics of the nonprobates, I do not feel justified in further refinement of the assumption. For those who may not find it entirely acceptable I show hereafter the conversion factors to determine the wealth values for only the probate-type wealthholders of each group. For corresponding regional figures, but pertaining only to probate-type wealthholders (sample data, w-weighted), the above figures may be multiplied by the following factors: New England, 1.49; Middle Colonies, 1.37; South, 1.32. For the thirteen colonies, reading down in column 1, the w-weighted figures are: £372.2, 999.8, 237.1, 38.1, 357.7, 538.0, 384.5, 201.7, 355.2, 374.8, 979.4, 658.0, 520.9, 382.9, 659.4, 281.5, 171.7, 97.6, 220.4, 76.7. In *American Colonial Wealth,* either edition, tables 7.9 and 7.12 and later tables for subgroups show w-weighted values for New England and Middle Colonies (including New York); tables 7.7 and 7.14 and later tables for subgroups show them for the thirteen colonies and the South based on Variant One weights. Figures for thirteen colonies and the South, w-weighted, Variant Two weights, are shown in *American Colonial Wealth,* 2d ed., tables A.7.7, A.7.14 and later tables for subgroups.

[a] Based on 3 cases: #01016, a mariner from Charleston, South Carolina, had £12 total physical wealth. #01071, a mariner from Charleston, had two land grants, totaling 300 acres, which gave him an estimated value in real estate of £270; his inventory listed no portable physical wealth but a bond owed him worth £355 sterling. #71037, coded a mariner from Queen Anne's County, Maryland, had £161 in inventoried portable physical wealth items, suggesting a planter, and real estate at an estimated value of £400. Genealogical research showed him listed as mariner on a deed and in some other records, but perhaps he would be more correctly described as a former mariner and should have been classified as a planter at the time of his death. There were no laborers in the southern sample.

Table 7.6
Percentage of Wealthholders Having Land (Real Estate)
by Socioeconomic Group, 1774

Wealthholder Group	Thirteen Colonies	New England	Middle Colonies	South[a]
All Wealthholders[b]	70.4	79.9	79.8	58.9
Total physical wealth £400 and over	92.3	99.6	100.0	88.9
Total physical wealth £100–399	86.6	98.4	92.6	67.0
Total physical wealth £99 and under	31.0	52.1	34.0	16.1
Younger (age 44 and under)	78.4	79.9	90.7	68.3
Older (age 45 and above)	80.3	84.2	85.5	73.1
Men	73.9	82.5	82.5	63.1
Women	21.2	38.6	29.0	11.0
Urban	68.2	69.4	64.7	62.5
Rural	70.6	83.4	81.9	58.8
Esquires, gentlemen, officials	94.7	97.1	91.4	92.1
Merchants	58.2	90.4	95.4	24.1
Professionals (including sea captains)	69.4	60.2	79.3	75.1
Farmers only and planters	78.8	86.3	95.4	65.5
Farmers plus other activity, vessel owners, fishermen	80.2	87.7	61.2	79.2
Shopkeepers, innkeepers	53.3	70.6	61.3	56.2
Artisans, chandlers	56.1	77.3	63.1	47.0
Mariners, laborers	46.7	55.2	22.5	93.2[c]
Women, occupation not determined	17.9	37.0	24.1	11.0
Men, occupation not determined	33.1	95.4	4.9	19.3

Source: Sample data, w-weighted, Variant Two. The same percentages are assumed to hold also for all living wealthholders (w*-weighted). For thirteen colonies and for line 1 of Middle Colonies, figures include an estimate for New York hybrid. All other Middle Colonies' lines include only New Jersey, Pennsylvania, and Delaware.

[a] See discussion in Note on Method and in appendix A regarding southern land regression for explanation of minimal figures for percentages owning real estate in the South.

[b] That percentages for all wealthholders appear low in relation to those "aged 44 and younger" and "aged 45 and older" is explained by the low percentage holding land of those with age not determined (age class 4); data for age class 4 are incorporated in the figures for all wealthholders but in this tabulation were not allocated to age classes 1 and 2 (aged 44 and younger) or age class 3 (aged 45 and older).

[c] See note b to table 7.7.

Table 7.7
Land (Real Estate), Average Value Held by Socioeconomic Group, 1774
(*In Pounds Sterling*)

Wealthholder Group	Thirteen Colonies	New England	Middle Colonies	South[a]
All Wealthholders	138.5	115.1	115.5	181.1
Total physical wealth £400 and over	394.5	388.5	378.1	400.5
Total physical wealth £100–399	96.3	99.9	103.6	74.6
Total physical wealth £99 and under	7.0	10.2	5.2	4.0
Younger (age 44 and under)	123.5	86.3	108.1	176.6
Older (age 45 and above)	222.5	191.9	182.6	301.3
Men	145.3	120.8	119.1	191.9
Women	42.2	25.7	37.5	57.2
Urban	152.4	129.7	197.0	225.1
Rural	136.3	110.5	100.6	180.6
Esquires, gentlemen, officials	346.0	242.3	920.9	547.4
Merchants	260.8	311.6	489.2	114.1
Professionals (including sea captains)	258.5	195.3	217.0	401.7
Farmers only and planters	139.1	115.1	102.8	181.1
Farmers plus other activity, vessel owners, fishermen	229.2	100.6	187.1	377.9
Shopkeepers, innkeepers	95.4	118.7	91.1	147.2
Artisans, chandlers	82.9	85.6	93.8	84.2
Mariners, laborers	32.0	26.7	30.9	276.8[b]
Women, occupation not determined	40.1	16.5	28.9	57.2
Men, occupation not determined	18.6	36.3	1.5	10.9

SOURCE: Sample data, w*-weighted, Variant Two. See source note to table 7.5.

NOTE: The general note to table 7.5 pertains to this table also, except that for the thirteen colonies reading down in column 1, the w-weighted figures are: £197.3, 534.5, 131.5, 8.6, 180.8, 319.4, 207.1, 61.6, 229.2, 193.4, 554.2, 335.1, 400.0, 196.3, 358.3, 129.2, 114.5, 50.9, 61.9, 22.6.

[a] See discussion in Note on Method and appendix A regarding southern land regression for explanation of minimal real estate values in the South. Percentages and values for the South are minimal, and the true figures would be somewhat higher.

[b] Average based on three mariners, one of whom held no land, one £400, and one £270 in land.

Table 7.8
Land (Real Estate) as Percentage of Total Physical Wealth
by Socioeconomic Group, 1774

Wealthholder Group	Thirteen Colonies	New England	Middle Colonies	South
All Wealthholders[a]	53.0	71.4	61.8	45.9
Total physical wealth £400 and over	53.5	76.5	70.2	47.4
Total physical wealth £100–399	55.5	68.9	56.4	42.9
Total physical wealth £99 and under	22.6	40.6	24.8	12.3
Younger (age 44 and under)	50.5	66.8	58.4	42.6
Older (age 45 and above)	59.4	76.2	66.7	50.6
Men	53.9	71.5	61.3	46.8
Women	30.5	60.6	36.4	26.6
Urban	64.5	67.8	68.6	35.1
Rural	51.6	72.9	58.2	46.1
Esquires, gentlemen, officials	56.6	77.3	75.3	42.7
Merchants	50.9	55.3	57.0	36.3
Professionals (including sea captains)	76.8	72.2	90.2	78.4
Farmers only and planters	51.3	74.1	57.2	45.7
Farmers plus other activity, vessel owners, fishermen	54.3	69.8	72.7	47.1
Shopkeepers, innkeepers	45.9	54.2	41.1	75.6
Artisans, chandlers	66.7	74.7	64.9	61.1
Mariners, laborers	52.2	51.1	46.3	72.2[b]
Women, occupation not determined	28.1	51.9	35.1	26.6
Men, occupation not determined	29.4	66.8	9.6	20.0

SOURCE: Sample data, w^*-weighted, Variant Two. See source note to table 7.5.

[a] Corresponding figures for all wealthholders for real estate as a percentage of total nonhuman physical wealth (which excludes value of slaves and servants) are: thirteen colonies, 68.4; New England, 71.7; Middle Colonies, 63.1; South, 69.1.
[b] See note b to table 7.7.

Table 7.9
Percentage of Wealthholders Having Slaves and Servants
by Socioeconomic Group, 1774

Wealthholder Group	Thirteen Colonies	New England	Middle Colonies	South
All Wealthholders	33.2	3.3	16.0	59.6
Total physical wealth £400 and over	72.6	13.7	22.7	96.6
Total physical wealth £100–399	28.3	0.4	21.9	61.1
Total physical wealth £99 and under	7.3	1.6	1.9	13.8
Younger (age 44 and under)	34.4	2.1	19.5	63.2
Older (age 45 and above)	33.7	6.2	15.9	67.4
Men	33.3	3.3	17.3	60.3
Women	32.0	2.6	16.0	50.7
Urban	11.6	7.9	14.9	24.0
Rural	35.8	1.7	17.4	60.0
Esquires, gentlemen, officials	42.5	7.7	82.8	93.3
Merchants	53.5	39.8	13.7	62.7
Professionals (including sea captains)	20.7	4.6	2.1	40.8
Farmers only and planters	37.6	1.2	15.8	63.4
Farmers plus other activity, vessel owners, fishermen	35.0	0.0	26.1	78.8
Shopkeepers, innkeepers	40.7	6.6	36.9	56.2
Artisans, chandlers	14.6	1.6	20.5	29.6
Mariners, laborers	14.7	10.0	15.5	86.4
Women, occupation not determined	37.3	0.0	16.6	50.7
Men, occupation not determined	20.6	0.0	0.0	24.9

SOURCE: Sample data, *w*-weighted, Variant Two. See source note to table 7.6.

Table 7.10
Slaves and Servants, Average Value Held
by Socioeconomic Group, 1774
(*In Pounds Sterling*)

Wealthholder Group	Thirteen Colonies	New England	Middle Colonies	South
All Wealthholders	49.4	0.7	7.2	132.6
Total physical wealth £400 and over	178.1	3.1	13.2	299.7
Total physical wealth £100–399	13.9	0.1	9.7	43.6
Total physical wealth £99 and under	1.6	0.4	0.1	4.1
Younger (age 44 and under)	48.4	0.4	8.8	135.1
Older (age 45 and above)	60.4	1.5	7.2	194.6
Men	49.6	0.8	7.5	135.6
Women	46.0	0.3	13.6	98.4
Urban	11.6	1.8	5.5	276.9
Rural	55.5	0.4	8.3	130.9
Esquires, gentlemen, officials	123.4	1.3	110.8	529.9
Merchants	39.3	7.0	3.8	97.4
Professionals (including sea captains)	19.1	0.8	0.3	61.6
Farmers only and planters	57.2	0.3	6.2	132.6
Farmers plus other activity, vessel owners, fishermen	71.3	0.0	6.7	252.8
Shopkeepers, innkeepers	10.2	4.2	9.0	28.2
Artisans, chandlers	8.6	0.6	10.6	20.8
Mariners, laborers	4.4	2.3	8.5	41.3
Women, occupation not determined	57.1	0.0	14.8	98.4
Men, occupation not determined	22.2	0.0	0.0	33.0

SOURCE: Sample data, *w**-weighted, Variant Two, See source note to table 7.5.

NOTE: The general note to table 7.5 pertains to this table also except that for the thirteen colonies, reading down in column 1, the *w*-weighted figures are: £82.2, 275.3, 23.0, 2.7, 81.7, 105.1, 82.8, 74.5, 22.8, 89.9, 257.1, 72.2, 37.3, 91.4, 127.8, 15.1, 14.0, 7.9, 95.2, 33.3.

Table 7.11
Slaves and Servants as Percentage of Total Physical Wealth
Held by Socioeconomic Group, 1774

Wealthholder Group	Thirteen Colonies	New England	Middle Colonies	South
All Wealthholders	22.1	0.4	3.9	33.6
Total physical wealth £400 and over	27.5	0.6	2.5	35.5
Total physical wealth £100–399	9.7	0.0	5.3	25.1
Total physical wealth £99 and under	7.1	1.5	0.6	12.4
Younger (age 44 and under)	22.8	0.3	4.8	35.1
Older (age 45 and above)	19.5	0.6	2.6	32.7
Men	21.5	0.5	3.9	33.0
Women	37.0	0.7	13.2	45.8
Urban	6.4	1.0	1.9	43.2
Rural	24.0	0.2	4.8	33.4
Esquires, gentlemen, officials	26.3	0.4	9.1	41.4
Merchants	11.0	1.2	0.4	31.0
Professionals (including sea captains)	7.2	0.3	0.1	12.0
Farmers only and planters	23.9	0.2	3.4	33.5
Farmers plus other activity, vessel owners, fishermen	19.4	0.0	2.6	31.4
Shopkeepers, innkeepers	5.4	1.9	4.1	14.5
Artisans, chandlers	8.1	0.5	7.3	19.3
Mariners, laborers	8.1	4.4	12.8	10.8
Women, occupation not determined	43.2	0.0	17.0	45.8
Men, occupation not determined	43.4	0.0	0.0	60.5

SOURCE: Sample data, w^*-weighted, Variant Two, See source note to table 7.5.

Table 7.12
Percentage of Wealthholders Having Business Inventory
by Socioeconomic Group, 1774

Wealthholder Group	*Thirteen Colonies*	*New England*	*Middle Colonies*	*South*
All Wealthholders	6.4	6.7	11.8	2.4
Total physical wealth £400 and over	7.8	12.1	28.0	2.4
Total physical wealth £100–399	5.1	6.0	6.9	1.8
Total physical wealth £99 and under	6.9	5.0	16.3	3.0
Younger (age 44 and under)	5.2	7.2	8.4	1.7
Older (age 45 and above)	4.2	5.0	8.7	0.1
Men	6.8	7.1	12.3	2.6
Women	1.1	0.0	4.3	0.0
Urban	19.2	16.7	24.6	6.5
Rural	4.7	3.4	9.3	2.4
Esquires, gentlemen, officials	2.3	4.0	0.0	0.0
Merchants	52.4	71.5	90.9	38.6
Professionals (including sea captains)	4.5	7.9	0.0	1.5
Farmers only and planters	0.4	0.0	0.0	0.0
Farmers plus other activity, vessel owners, fishermen	20.1	4.0	52.7	15.1
Shopkeepers, innkeepers	58.2	56.4	56.5	29.1
Artisans, chandlers	21.8	23.3	41.4	17.2
Mariners, laborers	? 1	0.0	7.0	0.0
Women, occupation not determined	0.0	0.0	0.0	0.0
Men, occupation not determined	1.6	0.0	0.0	0.0

SOURCE: Sample data, w^{+}-weighted, Variant Two, See source note to table 7.6.

NOTE: These figures pertain to only one part, the larger part, of the component "business equipment and inventory, nonfarm" of tables 7.13 and 7.14.

Table 7.13
Business Equipment and Inventory, Nonfarm, Average Value
Held by Socioeconomic Group, 1774

Wealthholder Group	Thirteen Colonies	New England	Middle Colonies	South
All Wealthholders	4.9	5.8	8.0	1.5
Total physical wealth £400 and over	13.7	21.7	51.1	1.3
Total physical wealth £100–399	3.3	4.2	2.7	3.5
Total physical wealth £99 and under	0.5	0.3	1.5	0.3
Younger (age 44 and under)	3.3	5.3	4.0	0.6
Older (age 45 and above)	8.6	7.9	18.3	1.5
Men	5.0	6.1	8.5	1.4
Women	4.1	0.0	12.0	3.1
Urban	26.0	19.2	43.7	22.7
Rural	1.5	1.3	2.2	1.3
Esquires, gentlemen, officials	1.7	2.4	0.0	0.0
Merchants	107.0	133.3	279.7	67.8
Professionals (including sea captains)	10.4	15.9	0.0	0.3
Farmers only and planters	0.2	0.5	0.0	0.0
Farmers plus other activity, vessel owners, fishermen	19.8	1.6	11.6	4.8
Shopkeepers, innkeepers	57.1	44.7	82.0	0.4
Artisans, chandlers	4.0	2.8	9.8	2.5
Mariners, laborers	3.0	3.5	0.9	0.1
Women, occupation not determined	1.8	0.0	0.0	3.1
Men, occupation not determined	—[a]	0.0	0.0	0.1

SOURCE: Sample data, w^*-weighted, Variant Two, See source note to table 7.5.

NOTE: The general note to table 7.5 pertains to this table also except that the w-weighted values for thirteen colonies in column 1, reading down, are: £6.4, 16.5, 4.5, 0.7, 3.9, 11.8, 6.4, 6.2, 40.4, 2.1, 2.0, 136.7, 11.8, 0.2, 32.1, 81.1, 5.9, 4.0, 3.0, 0.2.

[a] Less than one-half pound.

Table 7.14
Business Equipment and Inventory, Nonfarm, as Percentage of
Total Physical Wealth, Held by Socioeconomic Group, 1774

Wealthholder Group	*Thirteen Colonies*	*New England*	*Middle Colonies*	*South*
All Wealthholders	1.7	3.6	4.3	0.4
Total physical wealth £400 and over	1.7	4.3	9.5	0.2
Total physical wealth £100–399	1.9	2.9	1.5	2.0
Total physical wealth £99 and under	2.0	1.2	7.1	0.5
Younger (age 44 and under)	1.1	4.1	2.2	0.1
Older (age 45 and above)	2.2	3.1	6.7	0.3
Men	1.7	3.6	4.4	0.3
Women	3.1	0.0	11.7	1.4
Urban	11.3	10.0	15.2	3.5
Rural	0.6	0.8	1.3	0.3
Esquires, gentlemen, officials	0.2	0.8	0.0	0.0
Merchants	20.7	23.7	32.6	21.5
Professionals (including sea captains)	2.2	5.9	0.0	—[a]
Farmers only and planters	[a]	0.3	0.0	0.0
Farmers plus other activity, vessel owners, fishermen	4.8	1.1	4.5	0.6
Shopkeepers, innkeepers	28.9	20.4	37.0	0.2
Artisans, chandlers	3.4	2.4	6.8	1.8
Mariners, laborers	4.1	6.7	1.3	—[a]
Women, occupation not determined	1.3	0.0	0.0	1.4
Men, occupation not determined	0.2	0.0	0.0	0.1

SOURCE: Sample data, w^*-weighted, Variant Two. See source note to table 7.5.

[a] Less than 0.05 percent.

Table 7.15
Other Producers' Goods, Average Value
Held by Socioeconomic Group, 1774
(*In Pounds Sterling*)

Wealthholder Group	Thirteen Colonies	New England	Middle Colonies	South
All Wealthholders	39.3	20.4	38.0	57.2
Total physical wealth £400 and over	83.3	47.0	59.4	104.6
Total physical wealth £100–399	37.3	23.7	49.3	36.6
Total physical wealth £99 and under	9.6	5.4	6.1	16.7
Younger (age 44 and under)	41.6	19.4	45.4	62.9
Older (age 45 and above)	44.4	26.2	43.1	70.6
Men	40.6	21.6	40.9	59.2
Women	21.3	2.8	26.0	32.8
Urban	13.3	13.1	10.9	42.8
Rural	43.6	23.0	45.6	57.3
Esquires, gentlemen, officials	60.6	36.8	110.4	142.2
Merchants	25.2	22.2	15.6	9.7
Professionals (including sea captains)	17.8	18.3	4.7	19.2
Farmers only and planters	48.2	25.5	53.3	61.3
Farmers plus other activity, vessel owners, fishermen	57.7	19.9	38.4	123.6
Shopkeepers, innkeepers	15.3	14.9	13.8	2.9
Artisans, chandlers	13.2	11.9	13.9	12.6
Mariners, laborers	8.6	7.5	7.6	52.6
Women, occupation not determined	19.9	2.4	27.1	32.8
Men, occupation not determined	8.0	5.3	4.5	6.6

SOURCE: Sample data, w^*-weighted, Variant Two, See source note to table 7.5.

NOTE: "Other producers' goods," in this table, include livestock, crops, producers' durable equipment of farm and household, and producers' perishable materials of household. It excludes slaves, nonfarm business equipment, nonfarm business inventory. No table parallel to 7.6 is shown because the numbers having these goods are virtually 100 percent in all instances. The general note to table 7.5 pertains to this table also, except that the values for thirteen colonies in column 1, reading down, are: £58.7, 119.3, 54.5, 14.7, 63.1, 67.2, 60.6, 33.6, 19.4, 63.6, 102.2, 35.6, 24.8, 70.2, 93.4, 21.2, 18.4, 13.3, 32.5, 10.6.

Table 7.16

Other Producers' Goods as Percentages of Total Physical Wealth
Held by Socioeconomic Group, 1774

Wealthholder Group	Thirteen Colonies	New England	Middle Colonies	South
All Wealthholders	15.8	12.7	20.3	14.5
Total physical wealth £400 and over	11.9	9.3	11.0	12.4
Total physical wealth £100–399	22.9	16.3	26.8	21.2
Total physical wealth £99 and under	38.5	21.5	29.0	50.6
Younger (age 44 and under)	17.5	15.0	24.5	15.9
Older (age 45 and above)	12.4	10.4	15.7	11.8
Men	15.8	12.8	21.0	14.4
Women	16.6	6.6	25.2	15.3
Urban	5.6	6.8	3.8	6.7
Rural	16.9	15.2	26.4	14.7
Esquires, gentlemen, officials	10.4	11.7	9.0	11.1
Merchants	5.4	3.9	1.8	3.1
Professionals (including sea captains)	4.8	6.8	2.0	3.8
Farmers only and planters	10.4	10.4	29.6	15.4
Farmers plus other activity, vessel owners, fishermen	14.1	13.8	14.9	15.5
Shopkeepers, innkeepers	7.5	6.8	6.2	1.5
Artisans, chandlers	10.7	10.4	9.6	9.1
Mariners, laborers	13.7	14.4	11.4	13.8
Women, occupation not determined	14.9	7.5	32.9	15.3
Men, occupation not determined	14.2	9.8	28.7	12.0

SOURCE: Sample data, w^*-weighted, Variant Two, See source note to table 7.5.

NOTE: For definition of "other producers' goods" see general note to table 7.15.

Table 7.17
Consumers' Goods, Average Value Held by Socioeconomic Group, 1774
(*In Pounds Sterling*)

Wealthholder Group	Thirteen Colonies	New England	Middle Colonies	South
All Wealthholders	19.9	19.2	18.1	30.1
Total physical wealth £400 and over	40.9	47.4	36.2	39.1
Total physical wealth £100–399	17.1	17.2	18.1	15.5
Total physical wealth £99 and under	8.3	8.7	7.9	7.9
Younger (age 44 and under)	20.0	17.6	18.6	24.1
Older (age 45 and above)	24.7	24.4	22.5	27.2
Men	20.0	19.6	18.2	22.3
Women	18.0	13.7	13.7	23.3
Urban	29.4	27.6	30.1	73.3
Rural	18.4	16.5	16.0	21.7
Esquires, gentlemen, officials	40.6	30.6	80.8	61.8
Merchants	64.9	89.1	69.8	25.1
Professionals (including sea captains)	35.2	40.2	17.8	29.2
Farmers only and planters	17.5	13.7	17.3	21.3
Farmers plus other activity, vessel owners, fishermen	32.5	22.0	13.0	42.4
Shopkeepers, innkeepers	26.2	36.4	25.8	16.0
Artisans, chandlers	13.5	13.6	16.4	11.8
Mariners, laborers	14.0	12.2	18.9	12.5
Women, occupation not determined	19.0	12.9	12.1	23.3
Men, occupation not determined	8.0	9.0	9.7	4.1

SOURCE: Sample data, w^*-weighted, Variant Two, See source note to table 7.5.

NOTE: "Consumers' goods" includes apparel, other consumers' durables, consumers' perishables. No table is shown for "percentage having" the goods because the numbers are approximately 100 percent in all instances. The general note to table 7.5 pertains to this table also except that w-weighted figures for thirteen colonies in column 1, reading down, are: £27.6, 54.2, 23.6, 11.2, 28.3, 34.3, 27.7, 25.6, 43.4, 25.7, 63.7, 78.3, 46.9, 24.3, 47.9, 34.9, 18.9, 21.4, 27.8, 10.0.

Table 7.18
Consumers' Goods as Percentages of Total Physical Wealth
Held by Socioeconomic Group, 1774

Wealthholder Group	Thirteen Colonies	New England	Middle Colonies	South
All Wealthholders	7.4	11.9	9.7	5.7
Total physical wealth £400 and over	5.5	9.3	6.7	4.7
Total physical wealth £100–399	9.9	11.9	9.9	8.9
Total physical wealth £99 and under	29.6	34.7	37.6	24.2
Younger (age 44 and under)	7.9	13.6	10.0	6.2
Older (age 45 and above)	6.4	9.7	8.2	4.6
Men	7.2	11.6	9.4	5.4
Women	12.8	32.3	13.3	10.9
Urban	12.1	14.4	10.5	11.4
Rural	6.8	10.9	9.3	5.6
Esquires, gentlemen, officials	6.5	9.8	6.6	4.8
Merchants	11.9	15.8	8.1	8.0
Professionals (including sea captains)	9.0	14.9	7.4	5.7
Farmers only and planters	6.5	8.8	9.6	5.3
Farmers plus other activity, vessel owners, fishermen	7.4	15.3	5.1	5.3
Shopkeepers, innkeepers	12.3	16.6	11.6	8.2
Artisans, chandlers	11.0	11.9	11.3	8.7
Mariners, laborers	21.9	23.4	28.3	3.2
Women, occupation not determined	12.6	40.6	14.7	10.9
Men, occupation not determined	12.9	16.6	61.8	7.5

SOURCE: Sample data, *w**-weighted, Variant Two, See source note to table 7.5.

Table 7.19
Percentages of High-, Middle-, Low-Wealth Farmers Having
Selected Forms of Wealth, 1774

Wealthholder Group and Kind of Wealth	Thirteen Colonies	New England	New Jersey Pennsylv. Delaware	South
Total Physical Wealth of £400 and over				
Slaves and servants	81.6	7.6	9.6	98.4
Land (real estate)	92.1	100.0	100.0	90.3
Livestock	97.9	93.3	98.5	98.4
Crops	63.1	45.5	96.9	61.4
Business Inventory, nonfarm	0.0	0.0	0.0	0.0
Financial Assets	38.9	72.0	100.0	28.0
Total Physical Wealth of £100–399				
Slaves and servants	29.0	0.0	17.9	63.1
Land (real estate)	89.7	98.8	99.1	68.8
Livestock	95.2	99.3	93.8	95.7
Crops	64.0	22.6	86.0	50.0
Business Inventory, nonfarm	0.0	0.0	0.0	0.0
Financial Assets	66.1	62.9	79.1	46.0
Total Physical Wealth of £99 and under				
Slaves and servants	4.7	0.0	2.4	7.2
Land (real estate)	37.7	59.8	59.1	21.6
Livestock	83.5	79.6	56.4	90.5
Crops	47.8	12.2	60.3	61.0
Business Inventory, nonfarm	0.0	0.0	0.0	0.0
Financial Assets	42.6	45.1	75.4	32.5

SOURCE: Sample data w-weighted, Variant Two. The same percentages are assumed to hold also for all living wealthholders (w*-weighted). For the thirteen colonies the figures include an estimate for New York hybrid.

NOTE: Corresponding figures, in greater detail, for "all farmers" are found in tables 7.77, 7.87, 7.97, 7.107 of *American Colonial Wealth*, either edition, and for "farmers plus other activity" in its tables 7.78, 7.88, 7.98, 7.108. They are found with Variant Two weights for the thirteen colonies for merchants and one farmer group, and for the South for two farmer groups, in *American Colonial Wealth*, 2d ed., tables A.7.185 through A.7.196. "Farmers" and "all farmers" include planters and exclude farmers or planters with such side activities as blacksmith, cooper, merchant, fisherman, who are classed as "farmers plus other activity."

Table 7.20
Wealth Components of High-Wealth Farmers, Average Value, 1774
(In Pounds Sterling)

Kind of Wealth	Thirteen Colonies	New England	New Jersey Pennsylv. Delaware	South
Net Worth	637.2	396.0	519.2	707.7
Total Physical Wealth	676.3	428.9	359.1	776.7
Slaves and servants	203.2	2.0	3.2	277.3
Land (real estate)	350.3	346.4	235.6	366.0
Livestock	57.5	35.6	49.4	63.7
Crops	19.3	4.6	27.3	21.8
Business equipment and inventory, nonfarm	0.5	3.4	0.0	0.0
Other producers' goods	13.9	12.6	16.0	14.1
Consumers' goods	31.4	24.2	27.6	33.8
Financial Assets	41.6	32.6	235.6	16.0
Financial Liabilities	80.7	65.5	75.4	85.0

SOURCE: Sample data, w^*-weighted, Variant Two. For the thirteen colonies the figures include an estimate for New York hybrid.

NOTE: The general note to table 7.19 pertains to this table also. High wealth is defined as total physical wealth of £400 sterling or more. In this table and succeeding tables "other producers' goods" include producers' durable equipment of farm and household, and producers' perishable materials of household. For corresponding regional figures for only probate types (sample data w-weighted), the above figures may be multiplied by the same factors as in the general note to table 7.5. For the thirteen colonies, reading down in column 1, the w-weighted figures are: £880.4, 936.4, 296.8, 470.6, 79.4, 27.4, 0.4, 18.6, 43.1, 53.7, 109.7.

Table 7.21
Wealth Components of Middle-Wealth Farmers, Average Value, 1774
(*In Pounds Sterling*)

Kind of Wealth	Thirteen Colonies	New England	New Jersey Pennsylv. Delaware	South
Net Worth	171.0	110.5	204.0	173.0
Total Physical Wealth	171.6	151.1	180.6	177.2
Slaves and servants	14.9	0.0	7.2	45.9
Land (real estate)	96.8	108.9	100.9	76.3
Livestock	26.9	18.7	31.3	27.0
Crops	7.8	1.0	14.7	2.3
Business equipment and inventory, nonfarm	—[a]	0.0	0.1	0.1
Other producers' goods	9.2	8.2	9.0	10.5
Consumers' goods	15.9	14.3	17.4	14.9
Financial Assets	35.1	9.3	56.9	20.1
Financial Liabilities	35.7	50.0	33.5	24.4

Source: Sample data, w^*-weighted, Variant Two. For the thirteen colonies the figures include an estimate for New York hybrid.

Note: The general note to table 7.19 pertains to this table also. Middle wealth is defined as total physical wealth of £100–399 sterling. For corresponding regional figures for only probate types (sample data w-weighted), the above figures may be multiplied by the same factors as in the general note to table 7.5. For the thirteen colonies, reading down in column 1, the w-weighted figures are: £243.8, 239.0, 23.9, 130.4, 38.3, 11.6, 0.1, 12.9, 21.9, 51.4, 46.5.

[a] Less than one-half pound.

Table 7.22
Wealth Components of Low-Wealth Farmers, Average Value, 1774
(*In Pounds Sterling*)

Kind of Wealth	Thirteen Colonies	New England	New Jersey Pennsylv. Delaware	South
Net Worth	28.9	30.5	51.4	32.2
Total Physical Wealth	34.5	30.2	29.4	40.1
Slaves and servants	0.7	0.0	0.1	1.4
Land (real estate)	10.0	13.6	13.6	6.1
Livestock	9.3	4.2	3.6	15.3
Crops	1.6	0.1	1.1	3.0
Business equipment and inventory, nonfarm	0.0	0.0	0.0	0.0
Other producers' goods	4.7	4.2	2.4	5.9
Consumers' goods	8.2	8.0	8.5	8.3
Financial Assets	13.2	19.3	29.2	5.2
Financial Liabilities	18.8	18.9	7.1	13.1

SOURCE: Sample data, w*-weighted, Variant Two. For the thirteen colonies the figures include an estimate for New York hybrid.

NOTE: The general note to table 7.19 pertains to this table also. Low wealth is defined as total physical wealth of £99 sterling or less. For corresponding regional figures for only probate type (sample data w-weighted), the above figures may be multiplied by the same factors as in the general note to table 7.5. For the thirteen colonies, reading down in column 1, the w-weighted figures are: £42.3, 48.9, 1.1, 12.7, 14.4, 2.6, 0.0, 6.8, 11.4, 16.4, 23.0

Table 7.23
Wealth Components of High-Wealth Farmers, as Percentage of
Total Physical Wealth, 1774

Kind of Wealth	Thirteen Colonies	New England	New Jersey Pennsylv. Delaware	South
Net Worth	94.0	92.3	144.6	91.1
Total Physical Wealth	100.0	100.0	100.0	100.0
Slaves and servants	31.7	0.5	0.9	35.7
Land (real estate)	50.3	80.8	65.6	47.1
Livestock	8.6	8.3	13.8	8.2
Crops	2.9	1.0	7.6	2.8
Business equipment and inventory, nonfarm	—[a]	0.8	0.0	0.0
Other producers' goods	2.0	2.9	4.4	1.8
Consumers' goods	4.6	5.6	7.7	4.4
Financial Assets	5.7	7.6	65.6	2.1
Financial Liabilities	11.7	15.3	21.0	10.9

SOURCE: Sample data, w^*-weighted, Variant Two, from table 7.20. For the thirteen colonies, the figures include an estimate for New York hybrid.

[a] Less than 0.05 percent.

Table 7.24
Wealth Components of Middle-Wealth Farmers, as Percentage of
Total Physical Wealth, 1774

Kind of Wealth	Thirteen Colonies	New England	New Jersey Pennsylv. Delaware	South
Net Worth	102.0	73.1	113.0	97.6
Total Physical Wealth	100.0	100.0	100.0	100.0
Slaves and servants	10.0	0.0	4.0	25.9
Land (real estate)	54.6	72.1	55.9	43.1
Livestock	16.0	12.4	17.3	15.3
Crops	4.9	0.7	8.1	1.3
Business equipment and inventory, nonfarm	—[a]	0.0	0.1	—[a]
Other producers' goods	5.2	5.4	5.0	6.0
Consumers' goods	9.2	9.5	9.6	8.5
Financial Assets	21.5	6.2	31.5	11.4
Financial Liabilities	19.5	33.1	18.6	13.8

SOURCE: Sample data, w^*-weighted, Variant Two, from table 7.21. For the thirteen colonies the figures include an estimate for New York hybrid.

[a] Less than 0.05 percent.

Table 7.25
Wealth Components of Low-Wealth Farmers, as Percentage of
Total Physical Wealth, 1774

Kind of Wealth	Thirteen Colonies	New England	New Jersey Pennsylv. Delaware	South
Net Worth	86.5	101.2	175.1	80.2
Total Physical Wealth	100.0	100.0	100.0	100.0
Slaves and servants	2.4	0.0	0.4	3.5
Land (real estate)	25.9	45.0	46.2	15.3
Livestock	29.3	13.9	12.2	37.8
Crops	5.4	0.5	3.9	7.5
Business equipment and inventory, nonfarm	0.0	0.0	0.0	0.0
Other producers' goods	13.8	13.9	8.7	15.0
Consumers' goods	23.2	26.5	28.9	21.0
Financial Assets	33.5	63.9	99.3	12.9
Financial Liabilities	47.0	62.7	24.1	32.7

SOURCE: Sample data, w^*-weighted, Variant Two, from table 7.22. For the thirteen colonies the figures include an estimate for New York hybrid.

Table 7.26
Wealth Components of Farmers, Including Those with Side Activities,
at Three Wealth Levels, Average Value,
South, 1774

Kind of Wealth	High	Middle	Low
Net Worth	754.9	169.4	32.5
Total Physical Wealth	830.0	173.2	40.3
Slaves and servants	291.6	44.7	1.4
Land (real estate)	392.4	73.2	6.7
Livestock	65.9	27.2	15.0
Crops	25.7	2.2	3.2
Business equipment and inventory, nonfarm	0.8	0.1	0.0
Other producers' goods	16.6	11.1	5.9
Consumers' goods	37.0	14.8	8.3
Financial Assets	27.8	20.2	5.0
Financial Liabilities	102.9	24.0	12.8

SOURCE: Sample data, w^*-weighted, Variant Two.

NOTE: High, middle, and low physical wealth are defined as in tables 7.20 through 7.22. Only in this table "farmers" includes farmer or planter without side activity and also farmer or planter with side activity, such as farmer-merchant, farmer-blacksmith, farmer-tanner, farmer-fisherman. For corresponding figures for only probate types (sample data, w-weighted) the above figures may be multiplied by 1.32.

Table 7.27
Percentages of High- and Middle-Wealth Merchants Having
Selected Forms of Wealth,
Thirteen Colonies and Two Regions, 1774

Wealthholder Group and Kind of Wealth	Thirteen Colonies	New England	New Jersey Pennsylv. Delaware
Total Physical Wealth of £400 and over:			
Slaves and servants	44.7	51.6	15.0
Land (real estate)	99.3	100.0	100.0
Livestock	76.0	71.3	73.0
Crops	10.4	4.1	10.0
Business Inventory, nonfarm	68.8	75.4	90.0
Financial Assets	71.8	66.8	95.0
Total Physical Wealth of £100–399:			
Slaves and servants	64.3	0.0	0.0
Land (real estate)	28.8	100.0	50.0
Livestock	21.9	100.0	0.0
Crops	0.0	0.0	0.0
Business Inventory, nonfarm	100.0	100.0	100.0
Financial Assets	13.8	0.0	100.0

SOURCE: Sample data, w weighted, Variant Two. The same percentages are assumed to hold also for all living wealthholders (w^*-weighted). For the thirteen colonies the figures include an estimate for New York hybrid, and values for the South where numbers of cases do not justify separate presentation.

Table 7.28
Wealth Components of High-Wealth Merchants, Average Value,
Thirteen Colonies and Two Regions, 1774
(In Pounds Sterling)

Kind of Wealth	Thirteen Colonies	New England	New Jersey Pennsylv. Delaware
Net Worth	796.7	536.2	1,053.9
Total Physical Wealth	797.7	694.5	926.5
Slaves and servants	38.9	9.1	4.1
Land (real estate)	462.7	399.4	535.3
Livestock	18.9	18.5	13.8
Crops	1.8	0.1	0.3
Business equipment and inventory, nonfarm	179.8	146.5	301.4
Other producers' goods	11.9	9.5	3.0
Consumers' goods	83.7	111.5	68.4
Financial Assets	252.2	110.4	391.6
Financial Liabilities	253.2	268.7	264.2

SOURCE: Sample data, w^*-weighted, Variant Two. The averages for the thirteen colonies include the New York hybrid estimate and values for the South, where numbers of cases do not justify separate presentation.

NOTE: High wealth is defined as in table 7.20. For corresponding regional figures for only probate types (sample data w-weighted) the above figures may be multiplied by the following factors: New England, 1.49; New Jersey, Pennsylvania, Delaware, 1.37. For the thirteen colonies, reading down in column 1, the w-weighted figures are: £1,215.0, 1,163.5. 70.4, 675.5, 26.9, 3.1, 262.7, 17.7, 107.2, 400.8, 349.2.

Table 7.29
Wealth Components of Middle-Wealth Merchants, Average Value,
Thirteen Colonies and Two Regions, 1774
(In Pounds Sterling)

Kind of Wealth	Thirteen Colonies	New England	New Jersey Pennsylv. Delaware
Net Worth	149.5	56.7	158.1
Total Physical Wealth	235.9	207.0	175.1
Slaves and servants	20.8	0.0	0.0
Land (real estate)	14.4	30.1	28.9
Livestock	1.2	3.5	0.0
Crops	0.0	0.0	0.0
Business equipment and inventory, nonfarm	155.6	152.9	62.9
Other producers' goods	1.5	0.8	0.2
Consumers' goods	42.4	19.8	83.0
Financial Assets	2.3	0.0	17.7
Financial Liabilities	88.6	150.3	34.6

Source: Sample data, w^*-weighted, Variant Two. The averages for the thirteen colonies include the New York hybrid estimate and values for the South, where numbers of cases do not justify separate presentation.

Note: Middle wealth is defined as in table 7.21. For corresponding regional figures for only probate types (sample data w-weighted), the above figures may be multiplied by the following factors: New England, 1.49; Middle Colonies, 1.37. For the thirteen colonies, reading down in column 1, the w-weighted figures are: £226.9, 329.9, 34.1, 15.3, 1.1, 0.0, 214.6, 2.2, 62.4, 3.4, 106.3.

Table 7.30
Wealth Components of High-Wealth Merchants, as Percentage of
Total Physical Wealth,
Thirteen Colonies and Two Regions, 1774

Kind of Wealth	Thirteen Colonies	New England	New Jersey Pennsylv. Delaware
Net Worth	104.4	77.2	113.8
Total Physical Wealth	100.0	100.0	100.0
Slaves and servants	6.0	1.3	0.4
Land (real estate)	58.1	57.5	57.8
Livestock	2.3	2.7	1.5
Crops	0.3	0.0	0.0
Business equipment and inventory, nonfarm	22.6	21.1	32.5
Other producers' goods	1.5	1.4	0.3
Consumers' goods	9.2	16.1	7.4
Financial Assets	34.4	15.9	42.3
Financial Liabilities	30.0	38.7	28.5

SOURCE: Sample data, *w**-weighted, Variant Two, from table 7.28. For the thirteen colonies the figures include an estimate for New York hybrid and values for the South, where numbers of cases do not justify separate presentation.

Table 7.31
Wealth Components of Middle-Wealth Merchants, as Percentage of
Total Physical Wealth,
Thirteen Colonies and Two Regions, 1774

Kind of Wealth	Thirteen Colonies	New England	New Jersey Pennsylv. Delaware
Net Worth	68.8	27.4	90.3
Total Physical Wealth	100.0	100.0	100.0
Slaves and servants	10.3	0.0	0.0
Land (real estate)	4.6	14.5	16.5
Livestock	0.3	1.7	0.0
Crops	0.0	0.0	0.0
Business equipment and inventory, nonfarm	65.1	73.9	35.9
Other producers' goods	0.7	0.4	0.1
Consumers' goods	18.9	9.6	47.4
Financial Assets	1.0	0.0	10.1
Financial Liabilities	32.3	72.6	19.8

SOURCE: Sample data, w^*-weighted, Variant Two, from table 7.29. For the thirteen colonies the figures include an estimate for New York hybrid and for the South where numbers of cases do not justify separate presentation.

Table 7.32
The Richest Women
Three Regions, 1774

Name, I.D., Age, Place	Occupation	NW	TPW	RE	FA	SS	PD	LVK	CD
Kathran Upham 55044 52 Brookfield, Worcester County Massachusetts	Gentlewoman	501	657	552	0	18	28	18	58
Mary Hubbard 54045 70 Boston, Suffolk County Massachusetts	Widow	117	460	15	0	0	20	12	425
Abigail Bradley 42008 67 New Haven County Connecticut	Widow	278	335	256	59	0	15	11	65
Martha Beard 42006 (3) Milford, New Haven County Connecticut	Widow	163	196	196	0	0	0	0	0
Abigail Puffer 54071 70 Stoughton, Suffolk County Massachusetts	Widow	118	155	141	0	0	—[a]	0	14
Miriam Potts 13040 34 Philadelphia, Philadelphia Co. Pennsylvania	Shopkeeper	475	690	287	23	0	4[b]	0	64
Sarah Harper 13046 60 Oxford Township, Phila. Co. Pennsylvania	Widow	688	545	505	143	40	1	0	39
Elizabeth Vanderspeigle 13023 52 Philadelphia, Philadelphia Co. Pennsylvania	Widow	1,544	252	39	1,292	0	1	0	210

Name / Location	Status								
Margaret Williams 13049 (3) Radnor, Chester County Pennsylvania	Widow	3,412	29	0	3,383	0	12	11	17
Ann Stricker 13121 (3) Philadelphia, Philadelphia Co. Pennsylvania	Innkeeper	232	170	48	90	0	101	22	13
Abigail Townsend 01069 (3) Wadmellow Island, Colleton Co. Charleston Dist., S. Carolina	Widow	1,993	1,559	0	0	2,350	168	118	38
Sarah Baker 01005 (3) Charleston District South Carolina	Widow	1,350	1,618	450	0	1,051	3	0	63
Elizabeth Smith 01061 (3) Charleston, Charleston District South Carolina	Widow	2,439	269	0	2,229	86	14	14	169
Elizabeth Brown 72002 (3) Anne Arundel County Maryland	Widow	1,561	1,943	1,102	40	422	228	142	69
Ann Emory 71013 (3) Queen Anne's County Maryland	Widow	1,244	1,251	1,220	0	9	13	11	8

SOURCE: Sample data, unweighted.

NOTE: Portions of notes to tables 6.3 and 6.7 pertain to this table also. Wealth values are in pounds sterling. Following are the wealth abbreviations: NW = Net worth; TPW = Total physical wealth; RE = Real estate; FA = Financial Assets; SS = Slaves and Servants; PD = Producers' Durable Goods; LVK = Livestock; CD = Consumers' Durable Goods. Cases are shown in order of size of total physical wealth by region, except in the South by province. The fifth case for the middle colonies (Stricker 13121) is only the seventh richest, either by total physical wealth or by net worth, but is included because of interest—she was an innkeeper. Williams (13049) is included because she had greatest net worth in the region.

[a] Less than £0.5.

[b] She had £336 in business inventory and £2 in business equipment.

Table 7.33
Selected Individual Wealthholders, 1774

Name, I.D., Age, Place	Occupation	NW	TPW	RE	FA	SS	PD	LVK	CD
Thomas Gerry 51040 72 Marblehead, Essex County Massachusetts	Merchant	5,741	4,143	2,092	1,960	0	611[a]	6	370
William White 54096 58 Boston, Suffolk Co. Massachusetts	Esquire (Inventory mentions goods in store in Queen Street)	15,303	3,793	3,216	11,657	0	155[a]	0	252
Benjamin Coats 54016 (2) Boston. Suffolk County Massachusetts	Trader	482	683	263	162	0	142[a]	138	275
Samuel Neave 13048 68 Philadelphia, Phila. Co. Pennsylvania	Merchant	6,647	8,336	1,623	0	0	118[a]	79	450
George Mellichop 31022 n.d. Murtherkill Hundred Kent Co., Delaware	Merchant	811	471	338	403	0	47[a]	16	28
Edmund Kearney 13101 56 Philadelphia, Phila. Co. Pennsylvania	Merchant	270	362	0	3	0	4[a]	0	200
Alexander Michel 01046 n.d. St. Michael's Parish Charleston Dist., South Carolina	Merchant	2,210	1,453	1,116	757	214	5[a]	0	106

Name / location	Occupation								
Nicholas Fittig 01025 (2) St. George's Parish Charleston Dist., South Carolina	Merchant	454	503	280	0	119	25[a]	19	43
Hugh Houston 83025 n.d. Spotsylvania County Virginia	Merchant	278	356	0	0	53	3[a]	0	63
Roswell Woodward 42036 66 East Haven, New Haven County Connecticut	Farmer and large landowner	859	1,070	857	25	47	89	81	67
Peleg Bryant, Jr. 53007 56 Scituate, Plymouth County Massachusetts	Yeoman	208	201	161	60	0	17	13	20
Edward Breck 54010 36 Dorchester, Suffolk County Massachusetts	Yeoman	5	15	0	0	0	2	1	13
David Powers 52025 68 Greenwich, Hampshire County Massachusetts	Husbandman	−6	13	0	0	0	4	2	5
Charles Jolley 13099 (2) Lower Merion Township Phila. Co., Pennsylvania	Farmer-miller	472	1,638	1,446	49	29	107	15	75
Henry Gristman 11008 (3) Chestnut Hill, Northampton Co. Pennsylvania	Farmer	207	242	210	0	0	30	17	2

Table 7.33 (Continued)
Selected Individual Wealthholders, 1774

Name, I.D., Age, Place	Occupation	NW	TPW	RE	FA	SS	PD	LVK	CD
James Cox 71008 (3) Queen Anne's County Maryland	Planter	2,739	2,709	2,241	63	98	144	104	39
Henry Walthall 83016 36 Chesterfield County Virginia	Planter	3,878	4,021	3,372	0	481	100	85	40
Hugh James 81006 (2) Charlotte County Virginia	Farmer	162	206	99	3	83	9	6	13
Charles Gordon 82014 (2) Brunswick County Virginia	Farmer	-101	21	0	0	0	18	17	3
James Harris 91019 (2) Halifax County North Carolina	Farmer	2,317	2,028	316	351	1,240	386	351	50
Neil McCallister 92014 (2) Orange County North Carolina	Farmer	202	225	0	26	102	101	83	11
Edward Mickleberry 91029 n.d. Halifax County North Carolina	Farmer	16	20	0	0	0	13	10	7

Name / Location	Occupation								
Elijah Postele 01056 (3) Dorchester, Charleston District South Carolina	Planter (Esquire)	12,705	15,561	542	466	11,384	1,182	3	605
Daniel Lewis 01082 (2) Charleston, Charleston District South Carolina	Planter	160	205	0	0	147	30	19	29
Thorndike Proctor 51099 74 Salem, Essex County Massachusetts	Blacksmith	511	685	550	14	0	61	20	59
John Ruggles 54075 36 Boston, Suffolk County Massachusetts	Housewright	353	480	400	0	0	21	11	59
Titus Keyes 55026 35 Northbridge, Worcester County Massachusetts	Blacksmith	16	28	2	0	0	17	2	7
Jeremiah Blake 54008 67 Dorchester, Suffolk County Massachusetts	Weaver	17	26	17	0	0	0	0	10
David Dutton 42019 72 Waterbury, New Haven County Connecticut	Shoemaker	13	16	0	0	0	6	1	9
Jacob Chrystler 13012 43 Philadelphia, Philadelphia Co. Pennsylvania	Tailor	2,170	1,500	1,387	319	0	24	18	88
Samuel Rockhill 21014 (3) Mansfield, Burlington County New Jersey	Wheelwright	562	389	374	173	0	7	7 —[b]	7

Table 7.33 (Continued)
Selected Individual Wealthholders, 1774

Name, I.D., Age, Place	Occupation	NW	TPW	RE	FA	SS	PD	LVK	CD
John Paul Dulmen 13083 50 Philadelphia, Philadelphia Co. Pennsylvania	Baker	29	29	22	0	0	0	0	6
John Hilton 13071 49 Manor of Moorland, Phila. Co. Pennsylvania	Shoemaker	22	20	0	3	0	6	3	12
Sewell Long 71024 (3) Queen Anne's County Maryland	Shipwright	779	624	139	197	296	67	33	58
Robert Henwood 72011 n.d. Anne Arundel County Maryland	Carpenter	10	13	0	0	0	1	0	11
John Cooper 82004 n.d. Southampton County Virginia	Wheelwright	397	410	383	0	0	11	7	13
David Gordon 83018 69 Fairfax County Virginia	Cooper	27	35	0	0	0	16	0	18
Richard Hart 01079 n.d. Charleston, Charleston District South Carolina	Chairmaker	1,834	1,919	1,537	0	233	25	0	92
Ananias Sayrs 01058 (2) Charleston, Charleston District ...	Shoemaker	13	16	0	0	0	1	0	10

	Occupation								
Thorndike Procter III 51098 49 Salem, Essex County Massachusetts	Mariner	590	95	155	495	0	4	0	37
Jonathan Pierpont 54068 79 Boston, Suffolk County Massachusetts	Mariner	EJ	14	0	0	0	2	0	12
John Nickerson 53022 45 Scituate, Plymouth County Massachusetts	Mariner	11	7	0	7	0	1	0	5
John Giddings 51041 26 Salem, Essex County Massachusetts	Mariner	4	7	0	0	0	0	0	7
William Heaslton 13047 (3) Philadelphia, Philadelphia Co. Pennsylvania	Mariner	724	621	467	220	12	17	9	98
Thomas Hardy 13096 33 Philadelphia, Philadelphia Co. Pennsylvania	Mariner	24	24	0	0	0	0	0	24
William Wallace 01071 n.d. Charleston, Charleston District South Carolina	Mariner	625	270	270	355	0	0	0	0
Thomas Comb 01016 n.d. Charleston, Charleston Dist. South Carolina	Mariner	10	12	0	0	0	3	0	10

Table 7.33 (Continued)
Selected Individual Wealthholders, 1774

Name, I.D., Age, Place	Occupation	NW	TPW	RE	FA	SS	PD	LVK	CD
Thomas Ring 54073 21 Medway, Suffolk County Massachusetts	Laborer	15	14	0	10	0	9	9	5
Enoch Perkins 51087 43 Topsfield, Essex County Massachusetts	Laborer	5	11	0	0	0	6	4	5
Jacob Keyser 13009 44 Philadelphia, Philadelphia Co. Pennsylvania	Laborer	134	80	75	57	0	0	0	4
John Thomas 13122 63 Philadelphia County Pennsylvania	Laborer	4	4	0	0	0	1	0	3
Cyrus 01017 (3) St. Andrew's Parish, Charleston Dist., South Carolina	Free Negro	152	196	0	0	186	10	10	0
Margaret Crawford 55004 60 Rutland, Worcester County Massachusetts	Widow	160	142	100	23	0	28	22	4
Mary Dwinell 51030 90 Topsfield, Essex County Massachusetts	Widow	13	7	0	10	0	1	0	5

Sarah Draper 31016 n.d. Mispillion Hundred Kent County, Delaware	Widow	243	197	0	46	125	68	58	2
Mary Hardy 13037 (3) Horsham Township Philadelphia Co., Pennsylvania	Widow	53	7	0	29	0	34	26	15
Anne Middleton 72016 (3) Anne Arundel County Maryland	Widow	1,1-3	436	0	804	0	157	0 277	
Sarah Brown 71003 (3) Queen Anne's County Maryland	Widow	14	25	0	0	7	7	5	11
Martha Miller 92017 n.d. Orange County North Carolina	Widow	3	11	0	0	0	6	3	4
Mary Duva 01022 (3) Christ Church, Charleston Dist. South Carolina	Widow	37	45	0	0	0	16	15	29

SOURCE: Sample data, unweighted.

NOTE: Wealth values are in pounds sterling. Following are the wealth abbreviations: NW = Net worth; TPW = Total physical wealth; RE = Real estate; FA = Financial Assets; PD = Producers' Durable Goods; LVK = Livestock; CD = Consumers' Durable Goods. Number within parenthesis indicates age class: class 2 = age 26–44; class 3 = age 45 and over; n.d. indicates not determined. For caution in interpretation of occupational classification see chapter 5, text and notes. Portions of notes to tables 6.3, 6.7 and 7.3 pertain to this table also. Cases are shown in order of size of total physical wealth by occupation group, by region except in the South by province. There were no cases in the middle colonies or in South Carolina of farmers with total physical wealth under £30, and there were no laborers in the southern sample.

[a] The merchants had the following amounts of business inventory and business equipment, respectively: Gerry 1,040, 574; White 170, 0; Coats 0, 0; Neave 6,141, 18; Mellicho 53, 28; Kearney 158, 4; Michel 0, 0; Fittig 36, 2; Houston 237, 0.

[b] Less than £.05.

CHAPTER EIGHT

Inequality Compared with Other Times and Places

SOME judgment about the equality or inequality of a variable such as wealth is best gained by comparison with what prevailed at other times or places. What was the distribution of wealth in 1774 like compared with some other points in time, or with contemporary England or Europe? Unfortunately, other overall or macro studies are scarce, and mostly not closely comparable for a variety of reasons. We may, however, look at some that seem most interesting or relevant to the question of whether the rich have grown richer or the poor poorer.

As a point of departure, the high degree of wealth inequality reached in the colonies by 1774, especially in New England and the South, is summarized in tables 8.1 and 8.2 The first table shows the portion of wealth owned by the top 10 percent. If we focus on only free wealthholders, this figure may be said to have been roughly a little over 50 percent, but higher for net worth. In the middle colonies it was somewhat lower. When we include the adult male slaves and indentured servants in the universe considered, inequality was substantially greater. The proportion of total physical wealth held by the top 10 percent, on this basis, reached the figure of 56 percent in the colonies as a whole. This figure was heavily influenced by the South. In the two northern regions it was slightly higher than among

Table 8.1
Inequality Comparison,
Thirteen Colonies and Three Regions, 1774
(Percentage Share of Wealth Held by Top 10 Percent)

	Thirteen Colonies	*New England*	*N. Jersey Pennsyl. Delaware*	*South*
Free Wealthholders:				
Net worth	55	57	42	49
Total physical wealth	51	47	35	47
Nonhuman wealth	—	—	—	50
Free and Nonfree Potential Wealthholders:				
Total physical wealth	56	48	37	69

SOURCE: Sample data, w^*B-weighted. Tables 6.1, 6.2, 6.11, 6.14, 6.15, and *American Colonial Wealth*, tables 7.181 and 7.182.

only the free but still below 50 percent, whereas it reached a high of 69 percent in the South.

A similar general view of high American colonial wealth inequality in 1774 is given by the Gini measure of table 8.2. This value was 0.73 for total physical wealth for the universe of free and nonfree potential wealthholders in the thirteen colonies and 0.83 on that basis for the South. If we exclude slaves and servants from the universe of wealthholders, this value for the free wealthholders dropped to 0.66 for total physical wealth, and a higher 0.73 for net worth for the thirteen colonies.

The composite inequality figures for the thirteen colonies in 1774 reflect, in small part, the extremes of wealth and poverty in the relatively few large cities, which contained less than 5 percent of the population. They also reflect lesser but still substantial differences in some of the larger towns in New England, the region with the greatest number of urbanized places and relatively largest urban population. They further reflect differences in wealth of young and old, of men and women, among occupational groups, and the wide spread in wealth within the overwhelmingly largest occupational category, that of farmers. Such differences were examined in chapter 7. I defer discussion of the figures in table 8.3 and the lower panels of 8.2 for America at later dates until we have considered comparisons with England and with earlier times in the colonies.

Table 8.2
Inequality Comparison
National and Regional, 1774 to 1962
(Gini Coefficient)

	Thirteen Colonies, United States	New England	N. Jersey Pennsylv. Delaware	South
Free Wealthholders:				
(1) 1774—Net worth	0.73	0.80	0.60	0.68
(2) 1774—Total physical wealth	0.66	0.64	0.54	0.67
(3) 1774—Nonhuman wealth	—	—	—	0.67
Free and Nonfree Potential Wealthholders:				
(4) 1774—Total physical wealth	0.73	0.65	0.57	0.83
Free Adult Males:				
(5) 1860—Total wealth	0.83		0.81[a]	0.85[b]
White Adult Males:				
(6) 1870—Total wealth	0.81		0.81[a]	0.82
All Adult Males:				
(7) 1870—Total wealth	0.83		0.82[a]	0.87
Consumer Units:				
(8) 1962—Wealth (approximates net worth)	0.76[c]		—	—

SOURCE: Lines 1 through 4, probate data from the present study, sample data $w*B$-weighted, tables 6.1, 6.2, 6.11, 6.14, and 6.15, and *American Colonial Wealth*, tables 7.181 and 7.182. Lines 5 through 7, U.S. manuscript census data sampled by Lee Soltow: Soltow (1975a:103) and Soltow (1971b:838). Line 8, Household survey data Projector and Weiss (1966:30).

NOTE: Wealth in slaves is included in lines 1, 2, 4, and 5. Consumer units on line 8 comprise families of two or more persons and also unrelated (single) individuals. Soltow's Gini coefficient on line 5 of 0.83 for the United States compares with one of 0.82 for a preliminary tabulation from the 1860 census by Gallman (1969:6). See Jones (1972), table 6. The figure of 0.85 on line 5 for the South compares with one of 0.74 for Texas from a sample from the 1860 manuscript census by Campbell and Lowe (1977:133). See text for argument that the 1860 measures should include *all* adult males.

[a] In the North.
[b] Soltow (1975a:103) shows this number carried to three decimal places as 0.845.
[c] Soltow (1975a:115) suggests that in view of the fact there were fewer in the youngest age class in 1962 than in 1870, and in view of the age-wealth relationship he found in 1870 (ibid.:109–10), the Gini coefficient in 1870 might be construed to be 0.3 Gini points lower (i.e., 0.80) to allow for the younger population in 1870. He suggests (ibid.:183) that as a consequence the Gini coefficient in 1962 was only about 5 percent less than that of 1870. Paglin (1975:607) suggests that if complete allowance were made in 1962 for the age-wealth profile (i.e., plotting as the P curve in figure 20 the cumulative wealth from youngest to oldest by age class intervals) the true 1962 inequality due to factors other than age would be the lower Paglin-Gini of 0.50 rather than the Lorenz-Gini of 0.76. A similar calculation for 1774, shown in figure 12, reduced my Lorenz-Gini from 0.73 to a Paglin-Gini of 0.51. I have not attempted such Paglin-Ginis for 1860 or 1870, but we can be sure they would be substantially lower than the figures of this table. Williamson and Lindert (1977:51–3) tested but did not find that differing age composition of men from 1774 to 1860 accounts for the seeming increase in wealth inequality to that date.

Table 8.3
Inequality Comparison,
National and Regional, 1860 to 1962
(Percentage Share of Wealth Held by Top 10 Percent)

	United States	North	South
Total Wealth:			
(1) 1860—Free adult males	73[a]	68	75
(2) 1870—White adult males	68	67	70
(3) 1870—All adult males	70	67	77
Farm and Home Wealth:			
(4) 1890—Families	72[b]	—	—
Wealth (approximates net worth):			
(5) 1962—Consumer units	62[c]	—	—

SOURCE: Lines 1, 2, and 3: Soltow (1975a:99, table 4.2. Line 4: Holmes (1893:591–92) as articulated by Williamson and Lindert (1977:78–79), on the basis of 1890 census data on owned homes and farms net of mortgage for 22 states, extrapolated to a "guesstimated" national distribution. Line 5: Projector and Weiss (1966), interpolated.

[a] Gallman (1969:6) estimated 71 percent for the top 10 percent of free families in 1860.

[b] The Holmes figure was 71 percent, as presented by Gallman (1968:320–21), on the basis of Merwin (1939:3, 5–9, 13–17). Soltow also made calculations from the farm and home census for 1890 (1975a:116, 197 n. 25). He made similar assumptions to those of Holmes (e.g., that tenants had no wealth). Soltow does not show percentage shares but presents Gini coefficients of 0.79 for farmers, 0.89 for nonfarmers, and 0.85 for all. He compares these with his 1870 sample results for real estate for males of Gini coefficients 0.79 for farmers, 0.91 for nonfarmers, and 0.86 for all men, arguing that inequality in the United States in 1890 was about the same as it was in 1870.

[c] Interpolation from Federal Reserve study data points shown in note 52. Williamson and Lindert (1977:87–98) raise questions as to whether this figure is too high and discuss reasons for discrepancies. The basis of their questions is comparison with estimates for the entire population made from upper-wealth estate tax data by Smith and Franklin (1974, and unpublished estimates following Lampman 1962). Williamson and Lindert (1977) suggest that appropriate adjustments might greatly reduce the 1962 Federal Reserve survey figure to 46 or 36 percent (depending on wealth definition) as the share held by the top 10 percent (see their table 3, p. 44 and table 20, p. 90). The same adjustments would reduce to 21 or 15 the interpolated share held by the top 1 percent (as opposed to the 34 percent in my table 8.11).

A final resolution of this problem exceeds the scope of this chapter and the reader is referred to section 5.2 in Williamson and Lindert (1977) for some of the issues. In that and the following section, they conclude that the estimates by Smith and Franklin from 1958 on fit with those by Lampman from 1929 to 1956 (shown in my table 8.10), the entire series showing an increase from 1922 to 1929 in the wealth share held by the top 1 percent of the population, a downdrift from 1929 to the mid-1950s, and a rather steady figure from that time to 1972. (Williamson and Lindert 1977:88, table 19, based on Lampman 1962:202, 204, and Smith and Franklin 1974 and unpublished estimates). Soltow (1975a:102) graphs the 1962 Federal Reserve data as compared with his findings for adult males in 1860 and 1870; he compares 1962 data (ibid.:114) from the Internal Revenue Service for net estates over $60,000 with the upper portion of his 1870 distribution, and finds similar slopes. He concludes that his analysis confirms Lampman's findings concerning the shares of the top group of families, namely the top 1 and 2 percent. He suggests (ibid.:123) that perhaps the share of the top percentile in 1962 was 29.

CONTEMPORARY AND LATER ENGLAND AND EUROPE

In England, slavery was not practiced in the seventeenth and eighteenth centuries. Consequently, there is no problem there of inclusion or exclusion of a universe of nonfree persons or families. Any comparison is with a universe of free family heads or persons, as in Gregory King's (1936:31) famous income estimate for 1688. Lee Soltow[1] has graphed a Lorenz curve from King's data. He computed that they yield a Gini coefficient of 0.55, which might be increased as much as 10 percent (e.g., to 0.61) if dispersion within each of 26 socioeconomic classes were accounted for. Using Patrick Colquhoun's[2] estimates for 1801–3 for England and Wales, he found a Gini coefficient of 0.56, and for Great Britain and Ireland in 1812 of 0.54, again for income, not wealth. For other income estimates, mostly for the United Kingdom (one for Great Britain and Ireland, beginning in 1867, which used income tax data), he found Gini coefficients ranging from 0.52 down to 0.34 in 1962–63. There were some possible alternate high values for Arthur Bowley's estimates of 1880 and 1913 of 0.63 and 0.59, respectively. On the basis of this evidence, despite some changes in shapes of Lorenz curves, Soltow (1968:21–22) offered for the United Kingdom the tentative hypothesis that long-run income inequality did not change in the eighteenth and nineteenth centuries. He found no indication of increased inequality in the third of a century before the First World War. He noted that only since that war has there been more inequality, and this increase has been substantial. Williamson, using much of the same and some additional evidence, suggests that the peak of income inequality in the United Kingdom was reached in the Napoleonic era, followed by a downdrift over the balance of the nineteenth century.[3]

There has been more than a generation of debate among British historians as to whether the standard of living of the British (or the English) worker rose prior to 1795, declined to 1840, and has since increased. A useful summary is contained in A. J. Taylor's (1960:17, 28–31) reappraisal. He and others strongly suggest that English workers shared in the income gains at least from 1800 on. Among the works Taylor cites is that of Dorothy George (1925: chap. 1), who argued, largely on the basis of mortality statistics, that the standard of life of the London laborer improved considerably in the course of the eighteenth century.

Specifically on wealth, there have been studies of estate tax data in England for upper wealthholders, published annually since 1961 in the Reports of the Commissioners of Inland Revenue and previously by independent estimators, but limited mostly to the twentieth century. Williamson and Lindert (1977:84–85) suggest that shares held by the top 1 percent and top 10 percent estimated from estate wealth (and tax lists for Prussia) show that the United States in 1912, on the eve of World War I, had reached a level of inequality as great as that of such industrialized nations as the United Kingdom, France, and Prussia. Their sources were W. I. King (1915:86–95) and Lampman (1962:210–15). Some confirmation of high English wealth inequality, based on land ownership data in 1873 assembled by John Bateman from *The Modern Domesday Book,* is presented by Soltow (1971a:126), who calculates a Gini coefficient for private landholders of 0.82 excluding cottagers and of 0.94 including them. Soltow (Ibid.:89–90) also presents the upper part of a Pareto curve on wealth in *speciedalers* in Kristiansand, an important Norwegian port of emigration to the United States, based on a census in 1865. The *speciedaler* exchanged for very near one American dollar. His comparative curve for Milwaukee County, Wisconsin in 1860[4] shows wealth of approximately equal value held in Milwaukee and Kristiansand by the top 0.1 percent. However, at the 92nd percentile, average wealth in Milwaukee was four times greater, and the value disparity continued to lower portions of the curve. Soltow concludes that Milwaukee offered a wider base of opportunity for a middle-class or middle-rung group. Robert Gallman[5] presented estimates by Simon Kuznets of the percentage of national income (not wealth) received by the top 5 percent of taxpayers in Prussia, Saxony, and Denmark compared with the United Kingdom in the 1870s and 1880s and subsequent dates. The figure for the United Kingdom was the highest, whereas those for the three European countries were within the range of Gallman's estimates of such a figure for the United States in 1867. While wealth is not income, this comparison suggests, indirectly, that the high wealth concentration in the United States following the Civil War was lower than that of the United Kingdom and about the same as in some European countries. The same comparison, continued for more European countries, shows the share of the top 5 percent in the United States to be lower than that in the United Kingdom until the 1950s and close to that in Sweden in the 1930s and 1940s. It was slightly higher than in three Scandinavian countries and West Germany in the 1950s, in which decade it was higher than in the United Kingdom for the first time. The overall impression, insofar as shares of national income can suggest parallel relationships in concentration of shares of wealth, is that high American wealth inequality in 1860 and 1870 was less than that of the United Kingdom and rather like that prevailing in a number of European countries. This situation may have continued to the 1950s and beyond.

A recent British study by Harbury and McMahon (1973:810) with a good bibliography of previous studies, suggests that the distribution of personal wealth in Britain today is much more unequal than that of income and than that of wealth in other advanced countries. They further suggest that some reduction in wealth concentration in the present century indicated by studies based on the estate duty multiplier technique[6] may be misleading. They report that some observers note that the decline in the share of the richest percentiles in the wealth distribution may reflect merely a rearrangement of wealth within families, rather than a redistribution of wealth from rich to poor families. The sample data the authors present for the top wealth levels of 1965 compared with those for a decade earlier contribute to further understanding of the importance of inherited wealth in Britain, and the relation between size of inheritance and age at death of father. They do not afford a summary statistic specifically for wealth distribution that pertains to the entire British or English population, which we might compare with our colonial data. Perhaps the closest approach is the statement by Atkinson (1972:52) that the "conventional wisdom that the top one percent own a third of total wealth is well within the range of estimates, whereas the figure often quoted for the top five percent—half total wealth—is almost certainly too low."

Let us return to the estimate of Soltow of a Gini coefficient of 0.55 (or possibly as high as 0.61) for income in the United Kingdom in 1688. I conjecture that a Gini coefficient for wealth, based on the same data, would be considerably higher. The reasoning is that the wealth Gini would be considerably higher than the income Gini coefficient because the capital values of the landed estates and personal wealth of the lords, barons, knights, esquires, and gentlemen would often have been very high; and wealth would have been negligible or very small for a great many of the 62 percent of all families in 1688 whose annual expenses, according to King, exceeded their incomes. These he named as the common seamen, laboring people and out-servants, cottagers and paupers, common soldiers. Hence I suggest that American colonial wealth inequality in 1774, although high, was not as high as that in England three quarters of a century earlier. Nor, I suggest, was it as high as that toward the end of the eighteenth century, judging by corresponding Ginis of about the same magnitude calculated by Soltow from Colquhoun's income estimates. I have no way of saying by how much, but it seems likely that if we had it, a Gini coefficient of wealth for the figures of King or Colquhoun would be substantially higher than the 0.66 for total physical wealth of colonial free wealthholders. It might easily exceed our 0.73 for total potential wealthholders in the colonies, free and nonfree. Or, put another way, the percentage of wealth owned by the top 1 percent in England in the latter part of eighteenth century was probably considerably greater than our figure of 13 percent for total physical wealth of free wealthholders, or 15 percent for free and nonfree wealthholders, shown in tables 6.2 and 6.15.

THE PREVIOUS COLONIAL EXPERIENCE

For quantitative evidence on changes in wealth concentration during the century and a half of colonial development before the Revolution we have the variety of local and sometimes conflicting studies referred to in chapter 6.[7] Many of these are good or excellent so far as they go. They pertain usually to a town, a county, or at most several counties in a province. Most are for places in New England, a few for localities in New York, Pennsylvania, or Maryland, and virtually none for areas south of Maryland, save for some early Virginia tax lists. Not surprisingly we get some divergent answers. Some illustrative numbers are shown in tables 8.4 through 8.6. The answers may all be reasonable for the particular time, place, and methods used. Besides differences due to place or date, there are methodological differences in sources of data and their completeness, principally tax lists or probate records. Some studies have adjusted

Table 8.4
Inequality Comparison, Male Probate Wealth
Selected Places, Predominantly Rural, Pre-1774

Years	Place	Share of Top 10 Percent	Gini Coefficient
(1) 1635–60	Essex Co., Mass., excluding Salem	33	—
(2) 1661–81	Essex Co., Mass., excluding Salem	45	—
(3) 1650–54	Suffolk Co., Mass., excluding Boston	60	0.73
(4) 1685–94	,, ,, ,, ,, ,,	46	0.61
(5) 1715–19	,, ,, ,, ,, ,,	54	0.68
(6) 1750–54	,, ,, ,, ,, ,,	53	0.67
(7) 1760–69	,, ,, ,, ,, ,,	53	0.68
(8) 1695–97	Suffolk Co., Mass.	41	0.51
(9) 1715–17	,, ,,	36	—
(10) 1735–37	,, ,,	39	—
(11) 1755–57	,, ,,	56	0.64
(12) 1766–67	,, ,,	49	—
(13) 1670–74	Hampshire Co., Mass.	30	0.47
(14) 1705–14	,, ,, ,,	38	0.48
(15) 1750–54	,, ,, ,,	41	0.54
(16) 1760–69	Worcester Co., Mass.	39	0.50
(17) 1650–69	Hartford Co., Conn.	45[a]	—
(18) 1680–89	,, ,, ,,	47[a]	—
(19) 1715–19	,, ,, ,,	44[a]	—
(20) 1750–54	,, ,, ,,	37[a]	—
(21) 1770–74	,, ,, ,,	50[a]	—
(22) 1675–79	Six Maryland Counties	49	0.60
(23) 1685–89	,, ,, ,,	53	0.61
(24) 1715–19	,, ,, ,,	65	0.74
(25) 1750–54	,, ,, ,,	66[b]	0.80[b]

SOURCE: Lines 1, 2: Koch (1969:54–55, 59–60). Lines 3–7: G. Main (1977a:567, table 3). Lines 8–12: Warden (1976:599, table 2) for shares, based on Lockridge (1968a:62–80); Warden (1976:603, table 3) for Gini coefficients. Lines 13–16: G. Main (1977a:567, table 3). Lines 17–21: J. Main (1976:88) cited in G. Main (1977a:565 table 2). Lines 22–25: G. Main (1977a:567, table 3).

NOTE: New England probate inventories include real estate, the Maryland ones only personal wealth. Re lines 8–12, Warden (1976:597, 599) notes that Lockridge (1968a) used only an unspecified half of recorded Suffolk inventories for males only and that probate inventories omit many decedents, particularly at lower portions of the distributions. He also notes the omission of debts, which omission pertains to all probate inventories in the colonies, as I observed in the Note on Method and in chapter 5. So far as I understand, all values in this table are for probate wealth unadjusted for age of decedent or for estates not probated, except as noted in footnotes a and b. Probate wealth includes financial assets, and hence is not comparable to my total physical wealth. Since it does not subtract debts, it is also not comparable to my net worth. Re lines 17–21, Daniels, (1973–74:131) shows, for Hartford County, probate wealth minus debts where he could ascertain them, and the share of the top 30 percent of a consistent sample of probate inventories as follows: 1700–20, 74; 1720–40, 73; 1740–60, 77; 1760–76, 74. For selected middle-sized Connecticut towns he found definite trends toward increasing shares held by the top 30 percent from 1700–20 to 1760–76, and the same for small-sized Connecticut towns from 1740–60 to 1760–76. For Chester County, Pennsylvania probate inventories, D. Ball (1976:637, table 7) cited by Williamson and Lindert (1977:113, 117) shows the share of the top 20 percent of all probate inventories as follows: 1714–31, 46; 1734–45, 53; 1750–70, 53.

[a] Corresponding percentages by J. Main after adjustment to encompass living males, as shown by G. Main (1977a:565, table 2, column 4), are: 1650–69, 46; 1680–89, 47; 1715–19, 44; 1750–54, 39; 1770–74, 46.

[b] Corrected by G. Main for underreporting.

Table 8.5
Inequality Comparison, Male Probate Wealth
Selected Northern Cities, Pre-1774

Years	Place	Share of Top 10 Percent	Gini Coefficient
(1) 1635–60	Salem, Mass.	41	0.47
(2) 1661–81	,,　　 ,,	62	0.60
(3) 1650–54	Boston, Mass.	60	0.73
(4) 1685–94	,,　　 ,,	46	0.61
(5) 1715–19	,,　　 ,,	54	0.68
(6) 1760–69	,,　　 ,,	53	0.68
(7) 1684–99	,,　　 ,,	41	—
(8) 1716–25	,,　　 ,,	62	—
(9) 1736–45	,,　　 ,,	59	—
(10) 1756–65	,,　　 ,,	68	—
(11) 1766–75	,,　　 ,,	61	—
(12) 1684–99	Philadelphia, Pa.	36	—
(13) 1716–25	,,　　 ,,	47	—
(14) 1736–45	,,　　 ,,	51	—
(15) 1756–65	,,　　 ,,	60	—
(16) 1766–75	,,　　 ,,	70	—

SOURCE: Lines 1, 2: Koch (1969:54–55, 59–60) for shares; Warden (1976:603) for Gini coefficients. Lines 3–6: G. Main (1977a:567, table 3). Lines 7–16: Nash (1976a:553, table 3).

NOTE: So far as I understand, none of the above studies were adjusted for age of decedents or for non-probated estates. The Boston and Salem probate inventories include real estate, the Philadelphia ones only personal wealth. See note to table 8.4. Daniels (1973–74:132, table 4) found that the share held by the top 30 percent in Portsmouth, New Hampshire rose from 66 in 1700–20 to 80 in 1740–60 and 79 in 1760–76, whereas for Boston (ibid.:129, table 2), there was little change in higher concentration over the same span, the percentages for corresponding dates being 84, 82, 88, and 85.

for data limitations; most have not. Differences in the population universes included and the kinds of wealth covered also limit comparisons. Some of the dates occur in periods of relatively greater or less prosperity in different provinces, which some observers call cycles. These depend on such factors as disruptions due to British wars into which the colonists were drawn, weather conditions, and varying prices and demand in Europe for such important colonial products as tobacco. These would affect income more immediately than wealth. However, Williamson and Lindert (1977:23) find that the particular initial date available or selected may affect judgment as to subsequent trends in a particular place.

I see no way to combine with any precision these methodologically diverse studies with appropriate weights to obtain macro results

Table 8.6
Inequality Comparison, Male Taxed Wealth
Selected Cities, Hingham, Massachusetts and Chester County, Pennsylvania,
Pre-1774

Years	Place	Share of Top 10 Percent	Gini Coefficient
(1) 1687	Boston, Mass.	42	0.53
(2) 1771	” ”	48	0.52
(3) 1759	Salem, Mass. Real estate	47	—
(4) 1759	” ” Personal estate	82	—
(5) 1769	” ” Real estate	52	—
(6) 1769	” ” Personal estate	82	—
(7) 1777	” ” Real estate	58	—
(8) 1777	” ” Personal estate	82	—
(9) 1754	Hingham, Mass.	37	—
(10) 1772	” ”	40	—
(11) 1695	New York	45	0.60
(12) 1701	” ”	46	0.59
(13) 1735	” ”	45	0.55
(14) 1693	Philadelphia, Pa.	46	—
(15) 1767	” ”	66	—
(16) 1774	” ”	72	—
(17) 1693	Chester Co., Pa.	24	0.26
(18) 1715	” ” ”	26	0.32
(19) 1748	” ” ”	29	0.35
(20) 1760	” ” ”	30	0.44

SOURCE: Lines 1, 2: Henretta (1965), adjusted by Warden (1976:601–2). Lines 3–8: Morris (1978:93, 95, tables I, II). Lines 9, 10: D. Smith (1973:90, table III-1), cited by Williamson and Lindert (1977:112, 115). Line 11: Goodfriend (1975), cited by G. Main (1977a:table 1). Lines 12, 13: Wilkenfeld (1973), cited by G. Main (1977a:table 1). Lines 14–16: Nash (1976a:549). Lines 17–20: Lemon and Nash (1968:11, table I), cited by Williamson and Lindert (1977:112, 116), except that the Gini coefficient for line 17 is from Warden (1976:303) and for lines 18, 19, and 20 from G. Main (1977a:560).

NOTE: Lines 1 and 2: Henretta's unadjusted figures for wealth shares were 47 in 1687 and 64 in 1771. Warden adjusted Henretta's figures for varying assessment rates and incomplete coverage in the Boston tax lists. Lines 3, 5, 7: Real estate does not measure ownership, but includes rented real estate which was taxed to the occupant. There is no adjustment for zero-property cases in lines 3–8. Lines 11: Nash (1976a:549) also shows 45 from New York tax lists for 1695 and 44 for 1730. Lines 14–16: noted by Williamson and Lindert (1977:116) as unadjusted for zero-property cases and for upward bias because the minimum assessment was lowered from £8 in 1756 to £2 in 1767 and £1 in 1774. Nash (1976a:552) also notes a problem on the 1756 Philadelphia tax list: it omitted all single persons, who ordinarily would have been assessed a head tax and counted in the lowest wealth bracket. Lines 17–20: noted by Williamson and Lindert (1977:116), as unadjusted for zero-property cases.

that would reliably pertain to the thirteen colonies as a whole.[8] Without such combinations or the execution of another cross-section study, somewhat comparable to mine, documentation concerning inequality over time in the thirteen colonies as a whole appears not to be available.

A Hypothesis

The hypothesis I find most plausible for the thirteen colonies as a whole is that wealth inequality rose, but not dramatically in the century and a half before the Revolution. I suggest that increasing inequality due to slavery overbalanced relatively stable trends in the middle colonies and in much of New England. The level of inequality was high in New England and in the South by 1774, as I have documented. It was more moderate in the middle colonies as a whole despite great disparities in Philadelphia. Was it initially high in New England and the South? Let us review a few well-known historic facts that, together with such evidence as in tables 8.4, 8.5, and 8.6, suggest some possible interpretations that bear on this point.

1.   The well-known accounts of the early group settlements in Virginia and Massachusetts Bay support the idea of comparatively equal wealth of the participants, at least at the start.

2.   In the proprietary colonies, there was more inequality at the start. The early settlers came with varying amounts of wealth, ranging from the negative obligations of indentured servants to the substantial wealth of those who came with assured large proprietary land grants. This meant fairly large initial inequality, except in Pennsylvania, where Quaker ideals played a large practical role. Even there, however, a favored few received very large land grants or opportunity to purchase large tracts for relatively small amounts.

3.   By the late seventeenth century, the periods of actual starvation and severe hardships in the first settlements were well over. Trade with Europe as well as intercolonial trade had reached considerable proportions.[9] The southern colonies were turning to importation of slaves to solve the shortage of labor not met by importation of indentured servants. Crop experimentation had reached the point where regional specialization in such valuable crops as tobacco and rice had developed in the South, and indigo became important in the eighteenth century. Grains were more predominant in the middle colonies, whereas New Englanders, with their relatively poor soil and climate, were forced more into the forests and onto the sea for livelihoods. The commercial and shipping possibilities, as well as the introduction of slaves, widened the range of wealth possibilities for individuals and hence of inequality.

4.   The comparative wealth of merchants in our sample, made more explicit in chapter 7, suggests that the more venturesome and

successful entrepreneurs in commercial activities would forge ahead of some of the small farmers. Shipbuilding and the maritime trade developed more in the North than in the South, and more specialized merchants appeared in the North, both tending to increase the inequality there, particularly in the cities and towns. However, the more enterprising southern planters also developed, in the eighteenth century, a variety of side commercial or other activities (Land 1965), which contributed to increased southern wealth inequality.

5.   Successful farming in the middle colonies and the South, more than in New England, was a major source of wealthbuilding. Real estate alone, assuming our estimates are not far from the truth, formed over half of total physical wealth (55 percent) in 1774 in all the colonies and two-thirds (68 percent) of nonhuman physical wealth. Those who could command large tracts of good land were in a position to increase their wealth. In the South, this was enhanced to the extent they could acquire slaves to work the land (Kulikoff 1975:chap. 5) Slave importations to Charleston remained heavy through the 1760s and to Virginia to the early 1760s. Acquisition of slaves was sometimes by inheritance. Purchase of slaves was facilitated by land ownership, and additional land purchase was facilitated by slave ownership.[10] The varying arrangements in the several colonies for original distribution of land grants, and the subsequent possibilities of purchase of desirable land by newcomers, as well as ability of fathers to provide land to sons, played a heavy role affecting wealth distribution. I am not aware of quantitative studies of land distribution over time,[11] other than the local studies cited. However, it would seem that whereas land wealth may have become more concentrated especially in New England, among those who remained in the older settled areas, the westward movement to newer counties of younger sons and new immigrants would work in the opposite direction. The landless who remained in New England's older areas also may have found wealth in artisan and commercial activities. The westward movement with repetition, at least for twenty or so years, of patterns of greater equality (Grant 1961; Daniels 1973–74) in newer counties would increase equality trends, whereas commercial activities would enhance inequality.[12]

6.   Colonial demographic trends, on which I am not expert, may have had mixed effects on wealth equality. Trends such as occurred in early Maryland, away from indentured single males to

free males in a population with more balanced sex ratios, permitted earlier marriage, earlier land acquisition, and hence a trend toward equality (G. Main 1977a:570). Conversely, a demographic trend toward slavery, as occurred after 1690 in much of the South, surely increased inequality. Blacks formed only 8 percent of the population in the colonies in 1690 but 14 percent by 1710 and over 20 percent by 1770. This trend would have enhanced southern wealth inequality by the early eighteenth century and the concentration probably continued through the century, though possibly at a slowing rate of increase. Immigration of free settlers was particularly strong in the middle colonies and the South, in the mid-eighteenth century. This resulted in rapid settlement of interior counties. Many of these experienced intensive growth. Overall, such settlement probably did not overbalance the inequality that existed in older areas.

Let us pull together some strands as to colonial wealth trends. It seems the social historians would agree that the level of wealth and its concentration was higher in the large cities than in the smaller towns, which latter were found chiefly in New England. I concur. They would also agree that, at least in the northern regions, the level of rural wealth and its concentration were lower in the newer or "frontier" areas than in the older settled areas. My evidence does not prove this view but is compatible with it. For some rural coastal counties of the Chesapeake area of the South the social historians would probably agree that there was initially a rather low wealth level but a higher concentration than found in rural Massachusetts at the same time. Again, my evidence does not prove but is compatible with this point. For the lower South, the social historians have virtually no information for us on wealth distribution, although many useful studies of Afro-American experience are appearing.[13] Putting these pieces together, with consideration of relative amounts of population involved, a hypothesis of stable or only slightly updrifting overall inequality in the colonial North emerges. This is the conclusion of Williamson and Lindert. It is supported by Gloria Main's analysis of work done with New England probate records. This still leaves us with the question of the impact of the South and slavery on the overall picture.

In light of the points enumerated above, I believe inequality came quite early, say at least by the 1690s, in New England as a whole and in the South as a whole. Further, I believe the larger cities such as Boston, Salem, New York City, Philadelphia, and surely Charleston, though we lack local studies of it, showed pronounced inequality by the late seventeenth century. The evidence for only one county, Chester, in Pennsylvania, plus our findings of low inequality in the middle colonies in 1774, suggests that the middle colonies' overall wealth was always less concentrated than that of the other two regions, with the rural areas outbalancing the high inequality in Philadelphia. I believe the overall trend to inequality accelerated slowly after 1690 in New England, but continued strong in the South, culminating in the inequality reported in this chapter and chapters 6 and 7, as of 1774. The net effect for the three regions combined would seem to have been a noticeable increase in overall colonial inequality up to the Revolution. The measures of inequality I find for 1774 are definitely high for New England and the South. Such inequality was possible from commercial developments in many lesser urban New England centers as well as Boston, and commercial and financial activities of the more enterprising southern planters, as well as the effects of slavery. All these effects could have been important well before signs of industrialization appeared. In the middle colonies, despite the stimulating effects of the busy seaport of Philadelphia and the wealth contrasts in that city noted by Nash,[14] the sturdy prosperity of middle-wealth farmers, demonstrated in chapter 7, seems to have held inequality there to the lowest measure in the colonies. In terms of population, however, these colonies were outweighed by the South plus New England. The net effect, influenced heavily by slavery in the South, must have been toward a somewhat greater inequality, overall, at the time of the Revolution, than was the pattern of the early communities in the mainland English colonies.

THE LATER AMERICAN EXPERIENCE

Overview

The high degree of inequality in the colonies in 1774 probably had increased in the United States as a whole by 1860 and 1870, as suggested by tables 8.2 and 8.3, but perhaps not so spectacularly as some scholars have believed.[15] Some studies suggest high wealth inequality in some localities between 1800 and 1860, particularly in large cities.[16] However, we lack consistent data on a nationwide basis until the United States' censuses of 1850, 1860, and 1870.[17] There seems to have been little change in the high concentration of wealth in real estate from 1850 to 1860[18] and possibly a slight increase in that in slaves over that decade.[19] These two were the only forms of wealth covered in the 1850 census. Surprisingly, the shape of a Gini measure of the distribution of total wealth among all adult males in the United States in 1870 remained virtually the same as for free males in 1860 (Soltow 1975a:102). This was so despite the tremendous upheavals of the Civil War, the loss of slave wealth by the former owners in the South, and introduction of former slaves for the first time into the distribution for 1870. This seeming paradox will be considered later. In both 1860 and 1870 inequality appears to have been slightly greater in the South than in the North[20] despite the fact that a higher proportion of the northern population was urban.

From 1870 to 1890 inequality may have increased still further. The increase may have continued to the World War I era, although the evidence between 1870 and 1922, when estate tax return data become available, is scanty and subject to uncertainty.[21] There seems clear evidence, from estate tax returns of large wealthholders, of increase in inequality from 1922 to 1929 among top wealthholders and of some decrease thereafter, especially from 1940 to the mid 1950s. Since the mid 1950s, there apparently has been little change in the shares of the upper 1 percent through the mid 1970s. The only year, since 1870, for which we have wealth data based on a survey of the entire population is 1962. In that year, wealth inequality was somewhat less than in 1860 and strikingly similar to that of two centuries ago.

A Hypothesis

For a general statement, it would seem that the most likely pattern of change in the United States as a whole over the past two centuries was: (1) some increase in wealth inequality to 1860–70, (2) possibly continued to a somewhat higher degree of concentration, which may have peaked around 1890 or 1929 or 1940, (3) a mild downdrift in inequality to the 1950s, and (4) little change since, at least among top wealthholders. This hypothesis is based on what I

judge to be the most convincing and generally acceptable indicators
we have, although they are far from infallible.

The Evidence: Trend Studies

It should be clear from the preceding several paragraphs that the
evidence on wealth inequality, starting with the nineteenth century, is
of varying quality and completeness, and that we cannot precisely
date turning points, or even know whether there have been such, in
nationwide wealth inequality for the entire population. My opening
generalizations depended on macro or nationwide studies or estimates[22] by Lee Soltow, Robert Gallman, G. K. Holmes, W. I. King,
Robert Lampman, D. S. Projector and G. S. Weiss, J. D. Smith, and
S. D. Franklin. Their data sources and methods vary. Consequently,
their results must be interpreted with care.[23]

There is by no means unanimity of interpretation among these
scholars, not to mention others whose views or partial studies are also
significant. However, I will note some chief aspects of their
interpretations, supporting evidence, or both. Method, data, and
validity of interpretation are so inextricably intertwined that I beg
my readers' indulgence for what may appear at times to be reverse or
circular order in the ensuing discussion. I present first some trend
hypotheses, and confirming evidence of Soltow, who has concentrated
for many years on studies of wealth and income and done a pro-
digious amount of analytical work on data from many sources. Also I
will note some conjectures by Robert Gallman, a leading scholar in
estimates of income and wealth in the framework of the national economic and social accounts. I will draw on a recent critical comparison
of many wealth studies by Williamson and Lindert (1977). These
include the work of Lampman, and subsequently Smith and
Franklin, who followed Horst Mendershausen in the application of
the estate multiplier technique to twentieth-century United States
estate data. They also include W. I. King, who earlier used probate
estate data but without an age correction, Holmes, who used census
and other data, the Federal Reserve study for 1962, and the work of
many social historians, some based on tax lists, some on probate
estate data, some on censuses and other sources. I present some highlights of coverage and method for a few of the major studies, espe-

cially that of the Federal Reserve Board in 1962, which I find of greatest interest for purposes of comparison with my own study.

Soltow's Views Lee Soltow in 1971 offered a hypothesis[24] that there was little change in wealth concentration in the United States from 1790 to 1860, and possibly from an earlier date. In 1975 he extended the same hypothesis to the late nineteenth century and possibly down to 1940.[25] His principal evidence for the first period for the South was the constancy he found in the concentration of slave holdings among slaveholders in the federal censuses of 1790, 1830, 1850, and 1860, with the Gini coefficient holding steady at 0.60 for each of those years.[26] Since he found close relationships between slave wealth and personal wealth of males in 1850 and of both to total wealth in 1860, he argues that slave wealth was, in the South, a good proxy for total wealth. Additionally, for Kentucky, his study of taxable holdings of males aged 21 and over resulted in his conclusion that wealth inequality in Kentucky was the same in 1800, 1860, and 1870 (Soltow 1975a:117–18). For the North, for the first period, he suggests that the evidence would be limited to assessed wealth and probate wealth. For Massachusetts probated estates with inventories,[27] he found similar slopes for 1829–31 and 1859–61 on the inverse Pareto curves, showing similar concentrations among upper wealthholders.

Between 1850 and 1870, he relies on his census samples, described in somewhat greater detail later in this chapter. The similarity of his Gini coefficients, shown in my table 8.2 for free men in 1860 and for all men in 1870, is the basis for his conclusion that emancipation of slaves had no effect upon the overall inequality of wealth for the United States as a whole. He explains this result as a combination of rearrangements in the South and of essentially no increase in wealth concentration in the North during this decade, as for example in Wisconsin, where slave wealth was nonexistent. His Gini coefficient for total wealth was 0.75 for 1860 and 0.74 for 1870 for men in that state as a whole; and for real estate, the only wealth value available for 1850, the Gini was 0.73 (Soltow 1971a:76). In the North as a whole, though there was a slight decrease from 53 to 51 percent in the share of wealth held by the top 5 percent, Soltow concludes that the distribution of wealth remained essentially unchanged during the Civil War decade.[28] In the South, the introduction for the first time of former slaves, most of whom had very small wealth by

1870, into the wealth distribution for all men in that year had a tendency to sharpen wealth inequality. This tendency, however, was offset by the great reduction in the wealth of former slave owners, particularly those at the top of the distribution, following the loss of their slaves, for which no compensation was given.[29] These two effects canceled out to yield an overall distribution very similar in 1870 to that of free men in 1860 at the start of the Civil War decade. The Gini coefficient for the United States was 0.83 for free men in 1860, 0.81 for white men in 1870, and 0.83 for all men in 1870. In the South, among white men only, there still remained more inequality among the top 2 to 5 percent of holders than in the North; but over the entire scale there was a little less inequality in 1870 than in 1860. It is worth quoting Soltow here (1975a:100–1):[30]

This is extraordinary when one considers that the real value of mean wealth dropped by two-thirds. Inequality then was a very robust phenomenon. It is doubtful that there will ever be such a revolutionary change again within our society—yet it left the relative hierarchy of whites as it was before. Some groups such as planters probably suffered while certain urban groups gained within the context of greatly deflated wealth values. . . . for the United States as a whole. The figures . . . for the free of 1860 and whites of 1870 indicate a significant decrease in inequality for the top decile class, more so than for the case of the North. The second decile group is the recipient of increased shares, and inequality remained essentially the same for the lower 80 percent of white males. Negroes, in accounting for about 11 percent of all free men in 1870, did have a measureable impact on inequality. Their presence meant that the top 20 percent had shares 2 points higher than otherwise. . . . The addition of nonwhites does not significantly alter the overall statistical picture of inequality. Of more impact on the picture in the United States is the fact that southern planters were a dominant influence among the economic elite in 1860 but not in 1870. This can be illustrated with the figures on residence in the accompanying table [8.7]. The statistics portray in a very dramatic way how the economic elite of the country was dominated by southerners in the antebellum period. Three of every five men [in the upper one percent] were from the South in 1860 compared to one of every five after the war. There were 70,000 Americans in 1860 with wealth of $40,000 or more [about $405,000 in 1976 dollars], and 40,000 of that number lived in the South. There were 7,000 Americans . . . with wealth of $111,000 or more [about $1,125,000 in 1976], 4,500 of whom lived in the South. The southern plutocracy was destroyed by the Civil War, at least in terms of the ownership of the country's private wealth.

Soltow's finding, overall stability, measures only the difference in inequality between free men in 1860 and a different set of free men

Table 8.7
Inequality Comparison
Proportions which Men from the South Comprised of Upper-Wealth Men of the United States, 1860, 1870

Rich of the United States Free Men 1860, All Men 1870 "Total Estate" Wealth, Percentile	Proportion of Men in the United States' Percentile formed by Men from the South	
	Free Men 1860 (Percentage)	All Men 1870 (Percentage)
100th (richest 1%)	59	18
99th (next richest 1%)	55	16
98th thru 95th (next richest 4%)	42	19
94th thru 91st (next richest 4%)	34	16
90th thru 81st (next richest 10%)	25	21
All	28	33

SOURCE: Soltow, 1975a:101. I rearranged the stub of the table to accord with presentation in this study.

(including the former slaves) in 1870. And the wealth definition changes. His 1860 wealth includes the value of slaves as part of the wealth of their owners, while his 1870 wealth has, of course, no slave value component. Soltow would have a higher measure of inequality in 1860 if he added to his 1860 distribution of free men the slaves, and attributed to them zero wealth, while still counting their asset value as part of the wealth of their owners.[31] Such a distribution would be comparable to the one I offer in table 6.15 for all free and nonfree potential wealthholders in 1774. This distribution counts slaves both as people and as assets belonging to others and is, I believe, the truest measure of inequality among the whole population, free and nonfree, in that year. My figures for that measure appear also on the last line of table 8.1, on line 4 of table 8.2, and are graphed in figure 19 for the South and in figure 21 for the thirteen colonies.

Williamson and Lindert (1977), in their table 3, measure inequality among adult males in 1860 in the way I consider most meaningful, counting slaves both as people and as wealth, comparable to my table 6.15. On this basis, they conclude there was a definite decrease in inequality of wealth among *all* adult males from 1860 to 1870. This argument is the one I find more convincing. Hence, I conclude that to compare wealth inequality of adult males in 1860 and 1870, we need for 1860 a measure of inequality for the total male population. It is clear that this would be higher than the measures shown on line 5 of table 8.2.

Census Samples   I digress here to discuss the method of samples drawn from the 1850, 1860, and 1870 censuses by Soltow, census samples by Gallman and ones for Texas by Campbell and Lowe. Of the various other studies I mention, only these samples, and that of the 1962 Federal Reserve Survey, are drawn from the entire population. The important studies by Lee Soltow,[32] selections from which are included in my tables 8.2 and 8.3, are based on carefully drawn samples from the manuscript U.S. censuses for 1850, 1860, and 1870, as is one by Gallman for 1860.[33] Careful samples for Texas were also drawn from the 1850 and 1860 censuses by Campbell and Lowe.[34] Soltow drew samples of free adult males, Gallman and Campbell and Lowe of free families headed by males.[35] In the 1850 census, the only information collected on wealth was value of real estate and of slaves. In 1860 and 1870, each respondent was asked the value of his real estate and his personal estate. Personal estate was to include value of intangibles (i.e., financial assets) and consumer durables, but not apparel. In 1860 it also included value of slaves. The standard of wealth valuation was to be the gross market value. Debts were not subtracted from either real or personal property. Holdings of personal property of less than $100 were not to be enumerated in 1870.[36] Persons with less than $100 personal estate in 1870 (and perhaps also frequently in 1860, depending apparently somewhat on the judgment of the enumerating marshal), if they also held no real estate, appear in the manuscript lists as holders of no wealth. Holders of no wealth formed 50 percent of Gallman's 1860 sample and, apparently, almost half of Soltow's U.S. samples,[37] both in 1860 and in 1870. They formed only 8 percent, however, of the 1860 Texas sample of Campbell and Lowe, while another 8.5 percent there held wealth of under $250.

Williamson and Lindert's and My Views to 1860   I am inclined to agree with Williamson and Lindert's demurral at Soltow's thesis of no trend in wealth inequality from the colonial period to 1860, although the increase may not be as sharp as their discussion implies.[38] Given the many problems of population covered, wealth definition, completeness and accuracy of reporting, and the like, there is plenty of room for difference of opinion. I am not fully persuaded that slaveholdings by the small percentage of free men who held slaves in the South and tax records for one state of Kentucky are sufficient to prove overall southern wealth stability among all free men. In the North, the development of manufactures and trade, the rising urban population, and the increase in immigration that tended to bring in young adults of low wealth[39] would seem to have contributed to rising inequality. Looking at the span 1774 to 1860, if we take the Gini coefficients at face value, a rise of 17 Gini points from my 0.66, or of 10 points from my 0.73 to Soltow's 0.83 in table 8.2 is not quite negligible. Nor is the rise for the South from my 0.67 or 0.68 to Soltow's 0.85. Hence, I prefer my characterization of some increase in wealth inequality to 1860–70.

Soltow's Hypothesis 1870 to 1890, Later and Long-term   For evidence on stability from 1870 to 1890, Soltow relies, in part, on the constancy of Gini coefficients for ownership of real estate, presented in my footnote *b* to table 8.3. He also finds (Soltow 1975a:117) stable Gini coefficients for 1870, 1880, 1890, and 1900, calculated as 0.68, 0.70, 0.71, 0.71, from distributions compiled by the Indiana Department of Statistics. These are based on quadrennial appraisement of real estate and annual valuation of personal property and improvements of all individuals in all the counties. A further argument made by Soltow (1975a:112–13) for believing that inequality did not change much, even on into the twentieth century, is that he found the numbers of millionaires in 1860 and 1870, in proportion to population, to be not greatly different from Lampman's findings for 1922, when Soltow allowed for differences in price level. He further noted the similarity in shares held by top wealthholders in the distributions he found and those of Lampman and that of the Federal Reserve Board for 1962.

We have determined that the rich held surprisingly large portions of wealth as early as 1850. The top 1 percent of realholders owned 20 and 29 percent of real estate, respectively, in 1850 and 1860, and the top 1 percent of wealthholders owned 29 and 27 percent of total estate in 1860 and 1870. Lampman's figures for this group are 32 percent for 1922 and 25 percent in 1953. Perhaps the share in 1962 was 29 percent.[40]

On the strength of the data named plus censuses of mortgages from 1880 to 1889, and United States inheritance and income tax data since 1914, Soltow (1975a:123) concludes:

The available evidence indicates that inequality of wealth remained the same from 1800 to 1940 and then decreased a little, particularly among middle-wealth groups. . . . A plutocratic elite emerged at the turn of the century but it did not fundamentally alter the share of wealth held by the top 1 percent of persons. The main point is that there already was strong inequality in 1860, 1870, and earlier.

Gallman's Surmise and My View 1860 to 1890   Gallman (1968) hazarded the surmise that there might have been further increases in inequality to 1890, drawing chiefly on the work of G. K. Holmes, with some consideration of Spahr's estimate. Holmes's estimate for 1890 is based on census data on farms and homes, which Williamson and Lindert report he used for twenty-two states. He subtracted mortgage data, available in the census, to give equity rather than gross estate value, and used supplementary material on millionaires to estimate wealth at the top.[41]

I incline to the Gallman view for the last third of the nineteenth century. I base this judgment less on the tentative figures of Holmes than on consideration of the extremely rapid rates of economic growth during the second half of the nineteenth century, which reflected the opening up of many new commercial, trade, and industrial possibilities for a growing population in the North. However, I cannot exclude the possibility, if we had more complete statistics for the late nineteenth and turn of the century, that the measure of inequality around 1890–1900 might not have changed significantly. As Soltow has at least partially demonstrated for the decade 1860–70, large changes can take place in an economic and social sense and yet the overall statistical measure of inequality may not change greatly, owing to a counterbalancing of many factors.

Studies of Locales

A number of partial studies, including some of the increasing number of excellent quantitative studies by social historians, are considered next for the further clues they offer in this elusive search for trends from colonial days through the nineteenth century. Though they are for limited locales and varying dates, and their methods are usually not strictly comparable, they nevertheless add useful depth to the general picture.

Probate Evidence for New England   One of these, which covers four three-year periods within the span 1829 to 1891, is Gloria Main's[42] analysis of decedent male wealth from probate inventories in Boston and separate Massachusetts counties. These can be compared with her findings,[43] partially shown in tables 8.4 and 8.5, from 1650 to 1788 from microfilmed probate records of Suffolk, Hampshire, and Worcester Counties, Massachusetts. Gini coefficients and shares of wealth held by the top 10 percent of probated males are her measures of inequality. Her conclusion is that there was little change in the colonial period and up to 1788 in the measures for Boston, Suffolk County excluding Boston, or for Hampshire or Worcester Counties. By 1829–31, however, the Gini for Boston had risen from 0.68 to 0.86, that for Worcester County from 0.50 to 0.63, and that for Hampshire County less noticeably from 0.54 to 0.56. The shares of the top 10 percent, by 1829–31, had risen well above the colonial levels, to 83 percent for Boston, 50 percent for Worcester County and 44 percent for Hampshire County. This increase reached a high for Boston in 1859–61, with taperings off to 1879–81 and 1889–91. For Worcester County, there was steady upward increase in inequality to 1889–91, whereas for Hampshire County, a maximum came in 1879–81. For eleven other counties, the three later three-year periods all showed higher inequality measures than 1829–31, with the maximum coming for Berkshire County in 1859–61, for six counties in 1879–81, and for four including Nantucket and Plymouth in 1889–91. For Massachusetts state totals as a whole, the highest inequality was reached in 1879–81. These results, though differing somewhat in dates of some peaks, are not unlike the findings in 1915 by W. I. King from the same source, Massachusetts probate records. Gallman (1968:325) reports that King's tables show a fairly marked increase in concentration between 1859–61 and 1879–81 and an equally marked decrease between 1879–81 and 1889–91, although King was not prepared to regard the changes as significant. The thing Main finds interesting is that, as early as 1829–31, before a significant start in industrialization, all the counties, with the exception of Plymouth and Dukes, showed higher shares held by the top 10 percent than noted for any of the three counties in the colonial period. Likewise, the Gini coefficients, again with the same exceptions of Plymouth and Dukes, were all higher than the highest levels found for the colonial period outside of Boston. We do not know whether Massachusetts' experience was duplicated elsewhere in the colonies. It might be reasonable to assume that it might have been approximated in Connecticut and Rhode Island, possibly also in New York, but the relatively larger urban population of Massachusetts makes it doubtful that the pattern would be applicable to the middle colonies and most particularly to the South.

Massachusetts Towns   Robert Doherty's study,[44] based on tax lists and 1860 census schedules for five Massachusetts towns Worcester, Northampton, Ware, Salem, and Pelham shows high concentration in 1860, in descending order as listed, in all but the hamlet of Pelham. The measure is the share of real and personal wealth held by the top 10 percent, and top 1 percent, of adult males, as compared with those in other deciles. The share of the top 10 ranged from 87 percent in Worcester and around 70 percent in Northampton, Ware, and Salem, to only 28 percent in the hamlet of Pelham situated in a region of self-sufficient agriculture. The change in Northampton was from 50 percent in 1800 to 72 in 1860. In the latter year, the richest 1 percent in each of Ware, Northampton, and Salem held about 25 percent of the property, and in Worcester, where there was more manufacturing, that group owned more than 40 percent of the town's wealth. Only in Pelham, where 4 percent of property was held by the richest 1 percent, was there anything approaching parity, although Doherty (1977:46) warns "no one should expect property to have been owned in absolutely equal shares in Pelham or anywhere else." He analyzes the data by age groups, economic activity, and property mobility groups, as well as hierarchical town location. He finds both rich and poor within an age group, but that, except within the 16–30 age group, wealth tended to be owned more equally among men of like age than in the population at large. He finds that one-third to one-half of males over 30 were unable to acquire real estate. The distribution of real estate among farmers was less unequal than that of total wealth among all males. Places of prominent commerce and manufacturing had higher wealth inequality. Agriculture produced greater equality, and the only communities that approached equal distribution of property were hamlets situated in less developed rural hinterlands.

Northeastern Cities   Edward Pessen (1973) gives a verbal, pictorial, and statistical description of great inequality of wealth in New

York City in 1828 and 1845, Brooklyn in 1810 and 1841, Boston in 1820, 1833, 1848, and Philadelphia in 1846. The study undertakes to prove de Tocqueville (1840:2:250, 258) wrong in his statement that "in a democratic society like that of the United States . . . fortunes are scanty. . . . The equality of conditions (that gives some resources to all members of the community . . . also prevents any of them from having resources of any great extent."

Pessen uses data from tax lists to name the wealthiest 71 to 300 in the several cities on the various dates, on the basis of assessed wealth. He finds the Philadelphia tax lists unusable because property taxes were assessed against occupants rather than owners and for that city uses a list of Philadelphians reputed wealthiest in 1846 assembled from sources he considers reasonably reliable, though not verifiable from tax assessments. For Philadelphia wealth held by top holders, he uses Blumin's (1969:352) figure for 1860.

He argues (Pessen 1973:16) that though wealth shown on tax lists was too low and that the underappraisals were not the same in Boston and New York, there is no reason to believe that relative ranking thereon of rich men within a city was invalid. He sees no reason why one rich man would understate more than another, and in any case sees the tax assessments as at least a rock bottom minimum appraisal of their wealth. His rosters contain many names of recognizable influence. His thrust is to prove the existence of substantial American fortunes and opulent living by some of their holders, and also to show a high percentage of assessed wealth held by the upper 1 percent of taxpayers. Material is presented on occupations, marriages, social life of the wealthy, and the passing on of at least some fortunes intact or augmented. He proves that there were some very rich people in three or four large northern cities, but hedges on comparisons with Europe. He does not consider southern or western cities of the period, nor what might have been comparative levels of big city and rural wealth. He offers no Gini coefficients nor anything resembling a complete wealth distribution. For a methodologically sophisticated appraisal of Pessen's attack on "the egalitarian myth" I recommend a recent article by Robert Gallman (1978).

Southern and Western Cities and States When Pessen's findings are compared in table 8.8 with data for some southern and western cities in 1860, it is apparent that New York, Boston, and

Philadelphia were not unique in the degree of inequality exhibited before the Civil War. The Gini coefficients and the shares of wealth held by the top 1 percent, based on census data rather than on tax lists, measured as high as the northeastern cities or higher for Baltimore, New Orleans, Milwaukee, and St. Louis. For four large commercial towns in Texas, namely Galveston, Houston, San Antonio, and Austin, which though relatively young were main centers of transportation, communication, commerce, and government in a predominantly rural state, the Gini coefficient was somewhat lower. The share of wealth held there by the top 5 percent of free families was somewhat lower, but still approached 60 percent. Additional data for principal urban counties with major cities within them, shown in note a to table 8.8, indicate that Gini coefficients in the high 80s or low 90s were found in all, including Cincinnati, St. Paul, and San Francisco.

We can look at figures for some of these same states (table 8.9), excluding the large urban centers, with the exception of Texas, where the figure includes the data for the four large towns. Wisconsin and Texas were states somewhat similar in age and dates of settlement, one northern, one southern. The Gini coefficient for Wisconsin including Milwaukee county (shown in note a to table 8.9), was 0.75, compared to 0.74 for Texas, and the percentage of wealth held by the top 2 percent, 31 for Wisconsin, was very close to that for Texas. The Wisconsin rich held no slaves, whereas slave wealth was important among the rich of Texas as well as of Maryland and Louisiana. Wisconsin, on the other hand, received more foreign-born immigrants than did the southern states, and many of them were young adult males who tended to have low wealth for a time.

The Twentieth Century

Some pioneer estimates for 1912 and 1923 are based on probate samples drawn by the Federal Trade Commission.[45] The estimates from them derived by W. I. King, who made assumptions as to the wealth of the nonprobated and who excluded women, have been reworked by Williamson and Lindert (1977:80 ff) with somewhat larger numbers of nonprobated cases than assumed by King, but the general results remain close to his. So far as I am aware, King did not make corrections to the age structure of the living.[46] Gallman

Table 8.8
Inequality Comparison
Free Families in Selected Urban Places, ca. 1860
(Gini Coefficient, Percentage Shares of Wealth by Top Holders)

	Gini Coefficient	Percentage Share Held by Richest		
		1 Percent	2 Percent	5 Percent
Boston (1848)	0.86[a]	37	—	—
New York (1845)	—[a]	40	—	—
Brooklyn (1841)	0.87[a]	42	—	—
Philadelphia	—[a]	50	—	—
Baltimore	0.90	39	54	72
New Orleans	0.89	43	57	72
Milwaukee County[b]	0.89[a]	44	50	—
St. Louis	0.88	38	50	68
Large Towns of Texas[c]	0.85	21	34	58

SOURCE: Share figures for Boston, New York, Brooklyn from Pessen (1973:30–40); Gini coefficients for foregoing cities by Campbell and Lowe (1977:132, table 50). Figure for Philadelphia by Blumin (1969), cited by Pessen (1973:40) and Campbell and Lowe (1977:132). Share figures for Baltimore, New Orleans, St. Louis from Gallman (1969:22–23); Gini figures for those cities from Campbell and Lowe (1977:132). Figures for Milwaukee County from Soltow (1971a:3, 66), except the 44 percent taken from Campbell and Lowe (1977:132). Figures for Texas towns from Campbell and Lowe (ibid.).

NOTE: Except where indicated by parentheses, all figures pertain to 1860. See cautions in Gallman (1969:18–21) that samples may understate wealth of the richest.

[a] Gini coefficients for free adult males in 1860 for the following counties, identified by name of the major city within the county, were: Boston, 0.94; New York, 0.93; Newark, 0.90; Philadelphia, 0.93; according to Soltow (1975b:236–37, table 1). For additional urban counties, the same source and table give the following Ginis in 1860: Washington, D.C., 0.90; Pittsburgh, 0.89; Cleveland, 0.86; Cincinnati, 0.93; St. Paul, 0.92; San Francisco, 0.92.

[b] Milwaukee county figures are for adult males, and "stem largely from persons living in the city of Milwaukee," according to Soltow.

[c] Galveston, Houston, San Antonio, and Austin.

(1968:321) compares, with reservations for differing methods, the Holmes 1890 estimate for families with two 1921 estimates by King for property owners and finds them rather similar. Holmes shows a larger share of wealth held at the top and less at the bottom, but is very close to King in the figure for the middle-wealth groups.

1922 to 1956 and Later: Lampman's Estimates and Smith and Franklin's   Data for upper wealthholders by years beginning with 1922 come from national statistics of estate tax returns published without personal identification by the Bureau of Internal Revenue. These are available only for estates larger than the required filing minimum, which was $60,000[47] for data used by Lampman and for the estimates by Smith and Franklin. Both Lampman and Smith and

Table 8.9
Inequality Comparison
Free Families, Selected States, 1860
(Gini Coefficient, Percentage Shares of Wealth by Top Holders)

	Gini Coefficient	Percentage Share Held by Richest	
		1 Percent	2 Percent
(1) United States (Soltow)	0.83	27	40
(2) United States (Gallman)	0.82	24	35
(3) Wisconsin, except Milwaukee Co.[a]	0.72	—	—
(4) Texas	0.74	—	33[b]
(5) Maryland, except Baltimore	0.80	16	26
(6) Louisiana, except New Orleans	0.83	24	37

SOURCE: Samples drawn from the 1860 manuscript census. Line 1: Soltow (1975a:99, 103); line 2: Gallman (1969:6, 22–23); line 3: Soltow (1971a:66); line 4: Campbell and Lowe (1977:127); lines 5 and 6: share figures from Gallman (1969:22–23), Gini coefficients from Campbell and Lowe (1977:127).

NOTE: Lines 1 and 3 are based on samples of free adult males; lines 2, 5 and 6 on samples of free families, see note 35 regarding coverage of males in various studies. Line 4 is based on a sample of free heads of households. The caution in the note to table 8.8 pertains here also.

[a] The figures for the state of Wisconsin, including Milwaukee County, are Gini 0.75, and 31 percent held by the richest 2 percent, Soltow (1971a:5, 45, 66).
[b] Top 2.2 percent.

Franklin use the estate multiplier technique of age correction to move from estimates of the decedent population to that of the living, but their estimates are still limited to "upper wealthholders." Only for 1953 did Lampman attempt an estimate for the entire population, using supplementary data such as national accounts and the work of Raymond Goldsmith. Lampman's finding that inequality, judged by shares of the top 1 percent, increased from 1922 to 1929 and has decreased since, to 1956, is shown in table 8.10. The absence of any noticeable directional movement since 1956 found by Smith and Franklin is also apparent in that table of probated estates. A further comparison by Gallman (1968:319) of the King 1921 figures with those by Lampman for 1953 suggests a general movement in the direction of greater equality by 1953, with the lowest three out of six wealth classes gaining at the expense of the three highest. However, Gallman cautions that because sources and methods of the two men were entirely different, the comparison should not be taken too seriously. Nevertheless, to the extent that it can be given weight, he finds that the comparison tends to confirm Lampman's finding of a long-term decline in the share of wealth owned by the richest group.

1962 Nationwide Federal Reserve Survey: Comparison with 1774 The 1962 survey made for the Federal Reserve Board is based on a carefully designed and analyzed nationwide sample of households that yielded 2,557 consumer units. Segments of the population expected to have sizable amounts of wealth were sampled at much higher rates than the remaining population. This procedure yielded enough cases with wealth of $100,00 or more, and within that group enough with $500,000 or more, to supply data not hitherto available for the twentieth century on the size and composition of living upper-wealth groups as well as of the complete range of population at lower wealths. Weighting is necessary in this sample, not to correct for age structure of the living but to bring down the proportion of high wealth cases to the smaller numbers that would have been drawn if more uniform rates of sampling had been used.[48] The weighted figures yield nationwide estimates of the entire living

Table 8.10
Shares of Personal Wealth Held by Top Wealthholders
United States, 1922–1972
(Percentage)

	Shares in Total Equity of		Shares in Net Worth of	
Year	Top 1% of Adults	Top 0.5% of Population	Top 1% of Population	Top 0.5% of Population
1922	32[a]	30	—	—
1929	36[a]	32	—	—
1933	28[a]	25	—	—
1939	31[a]	28	—	—
1945	23[a]	21	—	—
1949	21[a]	19	—	—
1953	24[a]	23	28	22
1956	26	25	—	—
1958	—	—	27	22
1962	—	—	27	22
1965	—	—	29	24
1969	—	—	25 (26[b])	20
1972	—	—	27[b]	21[b]

SOURCE: Columns 1 and 2, Lampman (1962:204, 202); columns 3 and 4, Smith and Franklin (1974:166), except figures denoted "b."

[a] Lampman (1962:228) shows figures from 1922 through 1953 for "Gross estate, total wealth variant" as follows: 32, 38, 30, 33, 26, 22, 25. For the top 2 percent of families, he shows a figure on this basis only for 1922, 33; and for 1953, 29.

[b] From Williamson and Lindert (1977:88), attributed as unpublished estimates of Smith and Franklin.

population. Women as well as men are included, in the proportions in which they fell in the weighted sample. Likewise, consumer units included unrelated individuals, who often lived singly and in any case not with related family members. Families of two or more related persons residing together are also treated as consumer units (Projector and Weiss 1966:58–61). Wealth was ascertained in interviews, using trained personnel and a detailed form. It included separate questions on value of own home and other real estate, automobile, equity in business and profession (farm and nonfarm), liquid financial assets, "investment assets," and miscellaneous assets. Debts owed on each of these forms of asset were subtracted to obtain the equity values of each as components of wealth.[49] Hence the "wealth" figure for 1962 is a rather close approximation to our "net worth" in 1774. In the sense of being a carefully designed and weighted sample that yields an estimate for the entire population, and in its definition of wealth, this study is the most nearly comparable to mine.

Results from the two studies for the earliest and latest dates for which we have complete American wealth distributions are compared in table 8.11. Graphically, they are seen by comparing[50] figures 12, 20,[51] and 21. The curves are very similar at the lower end of the scale, up to about the seventh decile, but diverge more thereafter, exhibiting somewhat greater inequality in 1962 at the higher wealth levels. A somewhat similar view is obtained by comparing the percentile and decile shares as shown in the table.

Given the uncertainty noted in our consideration of table 8.3 as to the wealth of the richest 1 and 10 percent in 1962, not to mention the frailties of our 1774 estimates discussed in the Note on Method and in appendix A, the two-century comparison must be viewed as impressionistic rather than definitive. It can at least suggest that the wealth inequalities found in virtually all societies were not widely different in the American colonies at the close of the colonial era from that of the industrial and financial world power that was the United States of 1962. If we refer to the wealthiest 30 percent of the population as the "rich" and the other 70 percent as the "poor," then the distribution was about the same. Both in 1962 and in 1774, the richest 30 percent held about 85 percent of the wealth.[52] Perhaps it was chiefly among the richest 1 percent that the distribution of wealth became notably more unequal over the centuries. Their share appears to have increased substantially, even if we accept the lower estimate

Table 8.11
Inequality Comparison
Thirteen Colonies 1774, United States 1962
(Percentage Shares of Wealth, by Decile)

	All Potential Wealthholders TPW 1774	Free Wealthholders		Consumer Units Wealth 1962
		TPW 1774	NW 1774	
Percentage share held by:				
100th percentile (richest 1%)	15	13	15	34[d]
99th percentile (next richest 1%)	9	7	8	8
98th–96th (next richest 3%)	17[a]	15[b]	16[c]	11
Tenth decile (100th–91st, richest 10%)	56	51	55	62[d]
Ninth decile	18	17	18	16
Eighth decile	12	11	11	7
Seventh decile	8	8	7	6
Sixth decile	4	6	5	4
Fifth decile	2	3	3	3
Fourth decile	1	2	2	2
Third decile	—[e]	1	1	—[e]
Second decile	0	1	—[e]	—[e]
First decile	0	—[e]	−2	—[e]
Mean	£199.1	£252.0	£237.3	$20,982
Median	£ 47.7	£108.7	£ 83.8	$ 6,721
Gini coefficient	0.73	0.66	0.73	0.76

SOURCE: 1774 data, $w*B$-weighted, rounded, from tables 6.15, 6.1, 6.2 and underlying tabulations deposited at the Newberry Library. 1962 data interpolated from Projector and Weiss (1966) (see note 52) mean from their p. 110, median and Gini from their p. 30.

NOTE: "TPW" indicates "total physical wealth," "NW" denotes "net worth." See text for definition of "wealth" in 1962. "Consumer Units" in 1962 comprised families of two or more; they also comprised unrelated individuals who often lived singly. See Projector and Weiss (1966:49).

[a] Separate percentile figures are: 98th, 6.4; 97th, 5.8; 96th, 5.0.
[b] Separate percentile figures are: 98th, 6.4; 97th, 4.8; 96th, 4.0.
[c] Separate percentile figures are: 98th, 6.6; 97th, 4.8; 96th, 4.6.
[d] Figures for the top 1 percent and top 10 percent are questioned. See note c to table 8.3.
[e] Less than 0.5 percent.

of 21 percent made by Williamson and Lindert. Here, in the top 1 percent in 1962, would be the Gettys, Hunts, Rockefellers, to whom our closest counterpart in 1774 was a poor match. Manigault's net worth of £32,738 was the equivalent in 1976 dollars of $1,566,000, hardly a superfortune by today's standards.

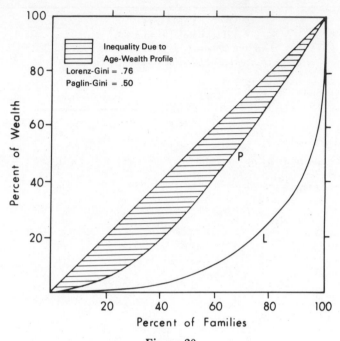

Figure 20.
U.S. Distribution of Wealth, 1962
SOURCE: Reprinted with permission from Paglin 1975:607; based on Projector and Weiss 1966:110, 151

The relatively lower shares in 1962 claimed by holders in the eighth and ninth deciles suggest some diminution, over the two centuries, of what we might call the upper middle classes. Their relative loss may reflect some intensification of inequality within the top decile.

There is great similarity over two centuries[53] in the lower wealth ranges. The shares held in the seventh decile and all lower ones, whether one looks only at free or at all potential wealthholders in 1774, diverge only slightly from the shares in 1962. Though the absolute content of the poverty level has unquestionably risen dramatically in two centuries, the relative shares of a larger total wealth held by the bottom half of the population, and by the next 20 percent, seem to have remained almost unchanged.

The length of the time span makes obvious what may also be true in some shorter time comparisons, that it is not the same individuals, nor even their posterity, who appear in corresponding positions on the wealth scale at differing times. The old saying "Three generations from shirtsleeves to shirtsleeves" may well be appropriate. A whole host of factors, of possibly quite differing intensity at different times and places, would be required to explain why particular individuals reached a particular wealth level at a particular time in their lives.[54]

The closeness of the inequality pattern two centuries apart is further confirmed by the Gini coefficients and the similarity in spreads between mean and median wealth. Two of the three colonial Gini coefficients, including the one for net worth, the most nearly comparable wealth definition, were 0.73, compared with that of 0.76 for 1962. That of 0.73 for total physical wealth for all potential wealthholders, including the nonfree males, would undoubtedly have

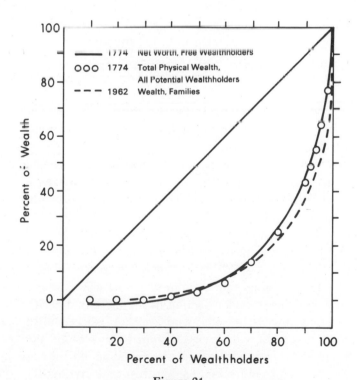

Figure 21.
U.S. Distribution of Wealth, 1774 and 1962
Source: 1774 Net Worth, table 6.1, data *w*B*-weighted; 1774 Total Physical Wealth, table 6.14, data *w*B*-weighted; 1962 Wealth, figure 20 and note 52

been still higher if we had computed it for net worth. Hence we
might assert that for comparable wealth and for the entire population, free and nonfree, inequality in 1774 was probably actually
greater than in 1962. Median total physical wealth was four times
that of the mean for the 1774 distribution, which includes the nonfree
as wealthholders, showing the greatest inequality by that measure.
The corresponding multiple of three for mean compared to median
net worth of free wealthholders in 1774 was about the same as that in
1962.

These similarities, by whatever measure of inequality we choose
to examine, occur notwithstanding the fact that the average age of the
population was higher in 1962. They occur also notwithstanding the
many changes brought about by the transformation from an agricultural and rural to an urban, industrial, and internationalized
financial economy, the abolition of slavery in the 1860s, and government tax and transfer policies, which have accelerated since World
War I. Some of the trends, such as to urbanization and to population
aging,[55] may have had offsetting effects on inequality.

There is surely no immutable law of an unchanging and
unchangeable pattern of wealth distribution in a society that permits
private property and relatively free enterprise. Nevertheless, in an
array, some will always be richer than others. Many elements must
have differing impact at different times and areas. On the other hand,
such factors as differences in natural endowments, willingness and
capacity to work, energy, drive, initiative, charisma as a word to
express attractiveness to and ability to cooperate with other people,
and plain luck, cannot have changed greatly in two centuries.
Influence of well-placed friends and family connections in making a
livelihood has been with us for centuries, and may not have changed
much in the past two. Even with great increase in medical care,
education, and training, reduction in sex and racial barriers to education and employment, and reduction in permissible inheritance, there
will seemingly always be some who are more successful than others
and many who, for a wide variety of individual reasons, do not make
it to the higher rungs of the wealth ladder. Though the absolute real
wealths involved are much higher than two centuries ago, the relative
shares of the larger pie are strikingly similar to the pattern I found
for 1774.

INEQUALITY AND ECONOMIC DEVELOPMENT

Except for the slave question, which admittedly is a large and troublesome exception, I would suggest that wealth inequality was not a bad thing for the economic development of the United States in the eighteenth and nineteenth centuries. First, as Paglin observed, it is not incompatible with a reasonable progression in wealth with advancing work experience and savings as a man matures. Second, the wealth of the richer in the upper deciles was available to furnish venture capital in lines other than agriculture. This was true more notably in the North, but also to some extent in the South, were some planters engaged in trade and various enterprises in addition to the raising of crops and cattle. Third, it should be recalled that wealth differs from income.[56] Some of those with zero wealth, including slaves, servants, children, and women, nonetheless shared to some extent in the real income or product resulting from the combination of labor with capital, including land, of their owners or family heads. They had shelter and some apparel and consumed food. Likewise, it should be recalled that wealth leveling proposals today, as in such countries as England, result in a higher share of national income (product) consumed, a smaller share saved, and a consequent diminishment at least in rate of accretion if not in total amount of national capital.

CHAPTER NINE

Summary and
Conclusions

O N the eve of the American Revolution, the American mainland
colonies that subsequently became the thirteen original states of
the United States of America had achieved an impressive amount of
privately held wealth. It totaled some £88 million sterling or £37.4
per capita excluding the value of slaves and servants. In the 150 years
since the first settlements by Englishmen, land had been cleared and
improved, livestock imported and bred, buildings erected, wharves,
docks, and some roads built. Towns had grown, particularly at
seaports and at strategic river locations. Crops had been experimented with to find those particularly suited to the New World,
among the more valuable being tobacco, indigo, and rice. Shipbuilding and shipping, both coastal and overseas, had developed, as well
as iron works, many grist and flour mills, some other manufactures,
and handicrafts. Fish, lumber, and other products of the sea and
forests were collected, processed, and traded. Slaves and indentured
servants had been imported to augment the relatively scarce supply of
free labor, and many blacks were colonial-born offspring of ancestors
imported directly or indirectly from Africa. The blacks comprised
one-fifth of the total population other than Indians, which had
reached almost 2.4 million (see table 2.4). The relatively small numbers of native Indians had been dispossessed of lands east of the Alle-
gheny mountains and many of them driven or maneuvered to the
west.

INSTITUTIONS

The institutional framework within which private wealth had
been accumulating for a century and a half came principally from

English heritage, with some influences from other European countries such as Holland, France, and Germany.

Law Law and government had developed from that of England. Provincial statute laws were subject to approval by the British crown, and colonial courts followed English precedents. The common law of England was followed. Private property, including ownership of slaves, was protected by law. Common law principles of fairness in market transactions prevailed.

Religion In religion (Hofstadter 1972:199–204) there was diversity. The Church of England never gained a strong foothold in New England, where, except in Rhode Island, the Puritan or Congregational was the established church. The Anglican Church had nominally more but not greatly more actual influence in New York, New Jersey, Maryland, North Carolina, and Georgia, where it was the established church, but where Anglicans were outnumbered by people of other denominations. In New York there were many of the Dutch Reformed Church, in New Jersey many Quakers, Presbyterians, and Puritans. Lord Baltimore brought Catholics to Maryland, but they were outnumbered by Puritans, Baptists, Presbyterians, Huguenots, and the German Reformed. In North Carolina many belonged to no church, and in Georgia there was a large group of German Lutherans. Only in Virginia and in South Carolina was the established Anglican Church the principal religious denomination. Quakers were prominent in Pennsylvania and Delaware, where there was never an established church and the official policy was religious freedom for all sects.

Education Education was limited principally to reading, writing, and arithmetic, often taught only to boys and for only a few years by schoolmasters paid by private fees. There were a few academies for boys and a few colleges: Harvard, William and Mary, King's College, which later became Columbia University, the College of Philadelphia, later the University of Pennsylvania, the College of New Jersey, later Princeton University, and the College of Rhode Island, later Brown University. Only men were admitted to the colleges.

Community Structures, Postal Service, Travel, Shipping There were virtually no hospitals save in Philadelphia. In New England the churches served as town meetinghouses and tax collecting units. Simple county courthouses were erected in most colonial counties, often adjacent to the town commons or market area. Shops, even of substantial merchants, were often located in one or more rooms of a dwelling. There was limited mail service on the post road from Boston to New York and Philadelphia. Most letters were sent by way of friends undertaking journeys, or by ship captains. There was expensive coach service a few times a week between major cities, but mostly travelers went afoot, by horse, or by private carriage for overland travel.

In the northern colonies, local trade centers developed where produce from farms or shops was assembled for further shipment by river to seaports, and manufactured goods from Europe or products from other colonies found their way back. In the South, there were so many rivers and creeks that crops for export could often be loaded onto boats directly at the site of the plantation, and these boats also brought in plantation supplies. In northern towns and county seats, and to a lesser extent at county seats in the South, there were market days where, at open air markets, farm and other produce could be purchased or exchanged. There was a substantial coastal trade, with exchange of products among the colonies, as well as overseas shipments (table 3.11; also Shepherd and Williamson 1972) to and imports from Europe, the West Indies, and Africa. Philadelphia, Charleston, Boston, and New York served as major centers both for coastal shipments and for overseas trade. Lesser ports including Newport, New Haven, Baltimore, Wilmington, Newport News, and Savannah played supplementary roles.

Money and Prices　　Money was complex and confusing even to the colonists. There were essentially no banks, in the modern sense, for deposit or loan of funds. Colonial coinage was forbidden by England. English coins and foreign coins circulated, but were scarce. Current money of each province was in the form of notes or promises to pay of the provincial legislature. Credit transactions were arranged by individual negotiation of notes or other financial instruments, or by book accounts carried by farmers as well as by merchants and tradesmen. These accounts were almost always in terms of the money of the particular province, that is, in provincial pounds, shillings, and pence, which varied somewhat in exchange value from one colony to another. Ine some colonies, as Maryland, there was one rate for "current" money, another for "common" money. The colonists measured their wealth in these local or provincial pounds, shillings, and pence. I have reduced all these to the common denominator of

British sterling (table 1.1), stated in pounds and decimal equivalents thereof for amounts smaller than a pound.

I calculate that a pound sterling in 1774 may be considered, in recent wealth purchasing power, equivalent to $47.84, or roughly almost $50 at the price level of 1976 and to $54 by 1978 (table 1.2). This price comparison is, at best, only approximate, since many real wealth items of two hundred years ago were vastly different from today's sophisticated products. Many items were hand fashioned and often sturdier than their modern mass-produced counterparts. Such possessions as a tailored-to-measure coat, a handcrafted saddle, a solid cherry tea table would be very exceptional and expensive today. And, in relative terms, such sturdy things as old iron or used apparel were more highly valued then than now. The differences reflect vast changes in technology, organization of production, and consumer demand over two centuries. The bundle of items in the wealth price index at the beginning and that at the end of the two-century period differ greatly. Nevertheless, such an index is our nearest approach to interpreting for twentieth-century readers the composite meaning of the real wealth values found in 1774. In chapter 1, I listed for various colonies in three kinds of money (local, pounds sterling, and 1976 dollars) the 1774 valuations from individual probate inventories of a varied range of goods. These included such things as a bushel of wheat, a horse, a cow, a plow, a hoe, a spinning wheel, a greatcoat, a mahogany bed, a silver spoon, a grindstone, and other items from which the reader can get some feel for relative prices of the period.

WEALTH DATA AND THE GENERAL CONCLUSION

From a statistical sample of probate inventories, supplemented where necessary with additional data evaluated in earlier chapters, we reach an approximate estimate of the amount and character of the private wealth held by the 2.35 million white and black inhabitants of the thirteen colonies. This population had been growing at the high rate of close to 3 percent a year (see table 2.1), most of which represented natural increase. A much larger proportion of the population than in the United States today were under 21—some 57 percent, or almost three fifths of the total.

Despite imperfections in the data, the evidence seems good enough to warrant the conclusion that the colonists in 1774 were relatively well off in comparison with the bulk of the population in Europe of that day and in comparison with much of the world's population in today's lesser developed countries. In terms of real wealth per capita, as we shall see, they had attained a level one-twelfth as high as that yielded two centuries later by the highly industrialized and complex economy of the United States in 1973. One may nevertheless wonder, without belittling the techniques of measurement of prices and real national product, whether such measures really tell us that we have twelve times as much consumption or are twelve times as well off today. Not all parts of the colonial picture were equally rosy. There were substantial wealth differences among the regions and among individual colonists within them. The range from rich to poor was great. As a painting is completed by what the viewer sees in it, the facets of emphasis will doubtless appear different to various readers, in the lights of their particular viewpoints. I offer, in this final chapter, interpretations of some of the specific conclusions which, to me, seem important and warranted by or suggested by the data.

AGGREGATE WEALTH IN 1774

Total private nonhuman tangible wealth in the thirteen colonies, by 1774, had reached the substantial figure of £88 million sterling (table 9.1 line 3). This translates, roughly, into $4.8 billion in dollars of 1978 purchasing power. This includes the value of privately owned land and improvements, which formed nearly seven tenths of the total. It also includes the value, as determined by contemporary appraisers appointed by courts, of livestock, farm, household, and business equipment, crops and business inventories and stocks of consumers' goods. Not included is a value of over £21 million sterling of 1774, roughly equal to $1.165 billion in 1978 dollars of private wealth invested in slaves and indentured servants, primarily slaves. The average value of a slave was £34 (table 4.9) or $1,845 in 1978 dollars.

The £88 million sterling may be considered as approximating, conceptually, the "national wealth," excluding human capital, of the

Table 9.1
Thirteen Colonies' Wealth Composition, 1774
(*In Pounds Sterling*)

	Total (Thousands of Pounds) (1)	Percentage (2)	Per Capita (Pounds) (3)	Per Free Wealthholder (Pounds) (4)
(1) Total physical wealth (2 + 3)	109,570	100.0	—ᵃ	252.0
(2) Slaves and servants	21,463	19.6	—ᵃ	49.4
(3) Nonhuman wealth, total (4 + 5 + 6 + 7)	88,106	80.4	37.4	202.6
(4) Land (real estate)	60,221	55.0	25.6	138.5
(5) Livestock	10,114	9.2	4.3	23.3
(6) Other producers' goodsᵇ	9,095	8.3	3.9	20.9
(7) Consumers' goods	8,677	7.9	3.7	20.0

SOURCE: Tables 3.1, 4.1, 4.2, 4.5, 4.7. Components may not add to totals because of rounding.

NOTE: Wealth per free capita was higher than that per capita. See tables 3.7 and 4.4.

ᵃ If the value of all slaves and servants is divided by the 2,354,000 total population, free and nonfree, the resulting figure for line 2, column 3 is £9.1 per capita. This figure added to £37.4 on line 3 yields £46.5 as the figure for line 1, column 3. We do not present these figures in the body of the table since we do not find useful the concept of private claims to wealth in the form of nonfree human beings divided as property among or available to such nonfree human beings.

ᵇ Includes crops.

thirteen colonies combined, except that it does not include any government or church wealth. Such wealth was, in any case, small in amount.[1] Most of the land was in the hands of private owners. Its value, including structures and other improvements, was by far the largest single component of colonial wealth. It formed 68 percent (see table 4.7) of "national wealth" excluding human capital. This percentage drops to 55 when the value of slaves is included in the total physical wealth (see tables 9.1 and 4.3). Again referring to the £88 million of total nonhuman "national wealth" (see table 4.1), livestock came second in importance, constituting 12 percent.[2] Other producers' goods of all kinds—including crops and merchants' or business inventories, farm implements, wagons, boats, artisan's equipment, household equipment and production supplies such as spinning wheels, wool, flax—at 10 percent, were valued almost as highly as livestock. The kinds of producers' goods aid in visualizing the kind of "national" productive capacity that was in place on the eve of the American Revolution. Consumers' goods, chiefly in such durables as furniture, household equipment for consumer use, and apparel, comprised 9 percent. Addition of another 1 percent in such consumers' perishables as food stored in households brings the total for consumers' goods up to equal value with that of "producers' goods other than livestock." It is the substantial size and character of wealth in consumers' goods, together with the high natural rate of population increase that prevailed, which suggest fairly high levels of living, particularly for the free colonists and their families.

PER CAPITA WEALTH, 1774

For the entire colonial population, man, woman, and child, whether free, slave or servant, white or black, private nonhuman tangible wealth averaged about £37.4 sterling in 1774. That amount of money in the colonies would buy about 310 bushels of wheat, 1,600 pounds of rice, a negro man, 11 cows, or 6 horses (see tables 1.3 through 1.7.). In dollars of 1978, it is roughly equivalent to about $2,030. Multiplied by 4 persons in a family, it yields an estimate of an average of about £150 sterling in 1774, or over $8,100 in 1978 dollars of wealth per family. This is for the value of the family's stock of physical assets, its wealth, not its income, and the figure does not include slave values.

If the same £88 million of nonhuman physical wealth is conceptually divided among only the adult males, the wealth per man, both white and black, averaged £172 sterling. (see table 3.6). Each man may be thought of, very roughly, as the head of a family, and this £172 pounds, translated into some $9,300 in 1978 dollars, though higher, is in the general neighborhood of the aforementioned average of around $8,100 for a family of four persons. Most of the black men were slaves who owned negligible amounts of private wealth. In fact, it was the white men, who outnumbered the blacks almost four to one (see table 2.4), who were the principal legal holders of wealth in colonial times. If, in deference to this historical reality, we conceptually divide the £88 million sterling among only the white men, the figure for average wealth per white man rises to £218 sterling, the equivalent of approximately $11,800 in 1978 dollars. This represents a substantial stock of real wealth per white family, achieved two hundred years ago in this newly developed part of the world.

Wealth in Slaves

At the 1774 point in American history, the institution of slavery was embedded in the legal and economic process, particularly of the South. Also the institution of indentured service remained important in the Middle Colonies and the South. The slaves and servants, in legal fact, had no claim to any of the wealth represented by the £88 million and hence any per capita figure is, in a sense, misleading. In their roles as producers, they did make use of property belonging to their owners or masters, and as consumers, they received such food, housing, and clothing as their masters provided or permitted. But they had no ownership claim to the wealth. If we then divide the total of £88 million of nonhuman physical wealth among only the free persons, men, women, and children, white and free blacks, the per free capita average becomes £48.4 (see table 3.7) or around $2,630 in 1978 dollars. There were comparatively so few free blacks (see table 2.4) that their inclusion or exclusion has slight effect on the average. The same £88 million divided among only the free whites yields almost as high an average wealth figure, £47.5 per free white capita (see table 3.6) or about $2,580 in 1978 dollars.

From the standpoint of the free wealthholder,[3] the foregoing figures do not encompass all the wealth, if the family owned slaves or had claim on the service of indentured servants. Such wealth was in a very real sense, economically as well as legally, a part of the total assets of the private owners in 1774. If we then add the value of holdings in slaves and servants, the total physical wealth per free wealthholder rises to £252.0 or nearly $13,700 in 1978 dollars (see tables 9.1, 3.7, and 3.8). Calculated on a per capita basis for only free persons, the same figure is £60.2 sterling or nearly $3,270 in 1978 dollars.

I argued in chapter 1 that slave and servant values are not properly included in a calculation of the aggregate or average wealth of a society, and especially not when one wishes to compare the wealth estimate with that for other places or times in which slavery did not exist. The best way to make an economically meaningful comparison for two dates or places, one of which included slave values, would be to extend the estimate for each date or place to include the value of all human capital, both free and nonfree. When we made such an estimate on a very crude basis (see chapter 3), we found that one might add some £63.2 million or 58 percent more for the value of free human capital in the colonies in 1774 to the aggregate wealth of £110 million shown in tables 9.1 and 3.1. This would raise total physical wealth (including human capital, both free and nonfree) to almost £173 million sterling in 1774, or about $9.37 billion of 1978. On a per capita basis, both free and nonfree, this crude estimate of total physical wealth is nearly double our estimate of £37.4 for nonhuman wealth, and reaches £73.4 pounds sterling, or nearly $4,000 per capita in 1978 dollars. Unfortunately, wealth figures for other times and places seldom give information on human capital values,[4] so we are not in a good position to make comparisons. Consequently, the comparisons here with other countries and discussion of economic growth over time will be made on the basis of nonhuman wealth.

Comparison of Per Capita Wealth With Contemporary England

Since slavery was not practiced in the British Isles, a comparison of wealth in the mother country with colonial wealth including slave values is not suitable. We can, however, compare the £37.4 per capita of nonhuman wealth in the colonies with per capita wealth estimates for England and Wales at around the same time. The £37.4 figure for the thirteen colonies in 1774 places them below the highly respected English estimate of £55 by Gregory King for 1688 and far below the more dubious estimate of £135 for 1770 by Arthur Young. (see table 3.13). An incommensurability still remains in that in the United Kingdom the estimates pertain to a population all of whom except prisoners were essentially free, whereas in the colonies some 23 percent of the population were not free and had no ownership claims to any part of their conceptual per capita portions of the aggregate nonhuman wealth. If we limit the comparison to the wealth owned only by the free colonists (nearly identical with the average wealth of the white colonists), the comparison with the mother country is more favorable to the free Americans. If we include colonial wealth in slaves, but exclude the slaves and servants as conceptual sharers of wealth, the resulting figure of £60.2 per free capita (see table 3.7) exceeds the 1688 per capita figure for England and Wales and comes closer to the questionable 1770 estimate of Young. In view of the doubts I expressed in chapter 3 as to the strength of the contemporary estimates for the mother country (see table 3.13 and notes) and in view of the strength of my colonial estimates, evidenced in part by their internal consistency and in part by their consistency with such external colonial data as we have, it is my opinion that the colonists in 1774 had an average per capita wealth that may have been lower but was of a very respectable order of magnitude in comparison with that of England and Wales.

Comparison of Per Capita Income With Other Places

When we convert the colonial wealth figures to annual income figures, the colonists in 1774 appear to have had real incomes per capita in excess of contemporary estimates for Holland, England, or France in about 1695 (see tables 3.10 and 3.12). They also appear to have been in excess of those of a group of developing countries today that include around half of the world's population (see table 3.14). They were around one-twelfth of per capita private real income in the United States in 1974.[5]

Per Capita Wealth by Region, 1774

Regional differences appear in our per capita estimates for 1774. The Middle Colonies were the richest in nonhuman wealth, with £40.2 per capita, while New England and the South were tied at an estimated £36.4 per capita (see tables 9.3 and 4.2). The South had almost half the total population of the colonies, but nearly 90 percent of the blacks (see tables 3.3 and 3.4). If the aggregate wealth is considered as owned only by free persons, and the value of slaves is included in the wealth total (see table 3.7), then the regional differences in wealth per free capita were much wider. The South was outstandingly the richest region in that sense. Its total physical wealth per free capita was £93, about double the £46 of the Middle Colonies, while New England was the poorest region, with £38.

Some factors other than the institution of slavery that may have contributed to regional wealth differences are discussed in chapter 3.

Colonial Economic Growth Prior to 1774

Our estimate for the thirteen colonies of £37.4 sterling per capita (see tables 9.1 and 3.5) of private, nonhuman, tangible wealth in 1774 suggests that there must have been substantial accretions in the intervening years from the relatively sparse beginning wealth of a few small colonial coastal settlements in the early 1600s (see appendix E). It seems likely that growth may have come in varying ways and at varying rates in the major regions and in particular counties or places within them. Such variations appear to be borne out by accruing quantitative evidence[6] from local studies and regional figures on exports and imports in the seventeenth and first three quarters of the eighteenth century. The figures range from estimates of negative growth rates for some times and places to ones as high as a positive 5 percent per year for others.[7] Exports[8] of such valuable products as tobacco, rice, grains, fish, lumber, cattle, furs, and skins as well as production of housing, food, clothing, and equipment for the colonists' own use were reflected in rather high estimates of wealth per probated wealthholder as early as the late seventeenth century, by scholars working with probate inventories in particular localities.[9]

A study of efficiency of tobacco production in some lower western shore Maryland counties (Menard 1975, 1980) suggests that a doubling of tobacco output per hand occurred between 1630 and 1670, but that there was little gain in tobacco productivity thereafter. Studies of agricultural productivity over the eighteenth century derived from data on crops and livestock from probate inventories in the counties of Worcester, Massachusetts (Anderson 1975a,b and 1979) and Chester, Pennsylvania (Ball and Walton 1976) suggest that there was little increase in northern agricultural productivity during the eighteenth century. Although there were some efficiency gains in shipping productivity during that century,[10] it has been suggested that these directly affected only a small part of the population and that the overwhelming predominance of the agricultural sector, in Pennsylvania, for example, held overall per capita productivity increases to something like 0.2 to 0.3 percent per year (Ball and Walton 1976).

What can we conclude from these diverse data and from the logic of my estimate of £37.4 pounds per capita nonhuman wealth in 1774? Despite varying local conditions in various earlier periods, and some changes in British imperial policy, there must have been some increase in wealth per capita in the colonies as a whole to reach the level attained by 1774. Rapid progress at times, particularly in the lower South, may have offset some periods of relative stagnation in some limited portions of the northern colonies. My conjecture, discussed more fully in chapter 3, is that for the colonies as a whole, per capita nonhuman wealth may have increased at a rate of around 0.3 percent per year from 1650 to 1725, accelerated to 0.4 percent in the next quarter century to 1750, and progressed at a rate of 0.5 percent from 1750 to 1774. These rates imply nonhuman wealth as high as £24 per capita in 1650, £28 in 1780, £30 in 1725 and £33 in 1750. If there was no great change in the general price level in the 125 years from 1650 to 1774 (see note to table 3.13), the £24 approximates a per capita wealth achieved in 1650 of $1,302 in dollars of 1978 purchasing power. This figure, give or take a little, suggests that the transplantation of Europeans and their knowhow, coupled with their eager use of the resources found in North America, resulted in early attainment of rather high wealth levels, once the hardships of first settlements were past. It approaches half of Gregory King's famous estimate for England and Wales in 1688 (see table 3.13). Depending upon what wealth-income or capital-output ratio is appropriate, it probably implies a real income per capita in excess of that of many underdeveloped countries today (see table 3.14). Despite possible local or regional spurts or lags or even declines in some subperiods after 1650, it seems likely that, for all regions combined, fairly steady intensive growth accompanied accumulating experience in the New World, learning-by-doing, increasing knowhow in shipping within the Atlantic community, and the enlargement in size of the market that came with growth of population and trade.

Growth in Per Capita Wealth from 1774 to 1973

The pace of American economic growth, measured by real, per capita, nonhuman physical wealth, accelerated markedly in the nineteenth century and slackened in the twentieth. The figure of $21,000 (see table 3.15 and figure 6) in 1976 dollars attained in the United States by 1973, compared with the estimate of about $1,780 for 1774 (see table 3.15; about \$2,030 in 1978 dollars), yields a longterm growth rate for the near 200-year span of a compounded 1.3 percent per year (see table 3.16 and figure 7). However, there were fluctuations in the rate among various subperiods, discussed in chapter 3. My estimates show some decline in real wealth per capita between 1774 and 1805, when the figure was a little over \$1,500 at 1976 prices. (For reservations as to the accuracy of this figure, see discussion in chapter 3, the section on United States wealth at benchmark dates since 1774.) The decline was likely a real event, considering the losses of the Revolutionary War, the great economic uncertainties, and difficulties in foreign shipping imposed by the groping through the confederation to a new national government and by the Napoleonic Wars, which commenced closely on the heels of the American Revolution. Some loyalists departed, taking movable wealth to Canadian provinces or to England, but I doubt whether, in aggregate physical terms, the amounts of what they could transport could have been large. From the low level in 1805, per capita wealth by 1850 on the eve of the Civil War reached a level double that of 1774. These figures yield a growth rate of 1.9 percent from 1805 to 1850. However, the rate from 1774 to 1850 (if we ignore the drop to 1805) was at the slower pace of 0.9. The drop to 1805 had a counterpart in the decline in real wealth per capita from 1929 to 1950 caused by reductions in production during the Great Depression, and then to interruptions due to World War II and subsequently the Korean War, so that the per capita real wealth level of 1929 was not regained until nearly 1960. The half century from 1850 to 1900 witnessed the spectacular growth rate of 2.4 percent per year, despite a slowdown[11] during the Civil War and its aftermath. This half century saw the freeing of the slaves, the coming of transcontinental railroads, the pushing of the frontier to the Pacific coast, and transformation from an agricultural to an industrial economy. By 1900, per capita wealth had increased to almost \$12,000 in 1976 dollars. By 1929, despite the disruptions of World War I, the figure reached over \$16,000. By 1973, after a depression, World War II, and the Korean War, and during the Vietnamese War, it was about \$21,000. Over the entire three quarter's century from 1900 to 1973, the latest wealth figure available, the growth rate averaged only 0.8 percent, close to the 0.9 from the late colonial period to 1850. However, for the shorter period within that time of 1950 to 1973 growth had regained the relatively high rate of 1.6 percent.

Rates of growth in per capita wealth are, of course, less volatile than those for income or product, since the latter are more vulnerable to extreme year-to-year or cyclical fluctuations. Since total wealth reflects not only the addition to (or subtraction from) stock of the current year's production minus consumption but also the base stock saved from all past production minus depreciation, its total moves more slowly than does current income in times of rising production and declines more slowly in times of falling production. Hence we do not expect close short-term parallels in rates of growth of per capita wealth and of per capita product. But over long periods, such as 200 years, the divergence should not be great. Our 200 year rate of 1.3 percent seems to be reasonably in accord with the average 1.6 percent rate in gross national product per head that Goldsmith (1959, 1965) found for the United States for the 120 years from 1839 to 1959, and the divergence to the low side is reasonable in view of our lower average rate of 0.9 from 1774 to 1850 (ignoring the possible wealth drop to 1805).[12]

INDIVIDUAL DIFFERENCES IN WEALTH IN 1774

A per capita wealth figure or an average per free colonial wealthholder is, of course, only a statistical construction that obscures all individual differences, all individuality. I noted earlier that slaves and servants did not, in fact, have claim to the wealth indicated by our per capita figures. Similarly, not all the free families in the colonies in 1774 had wealth of the amounts and kinds indicated in column 4 of table 9.1.

To get a more personal feeling for the wealth and life of colonial times, we can recall the diversities in the makeup of the population, review the regional differences and the ranges from rich to poor found in earlier chapters, and consider further their meaning. Likewise we can refresh our memories on the degree of urbanization and extent of occupational specialization reached by 1774, with their impacts on wealth production and life styles. A concrete way in which to approach some of these differences lies in summary sketches of the wealth and characteristics of some selected individuals (shown in table 7.33), with which this chapter closes.

Population Diversities

There were great diversities in the kinds of people who had come to the colonies in earlier years[13] and in their descendants. By 1774, relatively few of the population were foreign born, although there had been considerable immigration of whites in the 1760s into the Middle Colonies and South and importations of slaves at Charleston continued substantial in the 1760s and early 1770s. Nearly half the total population was in the South, with the balance almost equally divided between New England and the Middle Colonies (see tables 3.3, 2.5, 2.6 and 2.7). The two northern regions together had almost two-thirds of the free population, but only 15 percent of the nonfree. The slaves were concentrated heavily in the South, but there were noticeable numbers of them in the Middle Colonies, especially Delaware and New York. I found indentured servants most often in Pennsylvania, Maryland, and Virginia.

Regional Differences in Wealth

The South was outstandingly the richest region and New England the poorest, in aggregate wealth, when the value of slaves is included. The South had over half the total in the thirteen colonies, as shown in table 9.2. In slave values alone, it held 95 percent of the

Table 9.2
Regional Wealth Composition, 1774
(_Aggregates, in Thousands of Pounds Sterling_)

	New England	Middle Colonies	South
(1) Total physical wealth (2 + 3)	22,238	26,814	60,518
(2) Slaves and servants	101	1,032	20,330
(3) Nonhuman wealth, total (4 + 5 + 6 + 7)	22,136	25,782	40,188
(4) Land (real estate)	15,874	16,584	27,763[a]
(5) Livestock	1,703	3,059	5,352
(6) Other producers' goods[b]	1,911	3,550	3,634
(7) Consumers' goods	2,648	2,590	3,439

SOURCE: Table 4.1. Components may not add to totals because of rounding.

[a] For discussion of the real estate estimate for the South, see Note on Method and appendix A.

[b] Includes crops.

total. But, without slave wealth, the share of the South was reduced to some 45 percent of the aggregate. The South had nearly half the total real estate in the thirteen colonies and over half of the livestock and crop values. The Middle Colonies were a strong second in crops and livestock, with New England trailing especially far behind in crops. In all "producers' goods other than livestock" (including crops; see tables 9.2, 4.1, 4.6), the South and the Middle Colonies were virtually tied at 40 and 39 percent respectively of the thirteen colonies' total, while New England had only half as much, 21 percent. In consumers' goods, New England was nearly on a par with the Middle Colonies, each of them having about 30 percent, whereas the South had more, about 40 percent of all the consumers' goods in the colonies (table 4.6).

The wealth dominance of the South remains notable when we look at the average wealths of the free wealthholders (roughly the free family heads), as in the upper panel of table 9.3. The overwhelming dominance of the South's free families in slave assets is clear from the upper panel of table 9.3, as is the negligible character of such assets in the North. Of course, not all southern free families held slaves, as was made clear in chapter 8 (also see table 4.8), and most northern free families did not. The South also held a greater value of land (real estate) per wealthholder and outdid the Middle Colonies in livestock per wealthholder. Only in "producers' equipment and materials" did the Middle Colonies' free wealthholders outshine those in the South, and in this respect, even relatively poor New England equaled the South. This category includes the inventories of nonfarm businesses, which were small compared to farm inventories of crops and livestock, but which were of greater significance in the two northern regions than in the South. In consumers' goods, at £22 per wealthholder, free southern households had more, but not notably more wealth on the average than those in the two northern regions, which were nearly equal in this respect.

The wealth advantage of the South over other regions disappears completely when we consider only total nonhuman wealth as conceptually shared among the entire population. The per capita figure for the South is reduced to equality with that for New England and falls behind that for the Middle Colonies, as seen in the lower panel of table 9.3. In land, per capita, there was virtually no difference among regions. In livestock, at around £5, the Middle

Table 9.3
Regional Wealth Composition, 1774
Average Per Free Wealthholder, Per Capita
(In Pounds Sterling)

	New England	Middle Colonies	South
Per free wealthholder:			
(1) Total physical wealth (2 + 3)	161.2	186.8	394.7
(2) Slaves and servants	0.7	7.2	132.6
(3) Nonhuman wealth, total (4 + 5 + 6 + 7)	160.5	179.6	262.1
(4) Land (real estate)	115.1	115.5	181.1[a]
(5) Livestock	12.3	21.3	34.9
(6) Other producers' goods[b]	13.9	24.7	23.7
(7) Consumers' goods	19.2	18.0	22.4
Per capita:			
(8) Nonhuman wealth, total (9 + 10 + 11 + 12)	36.4	40.2	36.4
(9) Land (real estate)	26.1	25.9	25.1
(10) Livestock	2.8	4.8	4.8
(11) Other producers' goods[b]	3.1	5.5	3.3
(12) Consumers' goods	4.4	4.0	3.1

SOURCE: Tables 4.5 and 4.2.

NOTE: The general note to table 9.1 pertains to this table also. Figures corresponding to the last value shown in note a of table 9.1 for total physical wealth are: New England £36.6, Middle Colonies, £41.9; South, £54.7.

[a] For discussion of the real estate for the South, see Note on Method and appendix A.

[b] Includes crops.

Colonies were as well off as the southerners, and in "other producers' goods," with £5.5 per capita, they were ahead of the South, which at around £3 was in the same class with New England. In consumers' goods per capita, there being many fewer slaves in the North to share them with, both northern regions, with £4 or more, exceeded the South's £3.1.

Here, then, we see the crux of regional colonial wealth differences. We must acknowledge the southern wealth in slaves as an important, indeed as the important difference in its wealth as compared with that of the two northern regions. The free wealthholders of the South were most strikingly ahead of the North only if we count their wealth in slaves. Not counting such wealth, they remained still ahead of their northern counterparts but less overwhelmingly so. Not counting wealth in slaves, the South had no more nonhuman wealth for each man, woman, and child, white and black, free and nonfree, than had the northern regions; indeed it had less than did the Middle Colonies (table 3.5).

The slave economy was an established and integral part of the income and wealth production processes of the South by 1774. It was closely tied to the production of highly valued crops, tobacco in Maryland and Virginia, and rice and indigo in South Carolina and Georgia. Slavery was peripheral, however, in the Middle Colonies and virtually nonexistent in New England. The slave economy of the South provided a ready-made basis for the post-Revolutionary shift to a cotton economy after the invention of the cotton gin in 1793, and the subsequent rapid expansion of demand from the British textile industry. It permitted relatively high consumption and aristocratic life styles, especially for the richer landowning and slaveholding free southern wealthholders. It gave little impetus to the development of urban trade centers other than Charleston, which was an important metropolis for the lower South, including North Carolina. The northern regions, on the other hand, were dependent on more diversified crops and heavy use of family labor for farming. Northerners also supplemented farming with fishing, shipping, shipbuilding, the beginning of other manufactures, and commerce. They developed more urban trade centers, more skilled artisans, shopkeepers, and merchants, and relatively fewer aristocratic societies than the South. The substantial volume of shipping and commerce in the North, as well as some small beginnings of industry, laid a basis for subsequent expansion there of industrial and trade sectors. The evidence up to this point suggests that, in many ways, divergent regional economic interests and social structures that were later to culminate in the Civil War had already taken deep root in the colonies by 1774.

FINANCIAL ASSETS AND LIABILITIES

Credit of various kinds (see the discussion in chapter 5) was extended usually on an individual basis, from one colonist to another in this pre-banking era. Assets resulting from these transactions were in the form chiefly of entries in "book accounts" of amounts owing;

or there were privately signed notes and bonds and occasional mortgages. The same instrument or credit entry for a given transaction denoted a financial asset of the creditor and a financial liability of the debtor. For an individual, the total of his financial assets minus his financial obligations, when added to his total physical wealth, equals his net worth.[14]

I noted earlier that the data on location of creditors and on total debts owed are inadequate to determine whether there may have been a net external debt owed abroad in 1774, but I incline to the view that if there was such a debt, it was not very large, perhaps in the neighborhood of £6 million sterling, and perhaps owed chiefly by people in the South and in New England. By region, I noted that free wealthholders in the North, particularly in the Middle Colonies, held relatively more wealth in the form of financial assets than did those of the South. In New England and the South, these assets were more than offset by debts owed, so that in each of those two regions aggregate and average net worth were somewhat below aggregate or average physical wealth. The reverse was the case in the Middle Colonies, which may have been a net supplier of food to New England (Klingaman 1971) and which furnished substantial shipping service to the upper South. The relatively high financial assets of the Middle Colonies suggest that in 1774 this region was in the best relative position for financing commercial and industrial ventures.

SIZE DISTRIBUTION OF WEALTH

Many circumstances contribute to explain the great differences in amounts of wealth that individual colonists accumulated around 1774. One obvious factor was having or not having personal freedom. A second factor was sex. A third very significant factor was age. Children, who formed over half the total population, were supported by and may have contributed to the production of the family's income and wealth, but they did not hold property or become separate wealthholders until adulthood. Wealth frequently increased with age. Some free young men, just starting an independent household, were fortunate if their fathers could give them some land. Others worked first as laborers to acquire the means to purchase land and perhaps later a slave or servants (Kulikoff 1975; Menard, Harris, and Carr

1974). Others, for a variety of reasons, never became landowners. As free men progressed through the life cycle, their wealth accumulation tended to rise to middle age, then sometimes to fall in later years as they retired from active farming or other occupation and dispensed some assets to help their children get a start in life (see tables C.3, C.4, C.5, C.6).

As a proposition of fairness or equity, it seems just that older people who have worked longer and saved more should have more wealth than young adults just starting out. Hence the Gini coefficient of concentration, which measures the departure in wealthholding from a line of perfect equality, overstates the wealth concentration that would be found in a measure of departure from a line of rising wealth by age (see figure 12 and discussion of wealth by age in chapter 7 and appendix C). Nevertheless it is a widely used, standard measure, and is presented in this book for convenience of comparison with other studies.

Another circumstance that affected an individual colonist's wealth accumulation was his place of residence, whether urban or rural and in what region. His occupation, whether farmer, forester, or fisherman, merchant or tradesman, or professional, artisan, or laborer was closely related to his income and wealth accumulation. Land ownership, slave ownership, marriage, family size and connections, inheritance, education, training and experience, health, and still other factors helped to put some people higher on the wealth scale than others.

For Free Wealthholders

A summary picture of the way in which wealth (including value of slaves and servants) was shared among the free adult wealthholders (roughly heads of free families) on the eve of the Revolution is shown in table 9.4. The picture was shaped, in large part, by combinations of the explanatory factors mentioned above. It is one of substantial inequality, well before the transition to an industrial economy. There were many poor but also many who were well off. In all regions, the share of aggregate wealth held by the poorest 30 percent of free wealthholders was very small, less than 3 percent, while the shares of top wealthholders were much larger. This picture is not greatly different from that of the United States in 1962. The

Table 9.4
Distribution of Free Wealthholders by Size of Total Physical Wealth, 1774

	Thirteen Colonies (1)	New England (2)	N. Jersey Pennsylv. Delaware (3)	South (4)
Percentage share held by:				
100th percentile (richest 1%)	12.9	11.6	12.0	10.4
Tenth decile (richest 10%)	50.7[a]	46.8	35.1	46.9
Ninth decile (next richest 10%)	17.2[a]	19.1	17.6	22.7
Eighth-Sixth decile (next richest 30%)	25.4	26.5	36.1	24.6
First-Third decile (poorest 30%)	1.8	2.2	2.3	1.6
Gini coefficient	0.66	0.64	0.54	0.67
Value in pounds sterling at lower bound of:				
100th percentile (richest 1%)	£2,027.5	£1,174.7	£1,087.2	£2,646.8
Tenth decile (richest 10%)	609.4	401.6	379.9	1,140.1
Eighth decile (richest 30%)	241.7	163.6	246.8	390.5
Sixth decile (richest 50%)	110.6	74.5	154.6	148.1
Third decile (richest 80%)	18.1	15.9	16.5	24.2
First decile (poorest 10%)	0.0	3.0	0.0	2.6

SOURCE: Table 6.2.

NOTE: Total physical wealth includes values of slaves and servants. It excludes financial assets and liabilities. For a comparable table based on total net worth see table 6.1. The Gini coefficients from that table are, respectively: 0.73, 0.80, 0.60 and 0.68.

[a] Note a of table 6.2 pertains to this table also.

Gini coefficient for total physical wealth is 0.66 for the thirteen colonies, and noticeably lower only for the middle colonies, where the greatest equality prevailed.

Upper Fractions, Median, Gini Coefficient The richest in the South were much richer than the richest in the North, as can be seen in the lower panel of table 9.4. The poor had much closer wealth values, regardless of region. The median wealth, the value dividing the richer half from the poorer half of free wealthholders, was lowest for New England at £161.2, somewhat higher for the middle colonies at £189.2 and much higher for the South at £394.7 (see table 6.2).

The lesser aggregate wealth in New England was, nonetheless, about as unequally distributed as the greater wealth in the South. About the same fractions of the respective regional wealths were held by the top 1 and 10 percents in both regions, and the Gini coefficients for the two were only three points apart. The middle colonies showed the greatest equality, not only by the Gini measure but by the comparative boundary values of wealth and the relative shares held in the middle deciles. For free wealthholders in all regions combined, the top 1 percent held 13 percent of physical wealth, while the bottom half all together held less than 7 percent.

For All Potential Wealthholders

The foregoing discussion of table 9.4 has ignored the wealth-holding status of slaves and servants, who, nonetheless, were present in the colonial population. They have been added in table 9.5 to complete the picture. Their inclusion enhances the inequalities, particularly in the South.

For this comparison I include wealth in slave values[15] as part of the wealth held by the free owners of slaves, since such wealth was, in legal fact and in a real economic sense, a part of the total wealth to which those owners had claim and over the disposition of which they had the power of decision. We add adult male slaves and servants to the wealth distribution of the free adult wealthholder population, by considering them as potential wealthholders whose wealth in fact was zero in every instance. Thus they all fall toward the bottom of the wealth scales and fill up the lowest deciles in these distributions; the free wealthholders are consequently pushed upward into higher deciles. Since the nonfree were so heavily concentrated in the South, that is the region showing the greatest impact when they are included. The South's Gini coefficient rises from the 0.67 of table 9.4 to 0.83. The change is insignificant in New England and the middle colonies. The figures for the thirteen colonies show more inequality after the change, with a rise in the Gini from 0.66 to 0.73, because of the importance of the southern cases in the total.

The distributions in this table are the ones that I believe most nearly approximate the true wealth distributions among the total populations of the colonies and regions, and are the ones most appropriately compared with wealth distributions in the United States in

Table 9.5
Distribution of All Potential Wealthholders by Size
of Total Physical Wealth, 1774

	Thirteen Colonies (1)	New England (2)	N. Jersey Pennsylv. Delaware (3)	South (4)
Percentage share held by:				
100th percentile (richest 1%)	14.5	11.6	12.0	28.9
Tenth decile (richest 10%)	56.4	47.8	37.3	69.2
Ninth decile (next richest 10%)	18.0	19.1	18.2	18.2
Eighth-Sixth decile (next richest 30%)	22.7	26.4	35.8	12.2
First-Third decile (poorest 30%)	0.3	1.7	1.6	0.0
Gini coefficient	0.73	0.65	0.57	0.83
Value in pounds sterling at lower bound of:				
100th percentile (richest 1%)	£1,946.2	£1,174.7	£1,087.2	£4,021.7
Tenth decile (richest 10%)	482.1	397.2	378.5	903.7
Eighth decile (richest 30%)	190.7	156.6	241.7	184.0
Sixth decile (richest 50%)	48.9	68.4	151.7	23.1
Third decile (richest 80%)	0.0	12.8	13.9	0.0

SOURCE: Columns 1 and 4, tables 6.15 and 6.14 respectively. Columns 2 and 3, tables 7.181 and 7.182 respectively from *American Colonial Wealth,* either edition, pp. 2120–21.

NOTE: "Potential wealthholders" are defined as all free wealthholders plus all nonfree adult males. The latter are treated as holding zero wealth. Wealth in slave and servant values is included as part of the total physical wealth of their free owners.

1870 and 1962 shown in chapter 6, or with wealth distributions for other times or places that did not have slavery as an institution.

Comparison with Earlier and Later Dates

Some colonial historians[16] suggest that wealth at the mid-eighteenth century in the colonies was becoming somewhat less evenly distributed. However, a good deal of evidence from local studies is becoming available (summarized in chapter 8) which suggests that any increase in inequality, at least in the northern regions, must have been relatively slight during the colonial period. The studies further suggest that rather high levels of inequality were reached, at least in New England, quite early in the colonial period.[17] This seems to have been true notably in the large cities. Rather high inequality has also been found in the seventeenth century in some Maryland coastal counties.

We lack local studies of early wealth distribution in the lower South. It seems likely, if we had the evidence, that inequality was already great in Charleston also by the late seventeenth century. The inherent logic of the effect of slave wealth, together with the fact that slave importations into Charleston, the principal port of their entry, as well as into Virginia, were heavy in the 1730s to 1760s, suggests that wealth inequality may have continued to grow in the South even more than in the North in the eighteenth century, and that hence for the colonies as a whole the trend may have been toward slightly greater inequality.

Evidence on the distribution of wealth in England during the seventeenth and early eighteenth centuries is limited. For income there is an estimate of a Gini coefficient ranging from 0.55 to a possible 0.61 based on the 1688 figures of Gregory King.[18] I reason in chapter 8 that the distribution of wealth would have yielded a higher Gini than would the distribution of income, and suggest that the inequality which we find in the colonies in 1774, though high, was probably not so great as that in England three quarters of a century earlier.

The wealth inequalities in the thirteen colonies on the eve of the Revolution were about on a par with those in the United States nearly two hundred years later, and somewhat less than those prevailing one century later. A 1962 survey for the Federal Reserve Board showed a pattern of inequality strikingly similar to our 1774 findings, while some estimates from census samples for 1860 and 1870 show a higher degree of inequality.[19] Because of many technical questions as to comparability of wealth definitions and differing analytical procedures as well as differences in population universes sampled, these comparisons and ones with other studies must be considered as only tentative. To the extent that we can put credence in them, they suggest some nineteenth-century increases in inequality, which may have continued and peaked around the 1920s and declined thereafter.

Chapter 8 summarizes evidence from other studies and concludes that there was probably some increase in wealth inequality from the late colonial period to 1860 and 1870, and possibly on to 1890 and the early twentieth century. Shares of the top 1 percent of wealthholders appear to have increased from 1922 to 1929 and then decreased to 1956 (see table 8.10 and text discussion) and to have shown little directional movement since. Another comparison of data for 1921 with that for 1953 suggests movement toward greater equality during that period (Gallman 1968:319). In any case, by 1962, the inequality of 1860 and 1870 appears to have declined to very nearly that which prevailed in 1774.

Though the absolute content of the poverty level has unquestionably risen dramatically in two centuries, the relative shares of a larger total wealth held by the bottom half of the population, and by the next higher 20 percent, seem to have been about the same in 1962 as in 1774. The relative shares received in 1962 by the eighth and ninth deciles suggest a strengthening over two centuries of what we might call the upper middle classes. This seems to have come at the expense of shares held by the top 10 percent, notwithstanding a rise over the two centuries as a whole in the share of the top 1 percent.

The remarkable similarity of the two-centuries apart patterns of inequality of course do not signify that the "wealthy" and the "poor" of 1962 and later are the lineal descendants of the "wealthy" and the "poor" of colonial days. Much new immigration occurred in the nineteenth century. Many factors contribute to the wealth position of an individual at varying periods of his or her life, and there has been much shifting over the years both into and out of the ranks of the wealthy, the middle classes, and the poor. The particularly persistent problems of equalizing income and hence wealth opportunities for blacks, with which twentieth-century Americans are wrestling, may represent the only area within the pattern of wealth inequality where we are still visited by "the sins of our fathers."

We return in following sections to further consideration of the range in individual differences in wealth in the late colonial period, as evidenced by the findings of our sample of probated decedents, and to differences among various socioeconomic groups in the population of that time.

Range in Probated Wealth

The range in net worth among the free wealthholders in 1774, judging by the cases drawn into our sample (see table 6.3), was from the £32,700 of Peter Manigault in Charleston, South Carolina[20] to the $200 of negative net worth (excess of debts owed over his assets) by Samuel Brewster of Kingston, Plymouth County, Massachusetts. Manigault was an esquire, an attorney, an owner of several plantations and held a provincial colonial office. Brewster was a gentleman who held land, but owed debts of £363. In total physical wealth (see table 6.7)[21] Manigault was also the richest in our sample, with nearly £28,000, but Mr. Brewster, who, despite his large debts, owned £142 in real estate and £21 of household goods and livestock, was far from the lowest holder of physical wealth. That dubious distinction goes to William Janney,[22] a 64-year-old of Kent County, Maryland, whose estate was probated in Philadelphia, whose occupation I could not determine and who had no physical wealth. I believe that some living free wealthholders whose estates were not probated when they died also held very small or no physical wealth.

Lists of the ten richest and ten poorest cases in the samples for the thirteen colonies and for each of the three regions, with their ages, occupations and residence, are shown in chapter 6, both by net worth and by total physical wealth. Of the ten richest in the thirteen colonies, by either measure, nine were from the South. One Boston esquire, William White, with £15,300, was second to Manigault in net worth, and one Philadelphia merchant, Samuel Neave with £8,300 total physical wealth, was fourth on that list for the thirteen colonies. The richest case of physical wealth in the New England sample was the merchant Thomas Gerry[23] of Marblehead, Massachusetts, whose son Elbridge was subsequently to sign the Declaration of Independence. Thomas Gerry had over £4,100 of total physical wealth and a net worth of over £5,700. The list of ten richest cases by physical wealth in New England, headed by Gerry, runs through three esquires, a physician, a shopkeeper, two yeomen, a captain, and a gentleman. The list for New England of ten poorest free wealthholders by physical wealth includes three widows, two single women, a fisherman, a husbandman-chairmaker, a mariner, a tailor, and a yeoman; their total physical wealth ranged from £6.8 to £3.6 The ten poorest by net worth in New England include two mariners, a yeoman-blacksmith, two gentlemen, a cooper, a yeoman, a merchant-captain, a cordwainer, and a farmer-fisherman. All of these ten had negative net worth, more debts than the total of their physical plus financial assets; the amounts of the negative net worth ranged from minus £25 to minus £200.

Corresponding figures for the middle colonies were a highest net worth near £6,650 for the Philadelphia merchant Samuel Neave, closely followed by another merchant, Stephen Carmick, who had almost £6,200, then a farmer, a widow, a captain, a merchant, a farmer–large landowner, a tallow chandler with £2,100. The middle colonies' ten poorest by net worth ranged from a schoolmaster with a positive £8.6 in Burlington County, New Jersey to a chaisemaker in Kent County, Delaware who had minus £60 of net worth. By physical wealth, the next richest after Neave in the middle colonies' sample was the Philadelphia provincial officeholder and large landowner Lynford Lardner,[24] with over £7,600. Four merchants were found among the top ten there. Among the poorest ten were three widows, two laborers, a pilot, and a shoemaker. Their total physical wealth ranged from £7.6 to zero.

For the South, the ten richest by net worth were all esquires, planters, or farmers from Charleston District, South Carolina, except one Charleston District physician who also had a plantation. The tenth richest had almost £6,800 in net worth. The ten poorest by net worth ranged from a positive £4.2 to a negative £101, and included a tailor from Orange County, North Carolina, four farmers, a carpenter, and a merchant from Chesterfield County, Virginia. By physical wealth, after Manigault, the nine next richest in the South were also all from Charleston District—planters, esquires, the same doctor as on the net worth list, and one clerk who had over £5,800 in total physical wealth. The ten poorest by physical wealth ranged from a Charleston shopkeeper with £7.0 and a farmer in Orange County, North Carolina with £6.8 to a farmer with £2.6 in Halifax County, North Carolina.

WEALTH DIVERSITY BY SOCIOECONOMIC GROUP

The following paragraphs highlight some of the wealth differences among various socioeconomic groups that are discussed more fully in chapter 7.

Wealth Differences by Age

That older wealthholders, at least up to a point in middle age, were usually better off than younger ones is indicated in chapter 7, in appendix C, and in the earlier section on size distribution of wealth in this chapter. The colonial population had a higher proportion of younger adults than today's United States population, which makes even more interesting the finding noted earlier of similar patterns of wealth inequality in 1962 and 1774 (see tables 7.1, 7.5, figures 12 and 20 and appendix C).

Urban/Rural Wealth Differences

Urban wealth was plainly visible in such cities as Charleston, Philadelphia, and Boston. There also were urban poor in all these cities. The rich southern planters more than held their own in comparison with the richest in the North. Some of the top-ranking northern wealthholders also were farmers or other rural residents. Data from other studies suggest that wealth inequality was greater in the large cities than in rural areas.

The proportion of the colonists who lived in cities and towns was least in the South and greatest in New England. The differential in size of wealth between urban and rural was greatest in the South, influenced by the high wealth in Charleston.

Occupational Wealth Differences

Terms of occupation were not always clearly separable from terms of social status. Although I found frequent cases of males designated as "gentleman" or "esquire," they usually had an occupation in farming or as attorney or merchant, or perhaps had more than one occupation. I found the term "yeoman" used more or less interchangeably with the term "husbandman," "farmer," or "planter." I found it impossible to distinguish those terms in the 1774 colonial economies, either as to size of farm or as to social status.

No strong pattern of occupational differences in wealth was discernible in the three regions. In each region, farmers formed a large proportion of the total and in each they ranged from rich to poor. Those who called themselves "gentleman" or "esquire" tended to be rich farmers. In the middle colonies, farmers were predominant in the middle-wealth ranges. Fishermen and farmer-fishermen in New England tended to be of low wealth. Planters and farmers in the South ranged all the way from very wealthy, with several plantations and many slaves, to very poor with no slaves, no land, and small personal estate. In neither the South nor the North did I find evidence of a "farmer class" as opposed to urban dwellers, who were numerically still a very small minority of not over 10 percent. Urban dwellers were frequently also farmers.

I found "merchant" to be associated frequently with high wealth and social status, particularly in New England and Philadelphia, but also found some "merchants" of modest and even low wealth. I found fewer "merchants" in the South than in the North. Generally, the merchants in the North, both middle colonies and New England, tended to be of upper or middle wealth. In all regions, professionals, including lawyers, doctors, ministers, teachers, fell usually in upper to middle wealth ranges, particularly if they also owned farms or had side activities, but sometimes they were of very low wealth. Ship captains in New England and Philadelphia were usually among the richer persons, whereas "mariners" were usually sailors with lower wealth akin to that of laborers. Some Philadelphia and Charleston "mariners" had high wealth, however.

Artisans and shopkeepers fell usually in middle to lower wealth ranges, but there were important exceptions. For example, a "smith" or "carriage maker" sometimes had a substantial business inventory, owned land and a slave or two, and had wealth that placed him in the upper echelons.

Sex Wealth Differences

Prevailing colonial laws and customs meant that married women with husbands living were considered nonwealthholders. As widows, they usually had claim only to some personal estate, not to land, which generally went directly to their sons. There were exceptions, however, of widows who owned land specifically bequeathed to them by their husbands, and of single women who inherited land from their fathers. Miriam Potts, a widowed shopkeeper in Philadelphia, was a very rich woman, as were two widows, Elizabeth Smith and Abigail Townsend, in the South Carolina sample. Kathran Upham, "gentlewoman," was the richest person in the sample for Worcester County, Massachusettes.[25]

The personal estate of some widows was extensive and valuable, particularly of some southern widows with large numbers of slaves. Some northern widows owned cattle and farming implements and may have carried on farming operations themselves or with the help of sons or laborers. Many widows, however, in all regions, seem to have been left with only some household effects and apparel, and sometimes also financial assets. On average, women wealthholders held distinctly less wealth than men.

I believe these women must be considered as wealthholders when one considers the entire population. They formed something like 9 percent of the free wealthholders (see table 2.4); and they controlled wealth of the amounts and kinds indicated in the tables. Though widows frequently remarried, probably owing in part to economic need, there was always a group of them, unmarried, in the population.

Racial Wealth Differences

The discussion of slavery has pointed sharply to the racial differences in wealthholding in the colonies. Except for the free blacks, who formed less than 1 percent of the total population and less than 1 percent of the free wealthholders (see table 2.4), all blacks were slaves with no claim to wealth. They were, themselves, the legally owned property of others.

The one probate inventory of a free Negro, Cyrus,[26] in Charleston District of South Carolina, shows that free Negroes, influenced by the prevailing custom, sometimes owned other Negroes as a part of their wealth.

Here we had, clearly established and sanctioned, especially in the South, the institution that permitted the subsequent development of a cotton economy and later a sugar economy in parts of Louisiana. It also was the institution which, though abolished by a later Civil War, underlies the heritage of racial discrimination with which twentieth-century Americans are coping.

IMPLICATIONS FOR FUTURE ECONOMIC
GROWTH AND SOCIAL STRUCTURE

The substantial aggregate wealth accumulated in the thirteen colonies as a whole by 1774 consisted, in considerable part, of capital that was a foundation for future economic growth. Legally, it was predominantly owned and controlled by white, adult males. These males were ordered in social status considerably more by the size of their wealth than by their occupational or birth status. The deferential social class structure of European societies had not survived well in the colonies, as suggested by the section on occupational wealth differences.

Social Structure

As to social structure, we may summarize that by 1774 the pattern had been set for relative fluidity in status for free white males, dependent chiefly on their economic success. For free white women, social status was generally that conferred by father or husband, as it was to remain in the nineteenth century. Indentured white men, upon completion of their terms of servitude, were given outfits of new clothing and sometimes other remuneration and could generally get jobs as laborers if they had no artisan skill. Some set up successfully as artisans and some later acquired land and became farmers or found their way into other activities. The white indentured women, upon completion of their servitude, had little choice other than domestic service or marriage, and almost all married. Black men and women, except for the relatively few free blacks who appear to have been accepted in artisan or other employment, particularly in northern cities, were consigned to the lowest social and economic class by the institution of slavery.

Role of Women

The modest role of women as wealthholders in the colonies, following English and European custom, was a portent of their being denied political voting status until 1920 and continued limitations in their property rights in many states to the present day, and de facto in their access to preferred occupations. However, it belies the importance of their economic contributions to wealth production, in many instances in sharing with their husbands the responsibilities of farming and agricultural decisions as well as in performance of farm tasks. Wives of artisans and shopkeepers also frequently helped tend shop, and when their husbands died, they sometimes ran them on their own for a substantial number of years. Additionally women contributed very substantially to wealth creation through household production of such items as dried and preserved foods, making of cider, cheese, wine, soap, potash, spinning of thread and yarn, plucking and cleaning feathers, making cloth, making garments, sheets, bedding, and curtains. Many of these tasks moved from the home to the factory during the course of the nineteenth and twentieth centuries that were to follow, and then the value of the products appears as a part of the estimates of output or gross national product. Some of the nineteenth-century factories (such as textile mills, which were among the first), employed women workers, but rarely in supervisory or managerial positions. It seems likely that a case could be made that, in the nineteenth century, American women lost rather than gained in such economic control and management of wealth as they possessed in the eighteenth century.

Private Property, Law, Trade, Business Organization

Among the economic institutions, other than slavery, that carried over from 1774 to the next century were private property and the legal interpretation of property rights founded on English legal tradition, much of which remained influential in court decisions and legislation even after the adoption of the American constitution. Systems of credit transactions involved fairly complex financial instruments but had not yet become banks in the modern sense. These were to come mainly after the work of Hamilton and Gallatin in 1792. Considerable barter still prevailed, but prices were essentially determined in free markets for commodities and labor in the North. Marketing of crops and purchasing of many supplies in the South were done, in considerable part, through resident factors or agents of firms in England and Scotland. A legacy of knowhow of arrangements in the intercolonial coastal trade and overseas trade carried over to the late eighteenth century and the nineteenth, despite the interruptions of the Revolutionary War and conflicting new governmental policies of the states under the confederacy and the federal policies in the early Republic. The partnership, as a business form that helped to raise capital and share risk, was found in quite a few colonial enterprises. Corporations were not to be developed until the next century, but they were foreshadowed by the system of sharing in shipping ventures, suggested by such terms in the probate inventories as "one twentieth of a schooner" or "one third of a sloop."

Nonhuman Capital, Urbanization

The character of nonhuman capital in all regions showed the heavy predominance of agriculture. A somewhat larger role of financial and commercial capital in the middle colonies than elsewhere suggests that, as of 1774, they might have had the best base for financing industrial ventures to come. The shipping and shipbuilding capital were considerable in both northern regions. A somewhat greater tendency to artisan and shop capital in towns in New England, despite lesser financial capital than in the middle colonies, suggests a base there for future industrial and commercial diversification. In the South, despite the high wealth, there was less tendency to urbanization outside of a few major seaports, and the structure of wealth remained geared to agriculture.

The slave economy, fully developed in the South, was in place and ready for an easy transition to cotton culture after 1793. Although some southern planters had important economic side activities in 1774, involving financial transactions, and though considerable manufacturing was done on some plantations, there was nothing in the colonial southern situation in 1774 that was leading to the development of urban or manufacturing centers.

IMPLICATIONS FOR COLONIAL LEVELS OF LIVING

At wealth levels of £30 sterling, which I estimate were exceeded by some two-thirds of all free wealthholders, the colonists usually owned some basic farm and household producers' implements, often some livestock, a modest and functional assortment of consumers' durable goods, and occasionally some land or real estate. At levels above £240, which I roughly judge were surpassed by the richest third of the free wealthholders, their physical assets frequently included land, in the South slaves, extensive producers' goods, livestock, and some impressive items of consumers' durable goods. For the third of the free wealthholders with physical assets below £30, whom in relative terms I would call the colonial "poor," the wealth list was much less apt to include land or slaves, frequently not livestock, and often consisted chiefly of some rudimentary tools and equipment, functional furnishings as pots, dishes, and utensils, beds, tables, chairs, and a few sturdy garments. The slaves and indentured servants, in the nature of things, had claim to virtually no wealth other than the clothes on their backs and perhaps some bedding and a few utensils. They, however, had the use of housing, rudimentary furniture, and food furnished by their masters.

It is difficult to compare colonial levels of living with present day ones because the character of the wealth items has changed in so many ways, with industrialization and technological "advances." In some ways, the "advances" may only have substituted flimsy gadgets or mass-produced articles of short lifetimes, with a high proportion of their value claimed by the packaging, for carefully hand-made ones of sturdy and sometimes artistic quality produced by the colonists. In other ways, such as the amplification of man- and woman-power by steam and electricity, the wealth items of today yield benefits far beyond those available to the colonists. One may, nonetheless, question the advantage of the twentieth-century person who uses an automobile for daily commuting to work 20 or even 50 miles on crowded highways and whose food is raised 3,000 miles away. At both time periods consumers purchased "harmful" items such as sugar, tobacco, rum, tea, coffee.

The consumers' goods portion of the colonial wealth, which the probate inventories reveal often in intimate detail, tell us that many, at least of the free colonists, lived very comfortably and a few opulently, despite the lack of modern plumbing, refrigeration, and jet airplanes. On the other hand, there were some poor widows, some men whose occupations I could not determine, and others whose possessions at the time they died were limited to no more than a bed and a chair or table, a few utensils, and "apparel" of very small value.

It seems clear that there was ample plain food for all to be had by hard work. Wild berries and game and fish could be gathered. Many farms had swine, geese, and other fowl and many had hives of bees for honey. They also raised vegetables, grain, and sometimes fruits. Sugar, coffee, cocoa, tea, spices were expensive imports but were enjoyed by many of the middle- and upper-wealthholders and their families and guests. Cider was often home made. The well-off had Madeira or other imported wines from the wine islands; and rum, often made in New England from West Indies' molasses, was found in many households as well as in taverns.

Many of the household implements in the inventories give clues as to the preparation, storing, and processing of foods that went on in most colonial households. The breads were usually home made, indicated by such words as "dough trough," "bake trough." The many "kettles," "pots," "bake irons," "oven pans," "frying pans," "skillets," "flesh forks," "griddles," "tubs," "kegs," "bags," "boxes," "pails," "piggins," "firkins," "gallons," "bushels," "quarts," "pints," "gills," "scales," "steelyards" were used for preparing, measuring, and storing foods. There were for instance "cutting boxes," "cabbage planes," "cabbage tubs" for preparing and storing sauerkraut. There were "sieves," "sifters," "riddles," "searches" for screening meal or flour. There were "meal chests," "meat chests," "sugar boxes," "cheese tubs," "tea cannisters," "salt boxes," "butter boxes," "a box to put meal in," "cheese vats," "churns," "skimmers," "ladles," "bottles," "bottle drainers," "mortar and pestles," "chopping knives," "apple mills," "cider mills," "coffee mills" and many more such items for food preparation and storage.

Heating and cooking were chiefly by open fireplaces with adjoining ovens. The many entries of "andirons," often written "handirons," and sometimes called "firedogs," as well as of "fire tongs and shovels," "pothooks," "potracks," "trammels," "chimney chain," "iron grate," "pot and hangings," "bellows," "iron pot," "iron kettle," "warming pan" suggest the warm hearth scene in many kitchens. For living rooms and bedchambers there were "fire screens," "brass shovels and tongs," in addition to andirons or grates. There was wood for fuel, which required the cutting and chopping indicated by the "handsaw," "crosscut saw," "axe," "broadaxe," "iron wedge," "maul rings," "hatchet" found in many farm inventories in all regions. City families usually purchased firewood. There were metal stoves in a few of the Pennsylvania inventories, with designations such as "six-plate iron stove with pipes," "ten-plate stove," and Benjamin Franklin's stove had been invented in 1743. "Box irons" were a form of heater, in which warm coals were placed.

There was as yet no electricity for practical use and no indoor plumbing. Lighting was commonly by candles, as evidenced by "candlesticks," "snuffers," and "candlemolds" in inventories. Candles were generally homemade in the "candlemolds," usually from animal grease and fat and occasionally, as in some areas in New Jersey, from bayberry oil. There were also lamps and lanterns with oiled or greased rags or wicks that burned oily animal fats or, more elegantly and less smelly, whale oil. Outhouses, chamber pots, and in some richer households "necessary chairs," wash basins and pitchers on dressers or stands served for personal needs. Water for cooking and bathing was fetched in buckets from wells or springs. Fire fighting equipment was limited to "fire buckets" passed hand to hand from the nearest water source. Laundry was done with lye and homemade soap in "washing tubs"—sometimes specified as "cedar washing tubs"—and in "washing buckets" or "pails," sometimes "wooden pails." Ironing was done with "smoothing irons" "flat irons" on an "ironing board" or "ironing blanket." The inventory of Philadelphia merchant Thomas Gilbert[27] specifies "sundry things in the wash house" in addition to a "brass wash kettle" and a few more things "in the wash house chamber."

In household furniture and eating utensils, the differences in luxury of appoitments between the rich and the poor is evident from the content of the various probate inventories. Beds and bedding were basic and indicated in almost all cases, and finer ones were frequently bequeathed in wills. They varied from straw- or chaff-filled bed ticks without a bedstead to mahogany bedsteads with bedcords, feather beds, pillows, bolsters, and curtains worth as much as £25 sterling. Curtains were important to enclose warmth and keep out drafts in chilly rooms. There were also many "blankets," "coverlids," and other pieces of bedding, sometimes called "rugs." In the South, inventories frequently mentioned with the bedding items "pavillions," which were gauze curtain arrangements to keep out mosquitoes or other insects. Chairs and tables ranged from simple pine to elaborate mahogany, walnut, and in the South sometimes sycamore. There were "mahogany tea tables," "walnut chairs with needlework bottoms and claw feet," "backgammon tables," and other descriptions suggestive of some of the heirloom pieces of colonial furniture that are exhibited with pride in museums today. Chests, dressers, desks, cupboards, buffets or "bofats," stools, benches, boxes were hand made and ranged from crude to elegant. The middle- to high-wealth homes frequently had some pewterware, silverware, or "plate," as "pewter platter," "pewter bason," "pewter jug," "silver spoons," "silver tea urn," "silver pitcher," "silver cream jug," "silver tea set," Some of the wealthy had inported china such as "Delftware" or "Queensware," "lacquered ware," or ivory-handled knives and forks. The more ordinary homes sometimes had wooden trenchers, tinware, and earthenware plates and cups. The more elegant homes had paintings by European artists, "Wilton carpets," "painted floor cloths," "mahogany screens," "gilt looking glasses," "eight-day clocks." Guns, pistols, swords, powder horns were found in many homes and were useful both for hunting and for protection.

In apparel, also, the range of possessions from the rich to poor was great. Some had scarcely more than the clothes on their backs. Others had wardrobes of many coats, trousers, shirts, hats, gloves, shoes, stockings, dresses, bonnets, and jewelry. For ordinary wear there were leather breeches and aprons, boots and shoes, homemade woolen or linsey-woolsey (made of linen and wool threads) dresses and shirts and worsted stockings. Many households had a flax spinning wheel or "small wheel" and a "great wheel" or wool spinning wheel, and the implements that accompanied them, such as "wool cards," "flax cards," "flax hetchel," "reels." Linen, made of home-grown flax, was commonly used for underwear. Cotton remained an expensive, imported cloth. For the well-to-do there were "greatcoats" or "surtouts," "beaver hats," "waistcoats," "velvet coats," "brocade gowns," "silk gowns," "silk stockings," "silver knee buckles," "silver shoe buckles," "gold buttons," "silver buttons," "silver headed canes," "wigs," "gold watches," "gold rings," and other jewelry. These finer items were observed in the inventories of the middle- to high-wealth people in such cities as Charleston, Philadelphia, Boston, New York, and Salem, but also to some extent in all regions among well-to-do farmers, particularly in the South.

Sometimes all of a man's "apparel" was willed to a son, or a "velvet suit" to a favorite nephew. Sometimes a man's will specifically stated that his wife was to retain all her clothing, which suggests that otherwise it was included in his estate and might be sold to settle his debts.

A riding horse was the equivalent in function of today's automobile, and many but not all households had one. Oxen and sturdy horses were used for plowing and hauling and are present in many of the farm inventories. Carriages were expensive, and their ownership limited to the wealthy. Wagons were used for overland hauling and were found particularly in Pennsylvania farm inventories. Sleds were also used in the Middle Colonies and New England for transport. Boats and canoes were used for river and water transport, and some of the richer colonists were share owners in "sloops" or "schooners" that could make ocean voyages.

Copies of the Bible were found in a great many inventories, even of people of small wealth. Other books also were found in homes of middle- to well-to-do farmers, ship captains, and professionals and merchants. The titles, sometimes enumerated in the probate inventories, reveal much of the intellectual life of the colonies. They range through some of the Greek, Latin, and English classics to other literature. Many were on religious subjects, including prayer books and hymnbooks. There were some manuals of instruction in practical tasks, with titles such as *Young Man's Companion,* books on mathematics, chemistry, and science. There were also volumes on medicine, including remedies for sickness. Medical volumes were found in the inventories not only of doctors but of ministers, teachers, and others who were called on to help the sick.

A feel for many more details of the way the individual colonists lived can be gained by thumbing through the probate inventories published, by region and county, in *American Colonial Wealth.* Many of the household utensils are illustrated and their use described in Earle (1974). Some authentic ones are also found in Langdon (1937).

The range of individual colonist's levels of living is so great that it is hard to say what was "typical." I venture to suggest that, in degree of affluence of consumer living, we might rank subgroups of colonists in 1774 somewhat as follows:

Southern wealthy planters and farmers, including those resident in Charleston.

Philadelphia, Boston, Salem, and other major northern city merchants, esquires, and captains.

High-wealth Middle Colony and New England farmers and artisans.

High-wealth widows.

Middle- to high-wealth lawyers, doctors, ministers, if not included in the above groups.

Middle- to low-wealth farmers in the Middle Colonies, South, New England.

Middle- to low-wealth artisans and shopkeepers.

Laborers and mariners.

Low-wealth widows.

Indentured servants.

Slaves.

Some Illustrative Cases

Illustrations follow from selected probate inventories in several of these classes.

Thomas Gerry of Marblehead, Massachusetts, 72 years old, the richest merchant in my New England sample, had total physical wealth of £4,143 sterling but financial assets brought his net worth to £5,741. His real estate of £2,092 included a wharf, warehouse and land adjoining, three houses and land "under and adjoining them," half a dwelling house and land under it, a dwelling house exclusive of lot, an island with "two fish houses and a stage thereon," "his lower fish fence land . . . and fish thereon," four other pieces of land, and a "pew in the old meeting house in Marblehead" appraised at £15. His total business inventory and equipment were valued at £1,584. He owned two schooners, the *Charlotte* and the *Industry,* which "with appurtenances" were valued at £468, a one-fourth part of the "Brigg *Union* and appurtenances" valued at £85, and two other "boats" valued at £9. A large amount of Jamaica fish was in warehouses. The merchant goods "in the warehouse" also included Barbados sugar, salt beef, salt pork, "100 gallons of spirit," rum, casks of raisins and Malaga wine, molasses, many pieces of cloth of specified kinds, pins, lace, sewing silk, thread, gartering tapes, buttons, caps, handkerchiefs, gloves, shoe buckles, combs, fans, padlocks, cod hooks, mackerel hooks, nails, hammers, scales, lamp-black, salt, bar iron and bar lead. He owned one Negro man, Cato, valued at £37. Among his apparel were a silver watch, a pair of gold buttons, a pair of white silk gloves, black silk gloves, 20 shirts, gold jewelry such as a locket and 6 gold rings, 2 velvet jackets, 2 velvet breeches, women's apparel, a brocade suit, brocade shoes. Among the household effects were a looking glass, pictures, a tea table and set of china ware, 17 leather-bottomed chairs, "a dozen Harrateen chairs," "delf dishes," and "delf plates," enameled China bowls, glass beakers, wine glasses, a 124 lb. loaf of sugar, stone teapots, pewterware, brassware, copperware, 225 ounces of wrought sil- verware valued at £57, books on history, religion, and "sundry other books," 10 cords of wood in the cellar, together with 2 loads of hay, ½ a load of oats, brandy, rum, spirits, barrels, tubs, pots, funnels, boards, and more such items.

The richest merchant in the middle colonies, Samuel Neave of Philadelphia, age 68, had total physical wealth of £8,336, but financial liabilities which brought his net worth down to £6,647. His business equipment and inventory, the latter separated into "dry goods" and "wet goods," totaled £6,159. I estimated his real estate at £1,623. He had no slaves or indentured servants. His consumers' durable goods totaled £450. His listed apparel was valued at £41 and included silver spurs, silver knee, shoe, and stock buckles, a pair of gold sleeve buttons, a gold watch, and a gold-headed cane. Among his household goods were square, oval, and round mahogany tables, 8 mahogany chairs with claw feet, Windsor chairs, a Wilton carpet, a "large painted floorcloth," framed pictures and maps. He also had a walnut double chest of drawers, a red cedar chest, 6 walnut chairs with green bottoms, a large carved and gilt sconce looking glass, 8 clawfooted walnut chairs with leather bottoms and damask covers, walnut framed looking glass, large chimney dogs with brass fluted columns, and brass shovels and tongs, books on history, commerce, etc., with a closet shelf of pamphlets. He owned silverware such as 12 large silver-handled knives with 12 forks in a case, a bread basket which weighed 40 oz. 14 d.wt. (d.wt. — denarius weight, i.e., penny- weight), also silver (with weights specified) coffee pot, tankard, waiter, butter boats, salts, sugar dish, cream pot, 14 table spoons, 6 dessert spoons, 9 teaspoons, large waiter, a set of castors in a frame. There were also burnt china, a japanned waiter, Delft ware, Queensware, mahogany waiters, walnut trays, fruit plates, custard cups, pewterware, stoneware, an ornamented iron stove, a large cannon stove with pipes, and a copper Dutch oven.

References to a warehouse suggest that Roswell Woodward, age 66, a wealthy farmer in New Haven County, Connecticut, may also have performed merchant functions, although I coded him simply as farmer and large landowner. Of his total physical wealth of £1,070, £857 was in real estate. This included 112 acres "adjoining to the sea and the highway," the warehouse lot, the old warehouse, fresh meadow, 9 acres of salt meadow, the hill lot, the house and house lot, corn house and stable, the "lot north of the road and house called the frog pond." He owned 3 Negroes valued at £47. He had cattle, horses, hogs, sheep, geese, feathers, corn, rye, barley, cider, cheese, a gun, farm implements, containers and casks. His consumers' durable goods totaled an appraised £67. Included among the apparel items were a beaver coat, coats and vests with silver buttons, a velvet vest, velvet "britches" with silver buttons, "14 silver buttons for britches," silver shoe and knee buckles. There were also listed a woman's cap, gown, hood, shift, and stays, bed and table linen, blankets, bed curtains, a desk, a stand, a looking glass, 8 chairs, 6 broken chairs, 9 silver table spoons, a silver tankard, silver porringers, a silver milkpot, a chafing dish, a pewter teapot, pewter plates and basins, 4 brass kettles, a brass milk pan, a brass skimmer, earthen plates, platters and teapot, 2 china teacups and saucers, 1 law book and 1 great Bible.

A wealthy farmer-miller of Lower Merion township in Philadelphia County, Pennsylvania was Charles Jolley, aged between 26 and 44. His total physical wealth came to £1,698, of which real estate accounted for £1,446. He had one Negro man valued at £29 and cash of £27. Besides horses, cattle, and hogs, he had rye and wheat crops, "a quantity of hay," a wind fan, a cart, a "sleigh and harness," a "curricle and harness" (i.e., a two-wheeled chaise drawn by two horses abreast), a wagon, four sets of wagon gears, 28 pounds of tallow, and a gun. Among his household items were a walnut dining table, 2 tea tables, a walnut desk, a walnut table, "1 arm and 6 common walnut chairs," 3 rush-bottom chairs, a pine table, a stove and pipe, 6 pictures, and a map of England. He also had china bowls, cups, and plates, a copper coffee pot, 6 silver table spoons, 4 silver teaspoons, silver sugar tongs and cream jug, pewter dishes, plates, and spoons, 3 dozen knives and forks, a carving knife and fork. The list also includes an iron tea kettle, 7 earthen pans, 1 copper kettle, a small Dutch oven, a small brass kettle, a dough trough, casks, hogsheads, and barrels. There were 29 books specified only as "old and new" and worth £1.8 sterling.

The richest planter in my Maryland sample was James Cox, aged 45 or more, of Queen Anne's County. Of his total physical wealth of £2,709, real estate accounted for £2,240. His four Negroes were valued at a total of £98 and he had £39 in consumers' durables, which involved apparel appraised at £5. Among his possessions were a "riding chair and harness," 11 silver table spoons, 6 rush-bottom chairs, a maple table, a "high bedstead," feather beds, a walnut desk, a corner cupboard, a tea chest, a case with 12 bottles, a "Delph punch bowl," a "Queen china mug," a stone mug, a brass crock, an iron teakettle, a copper teakettle, a brass kettle, as well as a "tin sieve to clean flax seed." He also possessed a case of surveyor's instruments, plows and tackling and various farm implements, several guns and a pistol, crops of tobacco, wheat, oats, potatoes, corn, and 260 pounds of lard.

The richest planter I found in Virginia was Henry Walthall, aged 36, of Chesterfield County, with total physical wealth of £4,021 sterling. Real estate comprised £3,372 and he had 10 slaves valued at £481. Horses, cattle, hogs, sheep, and geese comprised another £85. He had 25 barrels of corn, 10 hogsheads of tobacco, 2 "slays and harness," casks, jugs, saws, reap hooks, and other tools, 2 saddles, and a gun. Among the household items were 2 black walnut tables, a looking glass, a sugar box, a small brass kettle, a "parcel of earthenware," a corner cupboard, a flax wheel, a cotton wheel, another wheel, and a loom. Very little apparel was itemized but there was mention of a pair of silver shoe buckles.

In South Carolina we find the second richest case in our southern sample, the planter Elijah Postele, Esq., aged 45 or over, of Dorchester, Charleston District. His total physical wealth came to £15,561 and his real estate to £542. At each of four named plantations, the Savannah, the Pine Hill, the Cane Acre, and the Round O, he had "plantation tools," 1 or 2 ox wagons or "oxcart and gear," 1 or 2 guns, cattle, oxen, horses, poultry, and hogs or sheep. There were substantial numbers of Negroes at each plantation, valued at a total of £11,384. There were grindstones, wind fans, and corn mills, 1 or 2 beds, mattresses and bedsteads, iron pots and similar items at each plantation. His dwelling house contained furniture of mahogany, including tea tables, oval table, table with marble slab, chests, dressing tables, looking glasses. There was a mahogany couch, arm chair, and 12 other mahogany chairs with "hair bottoms," 12 more with leather bottoms, walnut tables and chairs, some with "worked bottoms," 14 hickory chairs, Wilton and Scotch floor carpets, a mahogany case with two dozen silver table spoons, a mahogany bottle case, a complete set of "enameled table china," another of "tea china," a "japanned tea chest, tray and cake basket," silver bottle stands, silver teaspoons, silver chased castors, pewter ware, 12 loaves of sugar, 2 chariot horses, and a horse chaise. Wearing apparel was valued at £43 sterling and included a gold watch, gold shoe buckles, gold sleeve buttons, gold stock buckle, 3 gold rings, and a silver-hilted sword. There was also mention of "small rice and sundries in the rice store."

A "yeoman" in Scituate, Plymouth County, Massachusettes, Peleg Bryant Jr., aged 56, at a wealth level nearer that of the middle third of all living wealthholders, had total physical wealth of £201, £161 in real estate and £40 in movables. He had no slaves. His financial assets of £60 exceeded by nearly £8 his financial liabilities. The real estate comprised "the home place house and barn," 15 acres of pasture land and 5 acres of woodland. He had one old horse, 3 sheep, 1 swine, 2 cows, 2 yearlings, some farm implements, apparel worth £3, books worth one and a half shillings, a large round table, a tea table, 6 framed chairs, some pewter and earthen ware, beef, pork, flax, corn, and rye.

Henry Gristman, a farmer of comparable wealth of Chestnut Hill in Northampton County, Pennsylvania, aged 45 or more, had total physical wealth of £242, real estate estimated at £210, and movables of £31. Among the latter were 2 horses, 2 cows, 4 sheep, geese, an old wagon, a saddle, and bridles. There were a plow, a harrow, a gun, saws, axes, hoes, shovels, a frow, and a hatchel. No apparel or household furniture were listed other than 2 pewter dishes, 2 pewter plates, 8 pewter spoons, a table, an iron lamp, a dough trough, milkpots, a churn, iron pots and pans and similar items.

Hugh James, a farmer of similar wealth, aged between 26 and 44, in Charlotte County, Virginia, had total physical wealth of £206 and land estimated at £99. He had 4 Negroes, valued at £83. There was one horse worth £4, and also 14 hogs, corn worth 3 shillings, feathers worth 23 shillings, and 4 sides of leather appraised at £1. No apparel was listed. There was a gun, pewter worth 16 shillings, a punch bowl, two bedsteads, feather beds and "furniture," 2 tables, 2 chests, 6 chairs, a looking glass, a cotton spinning wheel and cards, an iron pot, pot hooks, a tobacco hogshead, casks, jugs, old iron, iron wedges, and a bell.

In Orange County, North Carolina, a farmer of about the same wealth was Neil McCallister, aged between 26 and 44. His physical movables or portable wealth came to £225. I found no evidence of land ownership (though I wonder if he may not have had some), so I treated that sum as his total physical wealth. Of this, £102 was invested in 4 Negroes. He had 16 head of cattle, 6 horses, 5 sheep, a wagon and gears. Oats, corn, and wheat in the ground were valued at a total of just under £4. There was also hay and some flaxseed. Besides saddles, a rifle gun, and a pair of stilliards (scales), there were a plow and other farm implements, a half bushel (container), and 4 bags. The inventory also listed "1 dresser of pewter and sundries," a chest of drawers, 2 tables, 5 chairs, a looking glass, 2 spinning wheels, a set of desk mountings, a watch, a lantern, 8 casks of flour, a dough trough, a potrack and hooks, a frying pan, and a grindstone.

John Nickerson, a 45-year old mariner of Scituate, Plymouth County, Massachusetts, had total physical wealth of £7 and another £7 of financial assets for "his wages for his last voyage at sea." He had consumers' durables of £5 and £1 of producers' durable goods. The former included apparel appraised at £0.2. A "bed, bedstead, and furniture," "another bedstead and some old feathers," and a "cupboard and old chests," summed in value to £2.4, and he had books worth £0.1. A "looking glass, spinning wheels, tables, and other household goods" added another £1.6. The inventory also enumerated pewter worth £0.2, "5 old razors," 5 large stone jugs, a quart jug, 6 cases of bottles, "other bottles," "some iron ware," and 26 gallons of molasses valued at £1.6. He had no real estate, no slaves, and no livestock.

Thoms Comb, a mariner whose age I could not determine, of Charleston, South Carolina, had total physical wealth of £12, principally in clothing. He owned no real estate, slaves, or livestock and had no financial assets. He owned two quadrants worth £2.1 and "5

Guinea mats" appraised at £0.4. He had "6 ivory teeth weighing 36" (I infer pounds avoirdupois) at 5 South Carolina shillings each, or a total of £1.3 sterling. He also had a silver watch worth £1 and gold and silver buttons and buckles worth £1.8. They included gold sleeve and breast buttons, a pair of silver shoe buckles, a pair of silver knee buckles and "3 old stone buckles." His apparel included 6 check and 2 white shirts, 8 pairs of old stockings, 2 pairs of trousers, "sundry old jackets," 2 hats, 4 striped jackets, a red jacket, and a blue cloth coat. No items of furniture were listed except "a chest and sundry articles in the file," and "1 chest and an empty case." The two chests, articles in the file, and empty case were worth all together £1.0.

Thomas Ring, a laborer of Medway, Suffolk County, Massachusetts, died at age 21 possessed of a horse and its equipment, a hog, his clothing, a small amount of household goods, and "notes of hand" valued at £10.4. His total physical wealth was £14, but estimated financial liabilities of £9.7 kept his net worth at about £15. He owned no real estate or slaves. Among his clothing, valued at a total of £7.9, were "the best suit of clothes" and "another suit of clothes" worth together about £2. There were "2 great coats, another coat, and 6 shirts" worth £1 and "a waistcoat, trousers, and sundry pairs of stockings" worth about £0.6. He also had "shoes, buckles, and sundry other small articles" worth £0.3. The household equipment included "2 pairs of sheets and pillow beers and a bedstead" worth £0.5, a warming pan, kettle, pot, frying pan, earthen ware, a bottle, tray, sieve, keg, and candlestick.

I give final illustrations of two widows, one in the South, one in the North. Sarah Brown, aged 45 or more, in Queen Anne's County, Maryland possessed, besides her apparel appraised at £2.2, some furniture and equipment, "1 old Negro man named Durham," valued at £7.5, a 16-year-old black mare appraised at £1.8, and a two-year-old colt worth £3.6. An "old riding chair and chair harness" were appraised at £0.15. The household furniture included a large walnut table valued at £0.9 and a "feather bed and furniture" (meaning accompaniments of the feather bed) appraised at £3.6. She had "an old woolen wheel" (spinning wheel) worth 2 Maryland shillings or £0.08. "6 silver tea spoons and 1 pair silver sugar tongs" were appraised at £0.6. Her other household items consisted of an old pine chest and padlock, 2 old chairs, a chest of drawers, an "old case of knives and forks," crockery ware, 1 wine glass, a vinegar cruet, a salt glass, a copper tea kettle, a bellmetal spice mortar and pestle, an iron potrack, an old iron skillet, an old frying pan, 1 and ½ dozen quart bottles, "2 old cypress piggins" (pails or tubs). Her total physical wealth came to £25. She had no real estate, crops, or financial assets. She owed £11 to four creditors named in the account filed by her estate administrator, William Brown, so that her net worth was £14.

Mary Dwinell, a 90-year-old widow in Topsfield, Essex County, Massachusetts had only £7 in total physical wealth but £9.5 "money due to the estate of the deceased." My estimate of £3.2 in debts brought her net worth down to £13. She had no real estate, slaves, or livestock, but had 25 pounds of pork appraised at 10 Massachusetts shillings or £0.4 sterling and 16 pounds of cheese at 4 Massachusettes pence per pound or £0.2 sterling and "5 feet and a half of wood" at 7 Massachusetts shillings 4 pence, or £0.3 sterling. I give a complete enumeration of her other possessions because they yield a clear picture of her living and show a large number of items encompassed in a low valuation. (This case, incidentally, is a reminder that the inventory items on which this entire wealth study is based are used ones, and that the appraised wealth values, as well as coinciding with actual estate sale values, may be on the low side. Also some of the other cases shown in table 7.33 suggest that the enumerated items in the probate inventories may not have included all possessions. For example, Cyrus the free Negro in Charleston, South Carolina and William Wallace the Charleston mariner must have had some consumers' durable goods, at least apparel, but none were shown in their inventories.)

The widow Dwinell's apparel totaled £1.4 and included "4 old pettycoats," a "quilted pettycoat," two gowns, a "riding hood and head," a pair of stays, 5 shifts, "caps and handkerchiefs," "gloves and mittens," a "fan and pocket," aprons, waistcoat, old stockings. There was a table worth £0.06 and 2 old chairs at 2 Massachusetts shillings or £0.08 sterling. A "feather bed with its furniture" was valued at £3.4, "one feather bed" at £0.7. There were besides a lookingglass, 3 old coverlets, 2 pairs of sheets, 2 pillowcases, 2 table-cloths, a little blanket, a towel, linen yarn, a clock reel, a large spinning wheel worth 1 Massachusetts shilling 2 pence or £0.04, an "old fashioned linen wheel," a "Dutch linen wheel" valued at 5 Massa-

chusetts shillings 4 pence or £0.2, and a flax comb. She also had a
fire shovel and tongs, a "box iron and heater," a warming pan, a frying pan, 2 trammels, "flesh forks," 2 iron pots, a small iron kettle,
"3 pounds of old pewter," 3 pewter platters, "2 plates and a por-
ringer," knives and forks, a box, a basket, wooden ware and a pail, a
lignum vitae mortar and pestle, a salt box, candlesticks, earthen
ware, "dealf ware" (the Delft valued at 8 Massachusetts pence or
£0.02), a funnel, a sauce pan, a small meat barrel, and 2 old cider
barrels.

What is the upshot of our investigation? I conclude that the level
of living attained on the eve of the American Revolution by typical
free colonists, even the "poor" ones, was substantial. It included sufficient food and drink, including meat, cider, and often strong liquors,
candles and sometimes oil lamps for lighting (though the number of
candles used was often closely limited for reasons of economy). Fire-
place equipment was found in nearly every household. Clothing was
sturdy and sometimes ornamental. Household furnishings and equipment met minimal functional needs and, even at some surprisingly
low wealth levels, articles of pewter, copper, crockery, chinaware,
and silverware allowed for amenities. Furniture was often made of
hard woods, handcrafted, and especially among the better off, was
quite ornamental and handsome. Cattle, sheep, hogs, poultry, and
geese provided meat, fats for soap and candles, wool for yarns and
cloth, feathers for bedding. Flax, grown on many farms, provided
linen for weaving cloth for household textiles and apparel, and the
spinning wheel was a near-universal item of household equipment.
At the middle to upper wealth levels, we see the enjoyment of more
imported goods, which extended the variety and heightened the
quality of articles used. Foot travel was still the common means of
locomotion on land, but virtually all the rich, many of middle wealth,
and some of low wealth had horses and accompanying harness and
saddles, if not riding chairs or carriages. Shares in ownership of large
vessels such as schooners were usually limited to the rich, but smaller
"boats" were owned by considerable numbers at middle wealth
levels, particularly in the South. This study does not furnish data on
the levels of living of the slaves or indentured servants, but it seems
reasonable to conclude that their apparel and house furnishings were
definitely more scanty or simpler than those of the free colonists,

though they obviously had to be sufficient to enable them to work effectively.

All together, I believe the evidence of this study shows that Americans of 1774 had attained substantial wealth which compared favorably with that of "ordinary people" in England and Europe and, on average, may have been not far behind that of England even when the wealth of the lords and barons is included. The level of living, even of the "poor," was usually sufficient for vigorous activity, and for the "rich," at least in such places as Philadelphia, Boston, and Charleston, might be called opulent. The economic sources of the wealth, in the capital goods and equipment of the colonists, their land and its improvements, their own and their slaves' and servants' working capacities, were in place as a base for the further economic growth of the nation that was to be.

APPENDIX A

Techniques Followed and Data Limitations

This appendix supplements the Note on Method and offers information helpful for assessment by the nontechnical reader of the results presented in this book. Part one condenses the more complete details regarding the sample design and related weighting that can be found in *American Colonial Wealth*. The scrupulous execution of the sample design, limited only by gaps encountered in the survival of records and their content, is basic to the entire study. Parts two through five offer essentially new material. The supplementation of data lacks in the probate inventories themselves with searches of tax lists, deeds, and estate accounts is covered in the Note on Method, as is the treatment of the severe problem of insufficient numbers of cases for New York counties.

Part one covers not only the initial sample plans, but also the successes, as well as the limitations due to obstacles noted, with which the plans could be executed, and the necessity for weighting at several levels. The first level, which takes account of differing numbers of cases obtained in various counties, is required to obtain unbiased regional estimates of wealth of probated decedents. The second and third levels of weighting expand the data beyond the bounds of the decedent sample to estimates of the wealth of living free wealthholders.

Part two treats more fully than does the second edition of *American Colonial Wealth* the problem of the highly atypical holdings of slaves in the Charleston District, one of the "counties" drawn in the sample. Post-weighing, using Variant Two weights for the South, which reduce the relative importance of data from Charleston and increase that of the remaining seven sample county groups, is my solution to this problem. The solution makes the best use of the results of the carefully drawn random sample, yet meets the requirement of reasonable conformity to independent data from outside the sample on a matter so important as the number of blacks in the South.

Part three gives an evaluation of the strengths of various portions of the estimates and some caveats as to their interpretation. Part four considers problems of replication of this study for other dates. Part five considers some of the limitations of the wealth-income or capital-output ratios used in chapter 3 to move, at the macro or "national" level, from wealth to income estimates for the colonies.

PART ONE:
THE SAMPLE DESIGN AND WEIGHTING, VARIANT ONE

First and Second Sample Plans Distinguished

When I refer to the first sample plan, I mean the design followed for the selection of counties in New Jersey, Pennsylvania, and Delaware, discussed in detail in Jones (1970:14–29) and in *American Colonial Wealth,* either edition, pp. 1813, 1820–21, 1833–35, 1837–40, 1843–44. The second sample plan is that followed for selection of counties in New England, New York, and the South, detailed in the latter work, either edition, pp. 1813–19, 1822–27, 1833–42, and 1845.

Both sample plans envisaged that approximately equal numbers of inventories be obtained for each cluster, that is, from each county or county group drawn in the sample. This feature—equal numbers of cases from each cluster—was designed to yield what statisticians call a "self-weighting sample." In my study, this would be one for which a simple sum, or average, of all the cases from all the clusters in a region would yield an unbiased estimate of the total, or average, wealth of all probated decedents in the region, that is, of the statistical universe represented by the sample. Such simplicity is highly desirable. Difficulties at the data collection stage, discussed in the next section, however, precluded obtaining such a sample.

Despite unequal numbers actually obtained, an unbiased estimate of wealth of decedents in a region was still obtained, but only by more cumbersome processes involving weighting the individual observations from each cluster.

Target Number of Cases In the first plan, executed for Pennsylvania, New Jersey, and Delaware, the target number of cases for each sample county was 83. The total number of inventories probated in 1774 for a county was to be determined when the investigator arrived at the courthouse or archival depositary of that county, and a sampling ratio was to be calculated to select 83 cases randomly from them. The cases were too few to follow this procedure in four of the five counties approached. In this situation, not a subsample but every case for 1774 was taken for each sample county. Yet these numbers were much smaller than the desired 83 except for Philadelphia County, where the number was 135. The sample size could be increased only by taking more counties or more years. No provision for alternate counties had been made in the first plan, for deliberate reasons presented in Jones (1970:16). For Westmoreland County, where there were only three 1774 cases, the number was increased to 7 by adding all the cases for 1773 and 1775, namely two each; this addition was made only because of the special problem of sparse data for that county. Despite the disparity in numbers of cases obtained in the five clusters, all the inventories obtained were tabulated and representative regional averages were computed, by assigning equal weight[1] to each cluster.

In the second sample design a revised and more flexible target number of cases per cluster was set, and a provision was made for alternate counties to be included in the event that the minimum number was not obtained from the first drawn county (or group of counties in the South) approached. For these regions, 25 cases (the approximate number obtained and found useful in three middle colonies' counties already studied) was set as the minimum number of inventories per cluster to be obtained from a single sample county or group of counties, or its alternate[2] if need be, and a maximum cutoff point was set at 100 cases.[3] If the numbers of cases obtained for each cluster proved reasonably equal, say none much below 25 nor over 50, serious consideration would have been given to treating the samples as self-weighting. In that case, the results, simply averaged, could be presented as unbiased estimates for New England, New York, and the South. Those unweighted estimates, when combined with the weighted estimate from the five counties for the middle colonies in the first sample, would yield an unbiased estimate for the thirteen colonies as a whole.

Actual data collection in New England, New York, and the South, however, also yielded substantially differing numbers of cases than the targets by county or county group. The range, except for New York counties, was less extreme than the experience in Pennsylvania, New Jersey, and Delaware. The range, New York excepted, from 23 to 102 per cluster, also required weighting to keep the results unbiased for these regions. Additionally, the severely limited 23 cases found in all of New York province required the development of the New York hybrid pattern (see section on New York hybrid in Note on Method).

County or c *Weights for Decedents' Wealth* Readers not interested in the technical aspects of weighting the sample data will, nonetheless, wish to know, in a general way, why an average of the raw data was not accepted as an estimate of wealth, and how we can infer wealth of the living from estate data of decedents. The why of weighting can be briefly stated. It is required, in view of the sample design and the unequal numbers of cases obtained in clusters from the various sample counties, in order to reach the first objective, an unbiased sample of probate inventories. Beyond that objective, to move to an estimate of wealth of the living, weighting is a means to counteract the too high proportion of older persons among decedents and to allow for the wealth of those whose estates never go through the legal process and hence are missed in our sample of decedents. The latter two points are discussed in subsequent sections.

I discuss here the county weights, or c weights.[4] These weighting factors have the effect of equalizing the contribution of each cluster to the regional average, regardless of the number of cases obtained for the cluster. Yet they utilize every case within a cluster, with each case contributing equally within its own cluster. They thus permit us to take full advantage of the information in all the inventories obtained, yet they prevent the large county clusters such as those from Philadelphia, Suffolk, and Essex Counties and Charleston District from dominating their regional averages. This redistribution, to achieve equal contribution from each cluster to the regional average, is appropriate because of the sample design, where each cluster was to represent an equal part of the total universe sampled, measured by approximately 20,000 living white "wealthholders."

The *c*-weighted results, together with their confidence intervals, are offered only in *American Colonial Wealth*[5] as an unbiased estimate of wealth of all decedents whose estates were probated in 1774 within the region, or for the thirteen colonies as a whole.

Construction of Estimates of Wealth of the Living

This study seeks information, however, regarding the wealth of all people living in 1774, not just the wealth of those dying. The information regarding the wealth of those who died, though it has its own interest, is sought chiefly as a means to the end. The *c*-weighted unbiased estimate of decedents' wealth cannot be intepreted directly as the wealth of the living for at least two important reasons. First, those who die comprise proportionately more older people than are found in a cross-section of living persons.[6] We might ignore this disproportion if it had no relation to wealth, but such is not the case. The colonial data,[7] as well as studies of wealth by age for more recent dates,[8] definitely show a positive correlation between age and wealth; older persons tend to have higher wealth, at least up to a plateau in late middle age. Second, the estate of not everyone who died went through the legal process of probate. How many of these nonprobates existed in 1774 and what was their wealth?

Wealth of Living "Probate-type" Wealthholders, w Weights The excess of older people is overcome by an age correction, achieved by modifying the *c* weights to reach what I call *w* weights. The appropriate *w* weight,[9] which depends both on the person's county and on his age class, is used as a multiplier for the data for each sample decedent. The *w* weights retain the effect of the *c* weights in keeping equal the contribution from each sample cluster to its regional total or average. In addition, they restructure those results (alter the proportions of older and younger) to reflect the age of the living, as determined in chapter 2. In effect the *w* weights, while still keeping equal the county contributions to the regional average, also pull down the influence of the older decedents and increase the influence of the younger on the results. This is tantamount to assuming that among the then-living wealthholders, the older, if they had died in 1774, would have had wealth like that held, on average, by the older probated decedents. Similarly, the younger wealthholders among the living, had they died in 1774, would have held wealth similar to the average wealth held by younger probated decedents. I find this assumption entirely reasonable for that segment of the living free wealthholders whose estates would have been probated when they died, the "probate-type" wealthholders. The w-weighted results accordingly, are presented as unbiased estimates of the wealth, or other personal characteristics, of all the living probate-type wealthholders within the region, or for the thirteen colonies as a whole. I present confidence intervals at this level also in *American Colonial Wealth*, and in appendix D of the present volume. This level still does not give us estimated wealth for all then-living wealthholders because it does not allow for the wealth of those whose estates were never probated.

Wealth of All Living Free Wealthholders, w^* Weights A third set of weights, designated w^*, moves the wealth estimates to a third, more interesting, level that pertains to all living wealthholders. These include both those among the then-living wealthholders whose estates would be expected to be probated when they died and those whose estates would not, the probate-type and nonprobate-type wealthholders, respectively. This level of estimate involves more than just getting an age-corrected unbiased sample of decedents. We must determine two further parameters not discernible directly from the sample data. We need to know the proportion of the living wealthholders who were of the nonprobate type, that is, the nonprobate ratio, as determined in the tables in chapter 2. Second, we must find a reasonable size of wealth of the nonprobate-type wealthholders. We cannot assume that their wealth is identical to, or only trivially different from, that of the probate types, for the very reasons that explain why some estates were not probated, discussed below.

To estimate the two required parameters, I lean in large part, on the sample data but also introduce some assumptions that I consider reasonable and as close to the truth as we can come with present knowledge. I believe that, with their use, our w^*-weighted[10] wealth values are much nearer the true values for the entire free wealthholder population of the colonies than either the c-weighted or w-weighted values. The latter two, are, however, independent of the nonprobate assumptions. The reader can find in *American Colonial Wealth*, either edition, table 6.1, 1866, a succinct summary of the weights and the populations to which the weighted sample results, at the three levels, pertain. The assumptions regarding wealth of the nonprobate types are summarized in succeeding paragraphs of the present appendix. It goes without saying that better knowledge to improve our probate-nonprobate ratio and our valuation of the wealth of the nonprobates would increase the accuracy of the w^*-weighted estimates of wealth of all living wealthholders.

Average Wealth of the Nonprobate-type Wealthholders (Value of h) What was the wealth of the nonprobate-type living wealthholders? Since their dying counterparts left no records, we can only infer it from consideration of the probable reasons for an estate's not being probated. We can be sure these reasons did not include estate or inheritance taxes, which were nonexistent in 1774. We may enumerate the following as among possible reasons. (1) The most obvious was that there was no wealth or so little as not to justify the bother. This would be true of the drifters and ne'er-do-wells, the infirm, the young who had not accumulated anything, the old who had already transferred all assets to their children, etc. Surely there were considerable numbers of these[11] among the living free population who legally might have held wealth, and so qualify as "wealthholders." But also, it seems reasonable that for not inconsiderable numbers of others of middle wealth and a few all the way to high wealth, an estate might escape the legal process for one of the following additional reasons: (2) The costs and inconvenience of travel by foot, horse, or boat to the county seat. (3) Desire to avoid the fees[12] and procedures of estate administration through the court. (4) Preference for a simple informal distribution of assets among heirs. This last reason for nonprobate would seem acceptable when there were no creditors or heirs demanding an accounting, and if, in New England, it were not desired to sell the land in order to settle the estate.[13]

The reasons 2, 3, and 4 suggested for not probating an estate preclude the simple assumption that all nonprobates had zero wealth. Striking something of a balance among the reasons for nonprobate, I assumed the average wealth of nonprobate-type wealthholders in a region to be a fraction of the average wealth (w-weighted mean) of probate-type wealthholders in that region. This fraction is denoted as h in section VI of *American Colonial Wealth,* either edition. The following values of h are assumed:[14]

New England	½ or .50
Middle Colonies (whether including or excluding New York hybrid)	¼ or .25
South	¼ or .25

The value of h set at one-quarter for the Middle Colonies[15] and the South seems reasonable. But for New England, where my estimate of the proportion of living wealthholders who were of the nonprobate type comes out at a high 66 percent (see chapter 2 and its footnote 24), I find the one-quarter assumption too low to be convincing and advance the alternative assumption that it might have been as high as one-half. (See comparison of the two assumptions in Jones 1972: table 6). To have assigned so many as two-thirds of the wealthholders only a quarter of the wealth of the "probate types" would have given us unconscionably low w^*-weighted wealth for all New England wealthholders. Even using the figure of one-half, the wealth of New England comes out as smaller per wealthholder than in any other region, as is apparent in chapters 3 and following. To have used a smaller value for h would have only aggravated the estimate of New England's relative poverty.

Conversion Factor for w^*-weighted Averages   The combination of the size of the probate ratio and the value of h for each region works out in effect to a simple conversion factor for each region, to move from a w-weighted average to a w^*-weighted average. This conversion factor, discussed in *American Colonial Wealth,* either edition, pp. 1887, 1888, is as follows:

New England		0.670
middle colonies (excluding New York hybrid)		0.730
Middle Colonies (including New York hybrid)		0.720
South[16]	(0.795)	0.760

This means that roughly (with slight discrepancies due to rounding), any figures presented only for probate-type wealthholders may be quickly reduced to their lower w^*-weighted levels for "all wealthholders" by multiplying each wealth value by the above factors. Conversely, if one is looking at a table for "all wealthholders," as in some tables in chapters 5 and 7, and wishes to know what the corresponding w-weighted higher average figure for probate-type wealthholders may be, one would multiply each w^*-weighted wealth value by the reciprocal of the above factor, that is, the decimal number that results from the number 1 divided by the factor. A single conversion factor is not available for the thirteen colonies because of the combining of regional weights, which yield differing factors for each wealth item depending on which region held more or less of that kind of wealth.

The foregoing conversion factors are not useful for estimating percentages of w^*-weighted wealthholders who held various forms of wealth, such as land, slaves, producers' goods, etc. Hence I carry such estimates only to the w-weighted or probate-type wealthholder level (see the discussion of reasons in part three).

Size Distribution of the Nonprobate-type Wealthholders (Assumption B) To estimate the concentration of w^*-weighted wealth among all wealthholders, we need not only the probate-nonprobate ratios and the values of h, but an answer to the further question: What was the size distribution among the nonprobate-type wealthholders? How many of them were rich, how many poor? In light of the possible reasons for not probating an estate, it is clear that some nonprobates would be richer than others. The question is by how much? Again we find an answer rooted in part in the sample data, in part in an assumption.

I present in chapter 6 the distributions under only my preferred assumption B.[17] This hypothesis is that some people at all wealth levels from zero to very high were not probated; that most of them were heavily concentrated in the lower-wealth levels; but that some, at a progressively decreasing rate, were found in all deciles even up to the highest. This permits a few cases of very wealthy nonprobate-types, but places the great bulk of them at lower wealth ranges. For the entire nonprobate distribution, I retain the constraint that the average wealth of all the nonprobate-types within a region must equal h times its w-weighted probate-type average wealth.[18] The wealth concentration figures of chapter 6 should, accordingly, be evaluated with the understanding that they depend not only upon the concentration found among the sample decedents but also upon the size of the nonprobate ratios in the regions, the assumed value for h, and the acceptability of assumption B. For the wealth concentration based more closely on only the sample of probates, the reader should seek the w-weighted size distribution in *American Colonial Wealth* or at the Newberry Library.

PART TWO: WEIGHTING, VARIANT TWO FOR THE SOUTH

The county weight assigned to the Charleston District in the regional average for the South, in the present volume, differs from that used in the first edition of *American Colonial Wealth,* as does the probate-nonprobate ratio for the South, for reasons discussed in this part. These changes yield alternative, or Variant Two–weighted, estimates for the South and consequently for the thirteen colonies. The Variant Two estimates for the South are used consistently in the present volume and are also presented in the appendix to the second edition of *American Colonial Wealth.* Values for the thirteen colonies in the present volume are comprised of Variant One–weighted figures for New England, Variant One–weighted figures for the Middle Colonies, and Variant Two-weighted figures for the South, combined in proportion to the numbers of living wealthholders in the respective regions. All tables for the South and for the thirteen colonies in section VII of both editions of *American Colonial Wealth* are Variant One–weighted tables, although those words do not appear there. Those tables remain correct, under the assumptions and weights of Variant One. These are clearly set forth in *American Colonial Wealth,* either edition, sections V on sampling and VI on weighting. They accord, except for the change in the southern probate-nonprobate ratio and the further change in Charleston's county weight, to the discussion in part one of this appendix.

Discrepancy in Slave Figures: The Reason for Variant Two

The compelling reason for change to Variant Two weights for the South arose from a data discrepancy noted in the course of completing the present volume and subsequent to publication of the first edition of *American Colonial Wealth.* Analysis of the weighted data revealed an unacceptable inconsistency between the known numbers of blacks in the South and the numbers implied by the calculation, presented in chapters 3 and 4, of aggregate wealth held in the form of slaves and servants in the South. The implied numbers of blacks, using Variant One weights, were over twice the best population estimates derived from *Historical Statistics*. Or, put another way, the implied average value per slave, using Variant One weights, was over twice what I obtained directly from values per slave tallied from my own sample of probate inventories. This tally was undertaken for the express purpose of checking on the black population figure, which I reached by dividing my estimated aggregate value of slaves by a value per slave.

Tables showing results of my unweighted tally of values per slave and per servant in the South are presented in chapter 4. Their average value of £34 for both sexes and all ages is less than half the result of the following calculations, which are based on the Variant One–weighted value of slaves and servants per wealthholder:

$$\frac{£245.7 \times 153,325}{433,106} = \frac{£37,671,952}{433,106} = £87 \text{ value per slave in the South}$$

or

$$\frac{£245.7 \times 153,325}{452,892} = \frac{£37,671,952}{452,892} = £83 \text{ value per slave and servant in the South.}$$

In the above calculations, £245.7 sterling is the Variant One w^*-weighted value of slaves and servants per wealthholder in the South, as presented in *American Colonial Wealth,* either edition, p. 1947, when the southern probate-nonprobate ratio is 73/27 and the county weight accorded the Charleston District is 0.125 or one-eighth of the southern average. The 153,325 is the number of all wealthholders in the South, including both probate-type and nonprobate-type, shown in table 2.7 and also in *American Colonial Wealth,* either edition, table 4.26. The 433,106 is the number of slaves in the South, shown in the same two tables, and 452,892 is the corresponding total of all nonfree persons, which includes also the indentured servants. The tallied values of slaves and servants, as presented in chapter 4, shows that the figure of £245.7 consists, for all practical purposes, only of slave values, since the number of indentured servants found in the southern sample was very small.

Ulrich B. Phillips found useful slave auction values from probate estates.[19] The values of my tally for adult male slaves (see table 4.11) are in reasonable accord with the £44.08 slave price for 1773–75 shown by Richard Bean[20] and with calculations of slave values by age made by Robert Fogel and Stanley Engerman.[21]

Outside Checks on the Discrepancy

To explain the discrepancy that troubled me and to satisfy myself that there was not a corresponding overstatement of my southern colonies' and thirteen colonies' estimates for other wealth categories than slaves, I sought outside data checks. However, aside from the figures on population and slave values already mentioned, I found little quantitative data, external to this study, that can be used as a check on the components of my wealth estimates. Figures on commodity exports and imports cover too small a portion of total wealth to be helpful for this purpose. Comparison was made, however, with some estimates by Samuel Blodget (1806:60) for 1774, with respect to total land acreage and value (for the colonies as a whole, which he was comparing with later dates for the United States), and with his numbers of horses and horned cattle. Although his figures are only rough guesses and not strictly commensurate with mine, the results from my study are of the same order of magnitude, though somewhat higher than his. Blodget's data, however, were not described with sufficient precision to justify altering my data to approach his results.

Checks for Possible Methodological Sources of the Discrepancy

Since I had the advantage of external checks on slave values and counts of total numbers of southern blacks, which were compelling, I turned to a review of my methods. I am satisfied that the sample is a good one and that the inventory values are reasonably accurate. I reconsidered my population estimates, exchange rates, and values of h without finding reason to change them. I found a change in probate ratio in the South to be in order, but the effect of this change, though in the right direction, was insufficient to yield a correction of the magnitude required to correct the discrepancy in slave figures. Since my slave tally pinpointed the Charleston District as the major source[22] of my high slave figure, I reviewed intensively my treatment of Charleston. This led to a revision of the Charleston county weight, after some other factors were eliminated as possible sources of the discrepancy.

Population The number of southern wealthholders could be shaved by lowering slightly the percentage of blacks calculated as free in table 2.7, but no change of major magnitude could result. The population figures presented in series Z of *Historical Statistics* have been reviewed by many authorities and are in a consistent relationship to the numbers actually counted only sixteen years later in the first census of the United States in 1790. The total numbers of blacks and of free blacks I show in table 2.7 cannot be far wrong. A slight revision in these figures would not eliminate the discrepancy.

Exchange Rates As to exchange rates, I noted on pages 1711–12 in *American Colonial Wealth* that David Wallace (1951:136) reported 763 South Carolina pounds equal to 100 pounds sterling as the exchange rate for South Carolina during the period 1770–73. If I changed to that rate from 700 to 100, it would reduce by some 9 percent all the South Carolina monetary values. This is still nowhere near the order of magnitude required to correct the slave figure that concerns us.[23] Since other sources, cited on pp. 1711–12 of *American Colonial Wealth*, support the exchange rate I had used and a change would require complicated retabulation, I retain the 700 to 100 exchange rate.

Value of h I am satisfied that nonprobate-type wealth must be included, and I find no convincing reason to alter my assumption[24] for the South that *h* equals one-fourth; i.e., that wealth of the nonprobate-type wealthholders, including wealth in slaves, might have averaged about 25 percent of that of the probate-type wealthholders.

Probate-Nonprobate Ratio I used a probate-nonprobate ratio of 68/32 in the preliminary paper on southern findings presented at the 1973 meeting in Chicago of the Organization of American Historians. This figure is closer to that of the Middle Colonies (64/36) and is more reasonable than the ratio of 73/27 used in Variant One weights, which gives the South the highest probate proportion of any of the regions and which was used in the first edition of *American Colonial Wealth*. I rechecked my worksheets and concluded that they verify the 68/32 figure. Hence I reverted to its use for the revised or Variant Two–weighted southern calculations. This revision, alone, results in about a 5 percent reduction in the average and aggregate values of slaves and servants for the South, as compared with the Variant One–weighted estimate. This change is in the right direction, and affects all the other wealth categories as well as slaves, but is insufficient to correct the discrepancy in the slave figure.

County Weight for Charleston District

I finally turned to consider the contribution of the Charleston District to my calculation of the average and aggregate value of servants and slaves in the South. Of the w^*-weighted value for slaves and servants of £245.7 per wealthholder, using Variant One weights, in the calculation where the Charleston sample observations were given a weight of one-eighth or 0.125 (i.e., the Charleston District was one of the eight areas drawn into the sample for the South),[25] the Charleston District still accounted for 47 percent[26] or nearly half of the weighted southern aggregate slave value. Although it will be seen from the tally tables in chapter 4 that the slaves in the Charleston sample had somewhat higher values, on average, than those in the other seven sample portions of the South, the principal source of the impact of the Charleston District on the slave values for the total South is the much larger number of slaves held by the average Charleston sample decedent than by the other decedents in the southern sample.

There is no denying that these slaves were, in fact, held by probated Charleston decedents, and that, with respect to other kinds of wealth as well, the Charleston District was rich. The problem therefore boils down to whether the Charleston District is a satisfactory representative of the wealth of one-eighth of all southern wealthholders, as envisaged in the sample plan. The stratum[27] from which it was drawn includes Savannah and parishes in Georgia, as well as other coastal and interior districts of South Carolina. I conclude that, in this particular sample, it is not, for two reasons. The first is the flagrantly high average wealth in Charleston District as compared with the other southern clusters, apparent in table A.1. The ratio of the average wealth in Charleston District to that in the seven other clusters is much higher than the ratio of the average wealth in Philadelphia County to that of the rest of the middle colonies and much higher than the ratio of the average wealth in Suffolk and Essex counties, which contain Boston and Salem, respectively, to that

Table A.1
Wealth by Cluster, All Regions, 1774
Average per Probate-type Wealthholder
(In Pounds Sterling)

Clusters	Net Worth	Total Physical Wealth	Slaves and Servants	Livestock	Crops
Litchfield, Conn.	131.9	173.4	0.0	21.4	1.1
New Haven, Conn.	139.7	190.0	1.8	15.4	0.4
Essex, Mass.	271.4	266.9	0.7	9.8	3.0
Hampshire, Mass.	178.2	207.6	0.6	24.0	0.9
Plymouth, Mass.	206.4	268.2	0.0	16.2	2.6
Suffolk, Mass.	312.4	322.9	4.3	11.6	1.2
Worcester, Mass.	202.3	255.4	0.2	30.7	1.0
New York[a]	425.5	279.2	11.5	16.6	6.2
Northampton, Pa.	246.6	254.1	0.8	28.6	10.3
Westmoreland, Pa.	158.6	182.4	0.0	30.9	1.4
Philadelphia, Pa.	396.7	386.5	7.3	15.2	6.3
Burlington, N.J.	341.5	191.5	18.7	53.4	26.6
Kent Del.	247.8	263.0	19.5	23.7	16.8
Queene Anne's, Md.	552.2	572.2	112.7	38.1	48.6
Anne Arundel, Md.	660.4	658.7	169.2	43.4	25.7
Charlotte-Halifax, Va.	546.5	600.5	214.8	51.3	3.5
Southhampton-Brunswick-Mecklenburg, Va.	311.3	348.8	92.6	24.8	2.3
Chesterfield-Fairfax-Spotsylvania, Va.	527.2	594.6	196.0	49.1	10.9
Halifax, N.C.	468.5	496.3	265.0	62.3	3.9
Orange, N.C.	227.5	236.4	89.6	52.3	1.9
Charleston District, S.C.	2,337.7	2,332.0	1,325.0	65.2	68.9

SOURCE: Sample data, *w*-weighted. Figures for livestock and crops include allocations from "mixed portable physical wealth," and "adjustments" shown separately in tables in *American Colonial Wealth.* If the reader prefers the lower *w**-weighted values for all wealthholders, he may multiply the above values by the conversion factors shown earlier in this appendix.

[a] Average of 23 sample cases. Corresponding values for New York hybrid are 278.0, 255.6, 8.0, 25.6, 9.5.

in the rest of New England. The table makes it clear that Charleston wealth, especially in slaves and the totals affected by the large slaves figures, is way out of line with that of the rest of the South. The second reason is that the Charleston District itself comprised only 1 percent of the total white population and 1 percent of the total white "wealthholders" of the South. (This can be seen in *American Colonial Wealth,* either edition, table 5.5.) In contrast, Philadelphia

County contained 12.8 percent of the total population of the middle colonies of Pennsylvania, New Jersey, and Delaware. Similarly, Suffolk County had 4.1 percent of the white "wealthholders" and 4.0 percent of the white population of New England, and Essex County had 7.6 and 7.5 percent, respectively. (The Philadelphia numbers are found in *American Colonial Wealth,* either edition, table 5.4, and the New England figures in its table 5.2.)

It is clear from table A.1 that the extreme wealth of Charleston was not found in samples anywhere else in the colonies. On the other hand, this wealth undeniably existed in the Charleston District and belongs in my estimates for its own sake, just as would the wealth in New York City or Chicago if we were taking a nationwide sample today. A procedure which I believe more nearly approximates the true value of the average wealth for the South as a whole is to reduce Charleston's weight to the relative importance of its white population in the South. This is 1 percent, whether measured by the total white population or by the white "wealthholder" population. Stated as a weight, it is 0.010. The other 99 percent of the southern white "wealthholders" are then represented equally by the remaining seven other clusters in the southern sample. Each of the eight clusters, Charleston included, originally contributed one-eighth to the southern regional total. That is to say, the county weight for each southern cluster in Variant One weights was $100/8 = 0.125$. When Charleston's county weight is reduced from 0.125 to 0.010, the remainder of its Variant One county weight, namely 0.115, is divided equally among the other seven clusters. Accordingly, each of their county weights, which under Variant One were also 0.125, are now increased under Variant Two to $0.125 + (0.115/7)$ or a total county weight of 0.1414 each. Note that 0.1414 is identical to 0.99 divided by 7[28] and is also identical to 0.125 plus 0.0164, which latter number is the value of 0.115 divided by 7. This revision, in effect, keeps the Charleston District in the sample, but representing only itself. The wealth in the balance of the stratum from which it was drawn is now represented by the wealth found in the rest of the South, that is, by the other seven clusters. This change, together with the change in probate-nonprobate ratio, gives us the results I call Variant Two-weighted (see table A.2). It brings the slave wealth figures down to values consistent with outside data checks and lowers all other wealth values for the South somewhat, though to a much smaller extent.

Table A.2
Wealth, South, Variants One and Two, 1774
Average per Probate-type Wealthholder and Average for
All Wealthholders
(*In Pounds Sterling*)

	Net Worth	Total Physical Wealth	Slaves and Servants	Livestock	Crops
w-weighted					
Variant One	703.9	729.9	308.1	48.2	20.7
Variant Two	489.2	519.3	174.5	46.0	14.3
w*-weighted					
Variant One	561.4	582.1	245.7	38.4	16.5
Variant Two	371.8	394.7	132.6	35.0	10.9

SOURCE: Sample data, *w*-weighted for probate-type wealthholders, *w**-weighted for all wealthholders. Variant One uses weights and assumptions in the first edition of *American Colonial Wealth*, namely the southern probate-nonprobate ratio of 73/27, and the county weight of 0.125 for Charleston District and for each of the seven other southern clusters. Variant Two uses the probate ratio of 68/32 for the South, and county weights for Charleston District of 0.010 and for each of the other seven southern clusters of 0.1414.

Effect of Using Variant Two Southern Weights

The range of wealth possibilities in the southern universe under Variant One is suggested by the size of the standard deviations and the confidence intervals shown in the upper panel of table A.3. The effect of the reweighting of the South, using Variant Two weights, is shown further in its lower panel.[29] It will be seen that all the means are lowered and that for slaves is nearly halved. Its Variant Two mean value falls below the lower bound confidence interval of Variant One. The same is true for the three totals of which slave value is a large component, namely portable physical wealth, total physical wealth, and net worth. The only other wealth category shown for which the southern mean in Variant Two falls outside the confidence intervals of Variant One is consumers' durables, also low. The consumers' durables include household furnishings and equipment for consumer use, and many Charleston District sample decedents had very fine articles in this category. For all the other wealth categories and subcategories, the various figures for which can be seen in the cited tables in *American Colonial Wealth* or in table D.6, the Variant Two means for the South lie within the confidence intervals of Variant One. The sharp reduction in the southern mean value of "financial assets" indicates that the Charleston component was large in this category also; nevertheless the impact was not as great as in the case of slaves, and the figure for Variant Two southern mean financial assets still falls within the confidence intervals of Variant One. Even for those wealth categories in the South where the Variant Two mean is below the lower bound for Variant One, the coefficients of variation drop at the most 3 percentage points, for "slaves and servants" and for "net worth." They drop only 2 percentage points for "total physical wealth" and for "porta-

Table A.3
Comparison of Means and Measures of Variance
Variant One and Variant Two
Probate-type Wealthholders, South, 1774
(In Pounds Sterling)

			Confidence Interval[a]		
Kinds of Wealth	*Mean*	*Standard Deviation*	*Lower Bound*	*Upper Bound*	*Coefficient of Variation*
Variant One Weights					
Net Worth	703.89	84.09	539.07	868.70	0.12
Total Physical Wealth	729.90	79.06	574.93	884.86	0.11
Land	295.94	40.91	215.75	376.13	0.14
Portable Phys. Wealth	433.96	47.43	341.01	526.92	0.11
Slaves & Servants	308.10	39.28	231.12	385.09	0.13
Producers' Durables	65.19	4.72	55.93	74.45	0.07
Consumers' Durables	34.06	3.04	28.09	40.02	0.09
Financial Assets	74.50	22.53	30.35	118.66	0.30
Variant Two Weights					
Net Worth	489.17	45.83	399.35	578.99	0.09
Total Physical Wealth	519.35	46.53	428.16	610.54	0.09
Land	238.25	30.67	178.14	298.37	0.13
Portable Phys. Wealth	281.09	24.34	233.38	328.81	0.09
Slaves & Servants	174.46	18.10	138.98	209.94	0.10
Producers' Durables	60.63	4.51	51.78	69.48	0.07
Consumers' Durables	26.35	2.06	22.32	30.39	0.08
Financial Assets	37.22	11.93	13.84	60.59	0.32

SOURCE: Sample data, *w*-weighted, Variant One, table 7.165, *American Colonial Wealth*, either edition; Variant Two, table A.7.165, *American Colonial Wealth*, 2d ed.

NOTE: Includes all cases in the sample, whether or not they held the kind of wealth (i.e., for which wealth is equal to or greater than zero). For corresponding figures, Variant Two, for some wealth totals that appear in tables of chapter 4, see tables D.6 and D.7.

[a] At .95 level of confidence.

Table A.4
Comparison of Means and Measures of Variance
Variant One and Variant Two
Probate-type Wealthholders, Thirteen Colonies, 1774
(In Pounds Sterling)

| Kinds of Wealth | Mean | Standard Deviation | Confidence Interval[a] | | Coefficient of Variation |
			Lower Bound	Upper Bound	
Variant One Weights					
Net Worth	458.82	39.08	382.23	535.41	0.09
Total Physical Wealth	466.96	36.11	396.18	537.73	0.08
Land	223.23	18.97	186.05	260.41	0.08
Portable Phys. Wealth	243.73	21.59	201.41	286.05	0.09
Slaves & Servants	142.34	17.70	107.65	177.02	0.12
Producers' Durables	48.66	2.50	43.76	53.56	0.05
Consumers' Durables	28.42	1.58	25.32	31.51	0.06
Financial Assets	74.10	11.85	50.88	97.33	0.16
Variant Two Weights					
Net Worth	362.27	22.84	317.50	407.04	0.06
Total Physical Wealth	372.28	21.86	329.45	415.12	0.06
Land	197.29	14.55	168.78	225.81	0.07
Portable Phys. Wealth	174.99	11.46	152.53	197.44	0.07
Slaves & Servants	82.24	8.21	66.14	98.34	0.10
Producers' Durables	46.61	2.42	41.86	51.35	0.05
Consumers' Durables	24.95	1.22	22.57	27.34	0.05
Financial Assets	57.34	8.16	41.35	73.32	0.14

SOURCE: Sample data, *w*-weighted, Variant One, table 7.162, *American Colonial Wealth*, either edition; Variant Two, table A.7.162, *American Colonial Wealth*, 2d ed.

NOTE: Includes all cases in the sample, whether or not they held the kind of wealth (i.e., for which wealth is equal to or greater than zero). For corresponding figures for some wealth totals that appear in tables of chapter 4, see appendix D, tables D.2 and D.3.

[a] At .95 level of confidence.

ble physical wealth," and only one for "consumers' durables." For most of the other commonly held wealth categories, the coefficients of variation, using Variant Two (shown in table A.7.165 of *American Colonial Wealth*, 2d edition), remain the same or are only slightly changed from those of Variant One in its table 7.165. The foregoing analysis of the location of the means, using Variant Two, with respect to the confidence intervals of Variant One is true also for the thirteen colonies, as can be seen in table A.4 and in tables A.7.162 and 7.162 of *American Colonial Wealth*. This is understandable, inasmuch as the southern region has such a large influence on the thirteen colonies' average. The changes in the coefficients of variation for the thirteen colonies are even less marked than was the corresponding comparison for the South.

PART THREE:
INTERPRETATION OF ESTIMATES

The Note on Method at the beginning of this volume and the foregoing discussion of techniques have been offered to alert the reader that some parts of my results are more firmly based than others. I hope that some of my roughest estimates may be improved by work of future scholars. In the meantime, I offer these wealth estimates as reasonable approximations to the unknown true figures.

Representativeness of Thirteen Colonies'
and Regional Estimates

As the sections on sampling and weighting in *American Colonial Wealth,* either edition, make clear, the simple average values from the cluster of inventories from one sample county (or group of counties in the South) do not necessarily epitomize the wealth of the particular province or colony in which the county lies. Irrespective of the sample design, the mean of a single cluster may deviate greatly from the true average wealth of its province. However, because of the sample design, the properly c-weighted results for all the sample clusters combined within a region yield an unbiased estimate of wealth for the region at the probated decedent level, and the w-weighted results yield an unbiased estimate for the region at the probate-type living wealthholder level. Likewise, the regional estimates, combined with regional weights proportional to the numbers of living wealthholders in the regions, yield unbiased estimates for decedents and for probate-type living properly attributable to the thirteen colonies. The same is true of my w^*-weighted regional and thirteen colonies' estimates for all wealthholders, subject to the acceptability of the probate/nonprobate ratios and of the values assigned to h.

Statements in the foregoing paragraph would hold completely if the records for New York had survived as well as those for the other provinces, and if wealth of Charleston District had been within reasonable range of wealth of the other seven clusters in the South. I take up these two questions in sequence.

New York and Middle Colonies' Estimates Because of the necessity to fill in the wealth measurement for New York with the New York hybrid wealth pattern, the above statements are true only so far as that pattern, described in the Note on Method, is found acceptable. The same qualification pertains to the Middle Colonies' estimate when it includes the New York hybrid figure. It can be seen from comparing *American Colonial Wealth* tables 7.11, 7.12, and 7.13 that inclusion or exclusion of New York hybrid, because of its definition, makes a relatively small difference in the Middle Colonies' figures. There are twelve colonies' totals that omit the New York hybrid in *American Colonial Wealth,* table 7.8, for those who wish to compare them with the thirteen colonies' averages. The differences are small. I believe that estimates including the New York hybrid make the best use of all available data and more nearly approach the true figures than estimates which omit it. The regional estimates for New England and those for the Middle Colonies, with or without the New York hybrid, retain the original Variant One weights.

Southern and Thirteen Colonies' Variant Two Estimates For the South, and for the thirteen colonies incorporating the southern result, acceptance of the Variant Two estimates depends on the reasonableness of reducing the population weight accorded to the Charleston district and of lowering the southern probate-nonprobate ratio. I have presented my arguments on these points in part two of this appendix. I should note, however, that while my solution to the Charleston problem may seem, at first glance, a violation of my random sample, I consider the post-weighting to conform to outside independent data to be rather the best correction for the fact that the random numbers happened to give us the rarely expected result of a sample with one cluster (Charleston, in slave values) that was an extreme "outlier," to use statistician's jargon. Post-weighting to bring the figures into line with known data external to the sample is an entirely different matter of principle than the initial selection of a sample by subjective judgment. It is the latter practice I condemn in the Note on Method and in previous publications. The change to Variant Two weights is more readily accepted if we reflect that the random numbers might just as likely have drawn into the sample a group of Georgia parishes or an interior district of South Carolina rather than Charleston District. In that event, I would have missed Charleston's wealth entirely and might well have underestimated total southern wealth.[30]

I believe the Variant Two–weighted results are a closer approximation to the unknown true values for the South and for the thirteen colonies than are the Variant One–weighted ones. Hence they are used as the preferred estimates in this volume. These weighted values at the w^*-weighted level for all living wealthholders underlie the estimates of aggregate and per capita wealth in chapters 3, 4, and 5 and are the values presented for "all wealthholders" in those and other chapters.

Measurement Strengths of Wealth Totals And Components

The deviations of individual observations from the mean, as measured in the standard deviation, reflect both sampling error and measurement error. The former arises because one sample differs somewhat from another drawn by identical procedures from the same universe—one decedent's wealth and other characteristics differ from another's. The latter arise because of difficulties of measuring precisely the variable in question, here wealth in its various forms. I have consistently tried to minimize both kinds of error through the sampling plans, weighting, and attempts to find correct values for the wealth items missing from the probate inventories. In the next few paragraphs I summarize my judgment of the relative strengths of the several measures of wealth.

Portable Physical Wealth, Financial Assets The portable physical wealth total and the financial assets total, summed from entries found directly in the sample probate inventories, are the strongest wealth totals from the measurement standpoint. They are firmer at the c- and w-weighted levels than at the w^*-weighted for reasons indicated in the Note on Method.

Net Worth Net worth, although it is the most comprehensive measure of total wealth, is the weakest total measure because it includes financial liabilities, which are subject to the qualifications discussed in the Note on Method. In addition, it includes real estate, which for New England comes from the inventories; however, for the

Middle Colonies and for the South, real estate is subject to the measurement qualifications treated in the Note on Method. I know, for the South, that I only roughly approximate the value of financial liabilities, and that my percentage of wealthholders having debts is not accurate; I show it as 99 or 100 percent. This results from the determination of financial liabilities as a function of portable physical wealth, the best estimator I was able to find. Likewise, I know that my calculated real estate value for the South may be on the low side for the sample decedents, and that it understates the percentage of them who owned real estate; yet I have not the means to improve these figures with present knowledge.

Total Physical Wealth Total physical wealth is a stronger total wealth measure than is net worth. Although it includes real estate, it excludes the less firm figure of financial liabilities. Being limited to physical wealth, it also excludes the firm figure on financial assets, which comes from the probate inventories. Because there are pros and cons, conceptually, for both as measures of total wealth, I offer in chapter 6 size distributions based on net worth and also on total physical wealth.[31] From the standpoint of measurement strength, I consider that primary reliance should be placed on the distribution by total physical wealth. For this reason, as well as for the further reason of the canceling nature of debts from and to all individuals within a society, I base the per capita wealth figures in chapter 4 on physical wealth alone.

Nonhuman Physical Wealth, Nonhuman Portable Physical Wealth Nonhuman physical wealth and nonhuman portable physical wealth are parallel in measurement strength to total physical wealth and to portable physical wealth. They differ only in that each excludes the capital value of slaves and servants. The preferability of nonhuman wealth figures for many kinds of economic analysis is suggested in chapters 1 and 3.

Subcategories of Portable Physical Wealth The figures for subcategories of portable wealth, whether in physical form or as financial assets, are as strongly based on the probate inventories, and hence as firm, as total portable wealth, at the c- and w-weighted levels. At the w^*-weighted level, however, we find the use of assumption h less satisfactory for subcategories. If nonprobate types were composed heavily of the less well-to-do, as I believe, is it likely that the proportionate composition of their wealth, in particular with respect to such subitems as servants and slaves, business equipment and inventory, livestock, and relative proportions of consumers' and producers' goods, would resemble that of the probate types, only with smaller amounts throughout? Is it not more likely that the proportions also would alter? I believe the proportions would alter, but in ways that depend upon precise reasons for nonprobate, which is what we do not know. Lacking solid ground upon which to base assumptions for varying these proportions for each component of wealth, I have preferred, but only by default, to use the same value of h for all wealth components, including the subitems of portable wealth.

Percentages of Wealthholders Having Various Kinds of Wealth   For the same reasons, I make no assumption, comparable to that of the size of h for value, as to the differential (in comparison with the probate types) in the percentages of nonprobate-type wealthholders who had various forms of wealth. I fall back here simply on known w-weighted figures for the percentages of the probate-type wealthholders having various forms of wealth. Consequently, the reader will observe in chapters 4, 5, and 7 that percentages having the various kinds of wealth are w-weighted. These values, shown in conjunction with w^*-weighted average values, are to be interpreted as the estimate that may pertain to all wealthholders if and only if it is true that the same percentages of nonprobate-type wealthholders as of the probate types held the respective forms of wealth. This condition is very closely true for totals such as total physical wealth, net worth, portable physical wealth, producers' goods, and consumers' goods, which virtually all wealthholders had, but becomes more doubtful in the finer subcategories.

Real Estate, Financial Liabilities, Slaves   The same reasoning and presentation is followed also for real estate and financial liabilities. With respect to real estate, the acceptability of h may be particularly questionable. May it not well be true that nonprobates held zero real estate more often than probates? For this reason, my real estate estimates at the w^*-weighted level may be somewhat high. And, reverting to the portable physical wealth subcategories, may it not be especially likely, in the South, that nonprobates were the very people who did not have servants and slaves? Disposition of slaves was often specified in wills, and filing the will insured its execution under supervision of the court. For southern wealth in slaves, in particular, should the assumed value of h, instead of being one-fourth, be much smaller on virtually zero? If so, is there some overestimate of southern wealth in slaves for "all wealthholders" at the w^*-weighted level? Our present limited knowledge of the nonprobates precludes a precise answer.

Strength of Probate Ratio and Validity of h *and of Probate Ratio for Subgroups of Wealthholders*

The calculation of the probate ratio, discussed in chapter 2, is one of the weakest links in the estimating chain. Such a ratio is essential, yet there are very great difficulties in making a correct estimate of the proportion of all dying wealthholders whose estates were probated. The precise ratios I have used may well be revised if better information on death rates becomes available. Additionally, they may need revision if industrious scholars make new and more extended counts of how many probate cases occurred, and surmount better than I was able to problems such as those mentioned in note 20 of chapter 2. Immediately preceding paragraphs discussed the possibility that a single value of h for all subcategories of wealth may be questioned.

Perhaps the same probate ratio and, additionally, also the same value of h may not be appropriate for all subgroups of wealthholders. Perhaps relatively more merchants and esquires were probated than, say, laborers. Also, perhaps h would be greater or less in some occupations than others, or would differ for men and women, for older and younger, for urban and rural. Again, all I can say is that present information is inadequate to attempt such refinements in either h or the probate ratio. I should add the further caution that, if such variations were made, weighting complexities would correspondingly increase, and they are already more than one wishes for the present study.

PART FOUR: REPLICATION FOR OTHER DATES

Replications of the present study for selected earlier dates would be highly desirable, to permit consistent comparisons. Aside from heavy money and time costs, investigators would face an even more serious problem in scarcity of surviving records than was encountered in this study. The random or appropriate selection of alternate counties to be substituted in proper sequence for first-choice counties for which data do not survive would be essential to success. Another big question would be whether population figures for all counties at the selected earlier dates could be established, adequate for the drawing of a random statistical sample of counties. If not, perhaps, as a minimum, complete lists of geographically contiguous counties then existing in all regions could be established, with some clues as to whether they had large or small populations. In consultation with a statistician experienced both in theory and practice of sampling, perhaps a way of drawing an unbiased sample of counties from such a geographic list could be worked out. Without reasonably good population figures, however, it would be difficult to establish reasonable target numbers of cases to be obtained from each stratum or subportion of the sample. It would also be difficult, without them, to have a proper basis to establish weights for combining the decedent data from the several sample counties into regional totals, and proper regional weights to combine regional totals into all-colony totals. Furthermore, lack of reasonable estimates of total numbers of living wealthholders and of total population by region (as in lines 1 and 21 of tables 2.4, 2.5, 2.6, and 2.7) would preclude convincing inflation of average data in the sample to estimates pertaining to the total population. Perhaps recent and future developments in demography can help to overcome such obstacles.

Replications of the present study for selected later dates are considerably more feasible from a data standpoint. Population figures by county for sample drawing would be available from censuses. Presumably, probate inventories are well preserved in many county courthouses or state archives for dates starting around, say, 1790, and many inventories and other probate documents have been copied by the Genealogical Society of the Church of Latter Day Saints and are filed in or near Salt Lake City. A question to be checked out would be whether the appraised values in probate inventories continued to be close to market values, or whether, after some dates and in some places, they became perfunctory. The more serious limitation would probably be the money and time cost of covering more territory and more counties, to keep up proportionately with the westward expansion of the population of the United States from 1790 onward. The cost problem would pose a serious challenge to the designer of the sample and the planners of the scope of the study. If nationwide samples prove too costly, perhaps more limited regional studies, with carefully drawn samples at various dates, could be useful.

PART FIVE:
WEALTH-INCOME OR CAPITAL-OUTPUT
RATIOS

Since we lack agreed-upon estimates of colonial output, in chapter 3 I estimated per capita income from my wealth figures by use of assumed wealth-income or capital-output ratios. The range in ratios there is somewhat narrower than the 3 to 1 or 5 to 1 which I used in earlier publications and excludes ratios suggested by some other writers. It is obvious that dividing our colonial wealth by a larger number than 3 or 3.5 would yield a smaller per capita income figure than that shown in chapter 3. The comparison in table 3.13 of my colonial estimates with those of Charles H. Feinstein for Britain underlines the key importance of the wealth-income ratio in reaching colonial figures useful for interpreting aspects of economic growth. Selection of the most convincing ratio for wealth to income that is applicable to the late colonial economy is a task that I believe requires considerably more data on both colonial wealth and colonial output than we now have, and more intensive scrutiny of the facts available.[32] I present here some considerations affecting my selection of the range of from 3 to 3.5 as the divisor of wealth to reach an income estimate.

In my pilot study,[33] I offered estimates of per capita income in the middle colonies in 1774 based on my preliminary estimate of £42 sterling wealth per capita and capital-output ratios of 5 to 1 and 3 to 1. These income estimates ranged from £8.4 to £14.0. In an earlier draft of chapter 3 of the present volume, I selected the ratio of 5 to 1, which yields a per capita income for the thirteen colonies in 1774 of only £7.5 sterling. In this choice, I was influenced by the higher wealth-income ratios implied by Gregory King and Arthur Young and other English estimators mentioned in a later paragraph, as well as by the ratios shown by Mulhall (see note 18 of chap. 3.) for various countries, including the United States around 1880. (I had not yet seen Feinstein's estimates for Britain presented in table A.5.)

Robert Gallman (1977b) and Stanley Engerman (1977b) both questioned the 5 to 1 ratio for this estimate. Gallman suggested that the resulting £7.5 per capita income is too low and that 3 or 2.5 to 1 would be more likely ratios for the late colonial period since "Goldsmith gets a value of 2.6 for 1850 and never gets much over 4, and Davis and Gallman" (1973:457, table 9) show ratios under 4 for the United States in the nineteenth century. I find for Goldsmith (1968:57, table 3) a figure of 2.8 for 1850, while Kuznets (1966:76, table 2.7), publishing earlier and using Goldsmith's data, shows 3.5 for the United States for that year. In a personal conversation with Messrs. Gallman and Engerman in Toronto in September 1978, we concluded that approximate ratios must serve for the present and that the determination of the best ratio for the late colonial period awaits further scholarly work.

I am unable to be comfortable with a ratio lower than 3 to 1, and I lean toward 3.5 to 1. Some reasons follow. The £12.5 of colonial per capita income implied by the 3 to 1 ratio appears to me too high, since I think the Arthur Young figure of £15.4 is too high (see note 16 of chapter 3) for contemporary England and Wales, and Feinstein gets a figure of only £10.0 for Britain. On the other hand, £12.5 seems not unreasonable in the context of the food estimates of Klingaman (1971:555 ff.), or as compared with the per capita commodity export figures of Shepherd and Walton (table 3.11). If we use the £12.5 figure for late colonial per capita income, the commodity exports form 10.6 percent of total income, and total exports (including shipping earnings) form 13.6 percent. The 10.6 is a little lower than the range of 11.5 to 13.5 percent mentioned by Shepherd and Williamson (1972:801–2) as the percentage of overseas commodity exports in relation to Gallman's estimate of total colonial commodity output. When we consider that total colonial real product included a year's food and housing for 2.35 million people, all the year's production of leather, fibers, yarn, thread, cloth, garments, shoes for that number, firewood and fuel, timber and other materials used for construction and repair, implements created during the year for household, farm, and business use, wagons, sleds, carriages, boats, ships created during the year, direct services (not embodied in products) from taverns, ferries, domestic servants, laborers, artisans, and professionals, it is credible that their total may have been seven to eight times as valuable as the exports of those crops and other products the colonists were able to create above their consumption needs. However, the £12.5 estimate of per capita income, translated into 1974 dollars and compared with a per capita figure for the United States in 1974 of $5,238 gross national product (see table 3.14 and text discussion), excluding the government sector, would give us an increase in income of ten and a half times over two centuries. This is lower than the twelvefold increase in real wealth that I find over that span (see table 3.15).

In contrast, the per capita figure of £10.7, which results from using the 3.5 to 1 capital-output ratio, has the virtue of yielding a twelvefold increase in per capita real income over two centuries. This coincides neatly with my estimate of increase in real wealth. While real income per head can increase more or less than real wealth, particularly in short periods, for a variety of reasons (see Gallman 1979 for some speculations), it seems more likely that over long periods the increases in both should be rather similar. In addition, the commodity exports (£1.32 per capita; see table 3.11) form 12.3 percent of this £10.7 estimated income, a percentage about in the middle of the range cited by Shepherd and Williamson (1972:801, n. 18). Finally, this per capita figure of £10.7 appears to me to lie within the range[34] of the estimate of Gallman (1972:24) of $60 to $70 per capita colonial output for 1774, expressed in dollars of 1840 purchasing power. Gallman's figures translate into the range of £22.5 to £26.5 million of estimated colonial output, or the range of £9.6 to £11.3 per capita.

Goldsmith (1952:297–99) suggests (referring to modern times) that when land is included in the numerator, the range for the ratio of total national wealth to income is usually between 4 to 1 and 6 to 1. In his encyclopedia article (1968:57, table 3), he computed two series of ratios for the United States, back only as far as 1850, the numerator being net national wealth and the denominator gross national product. For the series that includes land (i.e., nonreproducible assets) in the numerator, his ratios are: 1850, 2.8; 1900, 4.7; 1929, 4.2; 1945, 2.7; 1958, 3.8. His ratio, excluding land, is 1.6 for 1850, around 3 for 1929 and 1958, lower for the war year 1945.

Kuznets (1966:76, table 2.7 and discussion pp. 75–81) gives a ratio for the United States in 1850 of "total capital," including land, to output of 3.5 to 1. This is based on capital data, at 1929 prices, assembled by Goldsmith and product data from Kuznets' estimates extrapolated back to 1840 by means of Gallman's estimates of commodity output. In the same table he shows "total capital" ratios, at current prices, of 8.2 for Britain in 1885 and 9.3 for Belgium in 1846. For reproducible capital only, related to product, Kuznets' figure for the United States in 1850 is 1.9. Soltow (1975a:63, 64, and 193, n. 9) notes that Amasa Walker in 1866 estimated 3.7 for "total estate" in the United States in 1860. He also cites Kuznets' 3.5 ratio for the United States in 1860 and reads from Kuznets' table (Kuznets 1966:76) that "at the time several European countries had ratios of 5 to 1 or more." Kuznets notes (1966: 78; see also Kuznets 1971:61– 73) for five important countries for which we have data, Great Britain, Belgium, the United States, Australia, and Japan, that the ratio for total capital to output declines over time. He suggested that "with the marked decline in the proportion of land and other natural resources in total material capital which accompanies modern economic growth and industrialization, such total capital-product ratios should decline over the long period for all developed countries." Davis and Gallman (1973:454–57), on the contrary, seem to note generally increasing ratios for the United States since 1840. They show the following ratios for the United States of capital stock, including land and inventories, to decade averages of U.S. gross national product: 1840, 3.0; 1850, 3.3; 1860, 3.9; 1870, 3.7; 1880, 3.8; 1890, 4.6; 1900, 4.4.

Careful work by Charles H. Feinstein (1978a,b) revises British capital and income estimates from 1770 to 1870. He calculates ratios as shown in table A.5. Professor Feinstein remarked (1978b), "The obvious comment is thus that the movement and the level of the ratio depend very much on the definition [of capital, i.e. wealth], though all show a downward trend over the period."

Older English estimates for capital-output or wealth-income ratios, including land, suggest high ratios for the late seventeenth, the eighteenth and the nineteenth centuries. Petty's estimate for England and Wales in 1664 was 6 as calculated by Pollard (1968:336) from Mulhall (1884:71, table A). Gregory King's (1936:32, 55) ratio for

Table A.5
Ratios of Capital to Output
Great Britain (excluding Ireland), 1760, 1860

| | To Gross Domestic Product | | | To GNP[a] |
| | *(1)* | *(2)* | *(3)* | *(4)* |
	Fixed Capital[b]	*Fixed + Inventories*[c]	*Fixed + Inventories + Land*[d]	*National Wealth*
1760	3.2	5.0	10.1	10.1
1860	3.5	4.2	6.4	6.9

SOURCE: Feinstein, 1978b.

NOTE: The ratios are calculated from values at current prices. Feinstein (1978b) observed: "Given the trend in land prices relative to other prices (see [1978a] pp. 72–73 and note 188, p. 646) the movement in the ratio for assets including land would be somewhat different" at 1851–60 prices. For 1760 at 1851–60 prices he gets values of 5.4, 7.4, 18.1 and 18.1 respectively for columns 1, 2, 3 and 4 and his corresponding figures for 1860 are 3.6, 4.3, 6.4 and 7.1. These values, as well as ones for 1800 and 1830 assembled in his letter (1978b), are also found in Feinstein, 1978a:647, 216 (re. columns 1 and 4 above) and p. 84, table 25 (re. column 2). The 1761–70 British price indexes on an 1851–60 base, used by Mr. Engerman in the rough conversion to ca. 1770 wealth values which I show in table 3.13, are found in ibid., pp. 38 and 42 for fixed capital, pp. 38 and 68 for inventories or circulating capital, and on pp. 68 and 72 for land (implicit).

[a] Output measured as gross national product is equal to gross domestic product plus earnings on foreign assets, which were zero in 1760.
[b] Domestic, fixed, reproducible capital. Excludes military assets, consumers' durable goods, and works of art, plate, etc. Feinstein (1978a:642, n. 144).
[c] Includes farm crops, livestock, etc., and nonfarm stock-in-trade.
[d] This total is equal to national wealth, except that the latter includes the value of overseas assets, which was a net zero in 1760. Feinstein (1978a:68).

England and Wales in 1688, as I calculate it, was 7. Deane (1961, as reprinted in Crouzet 1972; 96) also calculated for him a ratio of 7, including land, and of 2.3 excluding it. Higher ratios were implied for the United Kingdom for eighteenth- and nineteenth-century dates by various estimators, as calculated and shown by Mulhall (1884:71, table A) and also shown by Pollard (1968:336) as follows: Davenant, 1701, 9; Young, 1770, 9.5; Pitt, 1800, 8; Colquhon, 1811, 9; Liverpool, 1822, 9; Pebrer, 1833, 11; Porter, 1840, 8.5; Levi, etc., 1860, 7.5; Mulhall, 1882, 7. These were not all independent estimates, in the judgment of Deane.[35] (The ratio, as I calculate it, for Arthur Young in 1770 is 9, but his figures are too sketchy[36] for this ratio to be taken seriously).

The considerations just presented, added to the discussion of income in chapter 3, suggest that the determination of the proper or best wealth-income ratio to use with a late colonial wealth figure is a matter that needs further critical consideration by scholars. In the meantime, considering that land in the colonies was relatively more abundant and cheaper than in Britain and that the value of roads and public improvements, which was relatively small in any case, is not included in my aggregate colonial wealth figures, I conclude that, with land included, a ratio of 3.0 or 3.5 wealth to 1 of income may be a presently useful approximation for the colonies in 1774.

APPENDIX B

Wealth Composition of Probate-type Wealthholders by County or Group of Counties, Three Regions, 1774

The sample was designed to yield reliable regional averages and a thirteen colonies' estimate (see appendix A). The figures for individual counties or county groups are not presented as reliable representations for any single province from which they are drawn. However, intermediate totals by county or county groups are required to reach combined regional and combined thirteen colonies' estimates. Because they have considerable interest in themselves, despite the foregoing caution as to their interpretation, they are presented here.

Averages in tables B.1 through B.3 are based on sample data, w-weighted, and hence pertain only to probate-type wealthholders and are higher than w^*-weighted values for all free wealthholders. We lack sufficiently reliable evidence on ratio of probates to nonprobates by individual county to vary the ratios and hence the calculation of w^*-weights county by county. To reach values at the w^* level of most text tables in this volume, the figures in tables B.1 and B.2 can all be multiplied by the conversion factor for the region shown in appendix A. This has been done in a column of the following tables, by county, in *American Colonial Wealth*, which also shows a column for "w-weighted percent having" various types of wealth and columns for average values (w or w^*-weighted) as "percentage of net worth" and as "percentage of total physical wealth":

7.122 through 7.128 for counties in New England
7.10   for New York, 23 cases
7.11   for New York hybrid estimate
7.12   for Middle Colonies' total (New Jersey, Pennsylvania, Delaware
       plus New York hybrid)
7.13   for New Jersey, Pennsylvania, Delaware, total
7.129 through 7.133 for counties in New Jersey, Pennsylvania, Dela-
       ware.

The stubs of those tables are in a slightly different form from tables B.1 through B.4 of this appendix. Table 7.6 of *American Colonial Wealth,* and its note on page 1929, give a key to the rearrangement.

Tables 7.134 through 7.141 in that volume show corresponding data by county or county group for the South. They are calculated under the procedures and assumptions of Variant One (explained in appendix A above). The change to Variant Two, the preferred treatment for the South for the present volume, does not change the "*w*-weighted average value" for individual southern counties, shown in table B.3, from those under Variant One in tables 7.134 through 7.141. However column 1 for All South of table B.3, under Variant Two, shows lower values than those in *American Colonial Wealth* table 7.14 for South, total, under Variant One. The complete computer printouts for individual southern counties, Variant Two, are deposited at the Newberry Library in Chicago. There is no change in some columns shown thereon but not included in appendix B tables, "percentage of net worth" or "percentage of total physical wealth" and only very slight change in the column "*w*-weighted percent having" from those in *American Colonial Wealth* tables 7.134 (Anne Arundel, Md.) through 7.141 (Charleston, S.C.). The figures for "*w**-weighted average value" are however slightly lower, under Variant Two, by individual southern counties, and are shown for convenience of the reader in table B.4.

Table B.:
Components of Private Wealth, New Eng and, By County, 1774
(Average Per Probate-type Wealthholder, in Pounds Sterling)

	All (1)	Litchfield (2)	New Haven (3)	Essex (4)	Hampshire (5)	Plymouth (6)	Suffolk (7)	Worcester (8)
Net worth	206.0	131.9	139.7	271.4	178.2	206.4	312.3	202.2
Total physical wealth	240.6	173.3	190.0	266.9	207.6	268.2	322.9	255.4
Human nonfree (slaves, servants)	1.1	0.0	1.8	0.7	0.6	0.0	4.3	0.2
Nonhuman physical wealth, total	238.3	173.3	188.2	266.2	207.0	268.2	318.6	255.4
Land (real estate)	171.8	120.5	139.4	188.1	143.4	204.2	222.8	184.1
Nonhuman portable, total	67.9	52.9	48.8	78.1	63.6	64.0	95.8	71.1
Producers' capital, total	39.2	34.7	25.1	41.9	41.1	31.5	47.7	48.8
Durable, total	29.0	28.7	22.6	25.3	33.9	27.7	20.2	42.1
Livestock	18.5	21.4	15.4	9.8	24.0	16.2	11.6	30.7
Equip. of household	8.2	7.3	7.2	8.1	9.9	7.7	6.7	10.7
Equip. of business	2.3	0.0	0.0	7.4	0.1	6.4	1.9	0.7
Perishable, total	10.2	6.0	2.5	16.6	7.2	3.8	27.5	6.7
Crops	1.4	1.1	0.4	3.0	0.9	2.6	1.2	1.0
Materials in household	2.4	4.9	1.4	0.3	6.3	1.1	0.9	1.6
Business inventory	6.4	0.0	0.7	13.3	0.0	0.1	25.4	4.1
Consumers' goods, total	28.7	18.2	23.6	36.2	22.5	29.9	44.2	22.2
Durable, total	27.3	17.4	22.4	34.9	21.7	27.8	42.4	20.4
Apparel	5.5	5.7	5.8	6.7	4.1	4.4	7.2	4.2
Equip., furn., other	21.8	11.7	16.5	28.1	17.7	23.4	39.1	16.2
Perishable	1.4	0.8	1.2	1.3	0.8	2.1	1.8	1.8
Financial Assets	42.2	12.1	3.1	88.4	17.0	38.1	91.2	42.4
Cash	2.7	0.9	.0	3.9	5.2	3.3	3.7	0.9
Claims, good	39.4	11.2	7.1	84.4	10.1	34.8	87.4	41.2
Claims, doubtful	0.3	0.0	0.0	0.0	1.8	0.0	0.2	0.3
Financial liabilities	77.1	53.6	51.4	83.8	46.4	100.0	101.8	95.6

SOURCE: Sample data, *w*-weighted.

Table B.2
Components of Private Wealth, Middle Colonies by County, 1774
(Average Per Probate-type Wealthholder, in Pounds Sterling)

	Total N.J., Pa., Del. (1)	Northampton Pa. (2)	Westmoreland Pa. (3)	Phil. Pa. (4)	Burlington N.J. (5)	Kent Del. (6)	New York Hybrid (7)
Net worth	289.2	246.6	158.6	396.7	340.8	247.8	278.0
Total physical wealth	259.0	254.1	182.4	386.5	190.8	263.0	255.6
Human nonfree (slaves, servants)	10.8	0.8	0.0	7.3	18.7	19.5	8.0
Nonhuman physical wealth, total	248.2	253.3	182.4	379.2	172.1	243.5	247.6
Land (real estate)	156.8	187.0	129.6	268.1	43.3	164.8	166.3
Nonhuman portable, total	91.4	66.3	52.8	111.1	128.8	78.7	81.3
Producers' capital, total	66.8	53.4	43.4	75.3	92.2	58.2	55.7
Durable, total	41.1	41.1	39.0	23.5	64.6	34.0	35.8
Livestock	30.8	28.6	30.9	15.2	53.4	23.7	25.6
Equip. of household	8.5	12.2	8.1	5.2	10.3	6.9	8.4
Equip. of business	1.8	0.4	0.0	3.0	0.9	3.4	1.7
Perishable, total	25.7	12.3	4.4	51.8	27.6	24.2	19.9
Crops	14.2	10.3	1.4	6.3	26.6	16.8	9.5
Materials in household	1.5	2.0	0.9	1.3	1.0	2.5	2.5
Business inventory	10.0	0.0	2.1	44.2	0.0	4.9	7.9
Consumers' goods, total	24.6	12.8	9.5	35.8	36.5	20.5	25.6
Durable, total	22.8	12.6	9.5	35.2	33.9	16.5	24.0
Apparel	6.8	3.3	3.8	5.8	16.0	3.1	6.1
Equip., furn., other	15.9	9.3	5.7	29.4	17.9	13.4	17.8
Perishable	1.8	0.2	0.0	0.6	2.6	4.0	1.6
Financial Assets	90.1	44.5	12.4	142.4	177.2	37.6	90.1
Cash	11.3	4.5	0.9	27.6	18.7	1.9	10.7
Claims, good	78.1	39.9	11.6	111.2	158.6	35.7	77.3
Claims, doubtful	0.7	0.0	0.0	3.6	0.0	0.0	2.1
Financial liabilities	59.9	52.0	36.1	132.2	27.3	52.8	67.7

SOURCE: Columns 1 through 6, sample data, *w*-weighted. For source of New York hybrid, column 7, see Note on Method. For values for New York sample see *American Colonial Wealth*, either edition, table 7.10.

Table B.3

Components of Private Wealth, South, by County or County Group, 1774
(*Average Per Probate-type Wealthholder, in Pounds Sterling*)

	All (1)	Q. Anne (2)	A. Arun (3)	CharHal (4)	SoBrMeck (5)	ChFaSp (6)	Halifax (7)	Orange (8)	CharDist (9)
Net worth	489.2	552.2	660.4	546.4	311.3	527.2	467.1	227.5	2,337.7
Total physical wealth	519.3	572.2	658.7	600.5	348.8	594.6	494.9	236.4	2,332.0
Human nonfree (slaves, servants)	174.5	112.7	169.2	214.8	92.6	196.0	265.0	89.6	1,325.0
Nonhuman physical wealth, total	344.9	459.5	489.5	385.7	256.2	398.6	229.9	146.8	1,007.0
Land (real estate)	238.3	323.3	352.1	281.6	205.4	286.3	123.2	60.7	734.9
Nonhuman portable, total	106.6	136.2	137.3	104.1	51.6	122.2	106.6	86.3	272.1
Producers' capital, total	77.0	103.6	94.4	69.4	34.4	82.6	80.4	69.6	173.0
Durable, total	59.9	52.4	64.2	65.8	31.0	61.4	76.1	67.5	93.2
Livestock	46.0	38.1	43.4	51.3	24.8	49.1	62.3	52.3	65.2
Equip. of household	13.4	14.3	18.5	14.3	6.2	12.2	13.8	13.9	26.9
Equip. of business	0.5	0.0	2.3	0.2	0.0	0.1	0.0	1.3	1.1
Perishable, total	17.1	51.2	30.2	3.6	3.4	21.2	4.3	2.1	79.8
Crops	14.3	48.6	25.7	3.5	2.3	10.9	3.9	1.9	68.9
Materials in household	1.3	0.1	4.5	0.1	1.1	2.4	0.4	0.2	8.0
Business inventory	1.5	2.5	0.0	0.0	0.0	7.9	0.0	0.0	2.9
Consumers' goods, total	29.5	32.6	42.9	34.7	17.2	39.6	26.2	16.7	99.1
Durable, total	26.4	25.4	36.7	31.2	16.7	38.0	25.3	15.3	92.8
Apparel	3.8	8.3	5.4	6.8	0.6	1.9	1.2	2.1	6.2
Equip., furn., other	22.6	17.1	31.3	24.4	16.2	26.2	24.1	13.2	86.5
Perishable	3.1	7.2	6.2	3.5	0.5	1.6	0.9	1.4	6.3
Financial Assets	37.2	94.1	53.3	15.6	0.0	0.6	36.1	38.2	358.2
Cash	9.8	18.2	28.1	0.0	0.0	0.2	18.7	3.4	12.7
Claims, good	19.4	21.8	23.0	15.6	0.0	0.3	17.4	34.7	344.5
Claims, doubtful	8.0	54.1	2.2	0.0	0.0	0.0	0.0	0.1	1.0
Financial liabilities	67.4	114.1	51.3	69.6	37.5	67.9	63.9	47.1	352.6

SOURCE: Sample data. Column 1, *w*-weighted, Variant Two. Columns 2 through 9, *w*-weighted Variants One or Two; the *w*-weighted results for individual counties or county groups do not change from Variant One to Variant Two. Full names of counties are: Queen Anne's Co., Md.; Anne Arundel Co., Md.; Charlotte-Halifax Cos., Va.; Southampton-Brunswick-Mecklenburg Cos., Va.; Chesterfield-Fairfax-Spotsylvania Cos., Va.; Halifax Co., N.C.; Orange Co., N.C.; Charleston District, S.C.

Table B.4

Components of Private Wealth, South, by County or County Group, 1774
(Average Per Wealthholder, in Pounds Sterling)

	All (1)	Q. Anne (2)	A. Arun (3)	CharHal (4)	SoBrMeck (5)	ChFaSp (6)	Halifax (7)	Orange (8)	CharDist (9)
Net worth	371.8	419.7	501.9	415.3	236.6	400.7	356.1	172.9	1,776.7
Total physical wealth	394.7	434.9	500.6	456.4	265.1	451.9	377.2	179.6	1,772.3
Human nonfree (slaves, servants)	132.6	85.6	128.6	163.3	70.4	149.0	201.4	68.1	1,007.0
Nonhuman physical wealth, total	262.1	349.3	371.9	293.1	194.7	302.8	175.8	111.6	765.1
Land (real estate)	181.1	245.7	267.6	214.0	156.1	217.6	93.6	46.6	558.3
Nonhuman portable, total	81.0	103.5	104.3	79.1	38.6	85.2	82.2	65.4	206.8
Producers' capital, total	58.7	78.8	71.7	52.7	25.5	62.7	61.2	52.7	131.5
Durable, total	45.7	39.8	48.9	50.0	22.9	46.6	57.9	51.2	70.7
Livestock	35.0	28.9	33.1	39.0	18.1	37.3	47.4	39.7	49.5
Equip. of household	10.2	10.8	14.0	10.8	4.7	9.3	10.5	10.5	20.4
Equip. of business	0.4	0.0	1.8	0.1	0.0	0.0	0.0	0.9	0.8
Perishable, total	13.0	39.0	22.8	2.7	2.6	16.1	3.3	1.5	60.8
Crops	10.9	37.0	19.5	2.6	1.7	8.3	3.0	1.4	52.4
Materials in household	1.0	0.1	3.4	0.1	0.8	1.8	0.3	0.1	6.2
Business inventory	1.1	1.9	0.0	0.0	0.0	6.0	0.0	0.0	2.2
Consumers' goods, total	22.3	24.7	32.6	26.4	13.1	22.5	21.0	12.7	75.3
Durable, total	20.0	19.2	27.9	23.7	12.7	21.3	20.3	11.6	70.5
Apparel	2.9	6.3	4.1	5.1	0.4	1.4	0.9	1.6	4.7
Equip., furn., other	17.2	12.9	23.8	18.5	12.3	19.9	19.4	10.0	65.8
Perishable	2.3	5.5	4.7	2.7	0.4	1.2	0.7	1.1	4.8
Financial Assets	28.3	71.5	40.5	11.8	0.0	0.4	27.4	29.1	272.2
Cash	7.5	13.8	21.3	0.0	0.0	0.2	14.2	2.6	9.7
Claims, good	14.7	16.6	17.5	11.8	0.0	0.2	13.3	26.3	261.8
Claims, doubtful	6.1	41.1	1.7	0.0	0.0	0.0	0.0	0.1	0.8
Financial liabilities	51.2	86.7	39.0	52.9	28.5	51.6	48.5	35.8	268.0

SOURCE: Sample data, w*-weighted, Variant Two. Full names of counties are: Queen Anne's Co., Md.; Anne Arundel Co., Md.; Charlotte-Halifax Cos., Va.; Southampton-Brunswick-Mecklenburg Cos., Va.; Chesterfield-Fairfax-Spotsylvania Cos., Va.; Halifax Co., N.C.; Orange Co., N.C.; Charleston District, S.C.

APPENDIX C

Relation Between Age and Wealth

I present here results of tabulations of age and wealth for subsamples of the cases for which the genealogists could determine age in actual years. There were 261 cases of such probated decedents in the New England sample, 112 in New Jersey, Pennsylvania, and Delaware. The 28 such cases for the South are too few to merit analysis.

A question arises as to whether these subsamples of decedents remain unbiased, since they comprise only a part of the carefully drawn full samples. The answer would seem to depend on whether persons of certain ages, or of higher or lower wealth at a given age, or living in one sample county as opposed to another, would be more likely to have left a trail whereby their exact age at death could be discovered today, as opposed only to clues whereby we could place them within one of three age classes but could not state their precise age. I am inclined to the view that such may well all be random factors and that these subsamples may be considered unbiased estimates of probated-decedent wealth for each region, after we weight them with modified c weights.[1]

A general pattern emerges of wealth rising to a peak or plateau in late middle age and declining thereafter. When the wealth values are plotted for each individual case and by single years, the pattern is obscured because of occasional outlier cases of extreme values, and because of differing wealth among two or more individuals of the same age. When the individual values are grouped for cases within 10-year age intervals, we get the smoothest results, shown in tables C.1 and C.2 and figures 22 and 23. We get more information, particularly as to the location of the middle-age wealth peak or plateau, when we group the cases by 5-year averages, as in tables C.3

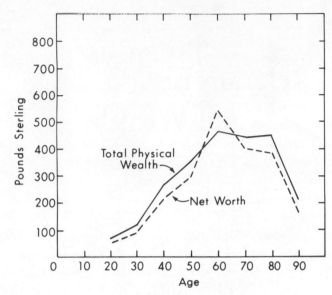

Figure 22.
Net Worth and Total Physical Wealth by
Ten-Year Age Brackets, New England, 1774.
Sample Decedents with Known Age in Years

SOURCE: Table C.1, data *c*-weighted

through C.6, even though there remain some irregularities explained by the small number of cases.

New England, with more cases of known actual age, gives a smoother result than do the fewer cases for New Jersey, Pennsylvania, and Delaware. In both regions, whether for net worth or for total physical wealth, there is a general rise to either a peak or a plateau at around age 60 and a falling off after about age 65. I do not consider the irregularities in the pattern statistically significant in view of the numbers of cases and their variability.

Somewhat similar patterns of relationship of wealth to age have been noted in other studies at various times and places. Waters (1976:156–59) found this for colonial Guilford, Connecticut. Menard, Harris, and Carr (1974:178) found it for the lower western shore of colonial Maryland in the early period. Soltow (1971a:37, 46) reported a similar pattern, but with peaks or plateaus at an earlier age, for both native- and foreign-born males in Milwaukee County in 1860 and for all Wisconsin adult males in 1860. For men in the United States, he (1975a:77) found rising wealth to age 40–99, which he treated as one age group. Campbell and Lowe (1977:58–61) found a similar pattern for men in Texas in 1860, with highest wealth in the 55 to 64 year age bracket. George Stigler (1952:274 n.) noted it for net estates before exemption in the United States in 1945, and Richard French (1970:51) for gross estates in Oklahoma in 1960. A similar pattern was reported by Projector and Weiss (1966:30–33) for wealthholders in the United States in 1962.

Gini measures of inequality within age groups in 1962 were found by Projector and Weiss to be largest for those under 35, next largest for those 65 and over, and nearly constant at ages from 35 to 64. Greater inequality in wealth of young males than those of middle years was also noted by Soltow for males in Wisconsin in 1860,[2] and in the United States for 1850, 1860, and 1870. It is to be expected that there should be greater extremes in wealth (more cases having very small wealth) for the very young and the very old than among those in the prime wealth-acquiring years.

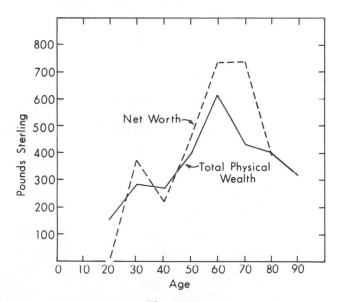

Figure 23.
Net Worth and Total Physical Wealth by Ten-Year Age Brackets,
New Jersey, Pennsylvania, Delaware, 1774.
Sample Decedents with Known Age in Years
SOURCE: Table C.2, data *c*-weighted

Table C.1
Net Worth and Total Physical Wealth by Ten-Year
Age Brackets
New England, 1774
(Subsample of Decedents, in Pounds Sterling)

Age	No. of Decedents	Mean Net Worth	Mean Total Physical Wealth
Under 25	7	49.2	64.2
25–34	25	91.6	116.0
35–44	51	215.5	255.8
45–54	45	297.3	349.8
55–64	41	541.0	462.8
65–74	48	407.7	442.9
75–84	31	388.4	449.0
85–94	12	163.3	218.3
95 and over	1	19.3	28.7

Source: Subsample of 261 cases for which age in years was determined, modifed *c*-weighted. See source note to table C.3.

Table C.2
Net Worth and Total Physical Wealth by Ten-Year
Age Brackets
New Jersey, Pennsylvania, Delaware, 1774
(Subsample of Decedents, in Pounds Sterling)

Age	No. of Decedents	Mean Net Worth	Mean Total Physical Wealth
Under 25	3	−0.7	150.9
25–34	13	369.7	281.5
35–44	21	218.3	272.7
45–54	23	457.7	399.8
55–64	27	736.5	618.3
65–74	16	737.1	433.1
75–84	8	394.2	402.8
85 and over	1	1,578.5	319.9

Source: Subsample of 112 cases for which age in years was determined, modifed *c*-weighted. See source note to table C.4.

Table C.3
Net Worth by Five-Year Age Brackets
New England, 1774
(Subsample of Decedents, in Pounds Sterling)

Age	No. (1)	Percent (2)	Mean (3)	Low (4)	High (5)	c-weighted Percent (6)	c-weighted Mean (7)
All	261	100.0	—	—	—	100.0	—
15–19	1	0.4	£10.4	£10.4	£10.5	0.5	£10.4
20–24	6	2.3	83.6	−13.5	326.8	2.1	59.1
25–29	13	5.0	97.0	−3.3	416.1	6.6	87.8
30–34	12	4.6	81.9	0.8	256.3	4.7	96.9
35–39	29	11.1	174.3	5.1	481.9	11.0	182.1
40–44	22	8.4	364.7	−78.3	4,071.2	8.2	260.2
45–49	24	9.2	268.3	2.8	1,694.3	9.2	285.4
50–54	21	8.0	401.1	−90.7	2,176.1	7.0	312.9
55–59	26	10.0	917.0	−26.7	15,303.2	11.2	634.5
60–64	15	5.7	354.7	−152.3	1,095.8	5.3	343.6
65–69	28	10.7	478.2	−6.3	3,235.2	12.0	403.3
70–74	20	7.7	524.4	12.4	5,786.2	6.2	416.3
75–79	19	7.3	483.0	−21.7	1,868.8	5.5	533.6
80–84	12	4.6	223.5	24.1	644.0	3.9	183.0
85–89	10	3.8	223.9	4.1	705.1	5.0	161.2
90–94	2	0.8	121.3	10.0	232.5	0.8	176.3
95–99	1	0.4	19.5	19.5	19.5	0.7	19.5

SOURCE: Subsample of those 261 cases in the full sample for which age in years was determined by a genealogist. Columns 1–5, subsample data not weighted, i.e., each case has equal weight, regardless of the county where the decedent dwelt. Columns 6, 7, subsample data modified *c*-weighted, i.e., each subsample case has equal weight within its county and each sample county represented in the subsample receives equal weight in the regional total. See *American Colonial Wealth,* either edition, Weighting Procedures, Section VI.

NOTE: Percentages do not sum to 100.0 because of rounding. For columns 1–6 the figures by 10-year age brackets may be computed simply by combining entries for two 5-year brackets.

Table C.4
Net Worth by Five-Year Age Brackets
New Jersey, Pennsylvania, Delaware, 1774
(Subsample of Decedents, in Pounds Sterling)

| | | | | | | c-weighted | |
Age	No. (1)	Percent (2)	Mean (3)	Low (4)	High (5)	Percent (6)	Mean (7)
All	112	100.0	—	—	—	100.0	—
15–19	1	0.9	£–59.6	£–59.6	£–59.6	1.5	£–59.6
20–24	2	1.8	74.4	40.0	108.7	1.8	49.8
25–29	6	5.4	224.0	14.3	656.3	2.9	428.8
30–34	7	6.3	281.0	69.6	492.3	4.4	331.0
35–39	7	6.3	156.5	–30.1	450.3	23.8	201.4
40–44	14	12.5	333.9	6.6	1,169.9	6.1	284.0
45–49	12	10.7	534.7	2.4	2,072.2	7.0	367.1
50–54	11	9.8	805.7	28.0	3,127.3	5.3	577.6
55–59	8	7.1	1,536.9	14.9	6,167.5	4.6	692.1
60–64	19	17.0	816.8	4.2	3,647.8	12.4	753.1
65–69	10	8.9	1,196.4	33.1	6,646.7	6.6	1,083.5
70–74	6	5.4	272.9	28.0	562.0	5.6	328.4
75–79	5	4.5	310.6	191.8	436.2	14.9	379.3
80–84	3	2.7	404.6	274.4	638.4	3.4	460.2
85–89	1	0.9	1,578.5	1,578.5	1,578.5	0.3	1,578.5

SOURCE: Subsample of those 112 cases in the full sample for which year of age was determined by a genealogist. Columns 1–5, subsample data not weighted, i.e., each case has equal weight, regardless of the county where the decedent dwelt. Columns 6, 7, subsample data modified c-weighted, i.e., each subsample case has equal weight within its county and each sample county represented in the subsample receives its Larntz county weight. See *American Colonial Wealth,* either edition, Weighting Procedures, Section VI.

NOTE: Percentages do not sum to 100.0 because of rounding. For columns 1–6 the figures by 10-year age brackets may be computed simply by combining entries for two 5-year brackets.

Table C.5
Total Physical Wealth by Five-Year Age Brackets
New England, 1774
(Subsample of Decedents, in Pounds Sterling)

Age	No. (1)	Percent (2)	Mean (3)	Low (4)	High (5)	c-weighted Percent (6)	Mean (7)
All	261	100.0	—	—	—	100.0	—
15–19	1	0.4	£3.7	£3.7	£3.7	0.5	£3.7
20–24	6	2.3	103.9	4.0	350.3	2.1	79.6
25–29	13	5.0	128.3	4.0	519.3	6.6	117.0
30–34	12	4.6	98.5	7.5	280.9	4.7	114.6
35–39	29	11.1	205.2	14.7	682.9	11.0	208.1
40–44	22	8.4	375.2	4.6	2,252.6	8.2	319.8
45–49	24	9.2	292.3	7.3	1,456.9	9.2	311.6
50–54	21	8.0	462.5	11.1	2,176.1	7.0	399.9
55–59	26	10.0	569.7	22.3	3,793.4	11.2	506.0
60–64	15	5.7	350.6	8.2	1,014.0	5.3	371.6
65–69	28	10.7	519.2	12.4	2,915.7	12.0	447.6
70–74	20	7.7	524.5	15.9	4,188.1	6.2	433.9
75–79	19	7.3	547.6	14.0	1,850.6	5.5	600.8
80–84	12	4.6	266.8	18.1	66.1	3.9	234.3
85–89	10	3.8	289.2	3.8	846.8	5.0	213.7
90–94	2	0.8	183.3	57.7	309.0	0.8	245.5
95–99	1	0.4	28.7	28.7	28.7	0.7	28.7

SOURCE: Source note for table C.3 pertains to this table also.

NOTE: Percentages do not sum to 100.0 because of rounding. For columns 1–6 the figures by 10-year age brackets may be computed simply by combining entries for two 5-year brackets.

Table C.6
Total Physical Wealth by Five-Year Age Brackets
New Jersey, Pennsylvania, Delaware, 1774
(Subsample of Decedents, in Pounds Sterling)

Age	No. (1)	Percent (2)	Mean (3)	Low (4)	High (5)	c-weighted Percent (6)	Mean (7)
All	112	100.0	—	—	—	100.0	—
15–19	1	0.9	£225.5	£225.5	£225.5	1.5	£225.5
20–24	2	1.8	196.7	43.2	350.3	1.8	87.0
25–29	6	5.4	206.0	10.5	609.5	2.9	211.7
30–34	7	6.3	412.0	57.0	1,048.2	4.4	327.3
35–39	7	6.3	224.2	7.6	446.0	23.8	269.8
40–44	14	12.5	347.1	6.6	1,500.0	6.1	284.0
45–49	12	10.7	544.6	3.8	1,579.5	7.0	369.9
50–54	11	9.8	448.6	28.8	1,566.8	5.3	403.7
55–59	8	7.1	1,491.5	20.7	7,601.8	4.6	671.6
60–64	19	17.0	600.8	0.0	2,395.7	12.4	598.4
65–69	10	8.9	1,112.5	32.6	8,335.6	6.6	597.5
70–74	6	5.4	258.0	23.3	395.8	5.6	239.1
75–79	5	4.5	372.6	266.9	550.8	14.9	431.4
80–84	3	2.7	271.6	168.9	394.5	3.4	276.1
85–89	1	0.9	319.9	319.9	319.9	0.3	319.9

SOURCE: Source note for table C.4 pertains to this table also.

NOTE: Percentages do not sum to 100.0 because of rounding. For columns 1–6 the figures by 10-year age brackets may be computed simply by combining entries for two 5-year brackets.

APPENDIX D

Measures of Variance

Table D.1
Means and Measures of Variance, Net Worth, Total Physical Wealth
Probate-type Wealthholders, 1774, Variant Two,
Thirteen Colonies, Three Regions
(*In Pounds Sterling*)

Kind of Wealth, Area	Mean	Standard Deviation	Confidence Interval[a] Lower Bound	Upper Bound	Coefficient of Variation
Net Worth					
Thirteen Colonies	362.27	22.84	317.50	407.04	0.06
New England	206.02	19.68	167.45	244.60	0.10
Middle Colonies	289.37	27.31	235.85	342.89	0.09
South	489.17	45.83	399.35	578.99	0.09
Total Physical Wealth					
Thirteen Colonies	372.28	21.86	329.45	415.12	0.06
New England	240.63	15.17	210.90	270.35	0.06
Middle Colonies	259.17	16.68	226.48	291.86	0.06
South	519.35	46.53	428.16	610.54	0.09

SOURCE: Sample data, w-weighted, Variant Two for South and thirteen colonies. Includes all cases in the sample.

NOTE: Corresponding figures, w-weighted, using Variant One weights, are shown in tables 7.162–7.165 of *American Colonial Wealth,* either edition. Corresponding figures, c-weighted, using Variant One weights, appear in tables 7.170–7.171 of *American Colonial Wealth,* either edition.

[a] At .95 level of confidence.

Table D.2
Means and Measures of Variance, Selected Totals
Probate-type Wealthholders, Variant Two,
Thirteen Colonies, 1774,
(In Pounds Sterling)

| | | | Confidence Interval[a] | | Coefficient |
| | | Standard | Lower | Upper | of |
Kind of Wealth	Mean	Deviation	Bound	Bound	Variation
Nonhuman physical, total	290.04	16.81	257.09	323.00	0.06
Nonhuman phys., portable	92.75	4.63	83.67	101.82	0.05
Producers' capital	63.38	3.83	56.38	71.39	0.06
Producers' durable goods	45.93	2.42	41.19	50.66	0.05
Producers' perishable	17.96	2.19	13.66	22.26	0.12
Perishable materials in					
household	1.71	0.36	1.02	2.41	0.21
Consumers' goods	27.20	1.31	24.64	29.76	0.05

SOURCE: Sample data, *w*-weighted, Variant Two. Includes all cases in the sample, whether or not they held the kind of wealth (i.e., for which wealth is equal to or greater than zero).

NOTE: The selected totals appear in tables in chapter 4. For relationship of the selected totals to subcategories, see table 7.6 of *American Colonial Wealth,* either edition. Corresponding figures, *w*-weighted, for other wealth totals and subcategories found in those tables appear in table A-7.162 of *American Colonial Wealth,* 2d edition. Corresponding figures, *c*-weighted, using Variant One weights, for the first two selected totals above, appear in tables 7.170 and 7.171 of *American Colonial Wealth,* either edition.

[a] At .95 level of confidence.

Table D.3
Means and Measures of Variance, Selected Totals
Probate-type Wealthholders, Variant One,
Thirteen Colonies, 1774
(*In Pounds Sterling*)

| Kind of Wealth | Mean | Standard Deviation | Confidence Interval[a] | | Coefficient of Variation |
			Lower Bound	Upper Bound	
Nonhuman physical, total	342.62	22.06	281.39	367.86	0.07
Nonhuman phys., portable	101.39	5.30	90.08	111.70	0.05
Producers' capital	68.90	4.18	60.71	77.08	0.06
Producers' durable goods	47.66	2.46	42.83	52.49	0.05
Producers' perishable	21.24	2.56	16.21	26.26	0.12
Perishable materials in household	2.07	0.50	1.09	3.06	0.24
Consumers' goods	30.83	1.73	27.44	34.22	0.06

SOURCE: Sample data, *w*-weighted, Variant One. Includes all cases in the sample, whether or not they held the kind of wealth (i.e. for which wealth is equal to or greater than zero).

NOTE: The selected totals appear in tables in chapter 4. For relationship of the selected totals to subcategories, see table 7.6 of *American Colonial Wealth,* either edition. Corresponding figures, *w*-weighted, for other wealth totals and subcategories, appear in table 7.162 of *American Colonial Wealth,* either edition. Corresponding ones, *c*-weighted, for nonhuman physical wealth, appear in table 7.170 of *American Colonial Wealth,* either edition.

[a] At .95 level of confidence.

Table D.4
Means and Measures of Variance, Selected Totals
Probate-type Wealthholders, *New England, 1774*
(*In Pounds Sterling*)

Kind of Wealth	Mean	Standard Deviation	Confidence Interval[a] Lower Bound	Upper Bound	Coefficient of Variation
Nonhuman physical, total	239.53	15.12	209.90	269.16	0.06
Nonhuman phys., portable	67.76	4.34	59.26	79.26	0.06
Producers' capital	38.54	3.04	32.58	44.50	0.08
Producers' durable goods	28.52	1.87	24.85	32.19	0.07
Producers' perishable	10.02	1.99	6.11	13.93	0.20
Perishable materials in household	2.37	0.44	1.50	3.23	0.19
Consumers' goods	28.21	1.98	24.34	32.08	0.07

SOURCE: Sample data, *w*-weighted.

NOTE: The general note to table D.3 pertains to this table also, except that corresponding *w*-weighted figures for other wealth totals and subcategories appear in table 7.163 of *American Colonial Wealth*, either edition.

[a] At .95 level of confidence.

Table D.5
Means and Measures of Variance, Selected Totals
Probate-type Wealthholders, *Middle Colonies, 1774*
(*In Pounds Sterling*)

Kind of Wealth	Mean	Standard Deviation	Confidence Interval[a] Lower Bound	Upper Bound	Coefficient of Variation
Nonhuman physical, total	248.42	15.89	217.27	279.57	0.06
Nonhuman phys., portable	91.58	8.70	74.52	108.64	0.09
Producers' capital	63.83	7.55	49.04	78.63	0.12
Producers' durable goods	39.16	3.93	31.46	46.85	0.10
Producers' perishable	24.67	5.17	14.55	34.80	0.21
Perishable materials in household	1.55	0.40	0.77	2.34	0.26
Consumers' goods	23.54	2.25	19.14	27.94	0.10

SOURCE: Sample data, *w*-weighted, including New York hybrid.

NOTE: The general note to table D.3 pertains to this table also, except that corresponding figures, *w*-weighted, for other wealth totals and subcategories, appear in table 7.164 of *American Colonial Wealth*, either edition, and corresponding ones, *c*-weighted, for nonhuman physical wealth, appear in table 7.171 of *American Colonial Wealth*, either edition.

[a] At .95 level of confidence.

Table D.6
Means and Measures of Variance, Selected Totals
Probate-type Wealthholders, Variant Two,
South, 1774
(*In Pounds Sterling*)

| | | | Confidence Interval[a] | | Coefficient |
| | | Standard | Lower | Upper | of |
Kind of Wealth	Mean	Deviation	Bound	Bound	Variation
Nonhuman physical, total	344.89	34.84	276.60	413.18	0.10
Nonhuman phys., portable	106.63	7.96	91.03	122.24	0.07
Producers' capital	76.98	6.45	64.33	89.62	0.08
Producers' durable goods	59.79	4.50	50.96	68.62	0.08
Producers' perishable	17.18	3.06	11.18	23.19	0.18
Perishable materials in					
household	1.35	0.69	0.00	2.69	0.51
Consumers' goods	29.44	2.22	25.08	33.79	0.08

SOURCE: Sample data, *w*-weighted, Variant Two.

NOTE. The general note to table D.3 pertains to this table also, except that corresponding figures for other wealth totals and subcategories appear in table A.7.165 of *American Colonial Wealth*, 2d edition.

[a] At .95 level of confidence.

Table D.7
Means and Measures of Variance, Selected Totals
Probate-type Wealthholders, Variant One,
South, 1774
(*In Pounds Sterling*)

| | | | Confidence Interval[a] | | Coefficient |
| | | Standard | Lower | Upper | of |
Kind of Wealth	Mean	Deviation	Bound	Bound	Variation
Nonhuman physical, total	421.79	47.14	329.40	514.19	0.11
Nonhuman phys., portable	125.86	9.80	106.65	145.07	0.08
Producers' capital	88.12	7.44	73.54	102.71	0.08
Producers' durable goods	63.65	4.62	54.58	72.71	0.07
Producers' perishable	24.47	4.26	16.13	32.82	0.17
Perishable materials in					
household	2.15	1.05	0.09	4.20	0.49
Consumers' goods	37.51	3.36	30.93	44.09	0.09

SOURCE: Sample data, *w*-weighted, Variant One.

NOTE: The general note to table D.3 pertains to this table also, except that corresponding figures, *w*-weighted, for other wealth totals and subcategories appear in appendix A, table A.3, and in table 7.165 of *American Colonial Wealth*, either edition. Corresponding ones, *c*-weighted, using Variant One weights, for nonhuman physical wealth, appear in table 7.171 of *American Colonial Wealth*, either edition.

[a] At .95 level of confidence.

APPENDIX E

Two Lists of Recommended Supplies a Colonist Should Bring to Subsist for a Year

1622, JAMESTOWN, VIRGINIA

THE INCONVENIENCIES
THAT HAVE HAPPENED TO SOME PERSONS
WHICH HAVE TRANSPORTED THEMSELVES
from England to Virginia, without provisions necessary to
sustaine themselves, hath greatly hindred the Progresse of that noble
Plantation: For prevention of the like disorders heereafter,
that no man suffer, either through ignorance or misinformation;
it is thought requisite to publish this short declaration:
wherein is contained a particular of such necessaries
as either private families or single persons shall have cause
to furnish themselves with, for their better support
at their first landing in Virginia;
whereby also greater numbers may receive in part,
directions how to provide themselves.

(Seal)

		li.	s.	d.
	Apparrell.			
	One Monmouth Cap	00	01	10
	Three falling bands	—	01	03
	Three shirts	—	07	06
	One waste coate	—	02	02
	One suite of Canvase	—	07	06
	One suite of Frize	—	10	00
	One Suite of Cloth	—	15	00
	Three paire of Irish stockins	—	04	—
Apparell for	Foure paire of shooes	—	08	08
one man, and	One paire of garters	—	00	10
so after the	One doozen of points	—	00	03
rate for more	One paire of Canvase Sheets	—	08	00
	Seven ells of Canvase, to make a bed and boulster, to be filled in Virginia 8.s. One Rug for a bed 8.s. which with the bed serving for two men, halfe is	—	08	00
	Five ells coorse Canvase, to make a bed at Sea for two men, to be filled with straw, iiij.s. One coorse Rug at Sea for two men, will cost vj.s. is for one	—	05	00
		04	00	00
	Victuall.			
For a whole	Eight bushels of Meale	02	00	00
yeere for one	Two bushels of pease at 3.s.	—	06	00
man, and so	Two bushels of Oatemeale 4.s.6.d	—	09	00
for more after	One gallon of Aquavite	—	02	06
the rate.	One gallon of Oyle	—	03	06
	Two gallons of Vinegar 1.s.	—	02	00
		03	03	00
	Armes.			
For one man,	One Armour compleat, light	—	17	00
but if halfe	One long Peece, five foot or five and a halfe, neere [sic] Musket bore	01	02	—
of your men	One sword	—	05	—
have armour it	One belt	—	01	—
is sufficient	One bandaleere	—	01	06
so that all	Twenty pound of powder	—	18	00
have Peeces	Sixty pound of shot or lead, Pistoll and Goose shot	—	05	00
and swords				
		03	09	05

	li.	s.	d.

Tooles.

	li.	s.	d.
Five broad howes at 2.s. a piece	—	10	—
Five narrow howes at 16.d. a piece	—	06	08
Two broad Axes at 3.s.8.d. a piece	—	07	04
Five felling Axes at 18.d. a piece	—	07	06
Two steele hand sawes at 16.d. a piece	—	02	08
Two two-hand sawes at 5.s. a piece	—	10	—
One whip-saw, set and filed with box, file, and wrest	—	10	—
Two hammers 12.d. a piece	—	02	00
Three shovels 18.d. a piece	—	04	06
Two spades at 18.d. a piece	—	03	—
Two augers 6.d. a piece	—	01	00
Sixe chissels 6.d. a piece	—	03	00
Two percers stocked 4.d. a piece	—	00	08
Three gimlets 2.d. a piece	—	00	06
Two hatchets 21.d. a piece	—	03	06
Two froues to cleave pale 18.d.	—	03	00
Two hand bills 20. a piece	—	03	04
One grindlestone 4.s.	—	04	00
Nailes of all sorts to the value of	02	00	—
Two pickaxes	—	03	—
	06	02	08

For a family of 6. persons and so after the rate, for more.

Household Implements.

	li.	s.	d.
One Iron Pot	00	07	—
One Kettle	—	06	—
One large frying pan	—	02	06
One gridiron	—	01	06
Two skillets	—	05	—
One Spit	—	02	—
Platters, dishes, spoones of wood	—	04	—
	01	08	00

For a family of 6. persons and so for more or lesse after the rate.

	li.	s.	d.
For Suger, Spice and fruit, and at Sea for 6 men—	00	12	06
So the full charge of Apparrel, Victuall, Armes, Tooles, and household stuffe, and after this rate for each person, will amount unto about the summe of	12	10	—
The passage of each man is	06	00	—
The fraight of these provisions for a man, will bee about halfe a Tun, which is	01	10	—
So the whole charge will amount to about	20	00	00

Nets, hookes, lines and a tent must be added, if the number of people be greater, as also some kine.

And this is the usuall proportion that the Virginia Company doe
bestow upon their Tenants which they send.

Whosoever transports himselfe or any other at his owne charge unto Virginia, shall
for each person so transported before Midsummer 1625 have to him and his heires
for ever fifty Acres of Land upon a first, and fifty Acres upon a second division.
            Imprinted at London by FELIX KYNGSTON.   1622   *(Seal)*

SOURCE: A photocopy of the foregoing printed announcement was given to the author by Ethel D. Hoover, who obtained it at the 350th celebration of the founding of Jamestown at Jamestown, Virginia.

EARLY EIGHTEENTH CENTURY, CAROLINA

"Early in the Eighteenth Century, the author of *The British Empire in America* wrote that the cost of settling in Carolina was as follows:

4 cows with calves at 25s. each	£5 0s.
4 sows at 15s. each	3 0
A canoe	3 0
Axes, hoes, wedges, saws, hammers, etc.	2 0
A steel mill	3 0
A small house, hut or cabin for the first year or two	8 0
Corn, peas, beef, pork, tea for the first year	14 0"
[Total	£38 0]

SOURCE: Anonymous. *The British Empire in America,* 2 vols. London, 1741. Vol. I, p. 523, as cited by Sutherland (1967:72).

Notes

PREFACE AND ACKNOWLEDGMENTS

1. Since the publication of that work, the title and makeup of the present volume, which was mentioned therein, have evolved from their preliminary forms. Hence, references that appear in *American Colonial Wealth* to *"The Wealth of the Colonies on the Eve of the American Revolution"* should be read as references to *Wealth of a Nation to Be: The American Colonies on the Eve of the Revolution.* Similarly references in the first named work to "chapter 3 of *Wealth of the Colonies,"* which appear particularly in the appendix to the second edition, should be read as references to "appendix A of *Wealth of a Nation to Be."* References to other chapters of *"Wealth of the Colonies"* numbered 4 or higher should be read as the chapters one number lower in each instance. For example, the reference on page 1850 to "chapters 4, 5 and 6 of *Wealth of the Colonies"* should be read as "chapters 3, 4, and 5 of *Wealth of a Nation to Be,"* and that on page 2219 to "chapter 8" should be read as "chapter 7." Since table numbers correspond with their chapter numbers, the relatively few references to tables numbered 4 or higher to the left of the decimal point should likewise be adjusted. For instance the reference on page 1850 to "table 5.1 of *Wealth of the Colonies"* should be read as "table 4.1 of *Wealth of a Nation to Be."* The present volume does not show in footnotes to tables in chapters 3, 4, and 5 separate values for New York hybrid and the middle colonies of Pennsylvania, New Jersey, and Delaware, as is stated on page 1850.

INTRODUCTION:
A NOTE ON METHOD

1. See David 1967a and 1967b and discussion of David by Engerman 1967. See also G. Taylor 1964; North 1974:27; Goldsmith 1959; Bruchey 1975.

2. A question might be raised regarding the effect of a clerical error that occurred in drawing the sample for the five counties in New Jersey, Pennsylvania, and Delaware, discussed in Jones 1970:22, n. 34. If it had not occurred, one more county, York, Pennsylvania, would have been added to the sample for those middle colonies. Although I wish the error had not occurred, it was a random one. It would be interesting to see how different the results would be for a six-county weighted average, including York. I believe the answer is "not much." York was a prosperous well settled farming county and it would be most surprising if its wealth values fell outside the confidence intervals I have found for the Middle Colonies' regional average composed of the five-counties' average plus the New York hybrid (a term explained later in the introduction). A further question might be raised that the

frame from which the five counties were drawn was all 71 northern counties rather than the 28 within the boundaries of New Jersey, Pennsylvania, and Delaware. A study of *American Colonial Wealth,* either edition, section V should convince a skeptic that the five-county sample was randomly drawn, proportionate to population after use of Larntz weights (*American Colonial Wealth,* either edition, pp. 1874 ff.), and that all probate inventories in those three provinces had an equal chance to be included in the final results. For the effect of post-weighting because of slaves, see appendix A of the present volume.

    3. In this discussion a "decedent" refers to a deceased person whose estate was probated in 1774 or close thereto. A "sample decedent" is such a person whose records are included in my sample. The universe sampled was all inventories of estates probated in 1774 in the thirteen colonies. Each inventory was an element of the universe.

    4. Statistical advisers in designing the samples were Jerome Cornfield for the first sample for the middle colonies of Pennsylvania, New Jersey, and Delaware; Stephen E. Fienberg and F. Kinley Larntz for the second sample extended to New England, New York, and the South. See Jones 1970:14–33 for the first sample and *American Colonial Wealth,* either edition, section V, for a complete account of the sampling procedure for both samples.

    5. See *American Colonial Wealth,* either edition: sections I and II on documents; III.C on tax lists and deeds; and III.D on regression analysis.

    6. In the South, where county populations were smaller, several geographically contiguous counties were grouped to make one unit for sampling. A combination of such counties drawn into the sample is treated as one in the count of 21.

    This count also treats all New York province as one group of counties. In the second sample design, two sample counties, each yielding a cluster of inventories, were the desired target for New York. (See *American Colonial Wealth,* either edition, table 5.3). Two New York counties, each yielding a cluster of inventories, would have made a total of 22 county groups for the thirteen colonies. However, a special problem without parallel in any other province arose from the paucity of surviving New York inventories. Whether for reasons of war, courthouse fires, or official or custodial neglect, only one probate inventory could be located from the two primary counties, Suffolk and Albany, drawn in the sample, and only one from the two alternate counties of Queens and Ulster. (See Jones 1970:29 for a previous unsuccessful attempt to gather records for Dutchess and Westchester Counties drawn in the first sample.) Although the search was then extended to all counties of New York, a total of only 23 inventories for estates probated from 1773 through 1775 from seven counties could be found for the entire province. This number was too small to comprise two clusters to represent 41,577 white "wealthholders," in two strata. Special treatment was required to take advantage of such information as the 23 cases give us. The procedure adopted, after careful consideration of alternatives, was to utilize them as a single cluster and, in combination with data from the other middle colonies and from New England, to estimate for it a New York hybrid pattern of wealth. This hybrid pattern, when used in regional combinations, is weighted by the relative importance of the wealthholders in the entire province of New York, in a manner parallel to the weighting of the sample data for other regions by their respective relative wealthholder populations. See note 25.

    7. For the purpose of sample drawing, the ideal number of chances each county has to be drawn would be proportionate to its number of probate inventories made in 1774. This is the universe of elements we are sampling. As this number could have been determined only at great cost by visiting each county, it was not feasible to use

in setting up a sample framework; therefore proxies were used. In the first sample design, for northern counties, the numbers of the total living population were used as the proxy. If death rates and probate practices did not vary greatly from county to county, we could expect a close correspondence between proportions of the total population by county and proportions of inventories by county. In the second sample design, for New England, for New York, and for the South where there were many blacks, the numbers of white "wealthholders" were used as the proxy. Their proportions by county should have an even closer correspondence to the proportions of inventories by county.

8. 20,366 is the number of white "wealthholders" (see the next note) in the middle colonies of Pennsylvania, New Jersey, and Delaware that may be thought of, retrospectively, as a stratum represented by each of the five randomly drawn sample counties in those colonies. See *American Colonial Wealth,* either edition, tables 5.4 and 5.6. This stratum size determined how many counties or county groups were to be chosen for New England, New York, and the South, to keep those samples congruent with the one already executed for Pennsylvania, New Jersey, and Delaware. In the first sample frame, all counties north of Maryland were arrayed from large to small population size, without regard to region, and regional allocation was left to the chance of the draw. See Jones 1970:14–29 and *American Colonial Wealth,* either edition, pp. 1829–30. In the second sample frame, all the counties of New England, New York, and the South were arrayed, within region, by geographical contiguity. The arrayed, contiguous counties in the South were separated first into groups of counties such that each group contained as close to 4,716 white "wealthholders" as was possible without splitting a county. This was the average number in a New England county. See *American Colonial Wealth,* either edition, pp. 1827, 1840. These arrayed county groups in the South and counties in New England and New York were next separated into strata with a target total per stratum of 20,366 white "wealthholders," achieved as closely as possible without dividing a county (or contiguous group of southern counties) in two.

9. The figures for white "wealthholders," when the words are placed within quotation marks, include the relatively small numbers of indentured whites of appro priate age and sex. They do not include the relatively small numbers of free black adult males or 10 percent of free black females. The proportions for these two groups, by province, as determined from the secondary sources cited in *American Colonial Wealth,* either edition, pp. 1798–99 are:

	Percent of Blacks Free	Percent of Whites Indentured
Mass., N.H., R.I., Conn.	9.0	2.0
New York	9.0	2.5
Pennsylvania, New Jersey, Del.	10.0	4.0
Maryland	5.0	3.0
Virginia	3.0	3.0
North Carolina	3.0	3.0
South Carolina	1.0	3.0
Georgia	1.0	3.0

See also Cappon 1976:25, 100. There was insufficient information to vary these proportions further by province or county. Adjustment of the proportions for each county, using the same percentages for all counties within a region (or province for southern blacks), would have altered only trivially the county's chance of being drawn into the sample.

10. This count treats New York as one of the six. In the second sample design, alternate counties were drawn for each primary county selected to provide additional cases if needed; however, for New York, the two primary and two alternate counties yielded insufficient cases. See note 6 for discussion of number of cases in New York.

11. Except in New York, where use of all available inventories in any county of the province yielded only 23 cases, sufficient to form only one cluster. See note 6.

12. My experience, in collaboration with Jerome Cornfield and others, with small samples in the World War II era, when their theory and application were emerging, dramatically proved their usefulness. See Hanson, Cornfield, and Epstein 1942 and Hanson and Cornfield 1942. The U.S. census estimates of unemployment started with a small nationwide sample household survey in the late 1930s and have expanded into today's monthly Current Population Surveys, which make sophisticated use of small samples to estimate not only unemployment but other items relevant to national policy concerns. See references in note 15. Statisticians continue to make advances in the theory of small samples. See Barrett and Goldsmith 1976.

13. See *American Colonial Wealth*, either edition, pp. 1853–54.

14. The size of the decedent samples for each region, as well as for the thirteen colonies, justifies the use of the central limit theorem and the expectation that the distribution of successive sample means is approximately normal. For understanding of confidence intervals for samples measuring a variable with a skewed distribution, such as wealth, see Cochran 1963:38–43 and Barrett and Goldsmith 1976:68–69.

15. A brief definition of an unbiased sample is one where every element in the total statistical population or universe to be sampled has an equal chance to be drawn into the sample and where the elements actually drawn are determined by random numbers, not by any subjective judgment. See Cochran 1963; Cornfield 1944; Guenther 1965; Hagood and Price 1952; Kish 1965; Lazerwitz 1968. Such an estimate can, within specified confidence intervals, be properly attributed to the entire statistical universe from which the cases were drawn.

16. Many people unfamiliar with sampling theory have an intuitive feeling that a larger sample, no matter how composed, is better than a small sample. Further, they often feel that if the elements being sampled, in this case probate inventories, are grouped in the total statistical universe in bundles or clusters, in this case within counties or groups of counties, which have differing characteristics as older/younger in date of founding, inland/coastal in location, on major river/not on major river, densely populated/sparsely populated, urban/rural, "subsistence agriculture"/commercial agriculture, that a judgment sample, taking some from each of the differing characteristics, or taking more from those with the more "important" characteristics according to the judgment of the investigator, is better than a randomly drawn group. The sampling theorists and experienced practitioners tell us this is fallacious. The reason is that the investigator may be aware of only some of the variables that differ, in this instance from county to county. In his zeal to adjust to those he regards as "important," he may fail to give any chance, or a proper chance, to other variables of which he has not thought or which he could not know. Thus his "best judgment" introduces the very thing we seek to avoid, bias. The safest and only theoretically defensible way to let all the variables, known and unknown, come into the sample in correct proportions is to eschew subjective judgment selection and let random numbers do the determining; they have no bias. In our sample they selected one cluster, the Charleston District, the results from which gave special problems which required post-weighting of the data, discussed in appendix A. The post-weighting to bring the results into line with known data external to the sample is,

however, quite different in principle to an initial choosing of a sample county on the basis of subjective judgment.

17. That is, for the w^*-weighted estimates including nonprobate-type wealth-holders. I find standard deviations and confidence intervals appropriate for the w-weighted estimates of wealth of the age-adjusted probates. See appendix D and *American Colonial Wealth,* either edition p. 1853.

18. There were a few exceptions to the 1774 date detailed in section V of *American Colonial Wealth.* Principally, aside from New York, already mentioned in note 6, these were Hampshire County, Massachusetts, where some 1773 cases were included, Westmoreland County, Pennsylvania, where some 1773 and some 1775 cases were included, all these in order to obtain a sufficient minimum number of cases. Also in Essex County, Massachusetts, the number of 1774 cases was cut off at 102, which was in the P's of surnames arranged in alphabetical order of cases probated in 1774. All 919 inventories are reproduced in full in section II of *American Colonical Wealth,* either edition.

19. See Brock 1975:487, 496–97; Gray 1932:chapter 18; Land 1969:152–66; Sellers 1934:55–57. My perusal of some issues in 1774 of the *South Carolina Gazette and Country Journal* disclosed frequent advertisements by estate executors or administrators, often in connection with announcing a public vendue, which requested that creditors make known their claims against the estate and that debtors thereto make immediate payment. I have observed similar advertisements in Philadelphia and other colonial newspapers.

20. The cases involved are enumerated in *American Colonial Wealth,* either edition, pp. 30–31. The searches for land information on tax lists for the middle colonies and on deeds and land grants for the South are treated in its section III.C. Use of such information for regression analysis to estimate land values for individual decedents is covered in its section IV.D, as is the regression analysis to estimate financial liabilities for those cases where they are unknown to me. The real estate and liabilities regression analysis for New Jersey, Pennsylvania, and Delaware is also presented in full in Jones 1970.

21. For a table showing estimated rural land price per acre in the South in 1774 by province, by such categories as proved statistically significant, see *American Colonial Wealth,* either edition, table 3.10, p. 1750.

22. See *American Colonial Wealth,* either edition, pp. 1752–53. I might have gone on to estimate still further regressions, associating the regression-estimated real estate values with the personal and wealth characteristics of the decedent, similar to my regression equations for the middle colonies, and from these results have "predicted" positive real estate values for some of my southern real estate zero cases. The results did not promise, however, to be as reliable or useful as those for the middle colonies, and I did not take this added step.

23. They are taken into account by Daniels 1973–74 and discussed by Land 1965.

24. See *American Colonial Wealth,* either edition, table 7.10; for hybrid, 7.11.

25. The hybrid wealth estimate assumes that had more New York records survived, perhaps 10 percent would have had high wealth, such as that found in the 23 cases of *American Colonial Wealth,* table 7.10, but that 90 percent might have had wealth and other characteristics somewhat like the cases in the other middle colonies and in New England, and somewhat more like the former than the latter. Hence the New York hybrid estimate is composed 10 percent from the 23 cases, 60 percent from the findings of the sample for the other middle colonies of Pennsylvania,

New Jersey, and Delaware, and 30 percent from the findings of the New England sample. When data for New York hybrid are combined with those for the other middle colonies, as in chapters 3, 4 and 5 of this volume, they receive a weight proportional to the wealthholding population of New York as calculated in table 4.23 of *American Colonial Wealth,* and they receive this relative weight in a thirteen colonies' total. (See *American Colonial Wealth,* either edition, the portions on the New York sample in section V, on New York weights in Section VI.C, and on regional combination procedures and table 6.8 in section VI.D.)

26. New York hybrid figures are omitted from all "Middle Colonies" tables in both editions of *American Colonial Wealth.* All text references in those volumes to the "Middle Colonies" refer only to New Jersey, Pennsylvania, and Delaware.

1. MEASURES OF WEALTH

1. Smith 1776:538.
2. Stuart Bruchey in foreword to *American Colonial Wealth.*
3. Ibid.
4. See Blodget 1806:195: Gallman 1960, 1966, 1968, 1969, 1972; Gallman and Howle 1971; Lampman 1962; Martin 1942; Pessen 1973; Soltow 1971a, 1975a,b.
5. See Christensen and Jorgenson 1973; Goldsmith 1952, 1962, 1968; Kendrick 1967; Lampman 1962; Projector and Weiss 1966.
6. See Brown 1955; Crandall 1971; Doherty 1971; Henretta 1965, 1973; Kulikoff 1971; Nash 1970; Warden 1976.
7. See Sutherland 1936, 1967; Wells 1975.
8. See McCusker 1972; Shepherd 1970; Shepherd and Walton 1972, 1976.
9. See Anderson 1975; Ball 1973; Carr and Walsh 1976; Cook 1970, 1971; Daniels 1973, 1973–74, 1976b; Davisson 1967a,b; Demos 1970; Greven 1970; Land 1965, 1969; Lemon and Nash 1968; G. Main 1972, 1974, 1977a,b; Menard, Harris, and Carr 1974; Scott and Owre 1970; D. S. Smith 1975; Walsh 1977a,b.
10. See J. Main 1965; Kulikoff 1975, 1978; Menard 1975; Nash 1970.
11. The question is discussed in detail in Jones 1970:6–8.
12. See Cash 1966; Daumard 1963; De Smedt 1970; Goubert 1960; Mattoso 1976; Robbert 1977; Van der Wee 1963. Johnson 1977 and Thrupp 1962 use wills rather than inventories.
13. All probate documents, with the exception of a few printed bond forms, were handwritten, in ink, on paper of widely varying sizes. The inventory format was generally similar within the same colony or province, with variations, especially in style of opening and closing, from one colony to another. See the verbatim reproduction of 919 inventories and selected estate accounts in section II of *American Colonial Wealth,* and three examples of complete wills, inventories, and accounts in Jones 1970:152–66.
14. The inventory was exhibited in court sometimes by only one appraiser, or occasionally by the executor/administrator on behalf of the appraisers.
15. "d.b.n." is the abbreviation for *de bonis non,* literally "of goods not," which, in practice, meant "of goods not yet administered."
16. Hartsook and Skordas 1946:81–89.
17. Andrews 1918; Brock 1975; Ernst 1973; Weiss 1970.

18. For the method and philosophy see *American Colonial Wealth,* either edition, pp. 1718 ff. I am indebted to Robert Gallman for a letter of October 1, 1973 discussing the relevance as a check to my deflation calculations of the estimates of the real value of land and tangible, reproducible capital (excluding consumers' durables) that underlie tables in Gallman 1972. His approach involved both the rate of increase in supply of the factors and their relative contributions to total or per capita product. I believe such a check yields results fairly consistent with table 1.2.

Arthur Cole and David Landes separately suggested to the author that a day's common labor is an item whose price can be compared directly over long time periods. However, questions would still remain as to length and pace of the working day and as to relative prices of the various items the laborer could buy with his day's wage at widely separated dates.

19. Maryland widows could renounce their legacies and take their thirds if they wished (letter to the author from Lois Green Carr, dated October 26, 1977). I believe the same practice was followed in most of the colonies.

20. According to the index of Gilboy and Schumpeter (whose data—based on Beveridge et al. 1939 and additional unpublished material which is deposited in the library of the Institute of Historical Research at London University—are shown numerically in Gilboy 1936:137; Schumpeter 1938:35; also in Mitchell and Deane 1962:465, 468–69; Deane and Cole 1967), the cost of living in London rose about 18 percent from 1739 to 1774; consumers' goods excluding cereals rose about 19 percent; and prices of producers' goods 13 percent. Ippolito 1975:298 found, on the basis of Gilboy and Schumpeter data, that "the aggregate price level remained roughly constant over the period" from 1730 to 1750.

21. Calculated on the basis of 8 bushels in a quarter, from data in Mitchell and Deane 1962:487, 488 tables 9 and 10, whose source is data from the Beveridge group.

22. See discussion of problems in estimating output per acre and related issues, with additional references, in Overton 1979.

23. Becker 1975; Gallman 1977a; Schultz 1972:14, 1974; Uselding 1971.

24. The quotation continues as follows: "The position of fundholders, or owners of the public debt of a country is similar. They are mortgagees on the general wealth of the country. The cancelling of the debt would be no destruction of wealth, but a transfer of it: a wrongful abstraction of wealth from certain members of the community, for the profit of the government, or of the tax-payers. Funded property therefore cannot be counted as part of the national wealth. This is not always borne in mind by the dealers in statistical calculations. For example, in estimates of the gross income of the country, founded on the proceeds of the income-tax, incomes derived from the funds are not always excluded: though the tax-payers are assessed on their whole nominal income, without being permitted to deduct from it the portion levied from them in taxation to form the income of the fundholder. In this calculation, therefore, one portion of the general income of the country is counted twice over, and the aggregate amount made to appear greater than it is by almost thirty millions. A country, however, may include in its wealth all stock held by its citizens in the funds of foreign countries, and other debts due to them from abroad. But even this is only wealth to them by being a part ownership in wealth held by others. It forms no part of the collective wealth of the human race. It is an element in the distribution, but not in the composition, of the general wealth."

25. G. King calculated £30.5 million income or product per year "by trade,

arts, labour etc. at near eleven years purchase (which being the value of the 5 million and a half of people at £60 per head) comes to 330,000,000" (1936:32).

26. Kendrick 1974 values human wealth as discounted lifetime earnings minus discounted costs of future maintenance at a customary level of consumption. The capital value of an infant at birth, which may be thought of as its birthright in a society without slavery, can be estimated as the discounted stream of its anticipated lifetime earnings, minus discounted future costs of its rearing, education, and maintenance. See Bergstrom 1971:32; Engerman 1973a:46–48.

27. See Gray 1932:473; Gallman and Anderson 1977:25. Discussions by Uselding 1971 and Gallman 1977a have focused on human capital inflow in white immigrants. Fogel and Engerman 1974a:261–62 discuss black human capital. See also the discussion, although not in human capital terms, of white-black relations by Jordan 1968, and of the importance of blacks in South Carolina by Wood 1974.

28. The paragraph cited was added in the 6th ed. (1865).

29. Engerman 1973a; Fogel and Engerman 1974a; 233–34, Hast 1969; Jordan 1968:47–48; Kalm 1770:1:206–7; Sirmans 1962; Wiecek 1977.

30. *American Husbandry* 1775:1:121–22; Kalm 1770:1:204–5.

31. We might argue, as did Mill, that whether or not the labor force, or a part of it, was free makes no difference in the region's real wealth. But, in the case of the American colonies, I believe this would be true only if we could also successfully argue that free and nonfree labor were equally productive, had the same maintenance costs, and worked as effectively in one region as another, regardless of differing social organization and work arrangements. See Engerman 1973a:46.

32. It is possible and interesting to present a wealth size distribution with slaves and servants included as zero wealthholders, and their capital value still counted as part of the wealth of their owners. I do this in chapter 7.

33. Bergstrom 1971:32; Conrad and Meyer 1964:chap. 3; Engerman 1973a.

34. It might be argued that it was reduced if the former slaves ceased on the average to work so productively, and the rest of the working population did not begin to labor more productively.

2. HUMAN AND LAND RESOURCES

1. See titles on white servitude cited in *American Colonial Wealth,* either edition, pp. 1798–99. Also see Carr and Menard 1979.

2. Estimates of possible average lengths of terms of indentured servitude in the middle colonies are reported in Jones 1970:110. See also Galenson 1977, 1978a; Heavner 1978a,b. I am indebted to Carr 1977 for explanation of indenture terms in Maryland.

3. Robert Fogel and Stanley Engerman conclude that, by 1774, around 70 to 80 percent of the black population was native born. Telephone conversation with S. Engerman, July 1, 1977.

4. At a court held on February 16, 1773 in Fairfax County, Virginia, John Smith was charged with harboring a runaway slave, and after witnesses were heard, was required to "give security himself in fifty pounds and two securities in twenty-five pounds each for his good behavior for a year and a day and that he be committed to Gaol until he gives such Security and pays Costs." *Fairfax County Order Book* 1772–74:169.

5. Kalm 1750:1:206–7 (Benson ed). A letter from Robert V. Wells to the author, dated November 15, 1976, confirms that Quaker counties of Pennsylvania and New Jersey were prone to manumission.

6. Free Negroes were listed on the Constable's Returns for Philadelphia County, made in October 1775. See Jones 1970:111.

7. Probate inventories for women have been ignored by most analysts who have used American inventories. Their exclusion by W. I. King (see Federal Trade Commission 1926:58–68) in his studies early in the twentieth century was noted by Merwin 1939.

8. Probate documents for my sample rather frequently show a widowed executrix or administratrix who had acquired a new surname by the time she submitted her estate account to the court.

9. For example, Thomas Rakestraw, sample case 21012 in Burlington County, New Jersey specified that his widow was to have the use of the east room belowstairs and ordered a door be made in the same to go in and out; also that she was to get one cow, bed and bedding of her choice, her warming pan, six pewter plates "to her and her disposing"; also about one fourth acre of ground on the north side of the house for a garden "and liberty to put such of her goods or lumber as she sees cause in the smokehouse, and to bake in the oven," get water from the spring, have her firewood cut and hauled to the door; her cow to be kept on hay and grass "so long as she remains my widow and no longer." For the first year she was to be provided with 200 weight of pork, 10 bushels of rye, 2 of wheat, 5 of Indian corn.

10. The widow of William Diethard, sample case 11002, in Northampton County, Pennsylvania was to receive one-third of the whole estate, likewise the youngest mare (gray), a cow, two sheep, her bed, a sidesaddle, and to "keep her residence in the house as long as she bears my name." Alexander Sillman, sample case 11015 in Northampton County, Pennsylvania left his "dearly well beloved" wife Margaret "all her clothes that is her wearing apparel, her bed, bedstead and bed clothes and spinning wheel and chest to have and hold without let or molestation during her natural life and then at her decease the chest to devolve to my son . . . the bed and spinning wheel before mentioned to devolve to my daughter . . ."; She "shall have the right to the place during her natural life. . . ." Also the Bible went to the wife for her natural life and then to son James.

11. For a brief description of the limited movable possessions held by Indians living north of Mexico, see Wright 1949:33–35. For analysis of their food see Bennett 1955. Alden Vaughan suggested to Stuart Bruchey that estimates are uncertain and there might have been roughly 100,000 Indians east of the Mississippi at about the time of the Declaration of Independence. Letter from Bruchey to the author, April 8, 1976. Robert V. Wells in a letter to the author of November 15, 1976 indicated absence of data for verification or contradiction.

12. The omission of Indians is in no way intended to denigrate their importance. It is a concession to the conceptual difficulties suggested in the text, which would fog interpretation of a figure of the combined portable wealth of the colonists and the Indians (see also note 11).

13. See *Historical Statistics* 1960 or 1975, General Notes to series Z; see also Wells 1975; Potter 1965.

14. Relative proportions in 1800, but not its absolute totals, were used together with the absolute population totals of 1774. The assumption here is that, despite intervening war, interruption in immigration, and some emigration of loyalists, these

basic demographic relationships of 1800 were a reasonably good proxy for those of 1774, and in any case were the best available to me.

15. Although I drew a few single women's probate inventories in New England and the South, my effort was concentrated on an estimate of the proportion of widows, women whom I am sure should be counted as wealthholders. I believe that the numbers of single women wealthholders were slight enough that the estimate of number of widows can encompass them as well. To estimate the proportion of the women who were widows, I considered data from the decennial censuses beginning in 1890, the earliest one reporting on widows. In the period from 1890 to 1940, widows were found equal to about 13 percent of the females 20 years old and over. I assumed that the percentage was probably somewhat smaller in the eighteenth century, in view of the excess of men, except in New England, and the economic necessity for women to remarry in the agricultural and frontier world of that day. I conclude that 10 percent is a reasonable figure for widows and single women wealth-holders. This coincides with the observation from the tax list for Philadelphia in 1774 that about 10 percent were women.

16. The age relationships in the 1800 census are given only for free whites and separately for males and females. For want of better data, I assume the same sex-age relationships pertain also to blacks in 1774. A tally of the ages of slaves held by my Maryland sample decedents checks quite closely with the 1800 census age distribution of Maryland free whites. The absolute numbers of free black wealthholders, for which these relationships are used, are quite small in any case, and hence slight errors in them could not greatly affect the total.

17. The calculation of white men and white women wealthholders, the only subtotals not readily calculable from the figures shown in tables 2.4 through 2.7, may be clarified by an example. The number of New England men (table 2.5, line 8) 129,989 times .975 (the percentage of white on line 2) times .980 (the percentage of whites not indentured) equals a number of free white men that differs from 124,247 (line 23) white men wealthholders by a small amount explained by rounding of multipliers. The calculation for white women is parallel, except for a third step of taking as wealthholders only 10 percent of the number of all free white women.

18. In some counties, particularly in Virginia, we must go to two or more files to match an estate inventory and the date it was taken or recorded. Also, depending on the county, or its clerk, the dates associated with a probate inventory may be variously: the date on which the will was exhibited in court and "proved"; the date on which letters of administration were granted and the estate executor/administrator was ordered to return a true and correct inventory in not less than a specified number of days; the date on which appraisers were appointed; the date of the actual inventory appraisal; the date of the "return to court" with an exhibited inventory that was then sworn to in court; the date on which the inventory was ordered filed. There was also sometimes evidence in court records that an estate was probated, although no inventory was ever filed; such evidence was in the proving of a will, the granting of letters testamentary or appointment of an estate administrator, the assigning of a probate case file number. Yet in all these instances either no inventory was filed or none has survived. I found several wills in Virginia where the maker specifically states that he does not wish his estate to be appraised. These are non-inventoried probates. Also there were in many courts probate case file numbers assigned for cases of guardianship of minors; yet these files contained no probate inventory of the wealth of the deceased parent, which was in a separate file. I con-

cluded that guardianship cases should not be included in a count of probate cases in my sense.

19. For the age correction with w-weights, discussed in appendix A, I was able to bypass the use of age-specific mortality rates by using instead the relative age structure of the living population in 1800 as an approximation to that in 1774. However, this happy solution does not answer the present question of number of nonprobated decedents.

20. This count is close to but not identical with the number of sample cases, all of which had inventories, and a few of which were probated before or after 1774. It excluded the guardianships but included the probate cases without inventories mentioned in note 18. It excluded a few cases of probate inventory filed, which, after genealogical search, turned out to pertain to a person dead several, or even many, years earlier. I found it necessary, in the Southern sample counties, to ask genealogists to review a year's court records, avoiding double counting of the same name, to determine the best count of the number of probate cases (whether or not an inventory was actually filed) in a year. I am indebted to Russell Glenn for a mathematical proof that if there tended to be a lag between date of death and date of inventory or first appearance in court records of an estate proceeding for a particular decedent, the carryover of probates from the previous year's deaths should balance the shortfall of deaths in the present year not yet probated.

21. The count of free wealthholders by county was derived from *American Colonial Wealth* tables 5.2 and 5.5 for New England and the South, with additional adjustments to subtract indentured whites and add free blacks. A corresponding estimate for the middle colonies of Pennsylvania, New Jersey, and Delaware was derived, with adjustments, from *American Colonial Wealth* table 5.4, using the 1800 census age proportions.

22. Death rates of 2.5 percent for ages 21–45, and 5.4 percent for 46 and over were calculated on the basis of survival rates for the City of Boston around 1811 from Richards 1909. (See note 1 on p. 1869 of *American Colonial Wealth*.)

23. Equal weights were used for New England and the South, and Larntz weights for the middle colonies of Pennsylvania, New Jersey, and Delaware. The use of Larntz weights accounts for the difference between the probate ratio for those middle colonies in this volume from that in Jones 1970. (See portion on Larntz weights in section VI of *American Colonial Wealth*.)

24. A comment from Gloria Main, in a letter to the author received July 7, 1978, suggests that Jackson T. Main found higher probate proportions for all of Connecticut in the late colonial period, and she found proportions approximating one-half at earlier dates for Suffolk County outside of Boston and about 40 to 45 percent for Hampshire County, Massachusetts. She states these are based on comparing numbers of taxables with numbers inventoried and using Model West Life tables with an adult mortality rate of about 2.0. See also varying proportions of male deaths for which probate inventories were recorded, ranging from 10 to 80 for individual counties in New England in three periods up to 1762, noted by Lockridge 1968b:516.

25. For New York, the paucity of surviving probate records, discussed in the Note on Method and appendix A, made the direct calculation of its probate and nonprobate ratios not feasible. Therefore a hybrid ratio was created for New York. A first approximation followed the same hybrid pattern as used for wealth, with the New England ratio given one-third and the ratio for the other middle colonies given

two-thirds weight. This yielded a low New York probate ratio of only .53 percent. This ratio, however, is estimating not wealth, but the percentage of all wealth-holders' estates in 1774 that reached the Surrogate Court, as the probate court in New York is called. I surmised that in probate procedures, even more than in wealth, New York might have tended to be more like the other middle colonies than like New England. Consequently, a rounded .60 was used as the New York probate ratio, instead of .53. (See *American Colonial Wealth,* p. 1906.)

26. The ratio used for tables for the South, using weighting Variant One, in *American Colonial Wealth* was .73/.27. My preferred variant of this ratio is .68/.32, which I use for tables for the South in the present volume. (See appendix A.)

27. There is a growing body of work by social historians dealing with land in the colonies, such as the hypothesis advanced by Lockridge 1968a, 1970, that land scarcity had become a severe economic problem to young families in the older portions of New England, causing strain in the social structure as well as forcing westward migration. See also Ball 1973; Berthoff 1960:501; Daniels, 1973–74; Demos 1970; Grant 1961; Greven 1970; Kulikoff 1975; Lemon, 1972; Menard, Harris, and Carr 1974; in addition to the older works of Gray 1932; Bidwell and Falconer 1941.

28. For maps showing density of settlement see Sutherland 1936; Friis 1968; Cappon 1976.

3. AGGREGATE AND PER CAPITA PRIVATE PHYSICAL WEALTH FOR THIRTEEN COLONIES AND THREE REGIONS

1. Excluding Indians, the reasons for whose omission are presented in chapter 2. The 2.35 million includes 0.53 million nonfree (see table 2.4).

2. I compute £61.881 million sterling as the minimum capital value of the 1,820,000 free persons, white and black, shown in table 2.4 plus £1.325 million as the additional value of servants not included in the servant and slave aggregate of table 3.1. The £61.881 million is the product of 1,820,000 times £34.0 sterling presented in chapter 4 as the tallied average inventory value per slave. The £1.325 million is the product of 53,016 servants times £25.0. This £25.0 is the differential between the £34.0 and the tallied £9 inventory approximate value per servant for the time remaining to serve. The difference is presumably the servant's capital value for the rest of his lifetime. The inventory values of slaves and servants are net of their consumption. A case could be made that these values should be raised by the value of slaves' and servants' consumption to reckon their total contribution to GNP. In that case £34.0 is too low for the human capital value of free persons, and the aggregate to add to table 3.1 is even greater than £63 million. The tallied values of £34.0 per slave and £9 per servant for remaining time to serve are lower than the average value of £40.2 per nonfree person, which results from dividing £21.5 million aggregate value of slaves and servants in table 3.1 by the total of 534,000 nonfree persons shown in table 2.4. (The aggregate value of £21.5 million is derived from the sample figures of wealth in "slaves and servants" per wealthholder, combined with our usual weighting procedures, using the Variant Two discussed in appendix A for Charleston and the rest of the South.) If we were to use the higher figure of £40.2 as the estimate of the average value of a free colonist, as well as of a servant, the additional free human capital value to be added to table 3.1 would rise to £73.165 million and the differential additional servant value would rise to £1.654 million,

adding a total of £74.819 million to table 3.1. Both £34.0 and £40.2 are well below the human capital value of £60 sterling per head that Gregory King estimated for the entire population of England and Wales in 1688; I infer that King capitalized their wages or output and hence included the value of their consumption (see G. King 1936:32). When he added £330 million by this calculation to his other figures, it doubled his total wealth estimate. Because of the highly tentative nature of both King's and my figures for free human capital, and because of the unsatisfactory economic analysis that results from valuing only the nonfree human capital, I prefer to limit the subsequent discussion of this chapter chiefly to nonhuman physical wealth.

3. See discussion of Mill in chapter 2. The inclusion or exclusion of slave wealth certainly affects a ranking of who was richer than whom. However, whether part of the labor force was free or nonfree is irrelevant to the productive potential of the economy, aside from the question of whether free workers were more or less productive than nonfree workers. This question is being debated anew as part of the vigorous revival in the past decade of interest in the economic interpretation of slavery. See Fogel and Engerman 1974a,b, 1977; Genovese 1974; and the October 1975 issue of *Explor. Ec. Hist.*, devoted to discussions of *Time on the Cross* and its assessment, in David, et al. 1976.

4. The consumers' goods proportion is around 10 percent, 9 of which is for durable goods, the use of which contributes to current consumption.

5. See the Note on Method. When the term "middle colonies" with small initial letters is used at any place in this volume it pertains to New Jersey, Pennsylvania, and Delaware only and excludes New York. Capitalized, the term includes New York.

6. Early studies probably grossly underestimated income in relation to wealth, since they probably underestimated income in kind. Such income includes the value of food and fuel produced or gathered, the preparation and preserving of foods, the making of yarns, curing of leathers, making of clothing, and other household production for consumption by the family members. If we were to raise the assumed capital-output ratio to the 7 to 1 implicit in Gregory King's 1688 estimate for England and in some later English estimates and in Mulhall's 1882 figures for the United States and some other countries, our 1774 per capita figure would be lowered to £5.3, the equivalent of around $115 in 1958 dollars, $253 in 1976, $288 in 1978) well below the 1776 Goldsmith projection, discussed in an ensuing subsection, but still above Fishlow's 1780s minimum. If we dropped the ratio to as low as 2.5 to 1, suggested as a possibility by Robert Gallman in a letter to the author of December 28, 1977 and in Gallman 1979, the per capita figure would reach £15 or $324 in 1958 dollars, more than double the Goldsmith projection and more than triple the Fishlow minimum. I believe the 7 yields an implausibly low income figure and a ratio of 2.5 to 1 yields one that is too high. I am inclined to believe that, before the outbreak of the Revolutionary War and after the relative prosperity, at least for some colonies, that followed the peace of 1763, the 3.0 or 3.5 to 1 ratios are more plausible. See further discussion in appendix A.

7. Klingaman 1971:568, table 5, calculated food consumption requirements and their wholesale market value in connection with his studies of coastal and intercolonial trade and shipping for the colonies in 1768–72. His range of possible per capita value of food consumed was from £4.5 to £7.5 sterling and he found £5.5 to £6.5 the most plausible. He also went on to estimate per capita income from the percentage of total income (or colonial output) that might have been comprised by food. His range of possible percentage of income spent for food, inferred from

present-day developing countries, was from 40 to 70 percent (the latter a figure for working-class families in India in 1968). Combinations of the two sets of ranges led to his per capita income estimates ranging from £6.5 to £19.0, with his preferred figures narrowed to the range from £9.0 to £13.0. This range of estimates, prepared quite independently and on a totally different basis, coincides strikingly with the range of my preliminary estimates for the middle colonies mentioned in appendix A, and encompasses both £10.7 and £12.5, the range of estimates I offer in the present chapter.

8. Goldsmith 1959. The projection is shown graphically in North 1974:27, and the text of the testimony is reprinted in Andreano 1965:337–361.

9. Fishlow 1964:566 suggested that for the United States in 1780 income per capita could not have been much less than $100 (at around the 1958 price level). He refers to North 1961b:390 and Parker and Whartenby 1960.

10. Christopher Collier (1978, 1979) estimates the labor cost of cutting, sawing and hauling a year's fuel supply for a household in Connecticut was about one-third of one man's time and that 20 to 40 acres of woodlot was needed for a perpetual supply, depending on the size of house. He is convinced that the shortage of woodlot was a significant element in migrations of people out of Connecticut after about 1760. See also Billy Smith (1979:40, notes 52 and 53) for estimates by others that 25 cords of wood a year were required for a "genteel" Philadelphia family and that an artisan in Charleston, where winters were warmer, thought firewood cost him £3 sterling each year.

11. Shepherd and Williamson 1972:801, using Robert E. Gallman's estimates of output in Davis et al. 1972:15–60 for 1774 (which latter draws on Jones 1970 data), find that overseas commodity (not "invisible") exports were in the neighborhood of 11.5 to 13.5 percent of total output during the later colonial period. This output excluded income or services from consumers' durables. Elimination of consumers' durables from our wealth and income figures would reduce wealth by 9 percent and income slightly. Commodity exports formed from 11.6 to 13.6 percent of such reduced per capita income estimates. Total export earnings per capita, including "invisible" earnings from shipping services, formed from 14.9 to 17.5 percent of such reduced per capita income estimates, or from 13.6 to 15.9 percent of per capita income including consumers' durables. Shepherd and Williamson suggest (1972:802) that coastal exports added a quarter more or about 3 to 3.5 percent of Gallman's estimate of total output for 1774, but that data on intercolonial flows and on subsistence production are not yet adequate to give a clear picture of regional balances. In a more recent article, Walton 1979 suggests that, on the eve of the American Revolution, income from overseas trade was probably in the neighborhood of 15 percent of total colonial income (source Shepherd and Walton 1972: chap. 6, 7, 8) and that coastal trade and other interregional and local trade within the colonies probably accounted for another 10 percent of income. My use of a 3 to 1 or 3.5 to 1 capital-output ratio yields an income that is in line with the 1774 output figure of Gallman as reported by Shepherd and Williamson 1972:801.

12. Klingaman 1971:555 ff.; Shepherd and Williamson 1972:801–2.

13. Deane 1955:28, 33. Deane 1961, reprinted in Crouzet 1972:95–101.

14. Walter Eltis (1975) remarked to the present author that the figures on France assembled by such Physiocrats as Quesnay, in his famous tableau economique, were only for illustrating their advanced theories and are not to be regarded as serious empirical estimates. Arthur Young toured France in 1789 and

made some estimates of its agricultural income, but none for the country's total national income, although he gave scattered figures for many categories of wealth, property and industrial activity. See Studenski 1961:61–68, 71–75.)

15. King 1936:61, 32, 34. Wealth estimate for 1688 excludes £16 million gold and silver coin, bullion, plate, jewels. Includes: land and buildings £234 million, livestock £25 million, consumers' (household) goods £12 million, producers' goods (shipping, stores, foreign or home goods, wares, and provisions for trade abroad or consumption at home, and all instruments and materials relating thereto) £33 million; total £304 million, which divided by 5.5 million equals £55. King 1936:30 shows a total yearly income of the nation in 1688 of £43.5 million, total population 5.5 million, total families, 1.36 million, and average income of 7 pounds 18 shillings per head or £32 per family. For discussion of the outstanding quality of King's remarkable estimates see Deane 1955:5–6; Deane and Cole 1967:1; Pollard and Crossley 1968:153 n. 3; Glass in Glass and Eversley 1965:162, 163, 167, 193, 203, 204, 216; Crouzet 1972: 20 n. 3, and Studenski 1961:30, 33. That King's wealth figures may be overestimates, however, is suggested by his own remarks, passim.

16. Young 1771:4:330–93 shows only income figures for England and Wales, with a total of £122 million for 1770. Excluding "public revenue" of £9 million and "sums at interest" of £5 million, which latter appear to me to be return on financial assets, which I have excluded from the colonial physical wealth figure, I reduce his total to £108 million, or 88.5 percent of £122 million. (See also Studenski 1961:41–43). Mulhall 1884:71 shows as corresponding to the $122 million or £16 per capita income a wealth estimate of £1,100,000 or £153 per capita, which he attributes to Young for 1770. Deane 1955:156, drawing on additional manuscript or printed sources attributable to Young, increases the income per capita figure to £18.5 (£17.6 excluding government and defense). Both Mulhall and Deane use a population figure of 7 million for England and Wales in 1770. Acceptance of Young's figures, in relation to others presented by Mulhall and discussed by Deane, as well as by Pollard and Crouzet, presents one with the apparent anomaly that growth of wealth per capita for England was very substantial before the industrial revolution but utterly lacking during the period of rapid industrialization from 1770 to 1840. It is my judgment that the impressionistic methods used by Young do not warrant placing much reliance on his aggregate figures. I am inclined to view the £108 million or £15.4 per capita as a sufficiently high and probably too high income figure. Correspondingly, I take 88.5 percent of Mulhall's figure for Young of £153 per capita to reach a very tentative per capita wealth figure of £135 for England and Wales in 1770, which I regard as probably still an overestimate, for comparison with colonial physical wealth. Deane notes that Young's estimate has been criticized as being too high, particularly in its agricultural component, and that the farmers he visited may have been of above-average wealth. See also Studenski 1961:42; Crouzet 1972:23; Pollard 1968:336 ff.; Feinstein 1978a.

17. The colonial income–recent GNP comparison can be made only if we are willing to accept the imperfections that underlie table 1.2, which makes a price comparison via intermediate linkages of very different bundles of commodities at the beginning and at the end of the 200 year period. (See *American Colonial Wealth*, p. 1718.) In addition, exchange rate conversions to U.S. dollars make for imperfect measures of present-day real product of various countries. The imperfections arise not only out of varying local tastes and consumption preferences, or varying natural resources for productive use, but also out of varying proportions of national product

entering international trade, where exchange rates are determined, and widely different cost-price relationships in centrally planned from relatively free market countries. (See World Bank 1976:21–22, 25–28.)

18. Mulhall 1884:470–73 published wealth figures in pounds sterling for the United States, by state and region for 1850, 1860, 1870 and 1880. He compared the 1880 figures with ones ca. 1882 for European countries, Canada, Mexico, Argentina, and Australia (ibid.:469, 473). In aggregate wealth he placed the United States first, United Kingdom second, France third, Germany fourth, Australia thirteenth, Argentina fourteenth. On a per capita basis, he ranked the United States sixth, topped by the United Kingdom, Holland, France, Denmark, Australia, in that order, and Argentina ninth. The figures presumably equated the currencies with British pounds sterling at prices of around 1882. he also (ibid.:473) estimated income as well as wealth for each country, in aggregate and per capita. The figures imply a wealth-income ratio for the United States ca. 1882 of 7, and the same for the United Kingdom, Germany, and Belgium. The highest ratio was 9 for Holland, Sweden, Norway, and Greece, and the lowest were 4 for Australia and 5 for Argentina. His comparison of component items of wealth ca. 1882 places land at about 22 percent of total wealth in Britain, 26 percent in the United States, and 33 percent in Australia. The wealth figures include values of railways, houses, furniture, merchandise, cattle, and at least for Britain, shipping, bullion, foreign loans, roads and public works. Assessing the reliability of these figures would require considerable further study.

19. Replications of the present study for selected earlier dates would be highly desirable, to permit such comparisons. Costs in time and money and difficulties would be great. See appendix A for discussion of some of the problems.

20. Basic figures for 1909 to 1959 from U.S. Department of Commerce; for 1879 to 1908 from Kuznets 1961; for 1839–79 from Gallman 1960.

21. Kulikoff 1979 deflates by the Carr group's price index, and makes age adjustments and reaches estimates of per capita wealth by dividing adjusted estate data by average household size.

22. Menard 1975:320, cited by Anderson 1979, and Menard 1978, 1979.

23. See also Anderson 1979, figure 1, based on his wealth data reduced to per capita income estimates.

24. To convert to dollars of other years, all numbers in column 3 may be multiplied by factors derived from table 1.2, using the preliminary value for 1976 of the index number 1,152.7 or $47.84 shown in its note a. These factors are: for 1978 dollars 1.1342; 1974, 0.8683; 1973, 0.7913; 1972, 0.7456; 1958, 0.4519; 1929, 0.1917; 1914, 0.1248; 1870, 0.1432; 1860, 0.0987; 1850, 0.0830; 1840, 0.1008. Since conversions are rough at best, the user may round the factors to two decimal places for convenience, with results that diverge slightly from some conversions I have made, and with greater divergence for years with larger factors.

25. The $21,130 is equivalent in purchasing power to $9,459 at the 1958 price level, to $15,755 at the 1972 level, to $16,720 at 1973 prices. See note 24 for the multipliers. Regardless of the price-level year selected, the increase in dollars of constant purchasing power remains twelvefold over the two centuries.

26. Decline in nonhuman wealth (including bonds, stocks, mortgages, notes), per adult male in the United States from 1860 to 1870 was reported by Lee Soltow on the basis of his samples from the census manuscripts (with adjustments to exclude value of slaves from the numerator and to include non free adult males in the denominator in 1860, for comparability with 1870. He calculated the decline for the decade

for the entire United States to be at the average annual percentage rate of −0.9 percent on the basis of values in constant dollars at 1860 prices (Soltow 1975a:65, 67). Virtually all of this decline occurred in the South, for which region the decline was at a rate of −4.0 percent (ibid.:182). He noted a strong parallel with Kuznets' drop for that decade in gross national product per worker to a rate of −0.1 percent in constant dollars and Robert Gallman's drop for that decade in commodity output per worker to the rate of 0.2 percent in constant dollars (Soltow 1975a:67; Kuznets 1965:305; and Gallman 1960:16, 17, 43). Gallman noted a negative rate in output per capita during the Civil War decade (Gallman 1960:15).

27. R. Martin 1939:6. See also Kuznets 1952:223–26; Goldsmith 1952; Parker and Whartenby 1960:205–7; North 1961b:387; Andreano 1965:139–41; David 1967a,b.

28. In Jones 1970:137 I calculated growth rates (for the middle colonies in 1774, the U.S. for subsequent dates) on the variant assumption that wealth in 1774 was as low as that of 1805. This gave a growth rate from 1774 to 1850 of 0.9 percent, and from 1774 to 1900 of 1.3 percent.

29. For growth rates from 1839 to the end of the nineteenth century, a principal source is Robert Gallman's estimates of commodity output, the high level of which in 1839, the starting date of his series, suggests that the rate of increase in income, with attendant possibilities of greater wealth accumulation, may have accelerated sometime around 1830 or 1840 (Gallman 1960:16, 41). In addition there are Gallman's series for gross national product (Gallman 1966:9), for net national product (Gallman 1972:34), and for capital stock (Davis and Gallman 1973:456, 457). (See also Towne and Rasmussen 1960:257, 280; Rezneck 1960:213–15; Goldsmith 1959:passim; Andreano 1965:150–51.) Fogel 1971:199 and David 1967b give some attention to the 1820s.

4. STRUCTURE OF PHYSICAL WEALTH IN THIRTEEN COLONIES AND THREE REGIONS

1. Goldsmith 1962, 1968; Kendrick 1974; J. Smith 1974; Lyons 1974; Podoluk 1974; Campbell and Lowe 1977; Soltow 1971a, 1975a.

2. The detailed county comparisons are found in *American Colonial Wealth*, tables 7.122 through 7.141, and in condensed form in appendix B.

3. They include some intergenerational studies of particular families or of population groups studied longitudinally through time. Most such studies are limited to one or at most a few towns or counties or one province. Most of the studies made thus far pertain to New England, though a few excellent ones have been done for the Middle Colonies and upper South. A useful bibliography is found in Henretta 1973. See also citations in Land, Carr, and Papenfuse 1977, and studies cited in chapter 1.

4. See Goldsmith 1962; Kendrick 1974; Christensen and Jorgenson 1973.

5. Sellers 1934:111 indicates that in South Carolina all owners of lands granted by the Lords Proprietor were required to take possession and begin cultivation within a reasonable time or forfeit their claims. Insofar as nonresidents owned land and other physical property, my study may underestimate the capital available to the production process in the colonies.

6. In the probate inventories the term "personalty" or "personal estate," as opposed to "real estate," covered not only portable physical nonhuman wealth but also slaves and servants and financial assets; for the analytical purposes here, I am

separating out the slaves and servants and reserving the financial assets for treatment in connection with net worth and size distribution (chapters 6 and 7).

7. Goldsmith 1952, 1962, 1968; Kendrick 1967, 1974; Christensen and Jorgenson 1973.

8. See the Glossary in *American Colonial Wealth,* section IX.

9. Scales were often called "steelyards," variantly spelled "stilliards" or "stillerts." See the Glossary in *American Colonial Wealth.*

10. For a complete enumeration of kinds of items classified as producers' and consumers' durables and perishables see the item codes p. 1646 ff. in *American Colonial Wealth.* Perishable materials are distinguished from durable materials in its tables 7.7 through 7.161. For the tables in the present volume all producers' materials in the household have been treated as perishables (see table 4.1 note). For comparability of stubs of corresponding tables in this volume and in volume 3 of *American Colonial Wealth* see table 7.6 of the latter.

11. The separation of producers' materials by perishability is shown by item code in *American Colonial Wealth,* pp. 1658–61, and in detail in its tables 7.7 through 7.161.

12. For an attempt to separate producers' or trade goods from consumers', household, or domestic goods, see Davisson 1967a.

13. See tables 1.3 through 1.7 and *American Colonial Wealth,* section II.

14. Frequently called "surtout," with such variant spellings as "situte" or "sertoat." See Glossary in *American Colonial Wealth.*

15. Gregory King (1936:32), when he arrived at a valuation for England and Wales in 1688 of £60 per inhabitant, seems to have made no subtraction for the cost of annual consumption. Kendrick 1974 subtracts from capitalized lifetime income the discounted cost of future consumption. Engerman 1977b points to the problem of the definition of human capital. He suggests that "the difficulty with the evaluation of slaves is that it is net of the slave's consumption, and gives the value of the individual to other members of the society. It is not the same as the value of an individual based upon his total output, which adds back his consumption to the slave price. This seems the better procedure to use to estimate the value of an individual when measuring per capita incomes and wealth, since properly discounted it would measure his per capita contribution to GNP. Thus I would think the addition of consumption useful to estimate the value of a free individual. Could this be why King gives a different number? In any case it might be useful to note the differences in value of an individual to: (1) a society which is defined to exclude him, and (2) one which includes him."

16. See *American Colonial Wealth,* tables 7.163, 7.164, A.7.162 and A.7.165.

17. See tables 4.10 to 4.12; also Davie 1936:35; Herrick 1926; Salmon 1911:21 ff.

18. See Clemens 1977:159–62; Galenson 1978a,b; G. Main 1977b:139; Menard, Harris, and Carr 1974; Sellers 1934:115, 119, 121–22; Walsh 1977a,b:111–15.

19. In my judgment, this estimate of the total value of land in the South is more likely under- than overestimated because of the data problem mentioned in the Note on Method and in appendix A and detailed more fully in *American Colonial Wealth,* section III.D.

20. I offer in table 3.10 of *American Colonial Wealth* some comparative values of rural land per acre in 1774 by province in the South, as revealed by my regression analysis. The Maryland tobacco land of Queen Anne's and Anne Arundel counties

and the South Carolina lower pine belt lands were the most valuable for which we obtained data. The Virginia land in interior counties in the southwestern and north central portions of the province was next most valuable and not far above the values in North Carolina's northern and eastern parts (see figure 4, map of southern sample). A possible further study might be made of the values per acre from the New England probate inventories in the sample, and from the worksheets of tax lists used to estimate land values for the sample in the middle colonies. I believe these latter for the Pennsylvania sample would be somewhat in line with the findings of Lemon and Nash 1968 for values in the late eighteenth century in Chester County, Pennsylvania.

21. See tables D.1 and D.2; also *American Colonial Wealth,* either edition, tables 7.163, 7.164, 7.167, 7.168 and 2d ed., tables A.7.162 and A.7.165.

22. For the possibility that the method of allocating lump-valued inventory items for New England and the South may have slightly overstated consumers' goods and correspondingly understated producers', see Jones 1972:110–11 and *American Colonial Wealth,* p. 1688.

23. See *American Colonial Wealth,* tables 7.163–7.164 and A.7.165.

24. It happens that the wealth of the richest merchants drawn in the sample in New England was below that of the richest merchants in Philadelphia. See tables 6.4, 6.5, 6.8, 6.9, and *American Colonial Wealth,* table 8.1.

25. See Sellers 1934:chaps. 3 and 4, esp. pp. 49, 50, 82–85.

26. It is appropriate to omit weights based on the decedent owner's age and county location when we are concerned only with values per slave or per servant. However, in table 4.9 (see its note) I use weights of relative frequency of slaves in the population. For reasons why the unweighted figure, tallied directly from inventory values of individual slaves, regardless of the w^*-weights of their owners, is somewhat lower than the implied average value per slave that can be inferred from the weighted aggregate slave value in table 4.1, see appendix A. I believe the figures of table 4.10 are the best estimates of individual slave values per se. In tables 4.10 through 4.14 no weights are used, other than those implicit in the presented numbers of slave cases or servant cases found in the sample.

27. Richard Bean estimates an average sale value for newly arrived prime males (aged 14–25) at Charleston, in 1772–74, of £49, which includes an average £5 transport cost from Jamaica. *Historical Statistics,* 1975, series Z 165–68, p. 1174 and telephone conversation of June 21, 1977. See also Fogel and Engerman 1974b:82 for slave prices by sex and age relative to prices of prime-age males 16–30. They found (Engerman 1977b) that the price of males peaked at about age 26 or 27. See also Sellers 1934:144, who reported for Charleston that in 1772 a cargo of slaves sold "for upwards of £45 sterling per head," and that in 1773 one merchant wrote to a correspondent "that prime men were selling for £350, prime women for £290 currency, and boys and girls in proportion, which expressed in sterling meant about £50 for men and £41 for women. . . . In a less favorable season the merchant was glad to get from £28 to £35 sterling for his Negro merchandise." See also Galenson 1979.

28. See end of general note to table 4.9. This is in contrast to tables 4.11 through 4.14, in which the "sample total" is a simple average of the numbers of cases tallied. In view of the limited data for subgroups of slaves in these latter tables, I do not believe it appropriate to use for them the slave population weights used for table 4.9.

29. Maryland is the province where slave ages were stated in inventories often enough to permit a distribution of slaves by age and sex. A comparison I made of

relative frequencies in the Maryland sample in the same sex-age groups as those shown for free whites in Maryland in the 1800 census reveals no statistically significant differences. (The 1800 census does not give age structure for blacks.)

30. The cases in New Jersey (Burlington County) are too few to be considered as an indication of interruption in the pattern.

31. The large numbers of Charleston holders of 26 and more slaves is directly related to the extremely high wealth in slaves that I found in the sample for the Charleston District, a wealth in slaves way out of proportion to that in any of the other southern counties sampled. This disproportion led me to make the Variant Two calculations for my wealth figures, discussed in appendix A and embodied in the tables in this volume with the exception of tables 4.9 through 4.14.

32. For nineteenth- and twentieth-century wealth estimates antecedent to and consonant with Jorgenson's work, see Goldsmith 1952, 1968 and Kendrick 1967. For figures roughly in line with Jorgenson's, by type of asset, in both current and 1958 dollars, for the years 1967, 1970, 1974, and 1975, see table 755 in the U.S. Bureau of the Census 1977:466, based on Kendrick, Lee, and Lomask 1976.

33. Since 1884 the annual value added in manufacture has exceeded the value of agricultural products. By 1923–25, exports of manufactures exceeded imports of manufactures. Since 1920 the proportion of urban population, defined as residents in places of 2,500 or more, has exceeded that of the rural population.

34. Jorgenson's $49.2 billion in current dollars of 1973 for "agricultural inventories" yields a per capita figure of $233 ($294 in 1976 dollars). The corresponding colonial per capita wealth in "crops and livestock" in 1774 was £5.6 ($268 in 1976 dollars). This calculation clarifies that there has been no absolute decline per capita in agricultural inventory over the past two centuries. Rather, there has been an absolute increase in other kinds of wealth.

5. NET WORTH: FINANCIAL ASSETS AND LIABILITIES

1. Data on financial assets but not on financial liabilities are found in probate inventories. See Note on Method for discussion of limitations in my estimates of financial liabilities, especially for the South and for New York. For reasons indicated there, as well as because of the limited numbers of cases, particularly when the small sample is subdivided into wealth classes or into socioeconomic groups by region, my findings in the later tables of this chapter should be considered suggestive rather than definitive. For sample size in subcategories, see tables 7.1 through 7.4.

2. It goes without saying that the potentialities for improving our understanding of the pace and character of colonial economic development would be enhanced if ways could be devised to determine more clearly than I have been able to do the origins of particular financial assets and the nature of particular financial liabilities. Some of this may come from probate inventories and estate accounts in more intensive studies of particular cities or counties, where the researcher becomes so familiar with the debtor and creditor names involved than he can deduce the likely purpose of a loan or a book debt from the amount involved and the name of the borrower or lender. He may also be able to determine from the name whether the borrower or lender lived nearby, in another colony, or overseas, and to infer the occupation of the borrower or lender. Some may come from scrutiny as to whether certain names appear sufficiently often as creditors in a given city or county as to suggest they may be large lenders beginning to perform almost banking functions. It is with this

thought in mind that in the summaries of the estate accounts in section II of *American Colonial Wealth,* where verbatim entries would have been too voluminous, I have frequently given the range in size of debts owed by the decedent and named one or more of the principal creditors.

3. Among repositories of colonial account books are the Baker Library at Harvard University, the Essex Institute at Salem, Massachusetts, and the Pennsylvania Historical Society, Philadelphia.

4. Brock 1975:4, 5, 7, 532; Ferguson 1953:168, 179; McCusker 1978:4–13. For an earlier period, see Nettels 1934:171, 175, 232, 236.

5. Andrews 1918:passim; Brock 1975:18–23; Ernst 1973:xvii, 50, 51, 97, 98; Ferguson 1953:168; McCusker 1978;121n, 126, 133, 136, 136n, 169, 170n, 175, 176, 190, 215, 215n, 232; Weiss, 1970.

6. The eighteenth-century spelling for this city was usually Charles Town or Charlestown, as can be seen for the Charles Town cases in *American Colonial Wealth,* but I use the modern version of Charleston for convenience.

7. When the pilot study figures were reweighted and age-adjusted using the Larntz weights (see note 2 of Note on Method), and adjusted for amounts written off as uncollectible or for other information that came to light in the subsequent accounts of estate administrators/executors (adjustments that have been made in the data in tables 5.1, 5.2, 5.4–5.6) the proportion of New Jersey-Pennsylvania-Delaware wealthholders who held "doubtful" or "bad" claims was reduced from the 1.7 of table 5.3 to 0.5 percent, and their average amount reduced to one-half pound. The dominance of claims of all sorts over cash remained for the middle colonies' sample after the adjustments.

8. Although I would like to have been able to present similar figures for other regions than the middle colonies, the time and money costs of coding and tabulating these separate entries for the other regions exceeded the resources of the expanded study. Comments for New England, New York, and the South are based on my general impressions from inspecting the documents.

9. Sellers 1934:56; Gray 1932:chap. XVIII; Price 1976a.

10. Adam Smith wrote: "I have never even heard of any tobacco plantation that was improved and cultivated by the capital of merchants who resided in Great Britain." Smith 1776:158.

11. Klingaman 1971:557–65; Shepherd and Williamson 1972:798–803. The network of trade flows among colonies documented thus far shows that the flows were in multiple directions, and net balances by region are not clear cut. Shepherd and Williamson 1972:803 show, for 1768–72, negative balances for both New England and the Middle Colonies for overseas plus coastal trade (not including earnings of sterling from the sale of ships abroad or from British defense and civil expenditures in the colonies). They also show on the same basis a positive balance for the southern colonies that does not, however, take into consideration expenditures made by the colonies for slaves.

12. Shepherd and Walton 1972:135–36, 151–53, 165–66. Engerman 1973b: 334, and in a letter to the author of March 14, 1978, suggests there is nothing in Shepherd and Walton to preclude a succession of short-term foreign debts. Gary Walton (1979) summarizes a balance of payments for average yearly exchanges in 1768–72 that includes estimates for ship sales (from Price 1976a:715), for payments for slaves, and for sterling receipts in the form of payments to army, navy and British civil servants in the colonies, which works out to a difference of only £20,000

between the sum of all the credits and the sum of all the debits. James Shepherd is continuing his research into magnitude of external debt of the colonies.

13. For percentages holding financial assets by county, see *American Colonial Wealth,* either edition, tables 7.122–7.141. The Charleston figures in those tables are valid. They remain unchanged by the reweighting discussed in appendix A.

14. Baxter 1945; McCusker 1972; Price 1974:163.

15. These can be inspected, case by case, in table 8.1 of *American Colonial Wealth,* either edition.

16. See the Note on Method portion on regression analysis.

17. See the insolvent code in table 8.1 of *American Colonial Wealth,* and its explanation on p. 1643, either edition.

18. I have greatest confidence in the figures for percentage of wealthholders having liabilities in New Jersey, Pennsylvania, and Delaware. There the liabilities regression equation took account of wealthholder characteristics such as age, sex, occupation, and residence, as well as several wealth variables including financial assets. See Note on Method. The percentages of wealthholders in those middle colonies estimated to have had some financial liabilities were greatest at the two upper levels. The specific percentages from high to low physical wealth class were 92.3, 98.0, and 56.2, and when wealth is measured by net worth, 89.7, 97.3 and 67.8.

19. Bruchey 1966:passim. Schlesinger 1964:26–28, 30, 35–37.

20. Formann 1971. Formann reported that during the eighteenth century the designation "gentleman" often replaced the craft identification as craftsmen attained some degree of affluence or entered the merchant's trade. His article notes the specific occupational titles of some Salem decedents in this study. See also Katz 1972 on uncertainties of colonial occupational classification.

21. I am indebted for this coding to Professor Maurice A. Crouse, whose doctoral dissertation was on the Manigault family.

22. Codes 40 and 44 in the occupational codes in *American Colonial Wealth,* section III.A. The distinction between "farmer" and "planter" was not clear from many probate inventories. The cases that clearly stated "planter" were coded 44 (41 in the middle colonies), as were cases of "farmer and large landowner." Those that stated "farmer" or where I inferred farmer from tools and livestock were coded 40 or "farmer only." Codes 41 (except in the middle colonies) 42, 43, 45–49 were used for "farmers plus other activity." This included "farmer-merchant" and "farmer-cooper." A rather small number of cases with codes for fishing in New England and two for "vessel owner" (with no other ascertainable occupation) in the middle colonies were also classified, for the occupational tables, with the "farmers plus other activity." I found no fishermen or "vessel owners" (with no other ascertainable occupation) in the southern sample.

23. Baxter 1945; Bruchey 1966; Price 1974; Sellers 1934; White 1956.

6. DISTRIBUTION OF WEALTH: THE RICH AND THE POOR

1. Two examples of foreign visitors to Boston who were impressed with the absence of extremes in wealth may be mentioned: Lord Adam Gordon, visiting in 1764, remarked: "The leveling principle here, everywhere operates strongly, and takes the lead, every body has property, and every body knows it" (Mereness 1916:449). Brissot de Warville, a French visitor in 1788, "saw none of those livid,

ragged wretches that one sees in Europe, who, soliciting our compassion at the foot of the altar, seem to bear witness . . . against our inhumanity. . . ." (Brissot de Warville 1964:87).

I am indebted to Williamson and Lindert (1977:7) for these examples, the first used by Warden 1976:585 and the second by Kulikoff 1971:383. Of colonial Philadelphia in the two decades before the Revolution, several visitors pronounced, "this is the best poor man's country in the world" (Nash 1976a:545; Lemon 1973). See other quotations emphasizing poverty in Philadelphia in Nash 1976b.

2. Tocqueville 1835, 1840. See discussion of his views in Pessen 1973:1–5.

3. Beard 1913. See also Brown 1956, esp. 33 ff.

4. Lockridge 1968a, 1970. See also Greven 1970 and Koch 1969.

5. Bridenbaugh 1955; Henretta 1965; Kulikoff 1971; J. Main 1965, 1971; Nash 1976a, b. For other view see Brown 1955; Cook 1976; Daniels 1973–74; Demos 1970; Grant 1961; Henretta 1965, 1973; Land 1965; Lemon and Nash 1968; Price 1976b; Rutman 1975; Warden 1976; and Waters 1976.

6. Warden 1976:602 corrected the Boston tax lists for 1687 and 1771 for both underreporting and underassessment and found a slight decrease in the level of inequality in 1771, compared with 1687–1771 increases from 47 to 64 percent of taxed wealth held by the top 10 percent found by Henretta 1965. See Williamson and Lindert 1977:18 and G. Main 1977a:563, n. 6.

7. G. King 1936:31, Studenski 1961:30 ff.

8. W. King 1926, 1927; Lampman 1954, 1962; Mendershausen 1956; J. Smith 1974, 1975; Soltow 1971a, 1975a.

9. Free wealthholders are defined in chapter 2. See discussion there of the possibility of there being two or more wealthholders in one household or family, so that the number of wealthholders is somewhat larger than the number of families.

10. For a definition of net worth, see chapter 5; for problems of its measurement in this study and the consequent greater reliability of my figures on total physical wealth, see Note on Method and appendix A.

11. In some preliminary tabulations for New England and the South, I used only portable physical wealth for rankings. This gave a lower Gini coefficient for New England than that for the total physical wealth, but for the South a higher one. Considering that slaves formed a negligible part of portable physical wealth in New England but a large part in the South, and that ownership of slaves ranged from zero for some wealthholders to very large amounts for some, the higher Gini coefficient in the South for portable physical wealth including slaves is not surprising. The lower value in New England implies that landholdings there were more unequally distributed than other physical assets. The nature of the differences disclosed and the lack of comparability of the concept of portable physical wealth with readily available totals used in some other studies appeared to me not to justify further tabulations of size distribution by portable physical wealth.

The concept of portable physical wealth, which excludes land and structures and financial assets, is not identical with total personal wealth found on probate inventories in the Middle Colonies and the South, since these include financial assets. Nor is it identical with the total inventory wealth shown in New England probate inventories, since these do include land and structures and also financial assets. Nor is it identical with the definition of reproducible tangible wealth used by Goldsmith 1968, since the latter includes structures, which I am unable to separate from land.

12. Estimates for New York are incorporated in the totals for the thirteen colonies, but do not justify separate presentation. They are omitted from middle

colony totals in chapters 6 and 7 to facilitate discernment of patterns in the relatively firm data for New Jersey, Pennsylvania, and Delaware, without their being obscured by the hybrid New York data.

13. Morgan 1962, gives a lucid exposition of the relation of the Lorenz curve to the Gini coefficient, which he prefers to call the Lorenz measure. Bronfenbrenner 1972, especially chapter 3, gives a convenient summary of the characteristics of different measures of inequality. An older discussion by Bowman 1945, is comprehensive, clear, and useful. For some limitations of the Gini coefficient, see Michal 1973:409 and Paglin 1975, and the next two notes.

14. Michal 1973:409 ff. lists the following limitations of the Gini coefficient (1) that it does not show in what ranges the inequality lies; (2) that it is rather insensitive to fairly large changes, especially toward the lower end of the array; (3) that its computation on the basis of grouped data statistics is subject to a margin of error, being more accurate when computed from smaller intervals. On the plus side, he notes that it has the convenient property of 1.0 as an upper limit of complete inequality, independent of the number of observations or group intervals used.

Atkinson 1970 argues that the Gini coefficient is insufficient without knowledge of the social welfare function. He (1972:49) finds it preferable despite the use of the Gini coefficients by the Inland Revenue to summarize their results, to "adopt the time-honoured approach of comparing points on the Lorenz curves." He finds it conventional to take the top 1 percent, 5 percent, 10 percent, etc., but since he is particularly concerned with the top of the distribution or with high wealthholders, he finds it helpful to focus on the top 0.1 percent and 0.5 percent as well as the top 1 percent or 5 percent.

15. Paglin 1975:599, 607–8, summarizes his reasoning with regard to wealth as follows:

Simply stated, the problem is this: the 45 degree line of equality requires that wealth holdings among families be equal regardless of the age of the head of household. Given a typical age distribution of the population, this means that cumulative annual saving, plus interest compounded, can have no effect on individual family wealth. Again this is an added specification which most persons would consider an unnecessary and unrealistic constraint even in an egalitarian society. It would seem sufficient to define equality as a social condition in which inheritance of wealth is not a significant factor in the *relative* distribution of wealth, all lifetime incomes (for a given generation) are equal, and family wealth is a function mainly of saving and time, with everyone having the same rate of saving (or dissaving) at a given stage of the life cycle. These assumptions would produce equality of wealth for families in the same age bracket, but would allow differences of wealth based on age. With this definition, what would a P-reference function for the United States look like, using the average age-wealth profile derived from the Federal Reserve Board data (see Dorothy Projector and Gertrude Weiss)? The results are shown in Figure 4 [figure 20 of chapter 8 of the present volume]. The area between the 45 degree line and the P-reference function is hatched, and the Lorenz curve of wealth is also shown. It is apparent that a significant percentage of the total area of inequality (about one-third of it) would exist even in a rigidly egalitarian society, and therefore, this segment of wealth inequality reflects the age structure and the social savings function rather than fundamental (lifetime) inequality in the economic system. For the United States (in 1962) the Lorenz-Gini of wealth was .76 compared with a Paglin-Gini of .50; hence, the traditional measure has overstated the degree of interfamily inequality of wealth by about 52 percent.

He also notes, (ibid.:603) that the question of defining the consuming unit whose income or wealth should be made equal is not a minor technical question, but one which has substantial effects on the area of inequality, second only to redefining the equality line itself. For U.S. census data on income for 1972, he gets substantially different coefficients, both Lorenz-Gini and Paglin-Gini, for (1) households as consumer units, including single-person units and incomes of nonfamily members living in the unit; (2) families consisting of two or more related persons but excluding unrelated persons in the living unit; or (3) persons in families. Paglin 1977 effectively replied to several critics, whose objections all pertained to the income measure, not the wealth measure. I recommend particularly the first Paglin article to all concerned with clarity in interpreting Lorenz or Gini measures of inequality. See further clarification in Paglin 1979, esp. pp. 675–76. See also the point made by Waters 1976:156–58 that wealth inequality in Guilford, Connecticut in the eighteenth century is largely explained by age. For continuation of the discussion opened by Paglin see citations in Seiver 1979.

16. Young 1916. My former professor, Frank H. Knight, attributed to his former professor, Allyn A. Young, the comment that wealth inequality should be measured not from a line of perfect equality but from one reflecting a "reasonable" degree of inequality. See Moss 1978 and Gallman 1968. Also see Kuznets 1976 for an analysis suggesting that income size distributions are deficient unless they allow for family size and age of head. Kuznets notes that family size tends to be associated with age of head and that a large family is not as well off as a smaller family with identical income. See also F. Williams and Hanson 1941, for analysis of the 1934–36 U.S. Bureau of Labor Statistics' studies of incomes and expenditures of families of wage earners and clerical workers, with families classified on the basis of amount of total family expenditure per consumption unit within the family. The consumption unit measured differing requirements for food, clothing, and other consumers' needs depending on the age and sex of each family member.

17. Brady 1956:192–193 and Mendershausen 1956:367–81.

18. Projector and Weiss 1966:29–33, 110, 151.

19. Sample data for average net worth, $w*B$-weighted, of free wealthholders aged 21–25 was multiplied by the numbers of such wealthholders in the living population, table 2.4, and similarly for the group aged 26–44 and for that 45 and over.

20. In the left panels of tables 6.1 and 6.2 one sees the numbers which, when cumulated upward from the first decile, form the basis for the Lorenz curves, shown in figures 11 through 17. In my computations of the Gini coefficient, and in graphing the Lorenz curves, I also subdivided the seventh and eighth deciles by halves and the tenth decile by tenths or percentiles, thus giving more points at the shaping of the upper ends of the curves. These tabulations are deposited at the Newberry Library in Chicago. The ratio of the area of inequality bounded by the 45 degree line and the curve of actual distribution to the triangular area bounded by the 45 degree line and the bottom and right sides of the square is summarized in the Gini coefficient.

21. Soltow 1968; Williamson 1978. Also see the famous table of G. King 1936:31.

22. Cook 1976:chap. 3, esp. 63, 80–88; Daniels 1975b:471; J. Main 1965:211–13, 1976:183–84, 189, 192; Gross 1976:12, Waters 1976:156; Pessen 1973:295–97; Campbell and Lowe 1977:122.

23. I learned of Lardner's official position in a biography of him that I found in the library of the Daughters of the American Revolution in Washington, D.C., but neglected to copy the exact citation. He had been a friend of the Penn family in England before coming to Pennsylvania and he was given a post having to do with proprietary grants of land.

24. For my underlying sample of probate-type wealthholders (sample data, w-weighted, standard deviations and confidence intervals), there is a statistically signifi-

cant difference between mean net worth for the South and the means for the two northern regions. For total physical wealth, the difference between the southern and each of the two northern means is also significant. The differences in means between New England and the middle colonies are not statistically significant for either net worth or total physical wealth, since their confidence intervals are not mutually exclusive. (See *American Colonial Wealth,* either edition, tables 7.163 and 7.164. Corresponding figures for the thirteen colonies and the South, w-weighted, Variant Two are given in the present volume, tables D.1 and D.2 and D.6. I cannot give a corresponding measure of whether the regional differences in means at the $w*B$-weighted level are statistically significant for reasons given in appendix A. Hence I am not able to state whether the differences in size distributions at the $w*B$-weighted level are statistically significant. It seems reasonable to believe that such differences as between a northern region and the South are significant, but that less significance should be attached to the specific size distribution differences between New England and the middle colonies.

25. Mean physical wealth was not greatly different from mean net worth for the thirteen colonies as a whole, (tables 6.1 and 6.2 means) as would be expected from the discussion in chapter 5. Reasons for greater discrepancies between these two means within particular regions were discussed in chapter 5.

26. I found a Gini coefficient of 0.68 for the distribution by size of net worth ($w*B$-weighted) for my Philadelphia County sample, 1774. See *American Colonial Wealth,* either edition, table 7.185, p. 2126. Fifty-five percent of the wealth was held by the tenth decile. This result was presented in a paper at the meeting of the Organization of American Historians, New Orleans, April, 1971. This contrasts with a Gini coefficient of 0.60 in table 6.1 and 42 percent held by the top decile for the entire middle colonies' sample. See also in appendix B the higher average wealths in the sample counties that contained large cities, namely Suffolk (Boston) and Essex (Salem), Massachusetts, Philadelphia County, Pennsylvania, and Charleston District, South Carolina.

27. This possibility is in line with the hypothesis of Lindstrom 1978 that economic growth of a 46-county "Philadelphia region" during the second through fourth decades of the nineteenth century was due in large part to strong internal market demand and northeastern coastal trade.

28. See Note on Method and appendix A regarding probable understatement of land ownership in the southern sample.

29. This possibility was suggested by Stanley Engerman in a letter to the author of July 8, 1978. He remarked that the occupations of the ten richest in the South should demonstrate that slaves permitted wealth. He also commented that slave ownership meant an implicit commitment to slaves' future consumption. Also see Sellers 1934:56 for discussion of the circularity between slave buying and wealth creation, and *American Husbandry* 1775:291–300.

30. A question arises as to how many of the nonfree we should consider as potential wealthholders to whom we assign zero wealth, not even the ownership of themselves. For the present purpose of gaining some rough perception of what the addition of the nonfree as potential wealthholders at the bottom of the distribution would mean, I have simplified the calculation for tables 6.14 and 6.15 to consider only the nonfree adult males (most of whom can be considered as heads of families or households) as potential wealthholders whose actual, legally owned, wealth was zero. Inclusion also of 10 percent of nonfree females would make little difference in results in the South, and none in New England and the middle colonies.

31. This is in contrast to the procedure of Robert E. Gallman in a somewhat similar estimate for 1860. See Gallman 1969:8–9, where he introduces propertyless families (slaves) into the universe of families, but alters and narrows the definition of wealth by subtracting the value of slaves from the property of their owners. The effects of these two changes work in opposite directions to yield virtually the same degree of inequality, with or without the inclusion of slaves as potential wealthholders. See further discussion of this point in chapter 8, particularly its footnote 31.

32. See insolvency code in *American Colonial Wealth,* either edition, p. 1643. See also Note on Method and *American Colonial Wealth,* either edition, pp. 1756–59 for discussion of regression analysis to estimate financial liabilities for the sample cases with unknown financial liabilities.

7. WEALTH DISTRIBUTION AND COMPOSITION AMONG VARIOUS SOCIOECONOMIC GROUPS

1. Additional tables on average wealth composition, but not size distribution, for each separate sample county appear in appendix B.

2. It is necessary to limit the analysis of socioeconomic groups to probate-type wealthholders, since we lack information for the nonprobate-types (not drawn into my sample) not only as to their wealth, but also as to their individual characteristics by age, sex, occupation, and residence. This restriction places fewer wealthholders in the middle- and low-wealth classes and places the lower bounds of those classes at somewhat higher values than would be the case if we were able to differentiate nonprobate-type wealthholders by socioeconomic group.

3. The breaks at £100 and £400 roughly divide all probate-type wealthholders in the colonies into thirds. To find those divisions, all 919 sample decedent cases were arrayed by size of their actual unweighted wealth. Two arrays were made, one by size of net worth and one by total physical wealth. The count of cases, separately for each array, was made by summing from the bottom the associated Variant One w weights until the sum of the weights reached respectively .333 and .666. The numbers £100 and £400, rounded for convenience, are close to the two sets of actual division points by thirds located by this procedure.

When the preferred Variant Two w weights, explained in appendix A, are used, the resulting distribution, shown on line 1 of table 7.1, has somewhat under a third of the cases at the high level and somewhat over a third in the middle level, but I conclude the divisions are still useful for the analysis of this chapter. Their continued acceptance meant I could use the already completed tables for New England and the middle colonies of New Jersey, Pennsylvania, and Delaware, and needed to retabulate only those for the South and for thirteen colonies, using Variant Two weights. Use of the w weights, either Variant One or Variant Two, corrects for the age bias of a sample of deceased as compared with then-living wealthholders, if not for the higher wealth of probate-type wealthholders.

Limited sample size, especially among the smaller socioeconomic groups, does not justify preparation for each group of a Gini coefficient and wealth size distribution so fine as by decile, the procedure followed for the full sample in chapter 6.

4. This is best done, as in table 7.5, without a second breakdown by wealth interval, to avoid erratic influence of a few unusual cases among a small total number. However, I show in table 7.19 and following tables a two-way break for the largest occupational group, farmers, and for a small but economically very interest-

ing one, merchants, despite some minor irregularities explained by the small numbers of cases.

5. Regional differences in size distribution of all probate-type wealthholders are apparent from inspection of lines 1 of table 7.2 through 7.4. In particular, the New England cases fall heavily into the two lower-class intervals, those for the South into the upper interval, and those for the middle colonies into the middle interval. These proportions should be borne in mind in interpreting subsequent tables.

6. This is based on sample data, w^*-weighted, Variant Two, in table 6.2, which incorporates my best estimates for the nonprobate types, most of whom I believe fell in the lower-wealth brackets, with some but diminishing proportions in higher brackets.

7. For example, since average value of real estate declines from the high to the low intervals used here, one would expect its value to be still lower among a "poor" group with an upper bound of £30.

8. I believe all the sample cases were white except for one case, 01017 Cyrus, a free Negro, aged 45 or over, in the Charleston sample. His total physical wealth of £196 consisted of six slaves valued at £186 and five horses valued at £10.

9. In New England the general literature abounds with reports of men "lost at sea" and this was the cause of death, discovered by genealogical research, of at least one case in the sample.

10. The absolute numbers of cases drawn, before any weighting adjustment, were: New England, 20; New York, none; the middle colonies, 31; and the South, 30. These comprise an unweighted 9 percent of the total sample. Most of them were widows. The balance were single women, some of whom were drawn in the New England and the southern samples. No married women with husbands living were found to have probate inventories. After the appropriate w-weighting (see appendix A) the percentages of probate-type wealthholders who were women were reduced to the figures in column 1 of tables 7.1 through 7.4. These proportions are not far from those found by Soltow 1975a:200, for 1860.

11. Occupation was not always clearcut from the probate documents (see chapter 5). When no occupation was stated, but livestock, farm tools, etc. were noted in the probate inventory, the occupation of "farmer" was usually inferred and coded. The code for "planter" was used when the probate inventory or other document specifically used the term; however, I consider the terms "planter" and "farmer" as interchangeable and have made no distinction between them in analysis. Sometimes there were multiple occupations beyond the provisions of my codes, and in those cases the most reasonable one was selected. For instance, a wealthy doctor in South Carolina, Dr. Archibald McNeill (I.D. #01042), had such plantation items as horses, a small amount of livestock, one plow, many Negroes, also much shoemaking leather, saddle leather, vats, shoemaker tools, 92 pairs of black leather mens shoes, 368 pairs of "Negro shoes," and coopering tools. On several deeds his occupation was listed as "Physician." I therefore coded him "doctor," not farmer nor farmer with side occupation, but I treated the 92 plus 368 pairs of shoes as nonfarm business inventory, since they were clearly not his personal apparel. He thus makes a case of "professional" with nonfarm business inventory, and large amounts of artisan equipment, the latter treated as producers' durable equipment of household, since I do not find him to have been personally a cooper or a shoemaker. (See section III.A on codes in *American Colonial Wealth*, either edition.)

12. Some middle colony farmers in the sample had boats, "seines," or other

fishing equipment in their inventories, but none seemed to depend primarily on fishing.

13. Cf. Shepherd and Walton 1972; McCusker 1971.

14. Except in New England, where this category includes fishermen, who, in my sample, were usually poor, and where there were a number of farmer-fishermen, who also tended to be poor.

15. The insufficiency of cases for the smaller categories explains some other combinations that do not fit within sectoral boundaries. Thus two "vessel owner" cases, with no indication of other specific occupation, in the middle colonies, were placed with "farmers plus other activity, fishermen." Sea captains in New England and the middle colonies, being of substantially higher wealth than most mariners (a term commonly used for "sailor") were grouped there with the professionals rather than with the mariners. There were no sea captains in the southern sample. Mariners were grouped with laborers.

16. The reader is reminded of reservations in interpretation of occupational comparisons, which are in order because of varying usage in the American colonies in the eighteenth century in the application of such designations as "gentleman," "esquire," "planter," "farmer" and names of some other occupations or trades. These are discussed in the text and notes of chapter 5.

17. See *American Colonial Wealth,* section II for individual cases, arranged by county.

18. The full wealth stub for each socioeconomic group is given in tables 7.74 through 7.113 in *American Colonial Wealth,* either edition, and by three net worth classes and three physical wealth classes in its tables 7.15 through 7.38. The weights in those tables for the South and for the thirteen colonies are derived under Variant One assumptions. Variant Two weighted corresponding tables for the South and thirteen colonies are given in the appendix of *American Colonial Wealth,* 2d ed.

19. For holdings of financial assets and liabilities by these groups see chapter 5, and, for farmers and merchants, tables 7.20 through 7.31.

20. Hence the reader may assume that the true percentages having goods in these two categories approach 100 percent for all the socioeconomic groups.

21. This pattern for the South is the same as for the North, but starts from a lower initial figure, explained by technical problems of data collection discussed in the Note on Method and in appendix A.

22. In Maryland one sample inventory (#72004) listed a 25-year-old Negro man, a "Blacksmith" valued at £80 Maryland local currency (£60 sterling).

23. In only one or two instances did a group have nonfarm business equipment, usually of small average amount, without also having some nonfarm business inventory. Therefore I regard the percentage having nonfarm business inventory as an indicator, or proxy, for those who had both, that is to say, who engaged in economic ventures other than farming.

24. Occasional large departures from regularity in patterns of regional difference that the reader may observe within some of the smaller socioeconomic groups may sometimes be due only to one or a few unusual cases in the small cell of basic sample data rather than to a significant underlying divergence. They may, however, as in this case of tables 7.12 and 7.13, also suggest real diversity in activity regarding a rather rare wealth form. Though a larger sample might not yield the same minor bulges in pattern at exactly the same places, it seems likely that, in the case of business inventories at least, minor bulges would again appear here and there and that

my general deductions therefrom might not be greatly different from those suggested above. The general consistency of observable patterns, in tables from 7.6 on, abstracting from a relatively few erratic departures that should not be interpreted literally, is so reasonable and the general differences so economically sensible that I present regional detail, subject to the above caution.

25. This is even more true for some of the subcategories not shown in tables enumerated above but in tables of *American Colonial Wealth* listed in note 18.

26. That it is not repeated for New England and the middle colonies with respect to percent of total physical wealth (table 7.11) may be due to a few exceptional cases; or it may be due to the stronger tendency noted for land ownership to expand at higher wealth levels in the North. For slave ownership in Philadelphia, see Nash 1973.

27. There may be some bias toward land-holding women being probated in New England, since land was included in the probate inventories there and action by the probate court was necessary to effect subsequent sale of land. Conversation with Frank E. Tuitt, II, Register, Probate and Insolvency Courts, Hampshire County, Northampton Massachusetts, July, 1969.

28. With exception of one southern mariner who held valuable land and strikingly brought up the average.

29. I drew no low-wealth merchants in the middle colonies and only one each in New England and the South. The unweighted count of total merchant cases in the sample was 14 in New England, of which 8 (one a merchant-captain) were from Boston, 2 from Salem, 3 (one a merchant-captain) from Marblehead and 1 from New Haven, Connecticut; 1 from Ulster county, New York; 9 from the other middle colonies, of which 8 were from Philadelphia and 1 from Kent County, Delaware; 6 from the South, of which 3 were from Charleston, 2 from Chesterfield County, Virginia, 1 from Spotsylvania County, Virginia. The w-weighted counts round to 2 percent of the regional samples for each of New England and the middle colonies (tables 7.2 and 7.3) and to only 1 percent for the South (table 7.4). These numbers appear small because cases at older ages and from counties with larger numbers of sample cases are weighted down for both age and large county, as explained in appendix A. Following are the respective net worths and total physical wealths for each of the merchant cases not included in tables of this chapter: Ulster County, New York, £3,310, £1,518; three from Charleston, S.C.: £454, £503; £393, £505; £2,210, £1,453; two from Chesterfield County, Virginia: –£20, £16; £1,022, £1,135; one from Spotsylvania County, Virginia, £278, £356. Details concerning them can be found in table 8.1 of *American Colonial Wealth,* either edition.

30. Parallel arrays by net worth, using the same three class intervals, were tabulated and the computer printouts are filed at the Newberry Library. The general conclusions to be drawn from these latter tables do not diverge greatly from the patterns we see in tables 7.1 through 7.4, although there are a few interesting differences. In particular, for New England, an even larger proportion by net worth than by physical wealth fell in the low-wealth class. This was particularly so for "esquires, gentlemen, and officials" and also merchants, less notably so for professionals and for farmers. On the other hand, fewer in New England fell in the low net worth class (as compared with the low physical wealth class) among "shopkeepers, innkeepers," "mariners, laborers" and "artisans, chandlers," suggesting that these groups had relatively smaller financial liabilities than did the esquires and merchants.

31. The numbers of sample cases for which I was able to obtain age in specific

years was 261 for New England, 112 in the middle colonies, and only 28 in the South. Appendix C shows the results for New England and for the middle colonies.

32. The pattern is also consistent with findings for more recent dates from studies of probate or inheritance data, which show higher estate values at higher age levels. See Lampman 1962; Soltow 1971a; Gallman 1972:31; Lansing and Soderquist 1969:64–66; Projector and Weiss 1966:29–33; J. Smith and Calvert 1965; Podoluk 1974:190–92; Podder and Kakwani 1976:85–86; Campbell and Lowe 1977:58–61, 135; Stigler 1952:274 n.; Menard, Harris, and Carr 1974; Paglin 1975; French 1970:51.

33. Gallman 1969; Williamson and Lindert 1977; Soltow 1975a. See note 55 of chapter 8.

34. I have not calculated Gini coefficients nor average values for urban and rural subdivided by wealth class because of small numbers of urban cases and difficulties of separate arrays for subsets of the sample. If relatively enough "urban rich" cases of the New England sample were much richer than the "rural rich" cases, and enough of the "urban poor" were much poorer than the "rural poor," then we would get a stronger measure of urban inequality. Researchers who wish to pursue this possibility can work with the data tapes at Ann Arbor or from the I.D. codes and wealth summaries of table 8.1 *American Colonial Wealth.*

35. See note 29 for their wealths; all the Charleston and one of the Virginia merchants fell in the high-wealth class, measured by total physical wealth, but one Virginia merchant had only £16 of such wealth and negative net worth.

8. INEQUALITY COMPARED WITH OTHER TIMES AND PLACES

1. Soltow 1968:18. A rather similar figure for King's 1688 data has been calculated by Williamson 1978:6, table 1.

2. Colquhoun, 1815; Soltow 1968:19–21; Studenski 1961:102–6.

3. Some unpublished analysis of work of past authors by Williamson 1978 suggests that greatest income inequality in the United Kingdom was reached in the 1801–3 and 1812 estimates, and that there was some decline in inequality across the nineteenth century. He and Lindert are gathering sample probate data at five points in time in four regions and analyzing tax, pay, and earnings structure to refine these estimates. See Williamson 1979.

4. At 1865 prices, which Soltow arrived at by adjusting with a consumer price index.

5. Gallman 1972:50–51, table 2.15, and U.S. estimate for 1867, based in part on Seaman 1870:242.

6. The estate multiplier technique involves estimating wealth of living upper wealthholders from estates of the dying corrected by mortality rates. See citations to literature concerning this method in Lampman 1962, also in Smith and Calvert 1965. My method of estimating wealth of the probate-type living from a sample of probated estates with w weights approximates it. See appendix A and *American Colonial Wealth,* either edition, p. 1868.

7. For more complete tabular summaries than offered in tables 8.4, 8.5, and 8.6, see tables 1, 2, 3 in G. Main 1977a, and table A.1 in Williamson and Lindert 1977 and their source notes. Some trends, mostly very slight, to greater inequality by the mid- or late eighteenth century appeared in such northern rural areas as

Hingham, Massachusetts (D. Smith 1973), three frontier and three middle-sized towns in Connecticut (Daniels 1973–74), Suffolk County excluding Boston (ibid.) Hampshire County, Massachusetts (G. Main 1977), Worcester County, Massachusetts (Daniels 1973–74, G. Main 1977a), Chester County, Pennsylvania (Lemon and Nash 1968; Ball 1976). The degree of inequality (Gini coefficient) was quite low in Chester County. A sharper trend in early Essex County to 1681 was noted by Koch 1969. No trend in probate wealth concentration was evident for Hartford, Connecticut (Daniels 1973–74; J. Main 1976). Likewise, no clear trend in concentration was found for Boston by G. Main (1977a) or Daniels (1973–74) to 1776, though Nash (1976a) found an irregular upward trend for that city to 1765 and Daniels found an upward trend for Portsmouth, New Hampshire to 1776. An increase in inequality of taxed wealth in Boston noted by Henretta (1965) from comparison of tax lists of 1687 and 1781 and found continued to 1790 by Kulikoff (1971) has been found to be much reduced when recomputed by Warden (1976) to adjust for great variation in valuation ratios over time, across assets, and for coverage problems. As to some other cities of the North, an upward trend in wealth concentration was apparent for Salem, Massachusetts to 1681 (Koch 1969). In New York there was no clear trend from tax records as observed from tax lists for 1675 (Ritchie 1972) and 1695 (Goodfriend 1975) up to 1789 (Wilkenfeld 1973), though by 1796 the share of the top 10 percent had reached 61 percent. For six coastal counties in Maryland, Gloria Main (1977a:567) appears to have found from probate records high initial inequality and a slight upward trend from 1675 to 1754. For the City of Philadelphia, Nash (1976b) found a pronounced increase in trend to inequality to 1775.

The more consistent conclusion that seems to emerge from the local studies is that wealth concentration was higher in the large cities of the North than in its rural areas and than in some smaller towns of Connecticut. Also it was higher in settled farm areas than in newer "frontier" communities. Early wealth concentration in Maryland coastal counties appears to have been high. We lack data for other parts of the South.

8. The reduced inequality of my Variant Two wealth estimates for thirteen colonies, as compared with my Variant One, suggests only in part the magnitude of problems that might be encountered. Differences in the relative weights assigned to the high wealth of Charleston District, discussed in appendix A, cause the difference between Variants One and Two. The differences for measures of inequality of total physical wealth, w^*B-weighted, in 1774, may be summarized as follows:

	Variant One	Variant Two
Gini coefficient:		
All free wealthholders	0.71	0.66
Free and nonfree potential wealthholders	0.77	0.73
Share of top one percent:		
All free wealthholders	22.4	12.9
Free and nonfree potential wealthholders	24.6	14.5

Source of Variant One figures: *American Colonial Wealth*, either edition, tables 7.176 and 7.180. Source of Variant Two figures: tables 6.2, 6.15 and 8.2.

9. Gallman 1972:19, suggests that by the Peace of Utrecht in 1713, the value of colonial exports to England alone ran about £1 per head per year and that total trade, including intercolonial trade, must have been considerably larger. "At a time when national income per capita, even in the relatively rich countries of the world,

ran probably no more than £8 or £9, this volume of trade is very impressive. It suggests that the colonies were exploiting their natural advantages and were developing a complex and productive organization."

10. See *American Husbandry* 1775:291–300, and circularity in acquisition of land and slaves mentioned by Sellers 1934:56.

11. For early land distribution in Virginia and Massachusetts see Hughes 1976:55–56, 62–63, 65–68. Also see G. Main 1977a:571–72. Robert Gallman is undertaking analysis of trends in land and other wealth in Perquimmans, one of the older North Carolina counties.

12. Daniels 1973–74; Doherty 1977; J. Main 1965.

13. Wood 1978 has an exceptionally complete bibliography; Kulikoff 1978.

14. Nash 1976a. However, the convincing demolition by Warden 1976 of the hypothesis of increasing inequality of taxed wealth in Boston, because of flaws in tax lists, raises doubts about the value of unadjusted tax list data for Philadelphia as indicators of increasing wealth concentration. Nash also finds greater shares of Philadelphia probate wealth held at the top over time, and these data, even when unadjusted for age and nonprobates, do seem to me to indicate a high liklihood of rising total wealth and rising shares for the top group in the city of Philadelphia. This conclusion, in view of relative size of urban and rural populations, still is compatible with a low overall wealth inequality for the entire region.

15. J. Main 1971 reacted to the high inequality for 1860 estimated by Gallman 1969, as compared with Main's lower estimates for the colonies, with suggestions as to possible explanations for the very large increase. Pessen 1973 accented heavy inequality in four large cities by the 1840s. Williamson and Lindert 1977:48–54 conclude that there was substantial increase in inequality from the end of the colonial period to the 1860s. An opposite view, that there was little, if any, change in inequality at least from 1790 on through the nineteenth century, and probably to 1940, is taken by Soltow 1971b:825–26, 828–29, and 1975a:116–18. His argument for the steadiness from 1860 to 1870 is presented in a later section of the present chapter, and that for no change from 1870 to 1890 is presented in note b to table 8.3.

16. Soltow 1971a, Milwaukee County compared with other Wisconsin counties, and 1975a:196, n. 10; Pessen 1973, whose data are for Boston, New York, and Philadelphia; Doherty 1977:chap. 5, five towns in Massachusetts; G. Main 1977a:560, table 1, Boston, New York, and 1977a:567, 574, tables 3 and 4, for Boston, Suffolk County excluding Boston, other Massachusetts counties.

17. Soltow 1971a:6–7, found the 1870 census absolute wealth values less reliable than those of 1860 for Milwaukee County since reported wealth per capita did not increase as much as prices from 1860 to 1870. However, he considered the 1870 relative values to be useful. In his 1975a volume he uses chiefly 1860 data for detailed analysis. See note 36.

18. Soltow 1975a:96–97; Campbell and Lowe 1977:38 for Texas; G. Wright 1970:74–76 for farm operators in the cotton South.

19. Soltow 1975a:142, Campbell and Lowe 1977:44 for Texas; G. Wright 1970:79 for farm operators in the cotton South.

20. Soltow 1975a:103. Campbell and Lowe 1977:128, 129, found from Soltow's (1971a) data for rural Wisconsin in 1860 a Gini of 0.72 compared with theirs of 0.73 for rural Texas.

21. Soltow argues there may have been no increase from 1870 to 1890. See note b to table 8.3.

22. Soltow 1971a, 1971b, 1975a, 1975b; Gallman 1968, 1969; Holmes 1893

and as articulated in Merwin 1939, in Gallman 1968:320–21, and in Williamson and Lindert 1977:78–79, 132; King 1915 and in Federal Trade Commission 1926:58–59, as articulated in Gallman 1968 and in Williamson and Lindert 1977; Lampman 1959, 1962; Projector and Weiss 1966; Smith and Franklin 1974 and unpublished data supplied to Williamson and Lindert 1977.

23. Incomparability occurs in wealth definitions, populations covered, completeness and accuracy of underlying enumerators' or interviewers' reports or of probate or estate returns, as well as in adjustments or assumptions made by some investigators to correct for data deficiencies. The limitation of my sample to probated decedents has been rectified, to a substantial extent I believe, by weighting to the age structure of living wealthholders and allowance for wealth of the nonprobated; see appendix A. For census returns see discussions by Hoenack 1964:193, 198; Gallman 1968:322–34; Soltow 1975a:1–3; Campbell and Lowe 1977:19–25. See also note 36 re instructions to census enumerators. Gallman 1968 evaluated estimates by Holmes, King, and Lampman. At the time of that writing, the results from Soltow's studies were not yet available. Gallman gave greatest credence to the estimates of Lampman, but found useful and not unreasonable the estimates by Holmes and King. Williamson and Lindert 1977 present summary findings from most of the studies named in note 22, with analytical comment and evaluation.

24. Soltow 1971b:825–26, 828–29.

25. Soltow 1975a:116–18.

26. In the four-region area of Maryland, District of Columbia, North Carolina, South Carolina, for which 1790 census records of slaves survive, Soltow 1971b:828. Soltow finds the same Gini values for a 14-state southern area sample for 1830, 1850, and 1860; Soltow 1971b:825. When he adds more questionable estimates for Virginia for 1790, the 1790 figure for a five-region area becomes 0.57, and the figures for later dates for that five-region area become; 1830, 0.57; 1850, 0.58; 1860, 0.60; Soltow 1971b:829. For the entire South, in 1860, Soltow 1975a:136 states that the Gini coefficient for slave wealth among slaveholders was 0.62, but the fact that 80 percent of freemen in that year had zero wealth in slaves raised it to the very high value of 0.93 per free adult male. Gloria Main 1977a:table 1, shows Soltow's 0.93 for 1860 compared with an 0.83 in 1790 as Gini coefficients for slave wealth per free adult male in the South: I assume she computed the 0.83, which I am unable to find in Soltow 1971b or Soltow 1975a. Campbell and Lowe 1977:44 find a Gini coefficient for slave wealth held in Texas by free families of 0.86 for 1850 and 0.88 for 1860.

27. Soltow 1975a:118, 197 fn. 28, which gives as source the Massachusetts Bureau of Statistics of Labor, *Twenty-fifth Annual Report.* Public Documents no. 15 (Boston, 1895), pp. 264–67. The note states that the Pareto curves tested are those for males, and indicates that an alternative presentation is given in Watkins 1908:37.

28. Soltow 1975a:100. He cautions that one must be careful to note that this analysis treats a changing population that grew by 30 percent for all adult males and by 34 percent for foreign-born males in the ten years, and one whose native-born population was depleted substantially among younger age groups.

29. In his Annual Message to Congress, December 1, 1862, President Lincoln urged that the nation as a whole reimburse slave owners for their losses. He proposed articles to be ratified as parts of the constitution which would provide for bonds of the United States, bearing interest, to be paid to every state that abolished slavery at any time before January 1, 1900. The amount was to equal the aggregate sum of a value to be set (presumably by Congress) for each slave shown to have been

in the state according to the 1860 census. Basler 1946:680–81. I am indebted to Allen Wallis for this citation.

30. See also Soltow 1975a:99, 123.

31. Soltow's finding of overall stability from 1860 to 1870 is similar to a calculation by Gallman on the basis of his 1860 sample (Gallman 1969:6–9). This estimate was made on the basis of only 1860 data, as an exercise anticipating what might have been the effect on wealth distribution of freeing of the slaves. In his *A* distribution, like Soltow's for 1860, Gallman excluded slaves as people but included their asset value as wealth of their owners. Hence his "1860" distribution is only for *free* family heads. In his *B* distribution, simulating 1870 conditions, he included adult male slaves as holders of zero wealth, but subtracted slave asset value from the wealth of their owners. He, too, found almost no difference in the inequality of the two distributions, *A* and *B*. His explanation was similar to Soltow's, that the decrease in riches of those from whom the slave assets were subtracted offset the inequality introduced at the bottom by adding slaves (by 1870 they would have become former slaves) as holders of no wealth. But Gallman as well as Soltow did not give us a distribution for 1860 that measured the inequality of wealthholding among both the free and the nonfree in that year, and if he had made such a distribution, it would certainly have shown greater inequality than did his *A* distribution.

32. Soltow 1971a, 1971b, 1975a, 1975b. Since censuses deal with living people and his cases were randomly drawn by a spin process, Soltow has no problems of weighting or adjustment of data for his U.S. samples. He is free to divide his cases into subgroups by any desired socioeconomic factors with no procedural complications. He has subjected his data to many kinds of extremely interesting and useful comparisons and analyses, but for which the reader must dig.

33. Gallman 1969 combined various subsamples with appropriate population weights to reach his U.S. estimate for 1860.

34. Campbell and Lowe 1977 drew stratified samples from four Texas regions in such a way that weighting was not required to reach a total for the state. They provide very useful analyses of population subgroups, including farmers who owned real estate and farmers who did not, farmers who owned slaves and farmers who did not, nonfarmers who owned slaves, etc.

35. Most studies have limited their observations to wealth held by free adult males, many but not all of whom were heads of families or households. Wealth held independently by widows, single women, or orphaned minors has usually been ignored in historical studies of wealthholding. Soltow's spin sample took only men aged 20 and older (Soltow 1975a:2–5). His reasons for excluding women and for taking males over 20 rather than families as his wealthholding unit are given in Soltow 1971a:22. Gallman noted that the 1860 census unit was the (free) family, but that enumerators treated hotels, boarding houses, convents, military academies, and like institutions as families, and included as part of the family where they lived hired men, boarders, and married children. His sample excluded the institutions and counted as wealth of the family only that of the family head and his spouse (Gallman 1968:333). He found that such wealth comprised over 95 percent of the total in three of his 1860 manuscript census samples, 90 percent in a fourth, and over 85 percent in a fifth sample. Lee Soltow drew a separate random U.S. sample from the 1860 census of free women and children with wealth. He reports that "their aggregate wealth was 7.8 percent of men's wealth, and that the number of women and children with wealth as a proportion of the number of adult males for the United States, the North, and the South, was, respectively" 5.9 percent, 5.4 percent, and 6.9 percent.

(Soltow 1975a:200, note 12). He reports on women and boys with wealth in Wisconsin in 1860 in Soltow 1971a:52–53, table 10.

36. Wright and Hunt 1900:157, instructions to census enumerators in 1870. Schedules for the 1850 census are on p. 147, for 1860 and 1870 censuses on p. 154. Instructions to marshals regarding real estate, personal estate, and slaves for the 1850 census are on pp. 152–153, for real estate and personal estate for the 1870 census on p. 157. For comparison of census definitions in 1850, 1860, and 1870 see Soltow 1971a:18; Campbell and Lowe 1977:22–23. For excerpts from instructions to U.S. marshals in 1860 not found in the Wright document but in a surviving 1860 census publication in the library of the American Philosophical Society, Philadelphia, see Soltow 1971a:appendix 1, 141–45 and 163 note 1.

37. Soltow 1975a:99. However, Soltow 1971a:45, 49, 50, 52 shows that about 30 percent of Wisconsin males in 1860 had zero wealth, and Soltow 1971b:table 5 seems to show that 37 percent of free men in the South in 1860 had personal estate of under $100. Whether all or nearly all of the lower half of the free population in 1860 really held virtually no wealth has troubled me. I have discussed the question with both Gallman and Soltow, who have individually persuaded me, with arithmetic examples, that even if one were to allocate an arbitrary sum, such as $50, or even $100, to cover apparel and miscellaneous unreported personal property to each of these zero wealthholders, the aggregate wealth involved would be so small that it would have relatively little impact on the overall size distribution. It can be noted in my tables 6.1 and 6.2 that the comparable percentages of wealth held by free wealthholders in 1774 by the bottom five deciles are under 4 for net worth and less than 7 for total physical wealth, and in table 6.15 they sum to less than 3 percent of total physical wealth for all potential wealthholders, free and nonfree.

38. Williamson and Lindert 1977:48–54. See other estimates of high inequality in 1860 in note 15. Sturm 1977 suggests that inequality among upper wealthholders was greatest at about 1800, decreased by 1850, and increased somewhat from 1850 to 1890. He bases his conclusion on a sample of approximately 2,600 inventories probated in four time periods: 1798–1806, 1848–1856, 1868–1873, and 1888–1893. The sample estates belonged to prosperous decedents (worth over $10,000) who lived in 22 localities distributed among the various regions of the nation.

39. See North 1961a:98 for occupations of immigrants. See further discussion of Soltow on foreign born and wealth in note 54.

40. Soltow 1975a:123, citing Lampman 1962:228.

41. Holmes's work is favorably evaluated by Gallman 1968:320–21, who cautioned that Holmes, a very able quantitative worker, "surely did not intend that his distribution bear much analytical weight." Williamson and Lindert 1977:78–79, 132 n. 29 find Holmes' estimates useful and reasonable. They suggest that:

Professor Lampman (1959, p. 388, n. 14) was apparently in error when he rejected Holmes' estimate of the 1890 wealth concentration with the statement: 'It is difficult to believe that wealth was actually that highly concentrated in 1890 in view of the 1921 and 1922 measures.' This statement is apparently based on the mistaken impression that Spahr's (1896) allegation that the top 1% held 51% of 1890 wealth could be attributed to Holmes as well. On the contrary, Holmes' results are quite in line with Lampman's estimates.

42. G. Main 1977a:574–75, tables 4 and 5. Table 4 is adjusted for differences in various years in proportions of males whose estates were inventoried. Data are not adjusted for age and were drawn from inventory data published by Carroll D. Wright in the *Twenty-fifth Annual Report* of the Massachusetts Bureau of Labor Statistics (Boston, 1895), pp. 238–67. Lack of age adjustment may not hinder time

comparisons if the age proportions among the decedents did not change greatly over time.

43. G. Main 1977a:560, table 1. Data are not adjusted for age.

44. Doherty 1977:chap. 5, esp. tables 5.1, p. 47, and 5.3, p. 51. Also his 1971 paper arrayed 1771 taxpayers in 12 Massachusetts towns plus Boston grouped as urban, "regional market centers or commercial agriculture towns," "lesser market centers or commercial agriculture towns," and "subsistence agriculture towns." He found successively less wealth concentration as he moved down from urban to "subsistence agriculture." His data support the thesis of Jackson Main that the greatest concentration was found in urban places, the least in places of subsistence or self-sufficient agriculture. That thesis is also supported by findings of Daniels 1973–74 for Connecticut towns through the colonial period. Soltow 1971a:7, 56–57, 66 was unable to get a clearcut answer for Wisconsin in 1860 as to whether inequality was lower in "frontier" areas than in more densely settled ones; he attributed the weak correlation he found between density of settlement and inequality by county to a peculiarity in Wisconsin geography and areas of settlement at that time.

45. Used by W. King, as reported in Williamson and Lindert 1977:80. See Federal Trade Commission 1926.

46. A. A. Young 1916; Merwin 1939.

47. French 1970 gives estimates based on estate tax returns for Oklahoma in 1960, where the law required filing for estates valued as low as $100. This study used the estate multiplier technique, and is the first such for a single state, and the first to cover the entire wealth range. It accords with Lampman's results in many respects.

48. Projector and Weiss 1966:1. The sampling was developed in a pilot study made for the Federal Reserve Board by the University of Michigan Survey Research Center, and the final study was executed for the Federal Reserve Board by the U.S. Census Bureau. Careful analyses of response error had been made for predecessor interview surveys obtaining financial information, and the National Science Foundation furnished funds for a similar analysis of the 1962 survey, in which the Federal Reserve Board and the Census Bureau cooperated. Nonresponse errors were also evaluated by using all the information available about nonrespondents—age of head when available, income stratum, and region. Adjustments for nonresponse were made in the survey results; see Projector and Weiss 1966:58–61.

49. Not included in "wealth" but in "net worth" as used in the Federal Reserve study (Projector and Weiss 1966:45, 48) were equity values in life insurance and pension funds. There were, of course, no counterparts in 1774 for such forms of wealth.

50. I find that a convenient way to compare Lorenz curves is to trace one or two of special interest on onion skin paper and superimpose one on another.

51. The lower Paglin-Ginis shown for 1962 in Figure 20, for 1774 in figure 12, and the hatched areas in those graphs are discussed in chapter 6.

52. Lower figures than 34 and 62 for the shares of the top 1 and top 10 percent (lines 1 and 4 of table 8.11) may be reasonable. See note c to table 8.3. I am inclined to the view that the combination of intricacies in down-weighting for intended oversampling of the very rich plus some of the adjustments for nonresponse might account for a too-high 1962 estimate for the top 1 percent. Despite great and special efforts made to obtain data from the very rich, it would seem that the Federal Reserve survey figures are more accurate and can be more readily accepted for the portion of the sample with wealth below $100,000, roughly the division point

between the 98th and 99th percentiles. Figures were supplied to me by Professor Paglin in a letter dated December 1, 1975, based on published Federal Reserve figures (Projector and Weiss 1966:110, 151), showing cumulated percentages of consumer units and of wealth; from these I made my interpolations for table 8.11. They are as follows:

		Consumer Units	Wealth
$500,000 and over	(approximately)	100.00	100.00
$200,000–499,999		99.83	78.97
$100,000–199,999		98.97	66.44
$ 50,000– 99,999		97.76	58.68
$ 25,000– 49,999		93.34	44.29
$ 10,000– 24,999		82.73	26.08
$ 5,000– 9,999		59.76	8.27
$ 1,000– 4,999		44.04	2.75
$ 999 and under		25.39	.30

53. Soltow 1975a:102 shows the same Lorenz curve as mine for the 1962 data. He compares it, on the same graph, with the two more unequal distributions of free adult males in 1860 and all adult males in 1870. The Gini coefficients for both the latter are 0.83, and the two curves lie almost on top of each other. In that graph, the 1962 distribution is somewhat less bowed from about the 30th to 95th percentile than the lines for 1860–70.

54. See Soltow 1975a:108–9 for an interesting statistical demonstration of some interconnections between nativity, urban society, and upper wealth levels. He shows that although the foreign born in 1870 had lower average wealth than the native born, one cannot statistically cite the relatively greater presence of foreign born in cities as an explanation of greater inequality there. See also Lebergott 1976a, b, for evidence of greater mobility, at least since the World War I era, into and out of the ranks of top wealthholders.

55. See note 54 and Soltow 1975a:183. Williamson and Lindert 1977:51–53, calculated from my individual 1774 observations for males, what would have been my inequality level if in 1774 the male age structure of 1860 had prevailed. They found, despite greater longevity in 1860, virtually no difference from my findings.

Gallman 1978:196–98 postulates a model by age brackets for an egalitarian society where, for each member, income, consumption, and savings are identical within an age bracket for all those aged 15 or older. For each person, income rises with age to a plateau from age 40 to 59 and then declines. Consumption rises to an earlier peak at 40–49 and then slackens. Saving goes from negative at age 15–19 to small positive at age 20–29, reaches a maximum at 50–59, and then becomes negative with small withdrawals in the sixties, larger ones in the seventies. Thus age alone determines income, savings, and wealth in this model. With it, and with an age distribution of a society, one can compute the hypothetical share of wealth that would be held by a given fraction of the population had the society in which the population lived been of the egalitarian sort described by the model. Gallman introduced into the model calculations for the actual age distributions of five populations (age 15 and older), the United States of 1830, 1860, and 1950, Great Britain of 1861, and France of 1851. He found that the fraction of wealth held by the richest 30 percent of the population aged 15 and over varied substantially, owing only to this age factor. The hypothetical estimates are:

> U.S. 1830 96 percent of wealth
> U.S. 1860 92
> U.S. 1950 78
> G.B. 1861 84
> France 1851 81

There are, of course, in real life some wealth inequalities within each age group. Hence these calculations, while they make a useful point, may go too far and seem to suggest a stronger point than their author's intent.

56. See chapter 1 and appendix A, part five. Also Moss 1978.

9. SUMMARY AND CONCLUSIONS

1. Amounts of colonial government and church wealth would have been relatively small in 1774, consisting of such things as value of church buildings and of town meetinghouses, town or county jails, public wharves, county roads, and town common lands, to the rather small extent that these had not been subdivided among settlers. The provincial governments were under the British crown and such wealth as naval ships beyond to the Royal Navy, and probably such items as militia supplies of the provinces, should be considered wealth of the British crown, not of the colonies.

2. The figure drops to 9.2 percent in table 9.1, which includes the value of slaves and servants in the total physical wealth considered. Correspondingly, other percentages in table 9.1 are lower than the text figures, which can be found in table 4.7 where the total presented is nonhuman physical wealth.

3. From table 2.4 we see that there were a total of 1,820,000 free persons of whom nearly 435,000 were free adult wealthholders. The wealthholders were principally men, but included some women. Each such wealthholder may be thought of as roughly the head of a free family with an average size of 4.2 persons.

4. But see note 2 of chapter 3 for the remarkable estimate of Gregory King for England and Wales in 1688, where his addition of a value for human capital doubled his wealth estimate.

5. See part five of appendix A for discussion of conversion from wealth to income. Life expectancy has, of course, increased considerably in the United States since colonial days, particularly in reduction of infant and child mortality.

6. Summarized in chapter 3, in the section on the thirteen colonies in earlier periods.

7. Negative rates were found by G. Main 1972, 1973 in seventeenth century New England locales, by Anderson 1975b, 1979, in New England locales in the early eighteenth century, and by Kulikoff 1979, for Maryland for the first half of the eighteenth century. Rates of 5 percent per year were found by Egnal 1975 in per capita imports and exports from the lower South from 1720 to 1735 and rates from 3 to 5 percent from the northern colonies (New England plus the Middle Colonies) for 1745–60. McCusker 1971, 1972, found that the rate of growth in per capita imports plus exports in Pennsylvania was 1.6 percent per year for the period 1725–29 to 1770–74.

8. For values around 1770 see table 3.11. Also see Egnal 1975; McCusker 1971, 1972; Shepherd and Walton 1972.

9. Anderson 1979; Davisson 1967b; Koch 1969; Kulikoff 1979; G. Main, 1972, 1973.

10. North 1971; Shepherd and Walton 1972.

11. Estimates of wealth by Lee Soltow from census samples suggest there was a slowdown in per capita wealth from 1860 to 1870. His figures include financial assets while mine in table 3.16 do not. See note 26 of chapter 3.

12. See discussion of other estimates of pre-1840 growth rates in chapter 3.

13. See Hofstadter 1972; chaps. 1, 2; Galeson 1978a,b, regarding indentured servants.

14. Because of the effect of financial assets and liabilities, the same people found at the tops and bottoms of lists of wealthholders arrayed by size of net worth are not always similarly located on the corresponding lists by total physical wealth. Some of the same names however, appear on both lists, as shown in tables in chapter 6.

15. In table 6.11 I show a size distribution for the South of only the nonhuman physical wealth (excluding values of wealth in slaves) of the free wealthholders. The Gini coefficient, at first glance surprisingly, is 0.67, the same as in table 9.4. However, the median and mean values drop by large amounts (compared with those in table 6.2), as do the values at lower bounds of all ten deciles and the top two percentiles. This tells us that, even without the impact of wealth in slaves, there was great disparity in the South in 1774 in the holdings of land and other physical assets as between the rich and poor free wealthholders. See chapter 6.

16. For example, see Hofstadter 1972:138–39, 146.

17. Gini coefficients as high as in the 0.60s and some in the 0.70s were found for male probate wealth in the seventeenth and early eighteenth century. See table 8.4. The shares of taxed wealth held by the top 10 percent of taxpayers were 40 percent or more in Boston, New York, and Philadelphia in the late seventeenth century. See table 8.6.

18. Estimated by Soltow 1968.

19. See table 8.2 and text discussion in chapter 8, particularly of the comparison between 1774 and 1962. The Gini coefficients in 1774 of 0.73 for net worth held by free wealthholders and of 0.73 for total physical wealth held by all potential wealthholders were only 3 points below the 0.76 Gini of the 1962 nationwide study of "wealth." Gini coefficients in 1860 and 1870, for the United States as a whole for "wealth" as reported in those censuses, reached figures around 0.81 to 0.83 and even higher for the South. These national figures for 1860 and 1870 compare closely to the high degree of inequality found in the South in 1774.

20. It is statistically unlikely that the richest living person in the colonies died in our particular year 1774, or lived in our particular sample counties, and hence there may have been richer persons than Manigault.

21. Details of Manigault's and Brewster's wealth can be found in *American Colonial Wealth,* table 8.1 and on pp. 1543–54 and 850–52 respectively.

22. Janney had no physical wealth reported, but an estate account showed an amount due him equivalent to £74 sterling, which exceeded financial obligations equivalent to £67 sterling paid on his behalf by his estate administrator. Details are shown in *American Colonial Wealth,* table 8.1 and pp. 284–85.

23. See *American Colonial Wealth,* table 8.1 and pp. 1014–16 for details for White, pp. 190–98 for Neave, and pp. 678–95 for Gerry. See also table 7.33.

24. See *American Colonial Wealth,* pp. 232–46 for details for Carmick, and pp. 214–18 for Lardner.

25. See *American Colonial Wealth,* table 8.1 and pp. 169–79 for details for

Potts, p. 1587 for Smith, pp. 1595–98 for Townsend, and pp. 1089–90 for Upham. See also table 7.32.

26. See *American Colonial Wealth,* table 8.1 and pp. 1499–1500 and table 7.33.

27. See *American Colonial Wealth,* pp. 136–37.

APPENDIX A

1. See Jones 1970:18–19. Also see *American Colonial Wealth,* either edition, pp. 1810, 1834, 1847ff., 1873 ff. for the subsequently refined Larntz weights for Pennsylvania, New Jersey, and Delaware.

2. Aside from the special problem of New York, the use of alternate counties to achieve the minimum number of 25 cases per cluster proved necessary only in Virginia. A total of 23 cases was accepted for the cluster for Southampton-Brunswick-Mecklenburg, Virginia, since three counties had already been used to attain that number and the additional reliability that might be added by two more cases did not appear to justify the added cost of extending the search further.

3. Additional cases beyond that number, even if costless, would not contribute sufficient additional accuracy to be worth taking. The cutoff point was invoked only for Essex County, Massachusetts. It happened that the number of 100 cases for Suffolk County, Massachusetts was the exact total of the 1774 cases found for that county.

4. See the introduction to section VI and the portions therein on "*c*" weights (county weights) in *American Colonial Wealth,* either edition.

5. See *American Colonial Wealth,* either edition, tables 7.2, 7.3, 7.142–7.161, 7.170, and 7.171.

6. Allyn Young 1916:583, in reviewing W. King 1915, suggested that King "should have allowed for the much greater inequality of possessions among men at the close of life than among men with a normal age distribution." Mendershausen 1956:280 stated the problem as follows, invoking even stronger comment by Young (1917:106–7):

Since the early years of this century, economists and statisticians have pointed to the discrepancy between the wealth distributions among the living and those among decedents which is caused by differences in their age structure. The size of a person's wealth is naturally related to his age; and the age distribution of the living differs greatly from that of the decedents. This discrepancy forbids any direct inference from the wealth distributions of decedents to that of the living. Information on the age of decedents is needed if the former is to be used as a basis for an estimate of the latter, or as A. A. Young put it, "Statistics of the size of estates admitted to probate are nearly worthless, unless they are accompanied by statistics of the age of the decedents."

For a note on the extensive body of literature on wealth estimates from estate data and the method of age correction known as the estate multiplier technique, see *American Colonial Wealth,* either edition, p. 1868. This method was developed by contributions from such people as Bernard Mallet in 1908 in Great Britain, soon followed by Corrado Gini of Italy and G. H. Knibbs of Australia and more recent British work by G. W. Daniels, H. Campion, Kathleen Langley and A. M. Carter. It has recently been reappraised for Britain by A. B. Atkinson. Horst Mendershausen (1956) was the first to use the method on American data, and Robert Lampman as well as J. Smith and Calvert used it. Lampman 1962:13 cites the major previous literature. Smith and Calvert 1965 in their opening paragraph give the following presentation of the method:

The estate multiplier technique, as currently used, rests on the assumption that death draws a random sample, stratified by age and sex, of the living population. If one has available age-sex-specific mortality rates, an estimate of the wealth of the living in a given period of time can be made by stepping-up the wealth of decedents in each age-sex class by the inverse of the mortality rate associated with that age-sex class and summing the results across all age-sex classes. . . . This technique can also be used to derive distributions for the living by any identifiable characteristic of the decedents or their wealth.

For 1774, we lack sufficiently precise sex-age specific mortality rates to follow exactly this method, but I have achieved approximately the same result by using the sex-age structure of the living in 1800 in each region in forming w weights to correct for age of the sample decedents.

7. See Jones 1970: tables 30 and 31, *American Colonial Wealth,* either edition, tables 7.39–7.54 and 7.146–7.161, and chapter 7 and appendix C of this volume. Correspondence between age and wealth has also been found by G. Main 1974:13; Waters 1976:158; and other students of colonial wealth.

8. See Soltow 1975a:69–74, 85; Projector and Weiss 1966:tables A-1 and A-2.

9. Mechanically, to minimize operations, the age correction factor and the c weights required to keep the county contributions equal are combined into a single factor for each decedent. See *American Colonial Wealth,* either edition, portion on w weights of section VI. The 1800 census gives us three relevant age breaks: 21–25 (which I computed as one-half the census age group 18–25); 26–44; 45 and over. The w weights are constructed on the assumption that the living wealthholders in 1774 were distributed among those three age groups in the same proportions as were the white adults of their sex in 1800. The total numbers of 1774 wealthholders, both men and women, and of both probate and nonprobate type, nevertheless pertain to 1774, not to 1800. (See tables 2.4 through 2.7, lines 28 and 29.) The w-weighted values are essentially nothing but the c-weighted unbiased sample results for decedents, restructured to reflect the correct proportions in each age group of the free living.

10. These w^*-weighted values are shown in *American Colonial Wealth,* either edition, tables 7.7–7.141, on wealth composition, in a separate column, alongside the column of w-weighted values, and in the 2d edition, w^*-weighted Variant Two values for the South and for the thirteen colonies appear in tables A.7.7, A.7.14, and subsequent tables in its appendix. The w^*-weighted values are shown in the tables on size distribution in two separate columns, one for assumption A, one for assumption B, as to the most likely distribution of the nonprobate-type wealthholders by size of wealth. These size distribution tables are found in *American Colonial Wealth,* either edition, tables 7.172–7.179 and in the 2d edition with w^*-weighted Variant Two values for the South in tables A.7.172, A.7.175 and subsequent tables in its appendix. No tables on standard deviations and confidence intervals are offered, for w^*-weighted values comparable to *American Colonial Wealth* tables 7.162–7.169, since the w^*-weighted values depend not only upon sample values but on the additional assumptions. However, if the reader finds the assumptions reasonable, I believe he can accept the w^*-weighted values with considerable, though not measureable, confidence, since they are undergirded by the measurably acceptable w-weighted values. (See the portion on w^* weights of section VI of *American Colonial Wealth,* either edition.)

No tables on personal characteristics at the w^*-weighted level, comparable to tables 7.4 and 7.5 of *American Colonial Wealth,* either edition, and A.7.4, 2d edition, are offered, since my assumptions as to wealth of the nonprobate types do not carry over to their personal characteristics. We have no better assumption as to their personal characteristics than that they are the same as those of the probate types, although I do not regard this as a particularly satisfying assumption. Likewise, in tables 7.7–7.141 of *American Colonial Wealth,* either edition, and A.7.7–A.7.21, 2d edition, the column headed "w-weighted percent having" is accepted as my estimate of the percent of all wealthholders having the indicated category of wealth, only for want of information on this point for nonprobate-type wealthholders. This interpretation, though obviously limited, seems preferable to devising my own assumptions with respect to each wealth category and subcategory as to the percent of the nonprobate types who might have held each. Clearly, this interpretation is most reasonable with respect to the major categories of wealth, such as total physical wealth and net worth, and may not be too far afield for such totals as producers' and consumers' durables, household equipment, and apparel. It may be very unsatisfactory with respect to such special items as "servants and slaves," "business inventories," "livestock," and "financial assets." Improvement of our knowledge in this area is desirable, yet it is difficult to see how we can discover any systematic information on the characteristics and proportions holding selected kinds of wealth of the group of free wealthholders, the nonprobates, who left us no court records of their wealth and who can be discovered biographically only on a partial and likely biased basis.

11. W. King 1915, using nineteenth-century data for Massachusetts for three periods, assumed that the nonprobated estates were insignificant in value, with an upper limit of $500. For the 40 percent of the estates for which no inventory was filed, he assumed that these were of the same size and distribution as those filed with inventories. (He excluded estates owned by females from his analysis.) He found the number of nonprobated estates by observing from the census that the number of deaths of males aged 25 and over for the three periods exceeded the number of estates filed. This summary relies on Merwin 1939; the $500 limit is discussed in A. A. Young, 1916.

12. I observed that costs of probate, though not negligible, were small, and I believe they were probably not a major deterrent. Costs of estate administration for many of the sample cases are indicated in section II of *American Colonial Wealth* in editorially condensed estate accounts.

13. To transfer legal title to land in New England, probate was required, and this is the reason that sometimes, many years after death, a probate inventory was filed at a time when it was desired to convey the land to a new owner who required a legal title. This information was obtained in a conversation with Mr. Frank E. Tuitt, II, Register of Probate of Hampshire County, Massachusetts, at the county courthouse in Northampton, Massachusetts, in the late summer of 1969. Land in New England, apparently at least, sometimes descended to heirs informally and was sometimes purchased informally without legal title. In the other regions, title to inherited land was clearly not dependent upon its being included in a probate inventory, since, with a few exceptions in Pennsylvania, it was omitted in all the sample inventories south of New England.

14. For an expanded statement of the reasoning in reaching the fraction one-fourth for the middle colonies, see Jones 1970:117.

15. See Jones 1970:137–38 for a calculation of the effect upon the per capita wealth estimate when the size of nonprobate-type wealth is placed nearer possible outer limits, as low as 10 percent or as high as 50 percent of the wealth of the probate type. Under these two alternate extreme assumptions, per capita wealth for the

total living population in Pennsylvania, New Jersey, and Delaware could go down by as much as 7 percent or up by as much as 13 percent. Even if we were to adopt one of these changed wealth levels for our 1774 base point, however, the consequent change in the growth rate over a period of years is small, a revision on the order of 0.1 percent a year up or down.

16. The conversion factor for tables for the South in the first edition of *American Colonial Wealth,* using Variant One weighting, is 0.7975. Under our preferred Variant Two weighting for the South, discussed in part two of this appendix, it becomes 0.760, the number appropriate for tables in the present volume.

17. For an alternate assumption A, which places all the nonprobates in lower wealth levels, and a fuller statement of assumption B, see *American Colonial Wealth,* either edition, pp. 1889–99 and 1924.

18. The nonprobate-type distribution never appears separately as such. It is incorporated, weighted by the nonprobate ratio, with the distribution of the probate-types, weighted by the probate ratio, to yield a combined all-weathholder size distribution. All this is accomplished by the $w*B$ weights.

19. Phillips 1905 (1971 rpt.):51–52. Speaking of slave values in the antebellum period, he says: "appraisal values were . . . less accurate than actual market prices. . . . The majority of the sales of which records are to be found were those of slaves in the estates of deceased persons. These sales were at auction; and except in abnormal cases, which may often be distinguished, they may be taken as fairly representative of slave prices for the time and place."

20. Bean 1975:1174. Mr. Bean has stated that his values are for prime-age adult male slaves in Jamaica and that one would add an estimated £5 transport cost to get the corresponding figure at Charleston, through which port virtually all imports of slaves were coming at this period. Telephone conversation, June 21, 1977.

21. I am indebted to Mr. Engerman for telephone conversations of July 1 and 2, 1977, and for a confirming computer listing of slave values by age and sex from probate inventories of Anne Arundel County, Maryland from 1771 through 1778.

22. In the case of the slave figure, using Variant One weights, the Charleston District contributed 47 percent to the total for the South (see discussion of the Charleston contribution later in this appendix).

23. An exchange rate adjustment of 9 percent times the 47 percent mentioned in note 22 would lower the aggregate or average slave figures for the South as a whole by .09 times .47, or .0423; i.e., by about 4.2 percent, if the weight accorded to the Charleston contribution remained as in Variant One.

24. I recognize that that assumption is more acceptable for total wealth than for more specific wealth subcategories, as slaves, land, consumers' goods, and so forth. Perhaps nonprobates in the South had virtually no slaves, rarely held land, and had consumers' goods not far behind those of probates. We can dream up other possibilities to vary the figure for specific wealth categories. If any new source of systematic appraisal of wealth of nonprobate types could be found, it would improve our knowledge of wealth in the late colonial period. However, in view of the scant present basis for my value for h, not to mention the horrendous increase in complexity of weighting if it were to vary by wealth category, I conclude that no change is in order. See further discussion in part three of this appendix.

25. See discussion of county weights in section one of this appendix and *American Colonial Wealth,* either edition, table 5.5.

26. This percentage is different for each kind of wealth, depending on the amount of that kind held by Charleston vis-à-vis the other seven areas. The cor-

responding percentage contributed by Charleston using Variant One weights for "net worth" is 33, for "total physical wealth" 31, and for "total physical wealth minus slaves and servants" 20 percent.

27. The sample plan, which draws one county (or county group) from each stratum, does not imply that the wealth of each particular sample county epitomizes the wealth of its stratum. Rather, the choice of the random numbers for an entire region yield a group of counties, some perhaps of high, others of low wealth, whose combined wealth gives an unbiased regional average. If many samples were drawn from the same frame, varying counties, with varying wealths would be drawn each time. The central limit theorem mentioned in a footnote to the Note on Method tells us that the mean wealths of successive regional samples, when plotted, would approach the shape of the curve of a normal distribution.

28. It was possible to make the retabulation, still using the initially calculated w weight for each southern sample decedent, by an instruction in the computer program. The program simply calls for multiplying each former Charleston w weight by $.01/.125$ and multiplying each w weight in the other southern clusters by $(.99/7)/.125$.

29. Use of Variant Two weights does not affect the mean values within each county-cluster. That is, the w-weighted values by county, in tables 7.134–7.141 of *American Colonial Wealth*, either edition, are identical to those of table B.3 of the present volume. The w^*-weighted values (table B.4) within each cluster change slightly with the change in the probate ratio assumed for the South and used also for each cluster within the southern samples. The regional averages for the South as a whole change under Variant Two at all levels of weights, the c-, w-, and w^*-weighted levels. The c- and w-weighted averages are affected by the change in the county weight for Charleston. The w^*-weighted averages reflect that change and also the change in the probate ratio.

30. I still believe that I was fortunate to draw Charleston into my particular sample to learn what was probably near the upper limit of wealth in the colonies. Even with Charleston in, I may very well not have the richest fortune in the colonies in the sample, since small samples may easily miss the highest wealth individual cases. (See Gallman 1969:18–21; Kish 1965:410–12.) In this study, the chance not only of which counties should be drawn but, within the sample counties, of which rich people happened to die in 1774 affect the results. That wealth is a variable whose distribution is skewed is, however, a separate point from the one that this particular sample including Charleston was an outlier.

31. I do not offer size distribution by the stronger total of portable physical wealth (or portable physical wealth plus financial assets, which total in Jones 1970 I called gross portable wealth) for two reasons. The first is that, lacking the real estate component, it is only a partial total of physical wealth. The second is simply economy of space and effort. For researchers who may desire such figures, they can be calculated from the individual decedent values and weights available either on tape deposited at Ann Arbor, or from the values in table 8.1 of *American Colonial Wealth*, either edition.

32. A letter to the author from Simon Kuznets (1978) makes five interesting points. (1) He reminds me that the capital-output ratio varies considerably, depending on whether the reproducible wealth measured is gross or net of depreciation. (In this study, the inventory values, being resale values, are net.) (2) He notes need for clarity as to whether the wealth is domestically owned as well as located; and whether the product is domestic, originating from domestically located wealth, or

national, originating from wealth owned by the country's inhabitants. That is, are the capital-output ratios domestic or national ratios for the colonies or for the other countries? (3) He suggests that the "free" components of colonial income (gathered from the countryside) that I mention may affect the relevance of capital-output ratios for older countries that have no (or much smaller) "free" components in final output. (4) He reminds me that since income from consumers' durables (except housing) is not usually included under final output, these durables should be excluded from wealth (in the calculation of the capital-output ratios). (5) "There are, and must have been in the past, wide differentials in the capital-output ratios for various large groups of capital goods—with high ratios for housing, fixed capital utilities and the like, and low ratios for manufacturing and agriculture (if land is excluded). Since you have the components, and some information on the differences in capital-output ratios, why not try a disaggregated approach?" He concludes: "These are the questions that come to mind. Your ratios and conclusions are plausible, but if the estimate of income is to have some independent value, the precise coverage of the ratios and a more disaggregated approach would seem to me worthwhile." The magnitude of the task suggested by Kuznets is beyond my capacity within the limits of this study and I must leave it as a challenge for future scholars.

33. Jones 1970:129. The wealth figure was used by Gallman 1972 (his table 2.3, p. 24) together with other data to estimate factor inputs and economic growth rates for the United States from 1774 to 1840.

34. If I understand correctly his price conversions as traced by Shepherd and Williamson 1972:801, n. 18. Since my conversions in table 1.2 differ somewhat from the Warren and Pearson price index used by Gallman to move to 1840 dollars and from the conversion from pounds sterling to American dollars at the rate of the old Spanish dollars, I translate my £10.7 sterling for thirteen colonies in 1774 as $52 in dollars of 1840 purchasing power, a slightly lower figure than Gallman's conversion.

35. Deane 1956, quoted by Pollard 1968:337. See also Deane 1955:9–14; Deane and Cole 1967:271 ff.; Crouzet 1972:20–21, 27.

36. See his own statement as to the limitations of his income figures in Young 1771:4:393 and appraisal of the accuracy of his estimates by Deane 1955:24.

APPENDIX C

1. Since I am looking at the specific relation between age and wealth, and do not wish to bring in the age correction to the living age structure, I use c weights. These keep the estimates at the probated-decedent level, but prevent the domination of the results by cases from the counties where most cases were obtained in the sample (see appendix A). These counties were principally Suffolk and Essex in Massachusetts and Philadelphia in Pennsylvania. The modified c weights perform the same function but are slightly altered to permit the sum of the c weights of the subsample to sum to one.

2. Soltow, 1971a, p. 45, 46; 1971b, p. 839; and 1975a, pp. 109–110, 115, 183.

Bibliography

American husbandry. 1775. 2 vols. London: J. Bew. Reprint, 1939, Harry J. Carmen, ed. New York: Columbia University Press; 1964, Port Washington, N.Y.: Kennikat Press.

Anderson, Terry L. 1975a. Wealth estimates for the New England colonies, 1650–1709. *Explor. Ec. Hist.* 12:151–76.

—— 1975b. *The economic growth of seventeenth-century New England: A measurement of regional income.* New York. Arno Press.

—— 1979. Economic growth in colonial New England: "Statistical renaissance." *Jour. Ec. Hist.* 39:243–57.

Andreano, Ralph. 1965. *New views on American economic development.* Cambridge, Mass.: Schenkman.

Andrews, Charles M. 1918. Current lawful money of New England. *Amer. Hist. Rev.* 24.73–77.

Anonymous. 1741. *The British Empire in America.* 2 vols. London.

Atkinson, A. B. 1970. On the measurement of inequality. *Jour. Ec. Theory* 2:244–63.

—— 1972. Distribution of wealth in Britain—the estate duty re-examined. Paper prepared for Conference on Income and Wealth, National Bureau of Economic Research, July 1972. Mimeographed.

Bailyn, Bernard. 1962. Political experience and enlightenment ideas in eighteenth-century America. *Amer. Hist. Rev.* 67:339–51.

Ball, Duane, E. 1973. The process of settlement in eighteenth-century Chester County, Pennsylvania: A social and economic history. Ph.D. diss., University of Pennsylvania.

—— 1976. Dynamics of population and wealth in eighteenth-century Chester County, Pennsylvania. *Jour. Interdisciplinary Hist.* 6:621–44.

Ball, Duane E., and Gary M. Walton. 1976. Agricultural productivity change in eighteenth-century Pennsylvania. *Jour. Ec. Hist.* 36:102–17.

Barrett, James P., and Leland Goldsmith. 1976. When is n sufficiently large? *Amer. Statis.* 30:67–70.

Basler, Roy P., ed., 1946. *Abraham Lincoln: His speeches and writings.* Cleveland: World.

Baxter, William T. 1945. *The house of Hancock: Business in Boston 1724–1775.* Harvard studies in business history. Cambridge: Harvard University Press.

Bean, Richard N. 1975. British-American and West African slave prices, 1638–42 to 1773–75. Ser. Z-165-168. In U.S. Bureau of the Census, *Historical Statistics of the United States, colonial times to 1970, Part 2.* Washington, D.C.

—— 1977. Telephone conversation with author, June 21, 1977.

Beard, Charles A. 1913. *An economic interpretation of the constitution of the United States.* Reprint, 1960. New York: Macmillan.

Becker, Gary S. 1975. *Human Capital.* 2d ed. New York: Columbia University Press for the National Bureau of Economic Research.

Belz, Herman. 1965. Paper money in colonial Massachusetts. Essex Institute, *Histor. Collections.* 101:149–63.

Bennett, M. K. 1955. The food economy of the New England Indians, 1605–75. *Jour. Polit. Econ.* 43:369–97.

Bergstrom, Theodore. 1971. On the existence and optimality of competitive equilibrium for a slave economy. *Rev. Ec. Stud.* 38:23–36.

Berthoff, Rowland W. 1960. The American social order: A conservative hypothesis. *Amer. Hist. Rev.* 45:495–514.

Beveridge, Sir William, et al. 1939. *Prices and wages in England from the twelfth to the nineteenth century.* vol. 1. London: Longmans, Green.

Bezanson, Anne, R. D. Gray, and M. Hussey. 1935. *Prices in colonial Pennsylvania.* Philadelphia: University of Pennsylvania Press.

Bezanson, Anne, B. Daley, M. Denison, and M. Hussey. 1951. *Prices and inflation during the American Revolution, Pennsylvania, 1770–1790.* Philadelphia: University of Pennsylvania Press.

Bidwell, Percy W., and John T. Falconer. 1925. *A history of agriculture in the northern United States, 1620–1860.* Carnegie Institution of Washington Publication no. 358. Reprint, 1941. New York: P. Smith.

Billias, George A. 1976. *Elbridge Gerry: Founding father and republican statesman.* New York: McGraw-Hill.

Blodget, Samuel. 1806. *Economica: A statistical manual for the United States of America.* Washington. Reprint, 1964. New York: Augustus M. Kelley.

Blumin, Stuart. 1969. Mobility and change in ante-bellum Philadelphia. In Stephan Thernstrom and Richard Sennett, eds. *Nineteenth-century cities: Essays in the new urban history.* New Haven: Yale University Press.

Bowman, Mary Jean. 1945. A graphical analysis of personal income distribution in the U.S. *Amer. Ec. Rev.* 35:607–28.

Brady, Dorothy S. 1956. Family saving, 1888 to 1950. In R. W. Goldsmith, D. Brady, and H. Mendershausen, *A study of saving in the United States.* Vol. 3. Princeton: Princeton University Press.

Bridenbaugh, Carl. 1955. *Cities in revolt: Urban life in America, 1743–1776.* New York: Alfred A. Knopf.

Brissot de Warville, Jacques Pierre. (1791) 1964. *New travels in the United States of America, 1788.* Trans. Mara Soceanu Vamos and Durand Echeverria. Ed. Durand Echeverria. Cambridge, Mass.: Belknap Press of Harvard University Press.

Brock, Leslie V. 1975. *The currency of the American colonies 1700–1764: A study in colonial finance and imperial relations.* New York: Arno Press.

Bronfenbrenner, Martin, 1972. *Income distribution theory.* Chicago: Aldine-Atherton Press.

Brown, Robert E. 1955. *Middle-class democracy and revolution in Massachusetts, 1691–1780.* Ithaca, N.Y.: Cornell University Press for the American Historical Association.

—— 1956. *Charles Beard and the Constitution: A critical analysis of "An economic interpretation of the Constitution."* Princeton: Princeton University Press.

Bruchey, Stuart, ed. 1966. *The colonial merchant.* New York: Harcourt, Brace & World.

—— 1968. *The roots of American economic growth, 1607–1861.* New York: Harper & Row, Torchbook ed.

—— 1975. *Growth of the modern American economy.* New York: Dodd, Mead.

—— 1976. Letter to author, April 8, 1976.

Bureau of Statistics of Labor (Massachusetts). 1895. See Wright, Carroll D. 1895.

Campbell, Randolph B., and Richard G. Lowe. 1977. *Wealth and power in antebellum Texas.* College Station: Texas A & M University Press.

Cappon, Lester J. ed. 1976. *Atlas of early American history.* Princeton: Princeton University Press for the Newberry Library and the Institute of Early American History and Culture.

Carr, Lois Green. 1975. Letter to author dated December 4, 1975.

—— 1977. Letter to author dated April 21, 1977.

Carr, Lois Green, and Russell R. Menard. 1979. Servants and freedmen in early colonial Maryland. In Thad W. Tate and David L. Ammerman, eds. *The Chesapeake in the seventeenth century: Essays on Anglo-American society and politics.* Chapel Hill, N.C.: University of North Carolina Press for the Institute of Early American History and Culture.

Carr, Lois Green, and Lorena S. Walsh. 1976. How colonial tobacco planters lived: Consumption patterns in St. Mary's County, Maryland, 1658–1777. Paper delivered at the Southern Historical Association meeting, November 1976.

Cash, Margaret, ed. 1966. *Devon inventories of the sixteenth and seventeenth centuries*. Devon and Cornwall Record Society, n.s., vol. 11. Torquay: Devonshire Press.

Christensen, Laurits R., and Dale W. Jorgenson. 1973. U.S. income, savings and wealth, 1929–1969. *Rev. Income and Wealth* 19:329–62.

Clemens, Paul G. E. 1977. Economy and society on Maryland's eastern shore, 1689–1733. Aubrey C. Land, Lois Green Carr, and Edward C. Papenfuse, eds, *Law, society and politics in early Maryland*. Baltimore: Johns Hopkins University Press.

Cochran, Thomas C. 1975. The paradox of American economic growth. *Jour. Amer. Hist*. 61:925–42.

Cochran, William G. 1963. *Sampling techniques*. 2d ed. New York: John Wiley & Sons.

Cole, Arthur H. 1938. *Wholesale commodity prices in the United States, 1700–1861*. Cambridge, Mass.: Harvard University Press.

—— 1956. Letter to author dated March 5, 1956.

Collier, Christopher. 1978. Wood smoke nostalgia. In *Conoco* 9, no. 4: 17–18. High Ridge Park, Stamford, Conn.: Continental Oil Co.

—— 1979. Letter to author dated September 7, 1979.

Colquhoun, Patrick. 1815. *A treatise on the wealth, power and resources of the British empire*. London. 2d. ed.

Conrad, Alfred H., and John R. Meyer. 1964. *The economics of slavery and other studies in econometric history*. Chicago: Aldine. Chapter 3.

Cook, Edward M., Jr. 1970. Social behavior and changing values in Dedham, Mass. 1700–1775. *Wm. & Mary Quart*. 3d. ser. 27:546–80.

—— 1971. Local leadership and the typology of New England towns, 1700–1785. *Pol. Sci. Quart*. 86:586–608.

—— 1976. *The fathers of the towns: Leadership and community structure in eighteenth-century New England*. Baltimore: Johns Hopkins University Press.

Cornfield, Jerome. 1944. On samples of finite populations. *Jour. Amer. Statis. Assoc*. 39:236–39.

Crandall, Ruth, 1971. *Tax and valuation lists of Massachusetts towns before 1776: Finding list for the microfilm edition*. Cambridge, Mass.: Charles Warren Center for Studies in Amer. History.

Crevecoeur, Michel Guillaume Hector St. John de. 1782. *Letters from an American farmer*. London. Reprint, 1793, Philadelphia: Carey. Reprint, 1951, New York: E. P. Dutton.

Crouse, Maurice A. 1964. The Manigault family of South Carolina, 1685–1783. Ph.D. diss., Northwestern University.

Crouzet, François, ed. 1972. *Capital formation in the Industrial Revolution*. London: Methuen.

Daniels, Bruce C. 1973. Family dynasties in Connecticut's largest towns,

1700–1760. *Canadian Jour. Hist. Annales Canadiennes d'Histoire.* 8:99–110.

——1973–74. Long range trends in wealth distribution in eighteenth-century New England. *Explor. Ec. Hist.* (Winter) 11:123–36.

—— 1975a. Large town officeholding in eighteenth-century Connecticut: The growth of oligarchy. *Jour. Amer. Studies* 9:1–12.

—— 1975b. Democracy and oligarchy in Connecticut towns, 1701–1790. *Soc. Sci. Quart.* 56:460–75.

—— 1976a. Emerging urbanism and increasing social stratification in the era of the American Revolution. In John Ferling, ed., *The American revolution: The home front.* Carrollton, Ga.: West Georgia College Press.

—— 1976b. Probate court inventories and colonial American history: Historiography, problems, and results. *Histoire Sociale/Social History* 9:387–405.

—— 1977. Connecticut's villages become mature towns: The complexity of local institutions, 1676 to 1776. *Wm. & Mary Quart.* 3d ser. 34:83–103.

Daumard, Adeline. 1963. *La Bourgeoisie parisienne de 1815 à 1848.* École pratique des hautes études, 6ᵉ section, Centre de recherches historiques. Démographie et sociétés no. 8 Paris: SEVPEN.

David, Paul A. 1967a. New light on a statistical dark age: U.S. real product growth before 1840. *Amer. Ec. Rev.* 57:294–306.

—— 1967b. The growth of real product in the United States before 1840: New evidence and controlled conjectures. *Jour. Ec. Hist.* 27:151–97.

David, Paul A., et al. 1976. *Reckoning with slavery.* New York: Oxford University Press.

Davie, Maurice R. 1936. *World immigration.* New York: Macmillan.

Davis, Lance E., et al. 1972. *American economic growth: An economist's history of the United States.* New York: Harper & Row.

Davis, Lance E., and Robert E. Gallman. 1973. The share of savings and investment in gross national product during the 19th century in the U.S.A. In *Fourth International Conference of Economic History.* (Proceedings, Bloomington, 1968). The Hague: Mouton.

Davisson, William I. 1967a. Essex county price trends: Money and markets in seventeenth-century Massachusetts. Essex Institute, *Histor. Collections.* 103:144–85.

—— 1967b. Essex County wealth trends: Wealth and economic growth in seventeenth-century Massachusetts. Essex Institute, *Histor. Collections.* 103:291–342.

Deane, Phyllis. 1955. The implications of early national income estimates for the measurement of long-term economic growth in the United Kingdom. *Ec. Develop. and Cult. Change* 4:3–38.

—— 1956. Contemporary estimates of national income in the first half of the nineteenth century. *Ec. Hist. Rev.* 2d ser. 8:339–54.

—— 1961. Capital formation in Britain before the railway age. *Ec. Develop. and Cult. Change.* 9:352–68. Reprinted in Crouzet 1972:94–118.

Deane, Phyllis, and W. A. Cole 1967. *British economic growth, 1688–1959: Trends and structure.* 2d ed. Cambridge University, Department of applied economics, Monographs, no. 8. Cambridge: Cambridge University Press.

Demos, John. 1970. *A little commonwealth: Family life in Plymouth colony.* New York and London: Oxford University Press.

De Smedt, Helma. 1970. *Antwerpen en de opbloei van de vlaamse vérhandel tijdens de 16ᵉ eeuw: rijkdom en inkomen van de Antwerpse koopman Jan Gamel volgens zijn staat van goed, 1572.* (The growth of the Antwerp market and the revival of active international trading by Flemish merchants in the 16th century: Analysis accompanied by some wealth and income estimates for the Antwerp merchant Jan Gamel, derived from his inventory after death, 1572.) Licentiaat diss., University of Leuven.

Doherty, Robert. 1971. Property distribution in America, 1800–1860. Paper presented at meeting of the Organization of American Historians, New Orleans, April 1971. Mimeographed.

—— 1977. *Society and power: Five New England towns, 1800–1860.* Amherst: University of Massachusetts Press.

Earle, Alice Morse. 1898. *Home life in colonial days.* Reprint, 1974. Stockbridge, Mass.: Berkshire Traveller Press.

Egnal, Marc. 1975. The economic development of the thirteen continental colonies, 1720 to 1775. *Wm. & Mary Quart.* 3d ser. 32:191–222.

Eltis, Walter A. 1975. François Quesnay: A reinterpretation. 1. The tableau economique. 2. The theory of economic growth. *Oxford Economic Papers* 27:167–200, 327–351.

Engel, C. L. Ernst. 1883. *Der Kostenwerth des Menschen.* Berlin. Also 1931 article on Engel, Christian Lorenz Ernst in *Encyclopedia of Social Sciences* 5:539–40. New York: Macmillan.

Engerman, Stanley L. 1967. Discussion (of Paul A. David, The growth of real product in the United States before 1840). *Amer. Ec. Rev.* 57:307–11.

—— 1973a. Some considerations relating to property rights in man. *Jour. Ec. Hist.* 33:43–65.

—— 1973b. Review of Shepherd and Walton, Shipping, maritime trade, and the economic development of colonial North America. *Wm. & Mary Quart.* 3d ser. 30:332–34.

—— 1977a. Telephone conversations with author July 1 and 2, 1977.

—— 1977b. Letter to author dated December 2, 1977.

—— 1978a. Letter to author dated March 14, 1978.

—— 1978b. Letter to author dated July 8, 1978.

—— 1979. Letter to author dated April 7, 1979.

Ernst, Joseph. 1973. *Money and politics in America, 1755–1775: A study in the currency act of 1764 and the political economy of revolution.* Chapel Hill: University of North Carolina Press for the Institute of Early American History and Culture.

Explorations in Economic History. 1975. (October.) 12:333–457. Issue devoted to discussion of Fogel and Engerman, *Time on the cross.*

Fairfax County, Virginia. 1772–74. *Fairfax County Order Book.* Record book at county courthouse. Microfilm copy available at Virginia State Library, Richmond, Virginia.

Federal Trade Commission. 1926. *Report: National wealth and income.* 69th Cong., 1st Sess., Senate Doc. No. 126.

Feinstein, Charles H. 1978a. Capital formation in Great Britain. In *The Cambridge Economic History of Europe.* Vol. 7. Cambridge: Cambridge University Press.

—— 1978b. Letter to author dated December 19, 1978.

Ferguson, E. James. 1953. Currency finance: An interpretation of colonial monetary practices. *Wm. & Mary Quart.* 3d ser. 10:153–80.

Fisher, Irving. 1906. *The nature of capital and income.* New York: Macmillan.

Fishlow, Albert. 1964. Discussion (of Gordon Bjork's Weaning the American economy). *Jour. Ec. Hist.* 24:561–66.

Fogel, Robert W. 1971. Railroads and American economic growth. In Robert W. Fogel and Stanley L. Engerman, eds., *The reinterpretation of American economic history.* New York: Harper & Row.

Fogel, Robert W., and Stanley L. Engerman. 1974a. *Time on the cross.* Vol. 1. *The economics of American negro slavery.* Boston: Little, Brown.

—— 1974b. *Time on the cross.* Vol. 2. *Evidence and methods—a supplement.* Boston: Little, Brown.

—— 1977. Explaining the relative efficiency of slave agriculture in the antebellum south. *Amer. Ec. Rev.* 67:275–96.

Formann, Benno M. 1971. Salem tradesmen and craftsmen circa 1762. Essex Institute, *Histor. Collections* 107:62–81.

French, Richard Edward. 1970. *An estimate of personal wealth in Oklahoma in 1960.* University of Florida, Social Sciences Monograph no. 39. Gainesville, Fla: Starter Printing Co.

Friedman, Milton. 1957. *A theory of the consumption function.* National Bureau of Economic Research, study no. 63, gen. ser. Princeton: Princeton University Press.

Friis, Herman R. 1968. *A series of population maps of the colonies and the*

United States, 1625-1790. New York: Amer. Geog. Soc., Mimeo. and Offset Pub. no. 3 revised.

Galenson, David W. 1977. Immigration and the colonial labor system: An analysis of the length of indenture. *Explor. Ec. Hist.* 14:360-77.

—— 1978a. British servants and the colonial indenture system in the eighteenth century. *Jour. South. Hist.* 44:41-66.

—— 1978b. "Middling people" or "common sort"?: The social origins of some early Americans reexamined. *Wm. & Mary Quart.* 3d ser. 35: 499-524.

—— 1979. The slave trade to the English West Indies. 1673-1724. *Ec. Hist. Rev.* 32:241-2.

Gallman, Robert E. 1960. Commodity output, 1839-1899. In William N. Parker, ed., *Trends in the American economy in the nineteenth century.* Conference on research in income and wealth, Studies in income and wealth, vol. 24, National Bureau of Economic Research. Princeton: Princeton University Press.

—— 1966. Gross national product in the United States, 1834-1909. In Dorothy S. Brady, ed. *Output, employment and productivity in the United States after 1800.* Conference on research in income and wealth, Studies in income and wealth, vol. 30, National Bureau of Economic Research. New York: Columbia University Press.

—— 1968. The social distribution of wealth in the United States of America. In *Third International Conference of Economic History.* (Proceedings, Munich, 1965). The Hague: Mouton.

—— 1969. Trends in the size distribution of wealth in the nineteenth century: Some speculations. In Lee Soltow, ed., *Six Papers on the size distribution of wealth and income.* Conference on income and wealth, Studies in income and wealth, vol. 33, National Bureau of Economic Research. New York: Columbia University Press.

—— 1972. The pace and pattern of American economic growth. In Lance E. Davis et al., *American economic growth: An economist's history of the United States.* New York: Harper & Row.

—— 1973. Letter to author dated October 1, 1973.

—— 1977a. Human capital in the first 80 years of the republic: How much did America owe the rest of the world? *Amer. Ec. Rev.* 67:27-31.

—— 1977b. Letter to author dated December 28, 1977.

—— 1978. Professor Pessen on the "egalitarian myth." *Soc. Sci. Hist.* 12:194-207.

—— 1979. Comment (on papers by T. L. Anderson, J. D. Haeger, A. Kulikoff and D. Lindstrom). *Jour. Ec. Hist.* 39:311-12.

Gallman, Robert E., and Ralph V. Anderson. 1977. Slaves as fixed capital: Slave labor and southern economic development. *Jour. Amer. Hist.* 64:24-46.

Gallman, Robert E., and Edward S. Howle. 1971. Trends in the structure of the American economy since 1840. In Robert W. Fogel and Stanley L. Engerman, Eds., *The reinterpretation of American economic history.* New York: Harper & Row.

Genovese, Eugene D. 1974. *Roll, Jordan, roll.* New York: Random House.

George, M. Dorothy. 1925. *London life in the eighteenth century.* Reprint, 1951. Series of Reprints of Scarce Works on Political Economy, no. 12. London: London School of Economics and Political Science.

Gilboy, Elizabeth W. 1936. The cost of living and real wages in eighteenth-century England. *Rev. Ec. Stat.* 18:134–43.

Gini, Corrado. 1912. *Variabilità e mutabilità: contributo allo studio delle distribuzione e delle relazioni statistiche.* Bologna: Tipografia di Paolo Cuppini.

Glass, D. V. 1965. Two papers on Gregory King. In D. V. Glass and D. E. C. Eversley, eds. *Population in history: Essays in historical demography.* London: Edward Arnold.

Goldsmith, Raymond W. 1952. The growth of reproducible wealth of the United States of America from 1805–1950. In Simon Kuznets, ed. *Income and wealth of the United States: Trends and structure.* International association for research in income and wealth, Income and wealth series, vol. 2. Baltimore: Johns Hopkins Press. Cambridge: Bowes and Bowes.

—— 1959. Historical and comparative rates of production, productivity and prices. *Hearings* before the Joint Economic Committee, 86th Cong., 1st sess., pt. 2 (April 7, 1959), pp. 220–79. Washington: Government Printing Office. (Reprint, see Goldsmith 1965.)

—— 1962. *The national wealth of the United States in the postwar period.* National Bureau of Economic Research study. Princeton: Princeton University Press.

—— 1965. Long period growth in income and product, 1839–1969. In Ralph L. Andreano, ed., *New views on American economic development.* Cambridge Mass: Schenkman. (Reprint of testimony before the Joint Economic Committee, April 7, 1959.)

—— 1968. National wealth: Estimation. In *International encyclopedia of the social sciences.* 11:50–58. New York: Macmillan.

Goodfriend, Joyce D. 1975. Too great a mixture of nations: The development of New York city society in the seventeenth century. Ph.D. diss., University of California at Los Angeles.

Gottman, Jean. 1957. Megalopolis. *Econ. Geog.* 33:189–200.

Goubert, Pierre. 1960. *Beauvais et le beauvaisis de 1600 à 1730: Contribution a l'histoire sociale de la France du 17ᵉ siècle.* École pratique des hautes études, 6ᵉ section, Centre de recherches historiques. Démographie et sociétés, no. 3. Paris: SEVPEN.

Grant, Charles S. 1961. *Democracy in the Connecticut frontier town of Kent.* New York: Columbia University Press.

Gray, Lewis C. 1932. *History of Agriculture in the southern United States to 1860.* Reprint, 1958. Gloucester, Mass.: Peter Smith. Vol. I.

Greven, Philip J., Jr., 1970. *Four generations: Population land and family in colonial Andover, Massachusetts.* Ithaca, N.Y.: Cornell University Press.

Gross, Robert A. 1976. *The minutemen and their world.* New York: Hill and Wang.

Guenther, William C. 1965. *Techniques of statistical inference.* New York: McGraw Hill.

Gwyn, Julian. 1971. Money lending in New England: The case of Admiral Sir Peter Warren and his heirs, 1739–1805. *New Eng. Quart.* 44:117–34.

—— 1974. *The enterprising admiral: The personal fortune of Admiral Sir Peter Warren.* Montreal: McGill-Queen's University Press.

Hagood, Margaret J., and Daniel O. Price. 1952. *Statistics for sociologists.* Rev. ed. New York: Holt, Rinehart and Winston.

Hanson, Alice C., and Jerome Cornfield. 1942. Spending and saving of the nation's families in wartime. *Monthly Labor Review* 55:700–13. Rev. ed., U.S. Bureau of Labor Statistics *Bulletin* no. 724.

Hanson, Alice C., Jerome Cornfield, and Lenore A. Epstein. 1942. Income and spending and saving of city families in wartime. *Monthly Labor Review* 55:419–34. Rev. ed., U.S. Bureau of Labor Statistics *Bulletin*, no. 723.

Harbury, C. D., and P. C. McMahon. 1973. Inheritance and the characteristics of top wealth leavers in Britain. *Ec. Jour.* 83:810–33.

Hartsook, Elizabeth, and Gust Skordas. 1946. *Land office and prerogative court records of Maryland.* Annapolis: Hall of Records Commission. Reprint, 1967. Baltimore: Genealogical Publishing.

Hast, Adele. 1969. The legal status of the negro in Virginia, 1705–1765. *Jour. Negro Hist.* 54:217–39.

Heavner, Robert O. 1978a. Indentured servitude: The Philadelphia market, 1771–1773. *Jour. Ec. Hist.* 38:701–13.

—— 1978b. *Economic aspects of indentured servitude in colonial Philadelphia.* New York: Arno Press.

Henretta, James A. 1965. Economic development and social structure in colonial Boston. *Wm. & Mary Quart.* 3d ser. 25:75–92.

—— 1973. *The evolution of American society, 1700–1815: An interdisciplinary analysis.* Lexington, Mass.: D. C. Heath.

Herrick, Cheesman A. 1926. *White servitude in Pennsylvania.* Philadelphia: McVey.

Historical Statistics. See U.S. Bureau of the Census. (Historical Statistics).

Hoenack, Stephen A. 1964. Historical censuses and estimates of wealth in the United States. In *Measuring the nation's wealth*. George Washington University, Wealth inventory planning study. Conference on research in income and wealth, Studies in income and wealth, vol. 29. National Bureau of Economic Research. Washington, D.C.: Government Printing Office.

Hofstadter, Richard. 1972. *America at 1750: A social portrait*. New York: Alfred A. Knopf.

Holmes, George K. 1893. The concentration of wealth. *Pol. Sci. Quart.* 8:589–600.

Hughes, Jonathan R. T. 1976. *Social control in the colonial economy*. Charlottesville: University Press of Virginia.

Ippolito, Richard A. 1975. The effect of the "agricultural depression" on industrial demand in England: 1730–1750. *Economica* 42:298–312.

Johnson, Harold B., Jr. 1977. Death and society in Portuguese Estremadura, 1672–1707. Unpublished MS., University of Virginia. Professor Johnson indicates that there is a splendid collection of probate inventories in the Brazilian National Archives in Rio de Janeiro for the city and its region circa 1770–1900.

Jones, Alice Hanson. 1969. La fortune privée en Pennsylvanie, New Jersey, Delaware. 1774. *Annales: Economies, Sociétés, Civilisations* 24, no. 2 (March–April):235–49.

—— 1970. Wealth estimates for the American middle colonies, 1774. *Econ. Develop. and Cult. Change* 18, no. 4, pt. 2 (supp. 172 pp.)

—— 1971. *Wealth distribution in the American middle colonies in the third quarter of the eighteenth century*. Paper presented at meeting of Organization of American Historians, New Orleans, April. St. Louis: Department of Economics, Washington University. Mimeographed.

—— 1972. Wealth estimates for the New England colonies about 1770. *Jour. Ec. Hist.* 32:98–127.

—— 1977. *American colonial wealth: Documents and methods*. 3 vols. New York: Arno Press.

—— 1978. *American colonial wealth: Documents and methods*. 3 vols. 2d ed., rev. New York: Arno Press.

Jordan, Winthrop D. 1968. *White over black: American attitudes toward the Negro, 1550–1812*. Chapel Hill: University of North Carolina Press for the Institute of Early American History and Culture.

Kalm, Peter. 1770. *Travels into North America*. London: T. Lowndes. 3 vols. Revised and retranslated from the Swedish, 1937. Adolph B. Benson, ed. *The America of 1750: Peter Kalm's travels in North America*. New York: Wilson-Erickson. 2 vols.

Katz, Michael B. 1972. Occupational classification in history. *Jour. Interdisciplinary Hist.* 3:63–88.

Kendrick, John W. 1967. The wealth of the United States. *Finance,* January: 10 ff.

—— 1968. National income and product accounts. *International encyclopedia of the social sciences* 11:19–33.

—— 1974. The accounting treatment of human investment and capital. *Rev. Income and Wealth.* 20:439–68.

Kendrick, John W., Kyu Sik Lee, and Jean Lomask. 1976. *The national wealth of the United States, by major sector and industry.* New York: The Conference Board.

King, Gregory. (1688) 1936. *Two tracts.* Ed. by George E. Barnett. Baltimore: The Johns Hopkins Press.

King, Willford I. 1915. *Wealth and income of the people of the United States.* New York: Macmillan.

—— 1926. Tables 10 through 19 on distribution of wealth in the United States as indicated by estates of 43,512 decedents in selected counties (1912–1923). In Federal Trade Commission, *Report: National wealth and income.* 69th Cong., 1st sess. (1926), Senate Doc. no. 126, pp. 58–68.

—— 1927. Wealth distribution in the continental United States at the close of 1921. *Jour. Amer. Statis. Assoc.* 22:135–53.

Kish, Leslie. 1965. *Survey sampling.* New York: John Wiley & Sons.

Klingaman, David. 1969. The significance of grain in the development of the tobacco colonies. *Jour. Ec. Hist.* 26:268–78.

—— 1971. Food surpluses and deficits in the American colonies, 1768–1772. *Jour. Ec. Hist.* 31:553–69.

Koch, Donald W. 1969. Income distribution and political structure in seventeenth-century Salem, Massachusetts. Essex Institute, *Histor. Collections* 105:50–71.

Kulikoff, Allan. 1971. The progress of inequality in revolutionary Boston. *Wm. & Mary Quart.* 3d. ser. 28:375–412.

—— 1975. Tobacco and slaves: Population, economy, and society in eighteenth-century Prince George's County, Maryland. Ph.D. diss., Brandeis University.

—— 1978. The origins of Afro-American society in tidewater Maryland and Virginia, 1700 to 1790. *Wm. & Mary Quart.* 3d ser. 35:226–59.

—— 1979. The economic growth of the eighteenth-century Chesapeake colonies. *Jour. Ec. Hist.* 39:275–88.

Kuznets, Simon. 1952. Long-term changes in the national income of the United States of America since 1870. In Simon Kuznets, ed. *Income and wealth of the United States: Trends and structure.* International association for research in income and wealth, Income and wealth series, vol. 2. Baltimore: Johns Hopkins Press. Cambridge: Bowes and Bowes.

—— 1961. *Capital in the American economy*. National Bureau of Economic Research. Princeton: Princeton University Press.

—— 1965. *Economic growth and structure*. New York: W. W. Norton.

—— 1966. *Modern economic growth*. New Haven and London: Yale University Press.

—— 1968. Capital formation in modern economic growth. In *Third International Conference of Economic History* (Proceedings, Munich, 1965). The Hague: Mouton.

—— 1971. *Economic growth of nations: Total output and production structure*. Cambridge, Mass.: Belknap Press of Harvard University Press.

—— 1976. Demographic aspects of the size distribution of income: An exploratory essay. *Ec. Develop. and Cult. Change*. 25:1–94.

—— 1978. Letter to author dated December 13, 1978.

Kyrk, Hazel. 1923. *A theory of consumption*. Boston: Houghton, Mifflin.

—— 1933. *Economic problems of the family*. New York: Harper & Bros.

—— 1953. *The family in the American economy*. Chicago: University of Chicago Press.

Lampman, Robert J. 1954. Recent changes in income inequality reconsidered. *Amer. Ec. Rev.* 44:251–68.

—— 1959. Changes in the share of wealth held by top wealth-holders, 1922–56. *Rev. Ec. Stat.* 41:379–92.

—— 1962. *The share of top wealth-holders in national wealth, 1922–1956*. National Bureau of Economic Research, Study no. 74. Princeton: Princeton University Press.

Land, Aubrey C. 1965. Economic base and social structure: The northern Chesapeake in the eighteenth century. *Jour. Ec. Hist.* 25:639–54.

—— ed. 1969. *Bases of the plantation society*. New York: Harper and Row.

Land, Aubrey C., Lois Green Carr, and Edward C. Papenfuse. 1977. *Law, society, and politics in early Maryland*. Baltimore: Johns Hopkins University Press.

Landes, David S. 1974–75. Letters to the author.

Langdon, William C. 1937. *Everyday Things in American Life, 1607–1776*. New York: Charles Scribner's Sons.

Lansing, John B., and John Sonquist. 1969. A cohort analysis of changes in the distribution of wealth. Lee Soltow, ed., *Six papers on the size distribution of wealth and income*. Conference on research in income and wealth, Studies in income and wealth, vol. 33. National Bureau of Economic Research. New York: Columbia University Press.

Lazerwitz, Bernard. 1968. Sampling theory and procedures. In Hubert M. Blalock, Jr., and A. B. Blalock, eds. *Methodology in social research.* New York: McGraw Hill.

Lebergott, Stanley. 1960. Wage trends, 1800–1900. In William N. Parker, ed. *Trends in the American economy in the nineteenth century.* Conference on research in income and wealth, Studies in income and wealth, vol. 24. National Bureau of Economic Research. Princeton: Princeton University Press.

——— 1976a. Are the rich getting richer? Trends in U.S. wealth concentration. *Jour Ec. Hist.* 36:147–62.

——— 1976b. *The American economy: Income, wealth and want.* Princeton: Princeton University Press.

Lemon, James T. 1972. *The best poor man's country: A geographical study of early southeastern Pennsylvania.* Baltimore: Johns Hopkins University Press.

Lemon, James T., and Gary B. Nash. 1968. The distribution of wealth in eighteenth-century America: A century of changes in Chester County, Pennsylvania, 1693–1802. *Jour. Soc. Hist.* 2:1–24.

Lindstrom, Diane. 1978. *Economic development in the Philadelphia region, 1810–1850.* New York: Columbia University Press.

Lockridge, Kenneth A. 1968a. Land, population and the evolution of New England society, 1630–1790. *Past & Present* 39:62–80. Reprint, 1971, with an Afterthought, in Stanley N. Katz, ed. *Colonial America: Essays in politics and social development.* Boston: Little, Brown.

——— 1968b. A communication. *Wm. & Mary Quart.* 3d ser. 25:516–17.

——— 1970. *A New England town, the first hundred years: Dedham, Massachusetts, 1636–1736.* New York: Norton.

Lorenz, Max O. 1905. Methods of measuring the concentration of wealth. *Pub. Amer. Statis. Assoc.* 9:209–19.

Lyons, Patrick M. 1974. The size distribution of personal wealth in the Republic of Ireland. *Rev. Income and Wealth* 20:181–202.

McCusker, John J. 1971. The current value of English exports. *Wm. & Mary Quart.* 3d ser. 28:607–28.

——— 1972. Sources of investment capital in the colonial Philadelphia shipping industry. *Jour. Ec. Hist.* 32:146–57.

——— 1978. *Money and exchange in Europe and America, 1600–1775: A handbook.* Chapel Hill: University of North Carolina Press for the Institute of Early American History and Culture.

McMahon, Theresa S. 1925. *Social and economic standards of living.* New York: D. C. Heath.

Main, Gloria L. 1972. Personal wealth in colonial America: explorations in the probate records of Maryland and Massachusetts, 1650 to 1720. Ph.D. diss., Columbia University.

—— 1973. The comparative economic behavior of two American colonies before 1720. Paper presented at meeting of the Organization of American Historians, New Orleans, April 1973.

—— 1974. The correction of biases in colonial American probate records. *Historical Methods Newsletter* 8:10–28.

—— 1977a. Inequality in early America: The evidence from probate records of Massachusetts and Maryland. *Jour. Interdisciplinary Hist.* 7:559–81.

—— 1977b. Maryland and the Chesapeake economy, 1670–1720. In Aubrey C. Land, Lois Green Carr, and Edward C. Papenfuse, eds., *Law society and politics in early Maryland.* Baltimore: Johns Hopkins University Press.

—— 1978. Letter to author dated July 7, 1978.

Main, Jackson Turner. 1965. *The social structure of revolutionary America.* Princeton: Princeton University Press.

—— 1970. The composition of American State Legislatures, 1780–1786. Representative institutions in theory and practice. Historical papers read at Bryn Mawr College, April 1968. In *Studies presented to the International Commission for the history of representative and parliamentary institutions.* Brussels: *Les éditions de la librairie encyclopédique.*

—— 1971. Trends in wealth concentration before 1860. *Jour. Ec. Hist.* 31:445–47.

—— 1976. The distribution of property in colonial Connecticut. In James Kirby Martin, ed., *The human dimensions of nation making: Essays on colonial and revolutionary America.* Madison, Wis.: The State Historical Society.

Malthus, Thomas R. 1798. *An essay on the principle of population.* Reprint, 1960. New York: Random House.

Marshall, Alfred. 1920. *Principles of economics.* 8th ed. (First ed. 1890). London: Macmillan.

Martin, Edgar W. 1942. *The standard of living in 1860: American consumption levels on the eve of the Civil War.* Chicago: University of Chicago Press.

Martin, Robert F. 1939. *National income in the United States, 1799–1938.* National Industrial Conference Board Studies, no. 241. New York: National Industrial Conference Board.

Massachusetts. Bureau of Statistics of Labor. 1895. See Wright, Carroll D. 1895.

Mattoso, Katia M. deQueiros. 1976. Um estudo quantitativo de estrutura social: A cidade do Salvador, Bahia de todos os santos, no secolo xix. Primeiras abordagens, primeiros resultados. *Estudios historicos* 15:7–28. Marilia, Brazil. Universidade Estadual Paulista. "Julio De Mesquita Filho."

Menard, Russell R. 1975. Economy and society in early colonial Maryland. Ph.D. diss., University of Iowa.

—— 1976. Comment (on Ball and Walton, Agricultural productivity change in eighteenth-century Pennsylvania). *Jour. Ec. Hist.* 36:118–25.

—— 1978. Secular trends in the Chesapeake tobacco industry. In *Working papers from the Regional Economic History Research Center* (Greenville, Wilmington, Delaware: Eleutherian Mills-Hagley Foundation) 1, no. 3:1–34.

—— 1980. The tobacco industry in the Chesapeake colonies, 1617–1730: An interpretation. In Paul Uselding, ed., *Research in economic history: a research annual.* Greenwich, Conn.: JAI Press Inc. 5:109–77.

Menard, Russell R., P.M.G. Harris, and Lois Green Carr. 1974. Opportunity and inequality: The distribution of wealth on the lower western shore of Maryland, 1638–1705. *Maryland Historical Magazine* (Maryland Historical Society) 69:169–84.

Mendershausen, Horst. 1956. The pattern of estate tax wealth. In R. W. Goldsmith, D. S. Brady, and H. Mendershausen, *A study of saving in the United States.* Vol. 3. Princeton: Princeton University Press.

Mereness, Newton D., ed. 1916. *Travels in the American colonies.* New York: Macmillan.

Merwin, C. L., Jr. 1939. *American studies of the distribution of wealth and income.* Conference on research in income and wealth, Studies in income and wealth, vol. 3. New York: National Bureau of Economic Research.

Michal, Jan W. 1973. Size-distribution of earnings and household incomes in small socialist countries. *Rev. Income and Wealth.* 19:407–27.

Mill, John Stuart. 1848. *Political economy.* New ed. 1909. Reprint, 1973. Clifton, N.J.: Augustus M. Kelley.

Mitchell, Brian R., and Phyllis Deane. 1962. *Abstract of British Historical Statistics.* Cambridge: Cambridge University Press.

Morgan, James. 1962. The anatomy of income distribution. *Rev. Ec. Stat.* 44:270–83.

Morris, Richard J. 1978. Wealth distribution in Salem, Massachusetts, 1759–1799: The impact of the Revolution and independence. Essex Institute, *Histor. Collections* 114:87–102.

Moss, Milton. 1978. Income distribution issues viewed in a lifetime income perspective. *Rev. Income and Wealth.* 24:119–36.

Mulhall, Michael G. 1884. *Mulhall's dictionary of statistics.* London: G. Routledge.

Murrin, John M. 1965–66. The myths of colonial democracy and royal decline in eighteenth-century America: A review essay. *Cithara* 5:53–70.

—— 1972. Review essay (on studies of family, town, and county in colonial New England). *History and Theory.* 11:226–75.

Nash, Gary B. 1970. *Class and society in early America.* Englewood Cliffs, N.J.: Prentice-Hall.

—— 1973. Slaves and slaveowners in colonial Philadelphia. *Wm. & Mary Quart.* 3d ser. 30:223–256.

—— 1976a. Urban wealth and poverty in pre-revolutionary America. *Jour. Interdisciplinary Hist.* 6:545–84.

—— 1976b. Poverty and poor relief in pre-revolutionary Philadelphia. *Wm. & Mary Quart.* 3d ser. 33:3–30.

Nettels, Curtis P. 1934. *The money supply of the American colonies before 1720.* University of Wisconsin Studies in the Social Sciences and History, no. 20. Madison, Wis.

Nevins, Allen. 1927. *The American states during and after the revolution, 1775–1789.* New York: Macmillan.

North, Douglass C. 1961a. *The economic growth of the United States, 1790–1860.* Englewood Cliffs, N.J.: Prentice-Hall.

—— 1961b. Early national income estimates. *Ec. Develop. and Cult. Change* 9:387–96.

—— 1971. Sources of productivity change in ocean shipping, 1600–1850. In Robert W. Fogel and Stanley L. Engerman, eds., *The reinterpretation of American economic history.* New York: Harper & Row.

—— 1974. Growth and welfare in the American past. 2d ed. Englewood Cliffs, N.J.: Prentice-Hall.

Overton, Mark. 1979. Estimating crop yields from probate inventories: An example from East Anglia, 1585–1735. *Jour. Ec. Hist.* 39:363–78.

Paglin, Morton 1975. The measurement and trend of inequality: A basic revision. *Amer. Ec. Rev.* 65:598–609.

—— 1977. The measurement and trend of inequality: Reply. *Amer. Ec. Rev.* 67:520–31.

—— 1979. The measurement of inequality: Reply (to Kenneth L. Wertz, The measurement of inequality: Comment). *Amer. Ec. Rev.* 69:673–77.

Parker, William N., and Franklee Whartenby. 1960. The growth of output before 1840. In *Trends in the American economy in the nineteenth century.* Conference on research in income and wealth. Studies in income and wealth, vol. 24. National Bureau of Economic Research. Princeton: Princeton University Press.

Pessen, Edward. 1973. *Riches, class and power before the Civil War.* Lexington, Mass.: D. C. Heath.

Phillips, Ulrich B. 1905. The economic cost of slaveholding in the cotton belt. *Pol. Sci. Quart.* 20:257–73. Reprint, 1971, in Hugh G. J. Aitken, ed. *Did Slavery Pay?* Boston: Houghton, Mifflin.

Pitkin, Timothy. 1817. *A statistical view of the commerce of the United States of America.* 2d ed. New York: James Eastburn.

Podder, N., and N. C. Kakwani. 1976. Distribution of wealth in Australia. *Rev. Income and Wealth.* 22:75–92.

Podoluk, J. R. 1974. The size distribution of personal wealth in Canada. *Rev. Income and Wealth.* 20:203–16.

Pollard, Sidney. 1968. The growth and distribution of capital in Great Britain, c. 1770–1870. In *Third International Confernece of Economic History* (Proceedings, Munich, 1965). The Hague: Mouton.

Pollard, Sidney, and David W. Crossley. 1968. *The wealth of Britain, 1085–1966.* London: B. T. Batsford.

Potter, James. 1965. The growth of American population, 1700–1860. In David V. Glass and D. E. C. Eversly, eds., *Population in history: Essays in historical demography.* Chicago: Aldine.

Price, Jacob M. 1974. Economic function and the growth of American port towns in the eighteenth century. In *Perspectives in American history* 8:123–86. Cambridge, Mass.: Charles Warren Center for Studies in American History.

—— 1976a. A note on the value of colonial exports of shipping. *Jour. Ec. Hist.* 36:704–24.

—— 1976b. Quantifying colonial America: A comment on Nash and Warden. *Jour. Interdisciplinary Hist.* 6:701–9.

Projector, Dorothy S., and Gertrude S. Weiss. 1966. *Survey of financial characteristics of consumers.* Washington, D.C.: Board of Governors of the Federal Reserve System.

Rezneck, Samuel. 1960. Comment (on Parker and Whartenby, The growth of output before 1840.) In William N. Parker, ed. *Trends in the American economy in the nineteenth century.* National Bureau of Economic Research, Conference on research in income and wealth, Studies in income and wealth, vol. 24. Princeton, N.J.: Princeton University Press.

Richards, H. A. 1909. A study of New England mortality. *Publications of the American Statistical Association,* n.s. 11, no. 88:636–46.

Ritchie, Robert C. 1972. The Duke's province: A study of proprietary New York, 1664–1685. Ph.D. diss., University of California at Los Angeles.

Robbert, Louise Buenger. 1977. The inventory of Gratianus Gradenigo, 1176. Unpublished MS., St. Louis. (Based on Biblioteca Nazionale, Venice, Marciana, Latin MS., class XIV, codex 71.)

Rutman, Darrett. 1975. People in progress: The New Hampshire towns of the eighteenth century. *Jour. Urban Hist.* 1:268–92.

Salmon, Lucy M. 1911. *Domestic service.* 2d ed. New York: Macmillan.

Schlesinger, Arthur Meier. 3d ptg, 1964. *The colonial merchants and the American Revolution, 1763–1776.* New York: Frederick Ungar.

Schultz, Theodore W. 1972. Human capital: Policy issues and research opportunities. In *Human resources.* (Fiftieth anniversary colloquiam VI, Atlanta 1971.) New York: Columbia University Press for the National Bureau of Economic Research.

—— 1974. *Economics of the family: Marriage, children, human capital.* Chicago: University of Chicago Press for the National Bureau of Economic Research.

Schumpeter, Elizabeth Boody. 1938. English prices and public finance, 1660–1822. *Rev. Ec. Stat.* 20:21–37.

Scott, Kenneth, and James A. Owre. 1970. *Genealogical data from inventories of New York estates, 1666–1825.* New York: New York Genealogical and Biographical Society.

Seaman, Ezra C. 1870. *The American system of government.* New York: Charles Scribner's Sons.

Seiver, Daniel A. 1979. A note on the measurement of income inequality with interval data. *Rev. Income and Wealth* 25:229–33.

Sellers, Leila. 1934. *Charleston business on the eve of the American revolution.* Chapel Hill, N.C.: University of North Carolina Press.

Shepherd, James F. 1970. Commodity exports from the British North American colonies to overseas areas, 1768–1772: Magnitudes and patterns of trade. *Explor. Ec. Hist.* 8:5 76.

Shepherd, James F., and Gary M. Walton. 1972. *Shipping, maritime trade, and the economic development of colonial North America.* Cambridge: Cambridge University Press.

—— 1976. Economic change after the American revolution: Pre- and postwar comparisons of maritime shipping and trade. *Explor. Ec. Hist.* 13:397–422.

Shepherd, James F., and Samuel H. Williamson. 1972. The coastal trade of the British North American colonies, 1768–1772. *Jour. Ec. Hist.* 32:783–810.

Sirmans, M. Eugene. 1962. The legal status of the slave in South Carolina, 1670–1740. *Jour. South. Hist.* 28:462–73. Reprint, in part, 1971, in Stanley M. Katz, ed. *Colonial America: Essays in politics and social development.* Boston: Little, Brown.

Smith, Adam. 1776. *An inquiry into the nature and causes of the wealth of nations.* London. Reprint, 1937. New York: Random House.

Smith, Billy G. 1979. "The best poor man's country": Living standards of the "lower sort" in late eighteenth-century Philadelphia. In *Working*

Papers from the Regional Economic History Research Center (Greenville, Wilmington, Delaware: Eleutherian Mills-Hagley Foundation) 2, no. 4:1–70.

Smith, Daniel Scott. 1973. Population, family and society in Hingham, Massachusetts, 1635–1880. Ph.D. diss., University of California, Berkeley.

—— 1975. Underregistration and bias in probate records: An analysis of data from eighteenth century Hingham, Massachusetts. *Wm. & Mary Quart.* 3d ser. 32:100–10.

Smith, James D. 1974. The concentration of personal wealth in America, 1969. *Rev. Income and Wealth.* 20:143–80.

—— 1975. White wealth and black people: The distribution of wealth in Washington, D.C., in 1967. In James D. Smith, ed., *The personal distribution of income and wealth.* Conference on research in income and wealth, Studies in income and wealth, vol. 32. National Bureau of Economic Research. New York: Columbia University Press.

Smith, James D., and S. K. Calvert. 1965. Estimating the wealth of top wealth holders from estate tax returns. In Amer. Stat. Assoc., *1965 Proceedings of the Business and Economic Statistics Section.* Washington, D.C.: Amer. Stat. Assoc.

Smith, James D., and Stephen D. Franklin. 1974. The concentration of personal wealth, 1922–1969. *Amer. Ec. Rev.* 64:162–67.

Soltow, Lee. 1968. Long-run changes in British income inequality. *Ec. Hist. Rev.* 21:17–29.

—— 1971a. *Patterns of wealthholding in Wisconsin since 1850.* Madison: University of Wisconsin Press.

—— 1971b. Economic inequality in the United States in the period from 1790 to 1860. *Jour. Ec. Hist.* 31:822–39.

—— 1975a. *Men and wealth in the United States, 1850–1870.* New Haven: Yale University Press.

—— 1975b. Wealth, income and social class of men in large northern cities of the United States in 1860. In James D. Smith, ed., *The personal distribution of income and wealth.* Studies in income and wealth, vol. 39, National Bureau of Economic Research. New York: Columbia University Press.

Spahr, Charles B. 1896. *An essay on the present distribution of wealth in the United States.* New York: Thomas Crowell.

Stark, Harry. 1961. *Infirmities of per capita national income estimates when employed to compare levels of living between developed and retarded areas.* University of Miami publications in economics, no. 4. Coral Gables, Fla.: University of Miami Press.

Stigler, George J. 1952. *The theory of price.* New York: Macmillan.

Studenski, Paul. 1961. *The income of nations. Part one: History.* New York: New York University Press. Vol. 1.

Sturm, James Lester. 1977. *Investing in the United States, 1798–1893: Upper wealth-holders in a market economy.* New York: Arno Press.

Sutherland, Stella. 1936. *Population distribution in colonial America.* New York: Columbia University Press.

—— 1967. Colonial statistics. *Explor. Entrepreneurial Hist.* 2d ser. 5:58–107.

Taylor, A. J. 1960. Progress and poverty in Britain, 1780–1850: A reappraisal. *History* 45:16–31.

Taylor, George Rogers. 1931–32. Wholesale commodity prices at Charleston, South Carolina, 1732–1791. *Jour. Ec. and Bus. Hist.* 4:356–77.

—— 1964. American economic growth before 1840: An exploratory essay. *Jour. Ec. Hist.* 24:427–44.

Thrupp, Sylvia. 1962. *The merchant class in medieval London, 1300–1500.* Ann Arbor: University of Michigan Press. (First published 1948.)

Tocqueville, Alexis de. 1835, vol. 1, 1840, vol. 2. *Democracy in America.* Reprint, 1954. New York: Phillips Bradley.

Towne, Marvin W., and W. D. Rasmussen. 1960. Farm gross product investment in the nineteenth century. In *Trends in the American economy in the nineteenth century.* National Bureau of Economic Research, Conference on research in income and wealth, Studies in income and wealth, vol. 24. Princeton, N.J.: Princeton University Press.

U.S. Bureau of the Census. (Historical Statistics) 1960. *Historical Statistics of the United States, colonial times to 1957.* Washington, D.C.: Government Printing Office.

—— (Historical Statistics) 1975. *Historical Statistics of the United States, colonial times to 1970.* Washington, D.C.: Government Printing Office.

—— 1977. *Statistical Abstract of the United States: 1977.* (98th annual edition.) Washington, D.C.: Government Printing Office.

U.S. Office of the President. 1975. *Economic Report of the President, February 1975.* Washington, D.C.: Government Printing Office.

Uselding, Paul. 1971. Conjectural estimates of gross human capital inflow to the American economy, 1790–1800. *Explor. Ec. Hist.* 9:49–61.

Van der Wee, Herman. 1963. *The growth of the Antwerp market and the European economy, fourteenth-sixteenth centuries.* 3 vols. The Hague: M. Nyoff.

Wallace, David. 1951. *South Carolina, a short history, 1520–1948.* Chapel Hill: University of North Carolina Press.

Walsh, Lorena S. 1977a. The political and social structure of Charles County, Maryland, 1658–1705. Ph.D. diss., Michigan State University.

—— 1977b. Servitude and opportunity in Charles County, Maryland, 1658–1705. In Aubrey C. Land, Lois Green Carr, and Edward C. Papenfuse, eds., *Law, society, and politics in early Maryland.* Baltimore: Johns Hopkins University Press.

Walton, Gary M. 1979. Colonial economy. In Glenn Porter, ed., *Encyclopedia of American Economic History.* New York: Charles Scribner's Sons.

Warden, Gerard B. 1976. Inequality and instability in eighteenth-century Boston: A reappraisal. *Jour. Interdisciplinary Hist.* 6:585–620.

Warner, Sam. B. 1968. *The private city: Philadelphia in three periods of its growth.* Philadelphia: University of Pennsylvania Press.

Warville. See Brissot de Warville.

Waters, John J. 1976. Patrimony, succession and social stability: Guilford Connecticut in the eighteenth century. In Donald Fleming and Bernard Bailyn, eds., *Perspectives in American history* 10:131–60. Cambridge, Mass.: Charles Warren Center for Studies in American History.

Watkins, G. P. 1908. An interpretation of certain statistical evidence of concentration of wealth. *Jour. Amer. Stat. Assoc.* 11:37.

Weiss, Roger. 1970. The issue of paper money in the American colonies, 1720–1774. *Jour. Ec. Hist.* 30:770–84.

Wells, Robert V. 1975. *The population of the British colonies in America before 1776: A survey of census data.* Princeton: Princeton University Press.

—— 1976. Letter to author dated November 15, 1976.

White, Philip L., ed. 1956. *The Beekman mercantile papers, 1746–1799.* New York: New York Historical Society.

Wiecek, William M. 1977. The statutory law of slavery and race in the thirteen mainland colonies of British America. *Wm. & Mary Quart.* 3d ser. 34:258–80.

Wilkenfeld, Bruce M. 1973. The social and economic structure of the city of New York, 1695–1796. Ph.D. diss., Columbia University.

Williams, Faith M., and Alice C. Hanson. 1941. Money disbursements of wage earners and clerical workers, 1934–36: Summary volume. U.S. Bureau of Labor Statistics, *Bulletin,* no. 638. Washington: Government Printing Office.

Williamson, Jeffrey G. 1978. British income inequality, 1688–1913: Political, arithmetic and conventional wisdom. Unpublished MS., Madison, Wisconsin.

—— 1979. The distribution of earnings in nineteenth century Britain. *Discussion paper.* Department of Economics, University of Wisconsin, Madison, Wisconsin. Mimeographed.

Williamson, Jeffrey G., and Peter Lindert. 1976. *Three centuries of American inequality.* Institute for Research on Poverty, University of Wisconsin, Discussion Paper no. 333–76. Madison, Wis. Mimeographed.

—— 1977. *Long term trends in American wealth inequality.* Institute for Research on Poverty, University of Wisconsin, Discussion Paper no. 472–77. Madison, Wis. Mimeographed.

Wimmer, Larry T., and Clayne L. Pope. 1975. The Genealogical Society library of Salt Lake City: A source of data for economic and social historians. *Historical Methods Newsletter* 8:51–60.

Wood, Peter H. 1974. *Black majority: Negroes in colonial South Carolina from 1676 through the Stono rebellion.* New York: Alfred A. Knopf.

—— 1978. "I did the best I could for my day"; The study of early black history during the second reconstruction, 1960–1976. *Wm. & Mary Quart.* 3d ser. 35:185–225.

World Bank. 1974. *Atlas: Population, per capita product, and growth rates.* Washington, D.C.: World Bank.

—— 1976. *Atlas: Population, per capita product, and growth rates.* Washington, D.C.: World Bank.

(Wright, Carroll D.) 1895. (Massachusetts) Bureau of Statistics of Labor, *Twenty-fifth annual report.* Public Documents, no. 15. Boston.

Wright, Carroll D., and W. C. Hunt. 1900. *The history and growth of the United States census.* 56th Congress, 1st sess. Senate Doc. no. 194. Washington, D.C.: Government Printing Office.

Wright, Chester W. 1949. *Economic history of the United States.* 2d ed. New York: McGraw-Hill.

Wright, Gavin. 1970. Economic democracy and the concentration of agricultural wealth in the cotton South, 1850–1860. *Agric. Hist.* 44:63–93.

Young, Allyn A. 1916. Review of . . . [W. I.] King's *Wealth and Income. Quart. Jour. Ec.* 30:582–87.

—— 1917. Economic problems, old and new. Amer. Econ. Assoc. *Ec. Rev.* 4th ser., 7 (supp.; March 1917):106–7.

Young, Arthur. 1771. *A six months tour through the north of England.* 2d ed. 4 vols. Reprint, 1967. New York: A. M. Kelley.

List of Tables and Figures

TABLES

FIGURES

Name Index

Subject Index